The Challenge of Professional Practice, Third Edition

How can teacher and schools encourage more parental involvement? *See Chapter 7.*

How can schools be made safer places where all students can learn? *See Chapter 7.*

Should racial designation matter for purposes of education? *See Chapter 8.*

How do perceptions of physical attractiveness relate to academic success? *See Chapter 8.*

Is there a "cognitive elite" in society? *See Chapter 8.*

Do boys and girls use different kinds of moral reasoning? *See Chapter 8.*

Should there be separate programs for gay and lesbian students? *See Chapter 8.*

What is multicultural education? *See Chapter 9.*

Do alternative culture-based curricula encourage separatism? *See Chapter 9.*

What are some ways teachers can capitalize on student diversity? *See Chapter 9.*

Has multiculturalism become just another form of political correctness? *See Chapter 9.*

What does it take to make inclusion work? *See Chapter 9.*

What kind of curriculum is in the national interest? *See Chapter 10.*

To what extent should teachers and professional associations determine the curriculum? *See Chapter 10.*

To what extent does the textbook publishing industry determine the curriculum? *See Chapter 10.*

What ethical considerations should guide testing and grading practices? *See Chapter 10.*

What is the key to effective classroom management? *See Chapter 10.*

Can teachers use physical punishment on a child? *See Chapter 11.*

Can school administrators censor student publications? *See Chapter 11.*

Is posting grades an invasion of students' privacy? *See Chapter 11.*

Do teachers have to pay teachers' union dues if they are not members? *See Chapter 11.*

When can a teacher be sued for negligence? *See Chapter 11.*

What are the implications of joining education and technology on a global scale? *See Chapter 12.*

For what kind of future should schools in the United States prepare students? *See Chapter 12.*

What makes the propagation of culture through schooling a problem in any country? *See Chapter 12.*

Would other countries' solutions for multilingual education work for the United States? *See Chapter 12.*

Will accountability for national standards cause schools to "teach to the test"? *See Chapter 13.*

Is a focus on minimum competency a disservice to students? *See Chapter 13.*

How far should schools go in attempting to ensure gender equity? *See Chapter 13.*

How far should schools go in teaching moral values? *See Chapter 13.*

Can collaborative networks contribute to the professionalization of teaching? *See Chapter 13.*

Foundations of Education

Third Edition

Foundations of Education

The Challenge of Professional Practice

Robert F. McNergney
University of Virginia

Joanne M. Herbert
University of Virginia

Allyn and Bacon
Boston   London   Toronto   Sydney   Tokyo   Singapore

Executive Editor: Stephen D. Dragin
Senior Development Editor: Linda Bieze
Editorial Assistant: Barbara Strickland
Senior Editorial-Production Administrator: Joe Sweeney
Editorial-Production Service: WordCrafters Editorial Services, Inc.
Composition Buyer: Linda Cox
Manufacturing Buyer: Megan Cochran
Cover Administrator: Linda Knowles
Text Design: Cia Boynton
Photo Research: Kate Cook
Text Composition: Publishers' Design and Production Services, Inc.

Library of Congress Cataloging-in-Publication Data
McNergney, Robert F.
    Foundations of education : the challenge of professional practice / Robert F. McNergney, Joanne M. Herbert.—3rd ed.
        p.   cm.
    Includes bibliographical references and index.
    ISBN 0-205-31691-3
    1. Teaching—Vocational guidance—United States   2. Education—United States.   I. Herbert, Joanne M.   II. Title.
LB1775.2 .M32 2000
370′.973—dc21   00-032274

Printed in the Unites States of America
10 9 8 7 6 5 4 3 2 1 04   03   02   01   00

To our parents,
Quentin and Thelma McNergney,
and
Elmore and Arvilla May,
with love

Brief Contents

Contents

ix

Modern U.S. Education History, 1865 to the Present   77

CHAPTER 6

School Governance and Education Finance   *207*

CHAPTER 7

Social Issues and the Schools   *251*

Preface

Today, when the professionalism of educators is being challenged by such phenomena as teacher-competency tests, state-mandated evaluations of student performance, and the mounting social tensions that erupt in schools, we continue to advocate that future teachers be educated to be professionals.

Professionals, regardless of their fields, use knowledge to solve problems and to capitalize on opportunities. Teachers, physicians, lawyers, and others face the challenge of professional practice by acquiring and learning how to apply specialized knowledge. Even then, professionals often work in situations where their knowledge is tentative and incomplete. They must do the best they can with the knowledge they possess.

The Plan of the Book

The book's organization reflects our conception of teaching as a profession. To us, professionals possess foundational knowledge others do not possess and are able to apply that knowledge to do things others cannot do. Professionals in all fields can explain why they behave as they do. They also have the capacity to reflect on or evaluate their actions and thus to continue to progress professionally. These abilities set the professional apart from other people.

Professional teachers perceive problems that need to be solved and opportunities to learn as they interact with students. They recognize when their own values and the values of others influence education. Professional teachers know about teaching, about students, about learning, and about content so they can improve their chances for successful practice. Because professional teachers are always reinforcing and extending their foundational knowledge, they can act in a timely fashion and evaluate or reflect on their actions to advance their development.

Many people have a stake in our educational systems. Because we have a society of ethnic, racial, religious, and social diversity, we also have a tradition of pluralistic thought and action with respect to educational matters. The third edition reflects this tradition of working together to make the learning environment a better place for everyone.

The third edition contains 13 chapters. We have written to acknowledge the interdependence of knowledge in the disciplines and knowledge from the education profession. We also have incorporated some very useful ideas and suggestions from readers of the previous editions.

Chapter 1 communicates the theme of professionalism. Chapters 2 through 4 place education in historical and philosophical contexts. Chapter 5 explores the many meanings of the concept of school. Chapter 6 examines the governmental and economic contexts in which education for children occurs. Chapters 7 through 9 describe the challenges of meeting students' diverse educational needs. Chapter 10 explores curriculum and instruction. Chapter 11 explains the major legal issues before the education community. Chapter 12 stretches beyond our own borders to consider international and global education. Chapter 13 anticipates an exciting future for educators in an increasingly interdependent world.

New Features of the Third Edition

This edition incorporates the following major changes suggested by instructors and students who have used the book, as well as by our experiences using the book in our own teaching:

▌ We have sharpened the opening chapter, "Teaching—The People's Profession," to focus on the questions of what does and what does not make teaching a profession.

▌ A new chapter, Chapter 9, focuses on multicultural and inclusive education. This change reflects widespread concern in the teaching profession for two especially challenging issues.

▌ We have infused material on multicultural education and technology throughout the text to communicate how and why these concepts are stretching across foundational areas. Each chapter offers a Cultural Awareness section and a Using Technology feature to help meet these goals.

▌ In Chapters 6, 7, and 11, we have updated discussions of government, legal decisions, and social issues that affect teaching and schools.

▌ We have revised Chapter 12 on global education by emphasizing comparisons of education in other nations with education in the United States.

▌ The last chapter of the book has a strong foundations orientation that focuses on the broader effects of technology, government regulation, alternative schooling, and national goals and standards in a changing future.

▌ By deleting outdated material and adding current information, we have updated all references by 38%.

As we explain below, we have also strengthened existing pedagogical features and added some new ones.

Aids to Understanding

The third edition includes features in each chapter to help you understand and remember the material. We have retained features from the second edition that worked well, enhanced others to capitalize on strengths that our readers found especially helpful, and added new ones to reflect the challenges facing professional educators.

▌ **Overviews** set the stage for the material presented in the chapter.

▌ **Professional Practice Questions** communicate from the outset, and throughout the chapters, exactly what material will be presented, and why it is important.

▌ **Benchmarks** represent important conceptual points in time and appear in each chapter.

▌ **Terms and Concepts** denoted by bold print in the body of the text appear alphabetically at the end of each chapter.

▌ The **Glossary** at the end of the book defines the terms and concepts.

▌ **Figures and Tables** communicate in shortened form current theory, research, and background information noted in the text.

▌ **Cultural Awareness** features highlight the influences of culture, variously defined, on teaching and learning.

▌ **Voices** provide first-hand accounts, reportage, and professional writings. **Critical Thinking** questions guide your thinking about these excerpts.

▌ A new **Using Technology** feature in each chapter illustrates how educators can integrate technology in today's and tomorrow's classrooms.

▌ A new **School Reform** feature in each chapter stretches readers to consider issues, problems, and opportunities surrounding efforts to teach and learn.

▌ A **Summary** reiterates the main points made in each chapter.

▌ A **Reflective Practice** exercise at the end of each chapter takes the form of a "mini case" of real life that encourages you to apply knowledge from the chapter. As you engage in the exercise you will identify issues, problems, dilemmas, opportunities; perceive other's points of view; call up knowledge to inform actions you might take if you were in the situation; and forecast how you might evaluate your actions.

▌ The **Online Activity** at the end of each chapter points you toward resources and useful professional connections on the World Wide Web.

Instructor Supplements to Accompany This Text

Contact your Allyn and Bacon representative for more information about any of the following supplements.

▌ **Instructor's Resource Manual and Test Bank.** The IRM contains graphic organizers, transparency masters, teaching suggestions, case-based activities supported by handout masters, and other resources for teaching each chapter. A 1300-item **Test Bank** with answer feedback includes multiple choice, essay, and application items as well as a component for authentic assessment.

▌ **Computerized Test Bank** for IBM and Macintosh computers.

▌ **Allyn and Bacon Introduction to Teaching/Foundations of Education Transparency Package,** containing over 100 ready-to-use acetate transparencies.

▌ A **Digital Media Archive** of Power Point presentations, weblinks, video clips, and electronic transparencies.

▌ Two sets of **Videocases** with a comprehensive **Guide,** providing an in-depth look at teaching and learning in multicultural classrooms in the Midwest, the Washington, DC, area, New York City, and elsewhere in the U.S.

▌ A **CD-ROM,** "Educational Border Culture in New Mexico," designed for in-depth exploration of multicultural/multilingual issues in education.

▌ **A new CD-ROM, "Project New Delhi,"** designed to encourage careful study of issues of global and comparative education.

▌ Our own **Web page** within the Allyn and Bacon Web site (http://www.abacon.com/mcnergney).

Acknowledgments

We thank the people who devoted time and energy to help produce this book. The following reviewers offered helpful suggestions on various drafts of the manuscript: Charles E. Alberti, Bemidji State University; Deborah Copeland, Baylor University; Dorothy Valcarcel Craig, Middle Tennessee State University; Cornelia J. Glenn, Owensboro Community College; Frank Guldbrandsen, University of Minnesota–Duluth; and Marcie Misik, McNeese State University.

Our colleagues at Allyn and Bacon are simply the best. Nancy Forsyth, Vice President and Editorial Director, makes good things happen and does so with a rich sense of humor. Steve Dragin, our editor, directed every aspect of this edition from start to finish. We truly appreciate his support and his keen sense of what works in publishing. Our developmental editor Linda Bieze deserves special recognition. Linda brought a fresh perspective to this edition; she shared her special knowledge with grace and unfailing good cheer.

Our University of Virginia colleagues helped us many ways, time and again. Clare Kilbane found, tested, and developed material for this edition. Her assistance was invaluable, her presence a joy. Linda Price tracked permissions and checked references with great care. Teri Adkins performed library research that led us to new material. Marsha Gartland found and fixed broken links in web sites that support this edition. Kay Cutler led us to material that only a librarian could find. Peggy Powell and Sandy West performed a range of recordkeeping and management tasks that enabled us to meet deadlines.

Finally, we thank our families for their love and support.

Foundations of Education

1

Teaching—The People's Profession

Teachers are members of what might be called the people's profession. They come from and work for the people. Teachers apply specialized knowledge to solve educational problems and capitalize on opportunities to help young people live full, productive lives. Although teachers share many characteristics with other professionals, they are unique in their professional roles.

In this chapter we explore some aspects of a teaching career. We discuss what people must do to become teachers, factors that influence their prospects for employment, how teachers succeed once they are on the job, how their earnings compare with those of other professionals, opportunities that teachers have to collaborate with others, and how teachers advance in the profession.

PROFESSIONAL PRACTICE QUESTIONS

- What makes teaching a profession?
- What makes teaching less than a profession?
- What are the challenges of professional practice?
- What career issues must beginning teachers face?
- How are teachers evaluated?
- How are teachers supported and rewarded?
- How do teachers demonstrate professional leadership?

 ## What Makes Teaching a Profession?

Is teaching a full profession?

Teaching is a profession because its members possess specialized knowledge and can apply this knowledge to increase the chances of solving educational problems. Unlike other professions, the range of demands placed on educators, the numbers of people involved in the enterprise, and the public's common knowledge of life in classrooms combine to make teaching what might be called the **people's profession.** Teachers come from the people; that is, teaching has been viewed traditionally as a way for the children of working-class families to ascend the social ladder. Teaching has also been viewed as a socially acceptable means of retaining middle-class or upper-class status for those who already have it. This work is serious, important, and not readily accomplished by just anyone. Teachers must be able to take care of the people's educational business—a business that can appear simultaneously routine yet noble, genuine yet surreal. The people assign teachers as the caretakers of democracy. As such, teachers are supposed to prepare those within their borders to live and work together harmoniously. Members of the people's profession seek approval of and support for their practice from the people themselves.

▶ Characteristics of Teachers as Professionals

Teachers exhibit collegiality, interacting with others in a courteous, conscientious, and generally businesslike manner. These behaviors are observable indications of a social contract among teachers themselves and between teachers and the lay public. This agreement, most often left unspoken, governs teachers' interactions with one another and with the people they serve.

Teachers are professionals in part because they are salaried. Professionals may volunteer or donate their services to worthy causes, but this is the exception, not the rule. Professionals get paid for what they know and what they can do.

Teachers are achievement oriented and their professional history serves as a record of accomplishment. A teacher does not simply do a job; she or he leaves a legacy. Professional histories influence people's expectations in the present and live on in others' memories long after teachers have completed their work.

More important than one's place in history, however, is the power to add value to an organization. Schools staffed with accomplished professionals have greater capacity to produce desirable results—students who have been well educated—than schools short on professional talent. Teachers do not merely acquire and possess specialized knowledge; they apply what they know in real-life settings to solve problems and to capitalize on opportunities.

Many teachers feel called to the profession, compelled or driven by a sense of responsibility to perform their work. Knowledge informs teachers' actions, but the passion to make a difference in people's lives fuels teachers' careers in the beginning and keeps them going years later.

Teachers, like all professionals, abide by the technical and ethical standards of their profession. Both the **American Federation of Teachers (AFT)** and the **National Education Association (NEA)**—professional organizations for teachers, sometimes called **teacher unions**—acknowledge this responsibility in their codes of ethics. The NEA's 1975 preamble to its Code of Ethics (Figure 1.1) describes the responsibility as follows:

> The educator, believing in the worth and dignity of each human being, recognizes the supreme importance of the pursuit of truth, devotion to excellence, and the nurture of the democratic principles. Essential to these goals is the protection of freedom to learn and to teach and the guarantee of equal educational opportunity for all. The educator accepts the responsibility to adhere to the highest ethical standards.

The Code of Ethics of the AFT appears in Figure 1.2. Teachers practice decision making, thus shaping educational environments in schools and classrooms. As Table 1.1 suggests, teachers perceive their own influence as being greater with regard to classroom issues than school issues.

What Makes Teaching Less Than a Profession?

Some describe teaching as a semiprofession, that is, simply an occupation with the trappings of a profession (Meyer & Rowan, 1978). They observe that the large numbers of people hired to work in classrooms, the ease of entry into the labor force, salary schedules, control by the state, and educators' difficulty articulating an explicit knowledge base all argue against the concept of the teacher as a professional (Eraut, 1994).

FIGURE 1.1
NEA Code of Ethics

PRINCIPLE I

Commitment to the Student

The educator strives to help each student realize his or her potential as a worthy and effective member of society. The educator therefore works to stimulate the spirit of inquiry, the acquisition of knowledge and understanding, and the thoughtful formulation of worthy goals.

In fulfillment of the obligation to the student, the educator—

1. Shall not unreasonably restrain the student from independent action in the pursuit of learning.
2. Shall not unreasonably deny the student's access to varying points of view.
3. Shall not deliberately suppress or distort subject matter relevant to the student's progress.
4. Shall make reasonable effort to protect the student from conditions harmful to learning or to health and safety.
5. Shall not intentionally expose the student to embarrassment or disparagement.
6. Shall not on the basis of race, color, creed, sex, national origin, marital status, political or religious beliefs, family, social or cultural background, or sexual orientation, unfairly—
   a. Exclude any student from participation in any program
   b. Deny benefits to any student
   c. Grant any advantage to any student
7. Shall not use professional relationships with students for private advantage.
8. Shall not disclose information about students obtained in the course of professional service unless disclosure serves a compelling professional purpose or is required by law.

▶ Lack of Control of Entry and Exit

Unlike people in other professions, teachers have little say regarding guidelines for hiring or dismissing teachers. As surely as the opening of school follows the dog days of summer, calls for an "alternative route" into teaching can be heard with regularity. Some public figure or private citizen argues that teachers should be able to get **alternative certification,** that is, some preparation to teach short of completing an approved program of teacher education. Talented people should be able to bypass education schools and go directly into teaching, they say.

Virginia Governor James Gilmore and his staff are a case in point. In the spring of 1999, Gilmore sent a proposal to the State Board of Education to develop a new license allowing business executives, retired military personnel, and others to teach

FIGURE 1.1
NEA Code of Ethics *(Continued)*

PRINCIPLE II

Commitment to the Profession

The education profession is vested by the public with a trust and responsibility requiring the highest ideals of professional service.

In the belief that the quality of the services of the education profession directly influences the nation and its citizens, the educator shall exert every effort to raise professional standards, to promote a climate that encourages the exercise of professional judgment, to achieve conditions that attract persons worthy of the trust to careers in education, and to assist in preventing the practice of the profession by unqualified persons.

In fulfillment of the obligation to the profession, the educator—

1. Shall not in an application for a professional position deliberately make a false statement or fail to disclose a material fact related to competency and qualifications.
2. Shall not misrepresent his/her professional qualifications.
3. Shall not assist any entry into the profession of a person known to be unqualified in respect to character, education, or other relevant attribute.
4. Shall not knowingly make a false statement concerning the qualifications of a candidate for a professional position.
5. Shall not assist a noneducator in the unauthorized practice of teaching.
6. Shall not disclose information about colleagues obtained in the course of professional service unless disclosure serves a compelling professional purpose or is required by law.
7. Shall not knowingly make false or malicious statements about a colleague.
8. Shall not accept any gratuity, gift, or favor that might impair or appear to influence professional decisions or action.

—Adopted by the NEA 1975 Representative Assembly
From "The Code of Ethics of the Education Profession." National Education Association, Washington, DC.

in public schools. " 'There are many qualified people out there who have expertise to bring into the schools,' said Lee Goodman, the governor's education policy advisor. 'The idea is to establish some procedures to open the doors for these professionals'" (Associated Press, 1999).

Such proposals may be fueled not only by ideology, but also by teacher shortages and political pressure. School administrators, like Fairfax County School Superintendent Daniel Domenech, like the idea too, because it could help them deal with teacher shortages: "[T]he district hired 1,300 new teachers last year and may have to hire 1,500 this year" (Associated Press, 1999, p. B1).

FIGURE 1.2
Code of Ethics of the American Federation of Teachers, AFL–CIO

(Adopted February 10, 1971)

I. Teacher–Student Commitment

The Teacher works to develop each student's potential as a worthy and effective citizen.

The Teacher works objectively to stimulate the spirit of inquiry, the acquisition of knowledge and understanding, and the thoughtful formulation of worthy goals in each of his/her students for their advancement.

The Teacher works to develop and provide sound and progressively better educational opportunities for all students.

II. Teacher–Public Commitment

The Teacher believes that patriotism in its highest form requires dedication to the principles of our democratic heritage.

The Teacher shares will all other citizens the responsibility for the development of sound public policy and assumes full political and citizenship responsibilities.

The Teacher has the privilege and the responsibility to enhance the public image of his/her school in order to create a positive community atmosphere which will be beneficial to education.

III. Teacher–Profession Commitment

The Teacher believes that the quality of his/her service in the education profession directly influences the nation and its citizens.

The Teacher urges active participation and support in professional organizations and their programs.

IV. Teacher–District Commitment

The Teacher strives to do the job for which he/she was hired with honesty and to the best of his/her ability.

The Teacher pledges to communicate this code, along with a positive attitude toward it, to all teachers.

The Teacher discourages the breaching of this code and requests that all charges be presented in writing to the Union Executive Board for their deliberation and judgment.

Source: American Federation of Teachers, AFL–CIO.

▌ **TABLE 1.1**

Teachers' and Principals' Perceptions of the Amount of Influence or Control Teachers Had over Selected School and Classroom Decisions in Their Schools, by Control and Level of School: School Year 1993–94*

School and classroom decisions	All schools	Public			Private		
		Total	Elementary	Secondary	Total	Elementary	Secondary
Percentage of teachers who perceived that teachers had a good deal of influence in their school over:							
Setting discipline policy	38.0	34.9	41.9	27.3	59.2	64.6	51.7
Determining the content of in-service programs	31.2	30.6	32.6	28.5	35.3	36.4	33.7
Establishing curriculum	37.1	34.3	31.8	37.0	55.7	55.0	56.8
Percentage of teachers who perceived having a good deal of control in their classroom over:							
Selecting textbooks and other instructional materials	57.0	55.2	48.9	62.1	68.8	63.4	76.6
Selecting content, topics, and skills to be taught	62.4	60.5	54.3	67.3	74.9	69.7	82.2
Selecting teaching techniques	87.1	86.5	83.9	89.2	91.7	89.9	94.3
Evaluating and grading students	87.4	86.8	83.8	90.1	91.5	90.1	93.4
Disciplining students	70.9	68.9	73.4	64.0	84.3	86.2	81.8
Determining the amount of homework to be assigned	86.8	86.7	83.7	90.0	86.9	85.5	89.0
Percentage of principals who perceived that teachers had a good deal of influence over:							
Setting discipline policy	74.8	74.6	75.5	72.5	75.3	82.2	68.9
Determining the content of in-service programs	68.4	70.6	70.3	71.6	61.6	66.6	70.1
Establishing curriculum	64.1	61.5	59.7	66.2	72.1	74.0	76.9

*Respondents were asked about influence and control on a scale of 0–5, with 0 meaning "no influence" or "no control," and 5 meaning a "great deal of influence" or "complete control." Responses 4 and 5 were combined in this analysis.

Note: Data are revised from previously published figures.

Source: U.S. Department of Education, National Center for Education Statistics, Schools and Staffing Survey, 1993–94 (Public School Teacher, Private School Teacher, Public School Principal, and Private School Principal questionnaires).

Recently, a group of educators and policymakers funded by the Thomas B. Fordham Foundation has called for all states to de-emphasize the role of schools and colleges of education in the preparation of teachers and instead to give more authority to school principals to hire teachers (Basinger, 1999). They have issued their call in the form of a "manifesto," some of which follows:

> We conclude that the regulatory strategy being pursued today to boost teacher quality is seriously flawed. Every additional requirement for prospective teachers—every additional pedagogical course, every new hoop or hurdle—will have a predictable and inexorable effect: it will limit the potential supply of teachers by narrowing the pipeline while having no bearing whatever on the quality or effectiveness of those in the pipeline. The regulatory approach is also bound, over

What makes teaching a profession? What makes teaching less than a profession? What can teachers do to be considered more professional?

time, to undermine the standards-and-accountability strategy for improving schools and raising student achievement.

A better solution to the teacher quality problem is to simplify the entry and hiring process. Get rid of most hoops and hurdles. Instead of requiring a long list of courses and degrees, test future teachers for their knowledge and skills. Allow principals to hire the teachers they need. Focus relentlessly on results, on whether students are learning. This strategy, we are confident, will produce a larger supply of able teachers and will tie judgments about their fitness and performance to success in the classroom, not to process or impression. (Thomas B Fordham Foundation, 1999)

▶ Lack of Control over Schedule and Work Load

How does a teacher's workday compare to that of other professionals?

Debate about the professional status of teachers often revolves around the amount of time teachers spend working, the number of classes they teach, and the number of students they teach in each class. Teachers also spend time outside school hours working on school-related matters. The U.S. Department of Education (1998) notes the following:

▌ On average, full-time public school teachers are required to be at school 33 hours per week, yet they report working 45 hours per week. The figures are slightly higher for private school teachers. They must work 34 hours each, while they report working 47 hours per week.

▌ Full-time public and private school teachers report spending an extra 12 and 13 hours respectively each week working before and after school and on weekends; about one-fourth of this time is spent on student-related activities.

▌ Public school teachers' classes are typically larger than those of private-school teachers (24 versus 21 students per class).

▊ Teachers with 3 years or less of teaching experience work more total hours per week than do more experienced teachers.

▶ Lower Salaries

Many argue that until teachers earn as much as other professionals they will always be relegated to subprofessional status. Simple direct comparisons between teachers' salaries and those of other professionals are often misleading, however. They rarely account for benefits packages that may include health insurance, dental coverage, sick leave, worker's compensation, and retirement. Sometimes benefits for teachers are better than the benefits others receive, sometimes not. Teachers are under contract nine or at most ten months, not twelve—a point to which we shall return later.

Teachers typically do not invest as much money in their education as do other professionals, who must possess a graduate degree to begin practice. The additional time required beyond a bachelor's degree for those who attend law school, for example, means greater expenditures for their professional preparation and greater lost earning opportunities—often referred to as opportunity costs—during the years spent in law school. It can take years for professionals with education beyond the bachelor's degree to recoup out-of-pocket losses.

Are teachers so poorly paid as many people seem to believe? Given the importance and magnitude of their work, their capacity to help society prevent problems instead of cure them, and the time and energy they devote to their work both during and after official business hours, the answer is clearly yes. At least in the early years of their careers, however, teachers fare better than some professionals and people employed in highly skilled occupations and not so well as others. Bearing in mind the caveats noted above, some rough comparisons of salaries are instructive.

Beginning Teachers. The average salary in 1997 constant dollars for beginning elementary and secondary teachers across the United States in the year ending in 1997 was $25,462 (U.S. Department of Education, 1998). This salary was earned over a period of no more than 40 weeks. Professionals in other fields typically work 50 weeks per year. Potentially, then, the average beginning teacher might be able to earn another 20 percent of his or her salary in the summertime, or about an additional $5,000, increasing earnings to more than $30,000. Too often, of course, comparable work at the level of pay a teacher receives during the school year is not available. If we assume the worst-case scenario—a beginning teacher took a summer job in 1997 at minimum wage or $5.25 per hour for 10 weeks—he or she could earn another $2,100. The average beginning teacher, then, might reasonably be said to have had the capacity to earn about $27,562 per year in 1997. There is a great deal of regional variation in beginning teachers' salaries, just as there is in experienced teachers' salaries. Table 1.2 contains average salaries for all teachers by state. Note, for instance, the difference between average salaries in North Dakota and Connecticut in 1996–97.

Other Beginning Professionals.* As illustrated in Table 1.3, teachers' starting salaries sometimes exceed and other times fall below those of other professionals. For

*The salary figures in this section are from the Bureau of Labor Statistics (1999).

▌ **TABLE 1.2**
Estimated Average Annual Salary of Teachers in Public Elementary and Secondary Schools, by State

State	1996–97	State	1996–97	State	1996–97
United States	**$39,242**	Kentucky	34,400	North Dakota	28,205
Alabama	33,129	Louisiana	29,543	Ohio	39,366
Alaska	51,550	Maine	34,277	Oklahoma	30,911
Arizona	33,894	Maryland	41,882	Oregon	41,690
Arkansas	30,860	Massachusetts	43,411	Pennsylvania	47,988
California	43,759	Michigan	49,098	Rhode Island	43,786
Colorado	36,918	Minnesota	38,964	South Carolina	33,415
Connecticut	51,325	Mississippi	28,214	South Dakota	27,241
Delaware	42,175	Missouri	33,746	Tennessee	34,832
District of Columbia	45,815	Montana	30,492	Texas	33,627
Florida	34,493	Nebraska	32,335	Utah	32,435
Georgia	36,231	Nevada	38,006	Vermont	36,696
Hawaii	36,481	New Hampshire	36,672	Virginia	36,328
Idaho	32,385	New Jersey	50,674	Washington	38,489
Illinois	42,876	New Mexico	30,668	West Virginia	33,850
Indiana	39,538	New York	48,856	Wisconsin	39,754
Iowa	33,865	North Carolina	31,723	Wyoming	32,281
Kansas	36,376				

Header spanning: Constant 1997–98 dollars

Source: Digest of Education Statistics, 1998 (p. 86) by U.S. Department of Education, National Center for Education Statistics (1999). Washington, DC: U.S. Government Printing Office.

How do teachers' salaries compare to those of other professionals?

each group of professionals, however, salaries vary by the type of work that people do. In 1996, for example, the median starting salary for all lawyers six months after graduation from law school was $40,000. Lawyers in private practice averaged $50,000, while government lawyers earned $34,500. Public-interest lawyers, for instance those who work as public defenders for indigent clients, had a median salary of $30,000 (Bureau of Labor Statistics, 1999).

Starting salaries for engineers with the bachelor's degree are significantly higher than starting salaries of bachelor's degree graduates in other fields. According to the National Association of Colleges and Employers, engineering graduates with a bachelor's degree averaged about $38,500 a year in private industry in 1997. Starting salaries for petroleum engineers averaged $43,674. Civil engineers, in contrast, averaged $33,119.

Bachelor's degree candidates in accounting received starting offers averaging $29,400 a year in 1996; master's degree candidates in accounting, $33,000. In the federal government, the starting annual salary for junior accountants and auditors was about $19,500 in 1997. Candidates who had a superior academic record might start

▍ **TABLE 1.3**
Minimum Beginning Teacher Salaries, by State: 1996–97

State	Minimum (Beginning Salary)	State	Minimum (Beginning Salary)	State	Minimum (Beginning Salary)
United States	$25,012	Kentucky	23,018	North Dakota	18,889
Alabama	26,717	Louisiana	21,087	Ohio	22,146
Alaska	32,502	Maine	21,108	Oklahoma	23,847
Arizona	24,286	Maryland	26,548	Oregon	25,373
Arkansas	20,680	Massachusetts	26,445	Pennsylvania	29,426
California	26,684	Michigan	26,404	Rhode Island	25,497
Colorado	23,068	Minnesota	25,600	South Carolina	22,681
Connecticut	29,154	Mississippi	20,264	South Dakota	19,820
Delaware	24,349	Missouri	23,205	Tennessee	21,705
District of Columbia	25,937	Montana	20,592	Texas	24,079
Florida	24,736	Nebraska	21,189	Utah	21,475
Georgia	25,434	Nevada	28,538	Vermont	24,934
Hawaii	25,965	New Hampshire	23,690	Virginia	24,774
Idaho	19,715	New Jersey	28,039	Washington	23,933
Illinois	27,210	New Mexico	22,840	West Virginia	22,278
Indiana	24,172	New York	28,749	Wisconsin	24,830
Iowa	21,884	North Carolina	21,136	Wyoming	22,010
Kansas	21,909				

Source: Digest of Education Statistics, 1998 (p. 87) by U.S. Department of Education, National Center for Education Statistics (1999). Washington, DC: U.S. Government Printing Office.

at $24,200, and applicants with a master's degree or two years of professional experience might begin at $29,600. Beginning salaries were slightly higher in selected areas where the prevailing local pay level was higher.

Other occupations that require specialized knowledge and skills offer useful points of comparison for teachers, in part because their members must demonstrate some of the same skills as teachers. The Newspaper Guild negotiates with individual newspapers on minimum salaries for both starting reporters and those still on the job after three to six years. The median minimum salary for these reporters was about $22,400 in December 1, 1996. Salaries ranged from $17,100 to $34,900. Newspapers outside the Guild often have starting salaries lower than $17,100. In 1996, beginning salaries for editorial assistants averaged $21,000 annually. Those who had at least five years experience averaged more than $30,000. Senior editors at the largest newspapers earned over $67,000 a year—it takes a long time to become a senior editor.

Sometime, somewhere over Omaha at 30,000 feet, a teacher with a spirit of adventure has contemplated life as a pilot. According to the Future Aviation Professionals of America (FAPA), the 1996 average starting salary for airline pilots ranged from about $15,000 at the smaller turboprop airlines to $26,290 at the larger major airlines. Earnings depend on factors such as the type, size, and maximum speed of the plane and the number of hours and miles flown. Generally, pilots working outside the airlines earn lower salaries.

Given the increasing development of technical skills among the teaching ranks, the job of graphic designer also invites comparison. The Society of Publication Designers estimates that entry-level graphic designers earned between $23,000 and $27,000 annually in 1997. Median earnings for salaried visual artists who usually work full time were about $27,100 a year in 1996. The middle 50 percent earned between $20,000 and $36,400 a year. The top 10 percent earned more than $43,000, and the bottom 10 percent earned less than $15,000. Earnings for self-employed visual artists vary widely. Those struggling to gain experience and a reputation may be forced to charge close to the minimum wage for their work. Well-established freelancers and fine artists may earn much more than salaried artists. Unlike other workers, self-employed artists must provide their own benefits.

▶ What Are the Challenges of Professional Practice?

The most significant challenge of the professional practice of teaching can be stated in one simple command: Stay awake! There are so many developments in education that devoting less than complete attention to challenges and opportunities in the field means risking one's professional edge. As a wise old coach used to say to his eager but inexperienced players, "You have to play the ball . . . or the ball will play you."

Classrooms are busy places, and teachers can be consumed easily by everyday problems and issues. Those most successful resist being hypnotized by the details; they can step back from situations and think and behave in a variety of ways. Good teachers stay informed and interact with colleagues, parents, and administrators to maximize students' opportunities to learn. The action of teaching is simply too fast, the challenges too plentiful and varied, to permit anything less than complete intellectual commitment to the field.

Professionals possess knowledge that nonprofessionals do not possess. Professionals apply their knowledge to increase a venture's likelihood for success. As a general rule, people do not get paid, or at least not much and not often, to perform tasks that are meaningless. In education, there is no shortage of important tasks to be accomplished. A sample from *Education Week* (March 17, 1999) of one week's excerpts from newspapers across the nation describes or implies some of the challenges confronting teachers:

What educational challenges hit the news in your community?

▌ From the *New York Times:* Programs that seek to reduce violence, drug abuse, pregnancy and other dangerous or unhealthy activities among adolescents are notorious for doing too little too late and at too great a cost. But a new study has shown that by starting early—in grades one through six—to foster an interest in school and learning among children and to enhance their self-esteem, many of these risky behaviors can be averted and school performance and attendance can be improved through high school.

▌ From the *Los Angeles Times:* About a dozen Sunny Hills High School honors students have been disciplined for using e-mail to share information on a history final—a vivid example of how computer technology is making it easier to cheat in school.

- From the *Miami Herald:* State education officials are calling to the mat Florida high schools that are not meeting federal and state requirements that girls have the same opportunities in sports as boys. Letters are being sent to the superintendents of 12 school districts whose schools are making the least progress toward complying with gender equity laws.

- From the *Boston Globe:* Governor Paul Cellucci proposed legislation yesterday that would require all Massachusetts schools to have uniforms unless their local parent councils opted out. This would effectively force each school to at least debate the uniform issue.

- From the *Detroit Free Press:* Outrage is growing among school districts throughout Michigan over state takeover of the Detroit school district—an issue they fear could set a dangerous precedent. What districts fear, educators say, is that a Detroit takeover may spur the state to target other elected boards.

- From the *Dallas Morning News:* The SAT could face more legal challenges if appeals courts uphold a Philadelphia judge's ruling that the test is unfair to black students, some legal scholars and educators say.

- From the *Los Angeles Times:* The state labor commissioner says a Bakersfield school district violated California law by transferring 15 students from the eighth-grade science class of a teacher who was perceived to be gay.

- From the *Minnesota St. Paul Pioneer Planet:* Some 6,000 Minnesota 11th-graders—nearly one of every 10—still haven't passed the state's required basic skills exams and are in danger of not graduating next year. Final school-by-school figures released Tuesday by the state education department show 6,155 11th-graders failed the basic skills reading exam, and 5,739 failed the math exam. Although the numbers are small—54,000 11th-graders have passed—the students who have failed likely will consume plenty of teacher time and energy in the coming months.

- From the *Lexington (Kentucky) Herald-Leader:* In May, Oldham County will start a revolutionary experiment: Pay some teachers for their knowledge and skills, instead of merely rewarding them for the years they've taught. The county is modeling its program after the National Board for Professional Teaching Standards.

As these excerpts suggest, there are many issues and opportunities on which to test one's professional mettle. The challenge is to decide where to begin. Once professionals know where to start, they can behave in ways that are likely to influence a situation in a positive manner. The actions that professionals take yield opportunities to reflect on their successes and failures. In doing so, they can learn from their experiences and increase the probability they will be successful in the future.

John Dewey said it well:

> Every vital activity of any depth and range inevitably meets obstacles in the course of its effort to realize itself—a fact that renders the search for artificial or external problems quite superfluous. The difficulties that present themselves within the development of an experience are, however, to be cherished by the

Issues in School Reform

Standards and School Reform

Standards derived from national and state goals are driving school reform, and teachers are on the bus. But do teachers really understand where they are going and how to get there? The results of a U.S. Department of Education survey indicate they do.

Percentage of public school teachers reporting the extent to which they understood the concept of new higher standards and the percentage reporting the extent to which they felt equipped to set or apply new higher standards: 1996

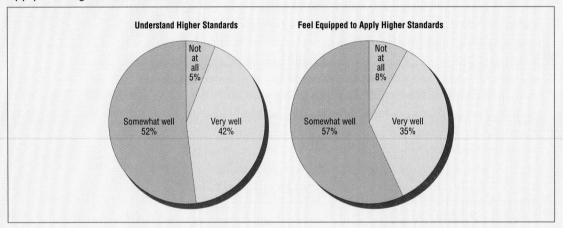

Note: Percentages may not add to 100 because of rounding.
Source: U.S. Department of Education, National Center for Education Statistics, *Fast Response Survey System,* "Public School Teacher Survey on Education Reform," FRSS 55, 1996. (Originally published as figure 1 on p. 4 of the complete report from which this article is excerpted.)

The survey also asked teachers to report the extent to which they were implementing seven specific activities associated with school reform. Teachers noted that they frequently incorporated the following two of these activities into their classes to a great extent: using instructional activities aligned with high standards and assisting all students to achieve high standards.

educator, not minimized, for they are the natural stimuli to reflective inquiry. (1910, pp. 64–65)

The issues we tend to learn most from are those we must grapple with in our own communities. They are closest to us both physically and emotionally. The fact that we often have a personal stake in local issues propels our involvement and stimulates our learning. But all our educational challenges are neither local nor unique. And if we relied only on our own circumstances to guide our education, we would be painfully provincial. In recent years, both educators and lay people have recognized

Percentage of public school teachers reporting the extent to which various reform activities were being implemented in their classes and areas for which information was most needed: 1996

Reform activity	Extent to which activity was implemented in class[1]		
	Great extent	Moderate extent	Information most needed[2]
Using instructional strategies aligned with high standards	56	35	34
Assisting all students to achieve to high standards	52	39	28
Using curricula aligned with high standards	38	45	31
Using textbooks or other instructional materials aligned with high standards	36	43	30
Providing students or parents with examples of work that meets high standards	30	42	33
Using authentic student assessments, such as portfolios, that measure performance against high standards	20	33	53
Using innovative technologies such as the Internet and telecommunications-supported instruction	7	20	79

[1]Percentages do not add to 100 because this table does not show the third response category (small extent) that was included on the questionnaire.

[2]Teachers could select up to three activities for information.

Source: U.S. Department of Education, National Center for Education Statistics, *Fast Response Survey System,* "Public School Teacher Survey on Education Reform," FRSS 55, 1996. (Originally published as table 2 on p. 6 of the complete report from which this article is excerpted.)

Discussion Questions: How well do you understand the concept of new higher educational standards? How equipped do you feel to apply these standards? How can you learn more about the current educational standards in the state in which you plan to teach?

Source: National Center for Education Statistics (1999, spring). *Education statistics quarterly: Elementary/secondary education* [On-line], *1*(1). Washington, D.C.: U.S. Department of Education. Available: http://nces.ed.gov/pubs99/quarterlyapr/4-elementary/4-esq11-g.html

the challenges we must face as a nation if our schools are to meet people's needs. Our country's national education goals embody these challenges most succinctly.

The idea of national goals was initially conceived at the 1989 education summit convened by President George Bush and all the nation's governors. At that session, six goals were designed as targets for the nation and the states to achieve by the year 2000. When President Bill Clinton signed the GOALS 2000: Educate America Act, two new education goals on teacher quality and parent involvement were added to the **National Education Goals** (Figure 1.3); grants were also established to help states set standards and create new student assessments. The National Education Goals and GOALS 2000 were endorsed by every major parent, education, and business group across the country. Although people realized that many of the goals would remain unmet by the year 2000, the goals themselves were credited with heightening citizens' concern for quality education and offering direction for educational change (Hoff, 1999). In 1999, members of the National Education Goals Panel recommended that the goals be renamed "America's Education Goals" and continue beyond the year 2000 (NEGP, 1999).

FIGURE 1.3
National Education Goals

 Goal 1: Ready to Learn All children in America will start school ready to learn.

 Goal 2: School Completion The high school graduation rate will increase to at least 90 percent.

 Goal 3: Student Achievement and Citizenship All students will leave grades 4, 8, and 12 having demonstrated competency over challenging subject matter including English, mathematics, science, foreign languages, civics and government, economics, the arts, history, and geography, and every school in America will ensure that all students learn to use their minds well, so they may be prepared for responsible citizenship, further learning, and productive employment in our Nation's modern economy.

 Goal 4: Teacher Education and Professional Development United States students will be first in the world in mathematics and science achievement.

 Goal 5: Mathematics and Science Every adult American will be literate and will possess the knowledge and skills necessary to compete in a global economy and exercise the rights and responsibilities of citizenship.

 Goal 6: Adult Literacy and Lifelong Learning Every school in the United States will be free of drugs, violence, and the unauthorized presence of firearms and alcohol and will offer a disciplined environment conducive to learning.

 Goal 7: Safe and Disciplined Alcohol- and Drug-free Schools The Nation's teaching force will have access to programs for the continued improvement of their professional skills and the opportunity to acquire the knowledge and skills needed to instruct and prepare all American students for the next century.

 Goal 8: Parental Participation Every school will promote partnerships that will increase parental involvement and participation in promoting the social, emotional, and academic growth of children.

Note: From National Education Goals Panel (1998). *National Education Goals: Building a Nation of Learners.* Available online: **http://negp.gov/webpg10.htm**

What Career Issues Must Beginning Teachers Face?

Teachers at the beginning of their careers face some issues that more experienced teachers do not encounter. These include becoming certified to teach, getting a first job, and successfully performing one's responsibilities.

▶ Teacher Certification

Requirements for teacher **certification,** also referred to as **licensure,** are established and monitored by each state. Certification is granted when teachers have met basic requirements and standards for becoming a practicing teacher. *Certification,* as the term is typically used in education, is not meant to convey the idea that a teacher is an expert or even exceptionally well qualified. Processes of certification are controlled by state governments to protect the public from harmful teaching practice backed by false claims of professional expertise.

Approved Programs.   Teaching certificates are typically granted in two ways: by transcript assessment and by completing an approved program. The transcript assessment process requires the candidate to submit his or her college transcript directly to the state education department. The department then compares the transcript to the state requirements and grants or denies the request for certification. The program approval approach requires completion of a teacher education program that has been approved or accredited by the state. **Accreditation,** then, involves processes of program review by outside experts and asserts that a program is worthy of preparing professionals. Approved programs submit transcripts of all graduates, and the state grants certification.

Reciprocity Agreements.   Certification requirements for teachers differ from state to state. When a college or university student graduates from an approved teacher education program, he or she receives certification to teach in the state where the program is located. But many states recognize one another's certification; that is, states have **reciprocity agreements** or pacts by which licensure in one state ensures eligibility for licensure in another state. Because states sometimes change their certification requirements, the list of states having reciprocity agreements can change. Even when one state does not recognize another's certification, however, the additional requirements to obtain a state's certification often can be fulfilled fairly easily by taking some additional college course work.

Alternative and Emergency Certifications.   Recently, several states have vigorously promoted the concept of alternative certification, or approval to teach without having participated in a traditional, state-approved teacher education program. New Jersey's alternative route into teaching, for example, allows people with college degrees, but no formal teacher preparation, to assume teaching positions and to take education courses as they teach. This alternative certification program provides supervisory assistance and formal instruction to people as they learn to teach on the

In what ways can teachers gain certification? Do you think each of these routes to achieving certification produces equally qualified teachers? Why or why not?

job (New Jersey Department of Education, 1999). About one-fifth of new teachers hired in the state enter the profession through this route (Feistritzer, 1997).

Some states, such as California, temporarily grant **emergency certification** until requirements are met. When school superintendents are unable to find a certified teacher to fill a position, they petition their state departments of education to hire an uncertified person on an emergency basis. This strategy buys time for the person to become certified or for the school district to find another teacher who possesses valid certification.

What are pros and cons of alternative certification?

Despite the appeal of alternative certification programs for the ease with which candidates can enter and exit, they have been roundly criticized for providing too little support to prospective teachers. Newly launched alternative certification programs include some that provide only a few weeks of training for entering teachers, skipping such fundamentals as learning theory, child development, and subject matter pedagogy. These programs place recruits in classrooms who have not had supervised clinical experience. More than 10 percent of individuals enter teaching on emergency and temporary certificates, without any preparation at all. Studies show that these teachers are less able to address students' needs and less effective in helping students learn (Darling-Hammond, 1995). In fact the evidence is clear that "more teacher education appears to be better than less—particularly when it includes well-constructed practical experiences interwoven with course work on curriculum, learning, and teaching" (Darling-Hammond & Berry, 1998, p. 48).

Internships for Uncertified Teachers.   The program Teach for America (TFA) provides college graduates who do not have teacher education backgrounds the opportunity to become teachers. Wendy S. Kopp's senior thesis at Princeton University stimulated the founding of this national teacher corps in 1989. Although early funding from foundations and corporations paid the salaries of TFA recruits, school systems employing these beginning teachers now assume financial responsibility, pegging wages to local rates (M. Albert, personal communication, May 20, 1999).

The Teach for America program began with 500 recruits from across the nation who were trained for eight weeks before assuming teaching responsibilities. TFA quickly grew to several thousand recruits with an annual budget of $8.3 million. Corporate and foundation sponsors liked the idea of putting bright young people into classrooms full of at-risk students and bypassing what they perceived as traditional and ineffectual teacher education programs. Others, however, have criticized TFA for putting ill-prepared teachers with students most in need of professionally strong teachers (Darling-Hammond, 1995). Because of increasing difficulty in attracting outside support, TFA reorganized itself in 1995 to seek support from local education agencies (Teacher Magazine, 1995). As of July 1998, TFA had taken 25,772 applications and placed 4,147 interns in schools (Teach For America, 1999).

Troops to Teachers.   In January 1994 the Department of Defense Troops to Teachers program was established. Authorized by Public Law 102-484, the program helps Department of Defense and Department of Energy civilian employees affected by military reductions to pursue new careers in public education. Other goals are to provide positive role models for young people in schools and to help relieve teacher shortages, especially in math and science (Department of Defense, 1999). The program is managed by the Defense Activity for Non-Traditional Education Support (DANTES), a Department of Defense agency located in Pensacola, Florida. A primary function of DANTES is to provide placement assistance, helping potential teacher candidates identify employment opportunities and teacher certification programs. State Support Offices have been established in twenty states to assist participants with both certification requirements and employment leads. Since the inception of the program, about 3,000 service members have made the transition from the military to classrooms across the nation (National Center for Education Information, 1998).

Since its inception, the Troops to Teachers program has been touted as a "rich source" of sought-after teachers. Recruits are much more likely than traditional teacher applicants to be male, members of minority groups, willing to work in hard-to-staff urban and rural schools, and qualified to teach mathematics, science, and special education (Bradley, 1998).

▶ Getting a First Job

Two interrelated factors influence the availability of teaching jobs: the number of properly qualified teachers available and the demand for these teachers. Both supply and demand, in turn, are subject to other societal influences. Factors that determine the demand for elementary and secondary teachers in any school year include enrollment changes, class size policies, budget considerations, changes in methods for classifying and educating special education students, and job turnover due to retirement or attrition. These factors influence decisions about hiring new teachers.

> **What will be the most important factor in your job search?**

Benchmarks

Teacher Education Reports and Reforms of the 1980s and 1990s

1985	A Call for Change in Teacher Education, National Commission for Excellence in Teacher Education of the American Association of Colleges for Teacher Education (AACTE)
1986	Tomorrow's Teachers, the Holmes Group
1986	A Nation Prepared: Teachers for the 21st Century, Task Force on Teaching as a Profession, the Carnegie Forum on Education and the Economy
1986	Time for Results: The Governors' Report on Education, the National Governors' Association (NGA)
1986	Visions of Reform: Implications for the Education Profession, the Association of Teacher Educators (ATE)
1987	National Board for Professional Teaching Standards (NBPTS) established
1989	National Education Goals issued from the White House after first Education Summit in Charlottesville, Virginia
1989	National Goals of Education issued from the White House
1994	Department of Defense Troops to Teachers established
1996	President Clinton, 40 governors, and chief executive officers of major corporations meet for second Education Summit in Palisades, New York
1999	National Education Goals Panel vote unanimously to rename the National Education Goals as America's Education Goals

Factors that determine the supply of teachers include salaries, educational and licensure requirements, interest in specific disciplines and geographical areas, the cost of living in some states, and other quality-of-life issues. The demand for teachers has gradually increased during the 1990s and is predicted to continue rising through 2008, primarily due to increases in school enrollment (U.S. Department of Education, 1998b).

Teacher Shortages. The nation's large cities experience teacher shortages more acutely than other parts of the nation. Why? Inner-city schools present special challenges, the working conditions often are difficult, and teaching opportunities in other settings often pull teachers away from cities. For example, 56.6 percent of public school administrators in Washington, D.C., reported difficulty finding qualified applicants (Choy, Bobbitt, Henke, Medrich, Horn, & Lieberman, 1993). The South and West also have unmet needs for teachers. Population growth in these sections of the United States is expected to increase steadily the national demand for teachers through 2008 (U.S. Department of Education, 1998b).

The need to provide bilingual education and special education services can also influence the demand for teachers. This demand varies, sometimes markedly, by state and locality. Demand for special education teachers is affected by the number of students with disabilities entering and leaving school systems and by changes in the criteria used to define specific disabilities. Demand for teachers is so great in some areas and in some specialties that school districts have offered cash bonuses, higher salary schedules, and other types of pay increases to attract and keep new teachers. Districts that offer these incentives want to attract teachers to less desirable geographical locations and into subject areas that have experienced shortages. About 15 percent of the nation's teachers work in private schools, including parochial (sectarian) schools affiliated with religious groups and independent (nonsectarian) schools (U.S. Department of Education, 1998b). Catholic schools employ more teachers than any other type of private school because the Catholic system is larger than any other private system.

Although states do not require teachers in private schools to meet the same level of certification as public school teachers, most private school teachers are fully certified. Operating without tax support, private schools are free from many state regulations governing curriculum and teaching. At the same time, because private schools are supported by private funds, average teaching salaries are far below teaching salaries in public schools. The average base salary for a teacher with a bachelor's degree in a private school is $21,968 (U.S. Department of Education, 1998b).

Some people with education degrees take jobs outside the school system. Indeed, people in many fields have been teachers at one time or another in their lives. Employers in business and industry and government agencies hire people with education degrees for various jobs. Strong educational programs that combine liberal arts and professional studies prepare people for a variety of technical and human service positions.

Projected Student Enrollments and School Budgets.   Enrollment trends vary for elementary and secondary schools, and they influence availability of jobs. In elementary schools, student numbers have been increasing steadily since the mid 1980s as a result of the "echo effect," as the offspring of the baby-boom generation began entering school. Projections suggest that enrollment in kindergarten through eighth grade will continue to increase up to the year 2008. In secondary schools, student numbers began declining in 1976, reaching a low of 12.4 million in 1990. Since that time, enrollment has steadily increased as the baby boomers' children grow older. Forecasters project enrollment in secondary schools to increase to 14.7 million by the year 2008 (U.S. Department of Education, 1998b). Between 1990 and 2008, enrollment patterns will look different across regions, states, and communities. As previously mentioned, the greatest increases in public school enrollment will show up in the South and West, but enrollments will decrease in the Northeast and Midwest (U.S. Department of Education, 1998b).

The federal government reports that by 2002 the student–teacher ratio in the nation's schools will be approximately 18 to 1 at the elementary level and 15 to 1 at the secondary level. These figures are lower than actual class size, however, because they are calculated by counting all the adults in schools, including many specialists who do not meet regularly with full classes. In 1993, for example, when the student–teacher ratio was a little over 17 to 1, average class size was 24 (U.S. Department of Education, 1996).

School budgets determine the school's capacity for hiring personnel. Personnel costs compose the largest category of expenditures in education budgets. Philosophy and mission drive budgets, but when times are financially lean, boards of education and school administrators often fall back on pocketbook considerations; that is, they choose to eliminate positions, most often through attrition. Teacher attrition is the largest single factor influencing the demand for additional teachers in the nation's schools. Studies over the years indicate that about 6 percent of full-time public school teachers and 10 percent of private school teachers leave teaching each year (U.S. Department of Education, 1998). Sometimes teachers are laid off. The term **reduction in force,** or RIF for short, became familiar to public school employees during the 1980s.

▶ Successfully Performing Responsibilities

What is your impression of tenure?

Teachers at the beginning of their careers work with probationary status. If they perform to standard, they may be granted **tenure** (continuing contract). In some school systems, tenure occurs automatically at the end of the probationary period; in other school systems, the school board determines whether tenure should be granted. Tenured teachers can only be released when it can be demonstrated that there is just cause; in most states, nontenured teachers can be released without cause. Thus tenure affords a teacher a measure of freedom to exercise his or her options without fear of being fired.

How Are Teachers Evaluated?

Teachers are evaluated mainly to help them grow professionally and to determine whether they meet minimum levels of competence (Duke & Stiggins, 1990). The first type of evaluation, called **formative assessment,** is done to shape, form, and improve teachers' knowledge and behavior. Formative assessment is not concerned with making judgments about salary status or tenure; instead, it is a helping process that provides data to teachers for making decisions about how they can improve their teaching techniques.

Evaluators concerned with formative assessment often concentrate on teachers' in-class performance by collecting data on teacher–student interactions during instruction and by helping teachers perceive what is happening during instruction. Formative assessment is based on the philosophical beliefs that (1) professional teachers constantly strive for continued individual excellence; (2) given sufficient information, professional teachers can and will evaluate themselves and modify their performance as well as or better than others; and (3) the evaluation procedures provide feedback designed to assist teachers in making judgments about how they can best improve their teaching (Barber, 1990, p. 217).

For instance, the California Formative Assessment & Support System for Teachers (CFASST) encourages beginning teachers to investigate their strengths and needs in a collaborative environment. Novices work with veteran teachers and with their peers to reflect on their own teaching as it relates to student achievement. They critique their lesson planning and in-class performance, and then they reflect in writing on their lessons (Olebe, Jackson, & Danielson, 1999).

▶ Accrediting and Approving Professional Programs

Evaluating teachers' competence and teaching outcomes are examples of **summative assessments,** in which data are collected and interpreted at the end of a specified period of time. Results are used to make decisions about teachers on matters such as hiring, compensation, status, tenure, and termination.

▶ Competency Testing

All states require some form of competency testing for preservice teachers. These tests provide perspectives on the effects of teacher education beyond that provided by teacher education programs. If prospective teachers do well on competency tests, teacher education programs can claim some of the credit for identifying and developing teaching talent. Likewise, when prospective teachers perform poorly on these tests, programs must take some of the blame. Makers of competency tests claim only that their tests reveal those who are minimally qualified to teach. The tests reveal nothing about one's capacity to be an outstanding teacher.

Control of teacher education through teacher competency tests is subtle but powerful. As preservice teachers exit their professional programs, they must demonstrate the knowledge, skills, and attitudes that such tests purport to measure. Teacher education programs will continue to experience pressure to make sure that beginning teachers excel on these tests. It can be said that the tests influence the curriculum of teacher education. States no longer rely strictly on schools, colleges, and departments of education to provide evidence of program quality. Competency tests provide alternative measures.

▶ Performance Evaluations and Portfolios

True performance evaluations begin in **student teaching.** Student teaching, that is, planning, organizing, and providing instruction to students full time over a period of weeks, typically occurs at or near the end of a preservice teacher's program. To prepare preservice teachers for student teaching, most programs require students to engage in a variety of field experiences. The types of assignments vary, but they are generally structured to help preservice teachers become familiar with various contexts in which teaching and learning occur.

Preservice teachers may be asked to maintain a journal in which they record

Voices

On Being a Student Teacher

In a letter to a student teacher, Margaret Metzger, a teacher at Massachusett's Brookline High School for 25 years, explains that teachers have to take care of themselves:

Dear Christine,
As you have begun to notice, some problems repeat themselves endlessly. This is probably true in all fields of work. As Annie Dillard observed about a bumbling church service, "You would think after 2,000 years, we could work the kinks out." We've been doing schools for centuries, and we still haven't worked out the kinks.

As soon as you see a repeating problem, think of a policy that is fair both to you and to the student. Just to help you along, here are a few inevitable problems: absenteeism, late papers, careless proofreading, missing homework, cheating, record-keeping. What happens when one group finishes group work before the others? How can you maintain discipline while you hold individual conferences?

You will exhaust yourself if you try to think of a solution to each problem individually. Your first year of teaching will be such a whirlwind that you won't be able to step aside and calmly write policy statements. You will barely survive. But notice what bothers you most or what is most easily solved, and write the policies covering those problems over the summer. Knock off the problems one at a time. Don't spend a lifetime complaining about the same issues. . . .

Insist on your own rights in the classroom. What do you need in order to maintain your own life and sanity? Although I hate dealing with late papers, my students may turn in one paper per quarter that is two school days late. I don't even want to hear the excuse, unless it is hysterically funny. My students receive no penalty for the first late paper. However, in exchange for the extra time that they get for the writing, I must get extra time as well. Otherwise, I will resent late papers. Thus I do not write a comment on any late paper, I merely give the paper a holistic letter grade. Late students get extra time, and so do I.

information about students' needs and abilities (for example, reading levels, mathematics proficiencies, and personal interests), classroom rules and routines, and the flow of instructional activities. Preservice teachers may also be expected to conduct one-on-one tutoring sessions or to assist the teacher with classroom activities. Classroom teachers and college instructors working together usually supervise student teachers.

How much work with children will you have done by graduation?

As preservice teachers separate from their previous roles as students and begin their careers as professional educators during student teaching, they gradually assume more classroom responsibilities. They grade papers, teach parts of lessons designed by the classroom teacher (sometimes referred to as the supervising or cooperating teacher), plan for and engage in whole-class instruction for one or two class periods, and eventually assume responsibility for the whole day's instruction. Because of the demands of student teaching, preservice teachers seldom enroll in academic courses during their field placements. Many teacher education programs, however, require student teachers to attend weekly seminars held on the college or university campus or in classrooms of student teachers. The seminars offer preservice teachers opportunities to discuss problems and issues of teaching and to share ideas about effective teaching strategies.

Here are four final bits of advice. I've failed at all of them for years—except the last one, which has kept me sane. When I follow my own advice, my teaching life feels happier.

1. Sign up for season tickets to cultural events; otherwise you'll think you are too tired to attend anything. Schedule regular social events with friends, even if it's only lunch in the cafeteria every week with your two favorite colleagues in the school.

2. Hunt for a place to work. Some schools spill over with technology, while others have no telephones or copying machines for teachers. Many schools don't provide desk space for teachers. Beg for some space in the school for yourself, even if it's an old closet. Try to get your own classroom. Moving all your belongings every 50 minutes will make you crazy. Imagine any office worker changing desks every hour!

3. Try to stay out of petty politics. There is more squabbling in schools than you can imagine. . . .

4. Find a friend with a sense of humor . . . who can laugh with you [about daily events]. . . . [Y]ou

cannot be a good teacher unless you are reading books, going to the movies, spending time alone, and maintaining a life. In order to give to others, you must take care of yourself. Teachers who generously support other people's growth also need to nurture themselves. Take care of yourself.

Love,

Margaret

CRITICAL THINKING

Metzger seems to argue that there are healthy and unhealthy ways for teachers to address problems and sources of stress. How might you recognize the differences between the two? Can you think of ways you might involve students in finding solutions to daily problems? What might be the upside and the downside of doing so? Do you agree with Metzger's advice? What other strategies might you add for your own situation?

Note: From "Maintaining a Life" by M. Metzger, 1996, *Phi Delta Kappan*, 77 (5), pp. 346–351.

Performance evaluations increasingly use observations and evidence that provide **authentic assessments** of teachers' knowledge and skills, or assessments directed toward producing information about teachers' abilities to perform their jobs in context. Authentic or realistic assessments are meant to augment or replace standardized assessments, such as examinations of subject matter and professional knowledge. Analysis of teaching performance on videotapes is an example of authentic assessment.

A **teacher portfolio,** a collection of artifacts that communicates a teacher's abilities to perform his or her job, is another example of an authentic assessment approach. A portfolio might contain tests and homework assignments the teacher gives students, samples of students' work, lesson plans, a videotape of a lesson, and so forth (Campbell, Cignetti, Melenyzer, Nettles, & Wyman, 1997). Teachers' portfolios provide opportunities for teachers to have input into their evaluations. They also provide excellent ways for a teacher to demonstrate his or her abilities to understand the links between educational theory and practice (Meyer & Tusin, 1999). Portfolios, however, are difficult to use in comparing teachers with one another.

According to reports by a national sample of public school teachers of kindergarten through grade 6, the practice of evaluating teachers is well established in the

Using Technology

Stephanie's Electronic Portfolio

Computers, CD-ROMs, facsimile machines, telephones, modems, calculators, overhead projectors, and video technologies such as televisions, video recorders, video disc players, and camcorders are just a few of electronic technologies available in schools. While the most common technologies are video and TV, more and more schools are increasing the availability of computer-based technologies in classrooms. With these changes, today's educators are expected to be knowledgeable about ways that technology might be used to enhance student learning. One way prospective teachers demonstrate their competence in this area is by creating electronic teaching portfolios.

Stephanie Britt, a fifth-year student in the University of Virginia's Curry School of Education, developed an online portfolio that includes her educational philosophy, a résumé, and a variety of instructional materials: goals, objectives, and lesson plans for a 13-day unit; criteria for judging the quality of students' work during the unit; and web-based resources. Britt also included a Hyperstudio project she developed for use with elementary-age students. You can find Stephanie Britt's portfolio on the web by visiting the Curry School of Education on the University of Virginia's web site.

A page from Stephanie Britt's electronic portfolio.

nation's schools. Evaluation of performance occurs for both formative and summative purposes. Evaluation criteria are known by most teachers prior to the process of performance evaluation, and most teachers are evaluated by their school principal, chiefly through formal and informal classroom observation. A large majority of teachers receive both written and verbal feedback following their evaluation, and most can submit a written response or file an appeal at their school (U.S. Department of Education, 1994, p. 14).

▶ National Teacher Examinations

More than 30 states require a national teacher examination as a test of teacher competency before granting initial certification. Although most states do not require people to reach minimum scores for certification, Delaware, Kentucky, New Mexico, Maryland, Montana, Oregon, Tennessee, Rhode Island, and West Virginia do require some minimum level of performance on a nationally marketed test for initial licensure (Tryneski, 1998).

The **Praxis Series,** a battery of tests developed and sold by the Educational Testing Service (ETS), purports to assesses skills and knowledge at each stage of a beginning teacher's career, from entry into teacher education to actual classroom performance. It measures teachers' basic skills in reading, writing, and mathematics, as well as professional education and subject matter knowledge. Teaching skills assessed include planning instruction, teaching, classroom management, and assessment of student learning. (Visit the ETS web site.)

How Are Teachers Supported and Rewarded?

All professionals must demonstrate minimum levels of competence to become certified to practice. But many drive themselves far beyond minimal expectations to excel in their fields. Teachers are no different. Many take advantage of every possible opportunity to acquire and demonstrate increasing levels of skill and knowledge. Mentor programs, career ladders, merit pay, national certification, and advanced college degrees may offer opportunities.

▶ Mentoring Programs

Some 30 states have required mentoring or **induction programs** of one form or another for new teachers up to the first 3 years on the job (Feiman-Nemser, 1996). These programs support experienced teachers, or "mentors" or "coaches," to work with beginning teachers to help them adjust successfully to full-time teaching. Mentoring programs typically call for high levels of collaboration between beginners and experienced teachers. Participants often share a vision of what constitutes good teaching and a commitment to inquiry. Policymakers argue for such programs because of the fairly high rate of attrition during the first 3 years of teaching and as a way of ameliorating some of the problems faced by beginning teachers (Little, 1990).

The practice of mentoring varies considerably from place to place. Some mentors promote conventional norms and practices, thus limiting reform (Feiman-Nemser, Parker, & Zeichner, 1993). Some foster creative, reform-minded practice. The privacy of teaching, the relatively few opportunities to observe and discuss each other's practice, and the ethic of treating all teachers as equals constrains what mentors can do, even when working with beginners (Little, 1990).

Some mentoring programs try to avoid misunderstanding and ensure effective operation by clearly specifying program operations. For instance, the Beginning Teacher Coaching Program of the Mt. Diablo School District (CA) and the Mt. Diablo Education Association spell out the responsibilities of the parties involved, that is, how and by whom full-time coaches are selected; how they are evaluated, rehired, and compensated; the eligibility of new teachers to participate in the program; how schedules of work are to be developed; and the like (National Education Association, 1999).

How can master teachers best be rewarded for their accomplishments? Why have some efforts, like career ladders and merit pay, been less successful than others?

▶ Career Ladders and Merit Pay

Career ladder programs are examples of incentive programs for teachers, offering advancement of status, increased responsibility, and extra pay for exemplary teaching practice. Supporters of career ladder programs assert that "the secret to improvement lies in bringing a change of focus into what one is doing" by motivating teachers to scrutinize their teaching, by encouraging them to think about alternative ways of teaching, and by focusing on what students are learning (Brandt, 1990, p. 222). Career ladders typically acknowledge differences in teachers' levels of accomplishment, as, for example, between beginners and master teachers. These programs come and go with the availability of funds to support them. In the 1980s, many career ladders failed largely because they were poorly designed; that is, they were not linked to the organizational needs of effective schools (Kelley & Odden, 1995).

What do you think about merit pay?

Like career ladders, **merit pay** promises to encourage teachers to strive for excellence by rewarding outstanding performance. The idea of merit pay for teachers began in the 1920s. Merit pay plans augment the lock-step progression of salary increases that characterize typical salary schedules by awarding either bonuses (one-time cash awards) or raises (financial increases added to teachers' base salaries). People have tried and usually abandoned various plans for awarding merit through the years.

Merit pay plans fail most often for three reasons. First, processes of identifying meritorious teachers are difficult to design and implement. Second, until recently, teacher unions typically oppose merit plans, because paying some teachers more might mean paying other teachers less. Third, particularly in difficult financial times, other school leaders, parents, and citizens often make other demands on funds that might go to merit pay plans. School systems often reward excellence informally through investment in professional development. Public recognition of teaching excellence is provided through state and national teacher-of-the-year programs, private organizations, grant foundations, and the mass media.

▶ National Certification

Teachers who possess a baccalaureate degree from an accredited institution and who have completed 3 years of successful teaching while holding a valid state teaching license may seek advanced certification through the **National Board for Professional Teaching Standards** (NBPTS). Created in 1987, the NBPTS is an independent, nonprofit, nonpartisan organization governed by a 63-member board of directors, most of whom are teachers. Other board members include school administrators, school board leaders, and business and community leaders.

Candidates seeking Board certification or **national certification** are evaluated on their knowledge of subjects, understanding of students and teaching, and actual classroom practice. In this instance, the term *certification* is meant to denote outstanding performance. To demonstrate their expertise, candidates complete a portfolio and then participate in a set of assessment exercises designed to assess their knowledge of teaching and learning. The portfolio includes documentation of work inside and outside the classroom. For example, candidates must provide videotapes of their interactions with students during instruction and samples of student work, as well as analyses of the videos and student products. Candidates must also describe their efforts to stretch beyond the classroom to involve parents and the larger community in the education of children. Teachers who successfully complete board requirements earn national certification. By 1999 a total of 1,835 teachers had achieved this goal (personal communication, L. Leyva, May 25, 1999).

In some localities, schools and districts assist teachers attempting to earn National Board Certification by organizing seminars, offering professional development days to allow teachers to prepare portfolio entries, providing technical support in the form of computers and video cameras, and organizing study and support groups. In some areas of the country, schools and districts also pay all or part of the $2000 assessment fee. If teachers achieve National Board Certification, their certificates are good for 10 years. Depending on state and local policy, certified teachers can receive salary increases, license renewal exemptions, and public recognition.

During the 1998–1999 academic year, Oklahoma was one of the most generous states, offering to pay full assessment fees for 100 teachers; to provide extensive support, including a $500 stipend during each teacher's candidate year; and to reward successful candidates with financial bonuses of $5,000 for each year that the National Board Certification is valid. Wyoming offered to support 20 candidates at 25 percent of the certification fee, noting that if only 10 to 19 teachers applied the subsidies would increase to 50 percent of the fee. The legislature established that certification fees would be reimbursed for up to 50 teachers achieving National Board Certification. Depending on the school district in which Wyoming teachers worked, successful candidates might be offered a $2,000 salary supplement or an annual $3,000 honorarium, or they might advance one step on the salary scale (National Board for Professional Teaching Standards, 1999).

▶ Advanced College Degrees

Many teachers acquire additional schooling and advanced degrees. When they do so, teachers enhance their salaries and may assume new responsibilities in the hierarchy of school systems. During the 1993–1994 school year, 42 percent of teachers held master's degrees, about 5 percent had education specialist degrees, and 0.7 percent had doctorates (U.S. Department of Education, 1998c).

 ## How Do Teachers Demonstrate Professional Leadership?

By definition, to be a teacher is to be a leader. Teachers demonstrate professional leadership in the normal course of their job by working with others and by modeling desirable behavior. They also often stretch beyond their own immediate circumstances to shape the behavior of a larger, more inclusive public. Teachers lead students, assistants, aides, parent volunteers, and many others who have a stake in schools. Teachers chair school and community committees organized to solve problems and capitalize on opportunities. Teachers create curricula. They lead workshops for their colleagues and other members of their communities. Teachers study for advanced degrees. They blaze new technological paths in education. They run professional associations. And much more. Sometimes teachers—Dennis Hastert, Speaker of the U.S. House of Representatives, for example—even wind up leading Congress.

▶ Working with Professional Organizations

How will you continue your professional development after you graduate?

As with other professionals, teachers' identities are shaped in part by the associations to which they belong and by the people and organizations that publicly represent them. Professional organizations and associations serve to educate members, provide a forum for discourse, lobby Congress and state legislatures on education issues, and offer a range of professional services.

Cultural Awareness

JoAnn Haysbert

JoAnn Haysbert, professor and provost, Hampton University, began her education career as an educational planner for the Macon County Public Schools in Tuskegee, Alabama:

As a planner, my job was to develop new programs and to seek funding to implement curriculum changes. At the time, I did not intend to stay in education; my undergraduate degree was in psychology, and I wanted to be a clinical psychologist. While working with the Tuskegee Schools, however, I learned quickly that if I stayed in the field of education I had the potential for making a difference in young people's lives. So you could say I entered education through the back door. Once there, however, I was hooked.

Haysbert earned a master's degree, served as the coordinator of research and program development in Alabama Schools, completed her doctorate, taught at a junior college, then began her career in higher education at Virginia State University as an assistant professor in educational leadership. She then went to Hampton University, where she served as the assistant vice-president of academic affairs for 10 years before going back into the classroom in 1990:

I picked up my teaching gavel and learned about new approaches in education, including case-based teaching, which I incorporated into my foundations of education classes. One year I organized a team of teacher-education students to participate in a national case competition, and our team won! I continued teaching with cases for the 7 years I taught classes. Now I am the provost at Hampton University. I like what I do, and I always have. What keeps me in education? The challenge to make changes, make a difference. Commitment is something I don't find readily in others. You've got to have commitment; you've got to believe you can make a difference in the lives you touch—students and colleagues. I know I can make a difference, my enthusiasm is deep-rooted. (personal communication, July 26,

Teachers, counselors, administrators, and others in education often belong to professional associations closely allied with their particular disciplines. These associations offer a variety of services: journals, conferences, and action committees designed to provide opportunities for interacting with others who have similar interests and to promote continuing professional development. The largest, most visible, and most powerful teachers' organizations are the National Education Association (NEA) and the American Federation of Teachers (AFT). Like labor unions, teacher unions protect members' rights to **collective bargaining** (negotiation of the professional rights and responsibilities of teachers as a group) in contract disputes and other job-related matters.

Teacher unions are controversial and are frequently criticized by outsiders for shielding their members from scrutiny and for maintaining the status quo. They are also praised, however, for exercising considerable power for the improvement of public education. Both the NEA and the AFT have helped shape conditions of schooling that promote child welfare. Both have fought for and won increases in teachers' salaries and improvements in working conditions. Both have heightened public awareness about the importance of involving teachers in decision-making processes and of cultivating concepts of teachers as professionals.

The National Education Association was founded in 1857 to advance the professionalism of teaching. It now boasts 2.3 million members, including teachers, school administrators, college and university faculty and students, guidance counselors, and librarians, as well as school secretaries, bus drivers, and custodians. Negotiating teacher salaries, reporting educational research, and supporting teachers' professional development are among the many services that the NEA provides. The NEA is one of the most effective lobbying organizations in the nation, stating views of educational matters to legislators in Washington, D.C., in state capitols, and in communities across the country.

In 1916 the American Federation of Teachers was founded from a merger of 20 small teacher unions that had begun to form after the turn of the century. More so than the NEA, the AFT has been closely allied with industrial labor unions and affiliated with the AFL–CIO (American Federation of Labor–Congress of Industrial Organizations). Like the AFL–CIO, in contract disputes the AFT has sometimes advocated withholding professional services through job actions—work slowdowns, sick-outs, and strikes. Today the AFT has more than 800,000 members, mostly in urban areas.

Although the AFT and NEA have a long history of competition for members and a record of disagreement on various issues, they have grown philosophically more compatible in recent years. NEA leaders have increasingly advocated political action on job issues, and AFT leaders have spoken out on issues of professional competence. Try as they might, the two unions have been unable to merge into one organization.

▶ Modeling Desirable Behavior

For the Council for Learned Societies in Education (1998), the capacity of teachers to behave professionally is defined as being able to interpret concepts and theories, to judge education in a normative context, and to think critically. Teachers' foundational knowledge helps them continue to develop these professional abilities.

In many observable ways, teachers use what they know day in and day out to learn from their work. They perceive and make explicit instructional issues present in educational life surrounding them—in the actions and interactions of students, the demands of curriculum, and the influence of colleagues and the many other concerns that affect the ebb and flow of classroom activity. Teachers must be able to perceive instructional issues, problems, and opportunities as they arise if they hope to maximize their chances for behaving in ways that make a difference in their students' lives. Teachers' attentiveness to people and to situations, then, is prerequisite to all other professional behavior.

Professional teachers value their own and others' points of view. What might be a compelling instructional problem to one teacher may be of little or no importance to another. When teachers pause to consider a student's, parent's, or colleague's perspective, they may find that their own concerns are not well formulated and that valuing the issues that the other individual deems important might be wise. When teachers take into account their own and others' values, the definition of what constitutes a problem or an opportunity can change.

Teachers call up the professional knowledge they possess to guide their actions. As professionals, teachers have specialized knowledge and skills acquired from long, intensive academic preparation and from practical experience in classrooms. Knowledge from theory, research, and practice informs teachers' decisions. Figure 1.4 suggests the complexity of the professional knowledge base on which teachers draw when they make decisions about teaching.

Teachers use what they know to take action. They apply their knowledge and skills imaginatively and deliberately as needed. If called upon to do so, they can articulate why they behave as they do. Teachers base their actions on knowledge of theory, research, and practice.

Teachers evaluate the consequences of their actions. Professional teachers equip themselves intellectually and emotionally to reflect on their experiences and thus to learn from what they do. Professional teachers develop their experience over time—a hallmark of professionals in all fields. This final step of evaluation leads back to the beginning of the reflective practice; that is, what teachers learn by thinking critically about their work enhances their ability to perceive issues and opportunities as they arise in the future. Taken together, then, the five steps of reflective teaching—perceiving, valuing, knowing, acting, and evaluating—form the foundation of professional practice.

One caveat bears noting. Professionals naturally tend to focus only or primarily on the problems of teaching and learning and to ignore what works well. This tendency is deeply ingrained in our professional cultures and for good reason: There is no shortage of problems to be solved, diseases to be cured, wrongs to be righted, good fights to be fought. The subtle danger in this way of thinking for teachers, however, is that the difficulties may seem to swamp the positive side of their work.

In contrast, Ruark (1999) draws attention to a fledgling but potentially important movement in the social sciences to look for success and for good organizational and personal behavior to guide professional thinking. This movement rejects professional practice of all kinds that focuses only on a "disease model" or on the kinds of personal and organizational behaviors that are ineffective. Instead, the emphasis is on moving away "from fixing what's wrong with people to developing what's right."

The connection to teachers and teaching seems clear. As teachers engage in the five steps given in Figure 1.4, they should take special care to look not only for "problems," but also for the kinds of experiences that fulfill people. They can ask themselves what human qualities and environmental factors enable students to flourish. When they do, teachers can begin to take the kinds of actions and to build the environments that support these experiences and qualities. As Ruark notes, professionals who engage in such thinking and behavior will essentially be asking a question that has intrigued philosophers for centuries: What is the good life? Not until teachers can imagine that life can they create it.

To every thing there is a season, "a time to laugh; a time to dance." Will you recognize the season in teaching?

FIGURE 1.4
Reflective Teaching Process   It is important for teachers to be able to reflect on their work so they can develop their professional knowledge and skills over time. Why is it also important for teachers to be able to explain their methods and the reasons underlying their behaviors?

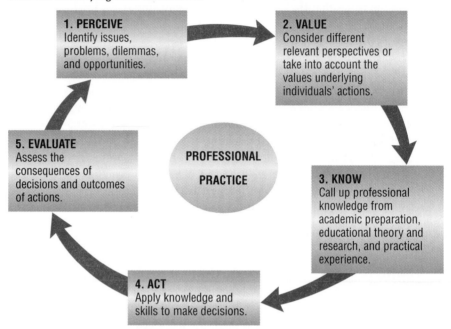

Note. From "Cooperation and competition in case-based teacher education," by R. F. McNergney, J. M. Herbert, & R. E. Ford, 1994, *Journal of Teacher Education*, 45(5), pp. 339–345. Adapted by permission.

SUMMARY

What Makes Teaching a Profession?

1. The range of demands placed on educators, the numbers of people involved in the enterprise, and the public's common knowledge of life in classrooms combine to make teaching what might be called the *people's profession*.

2. Teachers are professionals in part because they participate in their work for financial gain or for their livelihood. Professionals get paid for what they know and what they can do.

3. Teachers view their profession as a career characterized by consecutive progressive achievement.

4. Teachers do not merely acquire and possess specialized knowledge, but they also apply what they know in real-life settings to solve problems and to capitalize on opportunities.

5. Teachers, like all professionals, must conform to the technical and ethical standards for their profession.

6. Teachers' participation in making decisions about schools and classrooms affects educational environments for students and helps define one dimension of professionalism.

What Makes Teaching Less Than a Profession?

7. Some describe teaching as a semiprofession, that is, an occupation with the trappings of a profession. They argue that the large numbers of people hired to work in classrooms, the ease of entry into the teacher labor force, salary schedules, control by the state, and educators' difficulty articulating an explicit knowledge base argue against the concept of the teacher as a professional.

8. Debate about the professional status of teachers often revolves around the amount of time teachers spend working, the number of classes they teach, and the number of students they teach in each class.

9. Many argue that until teachers earn as much as other professionals they will always be relegated to subprofessional status. Simple direct comparisons between teachers' salaries and those of other professionals are often misleading, however. They rarely account for benefits packages that may include health insurance, dental coverage, sick leave, worker compensation, and retirement.

What Are the Challenges of Professional Practice?

10. The most significant challenge of the professional practice of teaching can be summarized in one simple command: Stay awake! There are so many simultaneous developments in education that devoting less than complete attention to the field means risking one's professional relevance.

11. Another challenge is to decide where to begin to apply one's knowledge. Once professionals know where to start, they can behave in ways that are likely to influence a situation in a positive manner.

12. All educational challenges are neither local nor unique. In recent years, both educators and lay people have recognized the challenges the United States must face as a nation if our schools are to meet people's needs. The National Education Goals embody these challenges most succinctly.

What Career Issues Must Beginning Teachers Face?

13. Teachers at the beginning of their careers face some issues that more experienced teachers do not encounter, or at least not to the same degree. These include getting certified to teach, getting a first job, successfully performing one's responsibilities, and planning for advancement in the profession.

14. Teaching certificates are typically granted in two ways: transcript assessment and program approval.

15. When one state does not recognize another's certification, teachers may have to take additional college course work to fulfill the requirements of the state to which they transfer.

16. People who wish to teach but are not certified or licensed may have to seek an emergency certificate or approval through an alternative certification program.

17. In order for people to be employed, jobs must be available. Two interrelated factors influence the availability of teaching jobs: the number of properly qualified teachers available and the demand for these teachers. Both supply and demand, in turn, are subject to other societal influences.

18. Factors that determine the demand for elementary and secondary teachers in any school year include enrollment changes, class size policies, budget considerations, changes in methods for classifying and educating special education students, and job turnover due to retirement or attrition.

19. Factors that determine the supply of teachers include salaries, educational and licensure requirements, interest in specific disciplines and geographical areas, the cost of living in some states, and other quality-of-life issues.

How Are Teachers Evaluated?

20. Evaluation of teachers is used mainly to help teachers grow professionally or to determine whether they meet minimum levels of competence.

21. One type of evaluation, called formative assessment, is done to shape, form, and improve teachers' knowledge and behavior. Formative assessment is not concerned with making judgments about salary status or tenure; instead, it is a helping process that provides data to teachers for making decisions about how they can improve their teaching techniques.

22. Another type of evaluation is referred to as summative. Evaluating teachers' competence and teaching outcomes are examples of summative assessments, in which data are collected and interpreted at the end of a specified period of time. Results are used to make decisions about teachers on matters such as hiring, compensation, status, tenure, and termination.

23. All states require some form of competency testing for preservice teachers. These tests provide perspectives on the effects of teacher education beyond that provided by teacher education programs.

24. Performance evaluations increasingly use observations and evidence that provide an authentic assessment of teachers' knowledge and skills. Such assessment is directed toward producing information about teachers' abilities to perform their jobs in context. True performance evaluations begin in student teaching.

25. More than 30 states require a national teacher examination as a test of teacher competency before granting initial certification.

How Are Teachers Supported and Rewarded?

26. Teachers often drive themselves far beyond minimal expectations to excel in their fields. Mentor programs, career ladders, merit pay, national certification, and advanced college degrees may offer opportunities for recognition.

27. Mentoring programs support experienced teachers, or "mentors" or "coaches," to work with beginning teachers to help them adjust successfully to full-time teaching.

28. Career ladder programs are examples of incentive programs for teachers, offering advancement of status, increased responsibility, and extra pay for exemplary teaching practice. Career ladders typically acknowledge differences in teachers' levels of accomplishment, as, for example, between beginners and master teachers.

29. Merit pay plans augment the lock-step progression of salary increases that characterize typical salary schedules by awarding either bonuses (one-time cash awards) or raises (financial increases added to teachers' base salaries).

30. National certification is intended to recognize a few outstanding teachers.

How Do Teachers Demonstrate Professional Leadership?

31. Teachers demonstrate leadership through their work in professional associations.

32. Teachers demonstrate leadership by modeling professional behavior on the job, that is, by recognizing problems and opportunities, by considering the values of stakeholders, by calling up professional knowledge, by applying that knowledge through action, and by assessing the consequences of such action.

TERMS AND CONCEPTS

accreditation   17
alternative certification   4
American Federation of Teachers (AFT)   3
authentic assessment   25
career ladder   28
certification   18
collective bargaining   31
emergency certification   17
formative assessment   22
induction program   27
licensure   17
merit pay   28
National Board for Professional Teaching Standards (NBPTS)   29

national certification   29
National Education Association (NEA)   3
National Education Goals   15
Praxis Series   27
professional   12
reciprocity agreement   17
reduction in force   22
student teaching   23
summative assessment   23
teacher portfolio   25
teacher union   3
tenure   22

REFLECTIVE PRACTICE

Janet Littlefield stood by the window watching droplets of rain roll down the panes as the last of the guests ran cackling to their cars in a flurry of umbrellas. For many students, she guessed, the end of the second year of college was supposed to be a time to decide on careers. But Janet's interactions with her family and friends that night had left her far from confident.

She had discussed the possibility of entering the education school, but they had said virtually nothing to help her clarify her thinking. Oh, everyone had been generally supportive, but that's not what Janet was looking for. She wanted strongly positive or negative comments that might galvanize her beliefs so she would feel certain about her decision. All she got was the kind of reaction her parents always gave her: "You do what is right for you and what makes you happy, dear." It was almost as if nobody really heard her.

In the quiet of the now empty room, Janet thought not so much about teaching as a career choice but about how she would feel standing before a classroom full of students. Did she have the right stuff to face them day in, day out? How would she know if the contract she signed was a good one? What might she find rewarding and discouraging about the work? Could she have a decent life, materially speaking, given her salary? Would someone be there to help her when she was unsure of herself? How would she know, once she took a job, if she was really succeeding? Would she find colleagues she would like as much as her college friends?

Issues, Problems, Dilemmas, Opportunities

What issues might be most important to Janet as she decides (1) whether to enter a program of teacher preparation and, eventually, (2) whether to stay in teaching or to leave?

Perceive and Value

How might Janet's view of teaching as a career be similar to and different from her parents' views? How might Janet's view of herself as a teacher be likely to change over time?

Know and Act

If you were Janet, what would you want to know about a teacher education program and about teaching as a career before you decided whether to enter an education school? How might you go about finding answers to your questions before you made a decision?

Evaluate

How might you decide if a career in teaching is a good idea for you? What factors might be most important to you as you considered a career in teaching?

 ONLINE ACTIVITY

Use a search engine to locate the Pathways to Improvement page on the North Central Regional Educational Laboratory web site, where you will find information on professional development for teachers. If you look for specific information on the critical issue of evaluating professional growth and development, you will see that a question at issue is whether "the ultimate worth of professional development for teachers is the essential role it plays in the improvement of student learning." What can you learn at this web site about how the professional development of teachers is evaluated and how it ultimately affects students in the classroom?

2

Historical Foundations of Education, 1600 to 1865

I n this chapter we describe American education from the arrival of European settlers in the 1600s to the end of the Civil War in 1865. We set the stage by noting the influence of European thinkers and events in history that influenced education. We also describe variations in educational opportunities extended to or denied different peoples living in the Colonies—opportunities that depended on people's ethnicity, gender, religion, wealth, and geographical location.

For many years, informal education—homeschooling, apprenticeships, and other educational activities outside school walls—were more important and more prevalent than formal processes of schooling. Formal education developed unevenly over time and across geographical regions. We examine both the structure and functions of education, broadly defined, in the Colonies and the new nation during this period.

Finally, we describe early reform movements that led to a universal tax-supported system of free schools and increased educational opportunities for women. During this time, people debated what a "good education" should be. As they struggled to define curriculum, people also considered the meanings of educational success and failure.

PROFESSIONAL PRACTICE QUESTIONS

- What European thinkers influenced education?
- What was the influence of informal education before the Civil War?
- What were the aims of education?
- How did formal education develop before the Civil War?
- What curricula and textbooks shaped education?
- How were educational success and failure evaluated?

What European Thinkers Influenced Early Education?

Although colonists were located far from England and Europe, immigration and overseas trade allowed for the exchange of goods and ideas between America and the larger world. Colonists' formal educational system was influenced heavily by European intellectuals.

▶ Comenius

John Amos Comenius (1592–1670), a Czech theologian and philosopher, viewed education as the primary means for improving society. All children—rich or poor, male or female—were to be instructed "thoroughly" by methodically trained teachers using quality textbooks in schools supported financially by state and city governments and the clergy. Educational programs were to be divided into four distinct "grades": the nursery school (birth to age 6), the elementary or national school (ages 6 to 12), the Latin school or gymnasium (gifted children ages 13 to 18), and the Academy (gifted youths ages 19 to 24). Children in each grade were to meet in a special school for 6 years. Their education would be "easy and pleasant" if the following conditions were met: (1) education began early, before a child's mind was "corrupted"; (2) a child's mind was "prepared" to receive instruction; (3) instruction moved from the general to the specific; (4) tasks were arranged from the easy to the more difficult; (5) the number of subjects studied was manageable for children; (6) teachers maintained a reasonable lesson pace; (7) instruction was age appropriate; (8) everything was taught through the senses; (9) material being learned was constantly before the children's eyes; and (10) a single method of instruction was employed at all times. To attain universal peace and progress, Comenius also advocated universal textbooks and schools, as well as a universal college and a universal language (Edwards, 1972; Ulich, 1968).

▶ Locke and Rousseau

John Locke (1632–1704), an English philosopher, argued convincingly that the human mind at birth is a blank slate (*tabula rasa*), not a repository of innate ideas placed there by God. He proposed that children should not simply read books but should also interact with the environment, using their five senses to accumulate and test ideas. Teachers should tailor instruction to the individual aptitudes and interests of each child; they should encourage curiosity and questions; and they should treat children as "rational creatures." Through reason, people might unlock life's mysteries. These ideas were consistent with the Age of Enlightenment, a period when application of reason was recognized as a virtue.

According to Locke, children learned through imitation; a good teacher taught by example and suggestion, not by coercion (Gay, 1964). Locke's belief in the essential goodness of people foreshadowed the development of a benevolent kind of education children should receive if they were to grow and prosper. To learn more about Locke's views, visit the web site of the Institute for Learning Technologies (ILT) at Columbia University.

Jean Jacques Rousseau (1712–1778), a Swiss philosopher, criticized educational methods that he believed were inconsistent with children's ways of thinking, seeing, and feeling. He contended that schools ignored the natural conditions of a child's growth, imposing books and abstract ideas on minds and bodies not yet ready to deal with such demands.

In *Emile,* Rousseau described the development of a human being from infancy to maturity—one who was educated in the country, away from the "vice and error" of contemporary social life. Emile's tutor provided experiences in harmony with the natural conditions of Emile's growth. From infancy through age 11, Emile's tutor dispensed a "negative" education, removing any obstacles that might impede development. Emile explored the environment with his senses, learning through trial and error and experiencing joy and pain from naturally occurring experiences. Between ages 11 and 14, Rousseau argued, education should become more intellectual, as Emile was introduced to geography, astronomy, and his first book, Daniel Defoe's *Robinson Crusoe.* Emile also learned carpentry, a practical skill that might serve him later in life. During adolescence, Emile began to compare himself with others, make abstractions, and probe secrets of the universe. Because his tutor had respected his human nature, removing obstacles that might hinder his development, Emile began to understand the meanings of love, justice, and duty as he entered into a deeper unity with the universe (Boyd, 1962; Ulich, 1968).

Johann Pestalozzi
(1746–1827)

▶ Pestalozzi and Herbart

Rousseau's ideas contributed to the child-study movement and to efforts to create child-centered schools. Johann Heinrich Pestalozzi (1746–1827), a Swiss educator, tested Rousseau's ideas with teachers and students at two schools for boys established in Germany. Pestalozzi (1898), like Rousseau, decried educational conditions that stifled children's playfulness and natural curiosity:

> At age five we make all nature . . . vanish from before their eyes . . . [and] pen them up like sheep, whole flocks huddled together, in stinking rooms; pitilessly chain them for hours, days, weeks, months, to the contemplation of unattractive and monotonous letters. (pp. 60–61)

Like Rousseau, Pestalozzi believed that children pass through a number of stages and that optimal growth occurs only when children fully master experiences and tasks of the previous stage. Such learning is facilitated by kind and loving educators who provide an array of sensory experiences when teaching concepts and skills rather than relying heavily on verbal instruction (Gutek, 1968). Pestalozzi wrote about his experiments with teaching and learning so parents and teachers might understand his simple methods for developing the inner capacity of the child. In *How Gertrude Teaches Her Children,* a book written for mothers, Pestalozzi (1898) illustrated why it was important to "always put a picture before the eye":

> It was inevitable, for instance, when [the teacher] asked, in arithmetic, How many times is seven contained in sixty-three? The child had no real background for his answer, and must, with great trouble, dig it out of his memory. Now, by the plan of putting nine times seven objects before his eyes, and letting him count them as nine sevens standing together, he has not to think any more about this question; he knows from what he has already learnt, although he is asked for the first time, that seven is contained nine times in sixty-three. So it is in other departments of the method. (p. 97)

How is Pestalozzi's "object lesson" in mathematics similar to or different from math lessons taught in today's elementary schools?

Pestalozzi's "object lessons" served as models for ways to facilitate step-by-step learning of abstract concepts. His ideas challenged educators in Germany and America to rethink methods of instruction that relied on repetition and memorization.

Johann Friedrich Herbart (1776–1841), a German philosopher, psychologist, and educational theorist, believed that a primary goal of education was to respect a child's individuality while conveying the discipline and consistency necessary to develop moral strength of character. A teacher should cultivate a child's interests while also introducing the child to a variety of human knowledge and experiences necessary for understanding and appreciating fundamental values of civilized societies. Herbart proposed several "steps of instruction" for developing a child's ability to concentrate, retain ideas, and participate in learning: (1) "clearness" (understanding of content); (2) "association" (connecting new ideas with previously learned content); (3) "system" (the analysis of new ideas and their relation to the purpose of the lesson); and (4) "method" (the ability to apply newly acquired knowledge to future problems). By the 19th century, teacher education programs stressed Herbart's methods of instruction (Ulich, 1968).

❱ Froebel

Friedrich Froebel (1782–1852), a German philosopher of education, established the first kindergarten in 1837 at Blankenburg. Froebel's **kindergarten** was not a school in the traditional sense but a "general institution" where young children could learn through the use of educational games and "occupations" (activities). A large portion of a child's school day was spent on gardening, an activity intended to help children see the similarity between the growth of plants and their own development (Downs, 1978).

Unlike Herbart, who explained the workings of the human mind as either associating or conflicting representations, Froebel viewed mental life as "the outgrowth of the incessant creativeness of the Divine" (Ulich, 1968, p. 287). To Froebel, a person's senses, emotions, and reason were the critical attributes necessary for learning to occur. Quality early childhood experiences that focused on play, music, and art allowed children to reveal their internal nature. Children were not "lumps of clay" to be molded; instead they were like plants and animals, which need time and space to develop according to natural law. Froebel recognized play as an important facet of learning and as the child's first sign of purposeful activity (Downs, 1978).

In 1855, Margaretta Schurtz, a German immigrant and one of Froebel's former students, established one of the first kindergartens in America in Watertown, Wisconsin. Schurtz's kindergarten was conducted in German, as were others founded by German immigrants. These early kindergartens were primarily meant to ensure that children would learn to speak German and to guarantee the preservation of their German heritage. The first kindergarten conducted in English was founded in Boston in 1860 by Elizabeth Peabody. By 1868 the first public kindergarten was opened in St. Louis, Missouri. It was a remarkable success and was thus imitated widely.

 ## What Was the Influence of Informal Education Before the Civil War?

European settlers who arrived on the shores of the New World in the 1600s had to adapt European ideas to their new environment as they struggled with themselves, with each other, and with outside forces to survive and prosper. Education both reflected and shaped people's values as they established their settlements along the eastern coast of America.

Students, young men called "scholars," were educated through a system of tutelage, in which the quality of education often depended entirely on the quality of the "master." In colonial times the schoolmaster typically was a member of the clergy and a prominent figure in the community. The purpose of education was to prepare young men for the ministry and for leadership. In their recollections, Meriwether Lewis, who later explored the Northwest Territories on the famous Lewis and Clark Expedition, and his younger cousin and classmate, Peachy Gilmer, complained about one of their schoolmasters and praised another. Lewis and Gilmer studied under Dr. Charles Everitt, of whom Gilmer said he was afflicted with very bad health, of an atrabilious and melancholy temperament; peevish, capricious, and every way disagreeable. . . . He invented cruel punishments for the scholars. . . . His method of teaching was as bad as anything could be. He was imparient [sic] of interruption. We seldom applied for assistance, said our lessons badly, made no proficiency, and acquired negligent and bad habits. (Ambrose, 1996, p. 27)

Lewis transferred in 1790 to Reverend James Waddell, who was a great contrast to the ill-tempered Everitt. Lewis called Waddell "a very polite scholar." He wrote to his mother in August,

I expect to continue [here] for eighteen months or two years. Every civility is here paid to me and leaves me without any reason to regret the loss of a home or nearer connection. As soon as I complete my education, you shall certainly see me. (Ambrose, 1996, p. 27)

▶ Education in the Southern Colonies

People who settled in the southern colonies of Virginia, Maryland, Georgia, and the Carolinas typically lived on large plantations where there were rigid class distinctions. A plantation was like a small community where crops such as tobacco, sugar, or cotton were raised. The owner's home often was at the center of the plantation and surrounded by a kitchen, smokehouse, stable, and sometimes a school, where a hired tutor taught the landowner's children. Around the periphery were tobacco fields and barns and cabins in which lived slaves from Africa and indentured servants from Europe. These people were the backbone of plantation life. They were trained as field workers, household workers, and skilled artisans—cobblers, carpenters, tailors, blacksmiths. Plantation owners were powerful people, directing both the lives of their servants and the lives of the numerous small farmers in the South.

Small farmers were isolated. Although they worked for themselves, their livelihood was often affected by plantation owners' willingness to purchase or sell surplus crops, rent their lands, and loan money. Farmers' decisions about where to settle were based mainly on the lay of the land, the quality of the soil, and the proximity of water. For these people who struggled to eke out a living from the land, there was no community of any sort, nor were there nearby schools or churches. For the most part, education was informal. Skills that boys and girls needed to learn were taught by the family. Families also taught their children to read and often conducted their own worship services until the middle of the 18th century, when itinerant missionaries began to minister to people in the backcountry.

▶ Education in the Middle Atlantic Colonies

People in the Middle Atlantic colonies (New York, New Jersey, Pennsylvania, and Delaware) were more diverse than were settlers in the Southern colonies. Although most Middle Atlantic colonists spoke English, there were also Dutch-, German-, French-, and Swedish-speaking families whose religious orientation varied greatly from one another. Among others, there were Catholics, Mennonites, Calvinists, Lutherans, Quakers, Presbyterians, and Jews, all diligent in their efforts to preserve their languages and beliefs. To do so, different groups established their own parochial schools. English, Irish, Welsh, Dutch, and German Quakers, for instance, who settled mainly in Pennsylvania, stressed the importance of formal education focused on religion, mathematics, reading, and writing. They also offered some vocational training to children. Teachers viewed children as inherently good and rejected use of corporal punishment. Their schools were open to everyone, including Native Americans and slaves (Bullock, 1967).

▶ Education in the New England Colonies

In the New England colonies of Massachusetts Bay, Rhode Island, New Hampshire, and Connecticut, there was less divergence in ideas and values, which made possible the establishment of town schools. Two school laws were instrumental in moving New Englanders in this direction. The Massachusetts Act of 1642 required that efforts of parents and master craftsmen who trained novices be monitored to ensure that children were learning to read and understand religious principles. The Massachusetts Act of 1647, sometimes referred to as the Old Deluder Satan Act, required towns to provide for the education of youth so that they might thwart Satan's trickery. To produce Scripture-literate citizens, every town of 50 households was required to employ a teacher of reading and writing, and every town of 100 households was to provide a grammar school to prepare youth for study at Harvard University.

In which area of the country would you have preferred to be educated during colonial times?

Many settlers were Puritans who followed the teachings of John Calvin, a Swiss religious reformer. Calvin believed that God was omnipotent and good, while human beings were evil and helpless, predestined for either salvation or eternal torment. The role of schooling was to produce literate, hard-working, frugal, and respectful men and women who might resist the temptations of the world. Children, perceived as savage and primitive creatures, were to be trained and disciplined for a life of social conformity and religious commitment.

Colonists living in northern cities experienced a lifestyle very different from other colonists. Cities were densely populated and built on trade. Merchants, who were key people in the community, made available an array of goods and services not found in other parts of the country. Cities also contained skilled craftsmen, barbers, wigmakers, and an abundance of schoolteachers better educated than those in other parts of the country. Ships arriving at port brought both goods and ideas from England and Europe. This meant city dwellers on the eastern seaboard were among the best informed and sometimes the most influential of the colonists (Blum et al., 1997).

▶ Education for Nationhood

Literacy was essential for democracy to work. Weekly newspapers and literary and political essays and verse were popular reading matter. The colonists understood how government worked, but they did not always agree on how it should work. Some colonists argued that they should rip themselves free from England; others counseled people to reconcile their differences with England and to remain a colony. The struggle for people's loyalties, both on and off the battlefield, shaped the talk and writings of the day. By the middle of the 18th century, almost every colony had a printing press churning out a daily newspaper containing not only local news and news from abroad but also literary and political essays. Printers also produced almanacs, flyers, and books. Thomas Paine's *Common Sense,* a compelling case for independence, sold 100,000 copies in its first 3 months of publication in 1776 and captured the minds and hearts of the delegates to the Continental Congress and of many others outside Philadelphia (Cremin, 1970). As Figure 2.1 shows, independence was one of several developments that significantly affected the American system of education.

As the country grew, competing forces continued to shape Americans' views of themselves and others. Plantation owners in the South protected their virtually self-sufficient communities with their permanent labor force, while abolitionists in the North battled covertly and openly to destroy the system of slavery that supported the plantations. The Cherokee, Creek, Iroquois, and others fought to preserve their lands and their physical and spiritual well-being, while European Americans took land by

FIGURE 2.1
Some Factors Affecting Education Before the Civil War   As you read, identify people whose contributions you might add to this figure under the heading "Influential Early Educators and Their Ideas."

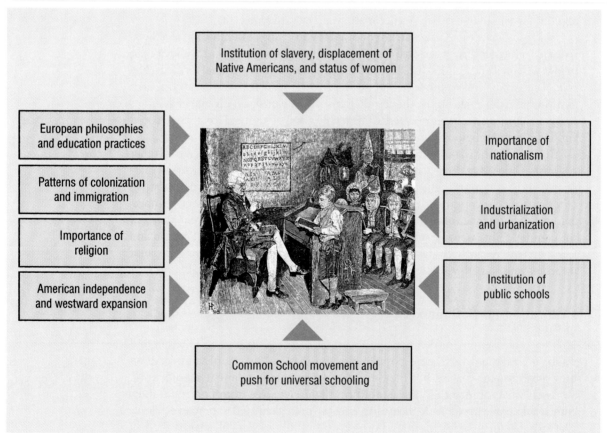

trickery and force to improve their own lives and to fulfill what they believed was their divine destiny.

Between 1800 and 1840, the value of agricultural products grew remarkably, largely due to westward expansion. The number of farmers increased from about 5 million to 15 million during this time. Only about one-seventh of the population lived west of the Appalachians in 1810, compared with one-third after 1840 (Blum et al., 1997).

The nation's founders believed that education was the best hope for the Republic. Freedom had to be tempered by the responsibility to maintain social order. Education would prepare good citizens. The virtuous, the disciplined, the intelligent would know how to participate responsibly in a democracy. Noah Webster in Connecticut, Benjamin Rush in Pennsylvania, and Thomas Jefferson in Virginia argued that the ability to read, write, and cipher would make the people and the nation strong. Jefferson (1931) viewed education as the key to advancing civilization:

> Education . . . grafts a new man on the native stock, and improves what in his nature was vicious and perverse into qualities of virtue and social worth. And it cannot be but that each generation succeeding to the knowledge acquired by all those who preceded it, adding to it their own acquisitions and discoveries, and handing the mass down for successive and constant accumulation, must advance the knowledge, and well-being of mankind, not *infinitely,* as some have said, but *indefinitely,* and to a term which no one can fix and foresee. (p. 250)

FIGURE 2.2
A Precedent for Public Education   Under the Northwest Ordinance of 1785, the sixteenth square mile of a township's land grant was reserved for town-supported education.

An expression of the desire to educate for nationhood may be found in the Northwest Ordinance of 1785, which sliced the Northwest Territories (now the states of Ohio, Indiana, Illinois, Michigan, Wisconsin, and part of Minnesota) into townships of 36 square miles each. As depicted in Figure 2.2, a township provided a section of land to be used for education. This first national education legislation established the precedent for financing education through **land grant schools.**

The Ordinance constituted what historians typically recognize as the greatest accomplishment of the government under the Articles of Confederation, or the governing principles established by the Continental Congress that preceded the United States Constitution. In fact, fear stimulated passage of the Ordinance—fear on the part of leaders in the East that those who moved to the Northwest would become less civilized than people on the East coast. The framers of the Ordinance wanted to be certain that residents of the Northwest did not undo democracy from their corner of the country. Education meant socialization.

 ## What Were the Aims of Education?

The main goal of education for European Americans was salvation of souls. Schooling began at home with the family. Father laid down the rules, keeping an eye on the King James Bible, and Mother enforced them. Formal schooling was patterned after English schools. In New England, legislatures reminded parents of their responsibility for their children's education, but laws were not well enforced. When families and communities organized themselves to provide schooling for their children, they sent them to inexpensive **dame schools,** or schools run by women, in the area. Dame schools offered training in rudimentary skills of reading, writing, and calculating. For some children, particularly girls, this was the only formal education they received. Schools were private, although some received town support, and attendance was voluntary. Wealthy Americans sent their children abroad for their education.

The term *educated* evolved rapidly to mean more than learning God's law, as people began to associate education with personal advancement. Moreover, government leaders promoted education as a way to develop informed, wise, and honest people who would help the fledgling democracy succeed. However, education for personal advancement and civic participation was rarely extended to women and to non-European populations such as Native Americans, Africans, and Mexicans. As the nation industrialized and urbanized, aims of education gave precedence to occupational training for immigrants and low-income citizens.

▶ The Role of Religion

A majority of colonists, particularly in the South, were Protestant and believed that the Scriptures were key to self-determination and to understanding God's will. Education should help save souls. As early as 1619, Virginia law made religious study on Sunday afternoons standard practice. The Bible typically was the medium for instruction.

What historical events have shaped religion as an issue in public education?

The King James Bible and other devotional literature instructed people on how to live and how to die. Written in the 1670s, *The Poor Man's Family Book* taught colonists how to attend to their private duties, as well as their duties to church, to rulers, and to neighbors. Early writers often taught by telling stories and applying religious and moral principles to particular situations. Children's schoolbooks reinforced these principles. Educators' methods of writing and teaching, a sort of case-method approach to divinity, was called "casuistry" (Cremin, 1970, p. 45).

Except in the New England colonies, where church, state, and school were closely related, there generally was a separation of church and state. Nonetheless, church leaders greatly influenced people's thinking. Some, like Cotton Mather, were among the most prolific writers in America, and some, like Michael Wigglesworth, enjoyed wide readership. Between 1662 and 1701, Wigglesworth's *The Day of Doom,* an account of the Last Judgment, went through five editions (Blum et al., 1997).

In the 1740s religious experiences were brought to thousands of people in every rank of society when George Whitefield, a traveling English preacher, prompted the Great Awakening with his religious revivals. Whitefield journeyed from the Carolinas to New England teaching the word of God to rich and poor, old and young, educated and ignorant. Whitefield combined Calvinism and showmanship as he dramatized in vivid detail the pain awaiting sinners, urging his audience to confess their sins and submit to God.

Jonathan Edwards, a minister from Northampton, Massachusetts, who was a staunch defender of the Awakening, preached an even stricter Calvinism. Edwards's Calvinist theology suggested that children were inherently evil and in need of strict

Voices

Ralph Waldo Emerson

Ralph Waldo Emerson (1803–1882) was the nation's leading essayist, poet, and moral thinker in the mid 19th century. When he gave a speech at Harvard entitled "The American Scholar" in 1837, Oliver Wendell Holmes, Sr., called it our "intellectual Declaration of Independence." Emerson urged the citizens of our youthful democracy to break intellectually with their European antecedents. He advised students, writers, artists, teachers, and moralists to break new intellectual ground, just as the founders of the nation had done in the political world. The American Scholar should be a pioneer, he argued, bent on exploring new-found intellectual and moral freedoms (Axelrod & Phillips, 1991).

There goes in the world a notion that the scholar should be a recluse, a valetudinarian—as unfit for any handiwork or public labor as a penknife for an axe. The so-called "practical men" sneer at speculative men, as if, because they speculate or *see,* they could do nothing. I have heard it said that the clergy—who are always, more universally than any other class, the scholars of their day—are addressed as women; that the rough, spontaneous conversation of men they do not hear, but only a mincing and diluted speech. They are often virtually disfranchised; and indeed there are advocates for their celibacy. As far as this is true of the studious classes, it is not just and wise. Action is with the scholar subordinate, but it is essential. Without it he is not yet man. With it

Ralph Waldo Emerson
(1803–1882)

thought can never ripen into truth. Whilst the world hangs before the eye as a cloud of beauty, we cannot even see its beauty. Inaction is cowardice, but there can be no scholar without the heroic mind. The preamble of thought, the transition through which it passes from the unconscious to the conscious, is action. Only so much do I know, as I have lived. Instantly we know whose words are loaded with life, and whose not." (1968, p. 52)

We will walk on our own feet; we will work with our own hands; we will speak our own minds. The study of letters shall be no longer a name for pity, for doubt, and for sensual indulgence. The dread of man and the love of man shall be a wall of defence and a wreath of joy around all. A nation of men will for the first time exist, because each believes himself inspired by the Divine Soul which also inspires all men." (1968, p. 63)

Some credit Emerson as the catalyst of the American Renaissance. Henry Thoreau, Walt Whitman, Herman Melville, and others were inspired by Emerson to leave their own marks on our nation's cultural and literary history.

CRITICAL THINKING

What might Emerson have had in mind when he counseled scholars to be people of action? Have you ever been particularly inspired by a speech? Does the spoken word have a more powerful effect on you than the written word, or vice versa? How might you decide whose words are loaded with life and whose not?

Source: The Selected Writings of Ralph Waldo Emerson. New York: Random House, Inc., 1968; and from Alan Axelrod and Charles Phillips, *What Every American Should Know about American History: 200 Events that Shaped the Nation.* Holbrook, MA: Adams Media Corporation, 1991.

discipline. His notions encouraged harsh treatment of children at home and at school (Blum et al., 1997).

By the 19th century the hard tenets of orthodox Calvinism began to soften, and Americans adopted more rationalistic and humanistic views. Many challenged the traditional methods of education and demanded secular curricula. Transcendentalist philosophers Henry David Thoreau, Bronson Alcott, and Ralph Waldo Emerson were among those who advocated the radical reform of education. They were concerned, in particular, with the stifling nature of education. According to Emerson (1884),

> Education has so cold, so hopeless a sound. A treatise on education, a convention for education, a lecture, a system, affects us with slight paralysis and a certain yawning of the jaws. . . . Education should be as broad as man. Whatever elements are in him that should foster and demonstrate. If he be dexterous, his tuition should make it appear; if he be capable of dividing men by the trenchant sword of his thought, education should unsheathe and sharpen it; if he is one to cement society by his all-reconciling affinities, oh! hasten their action! If he is jovial, if he is mercurial, if he is great hearted, a cunning artificer, a strong commander, a potent ally, ingenious, useful, elegant, witty, prophet, diviner—society has need of all these. The imagination must be addressed. (p. 133)

▶ The Impact of Industrialization

Forces of urbanization and industrialization shaped the character of the nation in the Northeast in the late 18th and early 19th centuries. After 1830, factories grew larger and more complex. As roads and shipping improved and as transportation costs decreased, people distributed their goods to mass markets. Hard work, inspiration, luck, and education all combined to influence these developments.

The Northeast had waterpower for factories and mills, iron and coal in Pennsylvania, and entrepreneurs ready to make the region the manufacturing center of the nation. The Erie Canal, an engineering marvel, symbolized people's technical capabilities and passion for economic prosperity. Federal law permitted people to patent their inventions, and many capitalized on this fact and on their inventiveness to pursue their fortunes.

As colonists migrated westward into Alabama, Mississippi, and Louisiana, King Cotton dominated southern agricultural life. Once Eli Whitney's cotton gin, a machine that separated seeds from cotton fibers, was invented in 1793, cotton production jumped from about 10,000 bales to about 500,000 bales in the 1820s (Blum et al., 1997). While the North propelled itself toward industrialization, the South remained rural and dependent on agriculture for its economic well-being.

Industrialization in the early 19th century led to an increasing emphasis on practical rather than theoretical learning. At the same time, demands for cheap, reliable labor had a direct effect on schools' enrollment. Women and children met the increased demands for labor in the Northeast by working long hours under extremely difficult conditions. Infant schools, a concept devised by a Welsh cotton-mill owner and social reformer named Robert Owen (1771–1858) to give child factory workers a minimal education, provided much-needed care for young children of working women. Such schools were designed to meet the mental, physical, and moral development needs of children not yet old enough to work in the factories.

▶ The Education of Slaves

When the Civil War began in 1861, there were 7 million slaves in the southern and western states. By the time the war ended in 1865, there were about 4 million, about 5 percent of whom could read and write (Blum et al., 1997). In the early 1600s, when the slave trade began, English clergy had expressed interest in providing religious training for slaves and had made some progress in achieving their goal. Presbyterians went a step further, providing formal training to African Americans to prepare them for religious leadership. In 1740 Hugh Bryan, a wealthy and pious Presbyterian, opened his school for African Americans in Charleston, South Carolina. By 1755, Presbyterian schools had extended to Virginia, where slaves were being taught to read and write. In an experiment to test African Americans' abilities to succeed in college, Presbyterians sent John Chavis of North Carolina to Princeton University. Chavis graduated and established a school in the South only to find that European Americans would not allow non-European American children to attend.

Slavery more than anything made the cultures in northern, Middle Atlantic, and southern colonies different from one another. In the northern states, many people, especially the Quakers, decried human bondage. By the early 19th century, antislavery groups had produced enough pressure to achieve abolition of slavery in the northern states. In the South, however, slavery continued to flourish. Slavery was recognized by the federal Constitution as a local institution within the jurisdiction of individual states; it was also a profitable fact of life for European American planters in the South. The practice provided a reliable pool of field hands, miners, craftsmen, and domestics. In the 1850s nearly half the populations of both Alabama and Louisiana were African slaves; more than half of Mississippi's population were slaves. Most slaves were owned by a relatively few people; three-fourths of southern European American families never owned slaves (Blum et al., 1997).

In the South teaching slaves constituted a violation of the law, although teaching one or two was not regarded as a serious crime. Teaching slaves in schools was another matter entirely; this practice typically was limited to household servants or to free African Americans. But some courageous Southerners did dare to teach slaves.

How was informal and illegal education for slaves a hidden passage to freedom for some African Americans?

Naturally, more care had to be exercised in the selection of students and in the dissemination of information concerning the schools, but there were blacks and whites who were willing to run the risk of legal prosecution and social disapprobation in order to teach slaves. Negro schools are known to have existed in Savannah, Georgia; Charleston, South Carolina; Fayetteville, New Bern, and Raleigh, North Carolina; Lexington and Louisville, Kentucky; Fredericksburg and Norfolk, Virginia; and various other cities in Florida, Tennessee, and Louisiana. (Franklin, 1980, p. 146)

European American missionaries and free African Americans established African schools and black academies in the North and the South during the 1800s. Christopher McPherson, a free African American, started a Richmond, Virginia, African school in 1811 to teach other free African Americans and slaves. From dusk until 9:30 each night, a European American teacher he had hired taught English, writing, arithmetic, geography, and astronomy for about $1.25 per month. Flush with success, McPherson ran an advertisement for his school in the newspaper. Southerners in positions of authority were not quite as enthusiastic about his efforts: They closed his school, proclaiming it a public nuisance, and sent McPherson to the Williamsburg Lunatic Asylum (Berlin, 1974).

In some southern colonies, such as South Carolina, laws forbade teaching slaves to read and write. Some colonists justified such laws by persuading themselves that slaves were incapable of learning any more than was required to perform their menial jobs. Others believed that education would produce a leadership that would encourage slaves to rebel against a life of bondage. In fact, such leadership did evolve. David Walker of Wilmington, North Carolina, for example, published his widely read *Appeal,* a spirited attack on slavery, in 1829 (Bullock, 1967).

Slave owners and African American preachers were also sources of education for slaves. Some slave owners placed their slaves under the tutelage of master craftsmen and even helped slaves establish small businesses to help them buy their freedom. Some slaves who did not receive formal education learned informally from their associations with literate European Americans. When assigned to houses, domestic workers might learn to read from the personal libraries of their masters and from studying recipes, music, and the Bible. Slave children also learned from their masters' children as they played school with one another, hidden from public view.

Some owners taught their slaves because they wanted to protect and enhance their investments; others educated slaves out of respect and caring. Henry Bullock (1967) called these educational activities the **hidden passage** to freedom—literacy helped slaves to escape bondage and to make lives for themselves after the Civil War.

Why might regional differences in students' academic achievements exist today?

Fear about educating slaves mounted in the years just before the Civil War. Well-educated, vocal freed men and escaped slaves were in a position to demand equal rights and privileges. In the 1840s fearful citizens created a list of "safe" books that reflected the Southern viewpoint. The South Carolina Legislature made it a misdemeanor "to learn a slave to write, subject to fine and imprisonment" (*The Sun*, 1833a, p. 2). Later safe reading lists included a Confederate edition of the New Testament. Many European immigrants in Northern cities also feared and resented Africans and non-European immigrants, perceiving them as threats to their jobs and way of life.

▶ Education for Native Americans

In Revolutionary times many settlers believed that Native Americans should be "civilized," or taught the ways of European Americans. Thomas Jefferson expressed the

Cultural Awareness

Frederick Douglass

Frederick Douglass learned the alphabet from his Maryland mistress until his master discovered that she was teaching the young slave. Douglass's master said, "If he learns to read the Bible it will for ever unfit him to be a slave. He should know nothing but the will of his master, and learn to obey it" (Douglass, 1974). Douglass (1882) became more determined than ever to learn to read:

> The plan which I mainly adopted, and the one which was most successful, was that of using my young white playmates, whom I met in the streets, as teachers. I used to carry almost constantly a copy of Webster's spelling-book in my pocket, and when sent on errands, or when playtime was allowed me, I would step aside with my young friends and take a lesson in spelling. I am greatly indebted to these boys—Gustavus Dorgan, Joseph Bailey, Charles Farity, and William Cosdry. (1882, p. 2)

Later, as an escaped slave, Douglass became one of the most eloquent orators against slavery in the United States. In his speeches and his newspapers, he advocated the destruction of slavery in the South and the achievement of voting and other rights for African Americans in the North. To help slaves overcome their lack of formal education, Douglass also ran a Sunday school in barns or outdoors (Bullock, 1967).

view that European Americans should intermingle with Native Americans and become one people. Paradoxically, he also believed that African Americans did not possess the mental capabilities to achieve equality with European Americans and should probably be resettled elsewhere. Jefferson wrote of Native Americans in 1803:

> In truth, the ultimate point of rest and happiness for them is to let our settlements and theirs meet and blend together, to intermix, and become one people. Incorporating themselves with us as citizens of the United States, this is what the natural progress of things will of course bring on, and it will be better to promote than retard it. (Cremin, 1980, pp. 231–232)

Assimilation, the process of educating and socializing a group to make it similar to the dominant culture, integration, and intermarriage with European Americans was rare, however. Some Native Americans who were self-educated in the European manner in turn advanced the European-style education of their people. In 1821 a Cherokee named Sequoyah devised an 86-character phonetic Cherokee alphabet. A press using Sequoyah's type churned out stories, hymns, and even a Bible in Cherokee. A newspaper, *The Cherokee Phoenix,* did much to advance literacy and knowledge among the tribe. Education of this sort, however, did not protect the Cherokees from the forced relocation and genocide that affected all Native American tribes and nations during the 19th century.

Sequoyah (1770?–1843)

During the early 19th century, Protestants and Catholics established **mission schools** among the Native Americans to teach English and to inculcate Christianity. One example was Brainerd Mission, established among the Cherokees in Georgia. Brainerd Mission tried to prepare the Cherokees for assimilation into the dominant culture. The schoolmaster even gave each child a new English name. The Mission became a self-sufficient society, producing nearly everything students needed to live. By 1830 there were eight such schools. The Brainerd Mission became the most common model for educating other eastern tribes and nations.

As far as the larger society knew, such schools were the best answer to "the Indian problem." The *Sun* newspaper carried this report in 1833:

> There is . . . an Indian School under the superintendence of Col R.M. Johnson, in Scott Co. which has one hundred scholars from the Choctaws, Creeks, Potawatomies, and Miamies, and supported chiefly by their own funds. This interesting school was established at the house of Col. Johnson, by the Choctaws, some years ago. It is very flourishing, and will do good. (*The Sun,* 1833b, p. 3)

Traditionally, Native American elders taught children by example, explanation, and imitation (Cremin, 1980). Schooling for Native Americans thus was a continuation of their education, not a beginning (Barman, Hebert, & McCaskill, 1986). Families bore the primary responsibility for education, but they assumed this responsibility in ways markedly different from European settlers. Native American children were surrounded by educators and caregivers—father and mother, grandparents, older siblings, uncles and aunts, other adults, and specialists, such as weavers, potters, warriors, and shamans (Coleman, 1993).

The roles of observation, practice, and self-discipline in traditional Native American education are evident in this account of learning beadwork by Zitkala-Sa (1921), a Nakota (Yankton Sioux):

> Close beside my mother I sat on a rug . . . with a scrap of buckskin in one hand and an awl in the other. This was the beginning of my practical observation lessons in the art of beadwork. . . . It took many trials before I learned how to knot my sinew thread on the point of my finger, as I saw her do. . . . The quietness of her oversight made me feel strongly responsible and dependent upon my own judgment. She treated me as a dignified little individual as long as I was on good behavior; and how humiliated I was when some boldness of mine drew forth a rebuke from her! . . . Always after these confining lessons I was wild with surplus spirits, and found joyous relief in running loose in the open again. (pp. 18–21)

▶ Education in Spain's American Colonies

Santa Fe (now New Mexico) was founded by the Spanish in 1609, only 2 years after the English settled Jamestown in Virginia. In 1790, in addition to many Native Americans, there were about 23,000 Spanish-speaking people in what is now the southwestern United States; they had migrated north from Mexico, the seat of the Spanish conquest. Most were of mixed Native American and Spanish descent, with a heritage that had come to be dominated by the Spanish language, religion (Catholicism), and social and political organizations. The Church and its missionaries provided what little formal education existed for Mexican Americans in those early years (Manuel, 1965).

Formal education was basic and heavily religious, conducted mainly by older men for younger men. Upper-class women, such as Sor Juana Ines de la Cruz (1648–1695), also had access to education:

> I was not yet three years old when my mother sent an older sister of mine to be taught to read at a school. . . . Moved by affection and a mischievous spirit, I followed her; and seeing her receive instruction, such a strong desire to read burned in me that I tried to deceive the teacher, telling her that my mother wanted her to give me lessons. . . . (Hahner, 1976, pp. 22–23)

How did Roman Catholic missions and a class system based on racial origins shape the educational experiences of Native Americans and Africans in Spanish colonies?

Sor Juana Ines later studied Latin and became a nun and a writer (Flynn, 1971). Her intellectual abilities made her a favorite of the Spanish viceroy and his wife in Mexico City, and she served as a court poet, successfully debating teachers from the university.

Spanish colonization of the Southwest fulfilled more than one purpose. Priests established mission schools to convert Native Americans to Catholicism, to effect a sort of peaceful conquest of the indigenous people (Fogel, 1988). But the missions also served to capture and hold territory and resources for Spain, while impeding any interests France and Britain might have had in these areas. Junipero Serra, a Franciscan priest, established missions in California territory in the 1770s.

> The missions were far more than religious outposts: They were social institutions, designed to transform the Indians from scattered hunting and gathering peoples into disciplined farmers, ranchers, and cloth weavers clustered around, and faithful to the church. (Fogel, 1988, p. 53)

From the outset, the Spanish- and English-speaking peoples in the Southwest fought for control of the land. English-speaking Texans achieved their independence from Mexico in 1836. The United States, in turn, annexed Texas in 1844. In 1846, the United States and Mexico commenced the Mexican War, which ended 2 years later with Mexico's defeat and the addition of California, Utah, New Mexico, and other Western territories to the United States.

▶ Education for Women

During colonial times women played a relatively insignificant role in the formal education of children. In just about every colony, however, there are records of one or more women having been employed as teachers. Most often, they instructed the younger children, and in many instances children of the poor, in dame schools. Generally, women taught during the summer months (April to September) and men taught during the winter. The Quakers in Pennsylvania did not discriminate against women to the degree that other religious sects did.

Emma Willard (1787–1870)

Catherine Beecher
(1800–1878)

While they were not compensated as well as Quaker schoolmasters, Quaker women accounted for a large proportion of the teachers in Pennsylvania (Elsbree, 1939).

Benjamin Rush's 1787 speech "Thoughts upon Female Education" marked a turning point in the education of women in the colonies. Rush contended that male heads of families were increasingly occupied with their roles outside the home and thus were unable to serve as primary educators of their sons and daughters. Women, who would necessarily assume such roles, were ill-prepared for the task.

Emma Willard was among several educators who developed programs for women that were more academically focused than schools of the past had been. In her speech to the New York legislature in 1819, Willard advocated the formation of schools that would teach geography, science, domestic skills, music, and other courses to women. Willard opened such a school in 1821 in Troy, New York. Her efforts stimulated others, such as Catherine Beecher, Zilpah Grant, Mary Lyons, and George B. Emerson, also to establish institutions expressly for the purpose of educating women (Deighton, 1971). During the mid-1800s Catherine Beecher borrowed concepts from Swedish gymnastics to introduce young women to calisthenics in order to improve their health, beauty, and strength (Steinhardt, 1992).

The literature of the early 19th century, as Patricia Mayer Spacks (1995) has argued, reinforced the "normalization of boredom" for women. Charles Bathurst wrote of young British women, who were emulated by women in upper-class American society, that their natural liveliness and feelings ought not to be encouraged. After all, "passion was passion"—one thing could lead to another.

> We often see girls . . . affect that behaviour which shows liveliness and quickness, even of temper, as well as of affectionate feeling, rather than sense and quietness; cultivate (in plain English) passion, feelings, and emotions, and what is called animation; not always meant to be confined to the kindly and affectionate feelings, but to nurse up, heighten, and exaggerate both likings and dislikings of any sort; as opposed to a cool, calm, peaceful state of mind, suited to reason, consideration, patience, and self-control. (Spacks, 1995, p. 184)

In studies of the foundations of education, the contributions of women traditionally have been downplayed or ignored. To see how history looks different when the contributions of women are included, visit the web site of the National Women's History Project.

▶ Education for People with Disabilities

How are people's attitudes toward individuals with special needs similar to or different from those of our ancestors?

The object of many superstitions, people with physical or mental disabilities were relegated to lives of confinement and idleness or were subjects of scapegoating and exploitation. The first permanent, state-supported school in the United States built expressly for the mentally retarded was opened in Syracuse, New York, in 1854. Clergymen and physicians were among the leaders in providing care and training for people with disabilities.

The assumption of the leaders in special education was that *all* handicapped persons could and should be provided with residential care that would cure their behavioral deficits and make them useful and productive citizens or at least improve their condition and skills markedly. (Kauffman, 1981, p. 5)

Lester Mann (1979) and others credit Jean-Jacques Rousseau for the ideas that stimulated the development of special education as it has become operationalized in modern times. Rousseau championed the idea of encouraging children to achieve the potential they possess inherently. He wrote of the importance of sensory–motor development in young children, followed by higher intellectual development in their later years. His ideas stimulated Jean-Marc Itard (1775–1838) and Edouard Seguin (1812–1880) in France, Johann Pestalozzi (1746–1827) in Switzerland, Friedrich Froebel (1782–1852) in Germany, and Maria Montessori (1870–1952) in Italy to fit education to a child's development.

Thomas Gallaudet (1787–1851)

Samuel Gridley Howe and Thomas Gallaudet both left the United States during the early 1800s to study abroad before establishing programs in the United States to educate children with disabilities. Howe taught Laura Bridgmen, a person without sight, hearing, or speech, and achieved international fame. He also taught Anne Sullivan, who later became Helen Keller's teacher. Gallaudet founded the first residential school for the deaf in Hartford, Connecticut. Named after the pioneer in education for people with hearing impairments, Gallaudet College for the Deaf in Washington, D.C., is the only college for the deaf in the world (Hewett & Forness, 1984).

Daniel Hallahan and James Kauffman (2000) contend that the development of education programs specially fitted to people's needs is deeply rooted in the past. Many of today's special education practices can be traced to ideas expressed much earlier, including prescribing instruction based on the child's characteristics, carefully sequencing tasks from simple to complex, emphasizing stimulation of the child's senses, and tutoring in functional skills.

How Did Formal Education Develop in America Before the Civil War?

Being a teacher in colonial America was much like being a lawyer: Neither required formal training. Academic qualifications of teachers, most of whom were men, ranged from mere ability to read and write to the scholarly attainments of a college graduate. The more rural the school, and the younger the children, the lower were the qualifications for a teaching position. In the North, particularly in Massachusetts, communities at the doorstep of Harvard were more selective, typically giving

How have the image, status, and roles of teachers changed since colonial times?

preference to college-trained men. For the most part, however, communities were not as interested in a candidate's scholastic preparation as in his character and religious orthodoxy. The Quakers of Pennsylvania, for example, stressed morality and membership in the Society of Friends. The Scotch–Irish in Pennsylvania insisted that schoolmasters be intelligent and sufficiently pious to teach the principles of Calvinism. In 1750, Pennsylvania Lutherans required the following qualifications:

> That the schoolhouse shall always be in charge of a faithful Evangelical Lutheran schoolmaster, whose competency to teach Reading, Writing, and Arithmetic, and also to play the organ (Orgelschlagen) and to use the English language, has been proved by the pastor; special regard being had at the same time, to the purity of his doctrine and his life. He shall be required to treat all his pupils with impartial

In 1829 Louis Braille adapted a system used by the French army for the exchange of messages by touch in war zones at night. Braille's raised-line system is a code that uses a six-dot cell to represent 63 alphabetical, numerical, and grammatical characters. By the end of the nineteenth century, "braille" was the universally accepted means of teaching blind people to read and write.

Grade 1   Braille grade 1 uses full spelling and consists of the letters of the alphabet, numbers, punctuation signs, and composition signs which are unique to braille.

YOUR FRIEND IS STANDING HERE.
capital   period

Grade 2   Braille grade 2 is a contracted system much like shorthand. It consists of grade 1 braille plus 189 contractions and short-form words.

Y R   F R   I S   (ST) (AND)(ING)   (HERE) .
capital   period

Source: "Special adaptations neccessitated by visual impairments" by M. D. Orlansky & J. M. Rhyne, 1981, in J. M. Kauffman & D. P. Hallahan (eds.), *Handbook of special education* (pp. 552–575), Upper Saddle River, NJ: Prentice Hall, Inc.

fidelity, and to instruct the children of other denominations, and of the neighborhood generally. He shall not allow the children to use profane language either in or out of school; but shall carefully teach them how, both in church and in school, and in the presence of others and upon the highway, to conduct themselves in a Christian and upright manner, and not like the Indians. (Elsbree, 1939, p. 39)

Benjamin Rush expressed another popular view of the roles of schoolmasters and their pupils. Rush believed that the teacher should be an absolute monarch: "The government of schools . . . should be arbitrary," wrote Rush. "By this mode of education we prepare our youth for the subordination of laws, and thereby qualify them for becoming good citizens of the republic. I am satisfied that the most useful citizens have been formed from those youth who have never known or felt their own wills till they were one and twenty years of age. . . ." (Tyack, 1967, p. 88)

▶ The Colonial Schoolhouse

Besides their teaching duties, schoolmasters were expected to perform a variety of duties outside school. In New England, some of the more common tasks included conducting religious services, leading the church choir, sweeping out the meetinghouse, ringing the bell for public worship, and digging graves (Elsbree, 1939). Schoolmasters usually juggled teaching and extra duties with one or more other jobs, ranging from surveying to innkeeping to artisanship. Teaching was often a stepping-stone for other careers, particularly the ministry; hence, teacher turnover was often quite high (Rury, 1989).

Schoolhouses were often one-room log or clapboard cabins containing students from the ages of 3 to 20 or more. Most often, teaching in these large-group settings meant making students memorize facts. To do so, students had to sit quietly for long periods of time on backless benches until called on by the teachers to recite. Teachers relied on whole-group instruction and choral responses in these mixed-ability classes. The entire system depended on repetition and drill, helped along with a more than healthy dose of punishment (Boyer et al., 2000).

When students misbehaved, the teacher punished them swiftly and often severely. Teachers used whipping, ear boxing, hand caning, and other terror tactics to control their charges. Although some educators expressed qualms about such brutality, most defended the use of corporal punishment. Punishment was an extension of authoritarian child-rearing practices and religious dictates.

> Use of corporal punishment was widespread. Eliphalet Nott, who grew up in Connecticut in the 1780s, said, "If I was not whipped more than three times a week, I considered myself for the time peculiarly fortunate." In 1819, six-year-old James Sims was sent to a boarding school in South Carolina where new boys were always flogged, usually "until the youngster vomited or wet his breeches." (Kaestle, 1983, p. 19)

During the mid-1800s teacher brutality decreased. Historians attribute this change to a number of events: (1) graded schools that separated older children from younger children evolved so that teachers who had once dealt with as many as 100 students now dealt with smaller groups; (2) women began entering the teaching profession; (3) educators such as Pestalozzi set out to enlighten teachers about the benefits of teaching students to behave in certain ways instead of beating or coercing them into submission; and (4) some school systems, particularly those in the cities, passed ordinances prohibiting harsh punishment. In 1867 Syracuse, New York, was one of the first cities to do away with corporal punishment (Elsbree, 1939; Kaestle, 1983).

Is corporal punishment still used in schools today?

▶ The Monitorial Method and the American Lyceum

Children started school at different ages. Abecedarians—beginners at school—often started as young as age 3. This meant, of course, that teachers often faced very large groups of students, composed of as many as 40 or 50 children, who differed markedly in abilities (Kaestle, 1983). The Lancasterian or **monitorial method** of teaching provided one response to this challenge.

Before graded schools were established in the cities, there were so many students crowded into a room that one teacher could not deal with all of them at once. In the 1820s Joseph Lancaster, a Quaker, found these urban classrooms to be fertile ground for the monitorial method of teaching used in Europe. In this educational pyramid scheme, the master teacher served as a "silent bystander" and "inspector." He instructed the monitors, and they, in turn, instructed the younger children. The older students also monitored attendance and kept order in the classroom. The approach made reading, writing, and arithmetic available to large numbers of children, and it was cheap. Lancaster also offered extensive and explicit directions on how to teach. If teachers followed his system, Lancaster argued, they could not fail (Reigart, 1969).

The monitorial system was one of the most successful and widely used educational methods of the first 30 years of the 19th century. Efficient, and easy to use, the monitorial method extended educational opportunities to increasing numbers of children from low-income families. Reformers concerned with the moral training of the poor believed the system might inculcate in these children obedience, industry, and promptness. At the same time, the Lancasterian system's use of monitors allowed for the training of future teachers (Kaestle, 1983).

Other types of schooling that developed during the 19th century included the **lyceum.** In 1826 a wealthy Connecticut farmer, Josiah Holbrook, founded the American Lyceum, an organization devoted to the advancement of education for children and adults. Holbrook wanted to provide an economical and practical education to American youth and to encourage the application of science and education in everyday life. People belonged to a lyceum for $1 a year. Some lyceums were reading circles, some debating clubs, and some concert bands.

The first branch of the American Lyceum was in Millbury, Massachusetts. By 1829 the lyceum had spread across the country. Ralph Waldo Emerson, a frequent lecturer on the lyceum circuit, considered the American Lyceum a new form of education and a broad cultural movement. This first formal adult and community education movement thrived in the late 1820s and 1830s and faded in the years following the Civil War.

▶ The Latin School and the English Academy

The **Latin grammar school,** the first formal type of secondary school in the colonies, was established in Boston in 1635. Boys entered the grammar school at age 9 or 10, if they could read and write English, and attended for 4 to 5 years. Although Latin grammar schools often offered arithmetic, geography, algebra, trigonometry, or rhetoric, their hallmark was the teaching of Latin and Greek and associated literatures. In other ways, the Latin grammar school was a conceptual leap backward to Europe, where money and social status meant power and privilege. The very few students who prepared to enter college went to these schools. Girls were not admitted.

In the belief that a more practical education was needed, Ben Franklin created an English-language academy in Philadelphia in 1749 (Best, 1962). Franklin recognized the need to prepare young people for highly skilled occupations and for the world of commerce. The classics were not neglected entirely, but the **English academy** emphasized the acquisition and application of practical knowledge thought to be most useful to the modern man.

The school originally taught practical subjects such as penmanship, arithmetic, and bookkeeping. Unlike in the Latin grammar school, English was the language of instruction, but students could study other languages related to their needs. Prospective merchants studied French, Spanish, or German. Prospective clergy studied Latin or Greek. Franklin's academy also taught many other practical skills, such as farming, carving, shipbuilding, carpentry, and printing.

▶ The Development of Public Schools

Perhaps most significant was the development of schooling based on the concept of free public education. This idea had its roots in the early Republic. Jefferson believed that it was to society's benefit to educate all of its citizens so they might provide leadership and support for the country. As a member of the Virginia Assembly's Committee to Revise the Laws of the Commonwealth from 1776–1779, Jefferson drafted the Bill for the More General Diffusion of Knowledge, a bill he considered one of his finest pieces of work (Cremin, 1980).

The bill proposed the establishment of **common schools,** tax-supported schools for reading, writing, arithmetic, and history, which children could attend free for 3 years and pay thereafter. The bill also proposed the establishment of 20 grammar schools, in which Latin, Greek, English grammar, and advanced arithmetic would be taught. The brightest students from the lower schools who could not afford to pay tuition would attend these grammar schools at public expense; children whose families could afford to pay would do so. From the grammar schools, 10 scholarship students would go on to the College of William and Mary for 3 years at public expense. Through such a system of education, Jefferson believed, society could safeguard liberty. To succeed, democracy needed the participation of educated citizens both to support and to restrict the power of its leaders. Although successful in establishing a public university, Jefferson did not live to realize his dream of publicly supported schools for Virginia's children (Cremin, 1980, pp. 440–441).

> **Why might some people have opposed the establishment of common schools?**

Benjamin Rush also advocated common schools. He argued that education should be organized to help prepare people to function effectively in a democratic society, which meant that education should encourage public over private interests. Moreover, education should be uniquely American, that is, practical and forward looking, particularly in light of the emerging sciences (Cremin, 1980).

The spread of common schools led to sweeping educational reform on a national scale. In the 1830s reformers in the common school movement pressed for a variety of measures: (1) taxation for public education (Horace Mann embarrassed Massachusetts towns into improving funding for education by publishing an annual list of all towns ranked by per pupil expenditures); (2) longer school terms; (3) a focus on getting particular groups of nonattenders enrolled in schools, particularly those living in urban slums and factory tenements and the children of free blacks; (4) hierarchical school organizations (e.g., state education agencies headed by a superintendent, schools headed by a "principal teacher," graded schools); (5) consolidation of small school districts into larger-scale school units so that per-pupil expenditures would be more uniform from district to district; (6) standardization of educational methods and curriculum; and (7) teacher training (Kaestle, 1983).

Primary school enrollment rates increased over time. In the late 18th and early 19th centuries, school attendance was higher in rural areas than in the cities. More girls began to go to school, particularly in the Northeast (Kaestle, 1983). Signs of literacy, such as the number of people able to sign their names and the number of newspaper subscriptions, pointed to rapid social change during this period (Cremin, 1970). From the 17th through the early 20th century, however, no more than 10 percent of eligible school-age children ever went beyond elementary school.

The public high school emerged in Boston in the 1820s as an alternative to the Latin grammar school and the English academy. High schools did not become important in American education, however, until the late 1800s, when courts ruled that people could raise taxes to support such schools (Krug, 1964). The high school was a public institution that provided an English or a classical secondary education. Lawrence Cremin (1980) described this early high school as one that "reproduced under public auspices the upper reaches of the academy, making available to day students at modest cost or gratis what had formerly been available to boarding students at more substantial cost" (pp. 389–90).

▶ Leaders in the Movement for Universal Education

A universal tax-supported system of free schools developed in the three decades before the Civil War. The Jeffersonian ideal of **universal schooling,** educating all citizens for the common good, came close to reality for those who were not of African, Native American, and Hispanic descent. At the same time, women became the backbone of the American educational system. First through their own schooling and then by assuming roles as teachers themselves, they capitalized on new and socially acceptable opportunities to assert their independence. Women benefited from the chance to fill jobs that men, for a number of reasons related to the expanding economy, no longer wanted.

Why and how did teaching evolve into "women's work"?

Horace Mann.   As secretary to the Massachusetts State Board of Education from 1837 to 1848, Horace Mann (1796–1859) aggressively promoted a sweeping transformation of schools. His goals included shifting responsibility for financial support for schools from parents to the state, establishing grades (classifying students by age and performance), extending the school term of two to three months to as many as ten months, using standardized textbooks, and making school attendance mandatory. With increased structure, Mann reasoned, schools might then be more than mere appendages of the family (Boyer et al., 2000).

Horace Mann also was instrumental in establishing public teachers' colleges, called **normal schools** (from the French *école normale*), in Massachusetts. Largely due to Mann's efforts, the state legislature passed a resolution accepting his proposal, and the first public normal school in the United States was opened in Lexington on July 3, 1839 (Elsbree, 1939).

In 1844, Mann promoted the idea of encouraging women to become teachers, although he did so with somewhat less than a ringing endorsement of their talents:

> There are thousands of females amongst us, who now spend lives of frivolity, of unbroken wearisomeness and worthlessness, who would rejoice to exchange their days of painful idleness for such ennobling occupations [as teaching]; and who, in addition to the immediate rewards of well-doing, would see, in the distant prospect, the consolations of life well spent, instead of the pangs of remorse for a frivolous and wasted existence. (p. 1317)

Horace Mann
(1796–1859)

Normal schools were educational programs dedicated solely to training teachers so that they could perform according to high standards, or "norms." Such institutes had existed in Germany for about 100 years and in France and England since the early 1800s. By 1850, there were only a few normal schools in the United States, mainly in the Northeast, preparing young women to become teachers. The curriculum consisted of courses in the history and philosophy of education, instructional principles and teaching methodology, and a period of practice teaching (Elsbree, 1939; Kaestle, 1983).

Henry Barnard.   With Horace Mann, Henry Barnard (1811–1900) was a leading proponent of the common school. A journalist by training, Barnard was secretary of the Connecticut Board of Education (1838–1842), state commissioner of the public schools in Rhode Island (1845–1849), chancellor of the University of Wisconsin (1858–1860), and U.S. Commissioner of Education (1867–1870). He wrote about public education and European educational reformers such as Pestalozzi and Froebel in the *Connecticut Common School Journal* and the *American Journal of Education.*

Barnard extolled the virtue of teaching civic values and basic skills, but to him the most important subject was the English language. He recognized the need for strong teacher preparation and for paying people enough to get them into teaching and to keep them there. This meant, of course, that he also perceived the importance of building public support for such actions: "The right beginning of this work of school improvement is in awakening, correcting, and elevating public sentiment in relation to it" (Barnard, 1857).

Henry Barnard also did much to promote the concept of the public high school. He argued that primary schools were not up to the task of providing the intellectually rigorous education that students needed. He also believed that by reaching out to students over a larger geographical area than did private schools, the high school would better serve the public. The high school "must make a good education common in the highest and best sense of the word common—common because it is good enough for the best, and cheap enough for the poorest family in the community" (Barnard, 1857, p. 185).

▶ The Proliferation of Parochial Schools

Although Protestants were the dominant religious group during colonial times, there was great diversity in religious preferences. Of the 260 churches existing in 1689, 71 were Anglican, 116 Congregational, 15 Baptist, 17 Dutch Reformed, 15 Presbyterian, 12 French Reformed, 9 Roman Catholic, and 5 Lutheran. There were also loosely organized groups of Quakers, Mennonites, Huguenots, Anabaptists, and Jews (Cremin, 1970). Depending on their religious beliefs, different groups had unique ideas about the education of children and so established **parochial schools,** or private schools with religious affiliations.

German Lutherans, for example, wanted to protect their language and way of life. By 1840 there were more than 200 Lutheran parochial schools in Pennsylvania. In 1856, in return for a rent-free house, firewood, a salary of $12 per month, and extra pay for baptisms and marriages, Lutheran minister Edmond Multanowski preached and taught members of his congregation for 6 hours a day, nearly 11 months a year in Carlinville, Illinois (Cremin, 1980). Groups such as the Amish and Mennonites also educated their own children, holding them out of the common schools. Parents were fearful that outside influences might corrupt their sons and daughters.

In the 1840s, Catholic leaders protested the use of the King James Bible in the common schools. They also fought against the religious and ethnic slurs aimed at Irish Catholics in particular in the common schools. The climate was right for the establishment of their own alternative school system—one that has grown to be the largest alternative to public education in the world. John Hughes, Bishop of New York, admonished his parishioners "to build the schoolhouse first, and the church afterwards" (Lannie, 1968). By 1865, Catholic schools were teaching 16,000 students, or about one-third of the Catholic school population, in New York (Dolan, 1985).

Why might some people have viewed parochial schools as a threat to democracy?

Catholics, Lutherans, Amish, Mennonites, and others wanted to protect their children and their ways of life, as did the general public. Reformers in the common-school movement viewed parochial schools as the greatest possible threat to democracy. In their minds, "the goals of a common-school system—moral training, discipline, patriotism, mutual understanding, formal equality, and cultural assimilation—could not be achieved if substantial numbers of children were in independent schools" (Kaestle, 1983, p. 116).

▶ The Growth of Institutions of Higher Education

FIGURE 2.3 Founding of the Colonial Colleges How was teacher education different from college education in the 18th century?

The colonists modeled their new colleges on Oxford and Cambridge. Only 6 years after the Puritans landed in Massachusetts, they founded the college that later assumed the name of its first benefactor, John Harvard (see Figure 2.3). Harvard students studied the liberal arts and sciences: Latin, Greek, Hebrew, mathematics, logic, rhetoric, astronomy, physics, metaphysics, and philosophy. Prospective ministers prepared for their callings only after they had graduated. The other colonial colleges also promoted the idea that higher education prepared young men for lives of leadership.

Teachers typically did not attend college. Most prepared to learn on the job in schools. They served as apprentices to teachers who had instructed them. Occasionally, they would read a textbook or attend a teachers' institute meant to transmit some new bit of scientific knowledge about teaching and learning. The first of these institutes, established by Henry Barnard at Hartford, Connecticut, in the autumn of 1839, provided 6 weeks of instruction focused on instructional strategies and curriculum to 26 young men (Cremin, 1980; Elsbree, 1939).

Founding of the Colonial Colleges	
1636	Harvard
1693	William and Mary
1701	Yale
1746	Princeton
1754	Columbia
1755	Pennsylvania
1766	Brown
1766	Rutgers
1769	Dartmouth

Private **seminaries**—academies for girls—were the primary means for advancing the skills of future teachers. In 1823 Samuel R. Hall opened a seminary with a model school at Concord, Vermont. That same year Catherine and Mary Beecher, sisters of Harriet Beecher Stowe, opened a seminary for young women in Hartford, Connecticut, that eventually became the Hartford Female Seminary. They taught grammar, geography, rhetoric, philosophy, chemistry, ancient and modern history, arithmetic, algebra, geometry, theology, and Latin (Cross, 1965). In 1827 James G. Carter, with the help of local citizens, established a teachers' seminary at Lancaster, Massachusetts. At about the same time, James Neef founded the New Harmony Community School in New Harmony, Indiana, where he introduced Pestalozzi's ideas about teaching and learning (Elsbree, 1939).

In response to the need for more teacher training programs, state-subsidized seminaries and academies began to evolve. Gradually private and semiprivate institutions gave way to public normal schools.

The growth of higher education was stimulated by the passage of the Morrill Act in 1862. The Morrill Act provided federal assistance for the establishment of public colleges of agriculture and the mechanic or industrial arts. The act granted each state 30,000 acres of public land for each of its congressional representatives. The income from the grant went to support at least one land-grant college in the state, which was devoted to agricultural and mechanical instruction. The Morrill Act emphasized the importance of applied science and made higher education accessible to millions of people in the years that followed. Like the Northwest Ordinance of 1785, it was also a precursor of federal involvement in education.

What Curricula and Textbooks Shaped Education?

Until about 1830, the curriculum, or what was to be learned, was driven by unswerving interpretations of God's preferences and the three R's. The Old and New Testaments, which were readily available in print, served as the main reading books in the late 18th and early 19th centuries. Arithmetic students learned from what was around them. Dealing with money, for example, reinforced the importance of numeracy skills. Many children studied whatever books their families sent to school with them—books that were jealously guarded. Sometimes teachers had to contend with as many different books as they had children in their schools (Kaestle, 1983).

Students learned to read by first learning their ABC's. They moved on to memorizing vowel sounds, such as "ab, eb, ib, ob, ub," then one-syllable words, and then longer words and sentences. They practiced on slates and worked their way up to quill pens and copybooks.

Hornbooks, Primers, and Almanacs.   The **hornbook** was the first reader for many students. It was a single piece of parchment imprinted with the alphabet, vowels, syllables, the doctrine of the Trinity, and the Lord's Prayer. To increase its durability, the parchment was covered with a transparent sheet of cow's horn, and the two were tacked to a board. The hornbook was eventually replaced with more elaborate books of several pages.

The *New England Primer* appeared in the late 17th century and was the prototype for **primers**—textbooks designed to impart rudimentary reading skills—used widely in the colonies through the 18th century. The *Primer* was a collection of rhymes for the letters of the alphabet, adorned with woodcut drawings. Each rhyme, an admonition or prayer, reflected the religious values of the colonies (Ford, 1899).

Benjamin Franklin left his imprint on the curriculum in the 18th century, as he did so often on anything in which he took an interest. His *Poor Richard's Almanack* extolled the virtues of thrift, hard work, and creativity. The *Almanack,* which became a mainstay in the classroom, served as a sort of philosophical touchstone for the self-made colonist.

Issues in School Reform

Noah Webster and Spelling Reform

The term *reform* as applied to education connotes that at one time something was established or fixed or concluded and that now or in the future that same something might or should be changed. That is not to say that (1) reform is always accomplished, or (2) if it is accomplished, even in part, it sticks for any particular period of time, or (3) a big name helps the cause, or (4) if the proposed reform fails, it goes away. The case of Noah Webster and the issue of spelling reform, juxtaposed with a recent article from *Teacher Magazine* seem pertinent.

In 1789, Webster argued:

It has been observed by all writers, on the English language, that the orthography or spelling of words is very irregular; the same letters often representing different sounds, and the same sounds often expressed by different letters.

The question now occurs; ought the Americans to retain these faults which produce innumerable inconveniences in the acquisition and use of the language, or ought they at once reform these abuses, and introduce order and regularity into the orthography of the AMERICAN TONGUE?

The principal alterations, necessary to render our orthography sufficiently regular and easy, are these:

1. The omission of all superfluous or silent letters; as *a* in bread. Thus *bread, head, give, breast, built, meant, realm, friend,* would be spelt, *bred, hed, giv, brest, bilt, ment, relm, frend*. . . .

2. A substitution of a character that has a certain definite sound, for one that is more vague and indeterminate. Thus by putting *ee* instead of *ea* or *ie*, the words *mean, near, speak, grieve, zeal,* would become *meen, neer, speek, greev, zeel*. . . .

3. A trifling alteration in a character, or the addition of a point would distinguish different sounds, without the substitution of a new character. Thus a very small stroke across *th* would distinguish its two sounds.

When and how did education based on European models become "Americanized"?

Geographies, Spellers, and Dictionaries. Jedidiah Morse provided an opportunity for children to think about their cultural identity as Americans when he produced his *Geography Made Easy* in 1784. The book focused on the geography of the United States rather than on that of Europe or Britain. Much like Franklin's *Poor Richard's Almanack*, it contained patriotic and moralistic themes.

In the late 1700s and early 1800s, Noah Webster promoted a common English language. Webster's *American Spelling Book*, sometimes referred to as the **Blue-Backed Speller,** was first published in 1783; by 1837, 15 million copies had been sold. Webster's magnum opus, *An American Dictionary,* first published in 1825, became the authoritative source on information about English words. Webster believed that power and prestige as a nation distinct from Britain would never come to the United States until it established its own distinctive vocabulary, spelling, and usage.

McGuffey Readers. William Holmes McGuffey, a clergyman and professor of philosophy, produced his legendary reader in 1836. It was the most widely used reading book in the United States in the 19th century. **McGuffey Readers** taught literacy skills

Webster advocated action: "*Now* is the time, and *this* the country, in which we may expect success, in attempting changes favorable to language. . . . Let us then seize the present moment, and establish a *national language,* as well as a national government."

In 1999, *Teacher Magazine* observed:

Advocates of whole language insist that it is not the death of phonics, which remains an important tool in the toolbox. But there is clearly a difference in priorities. Critics feel that whole language overemphasizes "understanding," at the expense of accuracy and correctness. A 1st grader in a whole-language classroom could come home with an essay full of "invented" spelling and fractured grammar—having received an "A" from a teacher impressed with the thoughts expressed and the overall use of language. Some parents feel that sort of laxity will lead to a generation of students who never learn how to spell properly. Advocates of the whole-language approach, by contrast,

say that an overemphasis on rules and rote learning has proven time and again to be stifling—and leads children to see reading and writing as arduous and arcane chores, rather than as an interesting way of gathering information.

The anonymous author proceeds to ask, "Which philosophy will win out?" . . . Indeed.

Discussion Questions: What concerns about spelling did Noah Webster voice? How does his view compare to that of advocates for whole language? As a classroom teacher, what is your perspective on this issue?

Source: N. Webster (1974). An essay on the necessity, advantages, and practicality of reforming the mode of spelling and of rendering the orthography of words correspondent to pronunciation (1789). In S. Cohen (ed.), *Education in the United States: A Documentary History* (Vol. 2, pp. 763–766). New York: Random House; also from *Teacher Magazine,* (August 16, 1999). Phonics and whole language. Available online at http://www.teachermagazine.org/context/topics/phonics.htm

and sought to advance the Protestant ethic through stories and essays that imparted values of thrift, honesty, and diligence. By including speeches of the nation's founders, McGuffey also used his book to promote patriotic nationalism. McGuffey Readers are still produced and sold.

How were Educational Success and Failure Evaluated?

Kaestle (1983) argues that before the Revolution and up until about 1840, local communities viewed their schools as quite successful. Because communities still depended on family and church to teach moral values and on work to train young people for occupations, schools did what they were supposed to do: provide rudimentary education in basic skills at low cost.

Was Alexis de Tocqueville right about American education?

FROM THE NEW ENGLAND PRIMER.

The *New England Primer* reflected the Puritan focus on religion as the point of education. Later, early textbooks in the United States reflected the importance of moral character and national pride. How do textbooks published today reflect certain educational objectives?

School is much more a part of life today than it was in earlier times. From the arrival of the colonists until the Civil War, few people went to school. Those who attended public schools got a dose of reading, writing, calculating, and the Protestant ethic, and then went their own way. Most acquired the knowledge necessary to survive and prosper from their families, churches, and work.

When the young Frenchman Alexis de Tocqueville came to this country in 1831 to see the new democracy in action, he observed that people in the United States influenced or taught one another informally and routinely through newspapers and voluntary associations. Tocqueville (1840) believed that the press, in particular, had great educational power:

> Nothing but a newspaper can drop the same thought into a thousand minds at the same moment. . . . I shall not deny that in democratic countries newspapers frequently lead the citizens to launch together into very ill-digested schemes; but if there were no newspapers there would be no common activity. The evil which they produce is therefore much less than that which they cure. (p. 116)

The narrowly defined and severely delivered education in the young nation helped those children who attended—most of whom were white, Protestant, and male—to learn the three R's and to assimilate Protestant or Catholic values. For other young people—Native Americans, African Americans, immigrants, and those living in poor, rural places—schooling, if it existed at all, was at best a mixed blessing. Public schools saved some from illiteracy but simultaneously reinforced the idea that one's worth was measured in terms of race and social class.

Using Technology

Making History Come Alive

Technology today allows high school teachers to make history more engaging than ever before. Videotapes and CD-ROMs, for example, depict historical events in realistic ways that allow students to imagine what life was like for people in earlier times. Materials on the web, depending on how they are structured, can also be powerful tools for making history accessible to young people. The "Valley of the Shadow," for example, a web site at the University of Virginia, is a large digital archive that focuses on two opposing communities from 1859 through the Civil War: Confederate Augusta County, in Virginia, and Unionist Franklin County,

in Pennsylvania. The web site includes lesson plans for teachers and a variety of online materials for students: newspapers, diaries, photographs, maps, church records, census information, and medical records. As students engage in online activities, they can write their own versions of history, reconstructing life stories of women, African Americans, farmers, politicians, soldiers, and families. Content is divided into two general sections, "The Eve of the War" and "The War Years."

According to Edward L. Ayers (1999), creator of the project, hypertext can be an effective medium for teaching history:

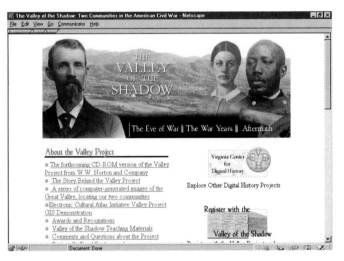

The web site for "The Valley of the Shadows" makes the Civil War come alive for students.

The computer provides a powerful environment for thinking more rigorously, revealing patterns we simply could not see before. The machine is equally felicitous with numbers and words and images, across time or space, in political, cultural, or social history. Students working with large but finite bodies of evidence experiment with various perspectives and questions. The computer amplifies students' critical abilities, allowing them to refine their questions and quickly follow up with new ones. It permits them to build archives and interpretations of their own and share them with others far beyond their own classroom.

As the nation grew, people debated what it meant to be American. As Riesman (1954) observed, in the early days, the idea of our nation as the melting pot was valuable. It forced people to think about equality and hospitality to culturally diverse peoples. But the early arrivals to our country narrowed the idea to try to produce a uniform variety of American, "freed of all cultural coloring, maladjustment, or deviation" (p. 60). This trend continued and even accelerated in the early 20th century.

Benchmarks

Historical Foundations of American Education, Colonial Times to 1865

1500s–1600s	Spanish conquer Native American peoples in Mexico and the American Southwest. Dutch, English, and French settle the Atlantic seaboard and explore North America. Dutch traders bring African slaves to plantations in the southern colonies. Such actions shape the people who will educate and be educated and will influence both individual and collective educational goals for many years to come.
1620–1630	Puritans and Pilgrims settle in New England, establishing the pattern of education for the New England and Middle Atlantic colonies.
1635–1636	Latin grammar school is established in Boston as a college preparatory school for young men. Harvard College is founded.
1642–1647	Massachusetts Act of 1642 makes citizens responsible for the education of their children and sets a precedent for the development of compulsory education. The Massachusetts Act of 1647, known as the Old Deluder Satan Act, is passed.
1788	U.S. Constitution is ratified. The framers of the Constitution give the power to establish schools and license teachers to the individual states rather than the federal government.
1803	Thomas Jefferson doubles the size of the United States with the Louisiana Purchase. During the next 100 years, Americans go west, building one-room schoolhouses across the country to preserve traditions of education.
1810–1811	The Shawnee under Tecumseh establish a confederacy of tribes to preserve their lands and way of life.
1819	Emma Willard asks the New York legislature to extend educational opportunities to women. First public high school opens in Boston.
1824	Federal government establishes the Bureau of Indian Affairs.
1825	First edition of Noah Webster's *An American Dictionary* is published.
1827	Massachusetts becomes the first state to require every town with 500 or more families to establish a public high school.

1833	First "penny press," the *New York Sun,* makes newspapers available to almost everyone. Popular literature aids the spread of literacy.
1836	First of the McGuffey Readers is published. About 122 million copies of the series are sold after this date.
1836–1837	Wesleyan College in Georgia and Oberlin College in Ohio become the first chartered colleges for women.
1837–1848	Horace Mann, secretary of the Board of Education in Massachusetts, calls for sweeping reforms based on the principle of universal free education for all citizens and the belief that teaching is a profession.
1839	First public normal school (teachers college) in the United States is established in Lexington, Massachusetts.
1848	Education issues are aired at the Women's Rights Convention in Seneca Falls, New York.
1852	Massachusetts enacts the first compulsory school attendance law.
1854	Lincoln University, the nation's first college for free African Americans, is established in Pennsylvania.
1855	Henry Barnard founds the *American Journal of Education,* the first educational journal in the United States.
1855	First kindergarten in the United States is established by Margaretta Schurtz in Watertown, Wisconsin.
1857	In the Dred Scott decision, the U.S. Supreme Court rules that African Americans, free or slave, are not citizens.
	The National Education Association (NEA) is established as a professional organization for teachers.
1860	Elizabeth Palmer Peabody opens the first English-speaking kindergarten in Boston.
1862	Morrill Land Grant College Act passes. Emancipation Proclamation passes.
1865	Civil War ends.

Heavy immigration from southern and eastern Europe and growing industrialization helped give rise to what Ezra Pound referred to as the "white alabaster cast," or the cultural mold that was used to produce the citizens of this nation.

When compared to education in other societies, however, education broadly defined in this country was remarkably successful. The nation's literacy rate climbed, industries flourished, people's standards of living increased, and governments usually changed hands peacefully.

SUMMARY

What European thinkers influenced early education?

1. Although colonists were located far from England and Europe, America's formal education system was influenced heavily by European theorists such as Comenius, Locke, Rousseau, Pestalozzi, Herbart, Froebel, and Spencer.

What was the influence of informal education before the Civil War?

2. Education both reflected and shaped people's values as they established their settlements along the eastern coast of America.

3. Education in the southern colonies was done on plantations by hired tutors and on small farms by the family.

4. Colonists in the middle colonies were more diverse than were settlers in the southern colonies. To preserve their language and beliefs, different groups established their own parochial schools.

5. In the New England colonies, the similarity of colonists' ideas and values made possible the establishment of town schools. Many settlers were Puritans who followed the teachings of John Calvin, a Swiss religious reformer.

6. Informal education for all people in early America meant learning from the family and from others in social situations and while at work in apprenticeships. People learned from each other as they interacted. As books and newspapers became widely available, people also learned from one another by reading.

7. As the country became industrialized and the population grew, the strength and diversity of American beliefs forced new meanings on schooling. Schools began slowly to broaden their focus from serving God, family, and narrowly defined communities to preparing greater numbers and more culturally diverse children for secular lives in the new nation.

What were the aims of education?

8. Most Colonists, particularly in the South, were Protestants who believed that the Scriptures were key to understanding God's will. To them, education should help save souls.

9. People began to view education as a means for personal advancement, primarily for European American men.

10. American industrialization in the early 19th century led to an increasing emphasis on practical rather than theoretical learning.

11. Religious groups played a major role in extending educational opportunities to oppressed groups, for whom individuals such as Frederick Douglass, Sequoyah, Sor Juana Ines de la Cruz, and Catherine and Mary Beecher were sources of inspiration.

12. Missionaries, freed blacks, religious groups, and slave owners were a source of education for slaves. The education of Native and Hispanic Americans took place at home and in mission schools established by priests who wanted to convert students to Catholicism. Until the 1800s, when formal schools were established for women, females were mainly educated at home or in dame schools, where they learned a variety of rudimentary skills. Clergymen and physicians, including Braille, Howe, and Gallaudet, developed educational programs for people with disabilities.

How did formal education develop before the Civil War?

13. During colonial times, academic qualifications of teachers, most of whom were men, ranged from bare ability to read and write to the scholarly attainments of a college graduate. Most often, teaching meant making children memorize facts. Teachers relied on whole-group instruction and choral responses in mixed-ability classes. In such settings, teachers frequently administered harsh corporal punishment.

14. In the 1820s, Joseph Lancaster, a Quaker, introduced to the United States the European monitorial method of teaching, an educational pyramid scheme in which the master teacher served as a "silent bystander" and instructed monitors, who in turn instructed small groups of children.

15. The spread of lyceums, common schools, land-grant schools, Latin grammar schools, English academies, and high schools expanded formal education at the primary and secondary levels.

16. The common-school reform program that began in the 1830s affected greatly the quality of education in the United States. Henry Barnard and Horace Mann were among those who aggressively promoted public schools for all children. Taxation for public education, longer school terms, and the emergence of teacher-training programs were among significant outcomes of reform efforts.

17. Private parochial schools attracted many colonists who wanted to preserve their languages and their religious and cultural beliefs. Educational reformers viewed such schools as a threat to democracy.

18. Within 6 years after the Puritans landed in Massachusetts, they founded the first college (Harvard), and by 1769 eight additional colleges had been established to prepare young men for lives of leadership. The Morrill Act of 1862 expanded educational opportunities even further by providing federal assistance for the establishment of public colleges of agriculture and colleges of mechanical or industrial arts.

What curricula and textbooks shaped education?

19. The Bible served as the main reading book in the 18th and 19th centuries. Hornbooks, primers, almanacs such as Franklin's *Poor Richard's Almanack,* geographies, spellers and McGuffey Readers were also used widely. These texts often contained patriotic and moralistic themes.

How were educational success and failure evaluated?

20. When schools provided rudimentary education in basic skills—reading, writing, and arithmetic—and religious ethics at low cost, they were usually deemed to be successful.

21. Those who were excluded from schools because of their race, gender, or social class may well have judged educational success and failure in other ways.

TERMS AND CONCEPTS

apprenticeships   40
assimilation   53
Blue-Backed Speller   66
common school   61
dame school   48
English Academy   60
hidden passage   52
hornbook   65
kindergarten   43
land grant school   47

Latin grammar school   60
lyceum   60
McGuffey Reader   66
mission school   54
monitorial method   59
normal school   62
parochial school   63
primer   65
seminary   64
universal schooling   62

REFLECTIVE PRACTICE

In the 19th and early 20th centuries, when people used the monitorial method to teach reading, a school was divided into eight classes. The classes focused on different topics: letters of the alphabet, words and syllables of two letters, words and syllables of three letters, words and syllables of four letters, reading lesson of one syllable, reading lesson of two syllables, the new Testament, and the Bible. A group of 10 children in the class, who were to receive instruction on the alphabet, sat at a table equipped with trays of sand. This table faced a large board or alphabet wheel that displayed the letters to be studied. Monitors then proceeded as follows:

> [E]ach scholar has a stick given to him about the thickness of a quill, and four inches long, with which he is to write the letters on the sand. The alphabet is divided into three parts, viz., the perpendicular letters, I H T L E F i and l, form the first lesson; the

triangular letters, A V W M N Z K Y X v w k y z and x form the second; and the circular letters, O U C J G D P B R Q S, a b o d p q g c m n h t u r s f and j, form the third class. These are in succession placed before the class, which is under the direction of a monitor, who, with an audible voice, desires them to form the first letter; each scholar now makes his best effort, which, perhaps, is a very awkward one; but the monitor pointing out the defects and occasionally printing the letter for them, teaches them to retrace it; after repeated trials upon the same letter, the class is soon able to form it readily, and with neatness. . . . The monitor then points to the first letter, and asks aloud, "What is that?" The boy at the head of the class answers first, when, if he should make a mistake, the question is put to the second boy, and so on until some one in the class answers aright; in which case the boy takes precedence in the class. This exercise soon perfects them in the knowledge of their letters and is also a pleasing relaxation. (Reigart, 1969, pp. 41–42)

Issues, Problems, Dilemmas, Opportunities

As we noted earlier in the chapter, many who promoted Lancaster's monitorial method believed that children would learn obedience, industry, and promptness. Whether or not they were right, what other outcomes might reasonably be expected from such a process of teaching and learning?

Perceive and Value

After reading some early accounts of schooling, one might imagine that monitors in these classrooms could easily have grown into self-important bullies. The chance to "be in charge" has corrupted more than a few people. But despite some pitiful historical and contemporary examples of misanthropic behavior, there is an ethic of caring that is alive and well in our public schools today that has evolved from the beliefs and practices of many early educators. Assume that some of the monitors did make school a valuable learning experience and a "pleasing relaxation" for all those present. What might these monitors have thought, what might they have felt about their fellow students and their teacher, that enabled them to perform their tasks effectively? In your own experience, specifically where and when have you encountered people with similar ideals?

Know and Act

The monitorial method is an excellent early example of a kind of "cross-age tutoring." If you wanted to learn more about other methods of encouraging students to work together—beyond your local library—where might you turn for information?

Evaluate

When it was used, the monitorial method's success was judged at least in part by how much it cost to deliver basic instruction and by how well participating students learned to read. Do you think these outcomes are more or less important today than they were in the 19th century? If you were to judge the monitorial method or some other cross-age tutoring program today, would you still be interested in these outcomes? What, if any, other outcomes might be of interest to you?

ONLINE ACTIVITY

We often ignore primary sources of information because they are too difficult to locate, or we are unwilling to exert the energy to find them. This activity will put you in touch with some primary sources that allow you to step back in time to learn more about how people thought about education prior to the Civil War. To find this information, go to the home page for the Library of Congress and click on "American Memory." If you search on the word "education," you will have access to more than 500 documents. For example, you will find a review of two lectures entitled "Hints to a Young Woman" that were delivered by Horace Mann in 1852. You can also read a report from the Board of Education for Freedmen that describes the creation and sustaining of the first public schools for children of freed slaves in and around New Orleans in 1864. Search through the list of documents for other readings pertinent to education before the Civil War. Discuss your findings with your colleagues.

3

Modern U.S. Education History, 1865 to the Present

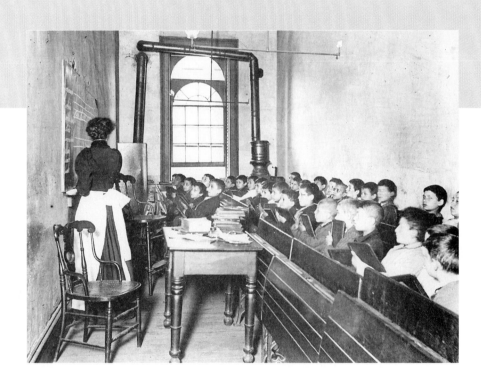

I n this chapter we describe education in the United States from 1865 to the present. We provide a historical overview of slavery and the reconstruction of the South after the Civil War, of calls for educational and social reform, of the influences of science, philanthropy, and the mass media on education, and of federal involvement in schooling.

We discuss the people who were teachers and students in this society, drawing attention to similarities and differences among them. We also note the gradual changes in how schools defined themselves and their missions as their leaders faced the demands of progress in its many forms.

Finally, we consider the evolution of teaching and curriculum. As curriculum and teaching have changed during this time, so too have society's expectations for educational success.

PROFESSIONAL PRACTICE QUESTIONS

▌ What changes after the Civil War affected the system of education in the United States?

▌ Who are "We the People"?

▌ How did teaching change after the Civil War?

▌ How did schools change during the modern era?

▌ What issues arose in curriculum development?

▌ How do people typically judge educational success and failure?

What Changes After the Civil War Affected the System of Education in the United States?

The end of the Civil War left people in the North and South seeking ways to build a nation. Slavery had ended and with it a set of social mores that had governed people's conduct. The nature of the Union was settled, but there was no blueprint for how that Union was to be operationalized in everyday lives. Leaders and ordinary citizens defined education by their actions both inside and outside schools. As illustrated in Figure 3.1, several events and reform efforts changed the nature of education in the United States.

▶ End of Slavery and Reconstruction of the South

Passion for intellectual freedom and civil liberties widened and deepened after the Civil War. The Thirteenth, Fourteenth, and Fifteenth amendments to the U.S. Constitution changed race relations legally by ending slavery, defining citizenship, and forbidding states to deny the right to vote. The customs of segregation and discrimination, however, remained entrenched. Northerners moved to reconstruct the South, often by trying to reeducate the vanquished. Not surprisingly, Southerners detested and resisted these actions.

The Bureau of Refugees, Freedmen, and Abandoned Lands, commonly known as the **Freedman's Bureau,** established 1 month before the end of the war, provided food, medicine, and seed to destitute Southerners. The Bureau secured legal rights for freed slaves and extended educational opportunities to them. Hundreds of northern teachers went south to teach African American children and adults. Despite opposition, the Freedman's Bureau succeeded in establishing and operating more than 4,000 primary schools, 74 normal schools, and 61 industrial schools for former

FIGURE 3.1
Some Factors Affecting Education in the Modern Era   Which factors do you think have had the greatest effect on your schooling?

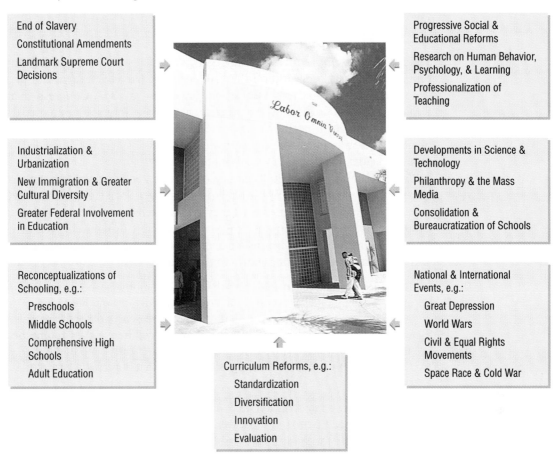

End of Slavery
Constitutional Amendments
Landmark Supreme Court Decisions

Industrialization & Urbanization
New Immigration & Greater Cultural Diversity
Greater Federal Involvement in Education

Reconceptualizations of Schooling, e.g.:
  Preschools
  Middle Schools
  Comprehensive High Schools
  Adult Education

Curriculum Reforms, e.g.:
  Standardization
  Diversification
  Innovation
  Evaluation

Progressive Social & Educational Reforms
Research on Human Behavior, Psychology, & Learning
Professionalization of Teaching

Developments in Science & Technology
Philanthropy & the Mass Media
Consolidation & Bureaucratization of Schools

National & International Events, e.g.:
  Great Depression
  World Wars
  Civil & Equal Rights Movements
  Space Race & Cold War

slaves and, in so doing, strengthened the role of the federal government in education (Degler, 1959).

Eager to keep "Negroes" in an inferior position, Southerners constructed the so-called **black codes** of conduct. These codes, or "halfway stations back to slavery," allowed African Americans to hold property, to sue and be sued, and to marry, but forbade them to carry firearms, to testify in court in cases involving European Americans, and to leave their jobs (Degler, 1959, p. 211).

The end of the Civil War did not end violence toward African Americans. Although precise numbers are impossible to determine, between 1865 and 1900, there were approximately 2,500 known lynchings, mainly of African Americans. Between 1900 and the start of World War I in 1914, more than 1,100 African Americans are known to have been lynched, mostly in the South, but also in some midwestern states (Franklin, 1967). Although rare, lynchings continued into the 1950s. In 1934 the **National Association for the Advancement of Colored People (NAACP)**, the first nationwide special interest group for African Americans, lobbied for an anti-lynching bill without success. Antilynching bills failed to pass throughout the Roosevelt and Truman administrations. Visit the NAACP web site to learn more about this organization.

▶ Calls for Educational and Social Reform

The push for universal education that began in the 1830s and 1840s gained momentum as the country moved toward the 20th century. Largely as a result of pressure from the National Teachers Association, organized in 1857, Congress created a Department of Education in 1867. President Andrew Johnson appointed Henry Barnard to assume the position of commissioner of education and to run the department. The commissioner collected statistics and facts on education and tried to promote the cause of education throughout the country.

By the beginning of the 20th century, critics initiated what was to become a sustained attack on public schools, particularly in the cities. Social reformers, sometimes called "muckrakers," bemoaned what they saw as mechanical teaching and learning, administrative ineptitude, and parents' lack of interest in their children's welfare. Joseph Mayer Rice (1969), for instance, thought that the environment of the New York City schools was nothing short of pernicious:

> It is indeed incomprehensible that so many loving mothers whose greatest care appears to be the welfare of their children are willing, without hesitation, to resign the fate of their little ones to the tender mercies of ward politicians, who in many instances have no scruples in placing the children in class-rooms the atmosphere of which is not fit for human beings to breathe, and in the charge of teachers who treat them with a degree of severity that borders on barbarism. (pp. 10–11)

Leonard Ayres's *Laggards in Our Schools* (1909) presented what he claimed was scientific evidence that the schools were filled with retarded children, or children who were overage for their grade. He blamed this consequence on the schools for creating programs for unusually bright children and ignoring the slow or average children.

In the early 20th century, many problems played themselves out in schools: an anti-evolution crusade, anti-immigration movements, organized campaigns against Roman Catholics, and increases in anti-semitism, to mention but a few. Urban poverty and the exploitation of children as cheap labor in the rapidly expanding industrial economy fueled the development of public schools and the organization of American labor; that is, schools protected children and prepared them for work later in life. In doing so, schools kept children out of the labor market, thus protecting jobs for adults.

▶ Influence of Science and Philanthropy

Education reformers in the early 20th century placed their faith in science to solve education and social problems. Frederick Taylor's studies on scientific management, or a system for getting greater productivity from human labor, appealed to businessmen who ran the school boards who, in turn, hired the superintendents who ran

Voices

Louis Terman

In 1916, Louis Terman published a book on the measurement of intelligence, one section of which explained his thinking about the utility of intelligence tests:

> [W]ithout such tests we cannot know to what extent a child's mental performances are determined by environment and to what extent by heredity. Is the place of the so-called lower classes in the social and industrial scale the result of their inferior native endowment, or is their apparent inferiority merely a result of their home and school training? Is genius more common among children of the educated classes than among the children of the ignorant and poor? Are the inferior races really inferior, or are they merely unfortunate in their lack of opportunity to learn?
>
> Only intelligence tests can answer these questions and grade the raw material with which education works. Without them we can never distinguish the result of our educational efforts with a given child from the influence of the child's original endowment. Such tests would have told us, for example, whether the much-discussed "wonder children," such as the Sidis and Wiener boys and the Stoner girl, owe their precocious intellectual prowess to superior training (as their parents believe) or to superior native ability. The supposed effects upon mental development of new methods of mind training, which are exploited so confidently from time to time (e.g., Montessori method and the various systems of sensory and motor training for the feeble-minded), will have to be checked up by the same kind of scientific measurement.
>
> In all these fields intelligence tests are certain to play an ever-increasing role. With the exception of moral character, there is nothing as significant for a child's future as his grade of intelligence. Even health itself is likely to have less influence in determining success in life. Although strength and swiftness have always had great survival value among the lower animals, these characteristics have long since lost their supremacy in man's struggle for existence. For us the rule of brawn has been broken, and intelligence has become the decisive factor in success. Schools, railroads, factories, and the largest commercial concerns may be successfully managed by persons who are physically weak or even sickly. One who has intelligence constantly measures opportunities against his own strength or weakness and adjusts himself to conditions by following those leads which promise most toward the realization of his individual possibilities.
>
> All classes of intellects, the weakest as well as the strongest, will profit by the application of their talents to tasks which are consonant with their ability. When we have learned the lessons which intelligence tests have to teach, we shall no longer blame mentally defective workmen for their industrial inefficiency, punish weak-minded children because of their inability to learn, or imprison and hang mentally defective criminals because they lacked the intelligence to appreciate the ordinary codes of social conduct.

Source: The Measurement of Intelligence by L. M. Terman, 1916. In S. Cohen (ed.), *Education in the United States: A Documentary History* (Vol. 4, pp. 2249–2250). New York: McGraw-Hill Companies, Inc.

CRITICAL THINKING

While Terman's thoughts in some ways sound strangely out of date, they seem remarkably prophetic. The intelligence tests Terman referred to have long since lost their luster in many venues, but the power of the intellect in our society reigns supreme. How might intelligence testing have opened doors for people in Terman's time? What opportunities did these tests create? How did these same tests make life difficult for others? The heredity–environment debate Terman describes continues today. Can you explain how a teacher's beliefs about the importance of heredity and environment might influence his or her teaching?

the schools (Callahan, 1962). Spurred on by grants from private foundations, leaders in school administration, including Elwood Cubberley, Frank Spaulding, and George Strayer, encouraged educational specialization and scientific management (Tyack & Hansot, 1982).

The seeds of basic research on teaching and learning also began to take root in schools at the turn of the century. James Cattell introduced "mental tests" to assess individual differences and encouraged counseling agencies and schools to incorporate such measures as part of their routine procedures. The work of Alfred Binet, Lewis Terman, and, later, Edward L. Thorndike on the measurement of intelligence was hailed as a great practical advance for schools (Travers, 1983). Psychologist Charles Judd emphasized the importance of viewing teaching and learning as social constructs, that is, as ideas that derive meaning from their use in everyday life. In contrast, John Watson's view of behavior and learning as mechanical phenomena—elements to be manipulated continually by outside sources—prompted a revolution in the way people thought about human behavior. Although strikingly different in philosophical persuasions, these researchers shared a belief in the power of science to improve the human condition.

If, as Walter Lippman argued in the popular press, science was our best weapon against ignorance, others recognized that there was money to be made from applying science to teaching and learning. Survey research and personality assessment centers sprang up in business and industry in the 1930s and 1940s and did much to shape people's thinking about what counted in life. For instance, Dale Carnegie (1936) reported that

> Investigation and research uncovered a most important and significant fact . . . about 15 percent of one's financial success is due to one's technical knowledge and about 85 percent is due to skill in human engineering—to personality and the ability to lead people. (p. 16)

He used this dubious claim to build a case for teaching others how to win friends and influence people. Carnegie sold about 1 million copies of his book in its first 2 years of publication.

From the late 19th century on, schools were embedded in a society that demonstrated in many ways the increasing value of education. In the 1870s fine-art museums opened—the Metropolitan Museum of Art in New York and the Museum of Fine Arts in Boston. The Library of Congress opened its Jefferson Building in 1897, permitting wide public access to its collection (Cole, 1979). By 1900 more than 45 million volumes were housed in the more than 9,000 public libraries across the country (Blum et al., 1997). Philanthropists such as Andrew Carnegie and Andrew Mellon donated money for promoting public access to books and art and for establishing philanthropic foundations. To upgrade educational conditions in the South, funding for the Southern Education Board (SEB), a philanthropic agency, was provided by northern capitalists, such as merchant Robert Ogden, railroad man William Baldwin, and oil magnate John D. Rockefeller.

In later years, other foundations rose to prominence in the promotion of educational causes. In 1936 the Ford Foundation, for example, began programs intended to strengthen democratic values, reduce poverty and injustice, and advance international cooperation. Since its inception, the Ford Foundation has given some $9.3 billion in support of educational and social causes. In June 1999, Bill Gates donated $5 billion to his family foundation. This gift vaulted the William H. Gates III Foundation to fourth place in the rankings of the biggest philanthropic institutions, with assets of $10 billion. It is believed to be the largest gift ever made by a living donor. The Gates Foundation supports many educational endeavors.

▶ Influence of the Mass Media

The press grew more powerful as an instrument of social education in the 20th century. Newspapers and magazines no longer served only the educated middle and upper classes; they now catered to the masses. The sensationalism of the "yellow press" of New York City—so called because the front pages of special editions were printed on yellow paper to catch the potential reader's eye—led by William Randolph Hearst and Joseph Pulitzer, shaped American opinion on education and many other matters, including its views of foreigners.

In the 15 years preceding the turn of the century, the number of periodicals published increased by 2200. By 1905 there were twenty 10¢ monthlies, with a combined circulation of 5.5 million (Blum et al., 1997). From 1920 to 1940, newspapers and magazines "continued to rival schools and churches as the chief instruments of mass education and the dissemination of ideas" (Link & Catton, 1963, p. 295).

By 1930, people in the United States were experiencing an economic depression. At the same time, new communications technology was fast becoming a part of daily life. Motion picture theaters spread across the country. About 23,000 theaters existed with a combined seating capacity of more than 11 million (Link & Catton, 1963). The entertainment value of the big screen was apparent immediately. The lure of escaping everyday troubles was too powerful to ignore. The more subtle educational influences of the movies—their power to compose the texts by which people lived or wished to live—would become an enduring national issue.

Radio captured the collective imagination of Americans in the 1920s, 1930s, and 1940s. The first broadcast was made in 1920. By 1922 there were 220 radio stations, and by 1923 there were some 2.5 million radios in the country. Approximately 80 percent of American families had radios in their homes by 1937 (Link & Catton, 1963).

While radio educated by delivering live voices of famous people into listeners' homes, television added images to those voices. The educational effects of seeing and hearing people and events that were discussed in school were profound. By January 1960, nine out of ten homes had television sets, competing with, contradicting, and complementing other sources of information, including teachers and parents. One study found that typical fourth-graders today watch between two and six hours of television daily (Daily Report Card, 1996). By high school graduation, some children have spent more time watching television than they have spent in school.

Unfortunately, public opinion on the effects of the press on education is routinely negative. David Berliner and Bruce Biddle report that roughly 95 percent of the people they surveyed at the 1997 annual meeting of the American Educational Research

Association believed reporting by the press about public education was unfairly critical of the schools (Berliner & Biddle, 1998). In a much more comprehensive survey, the Education Writers themselves found that 75 to 91 percent of educators thought the media covered education with an eye toward what sells, unfairly concentrated on conflict and failure, and contributed to the public's loss of confidence in schools (Public Agenda, 1997).

▶ Impact of Federal Involvement

Direct federal involvement in education increased after the 1950s, when the Supreme Court ruled that school racial segregation was unconstitutional. Schools became front-page news in the 1960s as battlegrounds in the war on poverty and the quest for racial equality. The federal government exerted its influence with money, legislation, and exhortation in many arenas: desegregation, aid to schools serving children of low-income families, legislation guaranteeing racial and sexual equity, new entitlements for students with disabilities, bilingual–bicultural programs, and career education. The compensatory and early intervention programs emanating from Washington, D.C., were aimed at meeting the basic needs of children living in poverty.

The most dramatic example of federal involvement was the **Elementary and Secondary Education Act (ESEA)** of 1965 (renamed the **Improving American Schools Act,** or **IASA,** in 1994). The ESEA changed the center of policy-making power from states and localities to the federal government and provided funds to alleviate the effects of poverty through a variety of programs. It supported school libraries, the purchase of textbooks and other instructional materials; guidance, counseling, and health services; and remedial instruction. The ESEA also established research centers and laboratories to advance educational practice.

Explore, for example, the Smithsonian Museum's offerings for elementary and secondary schools on the Web. See also "A Teacher's Guide to the U.S. Department of Education" on the Web.

The New Federalism of the 1980s returned to states and localities both power and financial responsibility for educational programs. As federal support for education shrank in terms of real dollars, the rhetoric of educational reform increased. National, state, and local commissions and task forces issued a spate of reports that called for changes in everything from how public schools are organized and schoolbooks are written to how teachers and students are taught and tested. Joseph Murphy (1990) described these reforms in terms of three goals: raising performance standards for students and teachers; decentralizing school management; and providing aid, such as preschool and nutrition programs to children in poverty-stricken areas.

As we enter a new century, federal involvement in public education means maintaining existing programs and attempting to improve educational practice via performance standards and other structural reforms. "The common view today is that the public schools are not good enough and that something must be done to make them better. Setting higher academic standards is one way to raise the educational achievement of students" (Jennings, 1998).

Who are "We the People"?

Concepts of federalism, the defining attributes of unity, have grown richer and more plentiful through the years. The United States is one nation out of many peoples—*e pluribus unum*. The people are similar because they are different (Fuchs, 1990). Nearly one in four Americans in the United States is a member of an ethnic or racial minority group.

After the Civil War, the population of the United States grew rapidly, most noticeably in the cities and industrialized areas. In the 1890s about 30 percent of the population of 63 million lived in cities; by 1988, 75 percent of the country's 245 million people lived in urban areas (U.S. Bureau of the Census, 1990). Although the population of the United States grew 200 percent between 1859 and 1914, the number of workers in manufacturing increased 650 percent (U.S. Bureau of the Census, 1975).

In 1910 about one half of men and women in the labor force lived in poverty. They worked long hours for meager wages, and their children often left school to work in factories. Only one-third of the enrolled children finished primary school; less than one tenth finished high school. Jacob Riis, a photographer who had an

Jacob Riis's 1890 photograph (left) shows people crowded into an urban slum in New York City. Although usually staged, as was customary in those times, Riis's photographs show the conditions in which migrant farmers and European immigrants lived in cities in the East. In other parts of the country, conditions for many African American, Chinese American, and Native American children were as difficult or worse. Walker

Evans's 1930 photograph (right) shows children from rural tenant farm families, or "sharecroppers," in Alabama during the Great Depression. As the 20th century wore on, social scientists and reformers talked about having discovered a new culture—a way of life shared by many people old and young, urban and rural, European and non-European in origin. They called it the culture of poverty.

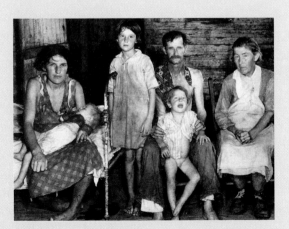

Have you seen "the culture of poverty" that exists today in the United States? Where is it? How does it look different from these photos? What appears to be the same?

agenda for social reform, found poverty and ignorance wherever he pointed his camera. In New York City's East Side, in a tenement building reported to house 478 tenants, Riis (1890) commented that the truant officer could find only seven children who said they attended school (p. 180). (See the accompanying box.)

Young social workers, nearly all women, took active roles in improving the deplorable living and working conditions of low-income people in New York City. Some ran charity nurseries, such as New York's Five Points Mission and the Five Points House of Industry. By 1890, an estimated 60,000 children had received assistance from these two institutions (Riis, 1890).

Other agents of change investigated sweatshops and tenements and established settlement houses in poor neighborhoods to help immigrants adjust to life in a new country. The first of these houses was established in 1886 in New York City; by 1910, there were 400 such houses (Carlson, 1975). Jane Addams's Hull House in Chicago had an education program that included playgrounds, a nursery, and a library.

Life was difficult in the rural areas as well, particularly where the tenant farmer population was large. The census of 1930 indicated that tenants constituted 64 percent of the population in Alabama and 66 percent in Georgia (Dabney, 1969). James Agee's account of the lives of three tenant farm families in Alabama, accompanied by Walker Evans's photographs, created a classic documentation of the period. Agee (Agee & Evans, 1960) described the families' educational needs:

> They learn the work they will spend their lives doing, chiefly of their parents, and from their parents and from the immediate world they take their conduct, their morality, and their mental and emotional and spiritual key. One could hardly say that any further knowledge or consciousness is at all to their use or advantage, since there is nothing to read, no reason to write, and no recourse against being cheated even if one is able to do sums. (p. 268)

Poverty has always been both stubbornly chronic and painfully acute in the United States. Even though more people go to school each year, poverty dominates the lives of millions. Daniel Weinberg of the U.S. Census Bureau described the situation:

> For the third consecutive year, households in the United States experienced an annual increase in their real median income. Between 1996 and 1997, median household income adjusted for inflation increased 1.9 percent, to $37,005. In addition, the poverty rate fell from 13.7 percent in 1996 to 13.3 percent in 1997. Despite this increase in income, however, the number of poor remained statistically unchanged—the number of poor in 1997 was 35.6 million people. (1997, p. 1)

▶ Native Americans

After the Civil War, military supremacy, the destruction of the buffalo, the expansion of railroads, confinement on reservations, and efforts to encourage individual rather than tribal ownership of land further eroded the traditional cultures of Native Americans. As Helen Hunt Jackson noted, the official abuse and neglect of Native Americans shaped *A Century of Dishonor*. Writing in the late 19th century, Jackson (1880/1977) estimated that 250,000 to 300,000 Native Americans lived in the United States, excluding those in Alaska:

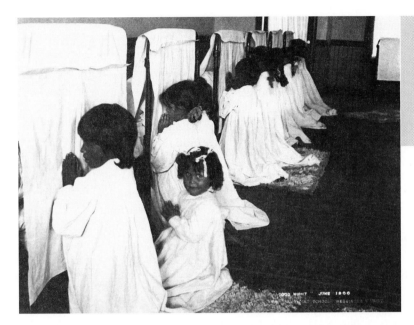

Indian boarding schools were conceived as a humanitarian way to help Native American children assimilate into the culture of the United States. How did these boarding schools do more harm than good?

> There is not among these . . . one which has not suffered cruelly at the hands either of the Government or of white settlers. The poorer, the more insignificant, the more helpless the band, the more certain the cruelty and outrage to which they have been subjected. . . . There are hundreds of pages of unimpeachable testimony on the side of the Indian; but it goes for nothing, is set down as sentimentalism or partisanship, tossed aside and forgotten. (pp. 337–338)

Government efforts to educate Native Americans were administered through the **Bureau of Indian Affairs (BIA).** Off-reservation boarding schools were meant to ensure the survival of Native Americans but were also instrumental in their destruction. These federal boarding schools took children away from their families and attempted—by way of food, dress, regimented schedules, religion, and job and language training—to impose on them the values and customs of the dominant European-American culture. Students were compelled to learn English and to "breathe the atmosphere of a civilized instead of a barbarous or semi-barbarous community" (U.S. Bureau of Indian Affairs, 1974, p. 1756). One such school, the Carlisle Indian School, established in 1879 by a young army officer named Richard Henry Pratt, educated approximately 4,000 children over a period of 24 years.

Boarding schools immersed Native American youngsters in the ways of a culture totally foreign to them.

> The first thing to do was to clean them thoroughly and to dress them in their new [military] attire. . . . [then] everything except swallowing, walking, and sleeping had to be taught; the care of person, clothing, furniture, the usages of the table, the carriage of the body, civility, all those things which white children usually learn from their childhood by mere imitation, had to be painfully inculcated and strenuously insisted on. In addition to this, they were to be taught the rudiments of an English school course and the practical use of tools. (U.S. Bureau of Indian Affairs, 1974, p. 1749)

Reservation schools had similar aims, which many Native Americans of the time accepted as valid. In the late 19th century, Princess Sara Winnemucca founded a school in California for Piute children. She taught them to spell, read, write, and calculate in English. She also taught drawing and sewing (Peabody, 1886).

The Dawes Act of 1887 had the effect of further undermining tribal authority by breaking up reservation land into smaller parcels and allotting them to individual Native Americans. These land allotments—most unsuitable for farming, particularly by people who had not been farmers—were initially held in trust and later transferred to individuals. Four out of five individuals were bilked of their property or lost it in other ways (Blum et al., 1997).

The "Indian Wars" as they came to be known were a series of bloody encounters between white settlers—sometimes with the aid of troops, sometimes without—and Native Americans. The gradual but deadly certain conclusion of these Wars was twofold: the death or subjugation of Native American peoples and their displacement from desirable lands.

Some historians have marked the conclusion of the Indian Wars at 1890 with the massacre at Wounded Knee, South Dakota. Among the Sioux, there had been a revival of ghost dancing (collective dancing that was supposed to bring back to life all the dead warriors and kin and all the dead buffalo and wild horses). Viewing these dances as a sign of resistance, the army was ordered to arrest and imprison any fomenters of disturbances. On December 15, 1890, a Native American policeman killed Chief Sitting Bull, and on the 29th, the cavalry surrounded Chief Big Foot at Wounded Knee Creek and slaughtered between 150 and 300 Lakota, or Sioux, men, women, and children. Native American resistance was crushed.

Native Americans were not considered citizens of the United States until passage of the Citizenship Act of 1924. At about the same time, the Meriam Report, a study conducted by the Brookings Institute, revealed the poor condition of education programs provided by the Education Division of the Bureau of Indian Affairs.

The 1930s and early 1940s were a period of gain for Native Americans. John Collier, commissioner of Indian affairs for Franklin Roosevelt, began to encourage preservation of Native American culture by permitting reservation schools to offer instruction in Native American languages and culture. Collier also promoted the idea of local self-government, hired Native Americans in his agency, and channeled millions of dollars into improving Native American lands. Passage of the Indian Reorganization Act of 1934 returned self-government to Native Americans, eliminated allotment policies that had reduced tribal land holdings, and prompted the study of ways to improve the poor economic, health, and social conditions of Native Americans.

Why might Native Americans as a group trail in levels of educational attainment today?

Coinciding with the onset of World War II, reduced funding for educational programs and a resurgence of assimilationist policies had a deleterious effect on the struggle for Native American autonomy. The National Congress of American Indians, founded during the war, was aggressive in its efforts to improve the lot of Native Americans. The American Indian Movement of 1968, composed mostly of militant urban Native Americans, resorted to violence. As Native Americans continued to press their case, Congress reversed its decision to terminate federal reservations and in 1975 passed the **Indian Self-Determination and Educational Assistance Act.**

Native American cultures are tremendously diverse. As a group, however, Native Americans are trailing others statistically in terms of income, life expectancy, and level of education. Unemployment is much greater than that for the total population, and poverty is rampant, particularly among widowed, divorced, and aged women (Goodman, 1985). In 1990, of the approximately 235,000 Native Americans ages 18 to 24, 63 percent had graduated from high school, and 2 percent held bachelor's degrees or higher (U.S. Census Bureau, 1995a). These figures are well below national averages for the general population.

▶ European Americans

After the Civil War, the population of the United States grew increasingly heterogeneous due to immigration. (See the accompanying box.) From 1880 to 1924, the majority of immigrants came from southern, central, and eastern Europe. Many settled in American cities and took jobs in industry. In Chicago in 1910, for example, 75 percent of the residents were immigrants or the children of immigrants (Cremin, 1988). In the 1930s and 1940s, Europeans fled the totalitarian regimes of Italy and Germany for the freedom and safety of the United States, and after them in the 1950s

From 1892 to 1954, some 12 million immigrants from many middle and eastern European countries entered America under the gaze of the Statue of Liberty in New York harbor. Emma Lazarus's (1888) poem "The New Colossus," inscribed at the base of the statue, welcomed all who arrived:

> Give me your tired, your poor,
> Your huddled masses yearning to breathe
>   free,
> The wretched refuse of your teeming shore.
> Send these, the homeless, tempest-tost [sic]
>   to me,
> I lift my lamp beside the golden door.

Lazarus's belief in the power of religious and ethnic tolerance, shaped in part by her own Jewish heritage, did not, however, convey the nation's long-standing ambivalence between accepting and rejecting foreign nationals. Many new immigrants met with the hostility of those who had preceded them. Nativism—formal policies and informal actions designed to favor the existing culture over immigrants—flourished. For example, a committee of the Fiftieth Congress appointed to investigate immigration viewed many immigrants with disdain:

> They are of a very low order of intelligence. They do not come here with the intention of becoming citizens; their whole purpose being to accumulate by parsimonious, rigid, and unhealthy economy a sum of money and then return to their native land. They live in miserable sheds like beasts; the food they eat is so meager, scant, unwholesome, and revolting that it would nauseate and disgust an American workman, and he should find it difficult to sustain life upon it. Their habits are vicious, their customs are disgusting, and the effect of their presence here upon our social condition is to be deplored. (Lodge, 1891, p. 33)

followed survivors of the Holocaust. The impact of new immigration on education was twofold: schools had to provide basic education to more people, and they had to socialize these new arrivals to the ways of the nation. Assimilation, therefore, again became a major goal of education.

As the population increased, then, it also diversified by religion and ethnicity. Differences in language and culture among the new arrivals, and between the immigrants and native born, made assimilation slow, difficult, and sometimes seemingly impossible.

Although many immigrants retain their ethnic identities through the years, many others willingly or unwillingly shed these identities. Based on a carefully selected sample of 524 households, Richard Alba (1991) found that almost no ethnic people were fluent in the language of their ancestral group. About 2 percent had ever received help in business endeavors from other members of their group. Only 2 percent were members of ethnic social clubs, while 1 percent ate ethnic foods daily, and 11 percent lived in neighborhoods having concentrations of their own ethnic group.

▶ African Americans

After the Civil War, African Americans began to take advantage of the citizenship they had gained via the Fourteenth Amendment by participating more fully in society, including attending public schools. In 1860, less than 2 percent of all school-age African American children were enrolled in school; by 1900 the figure had risen to 31 percent. Furthermore, illiteracy dropped from 82 percent in 1870 to 45 percent in 1900 (U.S. Bureau of the Census, 1990).

Emancipated slaves and European Americans established Sunday schools and universal public education during Reconstruction. Churches and ministers in African American communities often formed the nucleus from which educational campaigns spread. By 1868 the African Methodist Episcopal Church had already enrolled 40,000 pupils in Sabbath schools; by 1885, there were 200,000. African American teachers offered almost all the instruction. At its height, the Freedman's Bureau operated more than 4,000 primary schools, 74 normal schools, and 61 industrial schools for African Americans. Thousands of "Yankee school marms" ventured south to teach in needy schools established for African Americans (Degler, 1959).

Booker Taliaferro Washington was among the many African Americans who flocked to normal schools to gain an education that would enable them to be effective leaders of their people. Washington attended and later taught at Hampton Normal and Agricultural Institute in Virginia. In 1881 he went to Macon County, Alabama, to become principal of the newly created state normal school for African Americans, Tuskegee Institute. Washington built programs at Tuskegee in academics, agriculture, industrial arts, health, religion and music. His first students were public school teachers from Macon County. He even created a mobile school on a horse-drawn cart that delivered basic education to ex-slaves' door steps. Through Washington's leadership, the Tuskegee Institute became a national model for educating African American teachers, farmers, and industrial workers.

Booker T. Washington (1856–1915)

Washington believed that vocational or industrial education was the best way for African Americans to gain financial self-sufficiency and better their lives. According to Washington (1907),

Mental development is a good thing. Gold is also a good thing, but gold is worthless without an opportunity to make itself touch the world of trade. (p. 77)

The development of Washington's ideas about the need for practical rather than academic education is evident in his autobiography, *Up From Slavery*. In response to his own times and experiences, he discouraged African Americans from seeking education to become lawyers, doctors, or politicians. He believed that achieving respectability as a trained worker contributing to the economy, not upsetting the social order, was the key to advancement. Washington was working in a time when African Americans were perceived as inferior in ability, and an educated African American citizenry was perceived as a potential threat to white supremacy.

An opposite view was taken by Washington's severest critic, W. E. B. DuBois, an African American sociologist with a Ph.D. from Harvard. DuBois (1904) argued that African Americans would never achieve civil and political equality with industrial education alone and instead advocated a more academic approach to "train the best of the Negro youth as teachers, professional men, and leaders" (p. 240). On the difficulty of being both an American and a Negro, DuBois wrote:

> The history of the American Negro is the history of this strife,—this longing to attain self-conscious manhood, to merge his double self into a better and truer self. In this merging he wishes neither of the older selves to be lost. He would not Africanize America, for America has too much to teach the world and Africa. He would not bleach his Negro soul in a flood of white Americanism, for he knows that Negro blood has a message for the world. He simply wishes to make it possible for a man to be both a Negro and an American, without being cursed and spit upon by his fellows, without having the doors of Opportunity closed roughly in his face. (1903, p. 3)

DuBois advocated political activism and challenged the ideas of both African and European Americans, helping to found the Civil Rights movement that continued through the 1970s. As editor of *The Crisis,* the journal of the National Association for the Advancement of Colored People, DuBois helped formulate the educational policy of that body, which was that all American children and youth should have an equal opportunity to pursue an education.

Individuals such as Mary McLeod Bethune were also instrumental in promoting education. Bethune believed, as did other African American leaders of the time, that education was the means to better lives for all children. As an educator concerned with practical training for upward mobility and as a political activist, Bethune may be seen as representing a combination of the views of Booker T. Washington and those of W. E. B. DuBois.

In 1904 Bethune founded the Daytona Normal and Industrial School for Training Negro Girls, which was expanded in 1923 to become Bethune–Cookman College. During the Depression and World War II eras, she served in the administrations of Franklin Roosevelt and Harry Truman as director of the National Youth Administration and adviser to the United Nations.

W. E. B. DuBois
(1868–1963)

Mary McLeod
Bethune
(1875–1955)

The efforts of leaders such as DuBois and Bethune gave rise to the Civil Rights movement that grew over the next 50 years and beyond. For in the early 20th century, despite the efforts of the new leadership, education did little to improve economic opportunities or to create political and social equality. Because of segregated housing and voting districts, schools for African Americans were funded from separate tax bases, and African Americans' comparative poverty meant that their schools were usually underfunded.

In 1896, in *Plessy* v. *Ferguson,* the Supreme Court ruled that public facilities for European and African Americans could be separate but equal, which served to legalize school segregation. By 1917 the discrepancy in financial resources for European American and African American schools had jumped to four to one in favor of European American schools. In some rural areas, schools for European Americans received 15 times more support. In Georgia from 1928 to 1929, for example, 99 percent of the money budgeted for teaching equipment went to European American schools, even though African Americans composed 34 percent of the population (Bond, 1934).

By 1900, African Americans outnumbered European Americans in several southern cities, including Charleston, South Carolina; Savannah, Georgia; and Shreveport, Louisiana. African Americans had few opportunities for employment, however. Jim Crow—the colloquial name for laws and customs supporting racial segregation—sharply restricted opportunities. In 1907 in Alabama, for example, European American teachers were paid roughly five times more money than were African American teachers.

At the same time, in 1900, southern states spent an average of $9.72 per pupil, compared with $20.80 per pupil in the north-central states. Publicists such as Walter Hines Page admonished Southerners for such inequities and urged citizens to support increases in state and local taxes to narrow the gap. Although such efforts did not equalize funding for schools, between 1902 and 1910 appropriations for schools in the South doubled, enrollment of European American students increased by almost a third, and school terms increased from 5 to 6 months. Illiteracy among European Americans declined from 11.8 percent in 1900 to about 5.5 percent in 1920; during the same time period, illiteracy among African Americans 10 years of age or older declined from 44.5 percent to about 22.9 percent (Link & Catton, 1963).

Poverty forced many African Americans to live in squalor. As industrialization advanced in the post–Civil War period, many African Americans migrated north, hoping to find work and to avoid what they perceived as a trend toward economic reenslavement in the South. For instance, after the Civil War, approximately 6,000 freed slaves left Louisiana, Mississippi, and Texas for Kansas in what was called the "Kansas Fever Exodus." These "exodusters" and other African Americans leaving the South prized education and sought educational opportunities as well as land in Kansas, in the West, and in northern cities (Painter, 1977).

Despite hardships, freedom in northern cities brought a burst of creativity. In New York City following World War I, a group of African American writers, artists, jazz and blues musicians, and other performers shaped what became known as the Harlem Renaissance, a period of artistic expression that celebrated African American culture and protested against social and economic injustices. Among the leading

Cultural Awareness

Craig Barton

Craig Barton is a teacher and an architect. He believes successful architects are those who can imagine the future in appropriate historical context—a context rich in the history of our nation's struggle for civil rights. After visiting Charleston, South Carolina, his students worked long hours to render their visions of history and functionality as plans for the development of usable community space. Through the content he delivers and the education he models, Barton makes connections between the lives of historically marginalized people and the environments we occupy today:

I think what I offer students is a way of looking at a place that they're not used to; I want students to walk through a place as somebody who is black. There's a perception that it doesn't matter who you are, and I try to teach students that in fact it actually does. I set out in the project statement the criteria that I think are central issues—both architectural, and I guess just generally cultural. Students have to do some basic historical research, and usually that gets set around a series of architectural precedents that have to do with buildings that are distant from us temporally. I've taken students to places like Selma, Alabama; I haven't taken them to Money, Mississippi, but I've been there on my own. (1999)

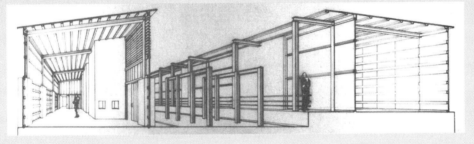

writers were James Weldon Johnson, Countee Cullen, and Langston Hughes. For further readings on the Harlem Renaissance, search the Web.

African Americans continued to struggle for equality and were heard. President Harry Truman acted to integrate the armed forces in 1948 and 1949. Many members of minority groups capitalized on their opportunities to go to college with expenses paid by the G.I. Bill. Thurgood Marshall of the NAACP argued constitutional cases, including the landmark *Brown* v. *Board of Education of Topeka, Kansas* in 1954. In this case, the Supreme Court ruled that segregation of students by race is unconstitutional and that education is a right that must be available to all people on equal terms. Martin Luther King, Jr. and others led the nationwide civil rights movement into the 1960s.

The economic, political, social, and educational conditions of African Americans have improved over the years. Although the physical separation of African American students is not legally sanctioned today as it was before *Brown* v. *Board of Education,* some people argue that public schools are being resegregated by economic and demographic factors, particularly in the cities. In Detroit's schools, between 1975 and 1996, for example, African American enrollment increased from 71 percent to about 94 percent (Harris, 1984; Kunen, 1996). In 1979 Linda Brown-Smith, who was 5 years old when her father filed the historic *Brown* case on her behalf, went back to court on behalf of her own child to charge that the Topeka, Kansas, public schools remained segregated, a consequence that years of forced busing to promote integration has not cured.

Today, many African Americans remain at the lower end of the economic scale, have more health problems, have a shorter life expectancy, and are statistically more prone to youth unemployment, teenage pregnancy, drug use, and violence. The percentage of high school graduates enrolling in college has consistently remained lower than that for European Americans. In 1976, 9.6 percent of the college population was African American. By 1996, this figure had risen only slightly to 11 percent (U.S. Department of Education, 1999).

▶ Hispanic Americans

Hispanic Americans constitute the fastest growing ethnic group in America. The term **Hispanic** means having Spanish colonial origins or being Spanish speaking. Hispanics include people of Native American, African, and European descent. People from Puerto Rico, Cuba, Central and South America, and Mexico have come to the United States to work and, in some cases, to find a haven from war and political repression.

Some groups in the Southwest prefer the name *Latino* (feminine: *Latina*) or *Chicano* (feminine: *Chicana*) to *Hispanic,* which originally described immigrants to urban areas of the eastern United States.

Most Cubans arrived in the United States as political refugees after Fidel Castro overthrew the Cuban dictatorship of Fulgencio Batista in 1959. Puerto Ricans, on the other hand, have migrated freely between the United States and Puerto Rico since 1917, when Puerto Rico became a possession of the United States with commonwealth status and its citizens became U.S. citizens. As pointed out in Chapter 2, Mexican Americans were absorbed into the United States through conquest and later through annexation of their lands. For decades Mexican nationals have attempted border crossings to the more affluent United States in search of economic opportunities. Today Hispanic peoples—Mexican Americans, Mexican nationals, Puerto Rican Americans, and Central Americans—constitute more than 70 percent of the migrant work force, which is made up mainly of farm workers (Bennett, 1999).

Like other immigrant groups, Hispanic Americans have had to struggle to overcome prejudice and discriminatory practices directed against them. Their struggles for civil rights and political representation during the 1960s resulted in four Mexican Americans winning election to Congress. By the 1980s, Hispanic Americans were seen as an emerging political force as they elected members of Congress, a governor in New Mexico, and mayors in Denver, San Antonio, Miami, Tampa, and Santa Fe.

In some states, such as California, Texas, and Florida, Hispanic Americans constitute the majority of public school enrollees. Overall, educational levels of Hispanic Americans have ranked somewhat lower than those of other groups. Comparisons of dropout rates indicate that, while only 7.6 percent of European American and 13.4 percent of African American 16- to 24-year-olds dropped out of school in 1997, 25.3 percent of Hispanic American youths failed to complete school. Income levels for Hispanic Americans averaged slightly higher than those of African Americans in 1996, but 39.9 percent of Hispanic American children younger than age 18 were living in poverty (U.S. Department of Education, 1999).

Some Hispanic and non-Hispanic Americans, including educators, have emphasized the need for bilingual education, in which children are taught in their native tongue as well as in English. Overall, research on the efficacy of bilingual education has yielded mixed results. Some studies conclude that students learn English at a much faster rate in bilingual classes, while other studies suggest that too many students languish in bilingual education too long, making little or no progress (Schnaiberg, 1999). Public debate centers on whether bilingual education leads to a lack of unity in American society or represents the best chance for immigrant students to succeed.

> **Does bilingual education slow the assimilation of immigrants? Should all immigrants be expected to want to assimilate?**

Sometimes public debate results in legislative action. In 1998, California voters passed Proposition 227, a law requiring schools in most cases to teach limited-English-proficient students almost entirely in English. The aftermath of Proposition 227 has been somewhat "dizzying," however. A clause in the broadly worded law allows parents the option of returning their children to bilingual education. "Everything from how a school or district has defined and presented parents their options under the law, to prevailing local politics, to the reputation of the school's or district's programs for limited-English students before Proposition 227 has shaped the way the law has played out at the local level" (Schnaiberg, 1999, p. 1).

▶ Asian Americans

Chinese immigrants began entering the United States in large numbers during the 1850s. Many of them settled in the West, where there was an acute labor shortage. They labored in gold mines and helped build the first transcontinental railway. Most of these early immigrants, typically men who planned to better their lot and then return to China, often lived in "Chinatowns," where they continued their traditional customs and cultural practices. Attempts by Protestant and Catholic missionaries to Americanize the Chinese were unsuccessful and prompted others to use forceful means—burning Chinatowns and cutting off the customary long braids of Chinese men—to try to destroy their "clannish" ways (Carlson, 1975).

Although these immigrants who seemed so resistant to assimilation composed less than 1 percent of the total population in 1870, Americans grew increasingly distrustful of them, particularly as union leaders began to paint the Chinese as "part of a diabolical plot to deprive white Americans of their rightful jobs and bleed the West of its wealth" (Brown & Pannell, 1985, p. 203). Congress passed **exclusion acts** based on race to stop unwanted immigration. The Chinese Exclusion Act was passed in 1882.

Japanese immigrants stepped readily into a number of agricultural jobs in California and Hawaii. Despite the fact that the Nipponese Empire of Japan and the United States were allies at the turn of the century, by 1924 the flow of Japanese into this country was halted with the passage of the Oriental Exclusion Act. With the onset of World War II, Asian immigrants, particularly those of Japanese descent, suffered the ire of Americans: more than 100,000 Japanese Americans were driven from their homes and placed in temporary assembly centers, relocation centers, and internment camps, and their property was confiscated. Many people believed that this was the worst domestic wartime mistake, but it was not until 1990 that the federal government officially apologized and offered Japanese Americans restitution for the internment.

Since the Korean and Vietnam wars, many immigrants from Korea and Southeast Asia have made America their home. The first Korean immigrants came to Hawaii and then the United States early this century. Most Korean Americans, however, are post-Korean War immigrants or their descendants, coming to the United States after 1970. Koreans have typically left their country for greater economic opportunities in the United States. More than 40 percent of Korean Americans live in the West, most notably in Los Angeles. Large Korean communities exist in New York, Philadelphia, and other cities.

Vietnamese Americans, one of the larger Asian groups to enter the United States in recent years, represent only 9.5 percent of the total Asian population (U.S. Census Bureau, 1995a). The first arrivals "were generals and peasants, schoolteachers and spies, physicians and fishermen, . . . [who] became in America a poignant symbol of the refugee's will to succeed" (Efron, 1990). Making up about one-third of the current Vietnamese American population, these early Vietnamese immigrants have generally done well by American standards. By 1980, their household incomes equaled the U.S. average, and, for the most part, their children were quite successful in American schools. Vietnamese who have been immigrating since the fall of Saigon in 1975, however, have not fared so well. The majority live in poverty, are poorly educated, and have less upward mobility than their predecessors (Zhou, in press).

Cambodians, Laotians, and Thais have also immigrated to the United States, but not in so many numbers as the Vietnamese. These tribal peoples were deeply affected by the war in Vietnam. In addition to facing physical separation from their homelands, they have had to adjust to a society that relies on the power of science and technology to solve human problems, educational and otherwise—a society that is truly foreign in character to that which they left behind.

In the 1950s the United States government began to lift restrictions on immigration by race. In 1965 Congress abolished the quota system that based annual numbers of people allowed to enter the United States on the basis of the proportion of their relatives who were already here.

By the late 1980s and early 1990s, Asian American students were being called the new "whiz kids." In 1997, Asian American students as a group had the highest SAT scores in the nation (U.S. Department of Education, 1999). If college admissions had not been influenced in part in recent years by racial and ethnic quotas, artificially depressing the numbers of Asian Americans admitted, they would have become a majority in some universities.

The size of the Asian American population is also increasing. The U.S. Bureau of the Census estimates that Asian and Pacific Islander populations in the United States will grow at a rate exceeding 2 percent until the year 2030. In comparison, even at the peak of the baby-boom era, the total U.S. population never grew by 2 percent in a year. The rate of growth of the population with Asian origins will be exceeded only by that of people with Hispanic origins. This growth is occurring not only on the east and west coasts but in other parts of the country (Nifong, 1996).

> **Why might Asian American students as a group have the highest SAT scores in the nation?**

▶ Exceptional Learners in America

Efforts to meet the educational needs of students with exceptional abilities or disabilities developed during the 1800s (Kauffman, 1981). Physicians, clergymen, educators, and social reformers such as Dorothea Dix were leaders in this movement. Between 1817 and the Civil War, their crusade resulted in the establishment of residential schools for people who were deaf, blind, mentally retarded, or orphaned. After the Civil War, many of these schools were deemed unsavory places—overcrowded, impersonal, and sometimes quite inhumane. At about the time reformers were calling for an end to such institutions, several states began to include special classes for students with disabilities in their public schools, and a number of professional organizations were formed to improve the care and treatment of children with disabilities.

The early 20th century also saw an upsurge in the scientific study of children, the scientific classification and measurement of types of disabilities, the establishment of the Children's Bureau in 1912, an increase in public school classes and resource programs for exceptional learners, and the emergence of new professional organizations and training programs for teachers. At the same time, the widespread institutionalization of people with disabilities in isolated special-care facilities led to social isolation and abuses, which sparked humanitarian reform movements in the 1950s and civil rights reform in the 1970s and 1980s.

> **Why should people with disabilities be more fully integrated into society today?**

Through federal involvement during the 1960s, a Bureau for the Handicapped was added to the United States Office of Education, which is now the Office of Special Education and Rehabilitative Services in the U.S. Department of Education. As Hallahan and Kauffman (2000) note, the field of special education has been changing dramatically in the 1980s and 1990s. Increasingly, people with disabilities are being integrated with the larger, nondisabled society. Greater emphasis is being placed on early intervention. And greater emphasis is being given to preparing people with disabilities for their transition from secondary school to adulthood.

▶ American Women

Women's place in society in the early 20th century remained restricted and confused. Some, following in the footsteps of Emma Willard—touted as having done more in the 19th century for the education of women than anyone in America—were determined that women should enjoy the privilege of education no less than men (Raven

& Weir, 1981). These women and others fought for and won an amendment to the U.S. Constitution granting women the right to vote in 1920. The suffragettes, as they were called, included Susan B. Anthony, a teacher; Elizabeth Blackwell, the first woman in the United States to qualify as a physician; Margaret Fuller, a teacher and foreign correspondent for the *New York Tribune;* and Elizabeth Cady Stanton, one of the organizers of the 1848 Seneca Falls Women's Rights Convention.

Women did not participate fully in society simply by virtue of winning formal recognition. During the Depression of the 1930s, they were often laid off from their jobs before men were, had greater difficulty finding jobs, and were rarely considered for supervisory positions. When World War II created a labor shortage, women were suddenly pulled into previously male-dominated jobs; they were just as suddenly discouraged from having careers when the war ended and the men came home.

After Congress passed an equal employment act in 1964, many types of job discrimination against women were eliminated. Women gradually moved out of what had become traditionally female-dominated jobs of teaching and nursing and into nearly all professional and occupational roles, including those traditionally held by men, such as firefighting, law enforcement, and military combat. In 1970, women accounted for approximately 5 percent of law school graduates; in the late 1980s, they constituted about 40 percent (Blum et al., 1997). **Title IX** of the Education Amendments Act, passed in 1972, guaranteed that "no person in the United States shall, on the basis of sex, be excluded from participation in, be denied the benefits of, or be subjected to discrimination under any education program or activity receiving federal financial assistance" (Title IX, Education Amendments of 1972). The greatest impact of Title IX has been on school athletic programs, which states that girls may not be excluded from any sport and must be given equal access to coaching and equipment.

Did the feminist movement help or hurt the struggle for equal educational opportunity for women?

The **Women's Educational Equity Act (WEEA)** of 1974 was a comprehensive attack on sex discrimination in education and had far-reaching effect on curriculum and instruction in the nation's schools. The law expanded programs for females in mathematics, science, technology, and athletics; mandated nonsexist curriculum materials; implemented programs for increasing the number of female administrators in education and raising the career aspirations of female students; and extended educational and career opportunities to minority-member, disabled, and rural women.

The struggle for equal rights for women has continued through the feminist movement and efforts to amend the Constitution. Meanwhile, women have been nominated for vice president of the United States; elected as mayors, governors, state legislators, and members of Congress; and appointed as ambassador to the United Nations, heads of cabinet posts, and heads of federal agencies. At the same time, sex discrimination and sexual harassment suits against school districts, corporations, and government agencies have increased.

Many women continue to battle poverty. Indeed, there appears to be what some have referred to as a "feminization of poverty." Between 1960 and 1980 the number of female-headed households increased twofold. By 1985 approximately 10 million children lived in such homes; about 6 million of them were with mothers whose incomes were less than $10,000. Today, on average, women earn about 74¢ for every $1 earned by men (U.S. Census Bureau, 1997).

How Did Teaching Change After the Civil War?

Following the Civil War most teachers were young, poorly paid, and rarely educated beyond elementary subjects. Teaching was not considered a desirable job, and the teacher turnover rate was high.

Discourse on teaching often reflected the traditional image of the teacher as a mentor, model of virtue, and disciplinarian, whose principal concern was the character of her pupils. Efforts to professionalize teaching began during the 19th century, as expectations of teachers broadened to include less subjective qualifications. By the 20th century teachers were supposed to be scientific experts with a mission to educate.

As thousands of immigrants streamed into urban schools in the late 19th century, teachers sometimes found themselves with classes of 70 pupils speaking dozens of different languages. The children often were poor, unbathed, and hungry (Tyack & Hansot, 1982).

▶ Shifts in the Status of Teachers

By 1920, 86 percent of teachers were women, but men controlled public education. In the early 1900s, women began to protest publicly about administrative edicts and the effects of decision making on life in schools. Women teachers fought for better working conditions and for pay that was equal to that received by men teachers.

Women such as Margaret Haley and Catherine Goggin, leaders of the Chicago Teachers Federation (CTF), an all-female teacher organization founded in 1897, drew attention to discrepancies in salaries between administrators and teachers. They also challenged the old male guard in the NEA and tried to force the association to focus on concerns of women teachers, who made up the majority of the teaching profession (Tyack & Hansot, 1982). The NEA reacted by offering symbolic gains, such as appointing a female president every other year. Ella Flagg Young, a brilliant scholar and leader in the women's movement, spoke against the psychological control that management exerted on teachers, in a sense treating them like "mere workers at the treadmill" (Tyack & Hansot, 1982, p. 181).

Although women gained positions as teachers during this time, they lost positions as school administrators. Decisions about who might be the best candidates for various administrative positions were less often based on performance records than on gender. Women were generally appointed to posts that men did not desire to fill. The absence of requirements for special credentials for school administrators continued until the 1930s.

Marriage typically was a liability for women in education but an asset for men. Even by 1940 only 22 percent of female teachers were married. In 1928 the NEA found that about three-fifths of urban districts prohibited hiring married teachers, and half forbade married teachers from continuing in their jobs. The situation grew worse during the Depression, as thousands of districts passed new bans against employing married women.

Margaret Haley

Helen Parkhurst

John Dewey
(1859–1952)

▶ The Progressive Movement

Between 1920 and 1945, educators were influenced by the progressive movement in American politics and social life. **Progressivism** called for the application of human and material resources to improve Americans' quality of life. Applied to education, progressive ideals meant that the needs and interests of students rather than of teachers should be the focus of everything that happens in schools. Progressive teachers relied more on class discussions, debates, and demonstrations than on direct instruction and rote learning from textbooks. Teachers also experimented with individualized instruction and curricula that involved students in practical experiences and relevant learning outside the classroom. Students were responsible for maximizing their own potential, with the teacher's role being that of a helper and guide.

In 1921, to encourage students' creativity, decision making, and independent thinking, Helen Parkhurst implemented what was to become known as the Dalton Laboratory Plan in Dalton, Massachusetts. The Dalton Plan organized the school day into subject labs. Students from fifth through twelfth grades set their own daily schedules. Officials turned off the bells, eliminated schedules, and disbanded traditional classrooms. The plan gave students some control over their learning and relied on their interests to promote learning (Edwards, 1991; Parkhurst, 1922).

The greatest proponent of progressive education was John Dewey (1859–1952), whose Laboratory School at the University of Chicago scientifically tested child-centered curricula and instructional approaches. As will be discussed in the next chapter in connection with educational philosophy, Dewey wanted to avoid teaching subjects in isolation, favoring the idea of integrating them during social activities, such as cooking, sewing, or building a playhouse, so that students might learn about cooperation among human beings (Kliebard, 1986).

Teachers practicing progressive techniques were not united by a single cohesive educational philosophy. After 1945 and until about 1960, critics expressed dissatisfaction with progressive education because it lacked a common set of principles and a body of knowledge. Some people said that progressivism risked pandering to individual happiness at the expense of intellectual rigor and placed Americans at a disadvantage in international competition. Nevertheless, the concept of child-centered education remained and has been revived in educational reforms of the 1990s.

Educational innovations have often been abandoned for more traditional instructional behavior. Industrial education, for example, was supposed to help students appreciate the philosophy and methods at the heart of industrial society; instead, it rapidly became vocational education, concentrating on transmitting skills. Activities intended to make learning concrete soon became substitutes for academics (Cremin, 1988).

Contemporary critics claim that teachers and teaching have been, and continue to be, virtually impervious to change. Larry Cuban (1984) wrote,

> I have been in many classrooms in the last decade. When I watched teachers in secondary schools a flash of recognition jumped out of my memory and swept over me. What I saw was almost exactly what I remembered of the junior and senior high school classrooms that I sat in as a student and as a teacher in the mid 1950s. This acute sense of recall about how teachers were teaching occurred

Why did progressivism enjoy a revival in the 1990s? Does the culture of teaching really discourage change?

in many different schools. How, I asked myself, could teaching over a forty-year period seem . . . almost unchanged? (p. 1)

Cuban outlined three reasons for the durability of teacher-centered instruction: (1) schools are a form of social control and sorting; (2) the organizational structure of the school and classroom drives teachers to adopt instructional practices that change little over time; and (3) the culture of teaching tilts toward stability and a reluctance to change.

▶ Education in the National Interest

World War II caused an exodus of men and women from teaching. By 1945 more than one-third of the teachers employed in 1941 had left for more lucrative professions in business, industry, and government. Approximately 109,000 individuals employed on emergency teaching certificates assumed some of those positions. Some schools were closed completely or open only for short terms. Some subjects had to be eliminated from the curriculum because there were no qualified staff to teach them.

From 1940 to 1960, many critics expressed dissatisfaction with American education by focusing on progressive education techniques that generally attempted to make education "practical" and relevant to daily life. Walter Lippmann, for instance, argued that progressive education had no common principles, no common body of knowledge, and no common moral and intellectual discipline (Adams, 1977). In 1957, the Soviet Union's launch of the first satellite, *Sputnik*, was taken as evidence of our intellectual and moral flabbiness and led to intensified efforts to beef up education in the United States. Schools, critics charged, simply had not been teaching students to think. What we needed was greater emphasis on mathematics, science, and foreign languages.

In the **National Defense Education Act (NDEA),** passed in 1958, the federal government took the lead in improving schools. The NDEA provided funds for upgrading the teaching of mathematics, science, and foreign languages, as well as for the establishment of guidance services. It also provided low-interest loans to college students. Not since the establishment of the National Science Foundation in 1950 had the federal government moved so decisively in education policy. The passage of the NDEA marked the beginning of a pattern of federal leadership in education. The Vocational Education Act (1963), the Elementary and Secondary Education Act (1965), the Higher Education Act (1965), the Education Professions Development Act (1967), the Education of the Handicapped Act (1975), the Individuals with Disabilities Act (1990), and other federal legislation emphasized our national commitment to public education.

In 1979 President Jimmy Carter and Congress split the Department of Health, Education, and Welfare into two federal departments: Health and Human Services and the Department of Education. President Carter appointed Shirley M. Hufstedler as the first Secretary of Education, thus raising the Department of Education to Cabinet level. As early as 1983, President Ronald Reagan was trying to dismantle the Department of Education, and in particular the National Institute of Education. Political conservatives aimed to curtail the federal government's involvement in edu-

Using Technology

Generation Why

Dennis Harper, colleagues, and students in the Olympia School District (Olympia, Washington) have created a program—called Generation www.Y—meant to stand traditional concepts of teaching and learning on their heads. Generation Why, as it is called, is now being copied in school districts across the United States.

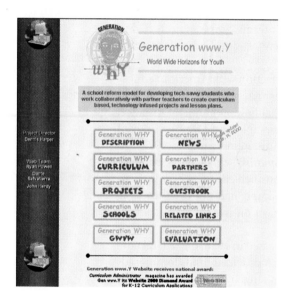

Generation Why involves students in collaboration with teachers, the local community, and corporate sponsors to assist in restructuring education through telecommunications. This model is being refined, documented, and extended to other schools throughout the country.

The backbone of the operation is the Generation www.Y Class, which you can read about on the Web. It is designed for students in grades 6–12 and runs for an 18-week semester. Students study the technology, mentoring, and lesson-planning skills necessary to mentor one of their teachers in technology use during the regular school day. Students learn to be change agents trained to transform education in their own school systems.

The Generation www.Y class has two major components. The first component—technology skills, presentation and communication skills, and teaching skills—prepares students to complete the second components. The second component prepares students to help their teachers incorporate technology into lessons. Subject matter experts from across the United States consult with the student–teacher teams to help them enhance the chances of creating successful lesson plans.

Why have presidential candidates focused on education?

cation matters they believed were better left to states and localities. President George Bush's Education Summit, planned and carried out in cooperation with the National Governors' Association, signaled that public education was to be largely a state, not a federal, matter.

President Clinton tried to expand the federal role. He created a new unit called the National Education School Improvement Council (NESIC) and charged the agency to promulgate and certify curricular content, student performance standards, and opportunity-to-learn standards. Congress passed Goals 2000, continued to reauthorize the Elementary and Secondary Education Act, and created a National Skills Standards Board to address vocational education. These actions were intended to encourage states and localities to address (1) what was to be taught in schools, (2) how student success was to be judged, and (3) how schools would be funded to create learning opportunities for children. Education was a key issue for both Republicans and Democrats in the 1996 and 2000 presidential campaigns.

 ## How Did Schools Change During the Modern Era?

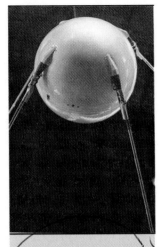

How did the Soviet Union's launch of the *Sputnik I* satellite in 1957 affect education in the United States?

The number of schools rose dramatically after World War I, but resources for funding schools rose and fell with the economy. The early Depression years (1929–1932) had a profoundly negative effect on funding for schools and colleges. By 1933–34, school expenditures had dropped more than 30 percent in many states. School funding in Michigan and Mississippi fell 41 percent and 52 percent, respectively. This meant that some rural schools' budgets were reduced by one-fifth to one-half. Teachers' salaries were cut, and some teachers were even paid in 4-year-maturity state bonds rather than by cash or check. Colleges and universities also were hurt by the Depression, particularly state-funded institutions, whose funding was cut by about one third. Between 1931 and 1934 total enrollment in higher education declined by 8.5 percent (Link & Catton, 1963). Changes in the modern era have aimed to make schools more efficient and cost effective while extending public education further and creating educational alternatives.

Good Question

▶ Consolidation and Bureaucratization

Most schools were small and rural until a program of consolidation began after World War II. Typically, one teacher taught all ages of students in the same room, and each student progressed at his or her own pace. Rural one-room schools were ungraded until about the 1920s, when they began to fall by the wayside as school districts were combined to concentrate resources and centralize administration. The number of separate school districts was reduced from about 130,000 in 1930 to fewer than 15,000 in 1997 (U.S. Department of Education, 1999). This consolidation meant that students had to be bused to central locations, such as huge regional high schools, often over long distances.

As consolidation increased in rural areas, bureaucratization became the hallmark of urban schooling. Boston, Massachusetts, and New York City developed complex networks of schools with distinct roles and rules, standardized curricula and procedures for each grade level, and administrative ideologies bent on efficiency, rationality, precision, and impartiality. Large cities patterned their school systems on the factory model: the single superintendent with a few foremen to supervise hundreds of operatives (Tyack & Hansot, 1982).

At the same time, many people within the system struggled against bureaucratization. Leonard Covello, teacher and principal in New York's East Harlem, for example, worked to connect schools to communities (Covello, 1958). He was among the pioneers of bilingual education, storefront schools, community advisory committees for schools, multicultural education, programs to prevent school dropouts, school-based community service, and political action programs. He also criticized the mis-application of IQ tests to culturally different populations. The debate over IQ tests still rages today.

▶ New Links Between Schools and Communities

Does equal educational opportunity mean the same opportunity for all people?

A sociological view of connections between schools and communities gained credence in the 1960s and 1970s. A survey conducted in 1965 by James S. Coleman, then of Johns Hopkins University, and Ernest Q. Campbell of Vanderbilt University suggested that disparities in students' academic achievement scores were due more to the racial composition of a school than to school facilities, teacher salaries, and per pupil expenditures. The 1965 Civil Rights Commission found that 75 percent of African American urban elementary students were in all-African American schools, while 83 percent of European American urban elementary students were in all-European American schools. Another finding was that African American students performed better in desegregated schools than in those that were "racially isolated" (Cremin, 1988).

As technological progress accelerated, people perceived more links between schools and society, specifically, the world of work. In 1986 the Carnegie Forum on Education and the Economy argued that weak schools threatened America's ability to compete in world markets: "Large numbers of American children are in limbo—ignorant of the past and unprepared for the future. Many are dropping out—not just out of school but out of productive society" (p. 2).

Schools that did work were thought to be alike in several ways (Bossert, 1985):

- They had climates that were safe and free of disciplinary problems.
- Teachers expected that students could achieve and communicated these expectations publicly.
- The schools emphasized basic skills with plenty of time for students to work.
- School personnel monitored and evaluated student progress.
- Successful schools had strong principals who served as program leaders.

By 1987, 39 million students were enrolled in elementary and secondary schools and more than 12 million in institutions of higher education. As in the past, the majority of these students attended public schools. In 1998, there were 46.8 million K–12 students in the public schools, another 5.9 million in private schools, and 14.3 million students in post-secondary institutions (U.S. Department of Education, 1999).

▶ Rise of Preschools

The preschool movement began anew in the United States in the 1920s and rapidly diversified. The American version of the nursery school, patterned on the earlier experiences of the British, stimulated interest in educating the whole child instead of simply providing custodial care. Inspired by the work of Rachel and Margaret McMillan in England, some farsighted teachers, such as Patty Smith Hill of Columbia Teachers College, created models that would guide the development of more schools.

By the depths of the Depression, the country needed good child care, and unemployed teachers needed jobs. Financial support from the federal government in the early 1930s stimulated the formation of many more nursery schools throughout the nation. By 1937 the Works Progress Administration (WPA) was responsible for 1,472 nursery schools with an enrollment of 39,873 children. At the same time, the WPA sponsored 3,270 parent education classes with an enrollment of 51,093 (Cremin, 1988).

During World War II the WPA programs were phased out and replaced by programs that were more oriented to child care than to education. By 1946 the majority of these child care centers closed when federal funds were withdrawn. As women continued to enter the workforce, the need for child care prompted the establishment of many private preschools. Today, enrollment in private prekindergartens continues to exceed that in public preschool programs.

When President Lyndon Johnson launched his war on poverty during the 1960s, education programs such as Head Start were the weapons he chose. Since its inception, **Head Start** has had a dual focus: to stimulate the development and academic achievement of 4- and 5-year-olds from low-income families and to involve parents in the education of their children. Head Start remains one of the most popular preschool programs. Head Start served about 794,000 children and their families in 1997, up from 752,000 in 1996 (U.S. Department of Education, 1999).

> **Why has the demand for preschool education increased dramatically in recent years?**

The growing interest in early childhood education and the success of experimental public kindergartens prompted many school districts to establish programs for 5-year-olds. At the beginning of the 20th century, there were 225,394 kindergartners in the United States, 58 percent of whom were in public schools (Cremin, 1988).

Preprimary education enrollment grew substantially from 1970 into the 1990s. In 1996, 37 percent of 3-year-olds, 58 percent of 4-year-olds, and 90 percent of 5-year-olds were enrolled in preprimary education. Similar percentages of European American and African American 3- and 4-year-olds were enrolled in center-based programs, while their Latino peers were less likely to be enrolled. In addition, 3- and 4-year-olds from families with incomes of more than $50,000 were more likely than their peers from families with lower incomes to be enrolled in preprimary education (U.S. Department of Education, 1998).

▶ The Middle School Movement

The housing of grades kindergarten through 8 in elementary school and grades 9 through 12 in secondary school, or the 8–4 pattern, was for many years the most common organizational scheme for schools in the United States. During the early 1900s, however, some school systems began to experiment with other ways of grouping their students. Although several organizational patterns were tested, the 6–3–3 pattern, or clustering of grades 7 through 9 in a junior high school—first tried in the cities of Columbus, Ohio, and Berkeley, California—proved to be quite popular in the years following World War I. By the 1950s and 1960s, many school districts began moving ninth-graders back into high schools and replacing their junior high schools with intermediate or middle schools (Cremin, 1988). Today many school systems continue to group ninth-graders with high school students in a 4–4–4 pattern. But their middle group of students (fifth- through eighth-graders) are clustered in a variety of ways with both the primary and high school grades. The middle-school movement has resulted in significant changes in curriculum and instruction for students in transition between late childhood and early adolescence (Walley & Gerrick, 1999).

▶ Comprehensive High Schools

After the 1870s private academies declined in number and were replaced by public high schools. A court case in Kalamazoo, Michigan, validated the right of school districts to establish and support public high schools with tax monies. By 1890 about 203,000 students were enrolled in public high schools, and 95,000 were enrolled in private academies. Together, these two groups made up less than 6 percent of the population of students 14 to 17 years of age, yet they constituted the entire potential pool of college entrants. By 2008, there will be some 16 million 14- to 17-year-olds enrolled in secondary schools (U.S. Department of Education, 1998).

Although every high school is unique, they all share a common feature—a multiplicity of course offerings for a student body having diverse needs, interests, and abilities. High schools are designed to be comprehensive in their offerings. Arthur Powell, Eleanor Farrar, and David Cohen (1985) liken the comprehensive high school to a shopping mall "governed by consumer choice" (p. 309). They see high schools wanting to maximize their holding power by satisfying consumers. In this metaphor, teachers are salespeople, classrooms are stores, students are customers. This outlook has led to a variety of course offerings, or "specialty shops" for high achievers, students with special needs, troublemakers, students with vocational and technical interests, athletes, and others.

▶ Homeschooling

An educational process reminiscent of colonial times, homeschooling is an alternative to on-site public education. Most states allow children to be taught at home, but, as will be explained in Chapter 11, such arrangements are regulated in various ways. Typically, parents must demonstrate that the education their children receive at home is equivalent to what they would receive in the public schools in terms of the books used, tests given, and time spent on studies.

Like private schools, home schools have grown in number for both pedagogical and ideological reasons. Estimates of the numbers of students served in such environments range from 200,000 to 300,000. The majority of these students tend to be from middle-class European American families located in the western and southern parts of the United States. The curriculum services used by homeschoolers indicate that the majority of families exercising the homeschool option do so for religious reasons. Not surprisingly, homeschooling appears to have gotten a boost from the telecommunications industry. A quick tour on the Web will reveal hundreds of sites related to homeschooling.

▶ Adult Education

Adult education took many forms in industrial America. Factories taught safety. Settlement houses taught immigrants and their children English and the skills needed to survive in a foreign culture. And beyond the cities, agricultural extension agents helped farmers improve their methods of growing crops and raising livestock.

The **Chautauqua movement** was the preeminent adult education movement of its time. What began as a Methodist Sunday School Institute in 1874 at Lake Chautauqua, New York, flourished as a secular educational institution through World War I. It was not "a single, unified, coherent plan, developed and directed by one man or a group of men. It was, fundamentally, a response to an unspoken demand, a sensitive alertness to the cravings of millions of people for 'something better' " (Gould, 1961, p. vii). Through the years, the Chautauqua movement pioneered the establishment of civic music associations, correspondence courses, lecture-study groups, youth groups, and reading circles. It responded to a vast need for adult education, particularly in rural areas of the United States. The movement may also have been, however, yet another indication of the American preoccupation with self-fulfillment and social advancement. Explore the history of the Chautauqua Institution online by visiting its web site.

Public schools and adult education became intertwined at the turn of the century. Progressives strengthened the philosophical and practical connections between community and school, perhaps most notably via the Gary Plan. After 1907, William Wirt, a school administrator in Gary, Indiana, worked to make public schools the centers of life in Gary neighborhoods. His intent was to unify the general, vocational, intellectual, and moral education of youth. By adhering to a "platoon system" of organization, students could be at gymnasiums, playgrounds, and assembly halls, as well as at schools. Gary schools could then accommodate twice as many students as did traditional schools (Cremin, 1988). By 1929 the Gary Plan had spread to more than 200 cities in 41 states. The plan faded a few years later when people opposed it as a form of cheapened education for their children.

More important than introducing progressive philosophy, the hard times of the 1930s forced people to use every resource at hand to help young and old alike work their way out of the Depression. Many programs made it appropriate for adults as well as children to congregate at school. The federally funded community education project associated with the Tennessee Valley Authority (TVA) in the mid-1930s, for example, tried to improve life in the rural TVA area by providing educational opportunities that directly related to community needs, and that served the entire community, not just its youth (Minzey & LeTarte, 1979). This meant helping adults learn basic literacy and job skills.

Adult education will likely become more important as we move into the 21st century. In the private sector, more and more corporations offer incentives for job-related education and for postsecondary adult education. Volunteer efforts such as Literacy Volunteers of America, Reading Is Fundamental, and AmeriCorps also underscore the importance of adult education. AmeriCorps, a national service program for adults initiated during the first Clinton administration, had 20,000 members by 1995. AmeriCorps programs address education, public safety, environmental, community, and human needs. In exchange for a year's service, members receive a living allowance, health insurance, child care services, and a cash benefit for further education (U.S. Federal Register, 1999).

While the private sector offers incentives for workers to further their education, it also offers training. For example, a for-profit education company, Kaplan Educational Centers, has 1,200 locations in the United States and abroad. Kaplan provides individuals a range of educational services. For some 60 years Kaplan has served 3 million students in its test preparation courses. The company also offers K–12 after-school programs at its Score! Educational Centers; customized education services for schools, universities, and businesses; books, software, and online services; and career and recruiting services.

▶ Opportunities for Higher Education

Ongoing pressures of industrialization in the North, the need for postwar development in the South, and the Morrill Act of 1862 combined to stimulate higher education in America. The higher education system offered a variety of alternatives for people who wanted to continue their education beyond high school. Technical training produced graduates for occupations and trades, while colleges and universities educated people for the professions, research, business and industry, and virtually every field that people would want to explore. Although higher education remained largely a man's world, by 1890 about 2,500 women a year were graduating from college.

The desires of the growing middle class for upward mobility stimulated colleges and universities to produce experts, specialists, and managers having greater skills and more degrees. Consequently, new professional schools—in dentistry, architecture, business administration, engineering, mining, forestry, education, and social work—emerged alongside the older professions of law, medicine, and theology and the newer disciplines of psychology, economics, and political science.

Why has the demand for higher education and adult education steadily increased?

The formation of the Association of American Universities in 1900 marked the beginning of nationwide efforts to raise academic standards in postsecondary education. Slightly fewer than 1,000 colleges and universities existed in 1900, with a combined enrollment of 238,000 students. By 1920 there were 1,041 institutions of higher education, but enrollment had more than doubled to nearly 600,000 students. The prosperity of the 1920s saw increases in state aid to public universities, colleges, and junior colleges, which made possible improvements in facilities for graduate and specialized training and technical education. (Link & Catton, 1963).

The years 1940 to 1960 yielded phenomenal growth in higher education. Enrollment increased from 1.5 million students to about 3.5 million. After World War II, with the passage of the Servicemen's Readjustment Act of 1944 (G.I. Bill of Rights), enrollment increased further. The McCarthy Era—so named for the anticommunist movement led by Senator Joseph McCarthy of Wisconsin—had a negative impact on academic freedom. In 1948 and 1949, many states imposed loyalty oaths on teachers and established committees to examine textbooks for subversive materials. Kansas, Massachusetts, and Pennsylvania authorized schools to dismiss teachers for disloyalty. Maryland, New York, and New Jersey forbade teachers to join certain organizations thought to be subversive.

Many Americans took advantage of higher education in the 1960s, 1970s, and 1980s. In 1996, there were 15 percent more students enrolled in all institutions of higher education than there were in 1981; 52 percent of those students were enrolled in public 4-year institutions (U.S. Department of Education, 1999).

The average annual earnings of college graduates compared to high school graduates indicates that postsecondary education remains a good investment. The U.S. Department of Education (1998) reports that in 1996 the median annual income of adults ages 25 to 34 who had not completed high school was substantially lower than that of their counterparts who had completed high school (31 percent and 36 percent lower for males and females, respectively). Young adults who had completed a bachelor's degree or higher earned substantially more than those who had earned no more than a high school diploma or GED (54 percent and 88 percent more for males and females, respectively).

 ## What Issues Arose in Curriculum Development?

Advocates for common schools after the Civil War tried to encourage citizens to send their children to public schools. But deep divisions along class, religious, and ethnic lines made the task difficult. No single philosophy seemed broad enough to permit the integration of all Americans into the schools. Social changes in the late 19th century—the growth of cities, popular journalism, and railroads—forced previously isolated, self-contained communities to live in a bigger world. As we shall discuss later, these conditions stimulated the struggle for control of American curricula. Figure 3.2 presents a sampling of influential books of the 20th century that stimulated debate about what and how students should be taught.

▶ Standardization of the Curriculum

In 1893 the **Committee of Ten on Secondary School Studies** (established by the National Education Association in 1892) attempted to standardize high school curricula. Chaired by Charles Eliot, president of Harvard University, the Committee of Ten prescribed four different academic courses of study for high school students: classical, modern languages, English, and Latin-scientific. The committee urged high schools to provide 4 years of English and 3 years each of history, science, mathematics, and a foreign language. Although the avowed intent of the curriculum was to put modern academic subjects and classical ones on an equal plane, not to sort students, critics viewed it as a program for failure for all but the college-bound student.

FIGURE 3.2
Some Books that Influenced the Development of Education in the 20th Century How might you use these resources to understand the curriculum you plan to teach?

John Dewey, *The Child and the Curriculum* (1902)

W. E. B. DuBois, *The Souls of Black Folk* (1904)

Booker T. Washington, *The Future of the American Negro* (1907)

Maria Montessori, *The Discovery of the Child* (1913)

John Dewey, *Democracy and Education* (1916)

H. Parkhurst, *Education on the Dalton Plan* (1922)

George S. Counts, *Dare the School Build a New Social Order?* (1932)

William C. Bagley, *Education and the Emergent Man* (1934)

Robert M. Hutchins, *The Higher Learning in America* (1936)

Harold Benjamin, *The Saber-Tooth Curriculum* (1939)

Ralph Tyler, *Basic Principles of Curriculum and Instruction* (1949)

Arthur Bestor, *Academic Wastelands* (1953); *The Restoration of Learning* (1955)

Theodore Brameld, *Toward a Reconstructed Philosophy of Education* (1956)

James B. Conant, *The American High School Today* (1959)

Hyman G. Rickover, *Education and Freedom* (1959)

Jerome S. Bruner, *The Process of Education* (1960)

A. S. Neill, *Summerhill: A Radical Approach to Child Rearing* (1960)

Paul Goodman, *Growing Up Absurd* (1960)

John W. Gardner, *Excellence: Can We Be Equal and Excellent Too?* (1961)

Robert M. Hutchins, *A Conversation on Education* (1963)

John Holt, *How Children Fail* (1964)

B. F. Skinner, *The Technology of Teaching* (1968)

Jean Piaget, *Science of Education and the Psychology of the Child* (1969)

Herbert R. Kohl, *The Open Classroom* (1969)

W. Glasser, *Schools Without Failure* (1969)

Alvin Toffler, *Future Shock* (1970)

Paulo Friere, *Pedagogy of the Oppressed* (1970)

Ivan Illich, *Deschooling Society* (1971)

B. F. Skinner, *Beyond Freedom and Dignity* (1971)

Charles A. Silberman, *Crisis in the Classroom* (1971)

John Holt, *How Children Learn* (1972)

Jonathan Kozol, *Free Schools* (1972)

Maxine Greene, *Landscapes of Learning* (1978)

Mortimer Adler, *Paideia Proposal* (1982)

Michael Apple, *Education and Power* (1982)

Diane Ravitch, *The Troubled Crusade* (1983)

John I. Goodlad, *A Place Called School* (1984)

Philip Coombes, *The World Crisis in Education* (1985)

A. G. Powell, E. Farrar, and D. K. Cohen, *The Shopping Mall High School* (1985)

Theodore R. Sizer, *Horace's Compromise* (1985)

Elliot W. Eisner, *The Educational Imagination* (1985)

Allan Bloom, *The Closing of the American Mind* (1987)

E. D. Hirsch, Jr., *Cultural Literacy* (1987)

Maxine Greene, *The Dialectic of Freedom* (1988)

Phillip C. Schlechty, *Schools for the 21st Century* (1990)

Jonathan Kozol, *Savage Inequalities* (1991)

In 1895, the **Committee of Fifteen** took on the curriculum of elementary schools. The chairman of the committee was William Torrey Harris, U.S. Commissioner of Education, who had established the first successful public school kindergarten in St. Louis in 1873 and gave America the graded school (Kliebard, 1986). Harris expressed strong belief in the value of a curriculum that focused on "the five windows of the soul"—grammar, literature and art, mathematics, geography, and history. Harris recommended that knowledge of Western cultural heritage be transmitted to students via standard literary works. He viewed the role of school as an efficient transmitter of cultural heritage through a curriculum that was graded, structured, and cumulative.

The tradition of local control over educational matters has remained strong throughout U.S. history. In the latter part of the 20th century, however, the National Education Goals, likely to be renamed America's Education Goals, has forced attention to common concerns (National Education Goals Panel, 1999). One way the United States might measure its maturity as a nation is to gauge the effort expended respecting differences and promoting a collective well-being.

▶ Diversification of the Curriculum

Efforts to diversify the curriculum paralleled efforts to standardize it. While some educators were out to safeguard tradition, others, such as G. Stanley Hall, pressed for making the curriculum responsive to stages of human development and to the process of learning. Social efficiency experts—David Sneddon, Ross Finney, and Franklin Bobbitt, for example—advocated training for specialized skills, much like industrial training. Social meliorists such as Lester Frank Ward viewed the curriculum as an instrument for producing social change.

Progressives, such as John Dewey, sought expanded, differentiated curricula; individualized school programs; and the use of schools to solve various social and political problems, such as those of racial, ethnic, class, and gender equality (Cremin, 1988). Progressive concerns were fueled by studies suggesting that the standard curricula did not fit the needs of increasingly heterogeneous classrooms. Dewey and others called for pluralism in curricula, meaning that all students were to learn a common culture, but other cultural views were to be both accepted and encouraged. By the late 1880s eight states had statutes permitting bilingual instruction in German and English in public schools. In 1872 Oregon legalized monolingual German schools (Tyack & Hansot, 1982).

> **Should the curriculum preserve traditional culture or be an instrument for change?**

Americanization efforts began to intensify in 1914 at the start of World War I and continued into the early 1920s. Schools treated southern and eastern European immigrants as a special group requiring a special, nonacademic education. The curriculum emphasized American government, home economics, and vocational training. During World War I, German was eliminated from the curriculum, and schools began to give report card grades not just for academic achievements but also for students' behavior. Citizenship grades were thought to be a "measure of [students'] dedication to the creation of a happy harmonious America" (Carlson, 1975, p. 123).

The Smith–Hughes Act, signed by President Woodrow Wilson in 1917, promoted job-skill training in public schools. The bill permitted federal funds to be used to train and pay teachers of agricultural, trade, industrial, and home economics subjects. Some saw Smith–Hughes as a natural link to the world of work. But Dewey, Harris, DuBois, and others argued that predetermining courses of study for students could restrict their choices and their natural potential.

The NEA's Commission on the Reorganization of Secondary Education in 1918 set a new direction for high schools. Its Cardinal Principles of Secondary Education called for comprehensive institutions that served all social groups and trained for many occupations (Commission on the Reorganization of Secondary Education, 1918). High schools were no longer to be just for the college bound. As the curriculum diversified, students took different courses and different programs depending on their abilities and interests, and schools assumed more responsibilities for student welfare and vocational training. If the history of high schools is a good predictor of their future, they are likely to become more not less diverse in both form and function as the new century unfolds.

▶ Core Curricula and Censorship

As the curriculum increasingly focused on progressivists' concerns with developing life skills, more people began to take the school curriculum to task for its lack of coherence. Robert Maynard Hutchins, president of the University of Chicago from 1929 to 1945, for example, advocated a core curriculum emphasizing grammar, rhetoric, logic, and mathematics. He also encouraged the study of the great books of the Western world so as to provide a common core of knowledge. This theme of a common core resurfaced periodically throughout the century in debates over what schools should teach.

Was God or Charles Darwin to be part of the common core? William Jennings Bryan led an anti-evolution crusade in the 1920s. Bryan was concerned about the possibility of atheistic evolutionists posing as teachers in public schools and undermining the Christian faith of American school children (Link & Catton, 1963). The 1925 Scopes trial in Dayton, Tennessee, upheld states' rights to ban the teaching of evolution. Although the forces of science would prevail in transmitting this Darwinian concept, to this day the teaching of evolution in the public schools remains a contentious issue. In the summer of 1999, the Kansas Board of Education voted to delete any mention of evolution from the state's science curriculum. Although the teaching of evolution was not prohibited, state assessments were redesigned to omit the topic. The decision was billed as "one of the most far-reaching efforts by creationists in recent years to challenge the teaching of evolution in the schools" (Belluck, 1999, p. A1).

Curriculum reformers in the 1930s disliked what they perceived as colleges' domination of the high school curriculum, a curriculum heavy on traditional academic subjects. The Progressive Education Association launched the Eight-Year Study to examine what was being taught in high schools. This investigation, directed by Ralph Tyler, involved 3,600 students in matched pairs—1 student from an experimental secondary school and 1 from a traditional high school—from 29 high schools. The results were published in 1942 and 1943 and suggested that students in experimental secondary schools (those having a more progressive or functional orientation) achieved as well in college as did students from traditional high schools. The 8-year study stimulated educators to modify the core curriculum to prepare students for "the duties of life." It also encouraged the use of behavioral objectives (statements describing what students should know or be able to do at the end of a lesson) when developing curricula. Such objectives were to have "a lasting and profound effect on the future course of curriculum development" (Kliebard, 1986, p. 220).

▶ Innovation and Reaction

By the 1950s, critics grew vitriolic in their attacks on education in America. Arthur Bestor's *Educational Wastelands* (1953) decried the anti-intellectualism he associated with education for "life adjustment." He advocated intellectual training for the masses, not just for college-bound students (Kliebard, 1986). Life adjustment education and other progressive strategies were blamed for America's perceived intellectual failures, following upon the USSR's launch of Sputnik. Critics such as Vice Admiral Hyman G. Rickover, credited with developing the atomic submarine, attacked what they believed was America's neglect of gifted and talented students. To Rickover, education was not rigorous enough to help the United States win the Cold War.

The 1960s and 1970s spawned a host of innovative curricula and instruction methods: School Math Study Group (SMSG), Man A Course of Study (MACOS), Physical Science Study Committee (PSSC), Harvard Project Physics, Biological Science Curriculum Study (BSCS), Chemical Education Materials Study (CHEM Study), Project English, audio-lingual language laboratories, and many more. Most of these efforts tried to involve students actively in their own learning by de-emphasizing teacher-centered instruction while concentrating on methods of inquiry.

> **How would you define educational rigor?**

Despite the creativity of many such programs, students, particularly low-income and minority students, seemed to be learning less in school year by year, while various estimates of the dropout rate climbed. As the country flirted with the possibility of becoming a second-rate economic power in the 1980s, everybody seemed to offer proposals for reform. The National Commission on Excellence in Education (1983) warned of a "rising tide of mediocrity." Many reform reports and proposals have offered to fix public education. And, often, proposed remedies come in the form of tests. The National Assessment of Educational Progress (NAEP) is referred to as the "nation's report card." The implication is clear: the way to reform education is to control the means of evaluating it (Bracey, 1998).

How Do People Typically Judge Educational Success and Failure?

Despite the implication that continual reform means continual failure, American education has improved dramatically during the modern era. Schools today educate and provide a variety of services to millions of children every year. Progress has been

Issues in School Reform

Educational Infrastructure

History seems to demand that we mark the end of one millennium and the beginning of another with bricks and mortar. And many school reformers who have their eyes trained on educational infrastructure argue that the United States should distinguish the new millennium by repairing and building schools.

How do renovations of existing schools and building new schools constitute an aspect of school reform?

The General Accounting Office (1995) surveyed school officials from some 10,000 schools in 5,000 school districts nationwide to estimate needs for school repair and replacement. The results suggest that the nation's schools need about $112 billion to repair or upgrade facilities. It would take about $11 billion (10 percent) immediately to comply with federal mandates that require schools to make all programs accessible to all students and to remove or correct hazardous substances.

About one-third of the schools, distributed nationwide, reported the need for extensive repair or replacement of one or more buildings. About 60 percent of the schools reported that at least one major building feature required extensive repair or replacement. Most schools had multiple problems. About half reported at least one unsatisfactory environmental condition in their schools. Lack of funds plague many efforts to maintain physical structures.

Discussion Questions   As the report from the General Accounting Office suggests, schools in many parts of the country are in no shape for the future. What do you know about the condition of schools in your own community? Are they able to accommodate student enrollment? Have they been renovated to use modern educational technologies? Do they have updated laboratories and libraries? If not, what if anything is being done to improve the schools?

Source: General Accounting Office (1995). *School facilities: Condition of America's schools. Report to Congressional requesters*. Washington, DC: General Accounting Office, Health, Education, and Human Services Division. Online (http://frwebgate.access.gpo.gov/).

uneven across regions of the country and across time, but there is no doubt that schools are better today than they were at the turn of the century.

Typically, judgments about educational success and failure have been guided by three factors: (1) the inputs into education, or, in a sense, the raw materials from which educated citizens are produced; (2) what occurs in schools and classrooms, or the processes of education; and (3) some measures of student learning. People have not always considered all three factors at once when judging education but traditionally they have relied on these concepts as indications of educational quality. For instance, the person who says the following is concentrating on inputs: "We have a good school. We built a new building, paid big salaries to hire the best teachers, and bought the newest books and equipment." Students' characteristics, like those of teachers, constitute another important input into the system. One who evaluates education in terms of processes might say, "The teachers and students in our school work together as inquirers. The curriculum is geared toward helping them identify important problems, collect information, and propose solutions. Teachers are always doing interesting things; it is a great school." Processes of schooling have most commonly been characterized in terms of effective teaching and delivery of the curriculum.

And the person who extols the virtues of schools because of "students' high test scores, winning football teams, and students' affection for the teachers" is judging success by outcomes. The quintessential measure of educational output is the standardized achievement test score. Joseph Rice developed the first educational achievement test in the United States in 1895. His spelling test, which he administered to more than 16,000 pupils in grades 4 to 8, consisted of 50 words. Stone's arithmetic reasoning test and Thorndike's scale for evaluating pupils' handwriting followed quickly. The Stanford Achievement Test, referred to as a "test battery," was published in 1923. It was designed as a group of survey tests in different content areas standardized on the same elementary school population. The Iowa High School Content Examination was published in 1925. Other test batteries, such as the Metropolitan Achievement Test and the California Achievement Test, followed shortly thereafter.

In the 1930s standardized aptitude and achievement tests and formal measures of school performance became the inexpensive and seemingly objective basis for making judgments about educational success or failure. Critics pointed out that the tests contained cultural biases and limited students' chances to demonstrate their true abilities. In addition, tests could be used to drive or control curriculum, instruction, teacher assessment, and school evaluation. The 1980s and 1990s saw renewed interest in comparing students, schools, and communities nationally and internationally. The **National Assessment of Educational Progress (NAEP)**, a battery of achievement tests administered nationwide, is used as a means of charting student progress, or the lack thereof, state by state.

> **Should judgments about measuring up as a nation rest on standardized test scores?**

Benchmarks

Modern U.S. Education History, 1865 to the Present

1865	Thirteenth Amendment to the Constitution abolishes slavery. Freedman's Bureau is established.
1868	Fourteenth Amendment grants citizenship to African Americans and guarantees that "No state shall make or enforce any law which shall abridge the privileges or immunities of citizens of the United States; nor shall any state deprive any person of life, liberty, or property without due process of law; nor deny to any person within its jurisdiction the equal protection of the laws."
1870	Fifteenth Amendment grants African American males the right to vote.
1874	Kalamazoo, Michigan, case specifies that states may establish and support public high schools with tax funds, which contribute to the secondary school movement and eventually to compulsory high school attendance laws.
1881	Booker T. Washington is named head of Tuskegee Institute in Alabama.
1890	Sioux men, women, and children are massacred by the U.S. Cavalry at Wounded Knee, South Dakota, which breaks Native American resistance to forced assimilation.
1893–1895	The Committee of Ten on Secondary School Studies and the Committee of Fifteen on Elementary School Studies attempt to standardize public high school and elementary school curricula, respectively.
1896	In *Plessy* v. *Ferguson,* the Supreme Court rules that states can provide separate but equal public facilities, legalizing racial segregation.
1898–1900	A period of American imperialism and statecraft exists, in which Cuba, Puerto Rico, the Philippines, Hawaii, Alaska, and Pacific islands such as Midway, Guam, and Samoa become possessions of the United States.
1909	First junior high schools are established in Berkeley, California, and Columbus, Ohio. The NAACP is founded through the efforts of African American leaders such as W. E. B. DuBois.
1910	Ella Flagg Young, Ph.D., the first female superintendent of schools of a large city (Chicago), becomes president of the National Education Association (NEA).
1914–1918	World War I and revolutions in Russia swell the ranks of immigrants from western, central, and eastern Europe in American cities and schools.
1916	American Federation of Teachers is formed as a labor union for classroom teachers.

1917	Congress passes the Smith–Hughes Act, which provides federal matching funds for vocational education in public high schools.
1919	Progressive Education Association is established to promote the educational philosophy of John Dewey and his followers.
1920	Nineteenth Amendment grants women the right to vote.
1925	Trial of John Scopes in Dayton, Tennessee, known as the Monkey Trial, upholds the right of states to ban the teaching of Darwin's theory of evolution.
1929–1936	Stock market crash precipitates the Great Depression. Franklin Roosevelt's New Deal provides federal aid for education of the unemployed and for school construction.
1939–1946	World War II era: Citizens of Japanese ancestry are dispossessed of their property and confined to relocation camps. Holocaust survivors and other war refugees come to the United States from southern and eastern Europe and from other countries touched by war.
1944 ✓	GI Bill provides financial aid for veterans to attend college.
1946–1953	The McCarthy Era, Korean War, and beginning of the Cold War period: The House Un-American Activities Committee (HUAC) abridges academic freedom and blacklists artists and intellectuals seen as communist sympathizers.
1950	National Science Foundation is founded.
1954 ✓	The Supreme Court rules in *Brown* v. *Board of Education of Topeka, Kansas* that separate but equal schooling is unconstitutional on the grounds that segregated schools generate feelings of racial inferiority and are inherently unequal.
1957	President Eisenhower orders federal troops to Little Rock, Arkansas, to enforce the Supreme Court's ruling against school segregation. The Soviet Union's successful launch of Sputnik I, the first artificial satellite, sparks a race for space and a movement for curriculum reform in the United States.
1958	National Defense Education Act (NDEA) provides federal funds to improve the teaching of science, mathematics, and modern foreign languages and to help schools provide guidance services.
1959-1961	Communist revolution in Cuba brings new wave of immigration; President Kennedy and Soviet Premier Khrushchev bring the world to the brink of nuclear war over the Cuban Missile Crisis and the Berlin Wall.
1963	President Kennedy is assassinated in Dallas, Texas.

1964	The Civil Rights Act of 1964 authorizes the federal government to compel compliance with school desegregation through lawsuits and by withholding federal funds from school districts that continue to discriminate. The era of busing to end racial segregation begins. President Johnson's War on Poverty begins to increase federal funding for school programs.
1965	Elementary and Secondary Education Act (ESEA) and subsequent amendments provide funding to aid students from low-income families through programs such as Title I (Chapter 1). The Economic Opportunity Act of 1965 creates Head Start as a compensatory education program.
1965–1973	Vietnam War era brings new waves of immigrants from Southeast-Asian countries. The antiwar movement leads to the "Kent State Massacre" in 1970 and profoundly affects curriculum and instruction in schools and on campuses across the United States.
1968	Dr. Martin Luther King, Jr., and Senator Robert F. Kennedy are assassinated. Bilingual Education Act enacted into law to address the special needs of students whose first language is not English.
1969	American Neil Armstrong becomes the first person to walk on the moon.
1972	Title IX of the Education Amendments Act prohibits sex discrimination in schools receiving federal funds. Indian Education and Self-Determination Act gives Native Americans more control over their schooling.
1974	Richard M. Nixon resigns the presidency of the United States as a consequence of the Watergate scandal.
1975	Education of the Handicapped Act (EHA) increases federal commitment to the education of children with disabilities and establishes a basis for subsequent special education legislation.
1979–1980	Department of Education is established; the U.S. Secretary of Education becomes a cabinet-level post.
1981	Educational Improvement and Consolidation Act (EICA) gives states greater power in allocating federal funds through block grants.
1983	National Commission on Excellence in Education issues a report, *A Nation at Risk,* which leads to new calls for educational reform to eliminate illiteracy and raise SAT scores.
1984	Perkins Vocational Education Act upgrades vocational programs in the schools.
1989	Carnegie Foundation's report, Turning Points: Preparing American Youth for the Twenty-First Century, calls for the elimination of tracking and creation of learning communities in the

	schools. Presidential Summit Conference on Education held in Charlottesville, Virginia, attended by President Bush and the 50 governors, who agree that "Good education makes good politics, good business, and good sense."
1992	Supreme Court rules that officially sanctioned prayers or invocations in public schools are unconstitutional.
1994	President Clinton and Congress cooperate to pass Goals 2000: Educate America Act.
1996	Second Education Summit held in Palisades, New York, attended by President Clinton, the nation's governors, and business leaders.
1997	Implementation regulations for the Individuals with Disabilities Education Act Amendments are finalized.
1999	National Education Goals Panel acknowledges that accomplishing the National Education Goals by the year 2000 is an impossibility. They recommend to Congress that the goals be renamed "America's Education Goals."

SUMMARY

What changes after the Civil War affected the system of education in the United States?

1. Passion for intellectual freedom and civil liberties increased greatly when the Civil War ended. Passage of constitutional amendments changed race relations legally by ending slavery, defining citizenship, and forbidding states to deny the right to vote. Nonetheless, the customs of segregation and discrimination remained entrenched. Intellectuals and ordinary citizens led organized efforts to combat racial, ethnic, and gender discrimination wherever they existed, including in schools. The federal government exerted its influence to educate ex-slaves and to reconstruct a war-ravaged nation.

2. By the beginning of the twentieth century, critics initiated what was to become a sustained attack on public schools, particularly in the cities. Increasingly educators looked to science for answers to their problems, engaging in research on teaching and learning and using techniques of scientific management to run the schools.

3. From the late 19th century on, schools were embedded in a society that demonstrated in many ways the increasing value of education. The increasing availability of newspapers, books, and magazines stimulated and supported people's desires to learn. The development of radio, motion pictures, television, and other forms of

mass communication made informal or out-of-school education more pervasive than ever before.

Who are "We the People"?

4. After the Civil War, the population of the United States grew rapidly, most noticeably in the cities and industrialized areas. As Fuchs (1990) observed, because America was meant to be inclusive of all, the country became a kaleidoscope of race, ethnicity, and civic culture. Schools were supported to shape the pieces into a coherent social design—a design that included Native Americans, European Americans, African Americans, Hispanic Americans, Asian Americans, other Americans, exceptional learners, and women.

How did teaching change after the Civil War?

5. Following the Civil War, most teachers were young, poorly paid, and rarely educated beyond elementary subjects. Teaching was not considered a desirable job, and teacher turnover was high. Efforts to professionalize teaching began during the 19th century, as expectations of teachers broadened to include less subjective qualifications. Teachers also gained a measure of economic independence. At the same time, they lost managerial and curricular control of schools and schooling.

6. Between 1920 and 1945, educators were influenced by the progressive movement. Progressive teachers served as helpers and guides, relying more on class discussions, debates, demonstrations, and individualized learning than on direct instruction and rote learning from textbooks. Nonetheless, innovations often were abandoned for more traditional instructional behavior.

7. In the 1960s, schools served as battlegrounds in the War on Poverty, in desegregation, and in the quest for racial equality. The federal government exerted its influence to end segregation, to support the needs of children living in poverty, to promote racial and sexual equity, to secure entitlements for students with disabilities, to promote bilingual–bicultural programs, and to provide career education opportunities. The New Federalism of the 1980s returned to states and localities both the power and financial responsibility for educational programs. This trend has continued through the turn of the century.

8. The Progressive Movement flourished in American education from about 1920 to 1945. Progressive teachers were not united by a single philosophy, but in general they tried to make the needs of students the focus of their instruction. They relied less on lectures and rote learning and more on class discussions, demonstrations, and other practical methods to encourage learning.

9. With the conclusion of World War II, a booming economy and the continuing spirit of nationalism fueled human and material investment in public education. The federal government exerted strong and continuing support for elementary and secondary schools and for a host of post-secondary and community education programs.

10. "Civilization" spread across the frontier in the form of one-room schools. As time passed and communities grew, people expected schools not only to eradicate igno-

rance but also to minimize differences among people and to ameliorate the effects of poverty and discrimination. Schooling was viewed as a way to get ahead.

11. Rapid industrialization in post–Civil War America created immense demands for workers who were willing and able to produce goods cheaply and quickly and to offer services efficiently. Public school teachers and school administrators taught immigrants, members of minority groups, and those from impoverished circumstances skills of literacy and numeracy as they transmitted the work ethic.

How did schools change during the modern era?

12. Wars and economic depressions have had dramatic effects on both the adults and the young in schools. Prior to World War II, for example, one teacher taught all ages of students in the same room, and each progressed at his or her own pace. These one-room schools began to fall by the wayside as school districts were combined to concentrate resources and centralize administration. Consolidation meant that students had to be bused to central locations, such as huge regional high schools, often over long distances.

13. The concept of school developed continually over time. Preschools acknowledged the special needs of young children. Middle schools were structured to help young people make the transition between childhood and early adolescence. Comprehensive high schools were established to meet the diverse needs, interests, and abilities of older students. Interest in home-schooling emerged in large part out of parents' desires to instill their own religious values in their children. Adult education grew and flourished as more and more people recognized needs for training and education that were not being met by traditional colleges and universities.

14. With technological advances, people have perceived more links between schools and the world of work. The 1986 Carnegie Forum on Education and the Economy argued that weak schools threatened America's ability to compete in world markets. Schools that worked were thought to be alike in several ways: (1) They were safe and free of disciplinary problems. (2) Teachers expected that students could achieve and communicated these expectations publicly. (3) They emphasized basic skills. (4) School personnel monitored and evaluated student progress. (5) They had strong principals who served as program leaders.

15. Higher education has grown continually, providing increasingly varied access to adults. Institutions of higher education provide technical training in occupations and trades and academic preparation in the professions, research, business and industry, and a variety of other fields.

What issues arose in curriculum development?

16. School curriculum has often reflected the nation's moods and values as well as its knowledge. Public schools, as defined in terms of teachers and curriculum, have been criticized routinely for trying to be and to do too much. Efforts to standardize the curriculum, to diversify course offerings, and to integrate different cultural views in course materials have been among major concerns.

How do people typically judge educational success and failure?

17. Those having responsibilities for regulation and control of public education have come to view educational success and failure in terms of what goes in, what goes on, and what comes out of schools.

■ TERMS AND CONCEPTS ■

black codes   79

Brown v. *Board of Education of Topeka, Kansas*   93

Bureau of Indian Affairs (BIA)   87

Chautauqua movement   107

Committee of Fifteen   111

Committee of Ten on Secondary School Studies   109

Elementary and Secondary Education Act (ESEA)   84

exclusion acts   95

Freedman's Bureau   78

Head Start   105

Hispanic   94

Improving American Schools Act (IASA)   84

Indian Self-Determination and Educational Assistance Act   88

National Assessment of Educational Progress (NAEP)   115

National Association for the Advancement of Colored People (NAACP)   79

National Defense Education Act (NDEA)   101

Plessy v. *Ferguson*   92

progressivism   100

Title IX   98

Women's Educational Equity Act (WEEA)   98

■ REFLECTIVE PRACTICE ■

The psychologist William James, professor at Harvard, was asked by the Harvard Corporation to give several public lectures on psychology to Cambridge Teachers. The passage below was taken from one of his talks to teachers.

In the general activity and uprising of ideal interests which every one with an eye for fact can discern all about us in American life, there is perhaps no more promising feature than the fermentation which for a dozen years or more has been going on among the teachers. In whatever sphere of education their functions may lie, there is to be seen among them a really inspiring searching of the heart about the highest concerns of their profession. The renovation of nations begins always at the top, among the reflective members of the State, and spreads slowly outward and downward. The teachers of this country, one may say, have its future in their hands. The earnestness which they at present show in striving to enlighten and strengthen themselves is an index of the nation's probabilities of advance in all ideal directions. The outward organization which we have in our United States is perhaps, on the whole, the best organization that exists in any country. The State school systems give a diversity and flexibility, an opportunity for experiment and keenness of competition, nowhere else to be found on such an important scale. The independence of so many of the colleges and universities; the give and take of students and instructors between them all; their emulation, and their happy organic relations to the lower schools; the traditions of instruction in them, evolved from the older American recitation-method (and so avoiding on the one hand the pure lecture-system prevalent in Germany and Scotland, which considers too little the individual student, and yet not involving the sacrifice of the instructor to the individual student, which the English tutorial system would seem too often to entail),—all these things (to say nothing of that coeducation of the sexes in whose benefits so many of us heartily believe), all these things, I say, are most happy features of our scholastic life, and from them the most sanguine auguries may be drawn (James, 1899, pp. 3–4).

Issues, Problems, Dilemmas, Opportunities

If you were asked to identify the one or two factors in society that have most influenced change in the education system James described, what might they be?

Perceive and Value

If you had ancestors who were educated in American schools at the turn of the century, do you think they might have agreed with James about the superiority of American schools? Why or why not? If some of your ancestors were in the United States at that time but were largely unschooled, what might they have thought about his perceptions?

Know and Act

How might you respond to someone who argues that the problems we face in public education today are not a result of changes in the schools over the last 100 years or so but rather the *lack* of change in schools? Where might you look for evidence to buttress your argument?

Evaluate

If we take James's remarks at face value, then we must conclude that he believed the American educational system was without peer. He seems to make that judgment based on several criteria. Can you identify his bases for the claim of American superiority? Which, if any, of these claims are made routinely today? Which, if any, seem hopelessly out-of-date, and why?

 ## ONLINE ACTIVITY

One's view of history often depends on where one stands. If you are stuck in one place, you might want to use the Web to help you take another perspective. We suggest that you stand at the site of the National Women's History Project and examine history from that vantage point. When you get there click on the button provided to learn more about a network of scholars in women's history and even a quiz of your own knowledge of the issues.

When you dig deeper in the "Ideas to Use" section, you will find suggestions for making women's history come alive in the classrooms. How might you use National Women's History Month to stimulate reflection on the history of women's contributions to society? Where can you get videos that highlight women's contributions? How might you have students examine their textbooks for attention to women's issues, and what might they do with the results of their work? What alternatives to the tried-and-true book report might you offer students as they explore historical influences on present practices? You will find possible answers to these questions and, in the process, perhaps reconsider the intellectual and practical value of studying history from different points of view.

4

Philosophical Foundations in Action

Philosophies live in people's minds and hearts and are made evident through their behavior. Although we rarely stop to notice, philosophy saturates our personal and professional existences. In this chapter we describe major philosophies that have influenced thought and behavior through the ages and that have special relevance for educators.

Francis Fukuyama (1992) has contended that people in the Western world have reached "the end of History," or the point at which all the really big philosophical questions have been settled. While communism is in decline and liberal democracy enjoys popularity, the increasingly complex problems and opportunities that present themselves in everyday life clamor for philosophical attention. No less than those who have preceded them, people today seek to understand who they are and who they might become.

Besides describing classical thought relevant to teachers and teaching, we suggest how philosophies are reflected in schools and educational programs. We explain why it is important to understand how people think about the means and ends of education, and we provide examples of how teachers' philosophies have been defined through personal and social action. Finally, we describe how you can begin to articulate your personal philosophy of education and to shape it over time.

PROFESSIONAL PRACTICE QUESTIONS

- What is philosophy, and what does it have to do with you as a teacher?
- What are the roots of American educational philosophies?
- What modern philosophies influence Western education?
- What non-Western philosophies influence American education?
- What factors shape teachers' personal philosophies of education?

What Is Philosophy, and What Does It Have to Do With You as a Teacher?

Philosophy can be defined as a set of ideas about the nature of reality and about the meaning of life. Ideas about being, knowledge, and conduct have evolved over time as philosophers have pondered such questions as the following: What is basic human nature? What is real and true about life and the world? What is knowledge? What is worth knowing or striving for? What is just, good, right, or beautiful? These questions, so central to life, routinely arise in many forms in the lives of teachers.

In the preface to a collection of essays, G. K. Chesterton, 19th- and 20th-century author, poet, social and literary critic, wrote:

> There are some people—and I am one of them—who think that the most practical and important thing about a [person] is still his view of the universe. We think that for a landlady considering a lodger it is important to know his income, but still more important to know his philosophy. We think that for a general about to fight an enemy it is important to know the enemy's numbers, but still more important to know the enemy's philosophy. (cited in James, 1907, p. 17)

As Chesterton suggests, there are some practical reasons why philosophy is important. If we know a lodger's or a general's or a teacher's or a student's philosophy, then we have some indication of how that person will behave, and why. The propensity for action inherent in one's philosophy gives it practical importance. John Dewey (1916) was more direct when he argued that "Whenever philosophy has been taken seriously, it has always been assumed that it signified achieving a wisdom which would influence the conduct of life" (p. 378).

▶ The Place of Philosophy in Education

Philosophy influences daily educational life in many ways. Parents may choose or reject a school for their children because they believe the school's philosophy will be translated into desirable or undesirable educational experiences. Principals run schools in keeping with their thoughts about managing people and administering programs—sometimes like businesses or factories, sometimes like churches, or colleges, or football teams. Teachers plan lessons, interact with students, and judge students' performances according to their views of knowledge, which may depend heavily on their idealized conceptions of the role of teacher. A professor requires a prospective teacher to learn a particular set of instructional methods based on her or his view of acceptable professional practice. Philosophy shapes the writing of curricula, the preparation and scoring of tests, and the architecture of school buildings.

▶ The Importance of Putting Educational Philosophies in Perspective

The potential for conflict in this philosophical potpourri is great. And from time to time, some person or some group tries to claim hegemony—the philosophical upper hand, the one best way to view the universe. But the one-best-way people do not seem to last long, particularly in public education. For public schools appeal to the general public for support. And sooner or later extreme ideas become unacceptable to the majority of people the schools are meant to serve.

Philosophies, or one's principles, as Noddings (1984) warned in her treatise on caring, can be wielded as bludgeons:

> Wherever there is a principle, there is implied its exception and, too often, principles function to separate us from each other. We may become dangerously self-righteous when we perceive ourselves as holding a precious principle not held by the other. The other may then be devalued and treated "differently." (p. 5)

Philosophical wars in education have become almost routine. People who adhere rigidly to philosophies often neglect to reexamine their views in light of changing conditions. Actions become habitual, out of touch with the present. Philosophies then can limit our visions of the future.

For example, it is possible to construct educational systems with a view of the "typical," "average," or "ordinary" person in mind and maintain these systems while they become populated with "extraordinary" people. When this phenomenon occurs, the systems do not work, because they do not "fit" the people they are supposed to serve. Martin Haberman (1995) has argued persuasively that the education of inner-city youth and teachers in the United States is a case in point. Colleges and universities recruit, select, and educate teachers with a vision of the suburban United States in mind. Inner-city students, however, do not conform to this vision; thus education programs for both teachers and the young people they will face are radically out of line with life in many communities.

Do educational philosophers relate to the realities of life in the United States today?

Philosophies different from our own force us to examine our thinking in a new light. Someone who calls herself an "idealist," cannot help but grow from a serious consideration of a "realist" view, and vice versa. There is almost always some room to change one's mind, but change is unlikely if people are unaware of the options. Big minds have room to consider more than one point of view; they are not constricted by real or imagined pressure to be philosophically correct.

Bill Pinar has been a leader in challenging traditional notions of philosophical and theoretical foundations of education in the United States by forcing attention to gay and lesbian cultures. Pinar's focus on "Queer Theory" goads intellectually complacent people, both heterosexuals and homosexuals, to rethink their assumptions about life in schools:

> As a gender ceremony of manhood, contemporary schooling compels heterosexuality . . . , implicating it in the complex configuration which is suffering in the West. Homosexuality as it now exists is implicated as well. Many homosexuals, like most oppressed groups in initial stages of political-rights work, tend to believe what their enemies say about them. Thus many homosexuals tend to believe in some measure that they are indeed a "third sex," unique, "queer." They tend to believe in a substantive category called *homosexual,* not seeing that it is in the service of their oppression, and in the heterosexual's self-delusion regarding his own gender composition. . . . (Pinar, 1998, p. 242)

What Are the Roots of American Educational Philosophies?

Western philosophies originated with the classical Greeks, who used a systematic method for addressing life's questions. Figure 4.1 shows how Greek thinkers divided philosophy into three branches:

1. **Metaphysics** and its two corollary areas deal with the study of reality. **Ontology** explores issues related to nature, existence, or being, while **cosmology** is concerned with the nature and origin of the cosmos, or universe.

2. **Epistemology** is concerned with the nature of knowledge or how we come to know things. We develop knowledge of truth through thought from observations and from logic—by reasoning deductively from a general proposition to a particular case and by reasoning inductively from a set of particulars or facts to a general principle. We also develop knowledge from scientific inquiry, intuition, and our senses.

3. **Axiology** seeks to determine what is of value. More specifically, **ethics** explores issues of morality and conduct, while **aesthetics** is concerned with beauty.

While some bemoan what they perceive to be the demise of classical education in the tradition of the Greeks, our education system remains rooted in the Western philosophies described in the following sections (Hanson & Heath, 1998). We also describe a number of non-Western philosophies held by people who attend and

FIGURE 4.1
Summary of Branches of Philosophy   How might each branch of philosophy be embedded in your role as a teacher?

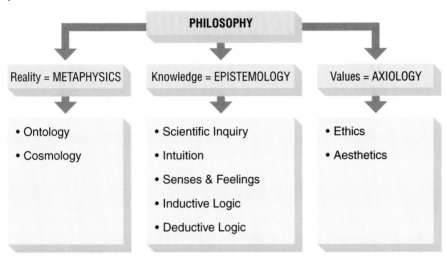

PHILOSOPHY

Reality = METAPHYSICS

Knowledge = EPISTEMOLOGY

Values = AXIOLOGY

- Ontology
- Cosmology

- Scientific Inquiry
- Intuition
- Senses & Feelings
- Inductive Logic
- Deductive Logic

- Ethics
- Aesthetics

work in public schools in the United States. These systems of ideas and beliefs will continue to affect education in this country as their adherents increase in number and influence.

▶ Idealism

Idealism suggests that ultimate reality lies in consciousness or reason. The progenitor of idealism, Plato (427?–347 BC), student of Socrates and citizen of Athens, imagined a society driven by the pursuit of knowledge. To search for truth, justice, and beauty in the world was to seek meaning in one's own life and in the collective life of the community. Plato envisioned this exploration as a shift of the mind away from the immediate physical world of what we can see, feel, smell, hear, and taste and toward a world of enduring ideas. Plato believed philosophy and philosophers should help people think clearly about these important ideas and aid people in governing themselves wisely. Perfect knowledge of the ideal resided outside humans as an absolute, or as God.

In his writings Plato explained his vision through imaginary conversations between Socrates and his students. These discussions, or dialogues, were written as poetry, science, and philosophy. They have guided thought and action in Western civilizations since Socrates died from drinking hemlock at about age 60. He had been convicted of corrupting the young and of not believing in the gods.

In the dialogues, Socrates asks questions of students that force them to examine critically their notions about life, truth, beauty, and justice. As they interact with Socrates, students discover the errors in their thinking and formulate clearer, more accurate ideas about life's questions. The **Socratic method,** then, is one of teaching through inquiry and dialogues in which students discover and clarify knowledge.

Plato (427?–347 BC)

The Republic is Plato's most celebrated dialogue. In it he described his ideal society—how people were to think, to value, to behave, to teach, and to organize and govern society. Plato knew that this utopia was unattainable. Yet for him, and for the idealists who followed, such visions of perfection serve as goals toward which we should strive in our own lifetimes and as benchmarks against which we should judge human progress over many lifetimes.

Plato, like Socrates, believed that people are born with knowledge and that the task of the teacher is to elicit this knowledge. The dialogues were teaching tools that forced people to consider ideas in relation to one another and to some idealized state.

How do idealists' beliefs reveal themselves in education today?

Plato promoted the idea of an aristocracy, not one based on wealth, brute power, or family influence but on wisdom and goodness. Although he believed men and women should be afforded opportunities to learn, he thought few would demonstrate the wisdom and goodness necessary to rule their fellow citizens. In Plato's utopia those tried and tested individuals who remained healthy, who thought clearly, and who were of high moral character would govern. They might arise from any segment of society, but in the end, the most talented among them would serve as philosopher kings.

An intermediate class of well-trained soldiers would safeguard the community. And a broad base of farmers, traders, and manufacturers would undergird society:

> In short, the perfect society would be that in which each class and each unit would be doing the work to which its nature and aptitude best adapted it; in which no class or individual would interfere with others, but all would cooperate in difference to produce an efficient and harmonious whole. That would be a just state. (Durant, 1961, p. 32)

For Plato, then, education was the vehicle of social mobility. It was also the key to creating and perpetuating the ideal society. Philosophers would train people to think clearly, and processes of education would screen people for their assignments to social classes. Plato's curriculum for this idealized society was straightforward, rigorous, and lifelong. He envisioned a kind of moral education that would make citizens realize they had responsibilities to one another.

▶ Realism

Realism is based on the idea that objects of sense or perception exist independently of the mind. Aristotle (384–322 BC), a student of Plato, differed markedly from his teacher in philosophical views. Plato, the idealist in search of truth, had turned away from the physical world toward the world of ideas. Aristotle sought truth by investigating the real world around him. His work reflected the philosophical orientation called realism and forms the basis for the scientific method.

Aristotle established a vast library of manuscripts, a collection of zoological and botanical specimens, and a lyceum in Athens, where he taught many young scholars. A staff of assistants helped him record raw observational information and synthesize the knowledge of the day. Despite the lack of scientific equipment and basic knowledge of the laws of nature, Aristotle pushed science forward by acting on the belief that the study of matter would lead to a better understanding of ideas. Aristotle and his students performed much of the intellectual spadework for Mendel's genetic the-

Issues in School Reform

The Philosophy of School Reform

Patricia Wasley, Robert Hampel, and Richard Clark (1997) studied 150 students from across the nation to learn more about how school reform affected their lives. The researchers explain just how important the philosophy of school reform can be on students' own philosophies of learning. They use the words of Alicia, one of the students they interviewed, to amplify this assertion:

> Rigorous work requires demonstrations of deep understanding. As Alicia put it, "You should be able to analyze stuff and draw conclusions based on what you read and what you see and be able to go somewhere with it, not just spit it back." Students echoed the definitions of teaching for understanding that are currently promoted by researchers and cognitive scientists. "[W]e're supposed to learn to use our minds well," said Alicia. "The teachers and the principal want us to work harder, think harder about stuff."
>
> Despite their clarifications, rigor is a tough word to define. In its original sense, rigor meant inflexibility, severity. Over the years, it has come to mean precision and exactness. When determining what it was that, when coupled with innovation, pushed these schools' reform efforts into the realm of important gains for kids, we chose the word rigor because it has embedded in it attention to quality—precision, depth of understanding—and attention to disciplined learning—practice, rehearsal, correctness. Rigor means that teachers require more precise and exacting work from students, work that demonstrates thoughtfulness, attention to detail, planning, revision, and solid effort. Rigorous work goes beyond mere effort to reflect high-quality performance. . . . Rigorous work meets and exceeds high standards. (1997, p. 106)

Discussion Questions: Why might it be important for teachers, administrators, and students to have similar understandings of "rigor"? What role, if any, do standards play in settings such as the one described by Alicia? Based on what you know about the effects of teachers' expectations, how do you suppose teachers in Alicia's school think about students?

Source: Kids and School Reform by P. A. Wasley, R. L. Hampel, & R. W. Clark, 1997, p. 106. San Francisco: Jossey-Bass Inc., Publishers.

ory, Darwin's theory of evolution, the science of embryology, and the disciplines of biology and psychology.

For Aristotle, Plato's ideals were real only insofar as they were actualized in material objects. He believed everything sought to fulfill its potential, or to take the form of what it was meant to be. He characterized this movement from potential to actual as involving four causes. If marble (material cause) was determined by the sculptor to be a statue of a woman (formal cause), and was shaped by the sculptor (efficient cause) to take the form of a woman (final cause), then the potential of the marble would be actualized. This same logical progression of causes, according to Aristotle, held for the development of humans.

Aristotle believed humans learn through their senses. As individuals experience the world, they develop and refine concepts about objects through direct experience. Unlike idealists, for whom truth resides within

Is happiness the ultimate aim of education?

Aristotle
(384–322 BC)

an individual, waiting to be discovered, realists believe knowledge exists independent of human knowing. The role of education, then, is to teach students about the world in which they live.

Aristotle contended that happiness is the ultimate goal in humans' lives. Unlike Plato, he thought goodness and wisdom were means to this end, not ends in themselves. People traversed the path to true happiness by stretching their minds to the fullest of their capabilities. "Virtue, or rather excellence, will depend on clear judgment, self-control, symmetry of desire, artistry of means" (Durant, 1961, p. 60). People were thought to demonstrate virtue through the achievement of experience; they did not simply possess virtue because of their intent or innocence.

But if excellence is desirable, excess is taboo. Aristotle counseled people to seek the middle ground, or Golden Mean, in matters of life: "between cowardice and rashness is courage; between stinginess and extravagance is liberality; between sloth and greed is ambition" (Durant, 1961, p. 60). Indeed, to Aristotle, the middle ground was fertile territory where training could make excellence flourish. As people practiced thinking and behaving in productive ways, they developed habits that would lead them to excellence.

Like Plato, Aristotle believed in government by an aristocracy of talented people. A government-run education system would emphasize balance in assigning people to the work of society and teaching responsibility to the state.

▶ Thomism

Thomism is a philosophical orientation that relies on faith and reason as complementary sources of truth. Thomism may rightfully be considered the religious form of realism (O'Neill, 1981). Named after Saint Thomas Aquinas (1225–1274), a Dominican theologian who taught at the University of Paris, Thomism advances the belief that the God of Christians created a knowable independent reality. Like Aristotle, Aquinas believed human beings use their senses and reason to understand the world. Aquinas also believed all people have a soul and the ultimate goal in life is to experience eternity with God. Truth, then, is both natural and spiritual. Natural truth is knowledge about the physical world gained through reason. Attainment of spiritual or supernatural knowledge is also dependent on reason:

> Supernatural knowledge is *nonrational,* but it is not irrational. Ideally, the teachings of faith should be presented through reason, as a logical inference from the known. When this is done, the supernatural pronouncements of faith become convincing beyond all doubt, because (a) they are the logical outgrowth of man's innate powers of rational inference and (b) they reflect a vision of reality that is so overwhelmingly meaningful as to be rationally irresistible. (O'Neill, 1981, p. 164)

To grasp truth, people combine reason with faith in the perfect knowledge that comes directly or indirectly from divine revelation or from the authority of the Church. The role of education is first and foremost to train individuals to understand the religious truths necessary for spiritual salvation. Secondary aims are to develop the intellectual, social, religious, and physical skills that will enable students to be effective and contributing members of society. Most often this is achieved through direct rather than indirect instructional methods; that is, information is conveyed through drill, lecture, recitation, teacher-directed questioning, and highly structured discussions. Catholics have used catechisms to teach students to reach their goals.

Thomism is the historical and philosophical foundation of Roman Catholic education, according to Lesko (1988). Prior to 1965, religion was the first subject of the day in Catholic high schools. "The class's prominent place in the schedule was intended to reinforce the preeminent position of religion in school and in a student's life" (Bryk, Lee, & Holland, 1993). Many Catholic schools today do not adhere strictly to the principles of Thomism but have turned their attention instead to secular issues common to the middle class:

> [R]eligious training is becoming secondary in Catholic schools; that is, these schools have become centrally concerned with preparing Catholic youth for contemporary life, i.e., facilitating their educational and social mobility. Catholic school administrators and board members are also prompted to emphasize the academic side of their schools as they develop strategies for the schools' economic survival. (Lesko, 1988, p. 18)

▶ Humanism

Humanism calls for respect and kindness toward students and developmentally appropriate instruction in liberal arts, social conduct, and moral principles. This orientation is grounded in the writings of Erasmus (1466?–1536), Martin Luther (1483–1546), and Jean Jacques Rousseau (1712–1778).

During the Renaissance in Europe, Erasmus advanced an enlightened view of the essential goodness of children. He advocated that the young be taught with kindness and gentleness. Children were to be nurtured, not scolded and abused.

Luther and others associated with the Protestant Reformation inspired the idea of public-supported education meant to prepare people to take responsibility for their own lives; that is, to help them read and interpret the Bible for themselves. As people defined the ways they would worship God, then, they also began to define how they would educate for character. Education was an essential ingredient in stimulating and sustaining both the Reformation and the Renaissance. Education empowered people to make their own decisions, thereby determining their own destiny on earth and thus in the afterlife.

Rousseau enriched Erasmus's humanistic perspective on the needs of children and the aims of education. He suggested children not be viewed as blank slates, or as miniature adults, but as individuals possessing natural goodness and needing continual support (see Chapter 2).

Jean Jacques Rousseau (1712–1778)

Is the basic nature of children good or bad?

In the 1950s, 1960s, and 1970s, humanistic psychologists, including Alfred Adler, Carl Rogers, Paul Goodman, and Abraham Maslow, extended humanist philosophy to education and schooling. They wrote and spoke often about the assumptions upon which a humanistic education should be based. Humanists have argued students should not be forced to learn; they will learn what they need and want to know. Processes of learning are thought to be at least as important as the acquisition of facts and skills. Students are assumed to be capable of evaluating themselves and so do not need to be judged by teachers or other adults. Students' emotional well-being is of critical importance for learning. Schools have to be free from threat if students are to take responsibility for their learning and to enjoy what they do. Self-fulfillment is the principal aim of education.

The work of Paulo Freire, a humanistic Brazilian educator, swept the developed world in the 1960s and 1970s. He has encouraged the teaching of illiterate, indigent workers in the developing world. With the abilities to read and write, Freire argues, people will become aware of their own essential humanness and their social situation. Education, Freire (1970) contends, will empower people to better their own lives and the lives of others:

> [W]hile both humanization and dehumanization are real alternatives, only the first is man's vocation. This vocation is constantly negated, yet it is affirmed by that very negation. It is thwarted by injustice, exploitation, oppression, and the violence of the oppressors; it is affirmed by the yearning of the oppressed for freedom and justice, and by their struggle to recover their lost humanity. (p. 28)

To learn more about humanism, visit the Library of Congress Vatican Exhibit on the Web.

Through the years classrooms have been influenced by idealism, realism, Thomism, and humanism. Each philosophy, as can be seen in Figure 4.2, reveals itself in educationally recognizable ways.

What Modern Philosophies Influence Western Education?

Educational philosophies have also been influenced by modern philosophies such as existentialism, Marxism, and others, as well as by philosophical orientations toward learning, such as behaviorism and cognitivism. The following sections describe modern philosophical orientations in education today, which are summarized in Figure 4.3.

▶ Existentialism

Sören Kierkegaard (1813–1855) is considered the originator of **existentialism**, a philosophy that emphasizes the subjectivity of human experience and the importance of individual creativity and choice in a nonrational world. Friedrich Wilhelm Nietzsche (1844–1900), Martin Heidegger (1889–1976), Jean-Paul Sartre (1905–1980),

FIGURE 4.2
Philosophies on Which Western Education Is Based   How might teachers who are idealists, realists, Thomists, and humanists differ in their philosophies of education, relationships with students, and approaches to teaching?

	IDEALISM	**REALISM**	**THOMISM**	**HUMANISM**
Philosophers	**Plato**	**Aristotle**	**Thomas Aquinas**	**Erasmus**
Metaphysics	Reality is an unchanging world of perfect ideas and universal truths.	Reality is observable events, objects, and matter independent of human knowing.	Reality is an ordered world created by God that people can come to know. People strive for eternity with God.	Reality is also humanity's creation. People strive for personal meaning in their experience and interpretation of life on earth.
Epistemology	Knowledge is obtained when ideas are brought into consciousness through self-examination and discourse.	Knowledge is obtained when students are taught ideas that can be verified and skills that enable them to know objects they encounter.	A combination of reason and faith enables students to acquire and use bodies of knowledge.	Exploration, questioning, and critical thinking enable students to discover or construct and use knowledge.
Axiology	Wisdom of goodness; discipline, order, self-control; preservation of cultural heritage of the past.	Self-control; clear judgment and rational thought; personal excellence; balance and moderation.	Knowing, loving, and serving God.	Knowing and loving God; serving humanity.

Albert Camus (1913–1960), Paul Tillich (1886–1965), Martin Buber (1878–1965), and others have developed existentialist thought by attempting to describe reality not as separate from or beyond the comprehension of humans, but as the result of individual passion and life experience.

Existentialists believe the physical universe has no inherent meaning apart from human experience. The world and forces of nature exist, but they are not ordered in some grand scheme in which humans play their appropriate part. Human life, too, exists; we are here, but we are only what we make of ourselves. Sartre's (1947, p. 28) often-quoted phrase states that "Existence precedes essence." We owe our existence to nature, but we define ourselves through our actions.

Nietzsche (1924, 1961)—a philosopher ignored in his own time—revealed the dark side of this view (Banville, 1998). He characterized life as a grim battle in which one requires strength, pride, and intelligence just to survive. Sensitivity, kindness, and consideration were signs of weakness. There was no God of mercy who ruled benevolently and rewarded the

Do we have free will to choose who we will be?

FIGURE 4.3
Philosophical Orientations in Education Today   What combination of philosophical orientations best matches your own beliefs and values?

	Goal of Education	Role of Students	Role of Teachers	Teaching Methods	Subjects Studied
Existentialism	Develop authentic individuals who exercise freedom of choice and take responsibility for their actions.	Develop independence, self-discipline; set challenges and solve problems.	Encourage students to philosophize about life and to recognize and fulfill personal freedom.	Discussion and analysis, examination of choice-making in own and others' lives.	Drama Art Literature Social Sciences History
Marxism	Shape people and institutions; change material conditions of society, producing classless society.	Live and work harmoniously with others, acquire and use knowledge that will enable them to transform natural and social world.	Lead and advocate change.	Scientific methodology, practical activity (problem solving).	Emphasis on science and history.
Behaviorism	Engineer environments that efficiently maximize learning.	Respond to environmental and behavioral stimuli; become self-regulated.	Manipulate the learning environment and present stimuli, using conditioning and social learning to shape student behavior.	Programmed instruction that provides feedback on performance, behavioral contracts, reinforcement.	Learning tasks in which behavior can be directly observed, measured, and evaluated.
Cognitivism	Develop thinking skills for lifelong self-directed learning.	Construct meaningful knowledge through experience and interaction.	Stimulate cognitive development; mediate student learning and monitor thought processes.	Use of manipulatives and real-life learning opportunities relevant to students' prior experiences.	Integrated curricula; emphasis on thinking and critical thinking skills, study skills, and problem-solving skills.
Pragmatism	Develop and apply practical knowledge and skills for life in a progressive democratic society.	Active learning and participation.	Teach inductive and deductive reasoning, the scientific method, and the powers of observation and practice.	Hands-on curricula, group work, experimentation.	Emphasis on citizenship, knowledge and skills applicable to daily life, and career or job preparation.
Perennialism	Acquisition of timeless principles of reality, truth, and value; learning for the sake of learning.	Receive knowledge and academic skills.	Guide to the classics; teach basic skills.	Teacher-centered direct instruction.	Emphasis on Great Books and core curricula in the arts and sciences.
Essentialism	Acquisition of culture; cultural literacy for personal benefit.	Receive knowledge; demonstrate minimum competencies.	Deliver a standard curriculum.	Subject-centered direct instruction.	Uniform curriculum for all students that emphasizes the essence of traditional American culture.
Social Reconstructionism	Solve social problems and create a better world.	Inquire, apply critical thinking skills, and take action.	Ask questions; present social issues and problem-solving challenges; serve as organizer and information resource.	Stimulate divergent thinking and group investigation.	Emphasis on social studies, social problems, global education, and environmental issues.

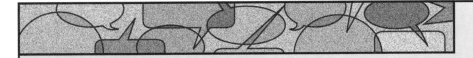

Voices

On the Existentialist Teacher

George F. Kneller, philosopher of education formerly at the University of California at Los Angeles, argued that if teachers were to adopt an existentialist view, their choices would be important and difficult and their pedagogical strategies would be clear.

If we accept [existentialism as a world view] . . . as free men and free teachers we must seek to expose and combat all those forces in culture and society that tend to dehumanize men by denying their freedom. We must repudiate the subordination of the person to economic "laws," the tyranny of the majority over the dissenting minority, and the stifling of individuality by social conformism. We must urge our students to recognize and fulfill the freedom that is theirs as persons. What we urge we must also practice by respecting their freedom as we value our own.

Most choices we make are admittedly trivial and inconsequential—choice of a necktie, choice of a restaurant, choice of a movie. A serious choice is a choice between actions involving fundamental values. It calls for deep concentration, a looking into oneself. However, I must not be content merely to apply an abstract moral principle. This is a weak choice, reliance on a rule rather than on myself. I should choose the course of action that seems uniquely right in this particular situation. I should seek not the way but my way. The hardest choices to make are often those between alternative goods. Two courses of action seem to have an equally good claim on us— which course do we take?

If I am an existentialist teacher, I urge the student to take responsibility for, and to deal with, the results of his actions. To act is to produce consequences. He must accept that these consequences are the issue of his choice, but at the same time he must not submit to them as unalterable, for this is to assume that freedom is exhausted in a single act. Freedom is never exhausted, and each consequence poses the need for further choice. I would teach him that his life is his own to lead and that no one else can lead it for him.

It is pointless to blame his failures on environment, family, temperament, or the influence of others. These conditions are for choice to challenge. Whatever may have happened to the student in the past, the future is his to make.

Does this attitude lead to a ruthless disregard for others, to my fulfillment at the expense of yours? Not at all. True freedom implies not egoism but communion. The egoist is driven by a narrow self-interest. With him choice is not self-fulfillment but self-limitation. Freedom, open and dynamic, longs for other centers of freedom, other persons. It does not calculate but gives. The fulfillment of freedom is communion with others.

If as a teacher I assume the style and gestures for which convention calls, I may touch only surfaces of my students' lives. I must go beyond familiarity and open myself to them. I must come to them unreservedly, creating the trust from which springs communion and true self-fulfillment.

CRITICAL THINKING

How might a classical idealist such as Plato respond to Kneller's declaration? How might a classical realist such as Aristotle respond? What examples of "dehumanizing" and "stifling" conditions in school cultures might Kneller accept as evidence of his claim? To what teacher "styles" and "gestures" might Kneller refer when he suggests that teachers risk touching only the "surfaces of students' lives"? How might teachers "open themselves" to students to create communion or mutual participation in educational life? How might "schools without walls" and "democratic classrooms" reflect values implicit in the philosophy of existentialism?

Note. From *Introduction to the Philosophy of Education* (2nd ed.) by Kneller, George F., © 1971. Reprinted by permission of Prentice-Hall, Inc., Upper Saddle River, NJ, pp. 72–76

worthy with eternal life in heaven. Indeed, there was no God at all. And if there ever had been, He was surely dead. Nietzsche believed we should strive not to better the majority of people, who were mostly worthless, but to promote genius and to develop superior personalities. From an aristocracy of talent and power—one cultivated by those who choose to restrain and discipline themselves—would arise the superman.

For existentialists, choice is a critical concept. People choose who they will be. Some allow others to decide for them, but exercising this default option is also a choice. Although existentialists do not reject morals or norms of behavior, they repudiate habitual adherence to them. Existentialists encourage people faced with a difficult conflict of values to concentrate seriously on their own situations and to choose what is right for them. When we are cut loose from restrictions, we assume responsibility for our own actions. We cannot simply rely on what we are told to do or on what some scripture directs us to do. And when we are free to choose our directions, we prize that freedom for others.

Martin Buber, existentialist and Hasidic Jew, assailed theologians' talk of God and their pretensions about knowing God. In *I and Thou* (1970), Buber did not try to support religion or to argue that God was present in all things. Instead, he raised the possibility that life without religion lacked an important dimension. Buber proclaimed that the secular was sacred and that God is present when people encounter one another in honest dialogue. Human relationships are central in creating meaning in our lives. Buber and other existentialists have influenced the development of humanistic psychology, in which relationships, free thinking, and action lead to self-actualization, or personal fulfillment.

A. S. Neill's Summerhill in England is a famous application of the existentialist–humanistic philosophy to schooling. Under Neill's direction, teachers encouraged students to philosophize about life, using their personal experiences as bases for examining individual choice making. Through dialogue with peers and instructors, students attempted to perceive and solve problems. The goal is to help students become cognitively equipped, "authentic" individuals having a deep commitment to the creation of a better world. Summerhill school continues today under the leadership of Neill's wife and daughter.

▶ Marxism

Marxism promotes the belief that the human condition is determined by forces in history that prevent people from achieving economic freedom and social and political equality. Karl Marx (1818–1883) was a historian, philosopher, and social theorist born to Jewish parents in Germany. In the main, his work was not taken seriously until after his death.

As a university student Marx was influenced greatly by the idealist Georg Wilhelm Friedrich Hegel (1770–1831), who at the time was the grand master of German philosophy. Although Marx grew to reject Hegel's political philosophy, he was influenced greatly by Hegel's thought, particularly his development of the concept of the dialectic, or the process by which human thought and human history progress.

The dialectic is a constant intellectual movement from thesis, to antithesis, and finally to synthesis. Movement in thought occurs, for example, when one plays a thesis or idea against its opposite, which for Hegel was the reality of nature. Thought moves along a continuum by way of the dialectic process to richer, more complex syntheses. Hegel argued that ultimately this process would reach the Absolute Idea, or an idea that bore close resemblance to idealists' conceptions of truth. He rejected the realist view that truth is independent of our minds. People become and remain alienated, according to Hegel, until they understand that they are thinking beings and that truth is a function of this self-realization.

> **How might our consciousness and progress be shaped by material conditions?**

The process, Hegel maintained, works also for history. Civilization progresses along a continuum toward richer, more complex syntheses. Culture moves forward, building on what has come before. To Marx, progress meant revolution. Marx thought of the dialectical process as a clash of economic forces in which the capitalist system exploited the worker. The ruling class seized workers' productive capacities and offered money in return, making workers subservient to the system.

Within this context, Marx saw progress as a mixed blessing. In capitalist society, the forces of production continually increase. Simultaneously, people create a more oppressive social organization as they characterize society by unequal classes. Capitalists, Marx contended, accumulate great wealth, but they create inequalities and dehumanize people. Marx thought that in time the exploited would rise up and overthrow the ruling class.

Marx recognized the value of science as a way to acquire knowledge. For Marx, human perception is based on sensory experience of the material world, and this perceptual experience shapes one's knowledge. The social order, therefore, is not fixed. Human nature is malleable—people and social institutions can be shaped and formed. A person's social class is a matter of education and circumstance. The aim of Marxism, then, is to change the material conditions of society. When these conditions change, consciousness changes; when consciousness changes, ideology changes, and the perfect, classless, communistic society will result.

In the 20th century, Marxism has been articulated and developed intellectually most notably by people referred to as the Frankfurt School—a school of thought based on Marxist assumptions about the social world, including Max Horkheimer (1895–1973), Theodor Adorno (1903–1969), Herbert Marcuse (1898–1979), and Jürgen Habermas (born 1929). Habermas in particular has exerted considerable influence on educational theory (Ewert, 1991). Critical theorists such as Habermas attempt to reveal the covert values in schooling and society, claiming that schools alienate students and "de-skill" them by establishing the goals of education instead of encouraging students to set their own goals. The process of schooling thus breeds dependency on authority, promotes top-down communication, and advances a distorted view of history (Apple, 1995).

▶ Behaviorism and Cognitivism

Behaviorism is based on the belief that human behavior is determined by forces in the environment that are beyond our control rather than by the exercise of free will. Behaviorism stands in stark contrast to **cognitivism**, a philosophical orientation based on the belief that people actively construct their knowledge of the world through experience and interaction rather than through behavioral conditioning.

B. F. Skinner
(1904–1990)

Several names are routinely associated with the development of behaviorism—Ivan Pavlov (1849–1936), John Watson (1878–1958), and E.L. Thorndike (1874–1949). But none is more prominent than that of B. F. Skinner (1904–1990).

Skinner was a psychologist who concentrated on scientific experimentation and empirical observation. Although he made his reputation with tightly controlled laboratory experimentation, he could let his mind roam freely over complex social problems. Skinner (1971) viewed our failure to solve social problems as a failure of the knowledge of human behavior:

> Physics and biology have come a long way, but there has been no comparable development of anything like a science of human behavior. Greek physics and biology are now of historical interest only . . . , but the dialogues of Plato are still assigned to students and cited as if they threw light on human behavior. Aristotle could not have understood a page of modern physics or biology, but Socrates and his friends would have little trouble in following most current discussions of human affairs. And as to technology, we have made immense strides in controlling the physical and biological worlds, but our practices in government, education, and much of economics, though adapted to very different conditions, have not greatly improved. (pp. 5–6)

Skinner would have placed science in the hands of those who would work for a peaceful and more just world. Science could be used to shape morality. To behaviorists, education conditions people to behave in more and less civilized ways.

Behaviorism is sometimes characterized as an "empty organism" theory of behavior; that is, behaviorists view the immediate world in terms of stimuli and responses to these stimuli without acknowledging what, if anything, happens in a person's mind. John Watson was extremely influential in this regard. In some of his experiments, he conditioned his son to fear small animals and then deconditioned him. Watson repudiated completely the value of introspection in psychology. He thought that because free will could not be measured, it did not exist.

Like other realists, then, behaviorists rely on knowledge derived from the physical world. To understand this world in relation to human behavior, they examine patterns of environmental influences on patterns of human responses to these influences. When students are not learning, behaviorists think there must be something wrong with the educational program. The way to solve the problem is to break down the program into its component parts and to fix the pieces that are broken, or to scrap the program altogether and try a new one. The challenge, then, is to engineer environments that produce desired results. This outlook has heavily influenced both the lay public's and educators' perceptions of educational problems and solutions.

The educational applications of behaviorism to enhance achievement and to improve conduct are many and varied. Schools use programmed instruction, both computer-based and print materials, to teach mathematics, reading, and other subject matter. These curricula are organized into discrete, sequentially ordered units of study, accompanied by unit tests, opportunities for feedback on performance, and chances to practice skills. Educators also advocate the use of behavioral contracts or contingency management schemes to influence student behavior. These are organized as "if . . ., then . . . "agreements between teachers and students: If you do your homework correctly, then you can spend the end of the class period reading whatever you wish in the library.

To what extent are we the products of behavioral conditioning?

The language of education is rife with behavioral terminology—*reward, punishment, contingency, reinforcer, shaping, fading.* Teachers speak of "reinforcing desirable behavior." They try to "ignore inappropriate behavior." People want student motivation to become "intrinsic" rather than "extrinsic," and so forth. Many educators use the words and phrases of behavioral engineering. They have incorporated the ideas, the language, and some of the practices into their own professional repertoires without abandoning strongly held beliefs about the importance of students' thoughts and feelings (Cohen & Hearn, 1988).

Alternatives to the behaviorist outlook take a variety of forms, loosely called cognitivism, from *cognition,* the process of thinking and knowing. On the basis of research on thinking, cognitive psychologists assert that people are not passively conditioned by the environment but rather are active learners. They mentally construct their knowledge of the world and beliefs about reality through their own direct experiences and interactions, and then they act upon those constructs. Cognitivists therefore focus on thought, which cannot be observed directly, while behaviorists focus on behavior that is observable and measurable.

Jere Brophy (1999) has observed that strict behaviorism, particularly as applied to classroom management issues, has incorporated ideas from the cognitivists to become "more realistic":

> Early behavioristic formulations were overly focused on specific behaviors and emphasized rather wooden and rigid technique prescriptions ("rules, praise, and ignoring") or converting classroom reward structures to token economy systems. As behaviorism developed and began to take into account human intentions and cognitions, behavioristic advice to teachers retained its emphasis on reinforcement but became more realistic, featuring such techniques as negotiated goal setting with students formalized through behavior contracts. (p. 45)

Like behaviorism, cognitivism is a philosophical orientation having implications for education. Educators who favor teaching models based on cognitivism often choose student-centered learning experiences. They assist students by teaching them study skills, thinking skills, and problem-solving skills. They try to provide conceptual bases or **scaffolding** upon which students construct meaning or make sense of information for themselves. In education, the movement to modify curriculum and instruction to reflect the cognitivist outlook is called **constructivism.**

Many people are associated with cognitivism and constructivism, most notably the Swiss developmental psychologist Jean Piaget (Perkins, 1998). Piaget tested children's understanding of basic logical structures by having them perform basic tasks. These included putting a series of sticks in order from smallest to largest and estimating how the shapes of containers influenced properties of liquids. Piaget encouraged teachers to become classroom experimenters intent on learning how students play active roles in their own development (Parziale & Fischer, 1998). Many modern constructivist teachers see themselves as action researchers seeking to understand how and why students construct knowledge as they do.

William James
(1842–1910)

▶ Pragmatism

Pragmatism is a philosophical method that defines the truth and meaning of ideas according to their physical consequences and practical value. An Englishman, Charles Sanders Peirce (1839–1914), is acknowledged as the originator of modern pragmatism. But pragmatism is so readily equated with the quality people refer to as "common sense" that many would claim it as the unofficial American philosophy. In the last 100 years or so, William James (1842–1910), John Dewey (1859–1952), and, most recently, Richard Rorty (born 1931) have used pragmatism to try to strike a philosophical balance between the realism of the natural sciences and the beliefs of idealists as expressed in art, religion, and politics (Rorty, 1991).

Like other philosophers, early pragmatists concerned themselves with the dualism of mind and matter: A subjective reality exists in our minds, an objective reality exists in the physical world around us. They agreed with the realists that a world exists and is not merely a figment of our imagination. In the objective–subjective dichotomy, however, objective reality has meaning only insofar as people ascribe meaning based on the consequences of the object. The goal of pragmatists, then, has been to seek wisdom, or truth, by examining the consequences of holding particular beliefs and acting on them.

William James emphasized the right of individuals to create their own reality. He (James, 1907) described the pragmatic method as a way to settle metaphysical disputes:

> Is the world one or many?—fated or free?—material or spiritual?—here are notions either of which may or may not hold good of the world; and disputes over such are unending. The pragmatic method in such cases is to try to interpret each notion by tracing its respective practical consequences. What difference would it practically make to any one if this notion rather than that notion were true? If no practical difference whatever can be traced, then the alternatives mean practically the same thing, and all dispute is idle. Whenever a dispute is serious, we ought to be able to show some practical difference that must follow from one side or the other's being right. (p. 42)

Other pragmatists have argued that the correspondence between human beliefs and physical objects is unimportant. If we believe with good reason that something is true, and there is some gap between our beliefs and truth, we can always improve our beliefs as new evidence becomes available. Truth is what is good for us to believe (Rorty, 1991). For all practical purposes, if something works, it is true.

Is pragmatism a convenient excuse for avoiding difficult moral issues?

John Dewey linked pragmatism to educational preparation for life in a democracy. When people are educated democratically, Dewey argued, they are prepared for life. And when education concentrates on real-life problems, that education prepares people for living fully and effectively in a democracy. Dewey believed that ordinary people possess the intelligence to govern themselves and to direct their own actions; the function of education is to enhance human potential.

Pragmatists thus believe that children should be encouraged to learn to make difficult decisions by considering the consequences their actions might have on others. Because democracy permits people to consider multiple points of view, pragmatic action and democracy complement each other. Education never ends—it is a process that continues throughout one's lifetime. People are instruments of change, capable of experiencing, experimenting, and testing their beliefs. Dewey believed that people can interpret the practical consequences of their actions; democracy demands as much (Westbrook, 1991).

Dewey criticized American public education as mechanical, mindless, and practically irrelevant—as little more than indoctrination. His progressive views (see Chapter 3) led him to argue for education that helps students realize their capacities to engage in activity that calls for genuine thinking and problem solving. According to Westbrook (1991),

> The youngest children in [Dewey's] school, who were four and five years old, engaged in activities familiar to them from their homes and neighborhood: cooking, sewing, and carpentry. The six-year-olds built a farm out of blocks, planted wheat and cotton, and processed and transported their crop to market. The seven-year-olds studied prehistoric life in caves of their own devising while their eight-year-old neighbors focused their attention on the work of the seafaring Phoenicians and subsequent adventurers like Marco Polo, Magellan, Columbus, and Robinson Crusoe. Local history and geography occupied the attention of the nine-year-olds, while those who were ten studied colonial history, constructing a replica of a room in an early American house. The older groups of children . . . [focused on] scientific experiments in anatomy, electro-magnetism, political economy, and photography. The search of the debating club formed by the thirteen-year-old students for a place to meet resulted in the building of a substantial clubhouse, which enlisted children of all ages in a cooperative project. (pp. 101–102)

Explore the Center for Dewey Studies at Southern Illinois University on the Web.

▶ Perennialism

A modern educational philosophy that looks backward through history and forward in time to shape thought about the goals and processes of education is called **perennialism.** Perennialists exalt the great ideas and accomplishments of Western civilization for their own sake and also for what Western classical writings can offer to future generations. Perennialists believe that the purpose of schools is to develop students' intellectual capabilities.

Perennialists contend that there are principles of education so important, so central to the development of culture that they cannot be ignored, such as the universality of truth, the importance of rationality, and the power of aesthetics and religion to encourage ethical behavior. Much like realists, perennialists believe that such enduring principles exist in the physical world and demand the attention of teachers and students. Culture is not relative, perennialists argue. That which is rational and intellectually self-disciplined is most desirable.

This philosophical view of what is important in education has been articulated most notably by Robert Maynard Hutchins (1899–1977) and Mortimer Adler (1902–). They have argued that in every important way, people are basically the same, regardless of where they live and who they are, thus all people need the same

Robert Maynard
Hutchins
(1899–1977)

basic education. This education should consist of a fundamental grounding in history, language, mathematics, science, literature, and humanities.

Hutchins and Adler introduced perennialism in the 1930s in reaction against progressive educational approaches that stressed the importance of change in society and the dynamics of teaching and learning. Progressives thought that education should be tailored to the times, the people, and the places it was offered. They advocated active learning, child-centered teaching, and problem solving as opposed to knowledge acquisition.

The perennialists, on the other hand, contended that people are rational animals having free will who learn to exercise self-control when their minds are disciplined by knowledge acquisition through basic education. Education implies teaching, teaching implies knowledge, knowledge is truth, truth is the same everywhere: therefore education should be the same everywhere (Hutchins, 1936).

Perennialists aver that schools are supposed to prepare students by putting them in touch with the classics of Western culture. A contemporary curriculum that disregards the classics does students and society a disservice. One must know the past if one is to be prepared to participate fully in the present and to contribute in the future. This view led to the development of the Great Books program at the University of Chicago in the 1950s.

Mortimer Adler's *Paideia Proposal* (1982), a more recent expression of perennialism, calls for a one-track system of public schooling. This single track would promote the same three learning objectives for all students. The first deals with mental, moral, and spiritual self-improvement. The second concerns civic education. The third addresses adults' needs to earn a living. In Adlerian language, these objectives are translated into goals. The goals and the means to their achievement are described in Figure 4.4.

The practical implications of perennialism for schooling are numerous. Perennialists prefer teacher-centered education; the teacher is the authority who must possess both the knowledge and responsibility necessary to teach a core curriculum to young people. Moral education, including Bible study, is important for what it communicates about self-control and social responsibility. Concepts of academic tracking and gifted education are acceptable to perennialists.

▶ Essentialism

Essentialism is a philosophical orientation that claims the existence of a body of knowledge that all people must learn if they are to function effectively in society. Like perennialists, essentialists acknowledge the timeless quality of great works, but they do not base their views on realist principles, and they do not agree on what constitutes the "essentials" that educated people should know. Essentialists agree that such essentials exist and that they ought to be represented in the curriculum. Like perennialists, essentialists have been criticized for defining the essentials in terms of Western history and culture. But, unlike perennialists, essentialists want students to study great works not for their own sake but to become better prepared to solve contemporary problems. The sciences, too, are useful and central to the process of knowing and improving one's world.

FIGURE 4.4
Adler's Recommended Course of Study   What might be some advantages and disadvantages of Adler's curriculum for a one-track system of public schooling?

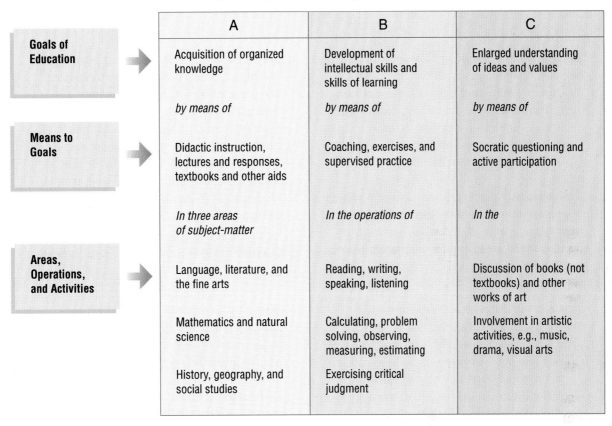

	A	B	C
Goals of Education →	Acquisition of organized knowledge	Development of intellectual skills and skills of learning	Enlarged understanding of ideas and values
	by means of	*by means of*	*by means of*
Means to Goals →	Didactic instruction, lectures and responses, textbooks and other aids	Coaching, exercises, and supervised practice	Socratic questioning and active participation
	In three areas of subject-matter	*In the operations of*	*In the*
Areas, Operations, and Activities →	Language, literature, and the fine arts	Reading, writing, speaking, listening	Discussion of books (not textbooks) and other works of art
	Mathematics and natural science	Calculating, problem solving, observing, measuring, estimating	Involvement in artistic activities, e.g., music, drama, visual arts
	History, geography, and social studies	Exercising critical judgment	

Note: Reprinted with the permission of Simon & Schuster from *The Paideia Proposal: An Educational Manifesto* (p. 8) by Mortimer J. Adler. Copyright © 1992 by Institute for Philosophical Research.

William Bagley (1874–1946) founded the Essentialistic Education Society as a reaction against progressive, pragmatic trends in education. Like the perennialists at the end of World War II, Bagley and his colleagues feared what they saw as an erosion of moral and intellectual standards in the young. To remedy this situation, they advocated that schools transmit a common essential core of knowledge to all students.

Essentialist Arthur Bestor (1879–1944), for example, also criticized the lack of rigor in American education. Bestor (1985) wrote:

To put the matter bluntly, we regard schooling as a mere experience, delightful to the recipient but hardly valuable to society. The school or college has become, to our minds, merely a branch of the luxury-purveying trade. Like the club car on a passenger train, it dispenses the amenities of life to persons bound on serious errands elsewhere. (p. 2)

In contrast to perennialists, essentialists place less emphasis on learning for learning's sake. They concentrate instead on the power of knowledge for solving contemporary problems and for preventing such problems from arising in the future.

Using Technology

Technology versus Social Learning

The Digital Age is spawning a class of what might be called "philosophers of technology" (Kent & McNergney, 1999). Among them, Lewis Perelman envisions dramatic changes in how students will approach their own education in the years to come. He foresees a time when students will purchase their own highly individualized education online.

Perelman's vision and the instructional philosophy behind his efforts have been criticized as emphasizing highly individualized, mechanistic learning at the expense of human contact in a social learning environment. He responds to this criticism:

> When I talk about hyperlearning and distance-learning and all this new-fangled stuff, somebody inevitably says, yes, that's very nice but it's never going to be as good as the gifted teacher in a classroom or the personal experience of going to Oxford or Harvard or whatever. They keep talking about experience, they love that word experience. Well look at this situation in 1952. . . . I put the pictures of the S.S. *United States* up on the wall, the picture of the Comet jet plane, and ask the question: Which is better? Well, it depends to what purpose. If you

need to be in Paris tomorrow morning to sign a contract, close a deal, there is no question; the plane is not just the better option, it is really the only option. If you want to enjoy the "experience" of luxury and entertainment, the steamship, with its swimming pools, restaurants, night clubs, movie theaters, sunshine, fresh air and all that, is incomparably better. (Horizon Instructional Systems, 1997, p. 2)

D. A. Norman, in contrast, argues for the preservation of the social environment in learning, at all costs:

> Experience with technology teaches us that once a technology makes something possible, it gets applied, whether good or bad. It makes sense to be able to show a sixth-grade play to interested relatives. . . . It makes no sense to destroy the experience through the act of recording it. It makes sense to have control over the viewing of records. It makes no sense to sacrifice human social relations in the process. Which will it be? I put my faith in people. Human social interaction is too important, too fundamental, to fall to obstructionist artifacts and event fanatics. (1992, p. 14)

How would essentialists encourage societal progress? They would have teachers instill in students the old-fashioned values of discipline, self-control, and hard work. Because essentialists view children as incapable of directing their own learning, teachers would direct it by structuring and pacing students' mastery of subject matter. Because much knowledge is abstract, practical problem solving, or "learning by doing," would not apply. Essentialists might well argue that details get in the way of seeing the big picture (Clive, 1989).

Essentialist curricula are rarely as specific as the recommendations of Hirsch (1987; Hirsch, Rowland, & Stanford, 1989). Hirsch argues that society cannot function properly without communication among its members, and communication cannot occur in the absence of literacy. But true literacy, Hirsch (1996) contends, is more than mechanical performance of the skills of reading and writing; it depends on people's shared information, or common knowledge of their culture.

Hirsch referred to this shared common knowledge as **cultural literacy** and developed an elaborately prescribed curriculum for students. He delineated exactly what he believed children need to know by the end of sixth grade in such categories as literature, religion and philosophy, history, geography, mathematics, science, and technology.

A criticism of Hirsch's work and that of perennialists and essentialists generally is that it is **Eurocentric;** that is, it is centered on the history and cultures of Europe. Such a curriculum is said to consist mainly of works by "dead white males." Cultural literacy becomes an exclusionary concept, one that does not include knowing the history and culture of non-European peoples. Defenders of essentialism, such as Allan Bloom in his book *The Closing of the American Mind* (1987), say that this is as it should be: "One should conclude from the study of non-Western cultures that not only to prefer one's own way but to believe it best, superior to all others, is primary and even natural—exactly the opposite of what is intended by requiring students to study these cultures" (p. 36). Michelle Fine (1987) and Henry Giroux (1984) contend that such an approach silences talk about instances of social, economic, and educational discrimination experienced by minority and low-income students. For these students, school "disconfirms rather than confirms their histories, experiences, and dreams" (Giroux, 1984, p. 189). In the United States, members of minority cultures are among those who bitterly oppose the essentialist interpretation of what is worth knowing. The countermovement of Afrocentrism makes the history and cultures of Africa and African Americans the focus of the curriculum.

> Should all students learn the same curriculum? What should a common curriculum include?

▶ Social Reconstructionism

Social reconstructionism promotes the belief that people are responsible for social conditions and can improve the quality of human life by changing the social order. Theodore Brameld (1904–1987) and George Counts (1889–1974) were instrumental in articulating social reconstructionism which advocates education as a means of preparing people to create a new society. Stimulated by progressivism, Brameld, Counts, and others pushed for rapid, sweeping changes throughout society to effect a new world order. Whereas the progressives and pragmatists of Dewey's day were politically moderate, urging gradual change, the social reconstructionists were provocative in advocating systemic change.

For example, social reconstructionists might attack the governance of schools to reorganize decision-making power, as they did in Chicago in the 1920s (Counts, 1928). They argued that every major legitimate interest in the city should be represented on the school board and that teachers should prepare themselves professionally to meet their responsibilities and guard their right to perform professional functions. Counts (1928) and other social reconstructionists argued that rebuilding public education was not going to be easy but was possible through courageous leadership and modern science. The optimism of early social reconstructionists was based on faith in the power of science to solve human problems, a faith others criticized as unjustifiable.

George Counts (1889–1974)

Unless the profession can develop a superior type of social leadership, a leadership at least equal in intelligence, courage, and power to the leadership in other fields of interest with which it must contend, the profession will find itself unable to incorporate in the systems of public education the findings of educational science. (p. 361)

The same kinds of arguments made by early social reconstructionists are advanced today to restructure schools and redesign professional education for teachers.

From the 1930s to the 1960s, social reconstructionists saw a world where confusion and crisis reigned. The Great Depression, World War II, the Nuclear Age, and the Cold War era stimulated and sustained concerns about world order. Rather than bemoan world conditions, social reconstructionists sought to define opportunities to build a good and just society. People cannot sit comfortably in their safe homes holding tightly to the good life while others less fortunate sit on the outside looking in. People have to act to bring the have-nots into a better society.

Therefore Brameld thought that the future could be bleak or promising: the choice belonged to all. People can take control of their lives and behave in ways that improve the human condition. But the education system itself needed to be reconstructed as a tool for transforming individuals' lives and shaping a new social order. Like the Platonists, social reconstructionists were utopian. As Brameld (1950) noted,

The common denominator of [social reconstructionism's] beliefs is a passionate concern for the future of civilization. It centers attention, therefore, upon clear-cut cultural goals, which, because they are idealizations of human and especially social potentialities, are in the historic stream of utopian philosophy. (p. 407)

How can education make the world a better place?

The spirit of social reconstructionism has been nurtured in the United States over the years by individuals and groups intent on creating change through social activism. The works of Saul Alinsky (1909–1972), Ivan Illich (1926–), and others embody this spirit. Social reconstructionists of the late 20th century press for schools to address many societal problems that occur because of ignorance, poverty, lack of educational and employment opportunities, and the like. This multiple-causation view of problems dictates a multifaceted approach to solving them. Social reconstructionists conceive of education, then, not so much as a linear response to a particular need but as the means to address an interdependent set of intellectual, emotional, personal, and social needs. Social reconstructionists' views of the interconnectedness of problems and solutions and of people's responsibility to society shape educational programs today.

What Non-Western Philosophies Influence American Education?

Eastern and Middle Eastern philosophies, religions, and cultures are gradually beginning to influence schools in the United States as the number of people having roots in Eastern and Middle Eastern countries grows. In cities across the country, there are many first-, second-, and third-generation American and foreign national public

Cultural Awareness

Vito Perrone

Vito Perrone is a faculty member in the Learning and Teaching Program and Director of Teacher Education at the Harvard Graduate School of Education. He describes how he has been touched and changed by a reformer from the past:

> I was first introduced to Leonard Covello's autobiography in 1969. In retrospect, I wonder why it took so long for me to hear about and read *The Heart Is the Teacher*. After all, I had, by then, been teaching for thirteen years and considered myself a serious student of teaching. Needless to say, perhaps, I was captivated immediately by the account, seeing in it a remarkable educator who comprehended well his East Harlem immigrant–migrant setting; articulated clearly a set of human, inspiring purposes for himself, his students, the schools, and those in the surrounding community; and exemplified in practice a large array of educational understandings that seemed so logical, so commonsensical, so right. I was attracted as well by the basic metaphors, especially the idea of teaching

> emanating from the heart, an antidote, it seemed, to the way teaching was (and still is) being described in the research literature. In a very large way, "Pop," as Covello was called by many of his students, affirmed much of what I understood teaching to be—essentially a moral and intellectual endeavor. Many of my colleagues at the time thought teachers needed to remain distant, involved exclusively with the content of their subject matters. My experience, as a student and as a teacher, was filled with other messages—that personal relationships and caring mattered, that the lives of the students, in and out of school, were never really apart from whatever was being studied. I was also drawn to Covello's work because he was Italian, a person who had struggled with the immigrant experience, something I understood well as the son of Italian immigrants. It was natural to see in Covello's life and work some of my own.

Source: Vito Perrone (1998), *Teacher with a heart: Reflections on Leonard Covello and community*, 1998. New York: Teacher College Press, p. 2.

school students who have Asian and Middle Eastern backgrounds. Groups such as Buddhist Vietnamese Americans in Los Angeles, Islamic Arab Americans in Detroit, and Hindu Indian Americans in New York often maintain private schools and educate children and adults through cultural festivals and religious celebrations.

In some nonsectarian private schools, students are guided in an exploration of world religions. Students are encouraged to develop secular spirituality, a personal ethical system, and inner peace. New multicultural curriculum materials also provide access to past and present ideas and expressions of spirituality, and in some alternative private schools, non-Western philosophies play a significant role.

In general, Western ways encourage people to look outward toward what they hope lies ahead in their personal and professional lives. One's sense of progress is rooted in work and one's place in society. Attendance at church or temple, the latest self-help book, or some traumatic event prompts people to think about "meaning" in their lives, but introspection may occur rarely for many. Non-Western philosophies can remind people that a long, focused gaze inward, often undertaken with the help of a spiritual guide or teacher, is essential if a life is to be fully lived.

▶ Hinduism

Hinduism is more than a religion. It is a philosophy, a way of life. To use the term *Hindu* as though it represents one particular philosophy or one way of life is misleading. Hindu beliefs and life-styles vary dramatically. Members of some Hindu sects are Stone Age animists. They believe that life exists in many forms. They worship trees, stones, snakes, and other objects and phenomena in nature. Other Hindus are sophisticated urban intellectuals. These accomplished leaders contribute to virtually all aspects of modern life (Organ, 1974).

Major Hindu writings began to appear in the form of hymns and chants, or mantras, about 1200 BC to AD 200. The three basic Hindu texts—the Vedas, the Upanishads, and the Epics—reveal a way of life that has evolved to guide believers through the years. The Vedas present a vision of the universe consisting of the earth, the atmosphere, and heaven. Vedic believers worship many gods, ascribing human characteristics to nonhuman things. Varuna, for example, is thought to control the changes in seasons. The Upanishads, or secret teachings, recognize a single god, Brahman, and established laws to govern conduct. These laws laid down rules for personal conduct and promoted the caste system. This system of social hierarchy, now outlawed, put the Brahmin, or priests, teachers, and other thinkers, at the top and relegated the Sudras, or "untouchables," to the bottom.

The Epics, which contain among other writings the Bhagavad-Gita, were written between 200 BC and AD 200. The Bhagavad-Gita is a poem of more than 700 verses that depicts a compassionate god who opens salvation to all devoted, dutiful souls. The Bhagavad-Gita also describes yoga as a means of uniting one's soul with the Absolute. Through yoga's teaching of right posture, correct breathing, and control of the senses, one learns to concentrate so as to free the mind and to attain enlightenment.

Mohandas Gandhi, a member of the Jain sect of Hinduism, was known as the Mahatma (the Great). His influence on Western thought included his advocacy of nonviolence as a means to social reform. Martin Luther King, Jr. (1964) wrote about the use of Gandhian nonviolent political action during the bus boycott in Montgomery, Alabama: "For Gandhi love was a potent instrument for social and collective transformation. It was in this Gandhian emphasis on love and nonviolence that I discovered the method for social reform that I had been seeking for many months" (p. 79).

To characterize Hindus as a single group having a monolithic set of beliefs is inaccurate and misleading. "Diversity is perhaps the first and most important feature of Hindu worship to be noted" (Rambachan, 1992). The beliefs, customs, and religious practices of Hindus vary widely from sect to sect and place to place. The life of a Bengali woman in rural India, for instance, can differ markedly from that of a Hindu woman in Calcutta, and even more so from the life of a Hindu woman in New York.

One example of Hindu education in practice is the Shishu Bharati School of Languages and Cultures of India in Burlington, Massachusetts, which was founded by a group of parents who had immigrated to the United States from India. They were concerned about preserving their languages and passing on their cultural heritages to their children. The school offers language programs in Bengali, Gujarati, Hindi, Marathi, Sanskrit, Sindhi, and Tamil. In addition to language classes, education programs address Indian arts, customs, religion, history, geography, and current events. The curriculum includes field trips to Indian cultural events, yoga, and advanced culture classes (Shishu Bharati, 1999).

▶ Buddhism

Having its roots in Indian Vedic culture, Buddhism is meant to help people recognize truth for themselves:

> Buddhism is not a fundamentalist religion. Its teachings are not dogmas or articles of faith that have to be blindly accepted at the cost of suspending reason, critical judgment, common sense or experience. Quite the contrary, in fact; their basic aim is to help us gain direct insight into the truth for ourselves. (Snelling, 1987, p. 51)

Buddha, or the Enlightened One, was born as Siddhartha Gautama (563–483 BC) to wealthy parents in Nepal. Although Gautama enjoyed a sheltered, opulent existence until age 29, tradition teaches that his life was immutably altered by three events. He saw an old man bent over a walking stick, a diseased man suffering with fever, and a corpse being carried to a funeral pyre. These experiences compelled him to seek a spiritual inner peace with which to face the ravages of old age, sickness, and death.

Gautama left his wife and son and lived an austere life of study concentrated on human suffering and its cure. The doctrine, or dharma, he taught consisted of four truths: life is full of suffering and dissatisfaction; suffering emanates from desire; suffering will cease when desire stops; and the cessation of desire can be accomplished through eight steps. These eight steps are right views, right aspirations, right speech, right conduct, right livelihood, right effort, right mindfulness, and right contemplation.

Buddhists think of life as a flowing stream. They believe in Hindu reincarnation, that is, rebirth in which people assume a new physical form and status depending on the quality of their deeds (karma). They also believe that with progress along Buddha's eightfold path people will reach *nirvana*, a state of serenity and wisdom in which they can escape the cycle of endless rebirth. Although Buddha did not believe in an Absolute or God, after his death he became revered as a god.

Zen, a sect of Buddhism, took root in Japan in the 12th century. Shinto, the traditional religion of Japan prior to the introduction of Buddhism and Confucianism from China, focused on worshipping nature and family ancestors (Holtom, 1984). Shinto philosophy encourages feelings of reverence toward all life, past and present. In feudal, patriarchal Japanese society, Zen Buddhist monks stressed the dignity of physical labor, the arts, swordsmanship, and the tea ceremony, emphasizing stern discipline, selflessness, and spontaneity. Zen beliefs and rituals became integral to Japanese culture.

▶ Islam

Islamic philosophy is based on the writings of the Koran (Quran), the holy or sacred book of Muslims. Muslims believe the word of God, or Allah, was revealed to Muhammad by the angel Gabriel. Abu-Bakr, Muhammad's father-in-law, collected Muhammad's words in the Koran. Muhammad (570–632), then, was a prophet, like Christ, who described Allah's will. Muhammad foretold of a world where Allah would come on the Last Judgment to appraise all souls by their abilities to live according to Allah's will. To those who succeeded, eternal reward would be granted in paradise; those who failed would be condemned to suffer the pain of eternal fire. The religion of Islam thus was rooted in both Judaism and Christianity and was strongly influenced by the Old and New Testaments (Corbin, 1993; Fakhry, 1983).

Al-Kindī (died after 870) expressed Islam's view of God as an absolute, transcendent being and the idea that revealed truth (that which emanated from philosophy and religion) and rational truth are the same thing. Al-Fārā bī (875–950) expressed the Islamic view that the goal of humankind is to attain immortality through education or the development of one's intellect.

In the ancient world Muslims made important advances in science and medicine. The physician ibn-Sina (980–1037), known as Avicenna, described concepts of matter, form, and existence in a way that allowed for a Necessary Being, or God, who was distinct from the world. To ibn-Sina, the prophets were teachers who used religion as philosophy for the masses to reveal symbolic truth—a kind of truth that helped people approach absolute truth, or God.

During the 1960s Islam gained large numbers of converts in the United States among African Americans, particularly among urban African-American males, principally because Islam is nonracist. The Koran, which includes both Judaic and Christian writings in addition to those of Muhammad and his disciples, expressly forbids discrimination in thought or deed on the basis of race. Submission to Allah and strict adherence to Islam's five pillars of faith guarantee automatic brotherhood and equality. In 1965 Malcolm X, an influential "Black Muslim," wrote bitterly about the need for Islam at a time when many African Americans felt disappointed that the civil rights acts of the late 1950s and early 1960s had not yet made much of a difference in people's lives:

> I am in agreement one hundred per cent with those racists who say that no government laws ever can *force* brotherhood. The only true world solution today is governments guided by true religion—of the spirit. Here in race-torn America, I am convinced that the Islam religion is desperately needed, particularly by the American black man. (pp. 368–369)

▶ African and Native American Philosophies

According to M. K. Asante, African and African American philosophies differ from European philosophies in important ways. Western thought is rational (I think, therefore I am), whereas African thought is based on feeling and sociality (I feel, and I relate to others, therefore I am) (Asante, 1987). Likewise, Sleeter and Grant (1993) describe a "synergetic" way of thinking among some African Americans—a preference for working cooperatively rather than independently and a desire to integrate personal relationships into learning tasks (p. 54).

This holistic view is expressed by the African writer Chinua Achebe. While no single scholar can claim to represent the African perspective, Achebe's *Things Fall Apart* (1968) has been translated into 50 languages and sold 50 million copies. He has "held fast to an African vision of the role of art, one that rejects the Western tradition of seeing the artist apart and alienated from society. In Africa's communal culture, 'art is intended to help society'" (Winkler, 1994, p. A9).

Asante (1992) writes of the importance of understanding an African American philosophy and its bearing on educational life in America. He advocates a curriculum that acknowledges African history and culture:

> The African-American children in your classrooms are not a black version of white people. They have different cultural and historical experiences that must be looked at and examined in a different way. To give an obvious example, African Americans did not come to America on the Mayflower. We recognize the Mayflower as part of the American experience, but our experience was different: We crossed the ocean packed in boats with as many as 1,000 other people, with only 18 inches of space between us and the deck above, and chained from neck to ankle. (p. 21)

Traditional Native American thought also emphasizes holistic, nonrational being and social relations. Reason and logic, for example, are not seen as superior to other explanations of events. Like African traditions, Native American traditions encourage spiritualism based on animism—belief in the presence of active supernatural forces in the natural world—and on the ideal of harmonious coexistence with nature. Truth comes not from great books or scientific inquiry but from personal introspection, oral traditions, and the values and knowledge handed down from ancestors.

Native American philosophies stress personal dignity, moral responsibility, and the mutual interdependence of all the people in a society or group. Group identity and well-being take precedence over individual needs and abilities. Traditional social values encourage silent reflection over verbalizing, cooperation over competition, stability over change, and continuity over progress (Banks, 1994).

Cherokee poet, author, and journalist MariJo Moore (1997) brings Native American philosophy alive through her stories and poetry. She demonstrates how Native American philosophy can be reflected in curricula for all learners:

> The History of Our Mothers' Dreams
>
> The deepest part of ourselves
> is formed before we are born.
> This is when the grandparents
> breathe into the dreams of our mothers.
>
> Heavy breaths colored by
> yellow black red and white.
> Sighing breaths sounding of
> poetry singing music and dance.

Falling breaths formed from
birds clouds trees and tears.
Yet we do not know
the history of our mothers' dreams.

The colored sounding forming dreams
holding the breaths of our grandparents.
It is time we begin to listen. (p. 18)

Source: From *Spirit Voices of Bones*, page 18, by MariJo Moore © 1997.

African and Native American thought, like the religious and secular philosophies of the Middle East, India, and Asia, influence the development of educational philosophies in the United States in two main ways: They broaden people's minds and they enlighten changes in curriculum and instruction that are designed to meet the needs of all students in our culturally diverse society.

What Factors Shape Teachers' Personal Philosophies of Education?

Individual educators draw upon various philosophies, both purposefully and casually, to fashion their own unique views of teaching and learning. Teachers are idealists, realists, pragmatists, cognitivists, and the like. They reveal their philosophical roots, both knowingly and unknowingly, through their interactions with students, parents, administrators, and others. Some hold classical positions on the nature of knowledge and of being—we think of a New York teacher we met who spoke a dozen languages and expressed a personal commitment to helping his students discover the universal truths we share as human beings. Others, like a teacher we encountered in New Mexico, describe the importance of their work almost strictly in terms of the practical value it yields in the lives of students. If asked to do so, many teachers might well articulate their philosophies as some amalgam of classical positions.

As a person, a teacher is changing and developing, advancing and regressing, experiencing the joys and disappointments of life just as all adults do. At the same time, a teacher is a powerful adult in a world of children. For most schoolchildren, their teacher is the adult with whom they have the greatest amount of daily contact. Teachers therefore have significant opportunities to influence the personal development of their impres-

Why does this teacher need to know her own philosophy of education? How can she develop a personal educational philosophy to guide her professional practice as a teacher?

sionable students. Teachers act as potential role models of responsible adult behavior, attitudes, and values. And the teacher is the architect of the social system of the classroom with its rules, norms, sanctions and rewards. The social system of the classroom sets the tone and context for human interaction for an entire school year. And the personality and values of the teacher are clearly reflected in how life in a classroom is lived out. Parents of schoolchildren know that who the teacher is as a person has a profound effect on the quality of education that their children experience. (Clark, 1995, p. 4)

> Should you teach from an educational philosophy or from a personal philosophy?

▶ Teachers' Theories and Beliefs

Clark and Peterson (1986) offer a model that attempts to account for the relationships between teachers' thought and action. In Figure 4.5, the circle on the left depicts how teachers think, or the unobservable. In this circle the terms *preactive*, *postactive*, and *interactive* refer respectively to thoughts before, after, and during teaching. Teachers' theories and beliefs evolve from these thoughts and also from teachers'

FIGURE 4.5
Teachers' Thought Processes in Relation to Teachers' Actions   In what ways might teachers' thought processes constrain teachers' actions? In what ways might teachers' thought processes provide opportunities for enhancing the effects of teachers' actions?

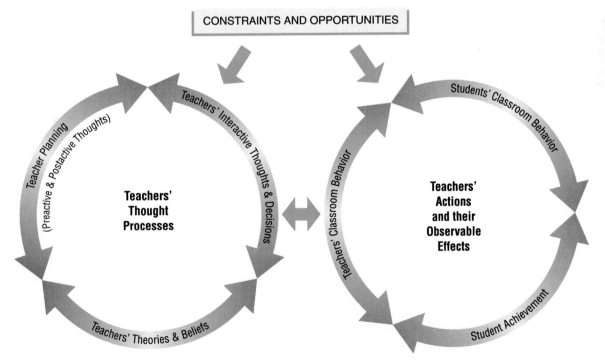

Note. From "Teachers' Thought Processes" by Christopher M. Clark and Penelope L. Peterson. Reprinted with permission of Macmillan Publishing Company from *Handbook of Research on Teach* (3rd ed.) Merlin C. Wittrock, Editor. Copyright 1986 by the American Education Research Association.

ideas about the nature of children as learners (metaphysics), ways of knowing (epistemology), and right content and conduct (axiology). The circle on the right—teachers' behaviors, students' behaviors, and students' achievements, such as test scores—represents the observable in classrooms. This circle represents where teaching actually occurs.

The arrows in the model show how teachers' thoughts and actions interact. For example, teachers' theories and beliefs affect their planning and their thoughts during teaching, which in turn, affect their theories and beliefs.

Effective teachers look for meaning in the events of teaching and learning. They are openminded and sensitive to new ideas. They resist simple explanations for complex problems and try instead to understand acts in the contexts in which they occur. They might be said to be more philosophical or theoretical than other teachers; they might also be said to be more practical.

How do teachers develop their habits of thinking, their personal philosophies? Although there are no simple answers, Hunt (1987), an instructional psychologist at the Ontario Institute for Studies in Education, has provided some intriguing leads. Hunt observes that most new ideas in philosophy, psychology, education, and social sciences are presented in orthodox fashion by making cases for them based on research results or on theoretical grounds. Teachers, for instance, take college courses designed to present them with the latest research and thinking on human behavior. They, in turn, are supposed to translate this knowledge into action with their students. Most of the time, then, teachers begin with someone else's ideas and try to make sense out of them in their own situations, a logical progression from philosophy to practice.

Hunt argues, however, that viewing the development of knowledge this way cuts people off from their own experiences. In effect, they must take information from outside themselves and try to integrate it, or to put it inside themselves. Hunt believes that people should begin constructing their philosophical and professional knowledge by examining their own personal beliefs. For teachers this means making explicit their own beliefs and values about teaching and learning by consciously considering their ideals about the nature of children as learners, what is worth knowing, and the purposes of education.

▶ Teachers' Personal and Professional Experiences

Teachers' experiences profoundly affect their educational philosophies. One beginning teacher, Marcia Sampson, is a good case in point (Herbert & Keller, 1999). We observed and interviewed Sampson during the second semester of her first year of teaching and the first semester of her second year. We selected her because she was known as an outstanding undergraduate education student and as an excellent beginning teacher.

Marcia remembered as a child playing school with her younger sister for hours. " 'I knew as early as age five or six that I wanted to be a teacher' " (p. 30). She went happily to college with little doubt about her future. When she had finished college and begun her first teaching position, however, the reality set in. Both Marcia and her principal described her first year in a fourth-grade classroom as a "real shock." Her students came from predominantly low income homes. They had histories of poor performance in school. She found herself applying "more structure" than she had done in student teaching.

She observed, " 'I didn't feel like I had to be so mean, or so tough [with students last year in student teaching] because I felt like we understood each other . . .' " (p. 31). Yet meanness was not part of her repertoire; she felt especially protective of her academically high risk students. She expended much effort each day to maximize their learning time—the kind of effort she did not always recognize in her colleagues: " 'It makes me angry to go by teachers' rooms and see the kids doing independent work first thing in the morning—that's the very time [students] are freshest. Also, some of the teachers often sit behind their desks while students are working. If you're not teaching, the students are not learning' " (p. 32).

Marcia believed she was shortchanging students if she did not expect them to perform to the fullest of their abilities: " 'Pacing slowly across the room, hands in pockets, a puzzled look on her face, Ms. Sampson continues to ask questions about concepts in the previous day's story. At one point, she calls on Tony, her student who is in special education. I want to see how much he knows because, of everyone in here, I think he might have a lower retention rate. . . . I just want to see how much he got from yesterday.' " (p. 37)

Marcia Sampson believed too many students like Tony had been allowed to sit and do nothing. She was eager to break the pattern. So she pushed and pulled and praised and prodded, always seeking to get the most from her students. Her tenacity seemed coupled with genuine concern for her students' emotional needs. Marcia never appeared to miss an opportunity to applaud her students' praiseworthy actions. She enjoyed being with them, and they seemed to enjoy being with her. " 'This is the best job I could have. . . . I could never sit behind a desk like you do at other jobs. Here I get to work with children, which is fun. It's hard to be in a bad mood when you are with them. Also, my day goes quickly, and I'm never bored.' " (p. 48)

▸ Teacher Reflection and Problem Solving

How do teachers achieve professional excellence?

Other researchers also have explored how teachers think on the job. Greta Morine-Dershimer (1990) has noted that teachers think about teaching in a variety of ways, illustrated in Figure 4.6.

First, some teachers base their thoughts on organized structures of knowledge that represent relationships among concepts. For example, sometimes they think in terms of scripts that summarize typical classroom routines. They envision scenes to organize information about people and objects in recurring classroom events. They also formulate propositions to summarize factual knowledge about students, subject matter content, and teaching strategies. Morine-Dershimer (1990) believes that this line of work "provides a very positive image of the mental functioning of teachers" (p. 5). Studies of experts and novices indicate that experienced teachers have acquired and systematically stored much useful information and can access this information when they need it (Clark & Peterson, 1986).

Second, teachers' thinking has been characterized in terms of artistry, or as reflecting in and reflecting on action. Reflection in action has been compared to having

FIGURE 4.6
Comparing Conceptualizations of Teacher Thinking

Conceptualizations	Types of information emphasized	Notable transformations of information	Ideal state	Possible use in teacher education
Thinking through schemata	Routines/scripts Classroom organizations/schemes Activity structures	Reorganization of new information according to existing schemata	Teacher manages flow of information to track pupil understanding of lesson content	Prospective teachers learn classroom routines
Reflecting in/on practice	Classroom events recalled from prior situations "Backtalk" of pupils in immediate situation	Reframing an ambiguous or problematic situation	Teacher reconceptualizes the situation and resolves the problem	Prospective teachers acquire experience in a variety of settings
Formulating pedagogical content	Subject matter content Pedagogical processes Pupils' common misconceptions of subject matter Pupils' real-life experiences related to subject matter	Transforming subject matter for presentation to pupils	Teacher uses appropriate analogies and varied examples to develop pupil understanding of concepts and relates topic to pupils' own experiences	Prospective teachers learn many alternative analogies and examples appropriate for use with basic concepts
Perceiving practical arguments	Experiential knowledge (situational premises) Propositional knowledge (principles of practice; empirical premises) Normative knowledge (value premises)	Recognizing "subjectively reasonable beliefs" and reformulating to arrive at "objectively reasonable beliefs"	Teacher's actions are consistent with objectively reasonable beliefs (research and "warranted practice")	Prospective teachers explore own beliefs in relation to research

Note. From *To Think Like a Teacher* by G. Morine-Dershimer, 1990. Vice Presidential address presented to the annual meeting of the American Education Research Association, Boston. Reprinted with permission.

a conversation with a situation (Schön, 1987). During *reflection,* a teacher perceives a problem, thinks about other past similar events, interprets the problem in light of this past knowledge, and takes action. The problem "talks back" by yielding information that causes the teacher to reframe the problem and to make another move. And so on. In contrast, reflection on action is after-the-fact analysis; that is, once an event has occurred, a teacher might think back on what he or she might have done differently and what effects such action might have produced. Such reflection is disconnected from present action. Because there is no need for a quick response, reflection on action is a more analytical process.

Vivian Paley (1979) demonstrated this type of thinking after a colleague accused her of reinforcing stereotypes. She reported, in *White Teacher,* how a middle-aged, Jewish woman learned to think about her own thinking as she interacted with her African American kindergarten students:

> "[T]he black girls" were, in fact, five separate girls who played together and copied each other a great deal. I could name five white girls who played together, but I did not call them "the white girls." I was starting to realize, with help of a good friend, that thinking of Ayana, Rena, Karla, Joyce, and Sylvia as "the black girls" kept me from seeing them always as individuals. (p. 135)

Third, Morine-Dershimer notes that teachers possess a unique form of knowledge, which exists at the intersection of content knowledge and knowledge of teaching or pedagogy, which Shulman (1987) calls "pedagogical content knowledge." Shulman has explored how teachers transform content and pedagogy by reading, discussion, observation, and practice into knowledge that is adapted to the abilities of students. Marcia Sampson, for example, sometimes role plays parts of stories so her students can "see" as well as read and hear interactions among characters.

And fourth, teachers' thinking about their work has been characterized in terms of Aristotle's concept of "practical argument," that is, an argument ending in action related to the logic of one's initial proposition. Tom Green (1976) suggested that good teachers can perceive the practical arguments of students. For instance, when students are incorrect or unreasonable, the teacher determines why students think as they do, then helps them reexamine their beliefs and formulate better responses. Gary Fenstermacher (1986) suggests that research on teaching can be used to influence teachers' beliefs, in a sense, to strengthen their practical arguments.

When teachers understand, articulate, and act on their philosophies, they, by example, encourage students to do the same. These consequences, some would argue, are enough to justify the study of philosophy for its own sake. But a teacher's philosophy serves other purposes as well. Philosophy provides the foundation upon which teachers construct knowledge about teaching and learning. Philosophy guides the professional rationale that supports reasoned and reasonable action. Philosophy helps teachers evaluate their work and thus assists them in their pursuit of personal and professional excellence.

Benchmarks

Developments in Western Intellectual Thought and Their Influence on American Education

The Classical Period 500 BC–AD 500

Greeks and Romans define the branches of philosophy and basic ideas on which Western intellectual thought is based. Socrates and Plato define idealism; Aristotle, realism. Quintillian establishes the Roman school system from which the American school system is descended.

The Middle Ages AD 500–1300

Arab scholars preserve the Greco-Roman intellectual traditions after the fall of Rome. Arab mathematicians, geographers, physicians, and scientists, such as Ibn-Sina (Avicenna), Ibn-Rushid (Averroes), and Ibn-Battuta contribute to Western learning.

In Charlemagne's empire, Alcuin establishes a prototype curriculum of seven "liberal arts." The first universities are established in medieval Spain, France, and England.

Thomas Aquinas formalizes scholasticism, later known as Thomism, an educational philosophy based on the logical study of beliefs of the Church. Thomism becomes the basis of Roman Catholic parochial education.

The Renaissance and Reformation 1300–1700

Humanism revives the classical philosophies of human nature. The humanist philosopher Erasmus calls for respect and kindness toward students and developmentally appropriate instruction in liberal arts, social conduct, and moral principles.

Developments in printing-press technology increase the availability of books and public demand for literacy. To the curriculum of humanism, Johann Comenius adds the study of science and the use of textbooks written specifically for students.

Martin Luther launches the Protestant Reformation, a reaction against some of the teachings of the Roman Catholic Church based on the idea that people should read and interpret the Bible for themselves. Luther and other Protestants call for universal state-supported liberal education.

Ignatius of Loyola founds the Society of Jesus (Jesuits), and Jean Baptiste de la Salle founds the Brothers of the Christian Schools, teaching orders devoted to furthering the cause of the Church and counteracting the Protestant Reformation.

In *Essay Concerning Human Understanding and Some Thoughts on Education,* John Locke expresses the realist view that reality and thought are separate. He describes a child's mind as a blank slate (*tabula rasa*) on which teachers must imprint an education.

The 1700s

In *Emile,* Jean Jacques Rousseau expresses a humanistic view of education in which children are not blank slates but possess natural goodness and freedom which must be nurtured so that individuals can express their greatest potentials. Educator Johann Pestalozzi puts Rousseau's theory into practice.

The writings of Voltaire and Descartes help to popularize scientific inquiry and spread commitment to rationalism and empiricism as philosophical orientations to education.

In his *Critique of Pure Reason,* Immanuel Kant reflects classical idealism in his definition of knowledge as the interaction of reason and experience. German idealist Georg Wilhelm Friedrich Hegel describes reality as a dialectic between thesis (idea), antithesis (nature), and synthesis (mind or spirit).

The 1800s	Karl Marx transforms Hegel's dialectic between ideas, nature, and mind into a dialectic between economic or material conditions and human choices. Dialectical materialism becomes the basis of the political philosophy known as Marxism.

Educators Johann Herbart and Friedrich Froebel develop Rousseau's philosophy into teaching methods that spread to the United States.

Charles Darwin's 1859 *On the Origin of Species* focuses attention on heredity, evolution, and natural processes of adaptation and change. His work stimulates the scientific movement and influences the philosophers and educators who come to be known as the pragmatists. Herbert Spencer's theory of Social Darwinism becomes the basis of a movement calling for utilitarian education. |
| **Around the Turn of the Century** | Charles Pierce and William James express the philosophy of pragmatism, based on the idea that the purpose of thought is to produce action. Practical knowledge and applied skills become a focus of educational reform.

Maria Montessori develops an educational philosophy in the humanist tradition that continues today through a system of private schools. |
| **1920s and 1930s** | John Dewey extends the philosophy of pragmatism in education. His views—that ideas must be tested through experimentation, that people learn best through questioning and hands-on experiences, and that the needs of the child are most important—become known as progressivism. Progressivism becomes the most influential educational philosophy in America until the 1950s.

Influenced by events of the Great Depression, Theodore Brameld and George Counts develop the philosophy of social reconstructionism, in which the aim of education is to reform the social order, fulfill democratic ideals, and improve the quality of human life. |
| **1940s and 1950s** | Progressivism underlies Jean Piaget's studies of children's cognitive and social development. |

Developments in Western Intellectual Thought and Their Influence on American Education *(Cont.)*

Opposing Dewey and progressivism, Robert Maynard Hutchins and Mortimer Adler promote the philosophy known as perennialism. They develop Great Books of the Western World, the study of selected classics to uncover enduring basic truths. Other perennialists call for reserving general education for the gifted and including character training and Bible study in the curriculum.

Other critics of progressivism, such as William Bagley and Arthur Bestor, promote essentialism, calling for a common core of essential knowledge that changes with the times and rigorous teacher-centered instruction in basic skills so that people can lead productive lives.

Influenced by events surrounding World War II, existentialist writers and philosophers such as Sören Kierkegaard, Albert Camus, and Jean-Paul Sartre popularize the idea that reality resides within the individual, that we are free to search for our own meaning in the world, and that we are what we choose to be.

Behavioral psychology emerges from experiments by Ivan Pavlov, John Watson, and others. B. F. Skinner improves this earlier work and develops principles based on the idea that behavior is determined by environment and that people are best motivated by rewards and punishments.

1960s and 1970s

In *Walden Two,* B. F. Skinner shows how behavioral engineering—the scientific control of the educative process—might lead to the creation of a utopian society. Behaviorism widely influences educational practice. Humanistic psychology develops from the work of Alfred Adler, Carl Rogers, Abraham Maslow, and others, partly as a reaction against behaviorism, and influences the open school movement. Experimental curricula, such as A. S. Neill's *Summerhill,* express the humanistic and existentialist views that the aim of education is to promote personal freedom and expression and individual self-fulfillment. Eastern philosophies derived from Hinduism and Buddhism influence curriculum in the United States and educational movements based on existential and reconstructionist philosophies. Social reconstructionism based on Marxist assumptions about the world is expressed in the writings of Herbert Marcuse, Jurgen Habermas, and others.

1980s through 2000

In *Paideia Proposal,* Mortimer Adler extends the educational philosophy of perennialism that he and Hutchins developed earlier in the century, calling for one course of study for all. The Back to Basics movement, the Essential Schools movement developed by Theodore Sizer, and E. D. Hirsch's curriculum for cultural literacy revive interest in essentialism. Constructivism and multiculturalism as educational movements have combined roots in the philosophies of humanism, progressivism, existentialism, and reconstructionism.

SUMMARY

What is philosophy, and what does it have to do with you as a teacher?

1. Philosophy is a set of ideas about the nature of reality and about the meaning of life. Both ancient and modern philosophies influence education today.

What are the roots of American educational philosophies?

2. The three main branches of philosophy are (1) metaphysics, which deals with the study of reality; (2) epistemology, which is concerned with the nature of knowledge; and (3) axiology, which seeks to determine what is of value.

3. Idealists are concerned with goals against which people can judge their own progress and the progress of civilization. Platonian idealists believe that education is the key to creating and perpetuating a society in which talent rises to the top.

4. Realists seek to discover truth in the world around them via methods of direct observation and scientific inquiry. Aristotle believed that excellence would flourish as one sought the middle ground between life's extremes. Realists believe that the role of education is to teach students about the world in which they live.

5. Thomists believe there is an independent reality knowable to man that is the creation of God. A combination of reason and faith enables people to discover truth. Thomists see the primary role of education as training individuals to understand the religious truths necessary for spiritual salvation.

6. Humanists reform people's perceptions of themselves in relation to teaching and learning. They also express their beliefs in the inherent goodness of children. Humanists believe that education should prepare people to take responsibility for their own lives.

What modern philosophies influence Western education?

7. Existentialists believe that people are free to define their lives as they choose. As such, existentialist educators prize individuality and resist social conformism.

8. Marxists believe that the human condition is determined by forces in history that prevent people from achieving economic freedom and social and political equality. When Marxists view public schools in the United States, they see evidence of the ruling elite, or the haves, in a capitalist society dominating the have-nots. This evidence, they contend, is often veiled by a curriculum that assumes the values of the ruling elite are viable for all.

9. Behaviorism explicates relationships between the environment and behavior. In America's schools, both curriculum and teaching reflect behavioristic philosophy in the use of conditioning and modeling techniques.

10. Cognitivism is based on the belief that people actively construct their knowledge of the world through experience and interaction rather than behavioral conditioning.

11. For pragmatists and progressives, truth is relative, or determined by science or by function. According to their philosophy, people are capable of experiencing, experimenting, and testing their beliefs, changing them if need be.

12. Perennialists and essentialists assert that there are some recurring principles of education so important that they should be learned for their own sake. Because people are basically the same, there must be constancy in the way they are educated. Essentialists also believe that some principles must be taught to all students so that they can solve contemporary problems. For essentialists, science is central to societal progress.

13. Social reconstructionists seek change in society. They would use education to reform not only schools but also the communities in which schools are embedded.

What non-Western philosophies influence American education?

14. Hinduism, Buddhism, and Islam influence contemporary American educational philosophies.

15. African American and Native American philosophies, based on feeling and sociality, influence the development of curriculum and instruction.

What factors shape teachers' personal philosophies of education?

16. Educators draw upon Western and non-Western philosophies, both purposefully and casually, to fashion their own unique views of teaching and learning. Teachers' theories and beliefs, personal life experiences, and reflection and problem-solving skills also help to shape their personal philosophies.

TERMS AND CONCEPTS

aesthetics   128
axiology   128
behaviorism   139
cognitivism   139
constructivism   141
cosmology   128
cultural literacy   147
epistemology   128
essentialism   144
ethics   128
Eurocentric   147
existentialism   134
humanism   133

idealism   129
Marxism   138
metaphysics   128
ontology   128
perennialism   143
philosophy   126
pragmatism   142
realism   130
scaffolding   141
social reconstructionism   147
Socratic method   129
Thomism   132

REFLECTIVE PRACTICE

Harry Shabanowitz, eighth-grade science teacher at Garfield Junior High School, served as managing editor of *The Garfield Gazette*, the school paper produced by students and faculty as part of an interdisciplinary unit. Shabanowitz thinks that students need to make logical connections between the subject matter and their own lives and to improve their work habits.

> I have watched them go through general science and biology, and in elementary chemistry, without understanding why they are here. They can't explain how an experiment relates to a concept in the text, or how a scientific concept in the text relates to a practical example of the concept in our lives. They just go through the motions—even the bright students. The other thing that worries me is their lack of general knowledge and the absence of pride in their work. They can't even keep a lab book so I can read it. Sloppy handwriting. Lousy grammar. They exhibit a casual disregard for self-discipline that would prevent them from ever being admitted to a decent college or university, let alone getting and keeping a job.

Steve Keegan, history teacher and entertainment editor for *The Garfield Gazette,* sees his teaching world in different terms.

> Our task is more than teaching our subject matter in interrelated ways. The kids come in here not knowing what they are going to do with their lives. They are too young really to know. But some are already failing—they are goofing up their chances for any kind of academic success in high school and probably for later economic success in life. Others are college bound. These students and their parents just naturally assume they will succeed. I think our work should suggest that interdisciplinary studies can help students connect with each other and link school work to real life.

LeRoy, a student who works on the newspaper, got caught in what might be termed a philosophical dispute between Shabanowitz and Keegan.

Scene: *Teachers had rolled back the accordion walls of their four classrooms in the west wing of Garfield Junior High in September and gathered 80 students. They were deep into production of the first issue of* The Garfield Gazette. *Harry Shabanowitz served as managing editor and held a meeting with his student science reporters.*

SHABANOWITZ: Okay, I want all you science reporters to tell me the name of the person you interviewed, the topic of your story, and how many manuscript pages you have written.

LEROY (student): Gretchen Vanderkellen. Astrology. Twelve pages.

SHABANOWITZ: LeRoy, this is supposed to be the science section, not the comics. Are you trying to roll in a story on the occult?

LEROY: You said we could identify a topic we were interested in, Mr. Shabanowitz. Astrologers predicted the future based on the mathematical positions of the sun, moon, stars, and planets. They also kept track of the movement of these bodies. Astrologers were practically worshipped by people. I think they were respected as much as our scientists are today. I read that astrologers even diagnosed diseases and prescribed medicines for the sick. See here, Mr. Keegan showed me how to take some things astrologers might say and to prove that their ideas are not that different from other people's ideas today. [LeRoy pulls a story outline out of his backpack and lays it on Harry Shabanowitz's desk.]

SHABANOWITZ: Look, LeRoy, that's all very interesting. I think I understand where you want to be going with this piece, but it does not belong in the science section. We can't have our readers thinking you believe astrology has the same credibility as physics or chemistry, or even as some social science.

LEROY: But Mr. Shabanowitz, I believe people thought about astrology and astronomy almost the same way for many centuries. You can even find astrology on the World Wide Web. I got this address from my older sister. [LeRoy puts a scrap of paper on the desk that contains the following address: **http://marilyn.metawire.com/stars**]

SHABANOWITZ: Sure, sure, LeRoy, but I think you had better find a new topic or try to convince Mr. Keegan to put your story in the entertainment section.

Note. From *All the news that's fit to teach.* by R. F. McNergney, 1996, Washington, DC: The Hitachi Foundation. Available at **http://casenet.edschool.virginia.edu**

Issues, Problems, Dilemmas, Opportunities

What problems or issues arise when Shabanowitz is talking with LeRoy?

Perceive and Value

Describe the similarities and differences in the views of Harry Shabanowitz and Steve Keegan. How might their personal philosophies influence their interactions with students?

Know and Act

Assume you were the managing editor in this situation. What more might you want to know if you were faced with the decision of running LeRoy's story? What might you do?

Evaluate

What might be the outcomes of publishing and not publishing LeRoy's story? What outcomes emanating from the publication or rejection of LeRoy's story might cause you to change your outlook on what is important for students to learn from their participation in the newspaper unit?

 ## ONLINE ACTIVITY

The American Philosophical Association challenges Web travelers to discern the relevance of philosophy to their lives. Use a search engine to locate their web site, where you will find newsletters, electronic texts, Web conferences, and even career opportunities for philosophers. When you arrive at the site, see whether you can find the link to "Exploring Plato's Dialogues: A Virtual Learning Environment on the World Wide Web," where you can read Plato's *Republic,* as well as other works.

5

Schools

The emergence of the common school marked the beginning of public education in the United States. Many people have viewed the common school as a great equalizing force having the potential to eliminate poverty, crime, and ignorance. Although schools have fallen short of these goals, we continue to pin our hopes for a better world on a place called "school."

In this chapter, we describe some of the ways schools differ from one another and what makes some schools more appealing to one group of people than to another. We also present research on more and less effective schools, which focuses on a number of attributes that seem to make a difference in students' performances and their attitudes toward school.

PROFESSIONAL PRACTICE QUESTIONS

- How is the school a social institution?
- How is public schooling organized in the United States?
- What are some schooling alternatives?
- How are schools administered?
- What organizational and policy issues do schools face?
- What makes some schools more effective than others?

How Is the School a Social Institution?

School is first and foremost a social **institution,** that is, an established organization having an identifiable structure and a set of functions meant to preserve and extend social order. Schools are structured to operate as relatively self-contained units, loosely coupled to other schools within a system. Schools have personalities that characterize daily life within their walls. Sometimes these personalities are visible in written mission statements, but more often than not they emerge in interactions with the members of the organization.

As a social institution, a school's primary function is to move young people into the mainstream of society. The curricula, teaching, processes of evaluation, and relationships among people reinforce a public image to which young people are expected to aspire. This image is concerned with preserving our heritage, adapting to social change, and making change happen where it is needed.

More and more people are recognizing the power of the school as a social institution. Recent reform efforts have tried to capitalize on the fact that schools are the places where people come together and stay together for an extended period of time in their lives. In such settings, educators work with parents, children, and outside agencies to ensure the psychological and physical well-being of students and to foster academic success. They also work collaboratively to build students' understanding and acceptance of others.

▶ School Districts

A **school district** is a state-defined geographical area assigned responsibility for public instruction within its borders. During the 1996–1997 academic year, there were 88,223 public schools serving a total of 45, 953,018 students in grades prekindergarten through 12. As illustrated in Table 5.1, the largest districts serve more than 31 percent of the total elementary and secondary school population in the country, yet they account for only 1.5 percent of all school districts. Three states—Florida, Texas, and California—account for over one-third of the 100 largest school districts. The New York City school district, the largest in the country, alone has 1,120 schools, 57,338 teachers, and 1,063,561 students (U.S. Department of Education, 1999a).

TABLE 5.1

Public School Districts and Enrollment by Size of District, 1996–1997

Enrollment size of district	Number of districts	Percent of districts	Percent of students
Total	14,841	100.0	100.0
25,000 or more	226	1.5	31.1
10,000 to 24,999	569	3.8	18.7
5,000 to 9,999	1,024	6.9	15.5
2,500 to 4,999	2,069	13.9	15.9
1,000 to 2,499	3,536	23.8	12.7
600 to 999	1,772	11.9	3.1
300 to 599	2,066	13.9	2.0
1 to 299	3,160	21.3	1.0
Size not reported*	419	2.8	

*Includes school districts reporting enrollment of 0.

Source: From *Digest of Education Statistics,* 1998 (p. 97) by U.S. Department of Education, 1999, Washington, DC: U.S. Government Printing Office.

Big school districts are very different from one another in a number of other ways. In Gwinnett County, Georgia, a small district, 10.3 percent of the students are eligible for free lunch, while 79.8 percent of those in San Antonio, Texas, qualify for the program (U.S. Department of Education, 1998a). Racial/ethnic compositions of school districts also show considerable variation. At least 87.3 percent of students in the District of Columbia are African American, while 86 percent in Jefferson County, Colorado, are European American. In Hawaii, 63.9 percent are Asian–Pacific-Islander American, while 76.2 percent in El Paso, Texas, and 83.7 percent in San Antonio, Texas, are Hispanic American. As noted in Table 5.2, six large school dis-

TABLE 5.2

Variation in Racial–Ethnic Composition of Student Populations in Six Districts, in Percent

School District	Hispanic	African American non-Hispanic	European American non-Hispanic	American Indian/ Alaska Native	Asian/ Pacific Islander
Dade County, FL	51.5	33.6	13.5	0.1	1.3
Dallas, TX	45.5	41.5	11.0	0.4	1.7
Fort Worth, TX	38.4	33.2	25.9	0.2	2.3
Austin, TX	41.7	18.0	37.7	0.3	2.2
Denver County, CO	47.5	21.3	26.1	1.4	3.7
Boston, MA	25.2	48.4	16.9	0.4	9.2

Source: Digest of Education Statistics 1998 (pp. 99–107) by U.S. Department of Education, 1999. Washington, DC: U.S. Government Printing Office.

tricts, three of which are in Texas, have student bodies composed mainly of three racial/ethnic categories (U.S. Department of Education, 1999a).

▌Types of Schools

Children in the United States have access to many types of public and private schools (see Figure 5.1). Schools are designed for different ages of students, from preschool

FIGURE 5.1

Examples of the Structure and Types of Schooling in America   You will learn as you read this chapter that it is difficult in many cases to draw solid lines between the three columns in this chart. Develop a hypothesis that you think might explain this difficulty.

PUBLIC SCHOOLS	PUBLIC ALTERNATIVE SCHOOLS	PRIVATE SCHOOLS
Kindergarten (K)	Head Start	Nursery Schools & Preschools
Elementary School (K/1–6 or K/1–8)	Prekindergarten Programs	"Concept School" Alternatives
• Primary (K–2)	Laboratory Schools	• Montessori Schools
• Intermediate (3–6)	Nongraded Schools	• Waldorf Schools
Middle School (5–8)	Magnet Schools	"Ethnic School" Alternatives
Secondary Schools	Charter Schools	• Afrocentric Schools (Black Academies)
• Junior High School (7–8 or 7–9)	Accelerated Schools	• Reservation Schools
• High School (7–12, 9–12, or 10–12)	Cluster Schools	Parochial/Religious Schools
Post-Secondary Schools	Vocational–Technical Schools	• Catholic Schools
• Community Colleges	Professional Development Schools	• Christian Academies
• State Colleges	Government-Run Schools	• Hebrew Schools
• State Universities	• Department of Defense Dependents Schools	• Islamic Schools
	• Native-American Schools	College Preparatory Schools
	• Career Academies	Trade Schools
	• Job Corps	Military Academies
	Home Schooling	Junior Colleges
		Colleges & Universities
		Adult Education Centers

to college. In many public school settings, there are magnet schools, charter schools, alternative schools, and vocational or trade schools. There are also rural schools, suburban schools, and urban schools. The various schools often differ in structure (organization) and function (programs and services).

A 1997 study by the Hudson Institute suggests that parents consider several attributes when selecting a school. When asked why they had chosen **charter schools** (independent public schools supported by state funds but exempt from many regulations), rather than traditional public schools, for example, 53 percent of parents cited small school size. This was the most frequent response, ahead of higher standards, educational philosophy, greater parental involvement, and better teachers. Andrew Rotherham, director of the 21st Century Schools Project at the Progressive Policy Institute in Washington, DC, notes that "it is also telling that urban parents, whose children are most likely to be in excessively large schools, are also the parents most likely to express dissatisfaction with their public schools" (1999, p. 76).

What do parents want in a school system?

How Is Public Schooling Organized in the United States?

Many children attend some form of preschool, but, as we explain later in the chapter, enrollment rates vary according to family income and race/ethnicity. Once children reach 5 years of age, nearly 72 percent enroll in one of the 61,805 public elementary schools (U.S. Department of Education, 1999a). Enrollees often are classified as primary (kindergarten through grade 2) and intermediate (grades 3 through 6) students. With increasing frequency, however, students in grades 4 through 6, 5 through 7, or 6 through 8 attend middle schools. In some school districts students in grades 7 through 8 or 7 through 9 are enrolled in junior high schools.

High schools, or secondary schools, usually include grades 10 through 12 or 9 through 12. In some states, such as California, Illinois, and New Jersey, where 4-year high schools are the rule, the high school may function as a separate entity, having its own board of education. For the most part, however, the trend has been to combine elementary, middle, and high schools into a unified district.

Because parents and school leaders want high school students to go on for more education, high schools try to prepare students to move up the academic ladder. As with preschool, however, access to higher education is influenced in large part by the cost of postsecondary education programs to students and their families. Among high school graduates' options are technical or vocation institutions, 2-year colleges, and 4-year colleges and universities.

▶ Early Childhood Education

Many of the first early childhood programs were in day nurseries funded by philanthropic organizations and associated with settlement houses. Today, preschool programs are more diversified and are supported by both public and private interest

To what extent should preschools be expected to assume child-rearing functions?

groups and sponsors. Project Head Start, infant intervention and enrichment programs, nursery schools, public and private prekindergartens and kindergartens, college and university laboratory schools, church-sponsored preschools, and parent cooperatives offer a variety of educational programs for young children. Although enrollment in such programs has gradually increased over time, not all children have access to preschool offerings. European American and African American 3- and 4-year-olds, for example, participate in early childhood programs at higher rates than do Latino children. Additionally, 3- and 4-year-olds from families with incomes greater than $50,000 are more likely to be enrolled in preprimary education than children from lower-income families. Enrollment is also affected by parents' education level; as parents' education attainment increases, so do enrollment rates of their children (U.S. Department of Education, 1998a).

With so many agencies sponsoring preschool programs, there is much variation in the types of services offered and in the types of families served. While some preschools offer full-day educational or custodial care, others offer only half-day programs. Preschools also may be restricted to children from low-income families, to children of adolescent parents, or to children with disabilities. Among the different preschools, program goals and philosophies about teaching and learning also vary considerably.

The professional preparation of early childhood education staff and the quality of programs vary greatly. This fact has fueled ongoing debates about whether early childhood programs should be school based or community based. Qualitative differences in programs also spurred the **National Association for the Education of Young Children (NAEYC),** the largest professional association for early childhood educators, and the National Association of Early Childhood Specialists in State Departments of Education (NAECS/SDE) to develop guidelines that could be used to ensure quality education of 3- through 8-year-olds (NAEYC & NAECS/SDE, 1992). Visit NAEYC's web site to learn more.

While many people tout the importance of philosophy and curriculum in preschool settings, others contend that increased funding for public preschool programs is crucial. In 1996 the National Center for the Early Childhood Work Force (NCECW) reported that the national average wage for a center-based early childhood teacher was only $7.50 per hour, or $13,125 per year. Such low wages make it difficult to attract and retain qualified staff—and it is staff who ultimately make the difference in what children experience at school (Whitebook, Howes, & Phillips, 1998).

▶ Kindergarten

While the number of students attending kindergarten on a full-time basis has quadrupled since 1969, only 54.7 percent of 5-year-olds experience full-time programs (U.S. Department of Education, 1999a). In some instances, children old enough to enter kindergarten programs are placed in one of two tracks, the regular kindergarten or a junior kindergarten. Those in junior kindergartens go to school for 1 year before being promoted to a regular kindergarten. This experience is supposed to help get them "ready" for kindergarten.

Placement in either setting is usually determined by students' performance on a variety of screening tests. Although screening policy and practice vary from district to district, low-income males have a tendency to score poorly on screening tests and thus are more likely to spend two years in kindergarten (Walsh, Ellwein, Eads, & Miller, 1991; Shepard, 1997). Boys' lower scores may be due in part to the fact that they develop more slowly than do girls in the early years and also that some cultures' expectations for young boys are not geared toward the development of attributes measured by such tests. Thus, some contend that using readiness tests to search for learning indicators in preschool children is an unproductive, often dangerous task, while others argue that discrete skill analyses are necessary

How is early childhood education organized in the United States? What alternatives exist for education at the preschool and kindergarten levels?

for maximizing students' success in school. Moreover, recent trends in the early identification of children with disabilities—"child find" provisions of the Individuals with Disabilities Education Act (1997), for example—encourage the use of detailed assessments of young children (Scarpati & Silver, 1999).

In some kindergarten programs, teachers are oriented to an academic curriculum, which often means extensive time spent in whole-group settings, didactic instruction, use of worksheets, and few opportunities for small-group, individualized, or hands-on activities. Other kindergarten teachers use a curriculum that is more student centered, or "developmentally appropriate," which usually means that students are expected to acquire skills and concepts at their own pace through exploration and free play.

To what extent should kindergartens focus on academics?

▶ Grades K through 6

Schools for elementary students typically have about 24 students working in a self-contained classroom with a teacher and sometimes, particularly at the primary level, with an aide. Classroom teachers usually focus on language arts, mathematics, science, social studies, and health, while specialist teachers offer instruction in art, music, physical education, and special education.

Despite many outward similarities, there are a number of curricular and instructional variations within and among elementary schools. Sometimes students are grouped homogeneously by ability or achievement for instructional purposes. Such grouping can occur within a classroom or across classrooms. In other settings, students work in **nongraded classrooms,** where they are grouped heterogeneously by ability, sometimes with students of various ages. Nongraded programs, also referred to as multiage, multigrade, or family grouping programs, are most prevalent in primary schools.

The popularity of multigrade or nongraded programs has waxed and waned through the years. During the 1950s and 1960s, nongrading was practiced in more

What are some advantages and challenges of multiage grouping in elementary schools? How would working in a nongraded classroom affect your role as teacher?

Should schools use multi-age rather than graded groupings?

than 7 percent of the schools. The popularity of the concept declined, however, when "back to basics" ideas took hold during the mid-1970s. Concerns about the strong correlation between retention in grade and the subsequent dropping out of a growing number of students have stimulated some elementary schools to revert to the one-room schoolhouse notion of multiage groupings of students.

Ideally, nongraded programs provide a developmentally appropriate curriculum. Such curriculum can be tailored to differences in students' stages of intellectual, emotional, physical, and/or social development, allowing for individualized, continuous progress for young children. While there are standards of performance to be reached by students, the time taken to reach those standards and methods for doing so should vary from student to student. Any grouping for instruction is said to be flexible and based on the abilities, interests, and needs of students. In these programs there is no formal promotion from one grade to the next. Instead, a student stays with a group of students until he has mastered necessary skills (Stone, 1998).

Research on nongraded elementary schools suggests that they can be quite effective when nongrading is used as a grouping method rather than as a means for individualizing instruction. Positive effects are greatest in situations where students are grouped across age lines in just one subject (usually reading) or in multiple subjects, with students receiving direct instruction for the majority of a class session. Experts agree that groupings should not be stagnant, however. They should be reassessed frequently and changed when student performance indicates a mismatch in instruction and achievement (Gutiérrez & Slavin, 1992).

▶ Junior High Schools and Middle Schools

In the fall of 1909, Columbus, Ohio, opened a new 3-year intermediate school, calling it a "junior high school." This was the first mention of such a school. In 1910, Berkeley, California, opened two 3-year intermediate schools and called them "introductory high schools"—a name that never caught on (Til, Vars, & Lounsbury, 1967). Junior high schools have been an important part of our education system since the 1930s. Junior high school programs are meant to help students make the transition from elementary to high school by concentrating on academic subjects and by exposing students to careers and occupations.

Although there are variations in enrollment patterns for junior high schools, most include students who are in grades 7 through 9. As in elementary schools, instruction occurs mainly in self-contained classrooms. Curriculum at the junior high school level, is usually more diversified, that is, there are more types of courses offered. Like their colleagues at the senior high school level, junior high school teachers generally specialize in the content and teaching of a particular subject area. Junior high schools typically use six class periods per day; instruction is usually teacher directed.

Middle schools, which emerged in the 1960s, aim to provide an educational environment less imitative of high school and better suited to the developmental needs of 10- to 14-year-olds in early adolescence. By the 1970s the number of middle schools (usually grades 5 through 8 or 6 through 8) had surpassed the number of junior high schools. Despite their continued popularity, particularly in the suburbs, middle schools for many years have been criticized for tailoring programs similar to the ones they were designed to replace. No doubt the preparation of teachers has been a factor in the way middle schools have operated. A study of the credentials of teachers in four junior high schools that were converting to middle schools (grades 6 through 8) during the 1995–1996 school year revealed that the majority of teachers (66 percent) were certified in secondary education. Only 21 percent of the teachers were certified in middle-grades education, and 13 percent were certified in elementary education (Hadley, 1996).

How are middle schools different from junior high schools? Why has the middle school movement spread so successfully nationwide?

Advocates for middle schools argue that the special needs of young adolescents require a school that is not as juvenile in its structure and approach as an elementary school and not as impersonal and demanding of independence as a high school. In a middle school, they contend, students should have a chance to mature before being thrust into the high school environment (Maehr & Midgley, 1999). Some believe that one of the best ways to encourage students to mature in the middle grades is to help them learn self-discipline (Wolfgang, Bennett, & Irvin, 1999).

Indiana's Harshman Middle School in downtown Indianapolis is an example of a middle school that shaped a program to meet the unique needs of young adolescents. Until 1992 Harshman had been a junior high school for students in grades 7 and 8. At the time, urban junior high schools in Indiana exhibited "violence; high rates of suspensions, expulsions, and absenteeism; low test scores; students with overwhelming social and emotional needs; and a general climate of disrespect for the teaching profession" (Ames, 1996, p. 4). When Indiana implemented its statewide Middle Grades Improvement Program, funded by Lilly Endowment, Inc., substantive changes took place in Indiana's middle schools.

Marcia Capuano, the principal of Harshman (the seventh principal in 5 years), first instituted a host of physical and mental health services for students. Next, she introduced a wide variety of reading initiatives and convinced her colleagues that teachers and students should be clustered in seven "houses," or teams, to create more personal units for teaching and learning. Finally, Capuano attempted to build community support for her programs.

Capuano worked with an existing parent–teacher planning group, Community Council 101, to arrange parent workshops, to create a parent–child reading program, and to sponsor a recognition evening for honor-roll students and their parents. She also started a GED (general equivalency diploma) class at the school. Other bridges to the community were formed through such programs as a buddy system, which linked students with key members of the community, and through "Just Say Grow," a project in which students worked with local residents to plant trees and other shrubs to help beautify the local neighborhood.

As these and other changes occurred at Harshman, attendance went up, and students' standardized scores in reading and math showed modest improvement. In 1993 Indiana reorganized its middle schools, moving sixth-graders in with seventh- and eighth-graders. Harshman continued to flourish—large numbers of students used the on-site health clinic, students were reading and writing more, and community volunteers were making frequent classroom visits. Parents new to the school proclaimed Harshman to be "the best kept secret in the district" (Ames, 1996). In 1997, Capuano received a presidential citation from the University of Delaware, her alma mater, for her outstanding achievement at Harshman Middle School (Information for Delaware Education Alumni, 1997).

▶ High Schools

High schools vary greatly in size. Enrollment in alternative schools may be as low as 200. Numbers of students in one out of four secondary schools nationwide exceed 1,000; enrollments of 2,000 and 3,000 are not uncommon. In New York City, nine schools enroll more than 4,000 students each; John F. Kennedy High School in the Bronx enrolls 5,300 (Rotherham, 1999). As noted in Chapter 3, comprehensive high schools—large high schools having a full range of programs—evolved over time from experimentation with concepts of the Latin grammar school, the academy, and the high school that emerged in the late 19th century. The comprehensive high school as it exists today was popularized in the late 1950s, largely through the efforts of former Harvard University president James B. Conant.

Large high schools are comprehensive in their educational offerings and also in their social mission. They educate in the general sense, they prepare young people for the world of work and for college, and they fulfill the civic mission of working toward the maintenance of a sense of community.

Are high schools too comprehensive?

Comprehensive high schools are not without their critics, however. In a study conducted by the Center on Organization and Restructuring of Schools, investigators discovered that large high schools can have deleterious effects on students. In fact, evidence suggests that "students learn more, and learning is distributed more equitably in smaller high schools" (Lee, Smith, & Croninger, 1996, p. 4). Critics also argue that the sense of alienation and purposelessness that plagues minority and other disadvantaged high school students, particularly those in urban areas, only deepens in huge, impersonal school settings. They point to high dropout rates, absenteeism, and classroom disorders as indications of the failure of large schools (Rotherham, 1999). School size may not cause such problems, but the problems of individual students are more difficult to identify and address in large schools.

In recent years several school districts have reduced the size of their secondary schools. In Columbus, Ohio, for example, educators reorganized several of their 17 high schools, creating "houses" of 250 students, each with an administrator, a team of teachers, and a guidance counselor who stay together throughout students' high school careers.

Other school districts have instituted magnet programs, or schools within schools, to create a more personal environment. Many high schools in New York

City, for example, include "clusters," or groups of programs in related career areas such as business, communications, law, and technology education.

Comprehensive schools can offer a wide variety of curricula fairly economically. They typically provide an array of courses to prepare students for vocational or technical areas and for college, but they also offer other experiences. Besides expecting students to have a certain number of credit hours in core courses, some, like Missouri's Pattonville High School, require students to spend 50 hours performing community service to graduate.

Depending on their academic needs, some high school students take courses at nearby colleges. In Minnesota, where state policy in 1985 enabled high school juniors and seniors to earn both high school and college credits at state expense, the line of distinction between the two institutions has become somewhat blurry. In 1998 about 800 students of high school age took classes at the University of Minnesota (S. Rye, personal communication, August 6, 1999).

▶ Higher Education

Between 1980 and 1996 the percentage of high school graduates who enrolled in college immediately after graduation increased from 49 to 65 percent. Only 48.6 percent of graduates from low-income families, as opposed to 78 percent from high-income families, were among this group. About 23 percent of graduates attended 2-year colleges, while 41.9 percent enrolled in 4-year public or private institutions (U.S. Department of Education, 1998a).

Curricular offerings in 2- and 4-year colleges are somewhat different. Two-year colleges typically offer basic undergraduate liberal arts and science courses while providing a wide range of vocational, technical, and adult education programs. They also offer a variety of professional and preprofessional programs. Four-year colleges and universities generally provide a full undergraduate program leading to a bachelor's degree as well as first-professional and graduate programs leading to advanced degrees.

As noted in Chapter 3, adult education programs have allowed many citizens to return to school. The increasing numbers of younger and older adults participating in such programs illustrate the possibilities for lifelong learning in our society. Adult education classes offer opportunities for young and old alike to develop interests and talents and to increase their literacy skills. According to the second report from the National Adult Literacy Survey, adults with higher literacy skills are more likely to work full time, to earn high wages, and to maintain better health (U.S. Department of Education, 1998a).

People are never too old to learn. Elderhostels provide educational opportunities for people age 60 and older. A network of some 800 institutions of higher education in the United States sponsors a wide variety of travel and study opportunities in every state and in many foreign countries. Students live in dormitories and study in college classrooms and conference centers. Even though elderhostels do not give college credit, the offerings range from oceanography to space science. The relatively low cost of elderhostels boosts their appeal.

What Are Some Schooling Alternatives?

An **alternative school** is any school operating within the public school system that has programs addressing the specific needs or interests of targeted student groups. Some alternative schools are self-contained structures; others are organized as schools within schools.

Although there are many models of alternative schooling in our country, alternative schools generally share many of the following attributes: small school size, small class size, voluntary membership, absence or minimization of ability grouping and other forms of labeling, school-based management, student involvement in governance, and extended roles for teachers that include counseling and guidance. Many people believe that alternative schools provide nonconforming programs for "at-risk" or "bad" students. As we explain below, alternative schools are for all types of students.

▶ Magnet Schools

Magnet schools are alternative schools within a public school system that draw students from the whole district instead of drawing only from their own neighborhoods. Magnet schools emerged in the 1970s, primarily as a means to desegregate schools. The intent was to avoid the divisiveness of mandatory busing by developing schools so appealing that a racial cross section of students would be drawn voluntarily to the schools. Despite the fact that many enrollees have to travel long distances for a longer and somewhat harder school day than they might have in typical public schools, the appeal of magnet programs is strong enough that schools usually have

long waiting lists for enrollment. Search for magnet school web sites on Yahoo! or a similar Web resource to learn more.

Magnet schools typically have three distinct features: (1) an enrollment policy that opens the school to children beyond a particular geographic attendance zone, (2) a student body that is present by choice that meets variable criteria established for inclusion, and (3) a curriculum based on a special theme or instructional method. Built into any level from preschool to senior high school, magnet schools may organize their curricula around mathematics and computers, the arts, the sciences, foreign language, or general academics, such as college preparation and honors courses.

For example, the Chicago High School for Agricultural Sciences (CHSAS), located in a working-class neighborhood of southwest Chicago, is a college preparatory magnet school that prepares students for professions in agriculture. Program objectives include providing opportunities to students from the entire city of Chicago to study agricultural sciences and producing graduates who are able to function

What are some alternatives to the comprehensive high school model? What are some distinguishing features of magnet schools? What other schooling alternatives exist for students in preprimary grades through grade 8?

on the cutting edge of science and technology. Classes are not tracked by ability level. First- and second-year students are exposed to intense career awareness and development activities and are required to choose a career major by the end of their sophomore year (U.S. Department of Education, 1998b).

Should all schools be magnet schools?

▶ Vocational–Technical Schools

As the phrase implies, vocational–technical high schools provide an education for students who wish to enter the trades or to develop technical skills for future employment. These schools offer programs in cosmetology; food production, management, and service; law enforcement; horticulture; automotive repair; tool and machine operation; air conditioning and refrigeration; building construction; masonry; graphic and commercial arts; drafting; electronics; data processing; a variety of health-related fields; child care; and many other areas.

Although vocational–technical high schools are designed to prepare people to assume jobs upon graduation, students who attend these schools may go on to community colleges or 4-year institutions. Vocational–technical schools that integrate academic work with technical training are thought to provide the best opportunities for continued development.

There are three general approaches to encouraging such integration (Grubb, 1996). Some schools simply exhort vocational instructors to use more reading, math, or writing in their courses; this is the least effective strategy. Other schools operate as academies, aligning the content of both types of courses so that they reinforce each other. Such approaches are fairly common in Philadelphia, Pennsylvania, and in California and appear to increase enrollments and decrease drop-out rates. The third approach is to organize and deliver academic courses on clusters of related occupations. For example, a manufacturing cluster might include mathematics and writing instruction relevant to future engineers, machinists, and production-line workers.

The Metropolitan Regional Career and Technical Center (Met) in Rhode Island offers a unique education program described not so much vocational as "avocational" (Keough, 1999). Teachers at the Met do not teach classes in the traditional sense. Instead, they work one-on-one with about 13 students, each designing curriculum and instruction appropriate to students' needs and interests. Met students are expected to take at least one college course before graduating; thus, a student's education plan may include one or more formal courses at nearby colleges, including Brown University. The heart of a Met student's plan, however, is a two-day-a-week internship. Other than required statewide exams, there are no tests; students demonstrate learning through the portfolios and projects related to their internships. The absence of a standard curriculum tied to assessment has raised more than one eyebrow. Nonetheless, Dennis Littky, founder of the Met, is confident that his brand of education will prove to be effective:

> In two years, when [the critics] see our kids in college, they'll really see. . . . People don't learn when you lecture to them. People don't learn facts that are disconnected. People learn when they construct knowledge, when they're passionate about something. . . . I'm an extremist in believing that there is no one

Voices

On Going to "Night High"

Manhattan Comprehensive Night and Day High School at Fifteenth Street and Second Avenue in New York City is an academic, accredited, diploma-granting high school that opened in 1989 with 25 students between the ages of 17 and 22. In 1999 Manhattan had 850 students from 42 countries and a waiting list for admission. Classes are offered year-round, Monday through Thursday. Sundays are devoted to athletics and cultural enrichment activities. This alternative high school is a school of choice, open to all New York City residents who have completed one year of high school and are reading at or above seventh-grade level. Before serving as its principal, Howard A. Freedman—the founder—was an English major at Hunter College and a teacher at New York's John Dewey High School and City as School. He also worked for the federally funded National Diffusion Network, helping others around the country start their own schools. Freedman described what makes Manhattan Comprehensive Night High School special:

When I worked at the high school division of City as School, one of the most well-known alternative schools in the nation, I wrote a proposal to create this high school designed to serve many young people who needed real flexibility in terms of time. Many had to support themselves and their children, whether they lived with their children or not. Many others traveled from school to school and never got their diplomas. They felt like they were too old to return to their neighborhood schools. The literature suggested that students over 17 or 18 should be treated differently from younger adolescents. And this moment in their lives was the last chance to educate

these youngsters. In New York you can get anything at any hour, why not school?

In the beginning we were open from 5:00 PM to 11:00 PM, Monday through Thursday, and on Sunday afternoon. I could write a book on working out agreements with unions, custodians, and others who were not used to working such strange hours. Now we start at 11:00 AM and go until 10:45 at night.

We are a full academic school. We are also an ESL school (more than 45 percent of the students are foreign born), but we are not a bilingual school. Our collaborative relationships are great. We have working relationships with 30-plus community-based organizations. Business and community leaders on our nonprofit board helped us raise about $300,000 for our library. A number of architects did a lot of pro bono work on the library too. We also started our student center with donations. It includes job counseling, medical referrals, job readiness training, and other services beyond our academic program. We have about 74 teachers and staff members. We have 140 mentor volunteers. Our next challenge will be to create a dormitory for the homeless students while we raise money for our science program.

CRITICAL THINKING

What are some of the special challenges students at Manhattan face? How might such a school create an environment in which school feels like "home" for its students? Are there specific activities individual teachers might use to foster a sense of community? *Source:* Personal interviews, Howard A. Freedman, June 24, 1996, and Iris Kupferstein, August 12, 1999.

content for every kid. Photosynthesis may be very important for you, but it ain't for me right now (Keough, 1999).

▶ Montessori and Waldorf Schools

Alternative schools, public and private, often reflect all-encompassing philosophies of education. Montessori and Waldorf schools are examples. Montessori preschools focus mainly on the development of children's perceptual, motor, intellectual, and social skills. Programs are based on the ideas of Maria Montessori (1870–1952), a physician who developed preschool teaching methods in the early 1900s focused on students' maturation levels and readiness to learn particular skills. Teachers trained in Montessori methods use a curriculum based on materials specifically designed to help children discover the physical properties of objects. As students interact with materials, such as the "pink tower" (blocks of graduated size), learning is self-directed rather than teacher directed. Teachers act as observers, assisting indirectly by asking questions or providing materials to optimize learning. Given that most instructional materials are graded and self-correcting, students experience liberty within structure in such settings. Search the Web to learn more about Montessori schools.

At the other end of the philosophical spectrum, Waldorf educators oppose a focus on the structured acquisition of specific learning skills. Waldorf education has its roots in the spiritual–scientific research of Rudolf Steiner (1861–1925), an Austrian scientist and educator. According to Steiner's philosophy, young children learn primarily through their senses and respond in the most active mode of knowing: imitation. In Waldorf preschools, creative play is viewed as the critical element in a child's development. Waldorf teachers believe that to draw the child's energies away from creative play to meet intellectual demands will rob the child of the health and vitality she will need in later life. They argue that, in the end, premature intellectual demands weaken the powers of judgment and practical intelligence the teacher wants to encourage (Barnes, 1991).

There are over 100 Waldorf schools, most of which are private, in the United States and Canada. Although the majority are elementary schools, there are also a few secondary schools that follow the Waldorf way. All Waldorf schools have a strong spiritual component, though they are nonsectarian. Ideally, teachers remain with the same group of students from 1st through 8th grades. To learn more about Waldorf schools, search the Web for "Waldorf Schools Worldwide."

▶ Private and Independent Schools

Private, or independent, **schools** are nonprofit, tax-exempt institutions governed by boards of trustees and financed through private funds, such as tuitions, endowments, and grants. Some are religiously affiliated while others are secular. All are accredited by state departments of education, must meet state and local health and safety rules, and must observe mandatory school attendance laws.

Despite many similarities, private schools differ from public schools in several ways:

- Public schools are tax supported while, in the main, private schools are not.
- Private schools can set their own admissions requirements, while public schools must accept all those who come for an education.
- Private school students are enrolled by parental or student choice, while, in the main, public schools serve only students in their districts.
- Private schools have the freedom to craft philosophies that appeal to specific groups of people, while public schools are driven by inclusivity.

As alternatives for schooling have increased, the distinction between public and private education has become increasingly vague. Although not a prevalent practice, the use of public revenues to fund private education has done much to blur the definition of a private school. In 1998, for example, Milwaukee students were allowed to use public funds to attend religious schools, and a private school was designated as a public school for one year (White, 1999).

Other actions obscuring the division between public and private education include (1) state loans of secular textbooks to church schools, (2) state reimbursement of funds for transportation to church schools, and (3) public funding for mandated standardized testing and scoring and for diagnostic, therapeutic, and remedial services in private and parochial schools. In 1999, Florida was the first state to enact legislation to permit the use of public funds for private schools.

Should distinctions between public and private schooling be dropped?

There are 27,686 private elementary and secondary schools in the United States (U.S. Department of Education, 1999a). The line demarcating public from private schools traditionally has been drawn in the source of funds and in the proscription against religious activity. That line, however, has continually been challenged. Although the number of initiatives to transform schools is small, the acceptance of new ideas about structuring schools seems to be growing. Ideas for private and quasi-private alternatives are based on the idea that market forces and competition will force public schools to improve or change (Kennedy, 1996).

There are a number of nonsectarian private school options in the United States. These schools vary in focus, structure, social organization, and size. Some, such as military schools, emphasize self-discipline while encouraging academic study. Others, such as elite college preparatory schools, place an unusually high premium on academic achievement. Some schools are less easily classifiable, developing their own unique personalities.

▶ For-Profit Schools

In the late 1980s and 1990s, concepts of for-profit schools have gained notoriety as alternatives to public schools. **For-profit schools** do not claim tax-exempt status because they are run by companies to make money. For-profit schools come in various forms, but the idea underlying their creation is that private enterprise can deliver better education to children than can public schools and can do so for the same or less money. Advocates of for-profit schools seek to privatize education, that is, to contract with private enterprise to perform educational services performed typically by public employees.

One of the most visible efforts to mount and sustain for-profit schools is The Edison Project, with headquarters in New York City. In 1995–1996, The Edison Project taught approximately 2,000 students in Boston, Massachusetts; Mount Clemens, Michigan; Sherman, Texas; and Wichita, Kansas. By 1999, the Edison Project managed 51 schools with an enrollment of about 25,000 students. Edison's school design is based on a set of curriculum standards, a longer school day and year, and heavy use of technology (Walsh, 1999). In April 1999, company officials reported rising student test scores in 17 of its schools, a statistic they contended was significant because 62 percent of Edison students are from low-income homes, compared to 33 percent nationwide. Although the company has invested $162 million in Edison schools, it has yet to make a profit. John Chubb, Edison's executive vice-president for curriculum and assessment, predicted that the company would become profitable once it gets beyond 100 schools and reduces its central administrative and research costs (Mathews, 1999).

> **Should schools be run as profit-making business enterprises?**

Another for-profit enterprise, the Minneapolis-based Education Alternatives, Inc. (EAI), signed and later lost contracts to run schools in Hartford, Connecticut; Baltimore, Maryland; and Dade County, Florida. The company started big and lost big. Apparently, EAI failed in Hartford not so much because of its educational program, although company claims of gains in achievement and attendance were not corroborated, but because of conflict over money. The schools and EAI could not agree on how much control a for-profit company should exert over a struggling city's school budget and how much it should be paid (Judson, 1996).

▶ Parochial Schools

As defined in Chapter 2, private schools that are maintained and operated by religious organizations are called parochial schools. Parochial schools vary in terms of their underlying philosophies, structures, and programs. Catholic schools account for the largest number of parochial school students. The majority of these students attend schools in New York, Pennsylvania, California, Illinois, and Ohio. Other areas of the country where Catholic schools are prominent include New Orleans, Louisiana, and Detroit, Michigan.

Sociologists have described the Catholic school as contributing heavily to the middle-class mores of our society. It teaches "respectability, cleanliness, conformity, ambition, patriotism" (Fichter, 1958, p. 451). A survey conducted by the National Catholic Educational Association (NCEA) indicates that today's teachers, 91 percent of whom are laypeople, are highly committed to inculcating values and morals. Respondents listed "gospel values" and "parental involvement" as the two most important benefits of a Catholic education. When asked to name five resources that were absolutely necessary for them to do their jobs in the year 2000, teachers named "parental support" first. Other choices were the Bible, finances, computers, and textbooks (Ponessa, 1996). You can visit a number of Catholic schools on the Web by searching on "Catholic Schools."

About 200,000 children attend some 650 Jewish day schools in North America, chiefly in the United States and Canada. Though the majority of them are Orthodox, many schools have been founded in the past 20 years by movements that once opposed the notion of separate schools for Jewish children. Jewish day schools are springing up not only in large Jewish population centers in the Northeast and Southern California, but also in Atlanta, for example, where there are seven schools representing every major movement. Each of the schools welcomes Jewish children regardless of their family's orientation.

At one of the K–8 Orthodox schools, Torah Day School, boys and girls are separated for prayer services and for Judaic and academic classes, enrollment permitting. Starting in the sixth grade, boys study the Jewish teachings, known as the Gemara, in

Cultural Awareness

Approximately 98 parochial schools in Ohio's Wayne and Holmes counties serve the largest Amish settlement in the country. In Holmes County, nearly 1,800 Amish youngsters walk or travel by horse-drawn buggy to one of the 60 schools in the area. They generally attend school for 160 days, finishing school in April, so that they can help with spring planting. Teachers, many of whom have only an eighth-grade education themselves, work alone or in pairs to instruct students in grades 1–8 in reading, writing, arithmetic, spelling, English, and geography or history. Methods and materials reinforce values taught at home—cooperation, humility, honesty, and hard work.

Schools are governed by individual school boards selected by the Amish communities. Although they are not connected to the public schools, committees representing the Amish schools report state-mandated statistics on enrollment and attendance to the Holmes County Office of Education. Most Amish attend school for 8 years, but recently students living in the East Holmes District have attended vocational education classes as well (Holmes County Chamber of Commerce, 1999).

their original Aramaic language, while girls' instruction focuses on the Bible. About 25 percent of Torah Day School's students are non-Orthodox Jews (Archer, 1998). Search the Web for "Jewish Day Schools Around the World" to learn more.

Other parochial schools—in particular, fundamentalist Christian schools—are growing in number more quickly than are other private schools, in large measure because of the popular appeal of their philosophies and curricula. Melinda Wagner's 1990 study of nine Christian schools in the southeastern United States suggests why this may be so. In examining the schools' philosophies, Wagner found that conservative Christians attempt to create an "ideal" culture to serve as a "crucible of change" for altering the inadequacies and evils in existing culture (p. 20).

▶ Charter Schools

Charter schools are independent public schools supported by state funds but exempt from many regulations. They are based on a contract, or "charter" between a group of school organizers (parents, teachers, or others) and a sponsor (usually a local or state board of education). Organizers generally have the power to hire and fire staff and to budget money as they see fit. In turn, they guarantee to sponsor certain academic outcomes.

Described as the "upstart reform idea of the decade," charter schools represent to some people the means for promoting school accountability and excellence in educational outcomes. According to Ray Budde, the originator of the charter schools concept, charter schools allow organizers autonomy and flexibility when determining how to respond to increasingly varied student needs. Thus they serve as the first real model of local autonomous control (Kennedy, 1996).

Like other reform initiatives, charter schools are meant to be innovative—to reach out to those not being served by the public schools. Other charter schools offer rigorous classical education; some integrate academics, counseling, technical training, and experiential training; other schools serve homeless children and wards of state; still others are for students who are deaf and hearing impaired and for dropouts and at-risk young people (Geske, Davis, & Hingle, 1997).

Will the charter school and home school movements damage public education?

In 1991 Minnesota became the first state to approve the concept of charter schools. According to Minnesota law, only certified teachers can contract with local school boards to create charters. While the board has a say in what outcomes charters must meet, it maintains a hands-off posture in their day-to-day operation. Within only 4 years after Minnesota's charter school legislation, at least 19 states had passed initiatives to allow charter schools.

One of the smallest and perhaps most unique charter schools is the Big Apple Circus's own One-Ring Schoolhouse, a formal independent school in New York state "where no one looks at you funny when you tell them your dad is a ringmaster" (Sommerfeld, 1995, p. 22). The school, an apple-red trailer that travels 5,000 miles a year, has only seven students, ranging in age from 6 to 14 years old, and one teacher.

Using Technology

Home Schooling Online

Following a midafternoon jewelry-making session with fellow home-schooling students, 11-year-old Janet Cooper and her younger sister shut down their computer and return to their "classroom" in one corner of their living room. Displeased with the education they were receiving at their school in Alaska's Kenai Peninsula, their mother has decided to teach her daughters at home. She is assisted in her efforts through the Interior Distance Education of Alaska program, a program that provides parents with access to state money for private online lessons, school supplies, and a personal computer. While Janet and her sister do not have face-to-face contact with teachers, they can connect online with teachers in the program's branch offices in Anchorage, Fairbanks, and the Kenai Peninsula.

The online program was started in 1997 by the tiny 240-student Galena School District on the Yukon River as a way to reach far-flung students not attending school. During the first year of operation, 3 families enrolled. By 1998, the numbers swelled to 3,000 and included many students who had left traditional public schools and district correspondence programs. Just 25 teachers serve the students. John Dahlgren, superintendent of the 10,000-student Kenai Peninsula Burrough, worries that students leaving his district to participate in the distance-education program may be receiving inadequate educational experiences. He criticizes the program's "loose accountability" and "shopping cart approach" to education. Supporters of the program, however, contend that students' high scores on standardized tests show that teachers' private online lessons and parents' instruction can be a winning combination (Sandham, 1998).

Source: Sandham, J. (1998, November 4). Program puts teachers online. *Education Week, 18* (10), p. 39.

The teacher—Leslie Martin—introduces basic concepts in reading, writing, math, science, and history and also works to incorporate the circus's theme in her lessons (Sommerfeld, 1995).

For more information about charter schools, visit the home page of the Center for Education Reform on the Web.

▶ Home Schools

The U.S. Department of Education estimates that more than 1 million primary and secondary students in the United States study at home, or in "home schools"; other estimates range from 700,000 to 2 million (Schnaiberg, 1999). Reliable numbers are hard to come by for a variety of reasons: states define and track homeschoolers differently, some parents do not comply with state rules requiring them to register their home-schooled children, and some parents do not joint home school support groups, another way of counting heads.

As described in Chapter 3, many homeschoolers are children of people who want to ensure that their religious doctrines are an integral part of daily lessons. Others educate their children at home to avoid what they perceive as lock-step learning practices sometimes used in schools. The Home School Legal Defense Association (1997) also suggests that a number of parents choose home schooling to avoid some of the social problems—drug use, violence, teen pregnancy, sexually transmitted diseases—prevalent in today's society.

How Are Schools Administered?

School administrators, from the **superintendent**—chief executive—on down, must operate in a world that has changed dramatically in the past 30 years or so. Today's school administrators have much less flexibility in making decisions than did their predecessors. As you will read in Chapter 6, they must contend with state-aid formulas, government mandates, external standards for educators' and students' performances, and a host of political pressure groups intent on sharing power. Administrators appear caught between the need to build consensus and the necessity to innovate—to raise expectations above the lowest common denominator.

Despite the fact that there are about 85,000 public schools in the United States, surveys indicate that the superintendents and their associates and assistants who compose the **central office staff,** along with principals, tend to view their worlds in remarkably similar fashion. The demands of their jobs and their training, no doubt, contribute to their common outlook. But administrators share other characteristics as well.

▶ The School Superintendent

Superintendents administer school systems organized to carry out line and staff functions. They do so with the approval of the board of education. The typical line and staff organization of public school systems is shown in Figure 5.2.

FIGURE 5.2
Typical Line and Staff Organization of Public School Systems What could you
say about the role of principals on the basis of this organizational chart?

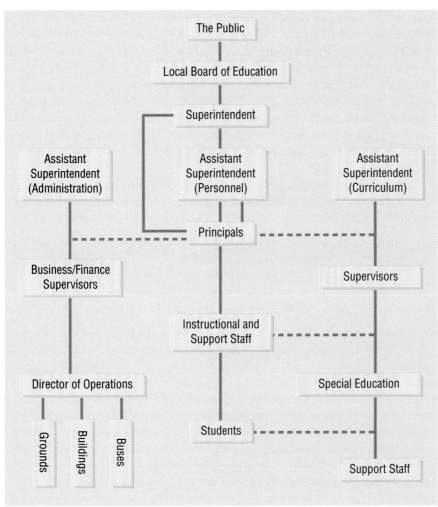

The superintendency can be an incredibly demanding job. The issues and challenges facing superintendents are many and varied: financing schools, planning and
goal setting, assessing educational outcomes, maintaining and enhancing accountability and credibility, evaluating staff and administrators, developing working relations with a school board, administering special education services, obtaining timely
and accurate information, negotiating labor contracts, dealing with changing enrollments, and so on (Norton, Webb, Dlugosh, & Sybouts, 1996).

In large U.S. cities, the superintendency has become an embattled
position. There are so many problems, so many constituencies with competing interests, and so few resources that city superintendents stay in
their jobs about 2.5 years on average, compared to the U.S. average of 5.5
years.

**Should school
superintendencies be
abolished?**

The chancellor of the New York City public schools, a sort of super superintendent, presides over 32 community school-district superintendents, 1,120 schools, 110,709 employees, and more than 1 million students. About 6.5 percent of students are Native American or Alaskan Native American, 10 percent Asian or Pacific-Islander American, 16.1 percent European American, 36.1 percent African American, and 37.3 percent Hispanic American (U.S. Department of Education, 1999).

Believed to have the largest and toughest urban education challenge in the country, the chancellor is expected to be (1) an educator well versed in instruction, supervision, and administration; (2) a leader who exhibits decisiveness, shrewdness, powers of consensus building, and a commitment to children; (3) a manager having skills to run a bureaucracy with more than 100,000 employees; and (4) a strategist, good at overcoming institutional barriers (New York City Public Schools, 1992; Litow, 1999).

No wonder superintendents face great pressure and are often forced out of their jobs. Raymond Callahan's 1962 description of the power of politics in school management still applies today:

> I am now convinced that very much of what has happened in American education since 1900 can be explained on the basis of the extreme vulnerability of our schoolmen to public criticism and pressure and that this vulnerability is built into our pattern of local support and control. This has been true in the past and, unless changes are made, will continue to be true in the future. (Eaton, 1990, p. viii)

Many more superintendents work in small communities than in large ones. About 4,000 districts enroll fewer than 300 students; only 24 districts enroll 100,000 or more students (U.S. Department of Education, 1999a). The superintendents in small communities must, however, fulfill many of the same responsibilities of educational leadership as do those in large districts. In many instances, their small and declining enrollments make opportunities to offer an intellectually rich, high-powered curriculum virtually impossible. Merely staffing the courses they must have to meet minimal requirements can be a major challenge. For rural school administrators to be successful, they must be a good "fit" with their communities. In small towns, educational leaders are not nameless, faceless bureaucrats. People know where to go and with whom they can speak if they are unhappy about educational policies and practices.

▶ Principals and Assistant Principals

Many scholars emphasize the importance of human relationships in successful school administration and programmatic change. Kathleen Sernak (1998), for example, calls for "balancing power with caring." She urges educators to examine the features of their organizations, so that structure functions to define and direct the patterns of human interaction in the organization. Human relationships and **collegiality,** or relationships based on a sharing of power, have been particularly effective in promoting and sustaining school improvement (Barth, 1990).

If any single individual is key to the everyday operation and tone of a school, it is the **principal,** the person responsible for managing a school at the building level. After formal training, one becomes a principal through a process of socialization, learning on the job (Leithwood, Steinbach, & Begley, 1992). Principals typically administer discipline to students, give guidance to students, deal with staff and faculty on simple to complex issues, locate substitute teachers, implement rules, conduct surveillance of halls, balance the school's budget, and maintain the building and equipment. High school principals may also spend 10 to 15 hours per week attending sporting events, fine arts performances, faculty socials, parent–teacher meetings, and dances (Hoy & Miskel, 1996).

Principals all perform similar everyday activities, such as visiting or observing classrooms, circulating through the building, and monitoring hallways. However, the ways principals interpret these activities can make a big difference in their effectiveness as leaders. More effective principals view everyday activities as opportunities for defining the school's goals, aiding student achievement, praising others' work, and practicing other characteristics of effective leadership.

How are schools administered and managed? In what ways do administrators and administrative teams influence the life of the school and school effectiveness? In what ways do teachers participate in the administrative process?

Building-level administrators' work lives can be defined by the tensions they believe they must resolve but more often must learn to live with. Some questions are never satisfactorily or permanently resolved (Ackerman, Donaldson, & Van der Bogert, 1996). Figure 5.3 identifies seven persisting questions that administrative teams face.

Terrence Deal and Kent Peterson (1991) have described the job of principal as one of shaping the culture by playing several important roles: symbol, potter, poet, actor, and healer. The principal's background, life-style, communication style, and management style strongly influence the culture of a school both practically and symbolically. Like a potter with a lump of clay, the principal shapes the shared values of the school. She emphasizes various school rituals—the pep rally, the reading of the honor roll, the stories told at public gatherings—to cultivate a sense of community. Like a poet and an actor, the principal expresses to everyone a shared vision of the school's philosophy and mission. Like a healer, the principal mediates among the groups that make up the school and responds to any criticism from the community about school operations or administrative decision making. If the principal has an assistant, the administrative team can reinforce even more effectively the school's values, norms, and goals.

The administrative team's relationship with teachers is a critical dimension of the job. The principal is in a position of middle management—between the superintendent and the teachers and school staff. As such, he must be able to follow and to lead. To lead the teachers and the support staff (guidance counselors, special education teachers, media specialists, librarians, custodians, bus drivers, and others), the principal must involve others in formulating and implementing ideas without sacrificing authority. Ultimately, the principal is responsible for what occurs in and around the school.

For more information about the roles of principals, visit the Web sites for the National Association of Elementary School Principals and the National Association of Secondary School Principals.

FIGURE 5.3
Persisting Questions that School Administrators Face   How might you answer these questions? Develop a set of guidelines for addressing the question that concerns you the most at this time.

1. The Justice Question

How can we be just to each child, as an individual and as a learner, and create a just and disciplined school as well?

2. The Teaching Question

How can we assure our children and the community that every staff member is performing effectively and value each individual staff member as well?

3. The Purpose Question

How can we produce measurable learning products and develop children who are capable of healthy learning, social, moral, and work processes as well?

4. The Resource Question

How can we encourage constant growth and improvement in our school and acknowledge the realistic limitations on our ability to meet such goals as well?

5. The Change Question

How can we foster improvement and change, and respect and value each staff member and citizen as well?

6. The Ownership Question

How can we honor the perspectives and purposes of multiple constituencies and work toward unified goals that will benefit all children as well?

7. The Autonomy Question

How can we honor teacher creativity and autonomy and share purposes, curricula, and equitable resources as well?

Note. From *Making Sense as a School Leader: Persisting Questions, Creative Opportunities* (p. 7), by R. Ackerman, G. A. Donaldson, Jr., & R. Van der Bogert, 1996, San Francisco: Jossey-Bass Publications.

▶ Site-Based Management

In the 1980s and 1990s, educators promoted the idea of involving people at the school level more directly in making decisions about teaching and learning, budgeting, and hiring personnel. This relatively new phenomenon in school governance is referred to most often as **site-based management**, sometimes as school-based management, or shared decision making. "For all its guises, site-based management is basically an attempt to transform schools into communities where the appropriate people participate constructively in major decisions that affect them" (David, 1995–1996, p. 4).

Reformers encourage these new governance and management strategies for two reasons. First, proponents believe that people who are most affected by educational decisions ought to be involved in those decisions. This belief is driven not only by a concern for fairness but by a sense that the people most intimately involved may also be most capable of rendering the best decisions. Second, proponents argue that once decisions are made, they are more likely to result in success if those who must live with the decisions helped make them. Or, at least, people who are involved in making the decisions may be less likely to undermine them.

> The composition of site-based management teams varies tremendously: In addition to teachers, parents, and the principal, they may include classified staff, community members, students, and business representatives. Educators may outnumber non-educators, or vice versa. States or districts may list constituencies who must be represented, or simply leave [this decision] to individual schools. (David, 1995–1996, p. 5)

Thomas Guskey and Kent Peterson (1995–1996) note that leaders of site-based management teams often face various problems, including, but not limited to, trying to fulfill an ambiguous mission, finding time for meetings, and motivating involvement. Effective leaders, however, are those who help the group set clear and specific goals, ensure that the decision-making process is not viewed as a goal in itself, and redesign schedules to give people time to participate (Glickman, 1998). Administrators who reward accomplishments and encourage genuine collaboration are more likely to enhance involvement than are those who neglect such opportunities (Guskey & Peterson, 1995–1996).

The job of leading site-based teams must also include attention to both classroom- and school-level measurement of students' performances (Popham, 1995). Measurement should be decision driven, that is, results should be geared to help administrators and teachers act as a result of what they learn.

> School-site assessment, because it's closer to children than district, state, or national assessment, should have a more decisive instructional payoff. It will succeed, however, only if principals realize that they must learn enough about it to supply the same sort of leadership in assessment that they possess in the realm of instruction. (Popham, 1995, p. 40)

In schools where there is site-based management, teachers have opportunities to serve in leadership roles that allow them to help shape educational programs to meet the needs of students. Some contend that

Can site-based management really work?

transforming schools into communities where everyone, including the students, has a voice increases a school's capacity to "effect powerful new teaching and learning practices and to change the lives of all students profoundly for the better" (Glickman, 1998, p. 168).

What Organizational and Policy Issues Do Schools Face?

As described earlier, schools have been organized in different ways to try to meet the needs of today's students. Decisions about such things as whether to establish separate grades or to implement multiage groupings shape the unique character of each school. School policies about issues from retention and tracking to class schedules and class size also affect life in classrooms. Regardless of school setting, these and other policies are regularly reviewed or revised. Changes might be prompted by teachers, administrators, parents, and students.

▶ Retention

Should students who fail be held back?

Flunking, to use the derisive term for failing a course or repeating grades in school—always an issue of concern, has taken on new urgency as education reformers tout the advantages of setting and maintaining high standards. In his 1999 State of the Union address, for example, President Clinton urged educators to practice **retention** and abandon the idea of **social promotion,** or passing children to successive grades to keep them with other children of their age. According to this view, it is only logical—and helpful to individuals and to the system as a whole—to retain children who do not reach set standards.

▶ Class Schedule and Class Size

One effort to restructure schools has involved changing factors such as class schedule and class size. **Block scheduling,** a method of organizing classes typically to provide longer instructional periods during the school day, is used in roughly 30 percent of the nation's secondary schools. Instead of the traditional seven- to eight-period day, various block schedules include four periods a day, each lasting 85 to 100 minutes. One model, the 4/4 schedule, allows students to complete four year-long courses each semester. Among the benefits of using the 4/4 schedule are declining failure rates, improvement in students' grades and an increase in the number of students on the honor roll, and greater instructional flexibility for teachers (Rettig & Canady, 1999).

Educators in Indiana have modified their school schedule by dividing the school year into three parts and offering five periods a day. This novel approach to block scheduling means that Westfield High School students can earn 15 credits instead of the usual 12 during an academic year. The 3 by 5 plan is touted as more than a schedule change; it is a way for Westfield to customize schedules to meet the needs of individual students. Potential advantages include (1) the high school can offer more dual-enrollment courses with nearby universities; (2) students can take up to three trimesters off for travel, work, or illness and still graduate on schedule; (3) specific subjects, such as calculus, physics and chemistry, can be enhanced by requiring an additional trimester without affecting electives; and (3) students can attend part-time and work part-time and still graduate with their class (Keen, 1999).

Sometimes fiscal woes are the impetus for changes in schedules. In 1994 the Animas Public Schools in New Mexico went to a four-day school week to save money. By 1999, 18 of the state's 89 school districts were on such a plan (Reeves, 1999). In other areas of the country, school districts may provide **year-round schools,** or programs that run through the summer months as well as during the academic year. In some instances, these programs are used to relieve space and budget concerns. In others, year-round schools are viewed as a means to improve student performance. During the 1997–1998 academic year, more than 1.9 million students were enrolled in over 2,800 year-round schools. By 1999, the number of students broke the 2 million mark (National Association for Year-Round School, 1999).

One of the more controversial issues in public education—and one over which teachers exert little or no control—is that of class size. How many children should be placed in a single room with one teacher? What happens to teaching and learning when a group becomes larger or smaller? Should the inclusion of one or more students with disabilities or students at risk in a class be weighted more heavily in the calculation of class size? How much does it cost to lower class size? How much money can a system save by increasing class size? What are the political costs to policy makers of increasing and decreasing class size?

In general, research supports the value of smaller classes (20 or fewer students), particularly in the early grades (U.S. Department of Education, 1999b). Younger pupils, especially those who are economically disadvantaged and ethnic minority-group students, have benefited from smaller classes, as demonstrated in reading and mathematics achievement and in terms of their attitudes and behavior (Finn & Achilles, 1990; Pate-Bain, Achilles, Boyd-Zaharias, & McKenna, 1992; Achilles, 1996). Critics are quick to observe, however, that simply lowering class size does not automatically lead to increases in learning (Hanushek, 1995).

> Are block schedules and year-round schools the answers to restructuring needs?

Districts vary in the way they report average class size. Surprisingly, just measuring class size can cause problems (Glass, 1988). Dividing the total number of students by the total number of staff (including noninstructional staff members) yields a more favorable **student–teacher ratio** than do calculations based on the number of actual classroom teachers.

▶ Tracking

Should students be grouped homogeneously or heterogeneously based on estimates of their abilities? Assigning students deemed to have similar abilities to certain instructional groups, class sections, and programs of study, a practice referred to as **tracking,** has been the focus of bitter debate throughout the twentieth century. Critics argue that students are tracked on flimsy, often biased evidence. Many assigned to "lower," or nonacademic, tracks may be placed there as much for behavior problems as for academic reasons. Those hurt most severely and most often are disadvantaged, minority-group students (Oakes, 1995). Students often get by in lower-track classrooms because teachers in lower-track classes may expect little of students. Students, in turn, develop a negative self-concept or lowered self-esteem, poor motivation, and even learned helplessness. Perhaps the most damning charge against tracking is the static nature of the assignments: once a student falls into the lower tracks, he or she seems caught in an academic tailspin from which few pull out (Pool & Page, 1995).

Rudolph Ford, middle school principal, remembers the feeling he had when a teacher helped him break out of the lower track.

> I remember being quietly told in the tenth grade by a blonde, middle-aged guidance counselor that I was college material and would be taken out of the general education track and would be placed in an academic track. . . . I had just been told by a white woman that I was as capable as the white students on the academic track, and that I deserved to be educated among the best children in school. This surprised me, because by tenth grade I had become accustomed to low expectations from school officials for students like myself—black males. I always knew that I was as capable academically as my white schoolmates—to have a white adult confirm this was an uplifting experience. She affected my self-esteem and shaped my later educational development more significantly than anyone else except my parents. (Ford, 1995, p. 161)

According to Loveless (1998), Rudolph Ford's experience is more the rule than the exception:

Why does the practice of tracking persist?

> For most of this century, schools used IQ tests to sort students as young as thirteen years old into classes of vastly different curricula that predetermined their fates. But today's tracking systems function differently. Grouping takes place within each subject, not across an entire regimen of academic courses. Track assignments are guided by successful completion of prerequisite courses, prior achievement, and teacher recommendations, not IQ tests. Students move from track to track based on their grades and performance. Permanent track assignment is a thing of the past, and almost all schools allow parents to overrule and change students' placements. (p. 1)

 ## What Makes Some Schools More Effective Than Others?

Effective schools, defined generally as those schools that can demonstrate student learning, allow substantial staff development time, some of which takes place during the regular workday. In these schools, improvement goals are sharply focused, attainable, and valued by staff members who receive in-class guidance and support from specialists. School needs, not standardized forms and checklists, guide staff. Methods for reaching goals often are based on techniques and materials that have proven successful in similar situations. Furthermore, a judicious mixture of teacher autonomy and central office control permeates improvement programs in effective schools. Figure 5.4 illustrates some of the elements that contribute to school effectiveness.

Standardized test scores are another criterion for identifying effective schools. When the Sandia National Laboratories in Albuquerque, New Mexico, evaluated student performance on the National Assessment of Education Progress (NAEP) and the Scholastic Aptitude Test (SAT), they found that student scores have steadily improved over time and that gains have not been at the expense of advanced skills. The previously supposed decline in test scores is due not to decreasing student performance but to the fact that more students in the bottom half of their class are taking the exam today than they did in years past. Although every ethnic group taking the test performs better today than it did 15 years ago, significant gaps in performance continue to exist among racially ethnic subgroups and between male and female students (U.S. Department of Education, 1999a).

FIGURE 5.4
Elements that Contribute to School Effectiveness   Identify specific examples for each of the nine elements. What other characteristics of effective schools might you add?

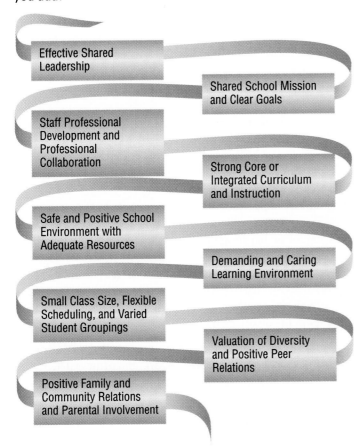

FIGURE 5.5
Some Characteristics of Effective Educational Leaders In what ways do these attributes contribute to effective leadership? What other attributes might you add?

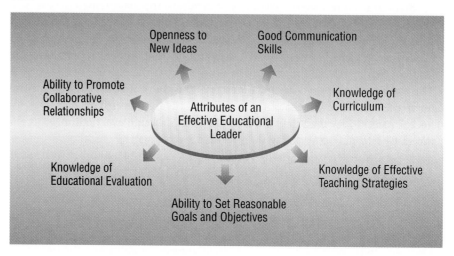

Effective schools are managed by effective leaders—individuals who provide the leadership necessary to create a strong curriculum and a safe environment in which students can achieve academic success. At the same time, effective leaders are concerned with the needs of faculty, promoting teacher recognition, and encouraging professional development. Good leaders also encourage parental, family, and community involvement in school activities (National Association of Elementary School Principals, 1994).

Many school leaders work in environments in which parents and teachers are assuming new and powerful leadership roles. In such situations effective leaders think of themselves as "leaders of leaders," creating conditions under which authority can be transferred to others (Parks & Barrett, 1994). Figure 5.5 identifies some of the attributes effective leaders share.

By 1999, 83 elementary schools were part of the Basic School Network—another conception of effective schools. This alliance was established by the Carnegie Foundation for the Advancement of Teaching in partnership with the National Association of Elementary School Principals (NAESP), the American College Testing Program, and the Ewing Marion Kauffman Foundation. These "Basic Schools" were based on Boyer's (1995) ideas on effective schools. The alliance's goals are to help students communicate effectively, acquire a core of knowledge, and become lifelong learners. Four key components distinguish these schools (Boyer, 1995):

1. The School as a Community—Separate classrooms are connected through a clear and vital mission. Teachers serve as leaders, and the principal acts as lead teacher. Parents are viewed as partners in the learning process.

2. A Curriculum with Coherence—There is an emphasis on language and on core subjects, which are organized around common themes.

3. A Climate for Learning—Class sizes are small, teaching schedules are flexible, and student grouping arrangements are varied. Students are provided with resources ranging from building blocks to electronic tools. They also have access to basic health and counseling services and afternoon and summer enrichment programs.

4. Character Development—The Basic School focuses on seven core values: honesty, respect, responsibility, compassion, self-discipline, perseverance, and giving.

At Mantua Elementary School in Fairfax, Virginia, sixth graders explore a single theme for an entire year. The theme integrates multiple strands in the Basic Schools philosophy:

> Activities within these strands connect social studies, language arts, math, science, the arts, and physical education in imaginative ways. Students learn about the Age of Discovery and Native Americans in social studies, while studying weather and its impact on migration. They discover the cultural roots of mathematical patterns as they learn about the navigational methods and computations used by early explorers. (Bafumo, 1998, p. 68)

▶ Positive School Environments

Interviews with 54 representative students from four comprehensive high schools in two California school districts suggest that students' views of positive school environments match those of contemporary theorists. Student measures include the following (Phelan, Davidson, & Cao, 1992):

- the level of visibility and accessibility of the principal,
- the amount of support students receive from teachers and staff members,
- students' perceived degree of personal safety,
- types of interactions between student groups,
- student behavior in general,
- availability of extracurricular activities,
- the physical condition of the school, and
- degree to which students can speak their native language in informal settings and the availability of at least one staff member who speaks the same primary language.

Students' opinions about schools are particularly strong when they have attended more than one high school or when their experiences in middle school are quite different from those in high school. One student, a sophomore, described vividly why her high school was special:

> **How should school effectiveness be judged?**

> I don't like it; I love it! This school is something else! The teachers, they're friendlier, they're easier to work with. If you need help, they'll bend over backwards to help you, if it's after school, before school, anything—they do it. I know just about every teacher here. I'm a really friendly person. And they're wonderful. I

Issues in School Reform

The Effects of Shifts in Policy

Larry Cuban, professor of education at Stanford University, has taken a hard look at efforts to reform schools. He contends that many changes have had little impact on teaching practices, particularly in big-city and rural school districts:

> Exactly two decades ago, I became superintendent of the Arlington, Virginia, public schools. Shrinking enrollments and increasing numbers of minority students had set off tremors in the community over falling test scores and a perceived decline in the school's academic quality. Mainstream wisdom among federal officials then was that schools do not make much of a difference in children's lives. Policy makers cited major research studies that supposedly proved that spending money on schools failed to yield returns in students' test scores.
>
> Just as other school boards around the country did, the Arlington School Board resisted that gloomy "wisdom" and made changes. All courses of study, texts, tests, and staff evaluations were aligned with the school board's instructional goals. Teachers and principals worked together in drawing up plans for their school's improvement. To be accountable to parents and taxpayers, each school published information about its enrollment and performance annually.
>
> What occurred in Arlington in the mid-1970s was a brief preview of coming attractions for the Effective Schools movement that swept across the nation in the following decade and continues today in many districts. The central beliefs fueling the Effective Schools movement became a national agenda for change: All children can learn; schools must have high academic standards; for a school to succeed, its goals, texts, tests, and the curriculum must be tightly coupled; and finally, published test scores will prove to a skeptical public that schools are accountable. That should sound familiar to ears attuned to the policy talk about schools in the mid-1990s. (p. 14)
>
> For those who appreciate irony, consider that within two decades policy-maker "wisdom" on schooling has flip-flopped from schools not making much difference

wouldn't trade them for nothing. I loved eighth grade, but that does not compare to Lincoln [High School]. I mean you would not believe it. This school is so dedicated. That's the word, dedicated, that's what this school is to their students. They would stop what they're doing to help you. This school cares about their students. (Wasley, Hampel, & Clark, 1997, p. 10)

A report by the National Association of Secondary School Principals (NASSP, 1996) suggests that small school size, or creating small units within a school, is one way to banish anonymity. Teachers' expectations for students, their willingness to be flexible—not equating seat time with learning and extending learning beyond the high school campus—are other factors that the NASSP considers crucial to the success of a school. Two programs that seem in keeping with principals' ideas about effective schools are Ward Melville High on the North Shore of Long Island and Ben-in children's lives to the school being the single most important instrument in securing equity and excellence for all children. But that 180-degree change in mainstream policy wisdom is not the only change that has occurred. In Arlington, as elsewhere in the country, there have been in the last two decades many changes in school governance, organization, and curriculum. . . . (p. 15)

I am convinced that frequent shifts in mainstream policy talk have coaxed both policy makers and practitioners into plunging head-first into school reform without regard to the underlying . . . system of schooling. Too often, they try to apply technical solutions to value-based problems. Such head-first plunges have produced changes in some aspects of schooling without clarifying why other reforms, such as the ones in the classroom, are much harder to secure. Schools are, indeed, change-prone, shifting in organization, governance, and curriculum over the last century. While there have been modest changes in classroom teaching over the decades, such changes have occurred very slowly, responding to a different clock. Some have survived when leadership was school-based and focused on the classroom. Cycles of policy wisdom and a lack of understanding or outright ignorance among reformers, particularly policy makers, about the world of school and classroom practices have often left a corrosive residue of disappointment among practitioners and parents. It is now time to say "enough." (p. 29)

Discussion Questions What concerns does Larry Cuban have about school reform efforts? What groups do you know of that have called for changes in education? How do their values and incentives compare to those of teachers and administrators? What measures are often used to judge the efficacy of school improvement? How do schools change reforms as they are implemented? Why might there be school-by-school variations in change?

Source: Reprinted by permission of the publisher from Kogan, B. S. (Ed.), *Common Schools, Uncommon Features: A Working Consensus for School Renewal* (New York: Teachers College Press, © 1997 by Teachers College, Columbia University. All rights reserved.), pp. 14, 15, & 29.

jamin Mays High in southwest Atlanta. Students at both schools must apply for admission, write an essay, and submit their grades. Mays takes about 175 of 300 applicants and Melville accepts about 35 of 65. Each program sends 100 percent of its graduates to 4-year colleges. Over the years, each school has also produced two members of the All-USA Academic First Team—students selected for national recognition by *USA Today* (Ordovensky, 1996).

When asked why students at the two schools have been so successful, winners of academic awards offered several reasons that sounded much like the NASSP's recommendations for creating effective schools. One student explained that teachers had high expectations, "paint[ed] pictures of the future," and encouraged students to excel. Another said that teachers allowed students to miss class if they needed to work on a project, for example, rather than "locking" them into class every day for the 50-minute period. Others noted the importance of strong parental support and

Benchmarks

The Development of American Schools from 1635 to the Present

1635–1636	Latin Grammar School is established in Boston as a college preparatory school for young men. Harvard College is founded.
1788	U.S. Constitution is ratified. The framers of the Constitution give the power to establish schools and license teachers to the individual states rather than to the federal government.
1801	First Roman Catholic school in New York is established.
1819	First public high school opens in Boston.
1824	Rensselaer Polytechnic Institute opens in Troy, New York.
1827	Massachusetts becomes the first state to require every town with 500 or more families to establish a public high school.
1836–1837	Wesleyan College in Georgia and Oberlin College in Ohio become the first chartered colleges for women.
1839	First public normal school (teachers college) in the United States is established in Lexington, Massachusetts.
1855	First kindergarten in the United States is established by Margaretta Schurtz in Watertown, Wisconsin.
1860	Elizabeth Palmer Peabody opens the first English-speaking kindergarten in Boston.
1865	The American Association of School Administrators is organized in Harrisburg, Pennsylvania.
1874	Kalamazoo, Michigan, case rules that states may establish and support public high schools with tax funds, which contributes to the secondary school movement and eventually to compulsory high school attendance laws.

positive role models who are "concrete examples of people achieving" (Ordovensky, 1996, p. 2D).

▶ Positive Family and Community Relations

Links between homes and schools have become more important in recent years because evidence suggests that connections between home and school help students adjust and learn. Parents influence their children's academic achievement by expos-

1901	First public junior college is established in Joliet, Illinois.
1907	Maria Montessori founds the first Montessori school in Rome.
1909	First junior high schools are established in Berkeley, California, and in Columbus, Ohio.
1916	The National Association of Secondary School Principals (NASSP) is founded in Chicago.
1917	Congress passes the Smith–Hughes Act, which provides federal matching funds for vocational education in public high schools.
1919	Rudolph Steiner founds the first Waldorf school in Stuttgart, Germany.
1921	National Association of Elementary School Principals (NAESP) is founded in Washington, D.C.
1964	Economic Opportunity Act establishes a Job Corps program and authorizes support of education and training activities and of community action programs, including Head Start.
1966	Adult Education Act (Public Law 89-750) authorizes grants to states for the establishment and expansion of educational programs for adults.
1991	Minnesota enacts the first charter school legislation.
1992	Chris Whittle announces his Edison Project, a plan to create 1,000 for-profit schools to compete with the public school system.
1994	Goals 2000: Educate America Act allows state education agencies to use federal funds for state planning and evaluation activities involving local efforts to contract with private management organizations to reform public schools.
1999	State of Florida enacts voucher legislation to permit use of public funds for private schools.

ing them to intellectually stimulating experiences, directly teaching them, monitoring homework, and communicating with the school. Parents also strengthen ties by volunteering at the school, attending school conferences, requesting information, and participating in school governance (Eccles & Harold, 1996).

The larger and more diverse schools are, the less likely parents are to be involved. As students are assigned to multiple teachers for various classes in middle and high schools, and as teachers teach large numbers of students in staggered classes, close teacher–student relationships are unlikely to develop (Dornbusch & Glasgow, 1996).

Teachers do not get to know their students well. And teachers are unlikely to encourage parental involvement because they find the idea impractical. In these situations, teachers tend to focus on the strongest and weakest students because they seem to require the most attention. The parents of the students of average achievement, then, may be among those least likely to be linked closely to schools (Dornbusch & Glasgow, 1996).

Some parents who live in dangerous or resource-poor neighborhoods have less time, energy, and resources available for parenting and for getting involved with schools. Indeed "family" involvement is probably a more appropriate term than "parent" involvement; in many communities children are raised by people who are not their parents (Decker, Gregg, & Decker, 1995). Children from single-parent families and stepfamilies are more likely than are children from two-parent families to experience school-based problems and are most in need of strong home–school ties (Zill, 1996).

Positive connections between home and school also may be influenced by social networks and social class. The social networks to which parents belong, which may be influenced by their linguistic and ethnic backgrounds, can affect their attitudes and beliefs about schools. Some research suggests that middle- and upper-class parents are more likely to think of education as a joint responsibility of school and home, while parents of lower socioeconomic status are more likely to view education as the teacher's job (Lareau, 1996). As children grow older, their parents become less likely to be involved in school activities. The gap that exists between socioeconomic status and children's academic achievement also widens with age, making it even more difficult for parents from low-income families to get involved (Alexander & Entwisle, 1996).

As Jeannie Oakes and Martin Lipton (1999) note, some school attempts at parent involvement only "scratch the surface of—and may actually work against—connecting schools and families" in productive ways. They describe first-year teacher Mary Ann Pacheco's efforts to overcome some common obstacles to communication:

> Generally, Latino parents hesitate to approach or question teachers because teaching is a highly respected position. I made myself very accessible and expressed my interest in their understanding bilingual education, student learning, and their voice in public education. I also built personal relationships, made phone calls, and made home visits. I reinforced their cultural beliefs but made them aware of certain characteristics that they might want to help their children develop. For example, during parent conferences, some parents were openly concerned with their child's tendency to talk excessively. Many times, I reminded them that in higher education, the willingness to initiate conversations, participation in group projects, and dialogue was required of students and highly valued. I told them about my own endless number of oral presentations, speeches, and debates I had to deliver throughout my educational career. I emphasized that they should not discourage their child's talk, but that together we could empower their children by helping them be responsible in [their speech]. I assured the parents that students need to converse by allowing for collaborative work, paired sharing, discussions, and oral presentations. (1999, pp. 354–355)

SUMMARY

How is the school a social institution?

1. Schools are organizations having an identifiable structure and a set of functions. Their primary function is to move young people into the mainstream of society. Educators work with parents, children, and outside agencies to ensure the psychological and physical well-being of students and to foster academic success. They also work collaboratively to build students' understanding and acceptance of others.

2. Schools differ in size, structure, and function. Their student populations are also quite diverse in terms of socioeconomic status and racial–ethnic composition.

3. Students have opportunities to attend many types of public and private schools. Parents base decisions about where their children go to school on such variables as class size and a school's scholastic ranking.

How is public schooling organized in the United States?

4. There are many types of preschools in the United States, and the professional preparation of staff and the quality of programs vary greatly. Programs are supported by both public and private interest groups and include Project Head Start, infant intervention and enrichment programs, nursery schools, public and private prekindergartens and kindergartens, college and university laboratory schools, church-sponsored preschools, and parent cooperatives.

5. About 55 percent of five-year-olds experience full-time kindergarten programs. While some programs focus on academics, others are more child centered, allowing students to acquire concepts and skills at their own pace through exploration and free play. Programs for children in grades 1–6 also vary. Sometimes students are grouped homogeneously by ability or achievement for all or portions of the school day. Students may also work in nongraded classrooms, where they are grouped heterogeneously by achievement.

6. Junior high and middle schools are meant to help students make the transition from elementary school to high school by concentrating on academic subjects and exposing students to careers and occupations. Some critics claim, however, that existing schools are too imitative of high schools and inappropriate to the needs of 10- to 14-year-olds.

7. Sizes of high schools vary, with enrollment in alternative schools being as low as 200 and enrollment in large "comprehensive" schools—high schools offering a full range of programs—being as high as 5,000.

8. In 1996 about 65 percent of high school graduates enrolled in college immediately after graduation. About 23 percent attended 2-year colleges, while 41.9 percent enrolled in 4-year public or private institutions.

What are some schooling alternatives?

9. There are a number of notable alternative programs that provide educational opportunities for people in the United States. Among these are magnet schools, vocational–technical schools, Montessori and Waldorf schools, private and independent schools, for-profit schools, parochial schools, charter schools, and home schools.

10. As alternatives for schooling have increased, the distinction between public and private education has become increasingly vague. Despite their similarities, public schools differ from private schools in several ways: (1) public schools are tax supported, while, in the main, private schools are not; (2) private schools can set their own admissions requirements; (3) private school students are enrolled by parental or student choice; and (4) private schools have the freedom to craft philosophies that appeal to specific groups of people.

How are schools administered?

11. Among those who are responsible for the administration of schools are superintendents, principals, assistant principals, and site-based management teams. These individuals and groups, from the superintendent down, operate in a world that has changed dramatically in the past 30 years or so. Today's school administrators have much less flexibility in making decisions than did their predecessors. They must contend with state-aid formulas, government mandates, external standards for educators' and students' performances, and a host of political pressure groups intent on sharing power.

What organizational and policy issues do schools face?

12. Schools have been organized in different ways to try to meet the needs of students. Decisions about such things as whether to establish separate grades or to implement multiage groupings shape the unique character of each school. School policies about a number of other issues, including retention, class schedules, class size, and tracking are regularly reviewed or revised. Changes might be prompted by teachers, administrators, parents, and students.

What makes some schools more effective than others?

13. Students seem to do better in schools where there is effective leadership and a positive relationship between school personnel and parents and other members of the community. Such schools are generally marked by substantial staff development time, a strong curriculum, and a safe environment. Teachers think positively about students' abilities to succeed, set high but reasonable standards for student performance, and maximize students' opportunities to learn.

TERMS AND CONCEPTS

alternative school   178
block scheduling   192
central office staff   186
charter school   171
collegiality   188
for-profit school   182
institution   168
magnet school   178
National Association for the Education
   of Young Children (NAEYC)   172
nongraded classrooms   173

principal   188
private school   181
retention   192
school district   168
site-based management   191
social promotion   192
student–teacher ratio   193
superintendent of schools   186
tracking   193
year-round school   193

REFLECTIVE PRACTICE

Pamela Piersol had lobbied the state legislature for 2 years on behalf of Citizens for Charter Schools (CCS). The group wanted the freedom to establish new schools that were free from most, if not all, state regulations but were supported with public funds. Pam and her colleagues contended that the public schools as they were presently run did not deliver the quality of education that students and taxpayers deserved or had a right to expect.

Piersol had taught public school for 6 years and served as a principal for 5 years before leaving to become headmaster of a private school. Her credentials were impeccable. She lobbied with considerable skill and managed to win a state-supported program of experimentation with charter schools funded for 5 years. Groups would write proposals for new charter schools, and, if the program were funded, parents could choose to send their children to one of the charter schools.

The new charter schools could serve any and all levels as the designers saw fit. The schools could not discriminate against students or staff by race, ethnicity, or gender, and they could not value one religion over another. Otherwise charter schools would be free to organize and run themselves in any fashion. Charter schools would not have to hire state-certified or -licensed personnel. They could include or exclude any grade levels. They could create their own admission standards and expel students. Most important, Piersol and her colleagues believed, they could craft their mission broadly or narrowly to shape the schools' structure and functions, which in turn would be used to attract and hold parents and students. At the end of the 5-year period of experimentation, those schools that got and kept students would continue to receive state aid; those that did not demonstrate holding power would lose funding.

Issues, Problems, Dilemmas, Opportunities

Assume Piersol and the CCS were located in your state. What specific problems, if any, might a new charter school be able to address more effectively than an existing public school? What opportunities, if any, might a charter school capitalize on to attract and hold students?

Perceive and Value

How might a proposal to create a new charter school written by a group of private school teachers and parents differ from one written by public school teachers and parents? In other words, how might the values of the people designing the school influence the school mission, its organization, and the activities in which faculty and students engage?

Know and Act

In 50 words or fewer, craft an advertisement that reflects your estimate of the defining characteristics of a charter school that might succeed in your community. Design the advertisement so that the attributes of the new school appear in descending order of importance.

Evaluate

In both the long and short term, a new charter school will be judged by its ability to attract and hold students. Are there other factors that might be used to judge the quality of a newly organized charter school? What might they be? How might you assess a school's ability to attend to these factors?

 ## ONLINE ACTIVITY

Search the Web for the "Virtual Schoolhouse" and then browse school Web pages. You will find more than 500 elementary schools, 300 high schools, and 50 international schools. You will also find the American School Directory that has listings and contact addresses for 106,000 K–12 schools nationwide. Look at five or six different school sites and identify some concepts that these sites share. To do so, you must read the school description and try to understand what the author wanted to convey. Why is school philosophy important? Which site seems to do the best job of expressing its philosophy in an appealing way? What makes you think so?

6

School Governance and Education Finance

We use this chapter to describe governmental influences on education and the characteristics of educational leaders and managers at federal, state, and local levels. We explain how special-interest groups influence the structure and functions of public schooling and discuss the interaction of public values and school funding. We also consider the chronic problems of increasing demands and decreasing resources and the challenges of site-based management and school choice.

PROFESSIONAL PRACTICE QUESTIONS

- ▮ What are school governance and education finance?
- ▮ How does the federal government influence education?
- ▮ How is education financed and controlled by the states?
- ▮ How are schools financed and managed at the local level?
- ▮ How are governance and funding related to educational success?

 ## What Are School Governance and Education Finance?

The power to establish and operate public schools is derived from the Tenth Amendment to the U.S. Constitution: "The powers not delegated to the United States by the Constitution; nor prohibited by it to the States, are reserved to the States respectively, or to the people." The power to educate is one reserved to the states; that is, the states are ultimately responsible for **school governance,** or for establishing and managing public education. States delegate many educational functions to local education agencies. Over time, a complex network of formal organizations and informal pressure groups at the federal, state, and local levels has made public education what it is today.

Governance controls finance, and finance shapes practice. For educational practitioners to exert some influence on these systems, they need to understand how public education is funded, where the money is allocated, and how it is eventually spent and accounted for. Some knowledge can be gained from examining the formal processes of governance and finance. But it is important to study informal processes, too.

▶ How Schools Are Run

Schools are run by leaders—you remember, the ones out front who look like movie stars, who take great risks, and who always win—whatever there is to win. Then, again, maybe they are following the parade, dressed in ill-fitting suits, doggedly determined to snatch whatever morsel they can get from wherever they can get it. Leaders run schools all right, but the definition of *leader* is subject to considerable debate.

What is good leadership?

To some, a leader is a person who takes on new tasks and pushes for change, someone who is proactive, not reactive (Zaleznick, 1977). To others, a leader is a system-oriented person who is concerned about production and a person-oriented manager who demonstrates consideration for staff members (Stogdill, 1981), or, similarly, a person who is concerned with tasks and people in the organization (Bales, 1954; Bowers & Seashore, 1966). Aristotle believed that leaders are born—people either have the capacity to lead or they do not, and some modern organizational theorists tend to agree. Yet others think that leadership is largely a function of the situations in which people find themselves (Fiedler, 1967). Kenneth Leithwood (1992)

Cultural Awareness

Joni Lucas

Joni Lucas, a former education editor, explains that Washington state is somewhat unique with regard to women's opportunities for school leadership positions:

> Keep an eye on school districts in the Puget Sound area of Washington state; they'll be the ones to watch in the next few years. That's the advice of incoming Kent, Wash., Supt. Barbara Grohe. Grohe says this not to be self-serving but as a way of acknowledging a distinctive group of female school leaders in the state and a departure from the norm nationwide—school districts headed by women.
>
> Washington state seems to be ahead of the curve when it comes to women in school leadership positions. Of the largest 24 districts in the state, eight have female superintendents at the helm, according to Doyle Winter, executive director of the Washington Association of School Adminis-
>
> trators. These eight districts are centered in the Puget Sound area near Seattle.
>
> But Puget Sound is not the only conclave of female leadership. Statewide, 15 percent of the top school leaders are female, Winter says. In the last several years, women have increasingly been moving into the larger districts in the state, reflecting a progressive mindset on education and other social issues.
>
> The Washington statistics suggest a state that may be a tad more welcoming when it comes to women in educational leadership posts. A 1998 study by AASA and Superintendents Prepared found that nationally only 12 percent of superintendents are female, up from 4 percent in 1985. (Lucas, 1999)

Source: Lucas, J. (1999, June 9). "Old girl" network of superintendents bucks prevailing statistics nationwide. *AASA Online. Leadership News.* Available online (http://www.aasa.org/LN/Misc/6-9-99oldgirl.htm).

has argued that school leaders are finding themselves more and more in the position of having to create conditions that enable staffs to find their own directions.

These leaders—school board members, superintendents, principals, department heads, and teachers—are responsible for the "governance" of schools: for controlling, directing, and otherwise influencing the actions and conduct of schooling. They do so within a system of institutions, laws, regulations, policies, politics, and customs. Leaders are designated and paid to exercise and delegate power to make schools work. To get a sense of school leadership today, visit the home page of a group dedicated to supporting leaders—the American Association of School Administrators.

▶ How Schools Are Funded

The total expenditure per pupil in public elementary and secondary school programs in 1997–1998 was $6,624. (U.S. Department of Education, 1998). As illustrated in Figure 6.1, public schools are financed primarily by localities, states, and the federal government. More than three-fourths of the 15,000 plus school boards in the United States have taxing authority. In economically troubled times, however, few

FIGURE 6.1
Sources of Revenues for School Funding What factors might alter the proportion of financial support that each level of government provides?

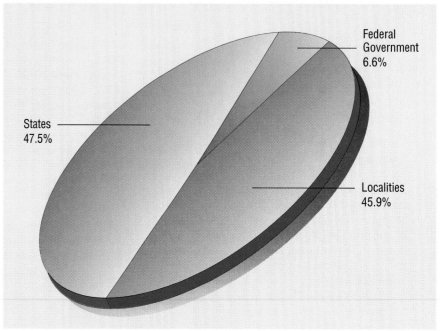

Note. From *Digest of Education Statistics, 1998,* by U.S. Department of Education, 1999, Washington, DC: Government Printing Office.

political leaders at any governmental level are willing to risk the ire of voters by raising taxes to support public schools. The chances for success of such a maneuver are diminished even further by the fact that an increasing number of voters no longer have children in the public schools. Those who are retired and on fixed incomes often are less willing and less able to support public education.

▶ Relationships Between Education and the Economy

Since before the founding of the republic, values and money have shaped public education into the system we have today. Values and money trigger all kinds of questions about the conduct of education. Does "equal" educational opportunity mean the same level of funding for all students? Or must some students and localities be afforded extra resources to put them on equal footing with others in their quest for educational success? Why and how should low-income communities be helped to provide adequate facilities and programs for educating their children? How can people recognize wasteful spending on schools? At what point do providers of money for education cross the line from being efficient to being stingy? Who decides how money will be spent at the school level? Should parents be allowed to choose what schools their children attend and use tax dollars to finance these choices? Contemporary leaders communicate their values through their answers to such questions.

Corporate values also shape education. Today, increasing computerization, the proliferation of services offered by businesses, a growing global economy, and decentralization of responsibility necessitate that workers and leaders possess a variety of skills (Glickman, 1998; Hambrick, 1998). Besides learning reading, communication, and mathematical skills, people must be able to reason, to direct their own work, to cooperate with others, and to adapt to change. These omnicompetent workers are in great demand. Because they may not need to defer to supervisors in the workplace, such individuals make production more efficient. As people become more educated, they also increase their work options. The more marketable skills a person has, the more likely she is to find a job.

To make a case for education spending, public leaders frequently point to connections between education and success in life and between lack of education and failure. "Would you prefer to pay to help a child learn how to read," a candidate for public office might ask, "or would you prefer to house an illiterate felon at three or four times the cost?" Illiteracy does not always lead to crime, just as education does not guarantee success, but there are strong links.

Increased educational opportunities also make democracy run more smoothly. Knowledge of history, geography, and culture enables people to gain a common perspective on current political and social problems. Development of language skills and interpersonal skills prepares people to communicate and work with others to reach common goals. Education programs convey from generation to generation more and less effective ways for conducting social and political discourse in a free society (Guthrie, Garms, & Pierce, 1988). These outcomes are essential for a democracy, and they make efforts to educate people worth the price.

Today's economists assess educational value in both public or social benefits and private returns. Many argue that the social benefits of education—reduced crime rates, inculcation of moral values, economic productivity—are most difficult to assess but also most important to achieve. Society as a whole, they contend, must benefit from money spent on public education because it requires redistribution of resources—taking money away from some to provide service to others.

Some view education as a means of developing human capital, much as businesses acquire and develop physical capital, such as buildings and equipment (Becker, 1964; Schultz, 1981). This view suggests that education should benefit both students and society. Students should have reason to expect that the time, effort, and money they invest in their education will yield some personal benefit, such as increased earnings and greater job satisfaction. Society should expect that public education will yield productive citizens with some sense of the common good.

What concept of the common good should education provide?

There is good reason to believe that education can help both individuals and communities. When people learn, they become more valuable to their neighbors. When all the neighbors are improving themselves, the neighborhood—regardless of whether it is defined locally, regionally, or nationally—is a better place for the individual.

Through the years, the challenge for policy makers has been to strike some balance among four ideals (Guthrie, Garms, & Pierce, 1988). Although the relative importance of these ideals has waxed and waned at different times and in different locales, all have figured prominently in shaping public education:

- *Equality,* or equal educational opportunity, typically has been defined in terms of providing equal access to schooling, making available to every student educational treatment tailored to his strengths and weaknesses and ensuring that all students acquire at least minimum or basic skills.

- *Adequacy* refers to the minimum resources sufficient to achieve some educational result (Clune, 1995).

- *Efficiency* connotes getting the maximum benefit from dollars spent on education.

- *Liberty,* or choice, implies control over where, how, and for what purposes students are educated.

▶ Political and Economic Influences on Public Education

Various individuals, groups, and organizations wield power to shape the course of events in schools. Formal sources of power reside in the organization itself—those in charge have final authority over salaries, make staff appointments, and the like. Increasingly, in restructured schools, this formal authority is being redefined to include parents and teachers. Others exercise power informally by virtue of the constituencies they represent or through the force of their personalities. Figure 6.2 shows some of the influences on education at the national, federal, regional, state, and local levels, which are discussed in this chapter.

Education Lobbies and Special-Interest Groups.   Public education, it seems, is everyone's business, and some people are more powerful in influencing its direction than are others. People often coalesce around specific interests and try to exert pressure for the advancement of their cause, hence the terms **special-interest group** and *pressure group*. These terms often are used pejoratively to communicate the idea that group members promote their own narrow point of view. But special-interest groups also educate the public about important issues and offer alternative solutions to problems.

While many education reforms in recent years have been initiated publicly by authorities at the state level, a variety of special interests has contributed informally to the reforms. Their members have worked publicly and behind the scenes to shape policy at the local, state, and national levels. For example, the largest volunteer education organization in the United States, the **National Congress of Parents and Teachers (PTA)**, has long supported legislation at the state and national levels designed to benefit children. Professional organizations such as the National School Boards Association, the National Association of State Boards of Education, and the American Association of Colleges for Teacher Education also support in spirit and with funds many education policy initiatives.

Interest groups often attempt to influence schools on ideological grounds. The Council for Basic Education, founded in 1956 by Mortimer Smith and Arthur Bestor, advocates curriculum in the liberal arts, much in keeping with Bestor's essentialist ideas (see Chapter 4). Since the 1960s, African Americans

Do special-interest groups have a positive impact on education?

FIGURE 6.2
Influences on Public Education   How might this figure change if you ranked the levels in terms of their power? Explain your reasoning.

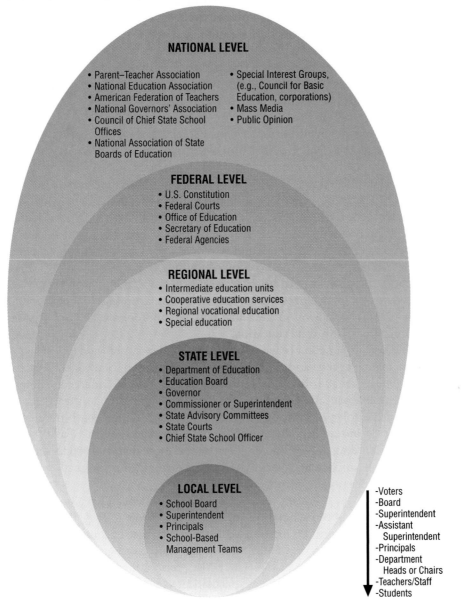

NATIONAL LEVEL
- Parent–Teacher Association
- National Education Association
- American Federation of Teachers
- National Governors' Association
- Council of Chief State School Offices
- National Association of State Boards of Education
- Special Interest Groups, (e.g., Council for Basic Education, corporations)
- Mass Media
- Public Opinion

FEDERAL LEVEL
- U.S. Constitution
- Federal Courts
- Office of Education
- Secretary of Education
- Federal Agencies

REGIONAL LEVEL
- Intermediate education units
- Cooperative education services
- Regional vocational education
- Special education

STATE LEVEL
- Department of Education
- Education Board
- Governor
- Commissioner or Superintendent
- State Advisory Committees
- State Courts
- Chief State School Officer

LOCAL LEVEL
- School Board
- Superintendent
- Principals
- School-Based Management Teams

-Voters
-Board
-Superintendent
-Assistant Superintendent
-Principals
-Department Heads or Chairs
-Teachers/Staff
-Students

and Native Americans have been increasingly active in demanding that schools respond to their needs and facilitate their participation in school activities. Hispanic Americans, too, have tried to establish *unidos,* or unity, among Spanish-speaking peoples to effect change in public schools. Such groups often are stimulated and sustained by their beliefs about school curricula and issues of social justice.

Interest groups advocate a wide range of activities aimed in one way or another at exerting control over curricular, instructional, and governance issues in public education. For example, the Americans with Disabilities Association, Inc., attempts to provide the community of individuals with disabilities with a political voice as an alternative to charity-based efforts (Americans with Disabilities Association, Inc., 1999). In addition to educating the public about issues that concern its members, the ADA works to influence political elections and legislative initiatives. This political action committee, or PAC, seeks to counter threats from other groups working against the interests of people with disabilities. The ADA conducts voter registration drives, promotes get-out-the-vote programs, and raises money for candidates who support positions favorable to people with disabilities. Search for and visit the web site of the ADA, Inc.

The American Civil Liberties Union (ACLU) has taken public positions on educational issues to defend people against what it has perceived as attacks on their civil liberties. One of its most notable involvements was in the Scopes trial of 1925; in fact, the ACLU stimulated the confrontation between Christian fundamentalists and evolutionists. The ACLU offered counsel to any Tennessee teacher who would test the law that forbade teaching in public schools any theory that denied the account of creation in the Book of Genesis. John T. Scopes took them up on the offer and was defended by Clarence Darrow. Scopes won. Visit the ACLU's home page on the Web, which contains position statements on education.

The ACLU also has filed briefs on legal issues as a "friend of the court" for the purpose of educating judges and lawyers; endorsed exempting students from the flag salute when their religion suggests that refusal is appropriate; and opposed the use of public funds for private education.

The Anti-Defamation League (ADL), organized in 1913 to end unjust and unfair discrimination against and ridicule of any religious sect or body of citizens, has 400 staff members in 30 field offices in U.S. cities. Its World of Difference Campaign, a comprehensive educational program for elementary and secondary teachers and students, fosters tolerance through teacher awareness training, youth training, classroom discussion guides, student after-school programs, and weekend awareness retreats. According to ADL figures, it has trained more than 100,000 teachers and 10 million public, private, and parochial school students. (More information about ADL activities can be obtained from their web site.)

For more than 100 years, the Daughters of the American Revolution (DAR) has promoted awards and scholarship programs in schools to foster patriotism. The group sponsors the Junior American Citizens program to encourage the teaching of good citizenship and gives Good Citizenship Medals to recognize qualities of honor, service, courage, and leadership. The DAR sponsors the American History Essay Contest for the middle grades, gives scholarships to college and university students in the Reserve Officer Training Corps (ROTC), and recognizes outstanding teachers of American history. Visit the DAR web site to learn more.

The Legal Defense and Education Fund (LDEF) of the National Organization for Women (NOW) sponsors a variety of actions to advance women's rights in education systems across the country. In St. Louis, Missouri, for example, the LDEF fought against the board of education policy to transfer pregnant elementary and junior high school girls to a less desirable school when their pregnancies became obvious. The board changed its policy, allowing girls to choose to remain in regular classes or to transfer (National Organization for Women Legal Defense and Education Fund,

1993, p. 2). For more information on NOW, visit their web site.

Since its founding in 1909, the National Association for the Advancement of Colored People (NAACP) has worked to ensure racial justice for all people and to improve the living conditions of low-income people. The association is the largest and most influential civil rights organization in the country. The NAACP has worked for open housing, job opportunities, prison reform, school desegregation, and education programs for youths and adults. For more information on the NAACP and its influence on education and society, visit its web site.

Business organizations also have left their mark on education. The National Association of Manufacturers (NAM), for example, believes that America's economic well-being and ability to compete in global markets depend on the skills of the nation's work force. No longer content to rely on old methods of lobbying to advance its mission, the NAM has joined forces with the General Physics Corporation to offer its own training online via NAM VIRTUAL UNIVERSITY (National Association of Manufacturers, 1999). They offer some 30 courses in general manufacturing, health and safety, human resources, leadership, information technology (IT), and quality assurance. While these courses are targeted at existing businesses and industries, it is clear that the NAM and other such groups seek to extend their influence on education well beyond traditional boundaries.

What effects do organizations such as the PTA, NOW, and NAACP have on the governance and finance of public education? What other interest groups influence public education policy and practice? How would you evaluate the benefits and disadvantages of these stakeholders' involvement in education?

Business–School Partnerships. Partnerships between public schools and private enterprises have existed for years. New York Alliance for the Public Schools, for example, was established in 1979. It includes business, community, and civic leaders, as well as school board members, representatives from the United Federation of Teachers, parents, and others. In the mid-1980s there were some 35,000 such partnerships (McCormick, 1984). By the 1990s the number had increased fivefold. Associations involving private businesses and corporations typically are driven by the idea that good schools yield good citizens, good employees, and good consumers.

Although partnerships between schools and businesses are not without critics—who wants budding scientists learning about nuclear power from the Detroit Edison Company?—such partnerships are popular. At a meeting of business and school leaders in Detroit, Naima Wartts, a reporter for the *Detroit Free Press*, noted the following:

What other special-interest groups can you identify that have had an impact on education in this country?

Is business involvement in education a wise idea?

> Detroit Superintendent Eddie Green has pushed the concept as a logical step in strengthening the public school system. "Community and business people will need to come together to prepare students to be gainfully employed and prepare students for secondary education," he said. . . . Molly Luembert-Coy, a supervisor at Detroit Edison and a member of the Schools' Partnership Advisory Committee, contends that the program has been rewarding for the schools and the com-

pany. "Detroit Edison began working with the public schools in the 1970s, and we've found the program to be very beneficial to us as a company as well as enriching for the schools," she said. Charles Katz, regional manager for the Copeland Co., invited financial players to consider the benefits of providing good public relations with the community, building company loyalty through paid internships for high school students, and tax benefits that result from financial investment in the schools. . . . "We must place the commitment to public school education in the heart of the community through opening communications and establishing ourselves as parts of one whole," Green said. "We all need each other to move forward." (Wartts, 1998)

Others insist that public education demands public involvement. Well-managed partnerships between schools and businesses can break down barriers between disparate groups of people. They also create opportunities for people to work together on common tasks that they want to see accomplished. When stakeholders in the success of public education work together to achieve common goals, the schools are bound to benefit.

Public Media.   One cannot ignore the influence of public opinion on processes of governing and managing public education in the United States. The press figures prominently in public opinion both by reporting on the state of the public mind and by suggesting what people ought to think.

| How do the mass media affect education? |

One view, expressed by Juan Williams, is that the job of the press is to watch governmental and educational leaders so that they do not cheat the public. This time-honored role of journalism is important. Williams (1992) describes the job of the journalist on the education beat:

The truth is, reporters and editors and, most important, readers are interested in education only as a function of political power. A major proportion of any jurisdiction's tax dollars goes into schools. Politicians have to make up those school budgets and defend them. The school or university budget has to be both sufficient to the task of educating young people and simultaneously able to withstand charges that it is really a pork-barrel project, wasting the taxpayer's money. Education budgets pay not only for teachers and books but also for construction workers, maintenance people, teachers' aides, administrators, union chiefs, and cooks. In other words, the tax dollars assigned to educate children are a major source of patronage and power in our society. Newspaper editors, as the public's watchdogs, want to know if the taxpayers are being cheated out of their money. (p. 179)

But too often, critics argue, the press goes out of its way to criticize schools. "We think that too frequently a story is found interesting to reporters only if it is critical of the schools, if it has some scent of blood about it. Using the news lingo, "If it bleeds, it leads" (Berliner and Biddle, 1998).

The press performs not only an informational function in society but a major educational functional as well. Television, newspapers, radio, and magazines touch more people today than at any time in our history, and they will reach more tomorrow than they do today. To make a positive impact, former U.S. Senator and presidential candidate Bill Bradley has argued, the media must be more civic minded.

At a time when harassed parents spend less time with their children, they have ceded to television more and more of the all-important role of storytelling, which is essential to the formation of moral education that sustains a civil society. But too often . . . the market acts blindly to sell and make money, never pausing to ask whether it furthers citizenship or decency. (Bradley, 1996, pp. 40–41)

How Does the Federal Government Influence Education?

Although there is no specific mention of public education in the Constitution, the federal government has always had a hand in shaping education. James Guthrie, Walter Garms, and Lawrence Pierce (1988) suggest that the federal agenda for education is shaped by the "Iron Triangle"—the combination of education interests in the executive branch, congressional committees, and interest groups outside government.

The executive branch combines exhortation and programs to influence public education. Presidential staffs and cabinets speak publicly about education issues, encourage states' attention to education reform, and earmark federal funds for education initiatives. The president is responsible for a comprehensive array of departments, agencies, and programs devoted to education.

Congress attends to public education by passing laws and appropriating funds. Although not part of the "Iron Triangle," federal courts also exert influence on the conduct of public education through their decisions. For instance, the courts play a continuing role in ruling on civil rights cases and controversial issues such as prayer in the public schools.

▶ Federal Funding for Education

Figure 6.3 illustrates trends in total federal support for education between 1965 and 1998. For elementary and secondary schools, for example, support increased by 144 percent between 1965 and 1975, rose only 2 percent between 1975 and 1980, declined 22 percent between 1980 and 1985, and then rose again 47 percent between 1985 and 1998 (U.S. Department of Education, 1999).

The **National Center for Education Statistics,** an arm of the executive branch responsible for collecting and analyzing education statistics for the nation, reported that the total federal support for education in fiscal year (FY) 1998 was $75.1 billion. As illustrated in Figure 6.4, a substantial portion of that money went to elementary and secondary education programs. Some 49 percent was allocated to elementary and secondary education, 21 percent to postsecondary expenses, 23 percent to university research, and 7 percent to "other" education programs, including libraries, museums, cultural activities, and miscellaneous research. Funds were distributed not only through the Department of Education but via the Departments of Health and Human Services, Agriculture, Defense, Energy, and Labor, as well as through the National Science Foundation.

FIGURE 6.3
Federal On-Budget Funds for Education by Level or Other Educational Purpose
1965 to 1998 Why might support for elementary, secondary, and postsecondary education have declined in the 1980s?

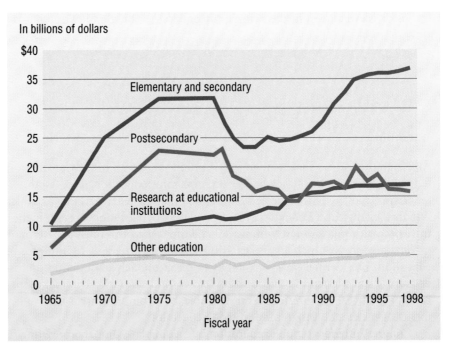

Note. From *Digest of Education Statistics 1998* (p. 396) by U.S. Department of Education, 1999, Washington, DC: U.S. Government Printing Office.

President Clinton requested money for a system of national standards and assessments for grades K through 12 and also boosted the Head Start budget in order to eventually provide educational services to all eligible preschool children in the nation. Among other programs for which Clinton achieved funding were school clinics; school-to-work programs; a national telecommunications network that would link schools, libraries, and other public institutions with individual homes; and educational research, statistics, and assessment.

Federal funding for education takes many forms: (1) major grant programs established through legislation such as the Vocational Act of 1963 (more recently the Carl Perkins Vocational Education Act of 1984) and the Education for All Handicapped Children Act of 1975 (renamed the Individuals with Disabilities Education Act of 1997); (2) aid to localities where there are large federal installations, such as military bases; and (3) **categorical grants** for funding of education programs designed for particular groups and specific purposes, including bilingual education (provided through the Bilingual Education Act of 1972) and compensatory programs for low-income children, such as Project Head Start and Title I.

Sometimes several education programs are grouped together as a **block grant** to localities. Chapter Two of the 1981 **Education Consolidation and Improvement Act**

FIGURE 6.4
Estimated Federal Education Dollar, 1998   What proportion of the federal budget
goes to elementary and secondary education?

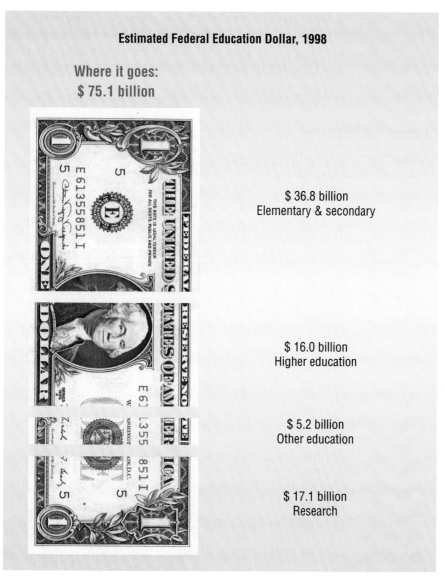

Estimated Federal Education Dollar, 1998

Where it goes:
$ 75.1 billion

$ 36.8 billion
Elementary & secondary

$ 16.0 billion
Higher education

$ 5.2 billion
Other education

$ 17.1 billion
Research

Note. From *Digest of Education Statistics* 1998 (p. 381) by U.S. Department of Education,
1999, Washington, DC: U.S. Government Printing Office.

(ECIA) combined 32 previously enacted education programs under one block grant
that state and local education agencies could use for general education purposes.
With this block grant, funds are allocated to states based on a student population formula. States then prepare a plan for using federal funds based on district enrollment
or on measures of student need. Finally, the state gives money to local school districts
for use in whichever programs need additional services.

Does federal funding improve state control of education?

Regardless of what type of federal funding a school district receives, the district is obligated to comply with federal guidelines when spending grant money. If a school district does not comply, that is, either does not spend the money the federal government allocates or misspends the money, one of several things can happen: the school system can be forced to return the money, it can be fined, and/or it can be prevented from receiving any federal funds in the future. States and school districts with educational programs or practices that are found to be in violation of federal laws also lose funding.

▶ National Goals

In the 1980s and 1990s, the federal government has influenced education at state and local levels by concentrating on the National Goals. Secretaries of education in the Reagan, Bush, and Clinton administrations have focused attention on states' performances on a variety of educational measures, including standardized achievement test scores, graduation rates, and teachers' salaries. States' progress toward meeting the Goals is made public through a national reporting system.

Table 6.1 shows how progress in one state, Illinois, was measured in 1998. For example, Goal 5, which calls for School Completion, shows that Illinois moved up from 85 percent in 1990 to 89 percent in 1996. The number of children with disabilities enrolled in preschool (Goal 1), however, decreased from 53 per 1,000 3- to 5-year-olds in 1991 to 50 per 1,000 3- to 5-year-olds in 1997 (National Education Goals Panel, 1998).

How Is Education Financed and Controlled by the States?

State governments exercise more influence on public education than does the federal government. They do so in a variety of ways. Figure 6.5 shows a typical organization of public education at the state level.

State governments influence public education most notably through taxation and distribution of revenues. States also set standards for building schools, educating teachers and school administrators, licensing school personnel, and establishing curriculum, the minimum length of the school term, attendance requirements, and school accreditation. States provide a host of other special services. While the structure of state bureaucracies and the relative influence of key officers vary from place to place, the role of state government in public education has become increasingly prominent through the years.

The states relate to the federal government in several ways. Education is recognized as a right reserved to the states under the Tenth Amendment to the Constitution. In addition, court cases have defined education as a property right or civil right under the Constitution and thus subject to the Fourteenth Amendment (Section 1: "No State shall make or enforce any law which shall abridge the privileges or immunities of citizens of the United States; nor shall any State deprive any person of life,

▌ **TABLE 6.1**
One State's Progress on the National Goals

Illinois placed among the highest-performing states in the nation on five measures of progress:

Goal 1: Ready to Learn

1. Percentage of infants born with one or more of four health risks (33%)

Goal 2: School Completion

2. High school completion rate among 18- to 24-year-olds (89%)

Goal 4: Teacher Education and Professional Development

3. Percentage of public secondary school teachers who hold an undergraduate or graduate degree in their main teaching assignment (72%)

4. Percentage of public secondary school teachers who hold a teaching certificate in their main teaching assignment (96%)

Goal 7: Safe, Disciplined, and Alcohol- and Drug-free Schools

5. Percentage of public school teachers reporting that they were threatened or physically attacked by a student from their school (12%)

Illinois improved on five measures of progress toward the Goals:

Goal 1: Ready to Learn

1. Illinois reduced the percentage of infants born with one or more of four health risks (from 35% in 1990 to 33% in 1996).

2. Illinois increased the percentage of 2-year-olds who had been fully immunized (from 68% in 1994 to 76% in 1997).

3. Illinois increased the percentage of mothers who received early prenatal care (from 78% in 1990 to 82% in 1996).

Goal 2: School Completion

4. Illinois increased the high school completion rate among 18- to 24-year-olds (from 85% in 1990 to 89% in 1996).

Goal 3: Student Achievement and Citizenship

5. Illinois increased the numbers of Advanced Placement examinations receiving a grade high enough to qualify students for college credit. (The number of AP exams receiving a grade of 3 or higher increased from 61 per 1,000 eleventh and twelfth graders in 1991 to 93 per 1,000 eleventh and twelfth graders in 1998).

There are six measures of progress where Illinois' performance became significantly worse:

Goal 1: Ready to Learn

1. The number of children with disabilities enrolled in preschool decreased for 3- to 5-year-olds from 53 per 1,000 in 1991 to 50 per 1,000 in 1997.

Goal 5: Mathematics and Science

2. The proportion of degrees earned by female students that were awarded in mathematics and science decreased from 35% in 1991 to 34% in 1995.

Goal 6: Adult Literacy and Lifelong Learning

3. The percentage of high school graduates who immediately enrolled in college in any state decreased from 63% in 1992 to 61% in 1996.

Goal 7: Safe, Disciplined, and Alcohol- and Drug-free Schools

4. The percentage of public high school students who reported using marijuana increased from 14% in 1993 to 25% in 1995.

5. The percentage of public high school students who reported that someone offered, sold, or gave them an illegal drug on school property increased from 19% in 1993 to 31% in 1995.

6. The percentage of public secondary teachers who reported that student disruptions interfered with their teaching increased from 40% in 1991 to 49% in 1994.

Source: National Education Goals Panel (1998). *Notes about the 1998 findings: Illinois.* Available online (http://www.negp.gov/issues/publication/98statefact/il.htm/).

FIGURE 6.5
Typical Organization of Public Education at the State Level Why are "The People" shown at the top of this figure? In what sense are the top and the bottom of this figure the same?

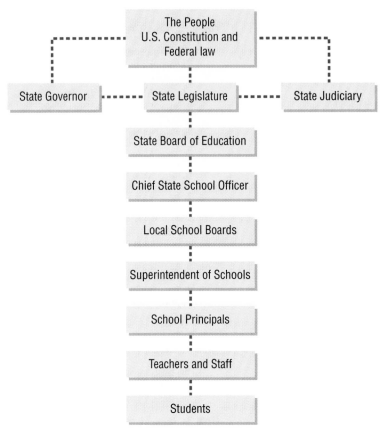

liberty, or property, without due process of law; nor deny to any person within its jurisdiction the equal protection of the laws."). The Fourteenth Amendment has allowed the federal government to intervene in ways that influence the education of children at the local level.

▶ State Funding

Much of the funding for public schools comes from the states. The state share of revenues for public elementary and secondary schools had grown steadily for many decades, but this trend began to reverse in the late 1980s. Between 1986 and 1987 and 1995 and 1996, the state share declined from 49.7 percent of all revenues to 47.5 percent, while the local share rose from 43.9 to 45.9 percent. The federal share was 6.6 percent in 1995–1996 (U.S. Department of Education, 1999). State funds earmarked for education are procured from a variety of sources other than the federal education budget, especially from taxes.

State Sales Taxes. Only Alaska, Delaware, Montana, New Hampshire, and Oregon have no sales taxes. The majority of their educational funds come from income or property taxes. However, numerous cities and towns in Alaska have their own local sales taxes. Furthermore, the other four states impose sales-type taxes on specific transactions, such as lodging accommodations (Business Owner's Toolkit, 1999). The 45 states with general sales taxes have rates varying from 3.5 percent in Colorado and Wyoming to 7 percent in Rhode Island and Mississippi. Of the 45 states, 31 permitted cities and/or counties to add local sales taxes to state sales taxes. New York City, for example, charged 4.25 percent in addition to the New York state sales tax of 4 percent for a total rate of 8.25 percent.

Sales taxes have great appeal because they are relatively easy and inexpensive to administer. Retailers collect sales taxes at the point of sale, and the state deals directly with retailers instead of collecting from individuals, as in the case of personal income taxes. Sales taxes raise large sums of money. The more money people earn, the more they spend, and the more tax revenue collected for the state. To ease the burden on the poor and the elderly, some items, such as food and drugs, can be exempt from sales taxes. Sales taxes on luxury items and so-called sin taxes—taxes on cigarettes and alcohol—are relatively easy to raise because most people do not object.

Sales taxes also have drawbacks. As long as the economy expands and retail sales generate more revenue, people come to expect that there will always be plenty of money. When retail sales decline, however, and there is less money rather than more, the downward adjustment in support for all public services, including education, can be painful. In addition, as more necessities are subject to taxation, sales taxes require people with limited incomes to spend a greater percentage of their income on taxes than wealthy people spend. This is referred to as **regressive taxation** (Burrup & Brimley, 1982).

State Income Taxes. State income taxes, both personal and corporate, are another source of revenue for education. Unlike sales taxes, income taxes are a form of **progressive taxation;** that is, people pay more as they earn more. But income taxes are only part of a state's education finance system, which is often a hodgepodge of revenue-producing and revenue-spending strategies.

Every state's financial situation is unique in some way, but in the 1990s, the battle over raising taxes and cutting services has been common to most states. Connecticut provides an especially useful example because it did not have an income tax until 1991. Public debate about establishing this tax helped frame the issues. The necessity of balancing the state budget required, in the minds of the governor, the legislature, and many citizens, a stronger source of income to underwrite basic services—education, roads, prisons, and health care.

> **Why do states need different ways to raise money for education?**

In 1992 Connecticut had to face the problem that new money raised from the income tax, combined with cuts in public services, was still insufficient both to meet the demands for basic services and to reduce its budget deficit. Unlike the federal government, Connecticut could not print more money with which to pay its bills. Like many other states it suffered from the economic recession of the 1980s; less business meant less money collected from all its taxes. Also like other states, Connecticut suffered from diminishing federal aid, yet it had to respond to federally mandated programs, such as Medicaid, that required major commitments of funds. The problem of too much money going out and too little coming in forced state leaders in Connecticut and elsewhere to make difficult choices about where to spend their limited revenues.

Why do so many state officials support lotteries?

State Lotteries and Other Sources.   Other sources of state aid for education include estate and inheritance taxes, miscellaneous user fees, licenses, severance taxes—fees for the privilege of extracting natural resources from land or water—and lotteries.

Early attempts to establish state lotteries were cumbersome and largely unsuccessful. New Hampshire, a state that had neither a sales tax nor an income tax, established a state lottery in 1964 to support public education and to hold down property taxes. New York followed in 1967. Neither state raised as much money as it had expected, because the lotteries were too costly and burdensome to operate. Tickets cost several dollars each, buyers had to register, and drawings were held only twice a year.

In the 1970s other states instituted lotteries having streamlined procedures and more frequent payoffs. Now 36 states and the District of Columbia have lotteries that, combined, put billions of dollars into state coffers. Only a small percentage of this money goes for state aid to education.

Lotteries have been criticized as inefficient ways to raise money (Webb, 1990). They are also frowned upon by some as immoral ways to raise money, even though the cause may be just. After payoffs the profit margin is immense. An average of about 40 percent of the money collected ends up in the state treasury.

State Aid Plans.   **Flat grants** are one type of financial aid provided by states to local communities; these grants are either uniform or variable in nature. States that provide flat grants usually give equal amounts of money on a per student basis to districts, regardless of district needs or financial capacity. States that use variable flat grants try to compensate for differing classroom needs. Typically, these needs are weighted to give more money to schools having more expensive services. For example, high schools with vocational programs can command more money than can elementary schools. Districts having high demands for bilingual or special education classes also may receive more aid.

When using a **foundation program,** the state guarantees a certain amount of money for educational expenditures (by pupil or by classroom) and determines what proportion of that cost should be shouldered by localities. The required local rate is usually expressed in terms of *mills.* (A mill is one-tenth of a cent.) A millage rate is the amount of property tax dollars to be paid for each $1,000 of assessed valuation. Foundation funding varies inversely with community wealth; that is, in poorer communities, where revenue from property taxes is low, the state contributes more money than in affluent communities, where revenue is high. School districts can supplement state contributions with local revenues.

Inequalities in **per pupil expenditures,** that is, money allocated for education services divided by the number of pupils to be served, vary from state to state, as shown in Figure 6.6. Variations in the way states distribute funds to localities depend mainly on money available, demand for services, and cost of living.

FIGURE 6.6

Expenditure Per Pupil in Average Daily Attendance in Public Elementary and Secondary Schools, by State: 1995–1996 What regional trends do you identify in per-pupil expenditures? What factors might account for differences?

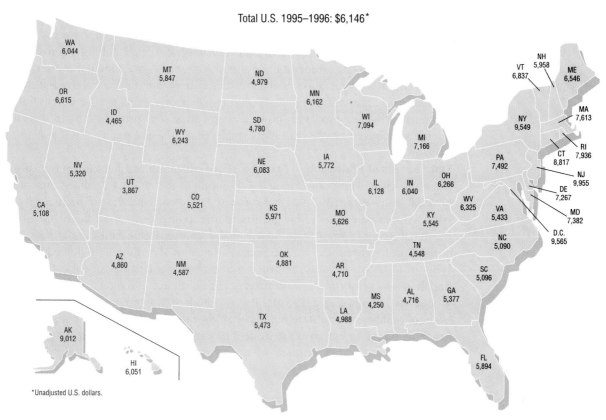

Total U.S. 1995–1996: $6,146*

WA 6,044
MT 5,847
ND 4,979
MN 6,162
NH 5,958
VT 6,837
ME 6,546
OR 6,615
ID 4,465
SD 4,780
WI 7,094
NY 9,549
MA 7,613
WY 6,243
MI 7,166
RI 7,936
NV 5,320
NE 6,083
IA 5,772
PA 7,492
CT 8,817
UT 3,867
CO 5,521
IL 6,128
IN 6,040
OH 6,266
NJ 9,955
CA 5,108
KS 5,971
MO 5,626
WV 6,325
KY 5,545
VA 5,433
DE 7,267
MD 7,382
D.C. 9,565
TN 4,548
NC 5,090
AZ 4,860
NM 4,587
OK 4,881
AR 4,710
SC 5,096
MS 4,250
AL 4,716
GA 5,377
TX 5,473
LA 4,988
AK 9,012
HI 6,051
FL 5,894

*Unadjusted U.S. dollars.

Note. From *Digest of Education Statistics* (p. 182) by U.S. Department of Education, 1999, Washington, DC: U.S. Government Printing Office.

Results from the 30th Annual Phi Delta Kappa/Gallup Poll indicate that lack of proper financial support for schools is the third greatest problem (following fighting and lack of discipline) facing schools today. Responses also suggest that some 50 percent of those polled believe the quality of schooling depends on the amount of money spent on students in schools (Rose & Gallup, 1998).

Under a **district power equalization** plan, localities establish the tax rate for educational spending, and the state guarantees a set amount of money proportional to local revenue. As in the foundation program, the state augments local revenue if it comes up short of the state guarantee. This program does not attempt to equalize expenditures on education; it merely equalizes access to funds for expenditures.

Hawaii, operating as a one-district state, provides **full state funding** for its schools—the state pays all educational expenses through a statewide tax. In this plan, then, all funding is equal and all taxation is equal. Although this plan is the most egal-

> **Why might states allocate money for education in different ways?**

itarian, in other states the desire for local autonomy causes many districts to reject the option of full state funding.

▶ State Education Oversight

State government has the responsibility to ensure that public education truly serves its citizens. The quantity and quality of educational services can and do vary across communities within a state, sometimes quite markedly. State government, however, must oversee educational operations to make certain that all communities receive at least the minimal level of services required to educate state residents. State government fulfills this mission by designing and implementing educational programs, by monitoring resources devoted to public education, and by evaluating the results of programs.

State Boards of Education.   **State boards of education** regulate educational practice and advise governors and state legislators about the conduct of educational business. All states except Wisconsin have state boards of education. The majority of states—35, to be exact—allow governors to appoint some or all board members (National Association of State Boards of Education, 1996). Some states have two boards, one for elementary and secondary education, the other for higher education. With the flurry of education reform in recent years, state boards of education often find themselves embroiled in controversy. For example, states establish requirements for homeschooling, creating possibilities for children to avoid ever setting foot inside a school building. Some state boards establish minimal standards for student performance that serve as barriers to student promotion and embarrass educators. State boards of education also regulate what teachers must do to get and keep their jobs,

How do the powers and responsibilities of state governments and the national government differ with regard to the governance and finance of education? How are the responsibilities of local boards of education or local education agencies different from those of state boards of education?

even though professional organizations and local education authorities may disagree with these requirements.

State board members also make momentous decisions about textbook adoption. Adoption procedures vary from state to state, but generally a state board approves a list of textbooks from which local school districts may select. If local districts expect to receive state funds for textbooks, they must buy from the approved list. State board members in densely populated states thus wield great influence by approving some books and banning others.

State board members in the populous states of Texas, California, and Florida influence schools in other states by shaping the content of textbooks that are sold across the nation. For example, when California state board members voice concerns about the lack of literature in elementary reading books or the sparseness of multicultural examples of family life, textbook publishers take notice because these populous states represent a huge volume in potential sales. Soon, the reading textbooks contain more samples of literature and focus greater attention on multicultural life. Often, children in less populous states, such as Montana, Kansas, or Vermont, for better or worse, use textbooks designed for other states.

State Education Departments.   A **state education department** (SED) is a bureaucracy organized to carry out a state's education business. An SED may administer programs directly, for example, schools for the deaf or blind. SEDs are directed by a state superintendent, a commissioner, or a **chief state school officer.** The organization regulates or oversees, among other things, the elementary and secondary schools' attention to curriculum and colleges' conduct of teacher preparation programs. An SED advises the executive and legislative branches of state government on a variety of issues, including school finance. It engages in staff development and public relations work for itself and for other governmental and nongovernmental agencies that have a stake in education. Over the years, SEDs have taken on more and more tasks. As laws have been passed and regulations established, SEDs have been expected to monitor schools' compliance. This has meant that the number of employees in SEDs has grown steadily.

Some states are trying to alter the way their state education departments are organized and the way they do their work. Michigan and Iowa, for instance, have moved to reduce the level of services provided at the state level and the number of employees in their state education departments.

> **Should teachers control the state standards boards?**

State Standards Boards.   All states now have **state standards boards** or commissions to regulate professional practice in education. In 13 states these boards have final authority; in the rest they serve only in an advisory capacity to policymakers. In Alabama, for example, the State Advisory Committee on Teacher Education and Certification is composed of about 30 members appointed by the state superintendent. As its name suggests, this Committee advises state policymakers. In contrast, standards boards in Minnesota, Nevada, Kentucky, West Virginia, and North Dakota have final authority concerning certification, entry, and exit standards for teachers, who make up a majority of the members.

The National Education Association and others have encouraged the establishment of standards boards to promote a concept of professionalism. Not until teachers control the state policy-making apparatus, it is argued, will teachers be able to control their own professional destiny.

The Governor's Influence. Historically, governors have relied on their appointees to formulate and implement educational policy in the states. Only in the past 10 to 15 years have governors themselves become personally involved in education issues.

The appointed leaders of state departments of elementary and secondary education in the 50 states, the District of Columbia, the Department of Defense Dependents Schools, and 5 U.S. jurisdictions—Virgin Islands, Puerto Rico, Northern Mariana Islands, Guam, and American Samoa—are tied to one another informally by an organization called the **Council of Chief State School Officers.** The Council provides a forum for education leaders and sponsors a series of special programs (international education, technology, national teacher of the year, etc.), a resource center on educational equity, and a state education assessment center. These programs and activities, plus an electronic network, provide opportunities for communication among leaders of state systems of public education.

In recent years the governors themselves have become major players in education reform through the **National Governors' Association (NGA),** founded in 1908 as a coalition of state chief executives. Many governors have come to believe that good education makes good politics. The problems in education are so intractable and so related to other facets of society that real reform demands strong, visible leadership from the very top of state government.

▶ Cooperation Among School Districts

Some educational services are so expensive, and both human and material resources so lean, that districts must band together to provide them. Such joint ventures are run by facilities most often called **intermediate educational units (IEUs),** educational service agencies (ESAs), or boards of cooperative educational services (BOCESs). For example, every high school in a state cannot provide the kind of vocational training that students need to be competitive in the job market. Several districts may join together to construct and maintain a technical training center for their students.

About three-fourths of the states mandate the creation of special units between the state and local levels and provide special support for the maintenance of these units. Special education services, particularly for children with severe and multiple disabilities, represent opportunities for such interdistrict cooperation or even for statewide cooperation.

Sometimes organizational units other than school districts cooperate with one another to increase their power, to reduce uncertainty, to increase performance by ensuring a steady flow of resources, and to protect themselves (Stearns, Hoffman, & Heide, 1987). They do so by sharing information, people, funds, and equipment. Schools contract with state and federal governments, universities, and private corporations to conduct research and to operate innovative educational projects. Projects Head Start and Follow Through are examples of such cooperative arrangements (Hoy & Miskel, 1996).

How Are Schools Financed and Managed at the Local Level?

Schools' personalities reflect the dispositions of the communities in which they are embedded. Some are dull, lethargic, and complacent; others bristle with activity and exude hopefulness. Citizen participation in and influence on educational matters are apparent at a variety of events—school board meetings, gatherings of parent–teacher organizations, and high school sporting events. People affect the schools, and the schools, in turn, influence constituents both inside and outside their walls.

Communities differ. Some are active, others are listless. In some communities the balance of power rests with a small number of people. At other times in other places, several factions compete to influence the focus and flow of educational policy. It is often possible to observe at the local level how money and personalities interact to yield a unique mix of educational practices.

▶ Property Taxes

In most states the local portion of schools' funds is derived almost exclusively from **local property taxes.** There are two kinds of property, real and personal. **Real property** is not readily movable; it includes land, buildings, and improvements. **Personal property** is movable; it consists of tangibles such as machinery, livestock, crops, and automobiles or intangibles such as money, stocks, and bonds. A community's ability to pay for education is dependent on its real assets, that is, on the assessed value of its property. To determine this figure, appraisers estimate the price that property would bring if placed on the market. This market value is then converted to an assessed value by using a predetermined ratio, which, in the majority of states, is now set at 100 percent.

> Should property taxes be abandoned as a way to fund education?

Use of property taxes as a source of revenue for public schools is a procedure that is widely criticized (Burrup, Brimley, & Garfield, 1999). One criticism is that homeowners shoulder a disproportionate amount of the cost for funding education. Lack of uniformity in schedules for conducting property assessments creates other inequities. While some communities reassess property every year, others reassess every third or fourth year. If the economy fluctuates greatly from year to year, some taxpayers pay more or less than their fair share of taxes because their property assessments remain the same over a long period of time. Furthermore, when localities within a state use different rates of assessment, a rich municipality having a low assessment rate may raise as much revenue or more than a property-poor area having a higher tax rate. Differences in revenue for education lead ultimately to educational inequalities.

Another concern about property taxes is that valuation procedures are inexact. When determining the market value of a house in a subdivision, assessors typically set a value based on what the house might sell for if it were on the market. This value is influenced in large part by recent sales of similar homes in the neighborhood. Such a strategy is difficult to use, however, in neighborhoods where houses vary greatly in age, size, and style. Assessment methods are also problematic in high-priced housing areas where real estate activity is minimal. When there are no benchmarks, some properties may be undervalued, thus masking the wealth of some districts (Cohn & Geske, 1990).

Property taxes, of course, are used to meet needs other than educational ones. This may be more problematic in some areas than in others, particularly in cities, where tax-exempt property (e.g., public buildings, churches, government property, and parks) can be a large part of the total. Cities, particularly those in high-crime areas, incur many expenses that suburbs either do not face or face on a more modest scale:

> Police expenditures are higher in crime-ridden cities than in most suburban towns. Fire department costs are also higher where dilapidated housing, often with substandard wiring, and arson-for-profit are familiar problems. Public health expenditures are also higher where poor people cannot pay for private hospitals. All of these expenditures compete with those for public schools. So the districts that face the toughest challenges are also likely to be those that have the fewest funds to meet their children's needs. (Kozol, 1991, p. 56)

Cities often provide services funded from property taxes to people who work in the city but live in the suburbs. When it snows, for example, the city must plow the streets so people can get to work. Workers who live in the suburbs benefit from the plowing of city streets, even though they do not support this activity with their own property taxes. While snow removal benefits many people, it uses up money that could be earmarked for inner-city schools.

Rural districts, too, may face considerable financial hardship because of higher per pupil costs (Appalachia Educational Laboratory, 1990; Verstegen, 1990). When a rural district must build a new school, for example, relatively few taxpayers share the cost of a building. To ease such inequities and the burden on property taxes, the trend in recent years has been to replace declining local revenues with state aid.

▶ Local School Boards

Local school boards are bodies of elected or appointed public servants with responsibility to provide advice and consent on the operation of public schools. Local school boards are one of the most common, visible examples of democracy in action. Because overseeing education is a power reserved to the states, local school boards are agents of the states.

The local school board is generally recognized as the policy-making body for public schools. For the most part, this means that school board members have the right to establish schools, to select the board's executive officer (the local superintendent of schools), to set rules to ensure the smooth running of schools, and to raise and spend tax dollars as they see fit.

Like all representatives in a republic, school board members try to interpret the public will and to exercise their own personal judgment in governing the public education system. On some issues, board members and the people they represent are out of tune with one another.

A recent poll conducted for the National School Boards Foundation revealed some points of tension between school boards and their constituents:

While more than two-thirds of school board members gave their local schools an A or B for overall performance, less than half the general public did so. Three-quarters of school board members said their teachers and principals were doing a good or excellent job. Among the public at large, just 43 percent rated principals that highly, while 54 percent gave teachers similar votes of confidence. More than 8 in 10 board members said their districts were doing a good or excellent job in combating violence and drugs, but only a third of the public agreed." (Hendrie, 1999a, p. 9)

When there is tension between school board members and their constituents, dissatisfaction can result in curtailment of power and, in some instances, complete disbandment of school boards. In Chicago, advocacy groups lobbied successfully for the establishment of popularly elected councils of citizens, parents, and teachers at each school who were given the right to select principals and to decide how discretionary funds should be spent. In New Jersey, dissatisfaction with the quality of education in the public schools resulted in state takeover of the Jersey City and Paterson districts.

▶ School District Budgets

The best way to understand local finance of public schools is to study a school district budget. Most school boards control the staffing of local schools and types of programs that are offered to students, so the budget represents a concrete statement of local values. To separate rhetoric about educational values from reality, look at the budget.

School districts develop long-term financial plans that represent predictions about the future. District employees craft a new budget for each fiscal year—a 12-month period covered by the annual budget, often corresponding with the state's fiscal year (e.g., July 1–June 30). Once an annual budget is adopted by local officials or approved by the voters, it guides school administrators' actions.

Who makes these plans, and how are they set in place? In most localities the budget-adoption process involves a number of steps (U.S. Department of Education, 1989):

1. District administrators led by the superintendent analyze needs and costs, set policies for the coming year, and plan an initial draft of the budget.

2. District administrators discuss this draft with the school board in one or more meetings.

3. District administrators publish a proposed budget, which is made available for public study.

4. The school board holds one or more public hearings, at which they receive comments from citizens on the proposed budget.

5. The school board adopts an official budget based on the proposed budget but with amendments it deems necessary.

6. In some districts the school board vote is the final decision. In other districts the budget must then be approved by elected officials or by voter referendum.

7. A budget that has received final approval takes effect in the district.

Using Technology

Understanding Education Finance

Technology is making it easier for schools and school districts to manage various aspects of education finance. From district-managed staff payrolls to revenue from cafeteria lunches, computerized record keeping increases the accuracy of financial accounting and reduces the amount of time required to administer such procedures. But software programs like spreadsheets and databases are not only valuable tools when trying to organize and monitor finances; use of these programs can also help teachers to understand how finances affect what happens in schools.

Clare Kilbane, a university instructor, uses a spreadsheet program to help students studying to become teachers to understand how school finance affects school quality, teachers' work environments, and classroom instruction. Using Excel, students organize budget information from a local public school district to see how money is spent. The annual district expenditures are broken down into different subcategories, including personnel salaries and benefits, student transportation, school operating expenses, instructional services, and human resources. A graphing feature in the software program allows students to create a visual representation of the total expenditures of the district. The resulting pie chart is used to determine whether the stated values of the school district correspond with spending priorities and to seek answers to difficult questions about budget cuts in tight financial times.

Students also use a spreadsheet to examine the components of two individual school budgets. Comparing the budgets of a private school and public school, they are better able to understand how school budgets affect the quality of school environments and teachers' classroom instruction. Line item allocations for textbooks, copy paper, lab equipment, computers, and other instructional supplies demonstrate ways that education programs in low-income areas and in some private schools compare to those in wealthier school districts. Information about number of personnel and average teacher salaries shows clearly the difference between compensation in school settings.

Students who use Kilbane's activity construct their own understandings of how school budgets and finance affect the lives of teachers and their students. Parenthetically, they also learn how to use spreadsheets for instructional purposes.

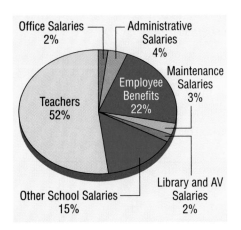

Public School Budget		
Fiscal Year July 1, 2000– July 1, 2001		
Salaries & Benefits	**Current Year**	
Administrative Salaries	$	62,431.00
Office Salaries	$	28,007.00
Teachers	$	917,004.00
Other School Salaries	$	264,327.00
Library and AV Salaries	$	32,268.00
Maintenance Salaries	$	51,149.00
Employee Benefits	$	389,311.00
	$	1,744,497.00
Other School Costs		
Office Supply & Expense	$	1,000.00
In-Service Fees, Meetings, Conventions	$	2,790.00
Media Supply and Expense	$	3,500.00
Student Transportation Costs	$	2,400.00	*Field trip transportation costs
New Equipment	$	600.00
Science Supplies	$	1,400.00
New Equipment–Science	$	600.00
Educational Supplies	$	16,700.00
Other Educational Supplies	$	2,400.00

In other areas where site-based management is the norm, people are experimenting with **school-based budgeting** or **site-based budgeting,** in which responsibility for allocating resources is fixed at the building level rather than at the level of central administration. Teachers, parents, and principals often are involved in making decisions about how money is spent on hiring staff, professional development for staff, and goods and services. To be effective, school-based budgeting requires that the principal and other staff members know the students well enough to match available resources to students' needs (Burrup et al., 1999).

Advocates of school-based budgeting think that efficiency will improve if decision-making authority is given to those who actually do the work (Levin, 1987). Budgeting, then, becomes responsive to the needs of those most immediately affected. School-based budgeting can also make it easier to hold people accountable for spending and for the results they produce, thereby helping to control costs.

People craft and adopt school budgets through processes of negotiation. Many people (taxpayers, teachers, administrators, and special-interest groups) have a stake in where the money to run schools comes from and where it goes. A school budget, then, represents a balance of values. It is a political document formed from compromise, one that should provide adequately for the educational needs of the school district's constituents.

Whose values and needs should a school budget represent?

When establishing their budgets, school officials sometimes justify only the increase that exceeds the previous year's request. In such instances, what the school district is spending is usually accepted as necessary. On occasion, however, schools must make a case for their entire appropriation request each year. Pyhrr (1973) calls this process **zero-base budgeting.** Although zero-base budgeting has not gained widespread use, many districts analyze and report past and budgeted expenditures on a program basis (Hentschke et al., 1986).

Once a budget is set, plans for spending can change for a number of reasons: enrollment figures may be higher or lower than projected, unexpected weather may affect utility bills, and unforeseen events (e.g., flooding of a school gymnasium during a heavy rain) can require emergency maintenance. School administrators sometimes have the authority to transfer dollars from one line item to another to take care of unforeseen needs. In other districts, administrators must first consult with the school board before making changes. When changes in budget are made, however, federal regulations prohibit the removal of money from federal grants designed to benefit specific groups of students or programs.

Most school districts use line-item budgets to explain their financial plans. These budgets include a beginning balance for the year, estimates of revenue by source, planned expenditures, and a projected balance at the end of the year. Sources of revenue may include moneys from federal, state, county or parish, and city government; income from local taxes or from the sale of bonds; payments of fees for meals and for use of sports facilities; and private donations expected during the year. Income often is earmarked for use with specific groups of students (e.g., students with disabilities) or special programs (e.g., library support or school nurse).

Planned expenditures represent the most detailed portion of a school budget. As illustrated in Table 6.2, a school system can incur a number of educational expenditures. In some states, regulations dictate which categories are to be listed in a budget; in other states, local districts can create line items as they see fit. Generally, districts

▌**TABLE 6.2**
Hypothetical Actual and Proposed School Budget Items

	Fiscal Year 2001 proposed budget	Fiscal Year 2000 actual budget
Instruction		
Salaries	$3,270,630	$3,014,110
Benefits	256,520	256,520
Purchased services	64,130	64,130
Supplies	128,260	192,390
Property	384,780	384,780
Total Instruction	4,104,320	3,911,930
Support		
Salaries	1,410,860	1,154,340
Benefits	128,260	128,260
Purchased services	192,390	64,130
Supplies	128,260	192,390
Property	192,390	128,260
Total support	2,052,160	1,667,380
Noninstructional services		
Salaries	64,130	128,260
Benefits	6,413	12,826
Supplies	19,239	38,478
Property	51,304	64,130
Total noninstructional	141,086	243,694
Facilities		
Salaries	192,390	153,912
Benefits	19,239	15,391
Supplies	256,520	153,912
Property	173,151	61,565
Total facilities	641,300	384,780
Total expenditures	$6,938,866	$6,207,784

Note. Adapted from *Making Sense of School Budgets* (p. 15) by U.S. Department of Education, 1989, Washington, DC: Office of Educational Research and Improvement.

categorize expenses in terms of "functions" (broad categories of purposes, such as instruction and support, to be served by spending) and "objects" (specific things to be paid for, such as personnel salaries and benefits).

Salaries and benefits for both instructional and noninstructional staff constitute the largest portion of any school budget. For this reason, and because they are visible in the budget, salaries often become sources of irritation in communities across the country.

 ## How Are Governance and Funding Related to Educational Success?

A nation needs strong public schools to ensure that children's futures will not be determined by their parents' wealth and influence. Public education uses public funds to provide access to education for all children. Funds relate directly to educational opportunities; that is, funds can buy equipment, materials, experiences, and the like. But the relationship between funds and learning as measured by standardized achievement tests resists simple explanation.

Eric Hanushek (1989) reviewed 38 research studies and concluded that there is no strong or systematic relationship between school expenditures and student performance. In contrast, Larry Hedges and his colleagues (Hedges, Laine, & Greenvals, 1994) reviewed the same studies using a different method, and they found that expenditures are positively related to school outcomes. Who is right? According to Michael Sadowski (1995), given their methods, both Hanusheck and Hodges are right. The question people should ask is, What do schools do with the money they have? When schools use money to reduce class size so that educators can change how they offer instruction, there are remarkable gains in student learning. In contrast, when decision makers simply reduce class size and hope for the best, while failing to adopt new curricula and methods that meet the needs of students, more money has little effect on student performance.

Unfortunately, more money is not always available. The press of debt and economic recession began to turn the education reforms of the 1980s into the retrenchment of the early 1990s. Even while tax revolt flourished at the state and federal levels in the 1980s, states experimented with a wide range of programs and organizational mechanisms to maximize the effect of the dollars spent on public education. These included site-based management, high-tech classrooms, career ladders for teachers, professional development schools, better and longer educational programs for teachers, innovative curricula, restructured school calendars, and new testing vehicles for both students and teachers.

But innovations can be expensive; and the political courage to stick with them long enough to obtain a fair test is difficult to come by. Many policymakers got nervous in the 1990s, as states faced budget problems. They wanted "hard evidence"—test scores—that demonstrated the money spent on education was not being wasted. If the public were to pay for education, but teachers and students did not produce, then why spend more money on people and systems that were failing? Or so went the public argument.

David Berliner and Bruce Biddle (1995) and others (Bracey, 1991; Carson, Huelskamp, & Woodall, 1991; Verstegen & McGuire, 1991) take issue with the position that schools are failing and that funding for education is not connected to success. They argue that people interpret test results incorrectly to suggest that student performance and educational quality are declining; moreover, they argue that test results fail to represent accomplishments or aptitudes.

How might this community support its schools? Why might this community have less money for education than other nearby communities or municipalities? Would funding relate to how well the students do? What measures might work to reduce disparities in funding from one school district to the next?

The highest spending states have, on average, eleven times higher percentages of their students taking the SAT than the lowest spending states. . . . Working under difficult conditions, with a greater at-risk population, the highest spending states posted a loss of up to ten items or about 7 percent of the raw score points on the SAT, but they posted an 1150 percent increase in the percent of high school seniors thinking about going to college. (Berliner, 1992, pp. 22–23)

Berliner and others contend that educational decline, if it exists, is educationally insignificant. Schools need funds to create opportunities for all students to learn and to succeed at a variety of challenges, and the schools are doing remarkably well, given their mission.

▶ The Issue of Funding Equity

People make trade-offs when education dollars are limited. Sometimes the trade-offs exist as choices between educational equity and educational excellence. Some people believe that efforts to promote educational excellence will swamp the poor, the weak, and the minority-group students, while others argue that money spent on equalization could be put to better use capitalizing on the strengths of outstanding students. Allan Odden (1984) contends that such choices are ill conceived, for there are more connections between excellence and equity than many realize:

On economic grounds, the simultaneous pursuit of excellence and equity is mandatory. If our national strategy for maintaining a competitive edge in the international market is to increase the per capita productivity of the U.S. work force, then all U.S. workers must have better-developed skills than their counterparts in other countries. In other words, it will not be enough for the top 10% of workers in the U.S. to outperform the top 10% of the workers in Japan. . . . The bottom 90% of U.S. workers will have to be better too. . . . (p. 316)

According to James Ward (1992), although the various state funding formulas are intended to provide some standardization of educational quality among communities, formulas are unable to do so for at least two reasons: (1) the level of funding from the state is seldom high enough to level the playing field, and (2) localities have discretion in setting local property tax rates for schools. James Ward contends that in many instances, "politics of privilege and exclusion" (p. 246) get in the way of changing inequalities. More affluent school districts can support high levels of education without much assistance from the state. They are reluctant to shoulder increased state taxes to benefit other districts in the state. Nor do such communities want to give up control of their ability to levy taxes, for to do so potentially reduces their ability to maintain a position of privilege (Ward, 1992, p. 246).

As we noted earlier, there are wide variations in expenditures and revenues among school districts across the country and within states. In some instances the differences between revenues available for education in school districts are so wide that the courts have been involved in settling issues of **funding equity**.

Some schools and school districts have much more money to spend on their students, staff, and facilities than do others. The disparities are so great in some parts of the country that those districts poor in property have had to

How can funding equity be achieved?

tax themselves three or four times as heavily as rich districts to raise revenue for their schools. On the average, however, the high-poverty districts receive much more of their revenue from state and federal sources than do low-poverty districts.

The big-ticket items—school buildings and building repair—can be incredible financial burdens, especially in urban districts where the infrastructure suffers from years of neglect. The upturn in the economy in the late 1990s has enabled many districts to undertake sorely needed construction projects.

> From June through August, Detroit officials are spending some $80 million to repair and restore the most ailing of the district's 263 schools. Workers are replacing roofs and windows, repairing restrooms, and painting and polishing hallways and classrooms. In addition to finishing three new schools and four multistory additions in Chicago this summer—part of a major capital-improvement plan there—officials are improving access for the disabled, modernizing high school science labs, refurbishing restrooms, painting classrooms, hallways, and cafeterias, and generally sprucing up schools. On any given day in New York City this summer, some 20,000 construction workers will be spread out over about 600 school construction or renovation projects. The New York City School Construction Authority is working on adding 16,000 new seats to the 1.1 million-student system by September, part of a five-year, $11 billion capital-improvement plan. (White, 1999, p. 1)

These figures sound astonishingly high until one considers the estimated needs for building construction. Cost estimates for constructing new schools are listed in Table 6.3.

Capital construction can be a heavy burden for any school district but especially for the poor district. When considering building a new school, district leaders must engage in an expensive and time-consuming process. This process begins with determining the need for a new building by examining other options, such as remodeling existing facilities, searching for other existing facilities, rescheduling instruction, or consolidating with other districts. A decision to build means determining location by

TABLE 6.3
How Much Does a New School Cost?

	Elementary	Middle	High
Cost/square foot	$114.29	$118.81	$123.08
Cost/student	$13,322	$16,325	$18,750
Square feet/student	105	143	167
Average no. pupils	600	788	950
Average size (sq. ft.)	71,000	113,750	160,000
No. classrooms	30	40	57
Total cost	$7,645,303	$12,690,637	$20,734,816

Source: From Agron, J. (1999). Official education construction study. Table 11. How much does a new school cost? Available online (http://www.asumag.com/ctable1199.htm). Reprinted permission of *American School & University Magazine,* May 1999.

studying possible sites for a new building and acquiring land through negotiation or through condemnation (sometimes referred to as eminent domain).

In the 1960s people thought that inequities in school finance might be corrected by appealing to the courts. The landmark 1971 case of *Serrano* v. *Priest* was the first case filed in state court (California) that declared unconstitutional a state public school finance system based on taxable wealth. By focusing on the link between educational expenditures and district property wealth, this case stimulated challenges to school district spending inequalities across the nation. William Thro (1990) refers to these cases as the "first wave" of public school finance reform litigation.

In *San Antonio Independent School District* v. *Rodriguez* (1973), a federal district court had ruled that the San Antonio, Texas, school finance system violated the equal protection clause of the Fourteenth Amendment because large disparities in school district expenditures existed across the state. The United States Supreme Court, however, ruled that education was not a fundamental right under the Constitution and was therefore not protected by the Fourteenth Amendment, a major setback for those who sought to reform school finance.

Thro (1990) noted three landmark school finance reform cases in 1989—cases in Montana, Kentucky, and Texas—in which school finance systems were invalidated in the same year because school funding disparities had grown dramatically. In part, these cases assert that a right to education is fundamental or of extreme importance under state constitutions. These cases may eventually serve as the basis for a revolution in school finance reform.

▶ The Issue of School Choice

Some people believe that **school choice,** the right of parents to choose the schools their children attend instead of being limited to schools in their immediate geographical area, should be common practice. Proponents of school choice argue that competition among schools would improve the public school system. Opponents contend that school choice would destroy the concept of a public education in which children of diverse backgrounds live and learn together. As illustrated in Figure 6.7, in 1998, 50 percent of public school parents who responded to a national survey indicated that they opposed allowing students and parents to choose a private school to attend at public expense (Rose & Gallup, 1998).

In a survey of parents who had "chosen" their child's school, the U.S. Department of Education (1996) reported that all parents selected a school primarily for academic reasons. For parents who chose a public school, the second-most important reason was convenience; among those who selected a private school, the second-most important reason was religious preferences.

People oppose concepts of "choice" for many reasons. They believe that if citizens can choose where to send their children to school, schools will become racially segregated, or, at the very least, the gains made by private schools will exacerbate class distinctions. A central purpose of public education is to prepare people to participate in our democracy, and school choice will allow people to opt out, thus subverting this goal. Also, children who most need their parents' involvement in order to make wise choices will be least likely to get it.

FIGURE 6.7
Public School Parents' Thoughts About School Choice   How might these percentages compare with the attitudes in your community? What is your opinion? What circumstances might make you want to change your opinion?

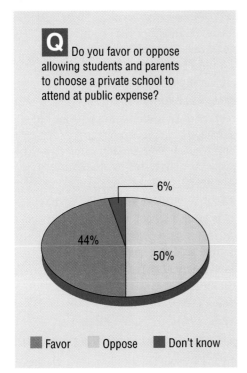

Note. From "The 30th Annual Phi Delta Kappa/Gallup Poll of the Public's Attitudes Toward the Public Schools," by L. C. Rose & A. M. Gallup, 1998, *Phi Delta Kappan,* 80(1), p. 43.

Opponents fear that in a deregulated market, one largely devoid of governmental control, for-profit schools will flourish largely unmonitored, reaping large profits at the expense of consumers (Putka, 1991). Others point out that the money available for most "choice" programs is far below costs; only wealthy individuals who can pay the extra will benefit.

Various plans are at issue in allowing parents to choose schools for their children, including providing for choices among public schools and between public and private schools. Chubb and Moe (1990) have outlined what they believe are the essential attributes for any choice plan. These attributes include defining "public school," monitoring the enactment of choice programs, informing parents about rights and responsibilities, having the freedom to expel students, and eliminating teacher tenure thus allowing for teacher dismissal. These last two factors, student expulsion and teacher dismissal, would enable schools to improve themselves by subtracting negative influences.

Historically, paying for private schooling has been a private matter. If parents wanted their children to be educated in a certain manner, to be inculcated with particular values, and to associate with certain other children, they paid for these privi-

Issues in School Reform

Top Ten School Choice Questions

School choice has been one of the most controversial approaches to reforming public education. Harvard professor Paul E. Peterson has identified what he believes are the "top ten" questions usually raised by critics of choice programs. We list the questions below. We also provide abbreviated versions of his answers, which were derived from his own and others' studies of choice programs around the country. Do not rely on these short answers, but read his full article.

1. What is meant by choice?
   ■ Charter schools
   ■ Tax deductions
   ■ Tax credits
   ■ Vouchers

2. Who supports school choice?
   ■ More Republicans than Democrats
   ■ Minorities living in central cities
   ■ De facto support from central-city public school teachers and members of Congress who send their children to private schools

3. Who takes advantage of the opportunity to choose schools?
   ■ Educationally disadvantaged
   ■ Economically disadvantaged
   ■ Hispanics and African Americans
   ■ Parents with education levels that are relatively high
   ■ People who are more socially connected than is sometimes suggested by studies of the urban poor
   ■ People with religious affiliations

4. When choosing a school, what do parents consider?
   ■ Improved academic quality (85%)
   ■ Greater safety (79%)
   ■ Location (59%)
   ■ Religion (37%)
   ■ Friends (19%)

5. Are parents more satisfied with choice schools?
   "Most participating families love their choice schools."

6. Do private schools retain their students or do they exclude and expel the disadvantaged?

> **Are school choice and tax credit plans the answer to funding inequities?**

leges out of their own pockets. Those who could afford to send their children to private schools continued to pay their taxes, which in turn supported public schools.

While some private schools have developed and maintained their reputations by appealing to the moneyed elite of society, others have attracted people from across the socioeconomic spectrum. The largest alternative school system in the United States, the Catholic schools, has high- and low-income students. Catholic schools may offer tuition endowments to encourage students from families with low incomes to attend. Other private schools, both religious and nonsectarian, may do so as well. Many parents over the years, even those who could least afford to do so, have been willing to sacrifice economically to send their children to private schools.

In the 1980s and 1990s, the debate about public support for private elementary and secondary schools has taken on renewed vigor, focusing in part on several mechanisms for enacting choice plans. The idea of using **vouchers,** or scrip, to purchase

"School mobility is less when parents are given a choice of school."

7. Do children learn more in choice schools?

"Unfortunately, most school choice experiments conducted thus far have not conformed to a classic randomized experiment. . . . Still, test score results from these programs are mainly positive."

8. Do private schools foster balkanization and intolerance?

"Despite the scare tactics and the rhetorical flourishes, choice critics have failed to offer much evidence that school choice will balkanize America."

9. What happens to the children left behind?

"[C]hoice critics often assume that the more able children from more privileged families will be the first to leave public schools, that children learn mainly from their peers, and that public schools will not respond to the challenge posed by choice. None of these assumptions is well supported by available data."

10. Is school choice constitutional?

Challenges are working their way through the state courts. They typically involve the First Amendment to the Constitution, which forbids any "law respecting an establishment of religion, or prohibiting the free exercise thereof." The Supreme Court tends to interpret this amendment by applying a three-pronged test to a choice law: (1) it must have a secular purpose, (2) it must not favor one religion over another or religion over nonreligion, and (3) it must not create an excessive entanglement between government and religion.

Discussion Questions   Where do you stand on the issue of school choice? How do your thoughts about choice compare to those of your colleagues? How are your views similar to or different from those of people in local school divisions?

Note: Peterson, P. E. (1999). Top ten questions asked about school choice. In D. Ravitch (Ed.), *Brookings papers on education policy 1999*. Washington, DC: Brookings Institution Press, 371–418.

public education was first offered by economist Milton Friedman in 1955. He argued that local government ought to create vouchers that provided parents with a sum of money in the form of scrip to pay for each of their children's education. Parents should be free to spend this money at any school they chose, as long as it met minimum governmental standards. "Such schools would be conducted under a variety of auspices: by private enterprises operated for profit, non-profit institutions established by private endowment, religious bodies, and some even by governmental units" (Friedman, 1955, p. 144).

A **tuition tax credit** allows a taxpayer to subtract educational costs from taxes owed. A **tuition tax deduction** allows a taxpayer to subtract educational costs from taxable income before computing taxes. Both credits and deductions resemble vouchers in that they are designed to give parents at least part of the money they spend on private schooling for their children. The appeal is obvious to parents who do so. Opponents contend that credits and deductions may encourage people to flee

Voices

On Privatization

Milton Friedman, a senior research fellow at the Hoover Institution, won the Nobel Prize for Economics in 1976. Excerpts from a paper he wrote on vouchers appear below.

Our elementary and secondary educational system needs to be radically reconstructed. That need arises in the first instance from the defects of our current system. But it has been greatly reinforced by some of the consequences of the technological and political revolutions of the past few decades. Those revolutions promise a major increase in world output, but they also threaten advanced countries with serious social conflict arising from a widening gap between the incomes of the highly skilled (cognitive elite) and the unskilled.

A radical reconstruction of the educational system has the potential of staving off social conflict while at the same time strengthening the growth in living standards made possible by the new technology and the increasingly global market. In my view, such a radical reconstruction can be achieved only by privatizing a major segment of the educational system—i.e., by enabling a private, for-profit industry to develop that will provide a wide variety of learning opportunities and offer effective competition to public schools. Such a reconstruction cannot come about overnight. It inevitably must be gradual.

The most feasible way to bring about a gradual yet substantial transfer from government to private enterprise is to enact in each state a voucher system that enables parents to choose freely the schools their children attend. I first proposed such a voucher system 40 years ago.

Many attempts have been made in the years since to adopt educational vouchers. With minor excep-

tions, no one has succeeded in getting a voucher system adopted, thanks primarily to the political power of the school establishment, more recently reinforced by the National Education Association and the American Federation of Teachers, together the strongest political lobbying body in the United States. . . .

Finally, as in every other area in which there has been extensive privatization, the privatization of schooling would produce a new, highly active and profitable private industry that would provide a real opportunity for many talented people who are currently deterred from entering the teaching profession by the dreadful state of so many of our schools.

This is not a federal issue. Schooling is and should remain primarily a local responsibility. Support for free choice of schools has been growing rapidly and cannot be held back indefinitely by the vested interests of the unions and educational bureaucracy. I sense that we are on the verge of a breakthrough in one state or another, which will then sweep like a wildfire through the rest of the country as it demonstrates its effectiveness. . . .

CRITICAL THINKING

How might you evaluate the success or failure of a voucher program designed to allow parents to send their children to any school of their choice, public or private? Try to synthesize what you have heard and read about vouchers into two crisp paragraphs, one for and one against.

Source: From Public schools: Make them private, by M. Friedman, 1995. Washington, DC: CATO Institute. You can get Friedman's complete manuscript online at **http://www.cato.org/**.

the public schools, leaving the public system for low-income families, who cannot afford to pay up front for the cost of education and wait to receive a deduction later.

Tuition tax credits, deductions, and vouchers must meet with state approval. Even if states adopt new funding mechanisms, they cannot contravene federal law in the process. For example, if a plan were enacted that denied persons their civil rights, the plan would be ruled unconstitutional by federal courts. If vouchers, deductions, and tuition tax credits continue to be part of the public debate on public and private education in the future, court challenges will surely ensue. Issues of the separation of church and state and of the possible establishment of a religion by allowing public funds to be spent on private schools will continue to make private schools a focus of public interest.

The most sweeping move toward the use of public funds for private schooling occurred in Florida in the spring of 1999 (Cooper & Pressley, 1999). The Florida legislature became the first in the nation to establish a statewide program of government vouchers to support students to leave what have been deemed failing public schools. Vouchers can be worth up to $4,000 to offset private school costs. The intent is to give students opportunities to enroll in private institutions, including religious schools, at public expense. But civil rights groups sued to stop Florida's school voucher plan one day after the program took effect. They fear the new law will harm existing public schools.

▶ The Issue of Site-Based Management

Increasingly, principals lead site-based or school-based management teams composed of teachers and parents—and sometimes students. The basic idea is that administrators, teachers, parents, and students best understand the school culture and have the biggest stake in outcomes and so must share responsibility for student learning and school decision making (Darling-Hammond & McLaughlin, 1995).

Reforms to institute site-based management have occurred most often in places where the schools are perceived as being in crisis. Chicago, Illinois; Dade County, Florida; and Rochester, New York, have tried to move educational decision making and control away from the superintendent's office and toward local schools.

Who could argue with the idea of involving in the formation of educational policies those affected by such policies? The nation's historical commitment to the common school has meant that public education should serve all the people by providing a central knowledge base and by involving people so as to form a community. Site-based, or school-based, management, then, has historical precedent and seems to make sense. But what appears reasonable in theory does not necessarily translate smoothly into practice. Moreover, other reform efforts, such as those aimed at professionalizing education, tend to conflict with participatory decision making.

Attempts to use site-based management to change the basic structure of schools have raised serious questions: Do people agree on the purposes and methods of restructuring schools? Are people clear about redefinitions of the roles of teachers, administrators, professional organizations, parents, and policy makers? Who will make what decisions? How will people decide if the changes are improvements over old ways of operating?

Like other educational innovations, site-based management must overcome a number of obstacles to succeed. One of the more prominent obstacles is inertia. When people are used to behaving in certain ways, it is difficult to change these patterns. Carol Weiss (1995) notes, for instance, that teachers often resist decisions that require them to make drastic changes in the way they teach. Moreover, Weiss argues, teachers

Why might teachers not want to participate in site-based management?

Benchmarks

Examples of Federal Government Involvement in Education, 1785–1997

1785–1890	Northwest Ordinances of 1785 and 1787 and the Morrill Acts of 1862 and 1890 stimulate the establishment of schools through land grants. The Department of Education Act authorizes the establishment of the U.S. Department of Education.
1887–1917	The Hatch Act and the Smith–Lever Agricultural Extension Act establish land-grant college extension services across the nation to improve agriculture and industry.
1917–1935	The Smith–Hughes Act marks first federal financial aid to public schools below college level. Funds are earmarked for vocational programs, including homemaking. Other acts fund vocational rehabilitation for veterans of foreign wars.
1935–1944	Congressional acts to cope with the Great Depression fund programs that benefit education, such as the Agricultural Adjustment Act (authorizes using funds for school lunch programs), Civilian Conservation Corps, National Youth Administration, Federal Emergency Relief Administration, Public Works Administration, and Federal Surplus Commodities Corporation.
1944–1964	The G. I. Bill of Rights assists the education of World War II veterans. Benefits are extended to Korean War veterans in 1952 and to Vietnam War veterans in 1966. Federal Funding increases for educational programs that contribute to national defense and economic security, such as the Vocational Education Act of 1963, the Manpower Development and Training Act, and the International Education Act. One of the most important is the National Defense Education Act of 1958, which extends financial aid to college students and funds research centers, foreign language study, and experimentation with media.
1964–1975	Congress funds equal educational opportunity programs and services as part of the Civil Rights Movement and War on Poverty. The Civil Rights Act of 1964 authorizes the Commissioner of Education to support educational institutions with problems caused by desegregation.

must be convinced that reform is permanent and real and that they can exert some power over events if they are to take collective action.

When Chicago began restructuring 32 schools in 1987 to encourage site-based management, teachers and administrators worried about blurring the distinctions between management and labor. And both were concerned about how to involve parents in decision making at the school level. In 1989 the Illinois legislature created

The Elementary and Secondary Education Act of 1965 creates grants for schools serving low-income children, strengthening state agencies, and enhancing educational research and development.

Federal funding also increases for higher education, adult education, elementary and secondary education, special education, and teacher education.

In 1966 the federal government funds a number of research, training and development, and dissemination agencies: the Office of Educational Research and Improvement (OERI), the Educational Resources Information Center (ERIC), Research and Development Centers, and Regional Education Laboratories.

In 1970 the Environmental Education Act and the Drug Abuse Act provide for the development of curriculum for schools.

The Education Amendments of 1974 establish a National Center for Education Statistics to track vital educational information.

1975–1997   The 1975 Education for All Handicapped Children Act (Public Law 94-142) provides a free and appropriate education for children with special needs.

The Indian Self-Determination and Education Assistance Act of 1975 gives Native Americans more say in the establishment and conduct of their education programs and services.

The Department of Education Organization Act (1979) creates a Cabinet-level department replacing the former U.S. Office of Education.

Presidential Education Summits with the nation's governors are held in 1989 and 1996.

The Goals 2000: Educate America Act establishes a new federal partnership through a system of grants to states and local communities to reform the nation's education system.

The Appropriations Bill of 1996 continues support for direct student loans, Americorps, and Goals 2000.

The Taxpayer Relief Act of 1997 enacts the Hope Scholarship and Life-Long Learning Tax Credit provisions into law.

local councils in each of Chicago's 589 schools. These councils were composed of six parents, two other community members, two school employees, and a principal. The councils were to govern the schools, managing the budget and hiring and firing of employees without regard to seniority. These restructured working relationships provided for shared authority and accountability among the stakeholders, but many became mired in the politics of the past and failed to deliver change.

Most recently, local school councils and central administration have fought over how principals are to be selected to run these urban schools. The principals are central characters in school reform. How they are hired and fired is an important issue. Central administration is citing abuses at some schools and wants to restrict the councils' authority. "The goal is to get the local school councils to make their decisions based on the quality of the principal as an academic leader and a manager," said Paul G. Vallas, the district's chief executive officer. "I think you can have a balance between local control and central-office control" (Hendrie, 1999b, p. 8). As Hendrie notes, some council leaders and their allies perceive this move as a power grab. Vallas would also subject council members to criminal-background checks for the first time, prohibit felons from serving on councils (never before done), and give central administrators the power to fire principals and remove councils in schools they thought were financially mismanaged.

Kentucky began site-based management in 1990 when its supreme court declared the public education system unconstitutional. The move was a bold attempt to reform a system rife with cronyism and nepotism by restructuring the way schools are funded, governed, and operated (Lindle, 1996). School-Based Decision Making (SBDM) councils were established, with authority to make decisions in 16 areas of school operations and policy, including hiring principals, selecting curriculum, assigning staff and students, setting the school schedule, formulating discipline policy, overseeing extracurricular programs, and aligning educational practice with state standards. All schools in Kentucky were required to be engaged in local decision making by July 1996.

At Cane Run Elementary in Louisville, Kentucky, parents help run the school. Through the school's PTA and site-based decision-making team, parents work with staff to set policy, raise funds, administer programs, hire new staff, and organize events (U.S. Department of Education, 1997).

About 80 percent of Cane Run's 450 students are eligible for the federal free or reduced-price lunches. The school's student population is 50 percent African American and 50 percent European American. The school has a Family Resource Center that serves families and members of the community. A coordinator links families with mental health counseling, medical services, social services, and other community resources. Staff and volunteers provide a variety of services, from collecting and distributing clothes and food to accompanying families to social service agencies.

The Family Resource Center sponsors an after-school program. Parent volunteers and staff tutor children in academic subjects, teach computer skills and karate classes, and offer other activities. In addition, Cane Run uses Title I funds for a preschool program for 3- and 4-year-olds.

Regardless of where site-based management occurs, lack of resources can be a serious impediment to effectiveness. With too little money, no matter how it is shared, even schools managed on site can remain dismal places to be. The schools most in need of a new lease on educational life may be least able to afford it. The ultimate intent of restructuring schools to encourage site-based management is to create environments that motivate and teach students to be successful. What Jonathan Kozol observed a decade ago may still be true: "In many cities, what is termed 'restructuring' struck me as very little more than moving around the same old furniture within the house of poverty" (Kozol, 1991, p. 4).

SUMMARY

What are school governance and education finance?

1. The power to establish and operate public schools is located in the Tenth Amendment to the U.S. Constitution: "The powers not delegated to the United States by the Constitution; nor prohibited by it to the States, are reserved to the States respectively, or to the people."

2. Governance is the web of laws, rules, regulations, and procedures by which schools must operate. Education finance is concerned with raising, allocating, spending, and accounting for funds for schools.

3. Educational leaders—school board members, superintendents, principals, department heads, and teachers—shape educational policy and practice. Corporate values also shape education. Increasing computerization, the proliferation of services offered by businesses, a growing global economy, and decentralization of responsibility necessitate that workers possess a variety of basic and work-related skills.

4. Public schools are financed primarily by localities, states, and the federal government. Contemporary leaders communicate their values in the ways they allocate resources for public education. The challenge for policy makers has been to strike some balance in public education among four dominant ideals: equality, adequacy, efficiency, and liberty.

5. There are many political and economic influences on public education. Special-interest groups influence the conduct of public education by lobbying for particular actions and by educating the public. Business–school partnerships can influence school values and the content and delivery of instruction. The public media both reflect and shape public opinion on education.

How does the federal government influence education?

6. The federal agenda for education is shaped by the "Iron Triangle"—the combination of education interests in the executive branch, congressional committees, and interest groups outside government.

7. Federal funding initiatives take many forms: major grant programs, aid to localities, and categorical grants for funding of education programs designed for particular groups and specific purposes. Sometimes several education programs are grouped together as a block grant to localities.

8. The National Goals are one of the most recent visible ways the federal government tries to influence education at state and local levels.

How is education financed and controlled by the states?

9. State funds for public education emanate from a variety of sources such as sales tax, income tax, lotteries, and various state aid plans. The expenditure of public monies for education is guided and monitored by various oversight groups—state boards of education, state education departments, and the governors themselves.

10. Because of the power reserved to states in the Constitution, state governments influence public education through taxation and distribution of revenues. They also set standards for buildings, personnel, and programs.

11. All states have state standards boards or commissions to regulate professional practice in education.

12. Many states support cooperative educational programs across local districts through intermediate educational units, or organizations that fall between state and local authorities.

How are schools financed and managed at the local level?

13. Communities vary in character and thus exert different types of influences on the schools and on those who run them.

14. In the majority of states, the local portion of schools' funds is derived almost exclusively from local property taxes.

15. Because overseeing education is a power reserved to the states, local school boards are agents of the states. The vast majority of local board members are elected to represent their constituents. These board members exercise power most explicitly through the decisions they make about the budget.

How are governance and funding related to educational success?

16. Funds relate directly to educational opportunities for students.

17. Some argue there is no strong or systematic relationship between school expenditures and student performance. Others contend that expenditures are positively related to school outcomes. The important issue is how schools use their funds to offer instruction for students.

18. Disagreements about school funding are often couched in terms of two positions: excellence and equity. Others argue that society cannot afford to have one without the other.

19. The idea of allowing parents to choose schools for their children has been a hot topic in the 1980s and 1990s. Advocates argue that competition for students will strengthen schools. Opponents worry that choice will destroy the concept of the common school.

20. Site-based management is an attempt to involve people at the school level more directly in making decisions. Reforms to institute site-based or school-based management occur most often in places where the schools are perceived as being in crisis.

TERMS AND CONCEPTS

block grant   218
categorical grant   218
chief state school officer   227
Council of Chief State School
    Officers   228
district power equalization   225
Education Consolidation and
    Improvement Act (ECIA)   218
flat grant   224
foundation program   224
full state funding   225
funding equity   236
intermediate educational unit
    (IEU)   228
local property taxes   229
local school board   230
National Center for Education Statistics
    (NCES)   217
National Congress of Parents and
    Teachers (PTA)   212

National Governors' Association
    (NGA)   228
per pupil expenditures   224
personal property   229
progressive taxation   222
real property   229
regressive taxation   222
school-based budgeting   233
school choice   238
school governance   208
site-based budgeting   233
special-interest group   212
state board of education   226
state education department   227
state standards board   227
tuition tax credit   241
tuition tax deduction   241
voucher   240
zero-base budgeting   233

REFLECTIVE PRACTICE

Harley Schumacher was recently elected for the first time to a local school board of a major metropolitan area. His community is economically depressed, and he feels honor bound to keep the promise on which he was elected, that is, to protect the quality of the schools regardless of the cost—within reason. Assuming a minimal level of public support, a new state law allows local school boards to augment the money they receive from local property taxes with local sales tax, local income tax, or local lottery. The tax measures would be add-ons to existing state sales and income taxes; that is, the state would administer the programs and return a percentage of money to the locality. Schumacher believes that he must work to encourage his colleagues on the board to put a proposal for revenue enhancement before the public at the coming election. Two of the board members have expressed their concerns about trying to raise taxes as they face reelection. Schumacher cannot decide on a course of action.

Issues, Problems, Dilemmas, Opportunities

What problems and opportunities do Schumacher and his colleagues face?

Perceive and Value

If you were a retired person in the school district, why might you oppose any attempt to raise additional funds for schools? If you supported any revenue enhancement measure, which one might it be, and why? If you were a beginning teacher, what might your preference be? Why?

Know and Act

List the general types of revenue-raising options the school board might consider putting before the voters, and discuss the pros and cons of each. If Schumacher and his colleagues want to seek public support for their proposal, where might they turn?

Evaluate

Assume that the school board and the voters decided to adopt a local lottery to raise revenue. What factors might you use to judge whether the lottery is successful? Would people's feelings about the morality of gambling enter into your assessment? Why or why not?

 ## ONLINE ACTIVITY

Visit the web site of the Education Commission of the States (ECS). The ECS is a national nonprofit organization that offers assistance to state leaders to improve their educational systems. The site contains information about a variety of current issues, policies, and programs. You will find information on school-to-work policies in various states, school governance, and school finance. See, for instance, how states compare in their approaches to establishing charter schools.

Visit the web site for the American Association of School Administrators. See "Current Issues and Ideas" for advice that the organization offers school administrators. Note in particular "Career Advice for School Leaders!" You will find "Do's and Don'ts" of handling school crises. You will also get advice on how to search for a superintendent's job—and how to survive if you land one.

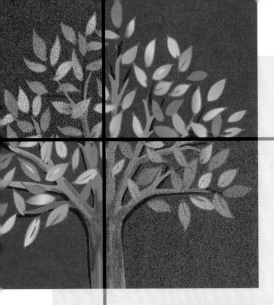

7

Social Issues and the Schools

We are social beings. Some of our problems have the capacity to impinge on every aspect of our lives and, to a great extent, on the lives of those around us. Some problems are shaped in part by who we are—our health, our attitudes, our beliefs, our dispositions. Other problems depend largely on the conditions in which we live—our home, our neighborhood, our community. Many problems are defined by the interplay of intrinsic and extrinsic forces.

When we can prevent problems instead of trying to solve them, our energies seem well spent. Schools exist in this reality.

Young people experience many problems, both acute and chronic. Adults express increasing concern about the variety of pressures on today's youth. In this chapter we explore some of society's most urgent problems and consider how they affect children. We describe some of the ways schools have stretched beyond their traditional missions to involve parents, social agencies, and private enterprise to counter threats to young people's lives.

PROFESSIONAL PRACTICE QUESTIONS

- What are society's expectations for schools?
- How does poverty place students at risk of school failure?
- How can schools intervene to help students at risk?
- How can schools get parents involved in their children's education?
- How can schools reduce risks that threaten children's health and safety?

 ## What Are Society's Expectations for Schools?

For many children, the years they spend in school are the best years of their lives. They interact with people who care about them and for them—people who help children to learn and to feel good about themselves in the process, and who nurture young people's hopes for the future.

In recent years, however, some have argued that schools have taken on too much. Educators' efforts to counter children's social problems while also trying to meet their academic needs have created for schools what amounts to a blueprint for failure. Students attending school from the beginning of kindergarten to the completion of 12th grade will have spent only about 9 percent of their total time on earth in the classroom (Finn, 1991). Nonetheless, expectations for schools usually exceed the "9 percent limit," as people look increasingly to schools to solve some of society's most difficult problems (see Figure 7.1).

When young people have problems, society has problems. Typically, different agencies address the plight of children. Because the public supports schools with tax dollars, people expect educators to help students succeed, regardless of circumstances.

The growing number of **at-risk students** who have "little or no hope of success in school or productivity in later life" (Barr & Parrett, 1995, p. 2) present unusually difficult challenges to educators. Generally, these students

- have failed one or more grades;
- have high rates of absenteeism and tardiness;
- speak a language other than English;
- are enrolled in special education classes; and/or

FIGURE 7.1
Some Social Issues that Affect Schools Think of other items that could be added to this figure. What effects might they have on teaching and learning?

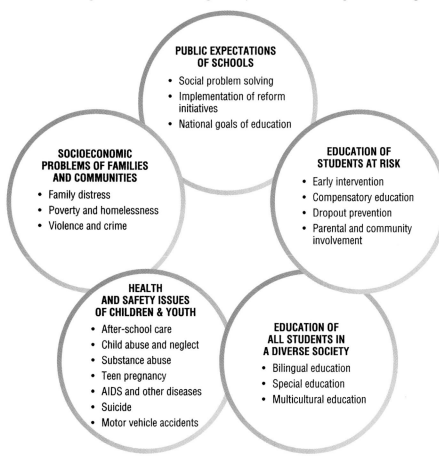

are affected adversely by health-threatening factors, such as poverty, disease, abuse and neglect, substance abuse, teenage pregnancy, and physical violence. (Waxman, 1992; Smith, Polloway, Patton, & Dowdy, 1995)

As these definitions suggest, students can be at risk for failure academically and socially due to intrinsic factors—motivation, ability, disability, and the like—or extrinsic factors—home and community environments.

Eventually, many students at risk drop out of school altogether. Communities across the country have structured schools and have advanced a variety of political initiatives to meet the challenge presented by school dropouts. School choice plans try to stimulate educators to make schools places where students want to stay. In some states, redrawing school attendance zones ("redistricting") is an attempt to prevent some schools from becoming way stations where students pause briefly before assuming a permanent spot on the streets. Efforts to equalize funding for public schools are also undertaken to help schools in poverty areas reduce their dropout and failure rates.

What is society's responsibility to students at risk?

How Does Poverty Place Students at Risk of School Failure?

Children—one in four of whom go to bed hungry, sick, or cold—are the people hardest hit by poverty (Sidel, 1996). Some 14 million children are victims of poverty; that is, they live in families that earn less than the 1997 federal poverty level of $16,400 (U.S. Bureau of the Census, 1998a, 1998b). This figure is calculated as three times the cost of a diet that would meet minimum nutritional requirements for a family of two adults and two children. The figure does not include other living expenses, such as housing, transportation, and health care.

A basic link exists between poverty and learning. Low-income communities mean underfunded school districts and poorer schools on virtually every index of quality. High-poverty schools exhibit diminished capacities to create educational opportunities for students. As Figure 7.2 indicates, when child poverty and poor school funding are combined, effects on student performance can be substantial (Payne & Biddle, 1999).

Generally, the sooner a child starts school, the longer she stays, and the greater the financial reward later in life. The social conundrum inherent in this statement is that more affluent parents send their children to school sooner and encourage them to stay in school longer.

Most affluent families are two-parent families. As Table 7.1 indicates, the percentage of children living in two-parent households varies greatly across racial groups. Many single parents cope admirably, but the demands they must face can be formidable. Moreover, those parents most in need of child care can least likely afford it. In 1993, for example, families below poverty level spent 18 percent of their weekly income on child care, while more affluent families spent only 7 percent of their weekly income on child care (U.S. Bureau of the Census, 1996). Sandra Balli (1996) relies on the results of a major study of migrant children to argue that socioeconomic status need not limit one's aspirations or level of achievement. When children have at least one parent who communicates high expectations for academic achievement, the children stay in school and perform well.

> **How might children in low-income neighborhoods get better schools?**

Conditions of life for many low-income families, many of whom are ethnic minorities, can be depressing. But these conditions are by no means characteristic for all minority-group members. It has been estimated that 50 percent of African American families and 53 percent of Hispanic American families generate incomes of $25,000 or more (U.S. Bureau of the Census, 1998d). Many more European American than minority group children in the United States live in poverty. All racial and ethnic groups are represented in all socioeconomic strata. Within minority groups, however, percentages of children from low-income families are higher.

Poverty leaves indelible marks on people. Some become trapped and embittered by it; others are resilient and motivated to defeat the circumstances in which they find themselves. In *Amazing Grace: The Lives of Children*, Jonathan Kozol (1995) describes vividly what he learned in New York City about being poor.

> The following day, I visit a soup kitchen where more than 200 people, about two thirds of whom are children, come to eat four times a week. The mothers of the

FIGURE 7.2
Average Number of Mathematics Problems Answered Correctly

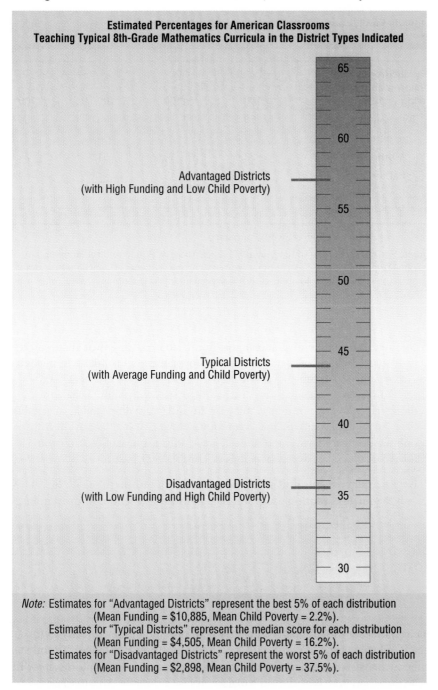

Estimated Percentages for American Classrooms
Teaching Typical 8th-Grade Mathematics Curricula in the District Types Indicated

Advantaged Districts
(with High Funding and Low Child Poverty)

Typical Districts
(with Average Funding and Child Poverty)

Disadvantaged Districts
(with Low Funding and High Child Poverty)

Note: Estimates for "Advantaged Districts" represent the best 5% of each distribution
(Mean Funding = $10,885, Mean Child Poverty = 2.2%).
Estimates for "Typical Districts" represent the median score for each distribution
(Mean Funding = $4,505, Mean Child Poverty = 16.2%).
Estimates for "Disadvantaged Districts" represent the worst 5% of each distribution
(Mean Funding = $2,898, Mean Child Poverty = 37.5%).

Note. Adapted by permission of the American Educational Research Association from "Poor
School Funding, Child Poverty, and Mathematics Achievement," August–September, 1999,
by K. J. Payne and B. J. Biddle. *Educational Researcher, 28*(6), p. 11. Copyright 1999.

▎ **TABLE 7.1**
Household Data, 1998, Families with Children

How do family configurations vary across racial groups?				
	All Races	**White**	**Black**	***Hispanic**
Family groups with children under 18 years living with:	100	100	100	100
Two parents	68.0	74.0	36.0	64.0
One parent	27.0	23.0	55.0	31.0
Mother only	23.0	18.0	51.0	27.0
Father only	4.0	5.0	4.0	4.0
Other relatives or nonrelatives	4.0	3.0	9.0	5.0

*Persons of Hispanic origin may be of any race.

Source: From U.S. Bureau of the Census (1998c). Table 4. Household relationship and presence of parents for persons under 18 years, by age, sex, race, and Hispanic origin: March 1998, p. 26. Available online: http://www.census.gov/population/www/soldemo/ms-1a.html

children seem competitive, and almost frantic, to make sure their children get their share. A child I meet, a five-year-old boy named Emmanuel, tells me he's "in kiddie garden." His mother says he hasn't started yet, "He starts next year."

"You have to remember," says one of the priests with whom I share my thoughts about these meetings, "that for this little boy whom you have met, his life is just as important to him, as your life is to you. No matter how insufficient or how shabby it may seem to some, it is the only one he has"—an obvious statement that upsets me deeply nonetheless. (Kozol, 1995, p. 70)

Explore the concept of at-risk students by going to the web site for the North Central Regional Educational Laboratory's Pathways to School Improvement.

How Can Schools Intervene to Help Students at Risk?

One response to the problem of poverty is to provide money directly to those who need it via some type of cash grant, tax credit, housing assistance, or food stamps. While such assistance can be aimed at families with dependent children, it is difficult to measure how much of the aid touches children directly. Another approach provides assistance indirectly through social or educational services.

Investing in education can foil the effects of poverty. For example, the U.S. Department of Education (1995a) notes that the availability of free or low-cost education can lead to a reduction in welfare or public assistance programs. People with

More people live in rural areas than in inner cities. Most of the poor in the nation are white, and most live in families with a wage earner.

more education rely less on welfare and public assistance than do people with less education. In 1992 high school dropouts were three times more likely to receive income from Aid to Families with Dependent Children (AFDC) or public assistance than were high school graduates who did not go to college (17 versus 6 percent).

Problems facing the young are interrelated. Many people advocate comprehensive integrated approaches to reduce the exposure of young people to high-risk settings. Such settings are characterized by poverty, substance abuse, parental neglect, and violence in many forms. According to the Panel on High Risk Youth (1993), "Reducing the risks generated by these settings is virtually a precondition for achieving widespread reductions in health- and life-compromising behavior by adolescents" (p. 235).

Often, helping students cope with serious social and personal problems falls to school counselors. In general, counselors try to enhance self-esteem, but many also foster career awareness and offer support groups for children affected by divorce or who need work on study skills or social skills. High school counselors, in particular, focus on college or job counseling (Gladding, 1996).

With funding through the National Defense Education Act (NDEA), counseling services moved beyond high schools to include elementary schools in 1964. This action acknowledged the importance of helping children succeed early in their educational careers, with "helping" defined increasingly in terms of preventing problems. Counselors typically perform the following functions:

1. provide inservice training and consultation for teachers in preventing serious student problems;

2. work with parents to promote understanding of child development;

3. identify and refer children with developmental deficiencies or disabilities to others who can offer assistance; and

4. help older children make connections between school and work (Gladding, 1996, p. 389).

Using Technology

Motivating At-Risk Students

 Many people believe that technology will offer new options for students at risk of failure. The web site sponsored by the North Central Regional Educational Laboratory (NCREL) has a particular interest in addressing these possibilities. In a sound file on the site, Professor Elliot Soloway of the University of Michigan discusses how new expectations for learning will change the look of classrooms and the ways that teachers teach and students learn. Instead of having children read a chapter and answer questions at the end, Soloway explains that students will take computers to bodies of water, collect and model data, and visualize their results. He and others argue that involvement is the key to learning for all children, but especially for at-risk children.

Judy Green, a former sixth-grade teacher at Abbott Middle School in Waukegan, Illinois, and currently a K–8 technology and learning coordinator at the Lincoln Center in Waukegan, discusses improvements in student motivation when students use technology tools for learning. Instead of dealing with students who resist learning, passively and actively, Green says that the technology "pulls them in."

What do successful teachers do to ensure that technology is being used to help all students succeed? Among other things, they:

- Seek opportunities to collaborate with other teachers and work in teams to design and implement technology-supported projects.
- Become comfortable learning about technology along with students, and repeatedly model higher-order thinking skills so that students can see positive ways to approach new learning challenges.
- Promote cooperative learning in the classroom so that students work together and learn from each other.
- Design activities so that every student has something to offer. Students who previously have had little success in learning activities may feel very successful in a technology-rich classroom that emphasizes meaningful, authentic tasks.
- Develop procedures and checklists to help monitor and document each student's progress.

For many children, these and other school-based interventions make a profound difference in their lives. Patsy Walker, a high school dropout with a family history of abuse and neglect, incest, prostitution, drugs, and incarceration, abandoned a lucrative career as a prostitute, got a job cleaning a store, completed high school, and at age 26 entered graduate school. Patsy Walker described the secret to her amazing turnaround:

> My secret was not so much liking everything we did in school . . . but I did like some of it, and a few of the teachers. Not a lot of them, but you don't need a lot of them. Fact is you only need a few. . . . 'Cause what they both were telling me was, okay, you want to make a secret out of it, that's cool. But we could either forget you and let you fall away like everybody else, or we can, like I say, plant a little seed in you.

That's what both of them did, too, plant little seeds. Took a long, long time for those seeds to grow into something, but they did. . . . What they were telling me, see, was you can play the game, but we want to tell you we'll support you playing a whole 'nother game if there ever comes a time you feel you might be ready. Maybe they were daring me. And the school, see, it stunk like it always stunk. Nothing changed. Wasn't like the day after they spoke with me everything was perfect again, and my mother was all good and my father flew out of prison. No magic. But the seeds. Two funny old ladies, two funny little seeds. So school didn't fail out like everything else. (Garbarino, Dubrow, Kostelny, & Pardo, 1992, 132–133)

Patsy Walker's experience points to the most important interventions that schools provide—caring teachers. These teachers collaborate with parents and other professionals to create conditions necessary for student success.

▶ Providing Early Intervention Programs

Early intervention provides desperately needed opportunities for student success in preschool and elementary school. The National Commission on Children recommended that "all children, from the prenatal period through the first years of life, [should] receive the care and support they need to enter school ready to learn—namely, good health care, nurturing environments, and experiences that enhance their development" (National Commission on Children, 1991, p. 187). The Commission's reasoning emanated from a set of facts that make evident the old adage: An ounce of prevention is worth a pound of cure.

There are many testaments to the value of early intervention. The Perry Preschool Program, begun in 1962 by David P. Weikart in Ypsilanti, Michigan, provided a preschool and home-visit program to 3- and 4-year-olds from economically disadvantaged families. The program captured public attention with results from a follow-up study of its students and a matched control group. A 22-year follow-up study done on 95 percent of the participants revealed that, in comparison to the control group, Perry Preschool graduates had a smaller chance of being arrested, earned approximately $2,000 more per month, were more likely to own a home, and had a higher rate of graduating from secondary schools.

The High/Scope curriculum used with Perry Preschool students exists today in all 50 states for children in preschools and the early elementary grades. Besides emphasizing connections between home and school, the curriculum stretches children to meet specific academic goals:

Based on Piaget's theories of cognition, the Perry Preschool curriculum seeks to increase academic achievement and reduce students' chances of being placed in special education classes by teaching them to become active learners. The teacher acts as a facilitator of knowledge who sets up the classroom in such a way that the student is provided with the opportunity to learn math, science, reading, art, music, social studies, and movement every day. Students choose what they wish to study or work with, but the teacher is expected to be available to answer any questions and clarify any misunderstandings that students may have. (Slavin & Fashola, 1998, p. 56)

What are the goals of early intervention programs? How effective is early intervention and in what ways?

Many programs help disadvantaged students enter school ready to learn. Data suggest, however, that lack of funding prevents such programs from reaching large numbers of children. In 1996, for example, only 26 percent of 3-year-old children from families earning $10,000 or less were enrolled in preschool, compared with 55 percent from families earning $50,000 or more (U.S. Department of Education, 1998).

Project Head Start, a federally subsidized preschool program for 3- and 4-year-old children from low-income families, tries to provide a curriculum fitted to students as well as deliver health, nutrition, and social services to their families. Head Start promotes parental involvement. Parents participate in program governance and parenting classes, and they also have opportunities to do volunteer work or to be hired as staff members in Head Start classrooms.

Amendments to the Head Start Act have required the Department of Health and Human Services to review, and to revise as needed, performance standards of local Head Start programs and to specify the minimum levels of accomplishment that must be achieved. Amendments also authorized funding for an initiative called Early Head Start, a program designed to provide comprehensive child development and family support services to low-income families with children younger than 3 and to pregnant women.

New standards for Head Start program operations help people chart progress in the following areas:

- Enhancing children's healthy growth and development
- Strengthening families as the primary nurturers of their children
- Providing children with educational, health, and nutritional services
- Linking children and families to needed community services
- Ensuring well-managed programs that involve parents in decision making

A field test conducted in the spring of 1997 concluded that (1) Head Start 4-year-olds perform above the levels expected for children from low-income families who have not attended center-based programs, and (2) almost 90 percent of parents are very satisfied with Head Start's program services, safety, and promotion of child growth and development (U.S. Department of Health and Human Services, 1997).

Some states and localities experiment with ways to supplement federal support for nutrition and health care to reach larger numbers of children. The state of Minnesota, for example, funded a pilot program that provides a free breakfast to all students, regardless of family income level. The intent is to help all children be nutritionally ready for learning and to avoid stigmatizing anyone as being low-income. Before the program began at Hans Christian Andersen Open Elementary

School in Minneapolis, only 42 percent of the 760 students who qualified for federally subsidized breakfasts ate them; now 99 percent participate in the free-breakfast program. Whole classrooms of children go to the lunchroom for breakfast instead of the typical practice of designating individuals who qualify for breakfast (Teri Edwards, personal communication, September 27, 1999).

The younger the child, the more important it is not only to support good nutrition but to encourage opportunities for human interaction—time to talk and listen. Researchers and practitioners agree that early intervention programs, coupled with parent action at home, can make a big difference in children's language skills.

> Children take their first critical steps toward learning to read and write very early in life. Long before they can exhibit reading and writing production skills, they begin to acquire some basic understandings of the concepts about literacy and its functions. Children learn to use symbols, combining their oral language, pictures, print, and play into a coherent mixed medium and creating and communicating meanings in a variety of ways. . . . Consequently reading and writing acquisition is conceptualized better as a developmental continuum than as an all-or-nothing phenomenon. (National Association for the Education of Young Children, 1998)

Researchers have concluded that if children are to enjoy the benefits of parental involvement in their education, professionals must be willing to try different teaching strategies congruent with family beliefs. Parents must be willing to participate in activities that enhance their role as educators of their own children. For example, when researchers studied 19 African American teenage mothers from low-income backgrounds whose children attended an early intervention program, they found considerable variation in the mothers' beliefs about learning and literacy. The mothers valued educational achievement, security and independence in learning, respect from and for teachers, and information that might help them help their children learn. While they shared such mainstream educational ideals, they also held very specific beliefs about how their children should be educated—beliefs that included the value of working with teachers.

> I'm a friend of Tameika's (her daughter) teacher. She know I'm a single parent and I'm young. She's working with me a lot, but I think that's helping me a lot, the way she teaches me how to. See, I don't have any patience, but she teaches me to "just sit down, and you do your homework while Tameika does her homework," and when you're finished you can recite words with her. And we worked it out, the way she told me to do. (Neuman, Hagedorn, Celano, & Daly, 1995, p. 820)

▶ Keeping Students in School

Educators cannot help young people avoid and face problems if they are not in school. Trying to determine who is not there and why, however, are major challenges for school officials. Some districts count as dropouts students who have died, left school to get married, taken a job, gone to vocational school, entered the armed forces, gone to jail, or been expelled. The federal government uses three measures to calculate dropouts: (1) an event rate, or the proportion of students who drop out in a single academic

How can we prevent students from dropping out of school?

year; (2) a cohort rate, or the number of students who drop out of a specific grade level; and (3) a status rate, or the percentage of people in a certain age range who are not enrolled in school.

Regardless of the confusion, educators are expected to keep students in school at least through twelfth grade, ultimately turning out literate, responsible, productive citizens. **Holding power,** or the ability to keep students in school until they receive a high school diploma or an equivalency certificate, has increased over the decades as youth have spent more and more years in school. Despite this positive trend, by 1997 about 4.6 percent of students between the ages of 15 and 24 failed to complete high school (U.S. Department of Education, 1999a).

▶ Providing Compensatory Education

A number of programs provide children from low-income families with additional educational opportunities beyond those offered in a school's standard program. These **compensatory education programs** attempt to compensate for important educational factors (e.g., teachers, curricula, time, and materials) that may be missing in young people's lives.

Title I.   Title I, one of the largest federally funded education programs for at-risk elementary and secondary students, began in 1965 as the first bill of President Lyndon Johnson's War on Poverty program. At one time referred to as Chapter 1, by 1999 the program provided approximately $100 billion to meet the educational needs of low-income, low-achieving students. For the most part, academic assistance to Title I students occurs in **pull-out programs;** that is, Title I children most often receive their services outside the regular classroom. Instruction usually lasts for 30 to 35 minutes and focuses mainly on reading, mathematics, and language arts. Some 60 percent of the teaching of Title I children is done by aides or paraprofessionals. About 41 percent of Title I aides spent half or more of their time working with children without a teacher present (U.S. Department of Education, 1999b).

> **How might you decide if a Title I program were successful?**

While the majority of the nation's school districts receive federal monies for such assistance, there is not enough money to fund instruction for all children who qualify for extra help under Title I guidelines. Early reports from the first large-scale longitudinal study of Title I indicated that almost one half of the elementary schools that served fewer than 10 percent low-income children participated in Title I, while one third of the low-performing children in high-poverty schools went unserved (U.S. Department of Education, 1993). A more recent study suggests, however, that conditions have changed. Between 1993–1994 and 1997–1998, the proportion of highest-poverty schools receiving Title I funds increased from 79 to 95 percent (U.S. Department of Education, 1999c). Federal dollars are reaching those who need them most.

Upward Bound.   Many older children also need all the help they can get. Upward Bound, a federally funded program, is structured to improve the academic performance and motivational levels of low-income high school students. Participants in the program receive tutoring, counseling, and basic skills instruction. The program encourages students to finish high school and win acceptance into college. At the end of the school year, students participate in a summer residential program focusing on the improvement of study skills and content knowledge. Established in the 1960s, Upward Bound programs continue to operate across the nation. Although Upward Bound programs are lauded by participants, these programs do not appear to affect the total number of high school credits earned, graduation rates, academic achievement, or college enrollment (U.S. Department of Education, 1999d).

▶ Providing Before- and After-School Programs

During the past 20 years, women have entered the work force in increasing numbers, with the sharpest increases being among married mothers of young children. By 1998, 63 percent of mothers with children younger than age 6 and 71 percent of women with children under 18 were employed or looking for employment (U.S. Bureau of the Census, 1998e). With more women in the workforce and thus unable to stay at home with their children, traditional roles and responsibilities of parents have changed. In some two-parent families, fathers assume child care responsibilities. In others, parents change their work schedules so that one or the other can be home with their children during the day. Working mothers of children between the ages of 5 and 14 most often hire someone to provide care in the child's home. Although most children under age 4 have some type of supervised care, nonrelatives typically provide this care outside the child's home. About 3.9 million children in the United States live with their grandparents (U.S. Bureau of the Census, 1997).

According to the Children's Defense Fund (1999), nearly 5 million school-age children go home each day to empty houses. Approximately 35 percent of 12-year-olds, for example, care for themselves on a regular basis while their parents are working. These **latchkey children,** many of whom live in low-income communities, may be without adult supervision for several hours each day when juvenile crime is at its peak. Several studies indicate that children who attend quality after-school programs demonstrate better behavior in school, make better grades, and spend less time watching television than those who are not enrolled in such programs. Moreover, children who participate in extracurricular activities are 49 percent less likely to use drugs and 37 percent less likely to become teen parents than young people who do not participate in such activities (Children's Defense Fund, 1999). Schools respond to needs for child care in many different ways. Buses transport children to school in the morning and home in the afternoon. Some children arrive early enough each day to receive a hot breakfast they would not get otherwise. For too many, national school breakfast or lunch programs offer the best meal of the day.

After-school programs across the country offer opportunities for supervised study, play, and participation in sports. In addition, bands and choruses and clubs of every kind meet in the late afternoons, evenings, and weekends. These offerings—billed as services, extracurricular activities, or enrichment programs—also amount to forms of child care. Unless schools provide transportation and equipment for such events, however, low-income children in particular are unlikely to benefit from after-school programs.

> **How might we meet the needs of latchkey children?**

Issues in School Reform

Peer Pressure

Some people argue that the major force in young people's lives is other young people. If so, the thinking goes, to reform schools young people need to support and emulate one another, provided, of course, that they model desirable behavior.

Hugh Price, president of the National Urban League, believes that African Americans can achieve far greater academic success than many people assume. He has acted on this belief by creating the Campaign for African American Achievement. The centerpiece of the effort is the Thurgood Marshall Achievers' Society. Designed as a national honor society for African American students from grades 3 through 11, it has inducted more than 5,000 youngsters since the spring of 1998. Price is telling everyone who will listen that "achievement matters:"

> "Vastly more of our kids can achieve at vastly higher levels," Mr. Price said, and ensuring that they do so is more urgently needed now than ever before.
>
> For one thing, he noted, the robust economy is opening new doors for blacks, but employers are demanding higher skill

levels than in the past. Competition in college admissions, meanwhile, is growing keener for all students, and affirmative action programs are under attack.

Public schools are adopting tougher academic standards at a time when the achievement gap between black and Hispanic students on the one hand and white and Asian American youngsters on the other has begun to widen again after nearly two decades of progress.

The achievement campaign, a collaboration between the Urban League and the Washington-based Congress of National Black Churches, is backed by a $25 million, five-year grant from the Indianapolis-based Lilly Endowment, as well as funding from other private sources. African American fraternities, sororities, and professional groups have also been enlisted in the cause.

One of the campaign's primary goals is to spur black parents and community members to demand more from their schools, and to press harder for changes that will translate into better student performance.

The campaign has mounted an advertising drive in black-owned newspapers around the country. And it has designated September as "achievement month," a period in which black clergy members are being urged

▶ Offering Incentives and Disincentives

Other tactics used to encourage academic success include **incentive programs.** These programs offer outside incentives—rewards for good attendance and good grades. For example, the HOPE Scholarship Program (Helping Outstanding Pupils Educationally), which is supported entirely by a state lottery, offers a free college education to all Georgia high school students with a B average who choose to attend a public college, university, or technical institute in the state. The HOPE Scholarship includes tuition, HOPE-approved mandatory fees, and a book allowance of up to $100 per quarter. Full-time enrollment in school is not required. Since its inception in 1993, the program has awarded scholarships totaling nearly $658 million to more than 358,000 Georgia residents (Georgia Student Finance Commission, 1999).

to preach about the importance of scholastic accomplishment.

Equally important is a drive to heighten expectations and support for students themselves. That's where the achievers' society comes in.

By serving as an "achievement gang," the society is designed to counteract the low esteem in which academically oriented blacks, especially boys, are often held by their peers.

"The whole point of the campaign is to fly into the eye of that storm: negative peer pressure," Mr. Price explained. "This has been a largely missing component of the education reform agenda."

To qualify for entry, students must achieve at least a B average. Modeled on a smaller-scale effort pioneered in Florida, the society has chapters run by Urban League affiliates in 35 cities around the country. Society members will be eligible for a pool of up to $10 million in college scholarships that the campaign plans to underwrite with the Lilly Endowment grant.

Each new member receives a custom-designed jacket garnished with the society's logo—a conscious echo of the gang-related garb and insignia that are fixtures in many inner-city neighborhoods. A highlight of the induction ceremony is the moment when the adults who are sponsoring the new members help them into their shiny black jackets.

The jackets were generally a hit with the 31 Jacksonville youngsters honored here in the June 26 ceremony, one of nearly three dozen such occasions taking place this year around the country. "It's cool," declared Victoria Hayes, 12, who said she would wear the jacket to the magnet school for gifted students she plans to enter in the fall.

Her father, Victor Hayes, was more interested in the less tangible benefits the society can offer his daughter, a straight-A student entering 6th grade. "Sometimes you can be the leader of your class and think you don't have to try too hard," he said. "She saw some competition out there today."

Discussion Questions Why did you admire some of your peers as you grew up? What qualities did they possess that made them special in your eyes? Can you think of ways that schools might encourage positive peer pressure without being heavy-handed and without placing too much responsibility on the young people who are good models?

Note. From "Urban League Effort Targets Young Achievers" by C. Hendrie, Education Week, *18*(42), pp. 6–7. Reprinted with permission from *Education Week*.

On September 16, 1999, Microsoft Corporation Chairman Bill Gates pledged to spend $1 billion over 20 years on college scholarships for thousands of academically talented but financially needy minority students. This represents the largest financial pledge ever made in education.

Gates said he believes too many minority students are not entering or finishing college, particularly in areas of medicine, science, and technology, because they cannot afford to do so. In his public announcement, Gates said, "This country is in an incredible time period. The advances in technology are really quite breathtaking. Is everybody getting a chance to benefit? The answer is really no" (Sanchez, 1999, A01).

In some instances punitive measures have been employed to reduce the dropout rate. Arkansas penalizes students with excessive unexcused absences and school dropouts by revoking their driver's licenses. From August 1997 through September

What are some tactics schools use to encourage academic achievement?

1999, the state revoked 1,609 licenses for these reasons (S. Sims, personal communication, October 1, 1999).

Since the establishment of Wisconsin's Learnfare program in 1987 and passage of the Family Support Act of 1988, several states have imposed penalties on parents who do not demonstrate "responsible" behaviors, including the completion of school. While the Family Support Act makes welfare payments

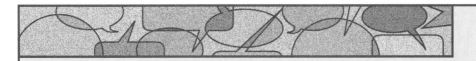

Voices

On Teachers' Perceptions of Students' Needs

Ms. Lori DeLuca began her career teaching low-achieving fifth graders who lived in poverty. She describes how another teacher's perceptions of students' needs influenced her own teaching behavior. What seemed to work for her colleague, however, did not work for Lori. She learned to rely on her own perceptions of her students' needs.

When I think of how my view of literacy has changed, I recall my first job with low-achieving fifth graders. As a new teacher, I was assigned to a very regimented veteran teacher who dismissed the ideas I learned in college and stressed instead phonics and vocabulary memorization. I was eager to follow her advice because she had a reputation in the district of getting results and improving her students' reading skills. I began my first year with phonics workbooks and vocabulary notebooks. I also imitated her strict discipline, even though I found it burdensome. By the end of the first month, I was overwhelmed, frustrated, and exhausted. It required so much energy to get my bored students to complete all their wearying work. I did read aloud chapter books and poems, but only after all the work was finished. When I expressed my discontent to the teacher I had emulated, she said, "These kids are tough. You've got to be tough to light a fire under them."

After a month of this, I decided that I was just not equal to the task of working with these students. I expressed my insecurities to my mother, a teacher in a different district. She encouraged me to have fun, to

"do my own thing." She said I needed to trust my own ability and discover my own style of teaching. I decided to take her advice to heart, and my classroom changed dramatically. I abandoned many of our workbook pages and encouraged children to respond to literature in a variety of creative ways. We read chapter books, researched topics of interest at the library, discussed books by favorite authors, used the computer to compose original stories, read picture books to the first graders, and went on a poetry picnic. To my surprise, when doing these supposedly less structured activities, I had fewer discipline problems and more on-task behavior from my students. I enjoyed my job so much more, and my students enjoyed reading much more. My sober, teacher-controlled classroom took on more of a workshop atmosphere as students grew motivated to become literate.

CRITICAL THINKING

Compare Lori DeLuca's beginning philosophy with her reformed outlook. How do her expectations for students differ? If you were asked to explain what Ms. DeLuca might have meant by the phrase *teacher-controlled classroom*, what would you say? Why is "having fun," as Ms. DeLuca describes it, as important for teachers as it is for students?

Source: Teachers' stories: From personal narrative to professional insight, pp. 157–158, by M. R. Jalongo, J. P. Isenberg, & G. Gerbracht, 1995. San Francisco: Jossey-Bass Publishers.

contingent on parents' efforts to obtain education, training, and employment necessary for breaking the cycle of welfare dependency, Learnfare-type programs such as those in Wisconsin, Maryland, and Oregon cut welfare payments to parents whose children are truant or drop out of school. An evaluation of Wisconsin's Learnfare program indicated that the program had no effects on students' school completion, on the amount of assistance received by Learnfare families, or on the length of time families received assistance, except in Milwaukee, where, on average, families received assistance for slightly shorter periods of time (Wisconsin Legislative Audit Bureau, 1997).

Ohio's Learning, Earning, and Parenting (LEAP) program blends penalties and rewards to encourage teenage parents to stay in school and graduate. Students can earn a $62 monthly bonus in their welfare benefits for staying in school, an additional $62 for completing a grade level, and a $200 bonus for graduating. LEAP deducts $62 from students' monthly benefits for poor attendance (Simich, personal communication, October 1, 1996). LEAP's short-term goals of inducing dropouts to return to high school or to enroll in General Educational Development programs and promoting better attendance among those already enrolled in school were accomplished. Longer-term goals of increasing the rate of high school graduation, GED attainment, and employment, and reducing welfare payments were only partly successful (U.S. Department of Health and Human Services, 1998).

▶ Providing Mentors and Tutors

Some programs try to enhance the academic success and self-esteem of at-risk students through the use of tutors and **mentoring programs**—efforts to model appropriate behavior in one-on-one situations. For example, in 1994 Donovan Steiner and Judy Mullet of Eastern Mennonite University (EMU) and Carole Groves of Bridgewater College began a tutoring program for high school students who had been suspended from school. For two days a week, these students go to EMU, where they work with college students specializing in education and counseling. They engage in a range of activities designed to enhance their academic success and to improve their attitudes toward learning. For suspended students, the program amounts to a kind of "homeschooling" at a university (Mullet & Groves, 1996).

Big Brothers Big Sisters of America (BBBSA) is the oldest mentoring organization serving youth in the nation. The BBBSA has provided one-to-one mentoring relationships between adult volunteers and children at risk since 1904. The organization currently serves more than 100,000 children and youth in 500-plus agencies throughout the United States.

The Big Brothers Big Sisters of America Diversity Initiatives promote racial, cultural, and ethnic diversity among the staff and volunteers of BBBSA and the children the organization serves. These initiatives are meant to respond to the growing number of minority children who need mentors. All the initiatives encourage people to search for solutions to problems facing minority youth, to become more aware of the influence of diversity in society, and to maximize volunteer involvement. For example, the purpose of Friends of Big Brothers Big Sisters initiative is to increase the involvement of people of color to serve as role models for youth.

Cultural Awareness

The Coca-Cola Valued Youth Program, created by the Intercultural Development Research Association (IDRA), is an internationally recognized cross-age tutoring program. The program is designed to increase the self-esteem and academic success of at-risk middle and high school students by placing them in positions of responsibility as tutors of younger children. Other goals of the Coca-Cola Valued Youth Program include reducing the drop-out rate of at-risk students, increasing students' sense of self-control, decreasing student truancy, reducing disciplinary referrals, and fostering home–school partnerships (Slavin & Fashola, 1998).

Tutors are paid for their work (4 hours of tutoring per week) with younger children. They are supported by teaching coordinators who work with tutors on a weekly basis to develop tutoring skills and to improve literacy skills. Tutors also go on at least three field trips during the year to learn about economic and cultural opportunities within their community. On five occasions, guest speakers model a variety of professions and experiences for the tutors. Speakers include individuals who are considered successful in their fields and who are representative of tutors' ethnic backgrounds.

According to data collected by the IDRA, the Coca-Cola Valued Youth Program has kept 5,500 students from 150 schools in 16 cities in school. Studies also indicate that tutors receive significantly higher reading grades, feel more a part of the school, and have better attitudes toward school than nonparticipants (Intercultural Development Research Association, 1999).

▶ Linking Home, School, and Work

Other efforts to help students at risk have tried to tighten the links among home, school, and the workplace to influence parents' and children's commitments to education. One of the most noteworthy efforts in recent years has been school-to-work (STW) programs. The School-to-Work Opportunities Act of 1994 provides seed money to states and local partnerships of business, labor, government, education, and community organizations to develop school-to-work systems. The law allows states and their partners to integrate efforts at education reform, worker preparation, and economic development to create a system to prepare youth for jobs of the future. Many who benefit most from STW efforts are in poverty-stricken areas. You can learn more about STW programs by visiting its web site.

Does the school-to-work concept have any drawbacks?

Sometimes local businesses and industries view their work with community schools as an investment in people. The Danville, Virginia, school board formed the Industry in Education group to involve local business and industrial leaders in the promotion of educational excellence. The group of about a dozen plant managers and executives uses a variety of means for stressing the value of education. At Goodyear Tire and Rubber Company, the public relations manager devotes one page of the plant's newsletter to accomplishments of employees' children and to other educational issues. Plant employees also work on a volunteer basis in the public schools, speaking to classes, participating in Parent–

Teacher Association activities, and tutoring students at the middle school level (L. Moran, personal communication, September 23, 1999).

Some view school-to-work transitional programs with skepticism. They argue that the major goal of public schools should be to prepare students to become informed participants in our democracy, not to produce workers for business and industry. The concentration on school-to-work, they fear, will drive school curriculum to become commercially oriented, while de-emphasizing the importance of a liberal education. Critics also contend that local and regional variations in resources will yield variations in schooling that will only exaggerate differences between more and less affluent communities.

How Can Schools Get Parents Involved in Their Children's Education?

Parents are teachers, too. To do their jobs well, they must ask good questions. How much television is Johnny watching? How much does he read? What should I do to help him with his homework? Is Johnny getting enough sleep? What does he eat? Parents can make the home-to-school connection an important factor in their child's success. When the link is weak or nonexistent, students' chances for healthy, productive academic lives diminish.

When schools are able to encourage parents to get involved in their children's education, the payoffs can be high. Research indicates that parent involvement in children's education from birth until they leave home has a major positive impact on children's achievement at school.

> However, there are discrepancies between teachers' and parents' attitudes and their practices. For example, the actual level of participation on the part of both parents and educators is low. Greater parent involvement is found among parents at higher SES levels; more involvement is needed among parents at lower SES levels. Both educators and parents are unsure how to practice parent involvement. . . . John Hollifield suggests that the involvement of parents depends more on how schools seek to involve parents than on the status of the parents. (Stein & Thorkildsen, 1999, p. 18)

Surveys indicate that many students lack the parental involvement needed to succeed in school. The 1990 National Assessment of Educational Progress (NAEP) of fourth, eighth, and twelfth graders indicated a relationship between literacy and school attendance, outside reading, homework, and television viewing (activities parents can control). Secretary of Education Richard Riley noted, "If all parents in America made it their patriotic duty to find an extra thirty minutes to help their children learn more—each and every day—it would revolutionize American education" (1996, p. 1).

Researchers have documented that younger children, ages 3 to 5, have changed their television viewing habits since 1981 (Hofferth, 1998). While preschoolers watched on average 11.5 hours of TV per week in 1981, in 1997 they watched 20 hours. The good news is that they also spend about 45 minutes more each week studying. Also, children ages 9 to 12 spent two fewer hours watching television in 1997 than they did in 1981. In general, researchers see children's lives as busier and more hurried than in earlier, simpler times (Elkind, 1988; Jacobson, 1998).

Follow-up surveys conducted since the National Education Longitudinal Study of 1988, which focused on 24,599 American eighth graders, revealed that regardless of subject matter, slightly more than 50 percent of 1988 eighth graders spent the same amount of time on homework in high school as they had in eighth grade. Of the remaining students, approximately 25 percent reported doing more homework in high school than in eighth grade and slightly more than 15 percent said they were doing less. Females, Asian Americans, students in the highest SES (socioeconomic status) quartile, and students scoring in the highest quartile on standardized tests were more likely to have increased their homework time since eighth grade than were other groups of students (U.S. Department of Education, 1995b, p. v).

▶ Implementing Parental Involvement Programs

For some parents, school involvement may seem like a luxury. Parents in poverty worry so much about making money to support their families that they may have little emotional energy left to devote to school activities. This is neither an indictment nor an excuse; poverty and worry are simple but hard facts of life for many people.

Schools have always tried to involve parents in the education of their children, but their efforts seem to have increased in recent years. Common and visible attempts are parent–teacher conferences, school open houses, parent–teacher associations and organizations (PTAs and PTOs), and school advisory councils. PTAs and PTOs vary in size and level of participation. Their goal is to bring parents into school activities to tackle virtually every kind of problem imaginable. In many instances, their fund-raising efforts allow schools to purchase classroom materials and equipment. PTA-generated funds also provide educational opportunities, such as field trips and theatrical performances. But despite its size—nearly 7 million members—the National PTA is not highly visible in debates about school funding, curricula, or school governance issues (Harp, 1994).

How can teachers and schools encourage more parental involvement?

Some of the more successful efforts to involve parents in schools have occurred where people might least expect to find them. At Fairbanks Elementary School in Springfield, Missouri, about 50 percent of the students come from single-parent households, about 88 percent are eligible for free or reduced-price lunches, and nearly 50 percent need remedial work on their math and verbal skills. Fairbanks parents tutor students during and after school, serve as classroom aides, participate in evening workshops to learn how to help their children succeed in school, and organize special events (Leighninger & Niedergang, 1995).

Sandra Balli (1996) suggests that some parents may not have had positive school experiences themselves and thus are reluctant to get involved in their children's schools. Melanie Stein's and Ron Thorkildsen's (1999) examination of research and practice reveals a variety of ways to begin to involve parents as volunteers in schools (see Figure 7.3).

FIGURE 7.3
Involving Parents as Volunteers

Ways Volunteers Can Help at Elementary School	Ways Volunteers Can Help at Secondary School
Tell stories.	Help in the office.
Listen to children read, and read to children.	Make attendance calls.
Lead flash card drills.	Help with school events.
Help contact parents about school or classroom activities.	Reproduce materials for teachers.
Reproduce materials for teachers.	Work in the library.
Help at recess.	Help in the lunchroom.
Prepare bulletin boards.	Tutor students who need extra help.
Reinforce spelling or vocabulary words.	Work on a school-to-home newsletter.
Help in the library.	Be a resource person for teachers.
Assist with arts and crafts projects.	Act as a liaison for non-English speaking families.
Visit with children; show that adults care.	Prepare bulletin boards.
Dramatize a story.	Participate in Saturday work parties.
Help children with handwriting.	Help with student clubs.
Help children with motor skills.	Gather resource materials.
Help non-English speaking children.	Volunteer as a hall monitor.
Share information about occupations.	Have a monthly parent–teacher or parent–student lunch period.
Help with special programs or assemblies.	Mentor students.
Give underachievers one-on-one assistance.	Provide homework help.
Work with gifted children.	Serve on advisory committee.
Help with field trips.	
Teach a skill.	
Gather resource materials.	

Note. From *Parent Involvement in Education: Insights and Applications from the Research* by M. R. S. Stein & R. Thorkildsen, 1999, Bloomington, IN: Phi Delta Kappa International, p. 54. Reprinted with permission from Phi Delta Kappa International.

Parental involvement figures heavily in efforts to reorganize schools. Concepts of parental choice, for example, are based on the idea that when parents can exercise some control over where their children attend school, schools become more responsive to consumers. Other strategies of school restructuring and school-based management draw upon parental participation in governing councils to bring about change in school systems.

Sometimes increased parental involvement is a serendipitous byproduct of another action. In Plainfield, Indiana, for example, when the middle school instituted a no-cut policy with regard to student membership on clubs and teams—anybody who shows up makes the team—parental interest jumped right along with student participation. With 50 cheerleaders and anyone who wants to play football suiting up

Why is parents' involvement in their children's education important? How do full-service schools support family-based education?

for games, parents have volunteered their assistance and bought tickets to games in record numbers. As Figure 7.4 illustrates, students in Plainfield participate in a number of activities in addition to football and cheerleading (J. Goldsberry, personal communication, September 23, 1999).

 Visit the National Parent Information Network (NPIN) online. There you will find reviews of books for family support personnel, descriptions of innovative programs for parents, and organizations that support parent education.

▶ Providing Family Services Through Full-Service Schools

As school budgets have dwindled in the past decade, the need to focus limited services has increased. Some health and social service agencies have begun to collaborate with schools to create a kind of one-stop shopping at what are being called **full-service schools** (Dryfoos, 1994; Calfee, Wittwer, & Meredith, 1998). These schools offer a range of services for children and their families while reducing bureaucratic overhead.

The challenges of dealing with students who have a variety of health problems have prompted the establishment of school-based health centers in a number of states. These centers allow schools to coordinate health care with health curricula emphasizing preventive care. Full-care clinics provide such services as physical examinations, weight and drug counseling, treatment of illness and minor injuries, and testing for pregnancy and sexually transmitted diseases. The first of these full-care centers was established in Dallas, Texas, in 1970. Now most states have such centers.

Should schools provide health and social services?

The success of these and related efforts depends on many people. Teachers, families, administrators, social service providers, health care providers, and others must collaborate to maximize the benefit of their energies. When

FIGURE 7.4
Plainfield Participation in Extracurricular Activities   How would you describe student participation in extracurricular activities at Plainfield Middle School? How does the level of participation compare with that in schools you have attended or observed?

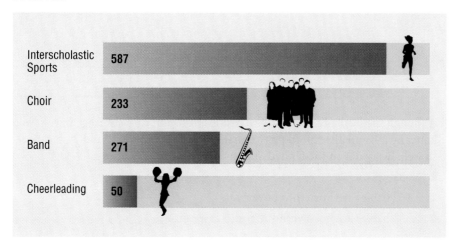

Interscholastic Sports   587
Choir   233
Band   271
Cheerleading   50

they do so, children's chances for living and learning in healthy environments are improved. Look for information about full-service schools on the Web at the North Central Regional Educational Laboratory Pathways to School Improvement site.

Northeast High School in St. Petersburg, Florida, is a full-service school that requires the cooperation of many people. Parents, students, health educators, and social service providers link students, families, and school faculty with needed resources.

The Clinic at Northeast High School began to offer services in August 1991. It is a community-based cooperative effort among the Pinellas County Schools and the Juvenile Welfare Board, Health Rehabilitative Services, and All Children's Hospital. The clinic is staffed by the Pinellas County Public Health Unit employees.

If parents give their consent, services provided at no cost to students include:

Health physicals (routine, school, and sports physicals)

Immunizations

Administration of prescriptions for routine medications

Health education

Care for acute illness and injury

Care for common adolescent physical problems

Follow-up as requested by a physician

Nutrition counseling

Social, emotional, and mental health counseling

Family counseling

Drug and alcohol counseling

Social service assistance

Pregnancy check-ups

Abstinence counseling and family planning information

Referral services

 ## How Can Schools Reduce Risks that Threaten Children's Health and Safety?

Although medical advances and extensions of health care coverage have resulted in better health and life expectancy for many Americans, today's children have not fared so well. Every day in the United States:

- 78 babies die
- 2,162 babies are born into poverty
- 1,353 babies are born without health insurance
- 415 babies are born to women who had late or no prenatal care
- 933 babies are born at low birthweight
- 1,377 babies are born to teen mothers
- 2,356 babies are born to mothers who are not high school graduates
- 3,453 babies are born to unmarried mothers
- 5,388 children are arrested
- 237 children are arrested for violent crimes
- 420 children are arrested for drug abuse
- 2,658 public school students are corporally punished
- 17,152 public school students are suspended
- 2,789 high school students drop out
- 2 young persons under 25 dies from HIV infection
- 36 children and youths under 20 die from accidents
- 13 children and youths under 20 die from firearms
- 6 children and youths under 20 commit suicide
- 11 children and youths under 20 are homicide victims
  (Children's Defense Fund, 1999)

At every age, among all races and income groups, and in communities throughout the nation, these and other problems threaten the well-being of young people.

▶ Preventing Child Abuse and Neglect

Many youngsters suffer from physical, emotional, or sexual abuse, and many more may be the victims of neglect by their parents or guardians. In 1974 Congress passed the **Child Abuse Prevention and Treatment Act** to provide financial support to states that implemented programs for identification, prevention, and treatment of child abuse and neglect. Congress passed the **Adoption and Safe Families Act of 1997** to enhance the services and extend the scope of child welfare agencies.

About 1.5 million children were the subjects of substantiated case reports of child abuse to child protective services nationwide (U.S. Department of Health and Human Services, 1988). Experts believe these represent only a fraction of actual cases, most of which go unreported. And this fraction would be even larger if homeless youth were accurately represented in the statistics (Russell, 1998). The most recent study suggests that the national annual incidence of neglect, physical abuse, and sexual abuse among reported and substantial cases of maltreatment among minor children were 52, 23, and 14 percent, respectively (U.S. Department of Health and Human Services, 1994).

Teachers are among those required by law to report instances of suspected child abuse. When teachers fail to do so, one or more things may happen: (1) they may be fined from $500 to $1,000, (2) they may be given prison terms of up to 1 year, (3) civil suits may be brought against them, and (4) they may be disciplined (e.g., demoted or dismissed) by their school system (McCarthy & Cambron-McCabe, 1998).

Problems of child abuse and neglect cut across all socioeconomic strata. According to the National Research Council (1993), however, financial problems may be the greatest contributor to the plight of children:

> [Child maltreatment] is disproportionately reported among poor families. Furthermore, child maltreatment—especially child neglect—is not simply concentrated among the poor, but among the poorest of the poor. Whether this association results from greater stress due to poverty-related conditions that precipitate abuse, or from greater scrutiny by public agencies that results in over-reporting, or whether maltreatment is but one characteristic of the pattern of disruption among the poorest of the poor continues to be debated. The link between unemployment and maltreatment is significant in understanding the relationship between poverty and maltreatment. Families reported for abuse often have multiple problems, and the abuse may simply be a part—or a consequence—of a broader continuum of social dysfunctions. (p. 9)

Because the physical and mental health of parents bears directly on the health and well-being of their children, many community-based programs try to provide parents with the skills and knowledge needed to cope more effectively with everyday stress and to care for and nurture their children. Parenting programs can help increase parents' involvement in their children's lives and also teach parents, particularly young, inexperienced ones, how to take care of themselves and their children. Schools often sponsor parenting programs within their own buildings. Some provide day care for infants and preschool children of high school students so the parents can complete their own high school programs and avoid the stunningly cruel conditions of life that breed child abuse and neglect.

▶ Preventing and Responding to Teen Pregnancy

Teenage childbearing correlates negatively with educational attainment, income, and participation in the labor force. Statistics indicate that for teens, having a child out-of-wedlock greatly increases the chance that a young mother and her child or children will live in poverty (Strapp, 1996). Many children of teenage parents wind up as teenage parents themselves, thus perpetuating the cycle of poverty and hopelessness.

The teenage birthrate declined steadily between 1991 and 1997. In 1997 the teenage birthrate was 52.3 per 1,000 births, 16 percent lower than the 62.1 rate in 1991 (U.S. Department of Health and Human Services, 1999a). Health and Human Services Secretary Donna Shalala stated that "this sustained national improvement is evidence that innovative programs to reach teenagers with information and support to make responsible choices is working." Not everyone shared Shalala's optimism. A separate report by the Child Welfare League of America indicated that Latino teenagers continue to have the highest birthrate of all ethnic groups. In 1997 the birthrate among Latino teenage girls ages 15 to 19 was 99.1 per 1,000. Among non-Latino whites, the rate was 36.4 per 1,000, and among blacks it was 89.5 per 1,000 (Coles, 1999b).

> **Should states mandate that all school districts provide sex education?**

The overwhelming majority of states encourage some type of sex education in schools, but the content and method of courses vary widely. Instruction runs the gamut from advocating abstinence from sexual contact to distributing condoms within the school. The high dropout rate among young mothers and, in many instances, the poor health of their babies have encouraged many school systems to alter their programs to meet the needs of adolescent parents and parents-to-be. In addition to standard curriculum, some schools offer home instruction to teenage mothers during their 4- to 6-week postpartum period. Schools may also provide teenage parents with child care, individual and group counseling, health care, parenting education, and vocational training.

In addition to support programs for teenage mothers, some schools offer services to young fathers and fathers-to-be. Boston schools, among the first to establish such programs, provide services through the nonprofit Crittenton Hastings House. During the 1999 academic year, two case managers worked with approximately 65 males from four high schools. Besides acting as mentors, case managers assist young fathers in more concrete ways by helping them find part-time jobs and steering them toward job-training programs (Sandham, 1999).

▶ Preventing the Spread of AIDS and Other Communicable Diseases

As Figure 7.5 indicates, citizens' support of sex education programs for young people has increased over the last few years. No doubt statistics on the general well-being of young people have affected shifts in attitudes. Students engaging in sexual relationships and students abusing drugs are especially susceptible to sexually transmitted diseases, including HIV (human immunodeficiency virus), the virus that causes AIDS (acquired immunodeficiency syndrome). Between 650,000 and 900,000 people in the United States are living with HIV. Nearly 690,000 people have been diagnosed with AIDS. Some 410,000 men, women, and children have lost their lives to this disease (U.S. Department of Health and Human Services, 1999b).

According to data collected by the Centers for Disease Control, 53 percent of students in grades 9 to 12 have had sexual intercourse. Almost 19 percent of these teenagers have had four or more sexual partners (Kann, Warren, & Collins, Ross,

FIGURE 7.5
The Public's Attitudes toward Sex Education   The Phi Delta Kappa/Gallup poll on the public's attitudes toward public education reveals educationally significant changes in recent years. In 1987, some 76 percent of respondents favored including sex education in the curriculum. In 1999, that support had increased to 87 percent. Support for the inclusion of specific topics also increased over that time period.

Do you feel the public high schools should or should not include sex education in their instructional programs?

	National Totals				No Children in School				Public School Parents				Nonpublic School Parents			
	'98 %	'87 %	'85 %	'81 %	'98 %	'87 %	'85 %	'81 %	'98 %	'87 %	'85 %	'81 %	'98 %	'87 %	'85 %	'81 %
Yes, should	87	76	75	70	87	73	72	66	89	82	81	79	78	81	80	79
No, should not	12	16	19	22	12	16	21	25	10	14	16	16	22	18	15	17
Don't know	1	8	6	8	1	11	7	9	1	4	3	5	*	1	5	4

*Less than one-half of 1%.

Which of the following topics, if any, should be included for high school students?

	Topics That Should Be Included			
	'98 %	'87 %	'85 %	'81 %
Venereal disease	92	86	84	84
AIDS	92	84	*	*
Biology of reproduction	90	80	82	77
Teen pregnancy	89	84	*	*
Birth control	87	83	85	79
Premarital sex	77	66	62	60
Nature of sexual intercourse	72	61	61	53
Abortion	70	60	60	54
Homosexuality	65	56	48	45

*These topics were not included in the earlier surveys.

Source: Rose, L. C. & Gallup, A. M. (1998, September). The 30th annual Phi Delta Kappa/Gallup poll of the public's attitudes toward the public schools. *Phi Delta Kappan, 80*(1), p. 54. Reprinted with permission of the *Phi Delta Kappan.*

Collins, & Kolbe, 1993). Although AIDS often has been characterized as a disease confined mainly to homosexual men and intravenous drug users, about 8 percent of HIV/AIDS cases result from heterosexual intercourse (Centers for Disease Control and Prevention, 1996).

Douglas Tonks (1992/1993) counsels educators to remember two important facts when developing programs to prevent HIV transmission. First, many students experiment with drugs as young as age 12. Sexual experimentation also begins at an early age, even though this may not include intercourse. HIV prevention programs, therefore, must begin in elementary school and continue through high school; they must also be flexible enough to meet the needs of all children.

One study of school-based HIV education programs revealed that the most effective interventions had the following characteristics:

- a narrow focus, emphasizing risk-taking behaviors that could lead to HIV infection;

- opportunities to acquire and practice refusal and communication skills through such activities as role playing and brainstorming;

- acknowledgment of social and media influences on sexual behavior;

- an emphasis on developing values and group norms regarding postponing sex, avoiding unprotected sex, using condoms, and avoiding high-risk partners; and

- inclusion of testimonials from respected peers to encourage a more conservative set of values (Landau, Pryor, & Haefli, 1995).

Childhood diseases also place at risk children who have not received preschool vaccinations on time and therefore enter school vulnerable to disease. Resurgences of preventable diseases such as measles, mumps, pertussis (whooping cough), and rubella are threats to both health and learning. The emergence and spread of drug-resistant strains of tuberculosis also threaten the children's well-being (Groopman, 1993). To stem outbreaks of childhood diseases, public health officials have expanded outreach programs to ensure the timely immunization of children. They have also increased several immunization requirements for school-age children. To enable all children to meet these requirements, many districts offer school-based clinics for youngsters.

▶ Preventing Suicide and Accidental Injury or Death

Adolescent suicide is a serious problem in the United States. Data from a national survey of students in all public, parochial, and private schools in grades 9 through 12 revealed that during the 12 months preceding the survey, 29 percent had thought seriously about attempting suicide, 18.6 percent had made a specific plan to attempt suicide, and 1.7 percent had made a suicide attempt that resulted in an injury, a poisoning, or an overdose that had to be treated by a doctor or nurse. Females were significantly more likely than were males to have thought about, planned, and attempted suicide (Kann, Warren, Collins, Ross, Collins, & Kolbe, 1993). An earlier study revealed that a number of factors led students to consider or attempt suicide: family problems or problems at home, problems with friends/peer pressure/social relations, boy/girl relationships, and feelings that no one cared (Gallup Organization, 1991).

Some groups of students are more prone to suicide than others. Data suggest that homosexual adolescents are two to three times more likely to attempt suicide than are their heterosexual peers (Green, 1991). Among ethnic groups, the suicide rates for African American males have risen dramatically. For African American males ages 15

FIGURE 7.6
Some Warning Signs of Suicide How might you respond to students who persistently exhibit these warning signs? What actions might you take?

Warning Signs:

Changing eating and sleeping habits

Withdrawal from friends, family, and regular activities

Violent or rebellious behavior

Running away from home

Unusual neglect of personal appearance

Radical change in personality

Persistent boredom, difficulty concentrating, or a decline in the quality of schoolwork

Frequent complaints about physical symptoms often related to emotions, such as stomachaches, headaches, or fatigue

Loss of interest in previously pleasurable activities

Inability to tolerate praise or rewards

Note. From "Counselors Can Make a Difference" by L. Peach and T. L. Riddick, 1991, *The School Counselor, 39,* pp. 107–111. Copyright by ACA. Reprinted with permission. No further reproduction authorized without written permission of the American School Counselor Association.

to 19, the rate jumped from 5.6 to 14.8 per 100,000 (Lawton, 1995). The leading cause of death of African American males ages 15 to 24, however, is homicide (U.S. Bureau of the Census, 1998f).

Addressing potentially suicidal students and acquaintances of suicide victims requires special attention to young people's concepts of themselves. Single suicides can stimulate imitation, or what some people have referred to as "cluster suicides." School-based programs on suicide prevention and suicide curricula advocate careful training for teachers who offer such programs.

For example, the California State Education Department has developed a program of worksheets, quizzes, and simulation games to address directly the threat of suicide. Other programs in other locales also address suicide more indirectly via drug education programs. In many of these programs, adults and students are taught to understand the myths, signs, facts, and symptoms of suicide. They may also concentrate on identifying the feelings of students at risk, thinking of ways to help students cope with stress and depression, and learning how to respond to a suicide crisis. In one study, young people who attempted suicide thought that being listened to was the most important experience they could have to prevent them from another attempt (Coleman, Lyon, & Piper, 1995). In another study, young people indicated that talking, being listened to, and listening to music are the best remedies for depression (Freidli and Scherzer, 1996). Figure 7.6 lists some of the warning signs of suicide.

Motor vehicle accidents are the leading cause of death among teenagers 15 to 19 years old (U.S. Bureau of the Census, 1998f). Many fatalities are alcohol related. Moving the minimum drinking age up to 21 in states where it was lower has resulted in a decline in arrests of teenagers for driving while intoxicated.

High schools offer driver education programs that precede the granting of a license to operate a motor vehicle. Insurance companies offer incentives to students for high scores in driver safety and to students who do well in academic courses. In combination with health education, driver education can potentially lower the incidence of the lethal habit of drinking and driving. Nonetheless, when school budgets are tight, driver education courses are among the first to be dropped.

Preoccupation with body image threatens the psychological and physical well-being of many students, particularly adolescents. A growing number of females from all races and socioeconomic groups experience anorexia nervosa (self-starvation) and bulimia (binging and purging). Eating disorders can cause serious consequences, including intermittent hospitalization and death (Loosli & Ruud, 1998).

▶ Preventing School Violence

Assault, homicide, vandalism, and related violent acts committed by and against young people are so shockingly high in the United States that they strain credulity. Since 1979, more children (60,008) have died from gunfire in the United States than did American soldiers during the Vietnam and Gulf wars and in U.S. engagements in Haiti, Somalia, and Bosnia combined. African American males ages 15 to 19 have suffered the greatest gun toll among children and teens. They are five times as likely as European American males to be gun victims. Gun violence is the leading cause of death among African American teens 15 to 19 years old (Children's Defense Fund, 1996).

Some assaults against young people result from gang warfare. While gangs are not confined to urban areas, big cities in particular experienced growth in gang membership and gang violence in the 1980s. Much of the gang-related violence that seeps into schools results from struggles between gangs for drug-selling "turf."

While some gang and individual acts of brutality seem random and baseless, others are the cold and calculated manifestations of hate against people who are different. "Different" can be defined in terms of religion, sexual preference, race, age, or virtually any characteristic. Attacks are aimed at specific people or perceived types of people. On April 20, 1999, for example, 13 students at Columbine High School in Colorado were killed by two members of the senior class. The gunmen, who ended the reign of terror by turning their guns on themselves, were described by classmates as members of a self-styled group of loners and outcasts calling themselves the Trenchcoat Mafia. "A student who was not a member of the Trenchcoat Mafia told ABC that students called members of the group 'dirtbags' and threw food at them" (Von Drehle, 1999).

Children's shocking violence toward other children, including hate crimes and firearm homicides, came to greater national attention during the 1990s.

About one in four students report some kind of social tension or violence in their schools (Louis Harris and Associates, Inc., 1996) including hostile or threatening remarks among different groups of students (25%); physical fights among members of different groups of friends (26%); threats or destructive acts other than physical fights (24%); turf battles among different groups of students (21%); and gang violence (26%). The same survey indicates that as students grow older, however, their concern for such problems diminishes. Some 30 to 36 percent of eighth graders surveyed perceive violence as a very serious problem, compared to just 11 to 15 percent of twelfth graders. Urban students are more like to report having serious problems with hostile remarks, physical fights, threats or destructive acts and gang violence (32% to 36%) than are suburban (20% to 24%) or rural (17% to 20%) students. African American and Hispanic students are twice as likely as are other students to report experiencing very serious problems with turf battles (32% and 33%, respectively, versus 16%) and gang violence (40% and 41%, respectively, versus 19%) (Louis Harris and Associates, Inc., 1996).

> **How can schools be made safe places where all students can learn?**

The central issue for educators is how to ensure children's safety. A number of efforts, many school based, aim to change the odds for children at highest risk. To deter crime and violence on buses and at school, some localities have turned to metal detectors and video cameras. Some schools employ police officers, sometimes referred to as resource officers, to help maintain order and to prevent nonstudents from going on to school grounds. In other schools, educators are eliminating teasing and bullying in the early grades and encouraging positive relationships and mutual respect among students. Using such activities as story time, meeting-time discussions, drawings, art projects, journal writing, and role playing, teachers help young children to explore stereotypes and behaviors that get in the way of friendship:

> The most important strategy is to talk about teasing and bullying, not just as incidents occur, but as a regular part of classroom life. As they talk about teasing and bullying, students learn to become critical thinkers. Through ongoing class discussions, they realize that the classroom is a place where they can talk about what makes them feel welcome, comfortable, and safe in school. (Froschl & Gropper, 1999)

Researchers are developing other techniques to prevent violence, such as interviewing students and mapping zones of danger in schools (Astor, Meyer, & Behre, 1999). Most often these zones include parking lots and rarely traveled hallways. Investigators argue that the best way to prevent violence, however, is to encourage and support teacher action. Violence occurs least often within classrooms occupied by teachers, and "in the final analysis, teacher-generated and implemented interventions hold the greatest likelihood of securing safety and preventing violence" (p. 36).

The American Psychological Association (APA) and Music Television (MTV) have collaborated to produce a Warning Signs guide to recognizing and dealing with violence in schools and in society more broadly defined. The following signs suggest that violence is a serious possibility:

▪ Loss of temper on a daily basis

▪ Frequent physical fighting

▊ Significant vandalism or property damage

▊ Increase in use of drugs or alcohol

▊ Increase in risk-taking behavior

▊ Detailed plans to commit acts of violence

▊ Announcing threats or plans for hurting others

▊ Enjoying hurting animals

▊ Carrying a weapon

When the following signs appear over a period of time, the potential for violence is real:

▊ A history of violent or aggressive behavior

▊ Serious drug or alcohol use

▊ Gang membership or strong desire to be in a gang

▊ Access to or fascination with weapons, especially guns

▊ Threatening others regularly

▊ Trouble controlling feelings like anger

▊ Withdrawal from friends and usual activities

▊ Feeling rejected or alone

▊ Having been a victim of bullying

▊ Poor school performance

▊ History of discipline problems or frequent run-ins with authorities

▊ Feeling constantly disrespected

▊ Failing to acknowledge the feelings or rights of others (American Psychological Association & Music Television, undated)

▶ Preventing Substance Abuse

Can schools prevent substance abuse?

Surveys conducted between 1975 and 1997 reveal high school seniors' reported use of alcohol and drugs (see Figure 7.7). Some 53 percent reported use of alcohol and 23.7 percent reported use of marijuana/hashish during a 30-day time frame (U.S. Department of Education, 1998). According to a study by the Center on Addiction and Substance Abuse at Columbia University, girls are 15 times more likely than were their mothers to have begun using illegal drugs by age 15 ("Girls' Substance Abuse," 1996).

Concerns about patterns of behavior that put students at risk have prompted parent groups in some school systems to band together to keep teenagers safe. The Boomerang Committee in Ames, Iowa, for example, was established more than 10 years ago. Members of the group sign a pledge, promising that parties held in their homes will be free from alcohol and drug use.

A variety of school-based programs also attempt to curb substance abuse. Project ALERT, a curriculum developed by the RAND Corporation, and Drug Abuse Resistance Education (DARE), a program that began as a joint effort between the Los

FIGURE 7.7
Alcohol and Drug Use Among High School Seniors   Describe the trends
indicated on this graph.

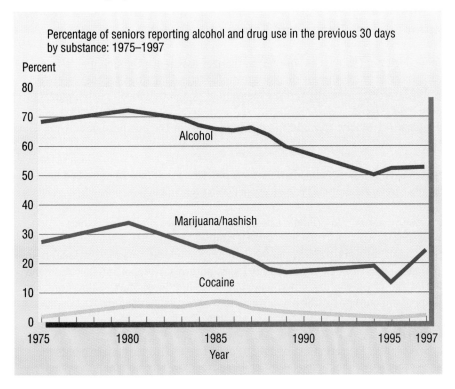

Percentage of seniors reporting alcohol and drug use in the previous 30 days
by substance: 1975–1997

Note. From *Digest of Education Statistics,* 1998, by U.S. Department of Education, 1998.
Washington, DC: U.S. Government Printing Office. Table 150, p. 158.

Angeles Unified School District and the Los Angeles Police Department, are two
examples of programs designed to help elementary and junior high school students
resist peer pressure to experiment with drugs and alcohol. Among program goals are
helping students learn to make their own decisions, learning drug and alcohol facts,
understanding peer pressure, and developing positive self-esteem. While such programs enjoy widespread use, they get mixed reviews (Coles, 1999a). Some educators
prefer to develop and use their own drug and health education programs.

Well-designed drug prevention programs have had positive effects. A 7-year study
indicated that seventh and eighth graders in 30 schools in California and Oregon
who were taught the Project ALERT curriculum reduced their use of illegal drugs,
particularly marijuana, by as much as 50 percent while enrolled in the program.
Once students left the program, however, positive effects all but disappeared. Such
results suggest that prevention programs are most effective if they are continued at
the high school level (Portner, 1993).

Benchmarks

Legislation for Student Health and Safety (1946–1998)

1946 National School Lunch Act (Public Law 79-396) authorizes assistance through grants-in-aid and other means to states to assist in providing adequate foods and facilities for the establishment, maintenance, operation, and expansion of nonprofit school lunch programs.

1954 School Milk Program Act (Public Law 83-597) provides funds for the purchase of milk for school lunch programs.

1958 National Defense Education Act (Public Law 85-864) provides assistance to state and local school systems for strengthening many services, including guidance and counseling.

1964 Economic Opportunity Act of 1964 (Public Law 88-452) authorizes grants for college work–study programs for students from low-income families; establishes a Job Corps program and authorizes support for work-training programs to provide education and vocational training and work experience opportunities in welfare programs; authorizes support of education and training activities and of community action programs, including Head Start, Follow Through, and Upward Bound; and authorizes the establishment of Volunteers in Service to America (VISTA).

1965 Elementary and Secondary Education Act of 1965 (Public Law 89-10) authorizes grants for elementary and secondary school programs for children from low-income families; school library resources, textbooks, and other instructional materials for school children; supplementary educational centers and services; state education agencies; and educational research and research training.

Higher Education Act of 1965 (Public Law 89-329) establishes a National Teacher Corps devoted to teaching in the nation's poverty-stricken areas.

1970 Drug Abuse Education Act of 1970 (Public Law 91-427) provides for development, demonstration, and evaluation of curricula on the problems of drug abuse.

1974 Juvenile Justice and Delinquency Prevention Act of 1974 (Public Law 93-415) provides for technical assistance, staff training, centralized research, and resources to develop and implement programs to keep students in elementary and secondary schools.

1977 Youth Employment and Demonstration Projects Act of 1977 (Public Law 95-93) establishes a youth employment training program that includes, among other activities, promoting education-to-work transition, literacy training and bilingual training, and attainment of certificates of high school equivalency.

1980 Asbestos School Hazard Detection and Control Act of 1980 (Public Law 96-270) establishes a program for inspection of schools for detection of hazardous asbestos materials and provides loans to assist educational agencies to contain or remove and replace such materials.

1986	Drug-Free Schools and Committees Act of 1986 (Part of Public Law 99-570), part of the Anti-Drug Abuse Act of 1986, authorizes funding for programs for drug abuse education and prevention, coordinated with related community efforts and resources.
1988	The Omnibus Drug Abuse Prevention Act of 1988 (Public Law 100-690) authorizes a new teacher training program under the Drug-Free Schools and Communities Act, an early childhood education program to be administered jointly by the U.S. Department of Health and Human Services and the U.S. Department of Education, and a pilot program for the children of alcoholics.
1990	Children's Television Act of 1990 (Public Law 101-437) requires the Federal Communications Commission to reinstate restrictions on advertising during children's television programs and enforces the obligation of broadcasters to meet the educational and informational needs of the child audience.
	National Assessment of Chapter 1 Act (Public Law 101-305) requires the Secretary of Education to conduct a comprehensive national assessment of programs, carried out with assistance under Chapter 1 of Title I of the Elementary and Secondary Education Act of 1965.
	School Dropout and Basic Skills Improvement Act of 1990 (Public Law 101-600) improves secondary school programs for basic skills improvements and dropout reduction.
1991	A bill making appropriations for the U.S. Department of the Interior and related agencies (Public Law 102-154) amends the Anti-Drug Abuse Act of 1988 to extend the authorization of appropriations for drug abuse education and prevention programs relating to youth gangs and for runaway and homeless youth. Directs the Secretary of Health and Human Services to report annually on the program of drug education and prevention relating to youth gangs.
1994	School-to-Work Opportunities Act of 1994 (Public Law 103-239) establishes a national framework within which states and communities can develop School-to-Work Opportunities systems to prepare young people for first jobs and continuing education. The act also provides money to states and communities to develop a system of programs that include work-based learning and school-based learning. School-to-Work programs provide students with a high school diploma (or its equivalent), a nationally recognized skill certificate, or an associate degree (if appropriate) and may lead to a first job or further education.
	Safe Schools Act of 1994 (Part of Public Law 103-227) authorizes the award of competitive grants to local educational agencies with serious crime to implement violence prevention activities, such as conflict resolution and peer mediation.
1995	House Resolution HR 1390—Children's Media Protection Act of 1995 makes the following requirements: *Establishment of Television Violence Rating Code*—In consultation with television broadcasters, cable operators, appropriate public-interest groups, and interested individuals by television broadcast systems and cable systems. *Television That Blocks Programs*—New televisions sold in the United States must (1) be equipped with circuitry

---

Legislation for Student Health and Safety (1946–1998) *(Cont.)*

designed to enable viewers to block the display of channels, programs, and time slots; and (2) enable viewers to block display of all programs with a common rating. *Prohibition on Violent Programming*—A commission shall . . . initiate a rule-making proceeding to prescribe a prohibition on the broadcast on commercial television and by public telecommunications entities, including the broadcast by cable operators, from the hours of 6 a.m. to 10 p.m., inclusive, of programming that contains gratuitous violence. *Educational and Information Programming for Children*—Broadcast and cable companies are required to provide a specific amount of "children's programming," as defined by the FCC.

1998 The Carl D. Perkins Vocational and Technical Education Act of 1998 (P.L. 105-332) is meant to increase the caliber of education provided by vo-tech programs by aligning them with state and local efforts to reform secondary schools. The Teen Drive for Employment Act changes child labor laws to prohibit 16-year-olds from driving on public roads for work purposes, while extending the amount of time 17-year-olds can drive as part of their workday.

SUMMARY

What are society's expectations for schools?

1. Americans have turned increasingly to schools to solve some of society's most difficult problems, many of which have devastating effects on children. The demands placed on schools often exceed their resources.

2. Of growing concern to educators is the increasing number of students at risk for failure both academically and socially.

How does poverty place students at risk of school failure?

3. Conditions of poverty or lower socioeconomic status (SES) are strongly and consistently related to school failure. Children from low-income homes often begin school less well prepared than their peers and have difficulty staying on grade level.

How can schools intervene to help students at risk?

4. Early intervention programs can help disadvantaged students enter school ready to learn. Some programs, such as Head Start, provide comprehensive child development and family support services to low-risk families with young children.

5. Compensatory programs provide children from low-income homes additional educational opportunities beyond those in a school's standard program. Before- and after-school programs can benefit children nutritionally, socially, and academically.

6. Establishing incentive programs; providing mentors and tutors; and linking home, school, and the workplace are other ways schools attempt to improve students' opportunities for success.

How can schools get parents involved in their children's education?

7. Parent–Teacher Associations and Organizations (PTAs and PTOs) provide opportunities for parent participation in school activities. The more successful parent involvement programs, however, are those in schools where parents are encouraged to participate in the education process.

8. Full-service programs and adult education programs also facilitate parental involvement by providing daycare services.

How can schools reduce risks that threaten children's health and safety?

9. The first demand schools face in reducing risks to children is to identify those risks.

10. Schools often are the first line of defense against child abuse; that is, educators have opportunities and responsibilities to identify and report suspected abuse and neglect.

11. Educational programs can make students and parents aware of a variety of risks, including but not limited to teen pregnancy, sexually transmitted diseases, suicide, and accidental injury or death.

12. School violence erupts for a variety of reasons. Increasingly, schools are taking measures to prevent violence at school that is initiated from within and outside school walls. In big cities, gang violence around the drug trade has grown even more vicious as young people have turned to weapons.

TERMS AND CONCEPTS

Adoption and Safe Families Act of 1997   275
at-risk student   252
Child Abuse Prevention and Treatment Act   274
compensatory education program   262
early intervention   259

full-service school   271
holding power   262
incentive program   264
latchkey child   263
mentoring program   268
pull-out program   262
Title I   262

REFLECTIVE PRACTICE

Before she got her doctorate, Ann C. Diver-Stamnes taught English in the Watts section of Los Angeles, an area of the city where for years gang warfare has been frighteningly common. The Crips and the Bloods claim this territory as home. In recent years routine violence in the community has been exacerbated by the drug trade. Combine drugs with the tendency to "come from the pocket," or to use knives and guns to settle scores, and anxiety is a fact of life for everyone within striking distance.

> When I first began to teach in Watts, I taught a senior remedial English class. We were discussing paragraph development one day when I heard a beeping noise. A student

stood up and began to sidle toward the door, saying, "I gotta go. No offense. I just gotta go now." He was very polite, attempting to make sure I knew it was not my lesson on paragraphs that caused him to leave the room. I was completely baffled and turned to my class for some explanation. They explained, amused by my obvious confusion, that the student who had left was a gang member and was selling drugs, and the noise I had heard was his pager or beeper. He had probably been paged, they told me, by either his supplier or a customer, either of which required his immediate response.

This young man, who was charming and warm in class, read and wrote at the fourth-grade level, carried a beeper, and had politely left my classroom to deal with a drug transaction.

Issues, Problems, Dilemmas, Opportunities

Diver-Stamnes notes that some people consider gang members to be expendable or "throwaway kids." Why is this attitude, particularly when held by teachers, a problem in itself? If you taught in a school in a community where drugs and violence were commonplace, beyond everyone's personal safety, what might be your major concerns?

Perceive and Value

Diver-Stamnes argues that the formation and maintenance of gangs is not a simple matter of too many "bad kids" in the same place at the same time. She characterizes gang membership as an almost logical response to a virtually hopeless situation—that is, the situation of being young and caught in the downward spiral of inner-city violence, poverty, and crime. Can you imagine why joining a gang might be viewed as a matter of self-protection? Why might a young person choose to sell drugs instead of working at a minimum-wage job?

Know and Act

If you had students in your classes who wore gang colors and emblems, what more might you want to know about these students? If you were the teacher, how might you respond to the student who excused himself from Ann Diver-Stammes's class to respond to a beeper? Diver-Stamnes described herself as feeling like a member of the "fashion police," always having students remove baseball caps and "rags" (bandannas), confiscating beepers, and instructing students to undo their braids, remove their earrings, or unlace their shoes. Why do schools have such rules?

Evaluate

Rightly or wrongly, we often evaluate people and situations by appearances. Diver-Stamnes describes how appearances affected her one day as she was walking near her school:

> As I walked down the street to the elementary school one day early in my second year at Medgar High, I noticed a large group of young men walking toward me, dressed in standard gangbanger attire. Although I had been given a walkie-talkie to carry on my frequent trips back and forth to the elementary school to drop off and pick up my

high school students who worked there with the younger children, I felt foolish using it for more than reporting my arrival at or departure from either school. As the group of young men drew closer, I forced myself to keep walking and to refrain from crossing the street, although I was very nervous. When they drew up in front of me, I gasped as one young man separated himself from the group and launched himself at me. He threw his arms around my neck, and yelled, "Dr. Stamnes! How you doing?!" In an instant, this frightening group of "gangbangers" was transformed into a group of laughing kids, one of whom had been a favored student of mine the previous year. Mingled with my relief was a profound sense of shame that I too had not seen beyond appearances.

Do you think Diver-Stamnes's "reading" of the students was typical of how you or other teachers might view the situation? Was her fear warranted? How might students' appearances influence teachers' judgments of students' capacity for violence and their capacity for success? How might such judgments vary by locale, that is, in inner-city schools, in suburban schools, and in rural schools?

 ## ONLINE ACTIVITY

Schools' abilities to help young people succeed might be judged ultimately by people outside of schools—that is, by employers. The School-to-Work efforts discussed in this chapter are evidence of such a view. If one were to take this position, as the federal government suggests on its School-to-Work web site, it would seem wise to consider how potential employers view students' performances.

Find *Hiring Smart: An Employer's Guide to Using School Records* online (http://www.bcer.org/macc/hiring_smart.cfm). The guide contains directions for helping business and industry use school records when they screen potential employees. It also suggests how schools can prepare their students to meet employers' needs. For instance, employers tend to believe that poor school attendance is a predictor of poor work attendance. So schools might avoid setting rigid attendance cutoffs for absences. There may be good reasons for such absences and being rigid may affect hiring decisions. Go to the site and speculate on how hiring policies and school policies might affect each other.

8

Influences of Diversity

I n this chapter we explore concepts of diversity and culture and speculate about their implications for education. As in preceding chapters, we assume that how people view society depends greatly on where they stand; thus we position readers to perceive concepts of cultural diversity from different points of view. We attempt to reduce some of the confusion in the language used to describe our common and unique characteristics. And we also try to suggest that the residents of this remarkable social experiment called the

United States of America have grown not simply to tolerate their differences, but to make the most of them.

PROFESSIONAL PRACTICE QUESTIONS

■ What is diversity?

■ How has diversity been defined in terms of development?

■ What other concepts define diversity?

 ## What Is Diversity?

The population of the United States is very diverse; that is, the people differ between and within groups on any number of characteristics. They vary by culture, ethnicity, race, ability, need, social class, and the like. This assertion seems simple and obvious, until one scratches beneath the surface.

What do people mean when they speak of *culture*? To what characteristics does one's *ethnicity* refer, and how is ethnicity different from one's *national origin,* if at all? Is *race* a concept with many connotations or only those limited to physical characteristics? When educators mention *minorities,* do they intend to refer only to the human attributes of race and ethnicity, or do they also mean gender, sexual orientation, disabilities, giftedness, and social class?

The language of diversity is perplexing. People speak and write about complex ideas of race, culture, and ethnicity as though there is agreement on the meaning of the terms. In some ways and in some places there is such agreement, but most often only in general terms. For instance, we may agree on something as seemingly obvious as concepts of gender by relying on a few physiological attributes to discriminate between the sexes. Try to enrich the concepts in terms of the intellectual, emotional, and social characteristics of the genders, however, and disagreement surfaces. When pushed, people often find their agreement on the complex concepts we use to describe human diversity exists at only a passive, unexamined level.

▶ Culture

Culture can be used in an inclusive or *macro* sense to refer to the sum of the learned characteristics of a people—language, religion, social mores, artistic expression, beliefs and values, and so on. In some cases a culture can be tied to a geographical region, while in other cases a culture exists largely irrespective of geography.

Culture also can be used in a *micro* sense to describe more conceptually discrete groups of people—cultures within cultures, subcultures, or microcultures. Users of illegal drugs are said to be part of the drug culture or drug subculture. Some people with hearing impairments choose to be part of the deaf culture. Some women consider themselves to be members of the feminist culture.

Culture is an important concept for educators to try to understand, because it influences students' lives. Culture teaches; it shapes learners' identities, beliefs, and behaviors. Understanding students' cultures is a prerequisite to valuing diversity and enlisting the force of culture as an instructional ally. To ignore or misunderstand students' cultures is to risk teaching at cross-purposes with them. In recent years, social scientists have begun to explore critically the influence of culture in classrooms.

Educational and psychological research used to be conducted routinely on the *mainstream,* the dominant ethnic and cultural group, typically composed of Anglo-Saxon Protestant males from middle or higher social classes. When results suggested that certain educational approaches were more or less effective, these results were translated into educational materials and programs for all students, including females, African Americans, and others. These approaches, however, often worked better with European American males than with females, people of other racial groups, and students from different cultures. Now, instead of assuming research findings hold up across genders and cultural groups, researchers typically investigate how such differences among people can affect learning and teaching.

Thoughts about culture in the United States have been characterized by the metaphor of the melting pot. Immigrants, like ingredients, were to be added to the great cauldron (public education) and simmered over low-intensity educational fire until a perfectly blended soup was achieved in which characteristics of the individual ingredients disappeared.

The melting pot metaphor, however, often gives way to the salad bowl (or salsa) metaphor. People in all their crisp, colorful, tangy ways, while tossed together, are said to retain their unique identities and essential differences. In similar fashion, the mosaic metaphor compares different shapes, sizes, and colors of tiles to the individuals and groups in our society.

Metaphors can be useful devices for thinking about culture in creative ways and for communicating social ideals. But a metaphor can become a hindrance when it is used as a prescription for practice. Although public education has been remarkably successful in many ways, it has not completely met the demands of the melting pot, the salad bowl, or the mosaic metaphors, nor is it likely to do so anytime soon. Our richness and diversity are too complex to be described fully by any metaphor. As a society, we seek a sense of **cultural pluralism,** that is, a state in which people of diverse ethnic, racial, religious, and social groups maintain autonomous participation within a common civilization.

> Is "salad bowl" a more apt metaphor than "melting pot" for cultural diversity in the United States?

How, then, are educators to view our sprawling, complex society to perceive the talents and needs of the people? There is no fail-safe plan, but the urgency to "decenter," to see and understand society from different points of view, is compelling. For the alternative is to be locked in an **ethnocentric** power struggle for the societal upper hand—a struggle based on the belief of the superiority of one's own culture.

You can explore online the complexities of diversity in the United States in its many forms by visiting the U.S. Census Bureau web site.

▶ Race and Ethnicity

Race is defined most often by physical characteristics, especially skin color, but sometimes also by ethnicity—ancestry in terms of national origin. A person of color might refer to himself or herself as black or African American or Latino (or Mexican,

Cuban, Haitian, or Puerto Rican); but depending on appearances, a Latino or a person with African ancestry might just as easily identify himself or herself as white or Caucasian (Banks, 1997). Robert Suro (1998) suggests that the current vocabulary of race, often couched in terms of black and white, is losing its meaning:

> The problem is not simply that we have added new groups to the mix. The language of black–white differences is losing its meaning because Latinos and Asians do not fit into a world in which people are permanently and definitively marked either as insiders or outsiders. (p. C2)

The term **ethnicity** refers to membership in a group with a common cultural tradition or common national origin. Ethnic groups function as subgroups within the larger society and may share a common language, religion, customs, or other elements of culture. While racial traits are heritable, cultural traits are learned in social contexts. The most important identifying characteristic of an ethnic group is the members' feelings of identification with the group, because ethnicity is largely a matter of self-identification (Banks, 1996).

When people complete forms for school enrollment, job applications, student loans, and the like, they are asked questions about racial or ethnic heritage. Usually students or their parents are asked to check one of four racial categories used by the United States federal government: American Indian or Alaskan Native, Asian or Pacific Islander, black, or white. They are also asked to note whether they are of Hispanic origin. This information serves many purposes—to monitor equal opportunities in education and employment and to track school desegregation.

Should racial designation matter for purposes of education?

The arbitrariness of racial classification categories is evident in the changes in Census Bureau questions asked since 1790 (Carey & Farris, 1996). In 1790, four categories were used to designate race: Free White Males, Free White Females, All Other Free Persons, and Slaves. In 1970, nine categories were used: white, Negro or black, Indian (American), Japanese, Chinese, Filipino, Hawaiian, Korean, and Other race. In the 1990 census the designation of Mixed Race was added, reflecting demographic realities and public discontent with the standard categories used by the government to collect statistics about the population. As Table 8.1 indicates, when diversity is defined in racial terms, numbers only hint at the richness of society.

While the same four categories noted above were used to designate race for 20 years, the population changed dramatically during that time. Immigration surged during the 1980s. Fewer of those immigrants came from Europe and Canada, and more came from Mexico, Central and South America, the Caribbean, and Asia (Harrison & Bennett, 1995). More than 40 percent of public schools report that there are students in their schools who are not described adequately by the current standard federal categories (Carey & Farris, 1996). Future reporting may be affected by the federal government's plan to allow individuals to report belonging to more than one racial group (Stroup, 1998).

Three important facts emerge immediately from a dispassionate examination of terms such as *race* and *ethnicity*. First, these classification systems are arbitrary—established capriciously or by convention or left generally ill-defined. Second, there may be as much or more variation within a group as there is between or among

▌ **TABLE 8.1**
Projected Population of the United States in 2005
Are figures lower, higher, or about the same as you would have estimated?

United States	Numbers in thousands	Percent
Total Population	285,981	100
White	232,463	81.3
Black	37,734	13.2
American Indian, Eskimo, or Aleut	2,572	0.9
Asian or Pacific Islander (Chinese, Filipino, Japanese, Asian Indian, Korean, Vietnamese, Hawaiian, Samoan, Guamanian, and other Asian or Pacific Islander)	13,212	4.6
*Hispanic Origin (Mexican, Puerto Rican, Cuban, and other Hispanic)	36,057	12.6

Note: Percentages total more than 100% due to rounding error and interaction of race (white and black) and Hispanic origin.

*Spanish origin and race are distinct; thus, persons of Spanish origin may be of any race.

Source: "Resident U.S. Population by Sex, Race and Hispanic Origin" by U.S. Census Bureau 1998. **http://www.census.gov/**

groups. For example, Matute-Bianchi (1991) found that "Mexican-descent students" as a group are very diverse in terms of their school performance. Thus the group requires more precise definition to help explain observed differences among Mexican-descent students relevant to their educational achievement. Mexicans tend to perform relatively well in school and, in many cases, outperform nonimmigrant Mexican American students. A simplistic classification scheme can mask important differences among people. When this happens teachers may be "pulled" to behave in ways that are consistent with that scheme but out of line with students' real needs.

The third fact that emerges from a consideration of the language of diversity, as Brian Bullivant (1993) observes, is that classifications can vary depending on who does the classifying. "The subgroups within a pluralistic society can be distinguished by outsiders, or they can distinguish themselves because of the characteristics their members share" (p. 36). Different perspectives, not surprisingly, often yield dissimilar concepts. When people behave in accordance with their differing expectations, as people often do, misunderstanding and conflict may arise.

Even the process of self-definition, while seemingly a reasonable way out of the semantic maze, can be problematic. For example, for census-taking purposes, the federal government defines "American Indian or Alaskan Native" as, "A person having origins in any of the original peoples of North America, and who maintains cultural identification through tribal affiliation or community recognition" (Office of Federal Statistical Policy and Standards, 1978, p. 37). People must define for themselves the meaning of "origins" and "maintains cultural identification."

▶ Prejudice and Discrimination

Providing equal educational opportunity in the classroom is complicated by continuing prejudice and discrimination in the wider society. **Prejudice,** an adverse opinion formed without just grounds or before possessing sufficient knowledge, underlies discrimination. **Discrimination**—differential treatment associated with labels—gives rise to conflict. People too often report and interpret information about groups as though all members conform to some mythical image of sameness, some average that, in turn, drives educational action. This tyranny of "average thinking" overwhelms good sense about the real people who are assigned to these groups.

Studs Terkel's (1992) description of C. P. Ellis, former Exalted Cyclops of the Durham, North Carolina, chapter of the Ku Klux Klan, demonstrates the kind of thinking that leads to racial prejudice and discrimination and also demonstrates the ever-present potential for changing one's attitudes toward others. Ellis told of growing up in abject poverty and quitting school in the eighth grade so that he could go to work when his father died. The degrading poverty was fertile ground for hate, and hate is the grist for the Klan:

> I began to say there's somethin' wrong with this country. I really began to get bitter. I tried to find somebody. I began to blame it on black people. I had to hate somebody. Hatin' America is hard to do because you can't see it to hate it. You gotta have somethin' to look at to hate. [Laughs.] The natural person for me to hate would be black people, because my father before me was a member of the Klan. As far as he was concerned, it was the savior of the white people. It was the only organization that would take care of the white people. So I began to admire the Klan. (Turkel, 1992, p. 272)

What issues relating to racial and cultural diversity might be played out among these students? In what ways might diversity issues affect what, how, and whom you teach?

Through the years, Ellis grew to believe that he and other people like him were being used as pawns by white businessmen. His confrontations with an African American woman named Ann Atwater and his eventual willingness to sit and talk with African Americans under the auspices of a federal program designed to solve racial problems in the schools led gradually to a change of heart.

One day, Ann and I just sat down and began to reflect. Ann said, "My daughter came home cryin' every day. She said her teacher was makin' fun of her in front of the other kids." I said, "Boy, same thing happened to my kid. White liberal teacher was makin' fun of Tim Ellis's father, the Klansman, in front of other peoples. He came home cryin'." At this point—[He pauses, swallows hard, stifles a sob.]—I begin to see, here we are, two people from the far ends of the fence, havin' identical problems, except her bein' black and me bein' white. From that moment on, I tell ya, that gal and I worked together good. I begin to love the girl, really. [He weeps.] (pp. 275–276)

Because some people are segregated from society, isolated by formal and informal means, they feel frightened, alone, and yet defiant. Nine teenagers experienced these feelings in the fall of 1957, when they entered Central High School in Little Rock, Arkansas, accompanied by 22 troopers from the U.S. Army's 101st Airborne as 350 more troopers surrounded the building. Hand picked by the Board of Education, these young people began putting an end to the era of school segregation.

For four decades court-ordered busing plans have signaled the nation's moral resolve to end de jure and de facto segregation (see Chapter 3). Nonetheless, informal or de facto segregation continues today. Many urban systems, such as the Kansas City, Missouri, School District, have lost European American students to the suburbs in droves, which has made impossible the task of achieving racial balance in the schools (Kunen, 1996).

> **Do you believe school integration is important?**

In 1995 the Supreme Court of the United States ruled in *Missouri* v. *Jenkins* that the state of Missouri and the school district did not have to pay for a school desegregation plan designed to attract European American suburban students to Kansas City schools. The Supreme Court held that the ultimate goal was to restore state and local authorities to the control of the school system, not to achieve racial balance. This meant that once the effects of segregation were eliminated, a district could operate schools that were either all European American or all minority.

One likely result of *Missouri* v. *Jenkins* is the resurgence of the concept of "neighborhood schools," or the idea that school assignment should be based on geographical location. In the summer of 1999, for example, the Boston school board voted to discontinue the use of race as a factor in determining where students go to school (Hendrie, 1999). Students who live near particular schools will be given preference to attend those schools. The likely practical effect will be that a disproportionate share of African American and Latino students will have to attend less desirable schools.

Harvard researcher Gary Orfield warns that the United States is moving backward toward separate and unequal education.

One of the great questions of the next generation is whether we ghettoize our Latino population or whether we open the doors of opportunity to them. . . . If we shut them out—and we can see evidence that we are in the employment, income, and school data—then we are facing a social catastrophe. (Hendrie, 1999)

Schools are resegregating at the fastest rate since the U.S. Supreme Court's historic 1954 decision to desegregate schools in *Brown* v. *Board of Education*. According to Hendrie, Orfield and his colleagues argue that the country is in danger of losing the monumental accomplishment of demolishing formerly legally segregated public school systems in the 17 southern and border states.

▶ Misunderstandings

Knowledge and attitude are joined in tangled, seemingly inseparable ways. Nowhere is this fact more obvious than in the relationship of what we know about race and social status and our attitudes about what we should do to educate people for full participation in society.

A national telephone survey of public perceptions of minorities in America sponsored by the *Washington Post,* the Kaiser Family Foundation, and Harvard University (Morin, 1995) suggests that unfortunately, much of what we "know" about race and ethnicity often is incomplete, biased by the language we use, or just plain wrong. A total of 1,970 randomly selected Americans were interviewed, including 802 European Americans, 474 African Americans, 352 English-speaking Asian Americans, and 252 Spanish- and English-speaking Hispanic Americans. Remaining interviewees were of other races or declined to identify their race.

> **What groups might be defined as minorities?**

In the survey a majority of European Americans said they believed that the average African American is faring as well or better than the average European American in jobs, health care, and education. But government statistics show that European Americans, on average, earn 60 percent more than do African Americans, are more likely to have medical insurance, and more than twice as likely to graduate from college. Most of those surveyed, regardless of race, also overestimated the number of minority Americans in the United States. African Americans constitute about 12 percent of the population, but all respondents said that the percentage was about twice that high (Morin, 1995).

The term *minority status* or **minority** carries both a quantitative, or statistical, meaning and a political connotation. Those groups or subgroups in society who are identifiably fewer in number than another group are said to be in the minority. This is a relative term, however. Nationally, African Americans are a minority compared to Anglo European Americans. In some states and cities, however, African Americans constitute a majority of the population.

Minority is also used to describe perceptions of the relative political power or influence that a group exerts in society. For example, because women do not hold public office in the same proportion as their number in the population, women are said to be a minority, that is, they are perceived to exert less influence on the operation of government than do men. The term *minority*, then, is defined comparatively.

How Has Diversity Been Defined in Terms of Development?

Historically, schools have relied to varying degrees on some common concepts to describe all students, most of which have evolved from the educational psychology literature. Students' similarities and differences have been defined in terms of physical development, intelligence, cognitive and moral development, and skills, attitudes, and values that we refer to collectively as *habits of mind*.

▶ Physical and Socioemotional Development

Children's patterns of physical, psychological, and social development and their individual differences in these areas have important implications for education. Between the ages of 2 and 5, preschoolers' control of their large and small muscles improves greatly. Teachers of young children optimize development of large muscles by providing a variety of activities that improve agility, strength, endurance, balance, rhythm, and speed. Teachers also incorporate diverse materials and activities, such as small-block play, clay manipulation, and puzzles to develop fine motor skills and to improve eye–hand coordination.

Some children develop abnormally because of the environments in which they live. One of the most insidious threats, lead, is present in the paint in many homes. Children who are poisoned by ingesting lead-contaminated dust and chips from lead-based paint may experience lasting developmental and health problems and, in extreme cases, comas, convulsions, mental retardation, even death (Children's Defense Fund, 1992).

Children experience a rapid increase in both height and weight that begins at about age 8 or 9 in girls and age 10 or 11 in boys. Although boys often are taller and heavier than girls at age 10, by age 13 girls usually surpass boys in height and weight. By age 16, this trend reverses and boys are once again taller and heavier than girls. The growth spurt young people experience during early adolescence is accompanied by a series of changes in all parts of the body as they begin to develop sexually.

Although children begin their school careers very interested in sports, their desire to participate declines over time. Some argue that one reason young people's enthusiasm wanes with age is due to the emphasis placed on winning. The keen competition it takes to produce champions drives off the majority of young people, who also need opportunities to learn about fair play and chances to practice teamwork skills.

As children grow and change, their body types influence developmental task achievement, self-image, and self-satisfaction. Students who are attractive and athletic typically are popular with adults and peers and are better adjusted than are unattractive students, particularly those who are overweight. Adolescents are particularly sensitive about their physical appearance and often have unrealistic expectations for physical attractiveness. Often **self-esteem,** or the value or sense of worth an individual places on his or her own characteristics, abilities, and behaviors, is affected by such expectations. In particular, girls who are dissatisfied with the way they look often

How do perceptions of physical attractiveness relate to academic success?

are self-conscious and may suffer from low self-esteem (Abramowitz, Petersen, & Schulenberg, 1984; Brooks-Gunn, Graber, & Paikoff, 1994). Many teenage girls who are unhappy with their bodies develop eating disorders. Girls who mature early exhibit more eating problems than do average- or late-maturing girls. Early-maturing girls also are at greater risk for depression (Brooks-Gunn et al., 1994; Rierdan & Koff, 1991).

For the past three decades, the percentage of very overweight children has roughly doubled. For children ages 6 to 11, the incidence of being extremely overweight increased over a 30-year period from 5.2 percent of the population to 10.8 percent for boys and 10.7 percent for girls. For 12- to 17-year-olds, the percentage increased a similar amount, but more dramatically for boys than for girls (Lawton, 1995, p. 6). Researchers have found that a multidisciplinary program of weight reduction, including diet, behavior modification, and exercise, is extremely effective with obese young people (Sothern, von Almen, Schumacher, Suskind, & Blecker, 1999).

Efforts to improve diet and exercise can make a difference in the overall health of young people. Researchers in four states studied the health and behavior of third-grade students over a 3-year period starting in 1991. They changed school lunches and physical education classes at 56 schools. By concentrating on eating habits and promoting exercise, they found that students lowered their fat and cholesterol consumption and increased their physical exercise (Lawton, 1996).

It is essential that adults be sensitive to what children do about their weight and say about their body images. Young people's comments and actions can provide valuable clues about their psychological well-being as well as about their physical health. But one must be careful when reading these clues. For example, what may appear as laziness in the behavior of students may in fact be a manifestation of poor nutrition.

▶ Intelligence

Robert Sternberg and Douglas Detterman's (1986) analysis of 24 descriptions of intelligence by leading experts in the field identifies many competing ideas about the nature of intelligence. Intelligence has been defined as a single, general trait and as a multidimensional set of traits that varies from time to time and from situation to situation. Intelligence also has been defined as error-free transmission of information through the cortex of the brain and as one's repertoire of intellectual knowledge and skills available at a particular point in time. In another definition intelligence is the combination of cognitive skills and knowledge demanded, fostered, and rewarded by one's particular culture.

Traditionally, intellectual aptitude has been measured with tests. Measurement is conducted by administering a number of tasks, observing responses to these tasks, and inferring intellectual capabilities from examinees' performances. Efforts to quantify aptitudes in this fashion began in the late 1800s, when Sir Francis Galton (1822–1911) devised a series of tests of reaction time and sensory acuity to assess adults' mental ability. By the early 1890s Alfred Binet (1857–1911) and Theophile Simon (1873–1961) of France had developed intelligence tests designed to discriminate between more and less able students. Diversity, then, was defined by test items that assessed intellectual abilities such as attention, verbal comprehension, and reasoning.

When Binet's tests were brought to the United States, translated, and revised for use with American children and adults, his detailed profiles of performance across a variety of measures were replaced with a single score, or **intelligence quotient (IQ)**. IQ scores were calculated by dividing an individual's mental age by his chronological age and multiplying the result by 100. Thus, IQ test scores compared individual mental ability to average mental abilities for other people of the same age.

What do intelligence tests measure, a single, general capacity or a combination of multiple abilities? Charles Spearman (1927) studied intelligence tests and determined that there was a *general factor,* or *g,* that all tests shared. He defined *g* as a general ability to form abstract relationships.

How should intelligence be defined?

More recently, J. P. Guilford (1988), Howard Gardner (1995, 1999), and Robert Sternberg and Wendy Williams (1998) have argued that there are many cognitive abilities, each slightly different from the next, that constitute one's intellectual ability. Guilford suggests that mental operations (ways of thinking), contents (what people think about), and products (results of thinking) define more and less intelligent people. Gardner contends that individuals possess **multiple intelligences** that include eight types of capacities and abilities: linguistic (verbal), logical-mathematical, musical, naturalist, spatial, bodily, knowledge of self, and understanding of others. In his triarchic theory of intelligence, Sternberg argues that intelligence is determined by the degree to which individuals demonstrate three processes: metacomponents (mental processes used to plan), performance components (processes used to execute a task), and knowledge-acquisition components (processes used to learn how to solve problems). All three theorists contend that people differ in the strength of these intelligences and in the ways that multiple intelligences are invoked and combined to perform tasks and to solve problems.

In recent years, however, Howard Gardner has expressed concerns about inappropriate applications of his work to classroom practice.

> My psychological work on multiple intelligences has had an unanticipated consequence. This is the assumption on the part of some critics that I am unsympathetic to a rigorous education, and that I eschew high standards. I suppose that is because the idea of multiple intelligences is rightly seen as a critique of the notion of a single intelligence, and of a school curriculum targeted exclusively to linguistic and logical capacities and concerns. . . . A belief in multiple intelligences, however, is in no sense a statement about standards, rigor, or expectations. I do not always succeed in my own life and work, but it is not for lack of trying. . . . It pains me to see my work aligned . . . with that of individuals who are apologists for low standards, low expectations, "anything goes." (1999, p. 25)

Other concerns have to do with the origins of intelligence. Is intellectual ability a result of one's biological inheritance or the product of one's environment? In other words, are people born with their intellectual abilities (endowed with them by nature), or are such abilities nurtured (developed by education and life's experiences)? Although it is impossible to answer the question with certainty, most experts agree that intellectual ability is a product of both nature and nurture. Many studies of twins who have been reared apart show that although genetic factors are strong predictors of intellectual functioning, other influences on intellectual ability, such as parenting and education, cannot be ignored (Bouchard, Lykken, McGue, Segal, & Tellegen, 1990).

Intellectual ability is certainly critical to one's academic success, but family income is also a powerful determinant of intellectual ability, particularly among young children. An analysis of longitudinal data from the Infant Health and Development Program, an eight-site study of low-birthweight babies that was launched in the 1980s, revealed that family income correlates more strongly with IQ at age 5 than do such factors as mother's education, child's ethnicity, or the fact that a child lives in a home headed by a woman. Among the sample of 900 low-birthweight children studied, those living in persistent poverty from birth had IQs about 9 points lower than did those who were not living in poverty during their first few years of life (Cohen, 1993).

Is there a cognitive elite in society?

Intelligence test scores, estimates of scholastic aptitude, and measures of general ability are widely considered good predictors of success in school and in the workplace, yet some people contend that test scores reveal relatively little about intelligence and even less about a person's creativity, wisdom, and intellectual style (Sternberg, 1996). Critics argue that tests unfairly restrict opportunities for growth and advancement (Hilliard, 1990). Employers who have worked with individuals with IQ scores below 100, for example, have found that low-scorers' abilities extend beyond what IQ scores predict (Ceci & Ruiz, 1993).

▶ Cognitive Development

Theories of cognitive development are closely related to concepts of intelligence. They too have been used to describe how people are alike and how they differ. Jean Piaget (1896–1980), a Swiss psychologist whose lifework was understanding how children at different ages perceive and know the world around them, is recognized as the most influential cognitivist. Piaget believed that children are born with the potential to develop intelligence and that the increasing complexity of children's thinking as they age is caused both by maturational changes in the nervous system and by direct experience as children interact with the physical world and with other people. Changes in cognitive development are based on the child's ability to change her ways of thinking about the world when existing ideas do not match new information and experience.

To explain how children perceive and structure reality at different points in their development, Piaget categorized children's ways of thinking into four qualitatively different stages: sensorimotor (birth to 2 years), preoperational (2 to 7 years), concrete operational (7 to 11 years), and formal operational (11 to 16 years).

According to Piaget, children may progress through the stages at different rates, but the order in which they do so remains constant. Decisions about a child's stage cannot be made on the basis of age alone, however. Children demonstrate inconsistencies in thinking; that is, a child may demonstrate one level of thinking in one situation and a different level of thinking in another.

Piaget's stage theory does not account for the effects of individual differences such as gender, personality, intelligence (as measured by IQ tests), or culture on students' cognitive development. Although Piagetians contend that the four developmental stages are universal, there is evidence that formal operations, the highest level of thinking, is attained by few adolescents, college students, or adults in the United States, Africa, or Europe (Mwamwenda, 1992). In some non-Western cultures that do not focus on abstract thinking, formal operational thought as defined by Piaget is not present. How quickly children move through the different stages also varies by culture, depending on environmental conditions. According to one researcher, children in Martinique, an island in the West Indies, were 4 years later developing operational thought than were their counterparts in Switzerland. In Tehran, the capital of Iran, children developed similarly to children in Switzerland, but in the rural villages of Iran, children developed 2 years later (Sutherland, 1992).

> **How do cultural factors affect cognitive development?**

▶ Moral Development

Moral development, or changes relating to age and intelligence in the way an individual makes reasoned judgments about right and wrong, has always been a concern of public schools. Despite disagreement over the meaning of the term, educators' goal has been to produce good people. Historically, programs in the United States have been structured to help students achieve a kind of American character, the particular variety of which was described early on by Horace Mann in terms of "veracity, probity, and rectitude" (Cremin, 1957, p. 100).

Too often, as Christopher Clark observes, concepts of moral development have been used by adults to describe children's shortcomings. Clark challenges adults to recognize that a young person's moral development depends in no small measure on the context in which the child lives, a context shaped and controlled by adults.

> Our culture of parenting and pedagogy invariably takes the side of the adult and blames the child for what has been done to him or her; for what was done to you and to me, when we were helpless children. Faced with the power of adults and the social conspiracy of denial, we and our children repress our feelings, idealize or excuse those parents and teachers who abused us, and, tragically, perpetuate the victimization of the next generation. (1995, p. 24)

Like Clark, Douglas Heath puts the responsibility for the moral development of children on adults, more specifically on educators. In any modern reform of schools, Heath would emphasize school accountability, but not merely accountability for academic success. "If they [schools] are to produce enduring effects on their students, they must educate for the healthy growth of mind *and* character, integrated by a maturing self" (1999, p. ix). For Heath, this means attending to such qualities as caring, honesty, courage, responsibility, integrity, fairness, and dedication.

Theories of character development and moral education have grown less absolute, less propagandistic, and more aligned with students' cognitive development. Beginning with his doctoral studies at the University of Chicago and proceeding through his career on the faculty at Harvard, Lawrence Kohlberg (1927–1987) shaped modern thinking about moral development and moral education. Much as Piaget described intellectual development, Kohlberg described moral reasoning in terms of six stages.

Kohlberg reasoned that, given opportunities, people's moral character grows more complex and more comprehensive over time. By studying how people think about moral questions, he recognized that simplistic terms such as *right* and *wrong,*

Issues in School Reform

Waging Peace

The 1999 shootings at Columbine High School have touched the public psyche as have few other tragedies in recent memory. As shock has settled into unwilling acceptance of a horrifying reality, educational leaders attempt, as best they can, to protect the safety of young people and adults in schools. Whether schools should have locks on doors, observation cameras, armed guards, and the like, is no longer debatable. These jailhouse accouterments are viewed increasingly as prerequisites for teaching and learning. But the physical trappings of violence prevention are only the most visible changes in schools. Because people's differences seem too quickly and easily translated into hate and then into violence, more and more educational leaders are advocating the reform of schools as a process of waging peace:

> As a nation, we need to take in the pain and suffering of the families and friends of Columbine High School and seek out ways to assure that others do not walk down the same path. There is no single, simple remedy to this problem. Our response to these complicated issues has to be a wide-ranging public response. When we think about solutions, our focus needs to be not on any one program or project, but rather [to]

include efforts involving the private sector, national and local governments, neighborhood organizations, religious communities, law enforcement, mental-health professionals, educators, researchers, and businesses. We must all mobilize our energies.

We need to question deeply what our vision of education is for our young people and what the role of schools is within that view. Schools are our society's primary formal institution for socializing children into their roles as concerned and responsible citizens in a democracy. This is a tremendous responsibility. It involves recognizing that our goals are not only to produce students with fabulous test scores, but students who become fabulous people. We want our children to become knowledgeable, of course, but also responsible and caring. We want our youths to have academic skills, but we also know that life success is based at least as much on emotional intelligence as on intellectual intelligence. We need academic standards to improve our students' skills in math, literacy, science, and social studies, but we also need standards in life skills so that we are effective in our interactions with others in the workplace, community, and family.

[In 1997] ASCD presented a list of 39 guidelines for providing effective social and emotional education. Several that are rele-

good and *bad* did not reflect the full range of people's capacity to judge moral issues. People at stages 1 and 2, or what Kohlberg called a preconventional level of morality, make decisions based on their own needs. People at stages 3 and 4 (conventional morality) weigh social mores and laws as they make judgments. And those who are at the most complex level of morality (stages 5 and 6, a level of postconventional morality) consider moral issues in keeping with abstract personal or universal principles.

The stories Kohlberg and his colleagues used to assess stages of moral develop-

vant to fostering a safer, more caring school climate follow:

▌ Build and reinforce life skills and social competencies; health-promotion and problem-prevention skills; coping skills; and social support for transitions, crises, and for making positive social contributions.

▌ Link efforts to build social and emotional skills to developmental milestones, as well as to the need to help students cope with ongoing life events and local circumstances.

▌ Emphasize the promotion of prosocial attitudes and values about self, others, and work.

▌ Integrate social and emotional learning with traditional academics to enhance learning in both areas.

▌ Build a caring, supportive, and challenging classroom and school climate to assure effective social and emotional teaching and learning.

▌ Integrate and coordinate social-and-emotional-learning programs and activities with the regular curriculum and life of the classroom and school.

▌ Foster enduring and pervasive effects in this type of social and emotional learning through collaboration between home and school.

The focus on reform and renewal among educators, politicians, and the public continues to miss the mark. To change a school's culture so all children can learn, we must address the relationships that exist in that school. Adults and young people who develop skills to communicate with one another, problem-solve together, believe in the richness of diversity, and embrace conflict as an opportunity to grow, can and do contribute to the kind of school culture we search for in schools today. But we can't change a school's culture unless we are willing and able to reflect on our own capacities to accept and respond to change ourselves. The problem is not "out there." It begins with each and every one of us. (Elias, Lantieri, Walberg, & Zins, 1999, pp. 45,49)

Discussion Questions What community-based and/or school-based programs are you aware of that focus on improving students' and teachers' relationships with one another? For what age groups are the programs designed? What role, if any, do parents play in the programs?

Source: Elias, M. J., Lantieri, L., Patti, J., Walberg, H. J., & Zins, J. E. (1999, May 19). Violence is preventable. *Education Week, 18*(36), 45,49. Reprinted with permission of Education Week.

ment are presented in the form of moral dilemmas—problems that force choices between unsatisfactory alternative courses of action. People's responses to these problems can be categorized into distinct types that represent the six stages in Kohlberg's theory. The following is an example of a dilemma used for assessment and educational purposes:

Before the junior class trip the faculty told the students that the whole class had to agree not to bring or use alcohol or drugs on the trip. If students were found using drugs or alcohol, they would be sent home. The students knew that without faculty approval they would not be able to have their trip. The students said in a class meeting that they all agreed to these conditions. On the trip, several students ask Bob, a fellow student, to go on a hike with them to the lake. When they get to the lake, they light up a joint and pass it around. What should Bob do? (Power, Higgins, & Kohlberg, 1989, p. 247)

Some social scientists have criticized Kohlberg for what they perceive to have been his bias in favor of males (Gilligan 1982; Gilligan & Attanucci, 1988). Carol Gilligan argued that Kohlberg's scoring system penalized females and that his level of postconventional morality excluded a dimension of human caring—a dimension upon which she believed females would excel. David Hansen (1996) argues, however, that such moral dimensions as justice and caring coexist in individual reasoning and development; they are not gender- or culture-specific but may be regarded as fundamental and universal. Regardless, Gilligan's claims have sensitized others to the importance of compassion as a dimension of morality.

Critics of Kohlberg also have focused on the absence of an explicit relationship in the theory between moral judgment and moral action (Sockett, 1993). Simply because people reason at higher levels of development does not guarantee that they will behave in moral ways.

Most stage theorists, such as Kohlberg and Piaget, hold that people only progress to higher stages when forced to confront situations that are slightly more complex than those with which they are prepared to deal. Generally, teachers who wish to encourage development try to understand how their students reason and to create learning opportunities that gently stretch the students to consider new possibilities.

When confronted with hypothetical moral issues, even young children display remarkable capacities to reason about justice and compassion. Experimenters in New England studied the reactions of children ages 5 to 13 to two fables, the "Porcupine and the Moles" and the "Dog in the Manger." The "Porcupine and the Moles" fable presents a family of moles who invite a porcupine to share the warmth of their cave.

Do boys and girls use different kinds of moral reasoning?

Unfortunately, the porcupine is so large that his sharp quills make the moles uncomfortable. When they courteously ask the porcupine to leave, he declines, because he likes the cave. The "Dog in the Manger" fable describes a hungry ox who returns to his stall after a hard day at work. There he finds a dog on the hay refusing to move aside so the ox can eat. The investigators asked the children how the animals should solve their problems.

Boys and girls tended to reason in similar fashion. As indicated in Figure 8.1, when asked for the best solution to the fables, children preferred "care-oriented responses." Children's ability to see more than one moral orientation depended on their abstract reasoning skills.

While not everyone agrees about what students should be taught to think, many agree that learning how to reason effectively about moral issues should be a high priority. People may favor contemporary moral orientations or prefer traditional values, but teaching children to handle the power to choose falls increasingly to schools and teachers.

FIGURE 8.1
Children's Responses to Fables   How do the justice-oriented responses differ from the care-oriented responses?

JUSTICE-ORIENTED RESPONSES	CARE-ORIENTED RESPONSES
If there's a whole messload of dogs and a whole messload of oxes, they should have a big war to see who gets the hay. (Boy, age 8)	The porcupine could make a wall across the cave. 'Cause then they'd both have a home. (Boy, age 5)
They should put out a sign and it has a circle and a cross on it and a porcupine in the middle. And maybe they write in red on it that says "No porcupines allowed." (Boy, age 6)	They should cooperate. Maybe like if there was more rock they could try and blast out some more, and they would all help. And a few of 'em, maybe, ought to take care of the babies if they have some. (Girl, age 6)
The porcupine should move because they [the moles] were there first, and if they left it wouldn't be fair, because they were there first. And the porcupine should move because they could hurt him, you know, really bad like that and stuff, and it's their home. (Girl, age 10)	They should all go on an expedition for marshmallows on the porcupine's quills and then the moles will really, really, really not get pricked. Then the porcupine would be happy because he could live in the moles' house that suited him just fine and the moles could have tasty tidbits as well as a warm home because of the porcupine's body heat... and all would be happy. (Boy, age 8)
If you want to be treated nicely, you got to treat the other person nice, too. (Boy, age 12)	The moles could dig another home for the porcupine. It would be generous of them, and they could make another friend if they did that. The more friends you have usually is the better. (Girl, age 12)

▶ Habits of Mind

Students' intellectual capacities and their abilities to reason morally influence both teaching and learning, but so too do what James Rutherford and Andrew Ahlgren (1994) and Melinda Fine (1995) call students' **habits of mind.** Habits of mind are the shared skills, attitudes, and values transmitted by custom or convention from one generation to the next. Many people other than teachers try to affect students' habits of mind. They do so by writing and selecting curricula, by funding or denying funding for educational programs, by creating employment opportunities for graduates, and by setting college admissions standards. Influencing students' habits of mind is serious business, for this set of values, attitudes, and skills relates directly to a person's outlook on education.

The habits of mind deemed important by parents, leaders in government and business, professors, and many others appear in public policy statements. The National Education Goals (Goals 2000), for example, contain references to skills, attitudes, and values that various people consider essential. But in many ways the informal, often implicit habits of mind, are those that shape the ethos of a community. They can be thought of as the attributes of the more abstract concepts that bind people together.

When people discuss education reform, talk turns to students' attitudes. Two attitudes in particular are often characterized as socially desirable: cooperation and competition. Adults argue that students need to cultivate the temperament to cooperate with one another. When they possess cooperative attitudes, and the concomitant skills needed to work together effectively, they will be prepared to compete with the nation's economic rivals.

When young people realize that cooperating and competing involve some personal risks and that working with and against others means not always getting one's own way and maybe losing more often than winning, they realize that the "winning-is-everything" attitude does not work. In fact, striving for success, failing, and coping gracefully with defeat yield an uncommon dignity that is widely admired.

Another attitude thought to be essential in a civilized society is compassion. Teachers encourage children to be kind to one another not because of the school mission statement or curriculum but because civilized people expect as much of each other.

People in North American middle-class society also expect each other to possess a variety of skills associated with science, mathematics, and technology that will allow them to participate fully in society. These include calculating skills, skills of manipulating and observing, communication skills, and critical response skills. Such skills are also recognized as habits of mind. Every day, particularly on the job, people need to be able to calculate. Simple paper-and-pencil arithmetic skills once were sufficient for most situations, but with the introduction of inexpensive electronic calculators, the workplace has changed. Operators must be able to read and follow step-by-step instructions in calculator manuals; construct simple algorithms for solving problems; determine what the unit (seconds, square inches, dollars per tankful) of the answer will be from inputs; round off answers; and judge whether an answer is reasonable by comparing it to an estimated answer. Each of these skills, in turn, involves other problem-solving skills (Rutherford & Ahlgren, 1994).

What habits of mind should teachers promote?

Mathematically and technologically literate people also must possess skills of manipulation and observation. These skills include distinguishing between observations and speculations; storing and retrieving computer information using standard computer software; using appropriate instruments to measure length, volume, weight, time, and temperature; troubleshooting common mechanical and electrical systems; and comparing consumer products.

Skills of reading, writing, and speaking have traditionally served as the hallmarks of literacy. The skill of listening—always crucial for learning but magnified in importance with the growth of modern technology—must be added to the list. People cannot take advantage of opportunities or advance their position in society without strong communication skills. Our information society demands ever-increasing levels of communicative sophistication.

The skills and attitudes society requires are worth little if young people do not develop a set of values. Some argue that public schools reinforce values of obedience and conformity to protect the status quo. Such skepticism expressed about educational intent is a widely accepted value. But the results of schooling as measured in bright, productive people who have emerged from the system stand as testament to the abiding importance of curiosity and openness to new ideas. When coupled with motivation or drive, good people resist being held down.

By placing people on a habits-of-mind continuum, from poor to admirable, we could see the considerable diversity among them. Some of the variation among individuals and groups might also be attributed to other cultural influences. The habits of mind valued by society are not always transmitted in ways that children from certain cultures are used to seeing and hearing. The style of communication to which they are accustomed is not congruent with that which they find in school. A study of Native American children, for instance, revealed that much of the formal learning that took place at home was nonverbal in nature. That is, children learned skills and values not from verbal instruction but from observing and sharing directly in the activities of others. While learning through observation and imitation is common across all cultures, Native Americans' predisposition to use this method of learning puts them at a disadvantage in schools, where learning socially desirable habits of mind often means being told (Henry & Pepper, 1990).

Many students express what they value through their participation in extracurricular activities and in how they choose to spend their free time. Table 8.2 shows how these choices compare by gender, race–ethnicity, and socioeconomic status of students. Low socioeconomic status (SES) students generally participate at lower rates in most activities, except for watching television and participating in selected school groups. To reinforce the value of participation, we must better understand how the constraints of poverty and family background and the influence of school community affect student choices.

We also need to understand what motivates students to get involved and stay involved. From the results of an analysis of 96 studies, Judy Cameron and David Pierce (1994) argue that reinforcement (verbal praise) and reward are what hook students and keep them coming back for more. Others (Kohn, 1996; Lepper, Keavney, & Drake, 1996) contend that the effects of rewards and verbal reinforcement are far too complicated to rely on them as simple prescriptions to guarantee successful teaching. Teachers must work to know their students' values, interests, and

TABLE 8.2
Participation of 12th-Graders in Extracurricular and Various Other Activities, by Selected Student Characteristics

						Percent who participated in school activities					
						1992 12th graders					
		Sex		Race/ethnicity					Socioeconomic status[1]		
Extracurricular activities	Total	Male	Female	White	Black	Hispanic	Asian	American Indian	Low	Middle	High
1	2	3	4	5	6	7	8	9	10	11	12
Athletics											
Interscholastic team sport	30.4	41.2	19.7	30.8	32.3	25.8	28.3	30.4	25.3	30.1	34.4
Interscholastic individual sport	20.3	26.8	13.9	20.9	21.2	14.9	21.6	20.7	13.6	18.7	27.7
Intramural team sport	22.7	31.8	13.8	22.3	25.8	20.8	24.9	27.9	20.4	22.9	24.1
Intramural individual sport	13.3	16.7	10.0	12.5	16.7	14.0	14.7	18.2	10.8	12.5	15.9
Performing arts											
Cheerleading	7.6	2.0	13.0	7.4	10.6	6.7	5.1	11.9	6.5	7.9	7.8
School band or orchestra	19.8	15.1	24.5	19.6	24.4	16.9	17.7	16.8	17.6	19.6	22.0
School play or musical	15.4	14.1	16.7	16.1	15.9	10.6	13.7	14.0	11.4	14.8	19.4
School government/clubs											
Student government	15.4	13.1	17.7	15.4	16.7	14.7	14.6	14.3	11.0	14.7	19.8
Academic honor society	18.5	14.4	22.7	19.6	14.0	12.5	27.2	13.6	9.6	15.9	29.5
School yearbook/newspaper	18.8	14.0	23.5	19.7	14.3	16.8	18.9	21.2	14.3	16.9	25.1
School service clubs	13.9	10.3	17.4	13.6	13.6	14.4	19.3	11.6	8.4	12.5	19.6
School academic clubs	25.1	22.9	27.4	25.8	20.7	22.6	32.3	17.7	18.8	24.1	31.1
School hobby clubs	7.7	8.1	7.4	7.4	6.6	9.1	11.3	10.8	6.7	7.0	9.3
School FTA, FHA, and FFA	17.7	14.7	20.7	17.6	22.5	16.4	8.8	22.1	24.8	19.7	9.9

At least once a week

Use personal computer	23.7	28.1	19.3	23.9	23.6	20.9	27.0	23.8	18.9	23.3	27.7
Work on hobbies	40.9	44.4	37.4	42.0	34.8	39.9	37.8	49.8	36.3	41.1	43.5
Attend religious activities	31.0	28.1	33.8	31.4	33.7	26.9	30.4	14.6	22.2	29.4	39.9
Attend youth groups	22.4	24.6	20.1	22.5	23.3	18.5	26.4	22.1	16.6	21.3	28.1
Perform community service	11.3	10.7	11.9	11.1	12.1	10.9	14.0	9.2	7.7	9.5	16.7
Driving or riding around	73.3	74.3	72.3	75.7	67.8	66.2	66.7	71.0	69.6	75.3	72.4
Do things with friends	88.1	88.2	88.0	90.7	79.8	82.4	85.9	77.2	80.8	88.1	93.2
Do things with parent	66.7	61.2	72.1	68.2	62.0	63.8	63.4	61.2	59.6	66.3	71.7
Talk with other adult	47.7	45.4	49.9	48.8	44.3	46.2	43.0	44.0	47.6	49.0	45.0
Take music, art, or dance class	10.1	7.9	12.2	9.9	9.7	9.8	14.0	10.6	7.1	8.8	14.0
Take sports lessons	7.3	9.7	5.0	7.0	7.4	8.2	9.4	11.6	5.6	6.6	9.5
Play ball or other sport	26.3	38.8	14.0	27.1	22.9	23.6	28.7	29.4	20.7	24.5	33.1

More than an hour a day

Reading for pleasure	55.4	53.1	57.7	56.3	51.0	53.5	54.4	59.3	51.6	55.0	58.6
Plays video games	13.0	19.2	6.8	11.7	19.9	13.0	13.5	21.1	16.9	13.7	9.4

Five or more hours on weekdays

Watches television	8.4	8.5	8.4	6.4	21.3	9.3	6.4	12.7	12.0	9.4	4.1

[1]Socioeconomic status was measured by a composite score on parental education and occupations, and family income. The Low SES group is the lowest quartile; the Middle SES group is the middle two quartiles; and the High SES group is the upper quartile.

Source: U.S. Department of Education, National Center for Education Statistics, "National Education Longitudinal Study of 1988," Second Followup survey, and "High School and Beyond," First Followup survey. (This table was prepared March 1994.)

Note: From U.S. Department of Education, 1999, Tables 144 and 146. *Digest of Education Statistics 1998.*

concerns—habits of mind—if they are to stimulate and maintain students' participation in school. Teachers themselves must be motivated if they expect students to be motivated, to care, to participate.

What Other Concepts Define Diversity?

As teachers plan for instruction, they may think about teaching and learning from the viewpoints of immigrants, language minority or bilingual students, and males and females. Educators may also consider exceptionalities (special abilities or disabilities) and sexual orientations that students bring to the classroom. How one views learners and the classrooms they inhabit depends entirely on where one stands. To be both successful and fair, teachers must be able to perceive situations from multiple perspectives.

▶ From Immigrants' Perspectives

In 1997, the foreign-born population of the United States numbered 25.8 million people or 9.7 percent of the total population (Schmidley & Alvarado, 1997). Five states had a larger percentage of foreign-born residents than did the United States as a nation: California (24.8%), New York (19.6%), Florida (16.4%), New Jersey (15.4%), and Texas (11.3%). Persons born in Central America, South America, or the Caribbean accounted for 51 percent of the total.

As illustrated in Figure 8.2, the percent of the U.S. population that is foreign born has continued to increase since 1970. More than 2 million immigrant children enrolled in U.S. schools in the 1980s and 1990s, more than at any other time since the early twentieth century. While immigration is still largely an urban phenomenon, it has touched suburban and rural communities as well. As Lynn Schnaiberg (1999a) notes, the ways in which schools deal with their changing populations is linked to society's attitudes about immigration; thus schools throughout the century "have found themselves in a recurring pendulum swing between assimilation and pluralism" (p. 34).

Immigrants' experiences vary widely and differ from those of other minorities.

How might the experiences of immigrants differ from those of other students?

Anthropologists John Ogbu and Herbert Simons have offered a controversial theory on these differences (1998). They describe "castelike minorities," or involuntary nonimmigrant minorities, as people who are Americans as a result of slavery, conquest, or colonization. Ogbu and Simons contend that, in addition to experiencing discrimination from others, involuntary minorities may also defeat themselves through feelings of inferiority.

When Ogbu and colleague Signithia Fordham studied bright African American students in Washington, DC, they found that the students did not live up to their potentials. Ogbu and Fordham claimed that these students did not want to be accused by their peers of "acting white"—speaking standard English, adopting certain clothing styles, listening to certain radio stations, or engaging in activities such as studying in the library or going camping (Hill, 1990). Ogbu and Simons argue that

FIGURE 8.2
Percentage of the U.S. Population That Is Foreign-born

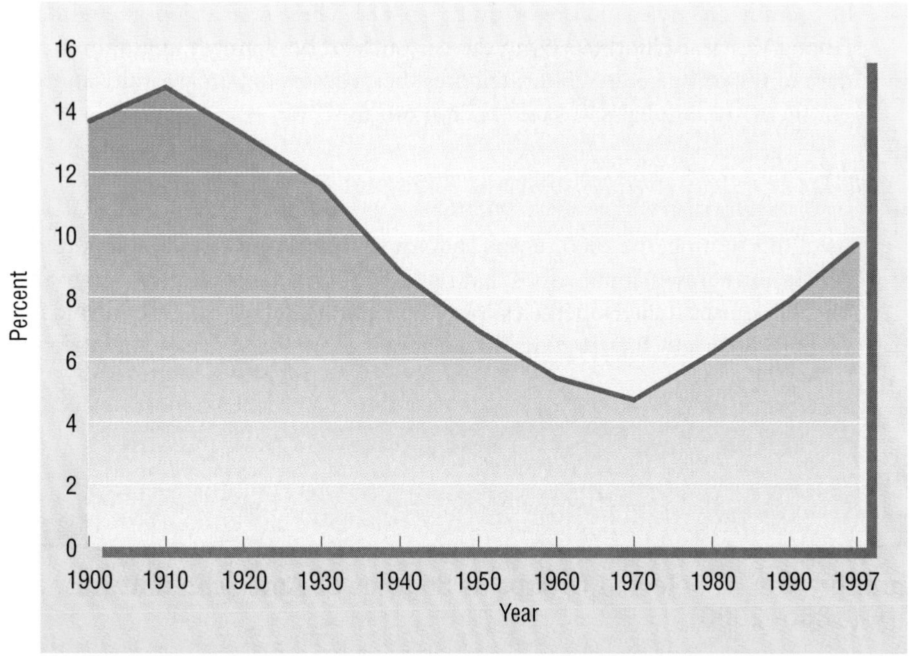

Source: From *Historical Census Statistics on the Foreign-born Population of the United States* by J. Gibson and E. Lennon, 1999. Washington, DC: U.S. Census Bureau.

as members of involuntary minorities, some African Americans, such as these students, see education as a "subtractive process" that forces them to lose their own cultural identity if they are to succeed. Furthermore, they contend that voluntary immigrant minorities tend to see education as an opportunity to get ahead and may not equate success in school with losing their culture.

Critics have denounced such theories as blaming the victims for their failures. They point out that many voluntary minorities also resist cultural assimilation. Although these minorities may value economic success, they do not view erasing or discarding all signs of native origin and cultural identity as a desirable outcome.

Nathan Caplan, Marcella Choy, and John Whitmore (1991) described compellingly the combined power of cultural factors and education in their discussion of "the children of the boat people." In 1981 these researchers began studying Vietnamese, Chinese, and Laotian immigrants to the United States and found among the children "high levels of achievement at the very outset of their formal education in America" (p. 20). Even when they attended low-income, inner-city schools, they earned uniformly high standardized achievement test scores. Kindergarten teachers' anecdotal records showed that the children were eager to learn and took pleasure from their work even before they entered first grade.

Why were these children so successful? The researchers attributed success on scholastic and economic measures to three factors they called "culturally based values, family life-style, and opportunity" (p. 88). These conclusions are reinforced by Duong Van Mai Elliott (1999) in the chronicle of her family's migration from Vietnam to the United States. She attributes their success to family loyalty and support. For them, the emphasis was on "us," not on "me."

▶ From a Language Minority or Bilingual Perspective

As of this writing, the 2000 census had not yet been conducted and reported, so the conclusions drawn about issues that revolve around language proficiency are based on 1990 census data. Nonetheless, we know that language can be a formidable barrier in U.S. society. Interpreting life as a language-minority person might do is some-

Benchmarks

Peak Immigration of Selected Groups as Sources of American Cultural Diversity (1800–2000)

Colonial Era & Early Republic	Spanish, French, English, Dutch, and Portuguese; African slaves.
1800–1860	Germans, Irish, African slaves, English, Swedes, Danes, Norwegians, Dutch, Belgians, Swiss, French. Peak immigration of people from western and northern Europe. One million Irish immigrate to the United States between 1847 and 1860. In 1854, Germans compose 50 percent of all immigrants.
1860–1880	Chinese, Poles, Russians, Hungarians, Serbs, Austrians, Scandinavians, Italians, Greeks, Canadians. By 1880, 4 of 5 New Yorkers are foreign born or first-generation American.
1880–1900	Japanese, Italians, Poles, Russians, Slovaks, Magyars, Czechs, Croats, Greeks. Four million Russians and Poles and 4.5 million Italians immigrate to the United States during these years.
1900–1930	Mexicans, Latin Americans, Canadians, Italians, Russians, Poles. Period of peak immigration from eastern and southern Europe. Puerto Ricans become U.S. citizens in 1917.
1930–1960	Cubans, Mexicans, Koreans. Period of peak relocation of Puerto Ricans. In the 1940s and 1950s, 3.5 million refugees come to the United States from all countries affected by World War II.
1960–2000	Vietnamese, Cambodians, Laotians, Thais, Guatemalans, and other groups from Central and South American countries, Ethiopians, Haitians.

thing most monolingual, English-speaking Americans never contemplate. Relatively few monolingual English speakers ever find themselves in situations where someone else does not also speak English. But many students who are categorized as **limited English proficient (LEP)** or qualify for instruction in **English as a Second Language (ESL)** view life in U.S. society from behind a language barrier.

According to the U.S. Department of Education (1996), there were dramatic changes in the numbers and characteristics of the non-English-speaking population between 1979 and 1989. The number of people in the U.S. population 5 years old and older who spoke a language other than English at home increased from 9 to 12 percent. Surprisingly, almost half of all non-English speakers were born in the United States. Spanish was spoken by 58 percent of all speakers of languages other than English.

About half of the non-English-speaking population has difficulty speaking English. In 1979, 53 percent of this group were enrolled below their expected grade level. By 1989, 38 percent were below grade level, compared to 34 percent for English-only speakers. Making placement decisions is difficult, however, because gauging the progress of students with limited English proficiency is challenging. No standard criteria exist by which specific forms of assessment can be selected or adapted to fit these students' language needs (U.S. Department of Education, 1996).

What are some implications of minority status for students and families? For teachers and schools? How might the experiences of immigrants differ from those of other minorities?

Students with limited English proficiency receive help in the form of **bilingual education,** or instruction in both English and their native language. Bilingual programs vary in the amount of support they provide. Some offer instruction to students in both English and their native language and culture throughout their school years. Other programs help students make the transition from their native language to English by offering ongoing, intensive instruction in English as a Second Language (ESL) classes. Yet other programs remove students from regular classes to receive special help in English or in reading in their native language. And some programs immerse non-English speaking students in English, sometimes providing an aide who speaks the native language, then place students in English-speaking classes.

Some people believe that teaching non-English-speaking children in their native language, the language they hear most at home, while easing them gradually into English is the only reasonable way to move these children into the mainstream. Make them "competent in two languages," argues Raul Yzaguirre, director of the National Council of La Raza in Washington, DC, an umbrella group of several hundred Hispanic organizations (Bernstein, 1990, p. 44). The most prominent concern of bilingual-education advocates appears to be retention of cultural identity. You can visit the National Council of La Raza online to learn more about this issue.

Others believe that teaching children in their native language is bad for them and bad for the country. They contend that bilingual programs hold children back by doing a substandard job of teaching children either in their native tongue or in English. "Bilingual education, they argue, is more likely to prepare minority children for careers in the local Taco Bell than for medical school or nuclear physics" (Bernstein,

Voices

On Passion

Passions underlying the debate about culture in our nation can be volatile and dangerous; at the same time, they can stimulate genuine human understanding where little or none has existed before. Philosopher Maxine Greene of Teachers College, Columbia University, reaffirms passion's correct place in the dialogue about cultural diversity in the United States.

There have always been newcomers in this country; there have always been strangers. There have always been young persons in our classrooms we did not, could not see or hear. In recent years, however, invisibility has been refused on many sides. Old silences have been shattered; long-repressed voices are making themselves heard. Yes, we are in search of what John Dewey called "The Great Community"; but, at once, we are challenged as never before to confront plurality and multiplicity. Unable to deny or obscure the facts of pluralism, we are asked to choose ourselves with respect to unimaginable diversities. To speak of passions in such a context is not to refer to the strong feelings aroused by what strikes many as a confusion and a cacophony. Rather, it is to have in mind the central sphere for the operation of the passions: "the realm of face-to-face relationships." It seems clear that the more continuous and authentic personal encounters can be, the less likely it will be for categorizing and distancing to take place. People are less likely to be treated instrumentally, to be made "other" by those around.

No one can predict precisely the common world of possibility, nor can we absolutely justify one kind of community over another. Many of us, however, for all the tensions and disagreements around us, would reaffirm the value of principles like justice and equality and freedom and commitment to human rights,

since, without these, we cannot even argue for the decency of welcoming. Only if more and more persons incarnate such principles, we might say, and choose to live by them and engage in dialogue in accord with them, are we likely to bring about a democratic pluralism and not fly apart in violence and disorder. Unable to provide an objective ground for such hopes and claims, all we can do is speak with others as eloquently and passionately as we can about justice and caring and love and trust.

We want our classrooms to be just and caring, full of various conceptions of the good. We want them to be articulate, with the dialogue involving as many persons as possible, opening to one another, opening to the world. And we want them to be concerned for one another, as we learn to be concerned for them. We want them to achieve friendships among one another, as each one moves to a heightened sense of craft and wide-awakeness, to a renewed consciousness of worth and possibility.

CRITICAL THINKING

Why might people who interact face-to-face continually and in genuine ways be less likely to categorize one another and to hold each other at a psychological distance? How might we use information we acquire about others not to understand them but to construct conceptions of whom we believe them to be? What guidelines would you develop for yourself to ensure that your classroom is "just and caring"?

Source: Freedom's Plow: Teaching in the Multicultural Classroom (pp. 193–194) by M. Greene, 1993, New York: Routledge. Reprinted by permission of the publisher.

1990, p. 44). Bilingual programs vary by the amount of English taught and the rapidity with which it is introduced. Definitions of program and student success vary widely.

Why might some people oppose bilingual education?

J. David Ramirez (1992) studied more than 2,000 students for 4 years. After examining data on the children, their families, classrooms, teachers, schools, school districts, and communities, he concluded that the more instruction children receive in their first language, the better they perform in their second language. Ramirez also found that children in all-English and bilingual programs showed comparable performances during the early elementary grades, and the students in immersion and early-exit bilingual programs began to fall behind in the upper grades. Other researchers have reached similar conclusions (Caudell, 1996).

Rosalie Pedalino Porter (1995) offers another view. Based on the findings of a study conducted over 4 years in the New York City schools, she argues there is strong evidence

> [that] the earlier a second language is introduced, the more rapidly it is learned for academic purposes. . . . Apparently, with appropriate teaching, children can learn a new language quickly and can learn subject matter taught *in* that language. Reading and writing skills can be mastered and math can be learned successfully in a second language. (1995, p. 2)

Should these students receive instruction in Spanish? In English only? What issues are involved? What does research suggest as the best way to educate students whose first language is not English?

Claims for and against the efficacy of bilingual education interact with feelings of ethnic pride. Some Latinos, for example, argue that a "white, Anglo" education damages students' feelings of self-worth. Others worry that bilingual education emphasizes differences in language, thus pushing people further apart when they need to come together as Americans. Anglos and Latinos can be found on both sides of the argument.

Independent of such disputes, schools often have great difficulty delivering bilingual services. There is a shortage of qualified bilingual teachers. Most are needed for Spanish–English classes, because most LEP students are Latinos. Increasingly, teachers are needed with combined skills in English and other languages. Fewer capable professionals means higher chances for misdiagnosing learning problems as special education concerns and lower capacity for teaching students with language needs. Hiring larger numbers of more highly qualified professionals is, unfortunately, a costly undertaking.

In California, the issue of how to teach students of limited English proficiency came to the forefront in 1998 with the passage of Proposition 227. This law requires schools to teach such students almost entirely in English, even though parents can opt out of English-only classes if they choose (Schnaiberg, 1999b). The issue of language instruction in California has become intertwined with the issue of educating the children of illegal immigrants. In 1994, 59 percent of the voters approved Proposition 187, which was meant to deny schooling to illegal immigrants. A federal court found the measure unconstitutional in 1998, but then governor Pete Wilson appealed that decision. In 1999, Governor Gray Davis asked a federal appeals court to mediate the dispute (Associated Press, 1999).

▶ From the Perspective of Gender

Girls consistently outscore boys on tests of reading and writing. Even though girls and boys are approximately equal in measured academic ability when they enter school, by age 12, girls perform less well than boys in such areas as higher level mathematics and measures of self-esteem, although the gender differences are declining in some areas such as mathematics (AAUW Educational Foundation & National Education Association, 1992; AAUW Educational Foundation, 1998; Pollina, 1995). Such differences may be due in part to **gender bias**—discriminatory treatment, often subtle or unconscious, that unfairly favors or disfavors individuals because they are females or because they are males.

Girls receive less attention from teachers than do boys, and the quality of attention boys get is better (Sadker & Sadker, 1993). The literature also suggests that teachers are prone to choose classroom activities that appeal to boys' interests and to use instructional methods that favor boys. Teachers foster competition, for example, despite the fact that many studies suggest that girls, and many boys, experience greater academic success when they work cooperatively (AAUW Educational Foundation & National Education Association, 1992). Teachers also ask boys more challenging questions, encourage them to work to get a correct answer, offer them more praise and constructive crit-

Are single-sex schools the answer to gender bias in the classroom?

Cultural Awareness

San Antonio, a crossroads between the United States and Mexico, is home for the International School of the Americas, a magnet school housing 460 first- through fourth-year high school students in a wing of the 2,200-student campus of Robert E. Lee High School. Students apply to the International School, but they are chosen by lottery. The principal, Shari Albright, also recruits foreign-exchange students. More than half of the local students are Latino, more than a third are European American, and the rest are African American.

The school's mission is to prepare students for a world in which "borders are blurred, speaking English alone won't do, and multicultural savvy is a matter of survival." Besides doing at least B quality work, students are expected to take four years of math and science (unless they can acquire precalculus and physics competence faster) and to stay abreast of international and national news. They are also required to be fluent in Spanish and English and conversant in a third language by graduation.

The school's Latin-American focus was motivated, at least in part, by NAFTA, the North America Free Trade Agreement. Two local Fortune 500 businesses are the school's partners. They have linked the school with the Mexican consulate and the Mexican university system to eventually enable teachers and students to take conversational Spanish and Mexican culture courses through interactive video. The school offers internships, both locally and abroad, for 100 to 120 juniors and seniors every year.

Source: Personal communications with Lucinda Puente and Liz Moore, August 12, 1999.

icism, and acknowledge their substantive achievement more than they do girls (Sadker & Sadker, 1993).

Are boys also victims of bias in the schools? Studies indicate that teachers consider boys in general to be significantly more active, less attentive, less dexterous, and more prone to have behavioral, academic, and language problems than are girls.

Judith Kleinfeld, University of Alaska professor, believes boys, particularly African American boys, have been shortchanged by schools. According to Kleinfeld, the myth that the schools shortchange girls is dangerously wrong, because it diverts policy attention from the group at genuine education risk—African American boys. They score lowest on virtually every educational measure (Lewin, 1998). When schools identify children with learning disabilities, mental retardation, and reading disabilities, boys typically are identified more often than girls. A study of 152 preservice teachers at the University of Minnesota during the 1990–1991 academic year revealed that the majority of teachers surveyed attributed disparities in academic achievement between boys and girls to society (87%) and school (71%). Other explanations for differences included family (25%) and genetics (21%) (Avery & Walker, 1993).

Research on the progress of young women and men in areas related to success in the labor market suggests that educational differences matter in their later lives—but not equitably. Female students are as likely as are males to take advanced math and science courses and are more likely to study a foreign language. Females are slightly more likely than are males to make an immediate transition from high school to college. Employment and earnings rates rise with educational attainment for both females and males, but earnings are lower for females than for males with the same education (U.S. Department of Education, 1999).

Public schools continue to experiment with the idea of single-sex education. Whether these experiments can survive legal challenges remains to be seen. University of Maine professor Bonnie Wood claims that an all-girl algebra class offered at the high school in Presque Isle, Maine, produces girls who are twice as likely to enroll in advanced chemistry and college physics.

Single-sex education also may benefit boys. Marsteller Middle School in Manassas, Virginia, offers single-sex classes in physics and English, claiming that separating the sexes eliminates distractions. Marsteller boys raised their average language arts scores by one grade after only one term. Robert Coleman Elementary School in Baltimore, Maryland, introduced single-sex classes to instill discipline in the boys.

But legal challenges could be on the horizon. Federal law does not allow segregation by sex in public schools, except for contact sports, human sexuality courses, and remedial classes. One middle school in Ventura, California, won a legal challenge by changing the name of its all-girl math class to Power Learning for Underrepresented Students (PLUS). No boys signed up.

Some critics are concerned that single-sex classes will "set back the cause for gender equity." Others claim that girls and boys must learn to work together in preparation for a coed world. However, some teachers counter that single-sex classes work because they "let kids think with something besides their hormones." "Impressing the opposite sex is a 14-year-old's reason for being. Take away that pressure, and miracles happen" (Daily Report Card, 1996).

▶ From Perspectives of Exceptionality

About 1 in 10 children has a special ability or disability that sets him or her apart from other children (U.S. Department of Education, 1999). Nearly 6 million **exceptional learners** across the United States possess one or more attributes that greatly affect the experiences they have at home, at school, and in the community.

Through the years, the knowledge of exceptionalities has grown. And with that growth has come public recognition of the importance of attending to exceptionalities in ways that maximize students' chances for success. Learner characteristics that were viewed as *handicaps* just 10 or 20 years ago are now characterized as *disabilities* that need not limit students' chances to advance or to contribute to the greater good.

How should exceptionality be defined?

Although there is widespread agreement that some children deviate from the norm, the definition of the norm can be debated. *Normal* means what is typically expected or desired in the context of a specific culture. Those who deviate from cultural expectations may possess one or more of the following characteristics.

Giftedness.   **Giftedness,** like other types of exceptionality, has been defined in several ways. According to the 1972 Marland definition (Public Law 91-230, Section 806), gifted and talented students are those children capable of high performance who excel in one or more of the following areas: general intellectual ability, specific academic aptitude, creative or productive thinking, leadership ability, ability in the visual or performing arts, and psychomotor ability. Traditionally, however, children have been labeled as gifted if they score above a certain level on an IQ test. A national survey indicated that 73 percent of school districts have adopted the Marland definition, yet few schools use the definition to identify and serve any area of giftedness other than high general intelligence as measured on verbal IQ and achievement tests (U.S. Department of Education, Office of Educational Research and Improvement, 1993).

As noted earlier, some contend that intelligence is not a general characteristic but instead a combination of several capacities and cognitive abilities that cannot all be measured through the usual types of testing (Gardner & Hatch, 1989; Gardner, 1999). Joseph Renzulli (1982) argues that giftedness is determined by high ability, high creativity, and high levels of motivation and task completion. Giftedness also has been described as "a sign of biopsychological potential in whichever domains exist in a culture" (Gardner, 1999, p. 51). Giftedness has important implications for differentiating instruction (Tomlinson, 1999).

High-Incidence Disabilities.   Many students qualify for special education services. The majority of these children have one or more of the following disabilities: speech and language disorders, learning disabilities, emotional and behavior disorders, and severe attention problems. Each of these conditions is defined by federal special education laws and regulations.

Speech and Language Disorders.   Children with **speech impairments** may have fluency disorders (such as stuttering), articulation disorders (abnormality in the production of sounds), or voice disorders (such as hoarseness or hypernasality—too many sounds produced through the nose). Some children may exhibit delayed speech; that is, they use communication patterns like those of someone of a much younger age (e.g., pointing at something they want rather than verbalizing what they want). Children with **language disorders** may have receptive, expressive, or language-processing problems, as well as combinations of these problems. In some instances they also have difficulty with the meaning of words (semantics), with the sequential organization of words according to their relationships to each other (syntax), or with the purpose of or uses for language (Palmer & Yantis, 1990).

Learning Disabilities.   Hallahan and Kauffman (2000) note that four factors have been used historically to define learning disabilities, and each has met with some degree of controversy: (1) a discrepancy between IQ and achievement, (2) a presumption of central nervous system dysfunction, (3) psychological processing disorders, and (4) learning problems not due to environmental disadvantage, cognitive disabilities, or emotional disturbance.

The National Joint Committee on Learning Disabilities, a group of representatives from eight national organizations that have a major interest in **learning disabilities,** defines the term as follows:

Benchmarks

Equal Opportunity for Americans with Disabilities

1973   Vocational Rehabilitation Act (Public Law 93-112, Section 504): People with disabilities cannot be discriminated against in any way in any federally funded program.

1974   Educational Amendments Act (Public Law 93-380): Federal funds are provided to the states for implementing programs for exceptional learners, including the gifted and talented. Rights to due process are granted to children with disabilities and their families in special education placement.

1975   Education of the Handicapped Law (Public Law 94-142, Part B, known as the Mainstreaming Law): A free and appropriate public education must be provided for all children with disabilities ages 5 and above. Education must be planned through an individualized education program (IEP) and carried out in the least restrictive environment.

1986   Education of the Handicapped Act Amendments (Public Law 99-457): A free and appropriate education must be extended to all children with disabilities ages 3 to 5, and early intervention programs must be established for infants and toddlers with disabilities.

1988   Technology-Related Assistance for Individuals with Disabilities Act of 1988 (Public Law 100-418): Provides financial assistance to states to develop and implement consumer-responsive statewide programs of technology-related assistance for persons of all ages with disabilities.

1990   Americans with Disabilities Act (ADA, Public Law 101-336): This law is essentially a national mandate to end discrimination against people with disabilities in private-sector employment, public services, public accommodations, transportation, and telecommunications.

Individuals with Disabilities Education Act (Public Law 101-476), or IDEA, replaces the Education of the Handicapped Act. Special education services are extended to children with autism and traumatic brain injury, and rehabilitation and social work services are included in the definition of special education.

1991   Individuals with Disabilities Act Amendments (Public Law 102-119): This law amends IDEA to extend authorization of appropriations and to revise the early intervention program of services for infants and toddlers with disabilities.

1994   Technology-Related Assistance for Individuals with Disabilities Amendments of 1993 (Public Law 103-218): This law amends the Technology-Related Assistance for Individuals with Disabilities Act of 1988 to authorize appropriations for each of the fiscal years 1994-1998.

1997   IDEA amendments focus on improving teaching and learning, emphasizing the Individualized Education Program (IEP) as the primary tool for enhancing children's involvement and progress in the general curriculum.

1999   U.S. Department of Education publishes federal regulations related to the 1997 reauthorization of the Individuals with Disabilities Education Act.

Learning disabilities is a general term that refers to a heterogeneous group of disorders manifested by significant difficulties in the acquisition and use of listening, speaking, reading, writing, reasoning, or mathematical abilities. These disorders are intrinsic to the individual, presumed to be due to central nervous system disorder, and may occur across the life span. Problems in self-regulatory behaviors, social perception and social interaction may exist with learning disabilities but do not by themselves constitute a learning disability. Although learning disabilities may occur concomitantly with other handicapping conditions (for example, sensory impairment, mental retardation, serious emotional disturbance) or with extrinsic influences (such as cultural differences, insufficient or inappropriate instruction), they are not the result of those conditions or influences. (Hammill, Leigh, McNutt, & Larsen, 1988, p. 217)

Emotional and Behavioral Disorders. Among terms used to describe those who have emotional, social, and behavioral problems are *behavioral disordered, socially maladjusted, emotionally disturbed,* and *emotionally or behaviorally disordered.* These problems can reveal themselves through behaviors such as phobias or depressions that are directed inward or by behaviors that are directed more at others (Wolf, Pratt, & Pruitt, 1990). The federal definition of "seriously emotionally disturbed" is as follows:

The term means a condition exhibiting one or more of the following characteristics over a long period of time and to a marked degree, which adversely affects educational performance: (1) an inability to learn which cannot be explained by intellectual, sensory, or health factors; (2) an inability to build or maintain satisfactory relationships with peers and teachers; (3) inappropriate types of behavior or feelings under normal circumstances; (4) a general pervasive mood of unhappiness or depression; or (5) a tendency to develop physical symptoms or fears associated with personal or school problems. The term includes children who are schizophrenic. . . . The term does not include children who are socially maladjusted, unless it is determined that they are seriously disturbed. (U.S. Department of Health, Education, and Welfare, 1977, p. 42478)

Attention Deficit Disorder. **Attention deficit–hyperactivity disorder (ADHD)** is a neurobiologically based disorder characterized by inappropriate levels of any of three observable behaviors: inattention, impulsivity, and/or hyperactivity (Friend & Bursuck, 1999). Attention deficit–hyperactivity disorder is sometimes referred to as attention deficit disorder (ADD). Classroom manifestations of the disorder include difficulty in staying on task, focusing attention, and completing work. Children with ADHD appear not to listen or not to have heard what they have been told. They may also display age-inappropriate hyperactive behavior, be easily distracted, and produce sloppy and careless work. Impulsivity can cause difficulty in accomplishing tasks that call for a delayed response, such as raising hands to answer questions, reading or listening to directions, asking questions to clarify information, planning, and organizing. Boys outnumber girls by more than three to one in the referrals made for this condition (Barkley, 1998).

Low-Incidence Disabilities. Some disabilities—cognitive disabilities, hearing and visual impairments, and orthopedic or other health impairments—are less prevalent among youngsters. As with more commonly occurring disabilities, teachers must often respond to these special needs as they occur in combination with other disabilities.

Cognitive Disabilities. According to the American Association on Mental Retardation (AAMR), cognitive disabilities manifest before age 18 and greatly limit personal capabilities. They are characterized by

> significantly subaverage intellectual functioning [an IQ standard score of 70 to 75 or lower], existing concurrently with related limitations in two or more of the following applicable adaptive skill areas: communication, self-care, home living, social skills, community use, self-direction, health and safety, functional academics, leisure, and work. (American Association on Mental Retardation, 1999)

Despite their limitations, those with cognitive disabilities who receive appropriate support over a sustained period will generally demonstrate improvement in their life functioning.

Hearing Impairment. **Hearing impairment** is a term used to describe degrees of deafness. While individuals who are hard of hearing can usually process oral language with the use of hearing aids, those who are deaf are unable to do so. Educators who work with hearing-impaired youngsters are concerned with the time in a child's development when hearing impairment occurred. They may describe hearing-impaired youngsters as *congenitally deaf* (born deaf) or *adventitiously deaf* (acquiring deafness sometime after birth). The main concern is the degree to which speech and language are affected by hearing loss and how best to facilitate communication skills (Hallahan & Kauffman, 2000).

Visual Impairment. A child who has **visual impairment** may be classified as legally blind, partially sighted, or educationally blind. According to the American Medical Association, a person is considered legally blind when visual acuity in the better eye does not exceed 20/200 with corrective lenses or when the field of vision is limited at its widest angle to 20 degrees or less. Those who are partially sighted have better visual acuity (greater than 20/200 but not greater than 20/70 in the stronger eye after correction.) Although some children with visual impairment use braille, increasing numbers of learners rely on tape recorders, letter magnifiers, and computer voice translators. According to experts, the move away from braille leaves the blind with a "shaky grasp" on the structure of language (Martelle, 1999).

Orthopedic Impairments and Other Health Impairments. Individuals with orthopedic and other health impairments include those with neurological impairment, or damage to their central nervous system; skeletal and muscular disorders; and congenital malformations. About half of the children with physical impairments in the United States have cerebral palsy, a neurological impairment characterized by weakness, lack of coordination, and/or motor dysfunction. Other neurological impairments include epilepsy (recurrent seizures), spina bifida (an improperly developed spinal cord that often causes paralysis of the lower body), and spinal cord injuries that occur when the spinal cord is traumatized or severed. Skeletal and muscular disorders include arthritis, a disease that causes inflammation around the joints, and muscular dystrophy, a degenerative disease that causes the breakdown of muscle tissues. Congenital malformations are abnormalities of any part of the body, such as the heart or the extremities, that are present at birth.

Using Technology

Assistive Technologies for People with Disabilities

When someone who works in the field of assistive technology, the application of technology to the general field of disabilities, says "technology," that person may be referring to an amazing array of devices. An assistive technology device is "any item, piece of equipment, or product system, whether acquired commercially off the shelf, modified, or customized, that is used to increase, maintain, or improve functional capabilities of individuals with disabilities" (Quist and Lloyd, 1997, p. 107). In the years ahead, teachers will only have more technology to help them reach learners.

Sources include: Regency Park Rehabilitation Engineering (1999, February). *Regency Rag:* Chapter 8. Assistive technology. Available online (http://regencyrehab.cca.org.au/regrag/chapt_08.htm); and Quist, R. W., & Lloyd, L. L. (1997). Chapter 8. Principles and uses of technology. In L. L. Lloyd, D. R. Fuller, & H. H. Arvidson (Eds.). *Augmentative and alternative communication: A handbook of principles and practices.* Boston: Allyn and Bacon, 107–126.

An electronic page turner

This electronic page turner provides full control for turning one or more pages forward or backward. The device is operated by activating a joystick or switch to select one of four modes to move a rubber roller that turns the pages. It can be used with paperbacks, hardbacks, magazines, or loose sheets that have been stapled together.

A portable environmental control system

This is a portable environmental control system, which may be controlled using voice input or switch access. It can be set up to control any infrared (TV, VCR, Stereo, etc.) or wired device such as lights, fan, or door latch.

A computer is required to set up and train the Pilot to recognize voice commands. It can then be unplugged and moved around the house on a wheelchair or be mounted near a bed or workstation.

A scanning director

The Scanning Director II is intended for people who can operate either a single or dual switch. Users scan through the menu of options on the back-lit display and activate the switch to send a signal. Scanning speed and access time are adjustable.

▶ From the Perspective of Sexual Orientation

Education for diversity often sparks disagreement and debate, especially on issues concerning which groups are to be identified as cultures, included in multicultural curricula, or educated separately in alternative or magnet schools. Consider, for example, New York City's controversial Harvey Milk School, opened in 1985 as the first and only high school in the nation for gay and lesbian youth. The school is jointly funded by the board of education and the Hetrick–Martin Institute, a nonprofit organization offering counseling and other services to homosexual youth. Named for Harvey Milk, the gay San Francisco supervisor murdered in 1978, the school is fully accredited and run through the board's Alternative High Schools and Programs division. The school is meant to provide an environment free from violence where gay and lesbian youth can work and learn with adults and peers who will not judge them by their sexual orientation. In 1999 the school limited enrollment to 50 students.

Should there be separate programs for gay and lesbian students?

Formal education through the Harvey Milk School is only a small part of the story of support for gay and lesbian youth by the Hetrick–Martin Institute. They offer counseling, informal education programs after normal school hours, a GED program, and a youth leadership training initiative that places interns in various agencies and organizations in New York City. Hetrick–Martin also seeks out homeless youth and offers them showers, clothes, meals, and contacts with case workers. This multiservice agency helped some 7,000 young people in 1999 (E. Lopez, personal communication, August 13, 1999).

Gay and lesbian issues seem to draw particularly vehement attacks. Not only do gay and lesbian students face harassment, but those heterosexual students who associate with them may be subject to abuse as well (Ruenzel, 1999). When the National Education Association passed a resolution in support of Lesbian and Gay History Month, a group called the Concerned Women for America (CWA) placed advertisements in newspapers around the country, condemning the NEA's action. They billed the resolution as a "threat to morality and decency." CWA's language was so strong that two newspapers in which the ads appeared later apologized for running inappropriate statements (Ponessa, 1995).

Initiatives such as the Harvey Milk School and the NEA resolution have been perceived by some people as responses to narrow and partisan interests in society. Historian Shelby Steele (1990) argues that a power base, a "new sovereignty," has been organized around the grievances of some interest groups. In higher education, for example, according to Steele, African Americans, women, Latinos, Native Americans, Asian Americans, gays, and lesbians press their agendas as "victims" of a racist, sexist, homophobic society to their own and to others' detriment. Separate dormitories, preferential admissions, campus study centers, fiscal aid policies, and faculty hiring quotas, Steele argues, make people concentrate on attributes such as skin color or sexual orientation first, before they assess the content of their own or others' characters.

But Steele's observations are not universally shared. Dennis Carlson (1998) describes the ethos with regard to gays and lesbians at one university in one point in time:

In the fall of 1995, a new float appeared in the homecoming parade at Miami University in Oxford, Ohio—a university known for its quiet conservatism. Wedged in between floats from Greek fraternities and sororities and from several other student groups on campus was a float representing the Gay, Lesbian, and Bisexual Alliance. In bold letters, the float proclaimed: "We're here, and we're queer, and we have a float." What is perhaps most remarkable about this event is that it created hardly a stir on campus. Gays and lesbians—or "queers" as an increasing number of young politically aware students refer to themselves—were becoming part of the new campus community, a community that (at least on the surface) was organized around the theme of respecting diversity. If multicultural education in the public schools does not yet include gay people as part of the diversity that is to be acknowledged and respected within the new American community of difference, this has not been the case in higher education. (1998, p. 107)

SUMMARY

What is diversity?

1. Diversity is defined in many ways in U.S. society. The language of diversity is characterized by terms relating to culture, race, ethnicity, and minority status. These classification systems are pervasive, yet they are often arbitrary, ambiguous, and changeable.

2. Culture can be used in an inclusive way to refer to the sum of the learned characteristics of a people or an exclusive way to describe smaller, more conceptually discrete groups of people.

3. Race is defined most often by physical characteristics, but sometimes also by ethnicity—ancestry in terms of national origin.

4. Prejudice and discrimination are unpleasant and morally unacceptable facts of life that affect teachers and students in many ways. Minorities, defined in terms of number and power, most often suffer the consequences.

How has diversity been defined in terms of development?

5. Traditionally, learners have been defined, both in theory and practice, in terms of their physical and psychological development, intelligence, cognitive development, moral development, and habits of mind. Although tradition supports these concepts, there is disagreement about the meaning of most of these terms and their importance for teachers.

What other concepts define diversity?

6. As teachers plan for instruction, they may think about teaching and learning from the viewpoints of immigrants, language-minority or bilingual students, and males and females. Teachers also consider exceptionalities (special abilities or disabilities) and sexual orientations of students.

7. Educators who work with immigrants from around the world try to help them understand culture in the United States so that they might participate successfully in society. At the same time, teachers encourage other students to learn about immigrant cultures and mores. Given their nations of origin, languages, religions, values, and ethnic identities, immigrants add to the richness that is public education in the United States.

8. Learners may be characterized by their facility with the English language. If students are thought to be limited-English proficient, they are likely to participate in a bilingual education program or to be immersed in English, depending on school resources and philosophies. Students often experience difficulty maintaining their native tongues and their family cultures.

9. Student gender influences teaching and learning. The likelihood of taking certain courses, speaking up in class, being classified as needing special help, and so forth, tend to characterize the sexes.

10. Students may be viewed from one or more perspectives of exceptionality. These include giftedness; cognitive disabilities; hearing, visual, or orthopedic impairments; speech and language disorders; emotional behavioral disorders; attention deficit disorder; and learning disabilities. Each exceptionality has implications for planning, teaching, and evaluating student success.

11. Increasingly, schools in metropolitan areas in particular are recognizing responsibilities to provide special services for gay and lesbian students. These may include formal instructional programs, informal educational activities, and health and social services.

TERMS AND CONCEPTS

attention deficit–hyperactivity disorder (ADHD)   323
bilingual education   314
cognitive disabilities   324
cultural pluralism   293
culture   292
discrimination   296
English as a Second Language (ESL)   314
ethnicity   294
ethnocentric   293
exceptional learners   320
gender bias   318
giftedness   321

habits of mind   308
hearing impairment   324
intelligence quotient (IQ)   301
language disorders   321
learning disabilities   321
limited English proficient (LEP)   314
minority   298
moral development   303
multiple intelligences   301
prejudice   296
race   293
self-esteem   299
speech impairments   321
visual impairment   324

▬▬▬▬ REFLECTIVE PRACTICE ▬▬▬▬

Teachers in the multicultural resource team at Columbus Elementary School, a public school in Columbus, New Mexico, discuss their work concerning parent involvement, family values, and multicultural education (Herbert & McNergney, 1996). Team members work with classroom teachers to enrich multicultural studies in the curriculum. Their school is unusual in that it serves children who live in the United States and children who live in Mexico. Columbus Elementary School is located in a small farming community 3 miles from the United States/Mexico border. As you read the account below, imagine why and how teachers "categorize" the people with whom they work and what effects such categorizations might have on teaching and learning.

CONSUELA: [*Describes parent education program.*] Our parents are coming to visit the computer lab now for ESL at night. I didn't think it was going to work, because some of the parents don't know how to read at all, and this requires some reading. But they don't even want to take a break.

OTHERS: Uh huh. . . . Parents love those computers.

MARIO: They don't even take a break. I know that Consuela tells them, "Okay, time to take a break. She has to tell them a couple of times."

CONSUELA: In both cultures, education is seen as something that is a necessity for the future.

OPHELIA: Education is a little bit different here. . . .

CONSUELA: I think that Anglo parents' expectation of a student is to excel, excel, excel in anything they do. This is from day one.

OPHELIA: The Mexican family, and I don't know if it is true any more, but their expectation is to just get enough education so they can go out there and work. Maybe it is changing a little bit. But in the United States, it is all college-bound. That is all you think . . . college, college.

CONSUELA: It is very evident too that the parents in Mexico take responsibility for the behavior or discipline part of the child's education. In the United States, a lot of parents say while students are in school, you teach them how to behave, you teach them what is right and what is wrong, all of that. In Mexico, I feel that is quite a bit different. Parents expect the child to come to school to learn subject matter. Discipline and behavior patterns are definitely the responsibility of the parent, but mostly of the mother.

Multicultural education takes advantage of a child's language. It is an asset to be able to speak a child's language, because the teacher can get so much more participation from the student if she can relate to the language.

Issues, Problems, Dilemmas, and Opportunities

What problems can arise when teachers expect too little or too much from students and their parents?

Perceive and Value

According to these teachers, how are Mexican/Latino and Anglo families similar? How are they different?

Know and Act

According to some of the models of multicultural education described in the chapter, what are some effective ways to integrate students of different cultures into schools? If you were going to teach in Columbus Elementary School and you were not bilingual or bicultural, what sort of information might you want about the students, the school, and the community? Where or from whom might you seek such information? What might you do to encourage parental participation?

Evaluate

One way to think about assessing education is to examine the resources, processes, and outcomes of education. Assume that you teach in a school on the border between the United States and Mexico and you are expected to provide an education for your students that is multicultural. What human and material resources might be useful? What learning activities would you provide, and what student outcomes would you encourage?

 ONLINE ACTIVITY

The Southern Poverty Law Center is an organization that works to combat hate, intolerance, and discrimination through education and litigation. The SPLC monitors the activities of the Ku Klux Klan and other hate groups. It also supports an array of curricular and instructional materials as part of its Teaching Tolerance program. It distributes a free magazine twice a year to more than a half-million educators throughout the United States and in 70 other nations. Its curriculum resources include free video and text teaching kits that address the history of hate and intolerance in the United States. The SPLC gives grants of up to $2,000 for K–12 teachers for implementing tolerance projects in their schools and communities. Be sure to visit the site. You can find a link to it on this book's web site, or you can use a search engine to find it. Once in the site, click on "What's New" to learn about center materials that teachers can use to fight hate and promote tolerance. Also investigate "Teaching Tolerance." Which of the resources and classroom activities listed on this page might be used in K–12 classrooms?

9

Multicultural and Inclusive Education

Teachers need more than ideas, enthusiasm, and love of children to be successful. They must be able to use educational strategies that can be fitted intelligently and sensitively to the diversity of their students' needs and abilities. Increasingly, educators are turning to concepts of multicultural education and inclusive education to provide such support. Great teachers do not have "a way" to behave toward all students or "a style" of teaching that works equally well with all people. Instead, these professionals adapt their teaching to help all their students succeed.

PROFESSIONAL PRACTICE QUESTIONS

▪ What is multicultural education?

▪ What types of multicultural education curricula exist and how are they evaluated?

▪ How are educational services adapted for students with exceptionalities?

▪ How can teachers create culturally relevant classrooms?

 ## What Is Multicultural Education?

The term *multicultural education* is used in a variety of ways. At its core, however, multicultural education attempts to alter existing education programs to respond more effectively to diversity in the United States:

> **Multicultural education** in the United States is an approach to teaching and learning that is based upon democratic values and beliefs, and that affirms cultural pluralism within diverse societies and an interdependent world (Bennett, 1999).

What is multicultural education?

Geneva Gay (1995) suggests that multicultural education is also a "concept, idea, or philosophy." As such, multicultural education both describes the way life is and prescribes what should be done to ensure equal access to education and treatment of diverse groups of students in schools. Diversity typically is addressed in terms of social class, gender, and disability, as well as race and ethnicity.

Christine Sleeter and Carl Grant (1998) note five general educational approaches to multicultural education, shown in Figure 9.1:

1. "teaching the culturally different" involves attempts to assimilate people into the cultural mainstream using transitional bridges in the regular school program;

2. "human relations approaches " try to help students of differing backgrounds understand and accept each other;

3. "single-group studies" encourage cultural pluralism by concentrating on the appreciation of the contributions of individuals and groups;

4. "multicultural approaches" promote pluralism by reforming whole educational programs—altering curricula, integrating staffs, and affirming family languages; and

5. "education that is multicultural and social reconstructionist" promotes active challenge of social inequality.

We examine each general approach in turn below.

FIGURE 9.1
Five Approaches to Multicultural Education   Think of one clear example of each
of the five approaches identified in this figure.

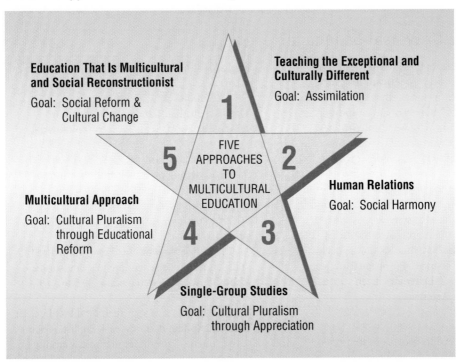

Source: Making Choices for Multicultural Education: Five Approaches to Race, Class, and Gender (3rd Ed.), by C.E. Sleeter and C.A. Grant, 1998, Upper Saddle River, NJ: Merrill/Prentice Hall.

▶ Teaching the Exceptional and Culturally Different

This approach attempts to assimilate students of different races, low-income students, and special education students into the "cultural mainstream" as it currently exists (Sleeter, 1993). These efforts may take the form of organizational or instructional changes intended to match students' learning styles and existing skills (Grant & Gomez, 1996).

For years this was the preferred approach to multicultural education. As immigrants arrived in this country, they were placed in programs designed to transmit the knowledge, skills, and attitudes deemed appropriate for successful life in the United States. Such programs often made their goals explicit. For example, students were to learn to read and write English, to master U.S. history, to adopt prevailing social customs, and so on.

Programs and processes of teaching the culturally different, however, have also been characterized by their implicit demands. Teachers' expectations for appropri-

Voices

English—The Universal Language?

Ellen Bigler (1999) asserts that Puerto Ricans and older, established European Americans negotiate visions of a multicultural society through the stories they tell. These stories "help us organize and make sense of our world and where we fit into it. They have strategic value as we attempt to move others to see our own visions of ourselves and our world" (1999, p. 91).

Conflict between these two groups erupted in the pseudonymous community of Arnhem, New York, over proposed changes in the state social studies curriculum. These changes promoted the use of Spanish and "Spanglish" in schools. Young Puerto Ricans supported the changes; European American senior citizens did not. One senior citizen wrote the following letter to the newspaper:

To the editor:

There is no need to debate or question which language should be spoken in these United States as the universal language. It is to the benefit of all nationalities to speak English, so that all can understand each other. . . .

The ambitious . . . built America. . . . They faced ridicule and name calling and survived . . . worked . . . for a few coins per hour. . . .

They asked for nothing. They spoke their native tongue in their homes, communities and business places. They had no modern schools, they learned to speak English from their coworkers . . . and [in the] streets.

My mother taught me to read and write Polish as a child. She sent me to a one-room schoolhouse to learn to read, write and spell English. . . .

The Indians . . . [lost] their land by force. Today the Indian nation speaks English. Their native tongue (I presume) they speak among themselves. . . .

It should be essential that all immigrants go to school to learn English, so they can read

ate behavior, for example, may subtly influence students to question their backgrounds or to view themselves negatively.

▶ Human Relations Approaches

Human relations approaches to multicultural education try to help students of differing backgrounds understand and accept each other. Encouraging cooperation and building self-esteem are activities integral to a human relations approach to multicultural education. These approaches take many forms and often are as informal as teachers assigning a "friend" to a new student in class or assigning work or play groups to facilitate understanding and acceptance. Human relations approaches also include formal procedures for accomplishing goals such as **conflict mediation**—formal efforts to help students resolve their differences peacefully.

Although program goals are the same in conflict mediation, the means for teaching students to reach these goals can differ. David and Roger Johnson advocate that teachers provide opportunities for students to practice skills involved in negotiating

and write, to vote and converse with their fellow men. . . .

If language becomes an issue, there will be hard feelings amongst all. . . . There will be the danger of dividing these United States into sections like Europe. Stand together and be an immigrant American under one God, one government, one flag and one universal language—English. Many speak English the world over. . . .

Let us lay aside our personal enmities. . . . (Bigler, 1999, p. 92)

The story expressed in this letter, Bigler argues, helps us understand some of the reasons underlying the conflict:

Seniors, raised on an ethos of ancestral sacrifice and hard work as the essential ingredients for upward mobility *and* having achieved something of the American dream (tenuous though their hold may be on it), unproblematically link hard work and conformity to white ethnics' successes in climbing the social class ladder. One consequence is to defend the individualistic "up by their own bootstraps" view of the American system and to situate themselves as resoundingly part of the mainstream white middle class, with its connotations of progress and order. For members of struggling minority communities for whom the "rags-to-riches" story has rarely applied, stories of hardship and discrimination . . . [have different meanings]. Linking racial oppression, past and present, to contemporary ethnic and racial socio-economic inequalities helps explain their current position in the social hierarchy and inspires members to challenge both the status quo and Seniors' classification of them as part of the "paradigmatic poor." (1999, p. 111).

CRITICAL THINKING

Have you ever heard opinions like those expressed by the senior citizen in the letter to the editor? By whom? When? Where? What is your impression of such "up-by-their-own-bootstraps" and "rags-to-riches" stories?

Source: Excerpted and reprinted from the chapter entitled "Telling Stories," included in *American Conversations: Puerto Ricans, White Ethnics and Multicultural Education* by Ellen Bigler by permission of Temple University Press. © 1999 by Temple University. All rights reserved.

and mediating differences among themselves. The Johnsons' approach proceeds through three steps (Johnson, Johnson, Dudley, Ward, & Magnuson, 1995). The first step involves negotiation. Here teachers try to "overteach" all students the skills for negotiating constructively. The intent is to keep these skills from being swamped by emotion when they will be most needed. Students learn to (1) state what they want; (2) state how they feel; (3) state the reasons for their wants and feelings; (4) summarize their understanding of the other person's wants, feelings, and reasons; (5) invent three optional plans to resolve the conflict; and (6) choose one plan and shake hands.

Did any of the schools you attended use human relations approaches?

The second step is to teach all students how to mediate the conflicts of their peers. This means asking the students in conflict if they want to solve the problem and not proceeding until both say yes. Then the mediator explains that (1) mediation is voluntary, (2) the mediator will not try to decide who is right or wrong, only to help solve the problem, and (3) each party will have the right to air his or her side of the problem. The parties to the dispute must agree to solve the problem, not to call each other names, not to interrupt, to be as honest as possible, to abide by the agreement if one is reached, and to keep confidential what is said in mediation.

In step 3 the teacher chooses two official mediators each day, rotating the assignments throughout the class. Any conflicts students cannot resolve themselves are referred to the mediators. The Johnsons advocate booster sessions from time to time to ensure that the skills are a natural part of a student's social repertoire. Peacemaking in this fashion can help young people learn to settle differences without resorting to violence.

The Johnsons (1997) conducted 11 studies that examined their Teaching to Be Peacemakers program. Among other things, they found that conflicts among students occur daily. Their training helped students to reject notions of winning disputes and to apply negotiation and mediation procedures to settle conflicts. When students were trained to be peacemakers, discipline problems handled by teachers decreased by about 60 percent. Richard Bodine and Donna Crawford (1998) believe these results support the importance of teaching students how to integrate negotiation strategies into their lives.

◗ Single-Group Studies

Single-group studies promote cultural pluralism by concentrating on individual and group contributions, emphasizing the importance of emulating the lives of outstanding people in various cultures. The intent is for young people to study the history of oppression, to feel proud of their heritage, and to recognize that human accomplishment transcends racial and cultural barriers.

Single-group approaches often address affective objectives (objectives aimed at influencing feelings, attitudes, or values), fostering appreciation and respect for other ways of life, or sometimes promoting the value of cultural relativism. In the simplest or most traditional approaches, students present or participate in activities that feature ethnic foods, dress, and customs of foreign countries. Sometimes single-group studies emphasize differences among groups to the extent that pluralism is celebrated over unity. Some curriculum reformers, for example, have taken a centrist, separatist, or particularist tack by emphasizing each of the primary ethnic–racial groups in the United States in separate courses. Others have advocated pluralist or infusion approaches by integrating information on these groups into all courses at all grade levels.

Do alternative culture-based curricula encourage separatism?

◗ Multicultural Approaches

Multicultural approaches try to reform education by revising curricula, integrating school staffs, and acknowledging the importance of families and family languages. Advocates of a multicultural approach "recognize, accept, and affirm human differences and similarities related to gender, race, disability, class, and (increasingly) sexual preference" (Sleeter & Grant, 1998, p. 167). In doing so, they encourage students to consider different viewpoints, drawing on content developed through single-group studies. Instructors also involve students actively in thinking about and analyzing real-life situations, attempting to make curriculum relevant to students' experiences and backgrounds. "This approach deliberately fosters equal academic

Cultural Awareness

The Algebra Project is an interactive curriculum designed to help inner-city and rural students better understand mathematical concepts. Developed by Bob Moses, a mathematician and civil rights leader, the curriculum calls for students to follow a five-step process in which they use their physical surroundings as tangible references for mathematical ideas.

As the first step in the process, students experience an event, such as a train ride or a field trip to several different places. Students then create a model or pictures of the event and write about it in an informal and creative manner. The language used to describe the event is then formalized so that it accurately depicts the activity. Finally, students develop a symbolic representation of the event using mathematical concepts.

The Algebra Project is being used in Chicago, Atlanta, Boston, and other urban school districts across the country, where it has benefited from the support of community organizations, and in rural areas, as in the Mississippi Delta Project. Many parents also have helped implement the project and have provided classroom support to teachers.

Algebra Project
National Headquarters
99 Bishop Richard Allen Drive
Cambridge, MA 02139
(617) 491-0200

Chicago Office
1603 S. Michigan Ave.
Chicago, IL 60616
(312) 427-8999

Source: Copyright 1999 by the North Central Regional Educational Laboratory (1999, August 2). *Algebra project. Pathways to school improvement.* Available online: (http://www.ncrel.org/ncrel/sdrs/areas/issues/content/cntareas/math/ma1algeb.htm)

achievement across groups; achievement does not take a back seat to interpersonal relationships" (Sleeter, 1993, p. 56).

Robert Moses teaches algebra to sixth-grade African American students in the Mississippi delta by drawing on examples from their everyday lives. A firm believer that algebra is the "gatekeeper" to the college prep math sequence, Moses uses a variety of strategies to help students succeed in school and to learn to view themselves as thinkers. He may teach the often-mysterious concept of ratios to students by contrasting rhythms of African drumbeats or by having students construct their own recipes. Or he may teach the concept of negative numbers by riding a make-believe subway and labeling the stops on the line. Kleinfeld (1995) calls this the "A Train approach" to teaching mathematics (after the A train on the New York subway system).

The A Train approach is appropriate for classrooms containing any mix of ethnic groups. The basic method—drawing on children's background knowledge, incorporating it into the curriculum, and creating concrete experiences for students to think about—is universal (Kleinfeld, 1995).

A set of 32 Tribal Colleges created during the past 30 years represents a comprehensive multicultural approach to postsecondary education. These colleges serve

FIGURE 9.2
Tribal Colleges The map outlines the geographic location of the 32 institutions that are a part of the American Indian Higher Education Consortium (AIHEC). How do Tribal Colleges exemplify a multicultural approach to education?

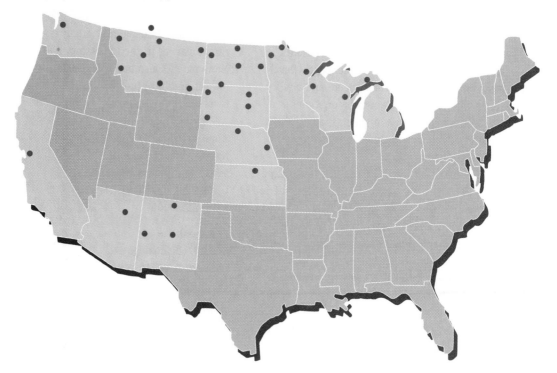

Source: "Tribal Colleges" by the American Indian Higher Education Consortium. Available online: http://www.aihec.org/college.htm#map

geographically isolated populations with limited access to education beyond high school. The Tribal Colleges combine personal attention with cultural relevance to encourage Native Americans, especially those living on reservations, to enter higher education (see Figure 9.2).

▶ Education That Is Multicultural and Social Reconstructionist

This general approach to educate for diversity actively challenges social inequality and seeks to restructure educational institutions ultimately to change society.

> **What standards should be applied to multicultural curricular reform?**

According to Sleeter and Grant (1998), teachers who want to achieve these goals use students' life experiences as opportunities to discuss inequities in society. They encourage students to think critically about information in textbooks, newspapers, and other print and media sources in which classism, sexism, racism, or other social issues might be evident. Students are encouraged to consider alternative points of view and to think about ways they might work constructively to achieve social justice for all peoples.

When studying United States history, for example, students might investigate how the racial category of "Other" evolved over time. They might begin by reading passages from Christopher Columbus' diary, in which he describes his encounter with the Taino Indians in the Caribbean. Through discussion, students could examine Columbus' perceptions of the Tainos and consider how his thoughts about these new peoples were influenced by European ideas and concepts. According to Banks (1996), one outcome of such a lesson would be to help students understand how Columbus began to think of the Tainos as the Other, "thus forming the basis for Indians to be perceived as a different and inferior race from Western Europeans" (p. 81).

Discussion of excerpts from Columbus' diary could serve as the springboard from which students move on to other activities. For instance, students might draw parallels to views of "others" in their extended families, or in the larger society, who have been characterized in specific ways. Teachers might then encourage students to speculate about personal, social, and civic activities in which they could engage to alter prevailing conceptions of these "others" to create a more democratic and just society.

What Types of Multicultural Education Curricula Exist and How Are They Evaluated?

The debate about multicultural education is neither new nor faddish. It is part of the larger, continuing dialogue about the meaning of *e pluribus unum,* or one out of many. As one country composed of many states and many peoples, the nation continues to struggle to define itself. How is the United States to conceptualize and deliver public education appropriate for all people? This question arises in many forms and many languages in political forums, churches, social organizations, and schools across the country.

> **What are the benefits of relating academics to students' lives?**

The appropriateness of multicultural education content and methods is defined most often at national and state levels. National and state initiatives related to multicultural education are numerous and varied. Donna Gollnick (1995) notes that both federal and state education laws are most often concerned with protecting the rights of cultural and ethnic minorities. This legislation is designed, however, to ensure equal educational opportunity, rather than to promote the preparation of all students to function effectively in a culturally diverse society. At the federal level, this has meant focusing on providing equal educational opportunities for female students, students of different races, LEP students, students from low-income families, and students with disabilities.

Through their professional literature, programs, and publications, national educational associations encourage attention to multicultural education, equity, and educational opportunity by advocating direct educational intervention at all levels of the public education system. National accreditation standards for teacher education programs and national certification programs for teachers also acknowledge the importance of multicultural education. Prominent among such standards are those promoted by the National Council for the Accreditation of Teacher Education (NCATE).

James Banks's (1997) levels of integrating ethnic content into elementary and high school curricula offer a practical guide that teachers might use to judge multicultural approaches (see Figure 9.3). Banks envisions a taxonomy of approaches to multicultural curricular reform, in which the lowest level is represented by "The Contributions Approach" and the highest level is "The Action Approach."

FIGURE 9.3
Bank's Approaches to Multicultural Curricular Reform   How is Banks's model similar to and different from the five approaches to multicultural education identified by Sleeter and Grant? (See Figure 9.1)

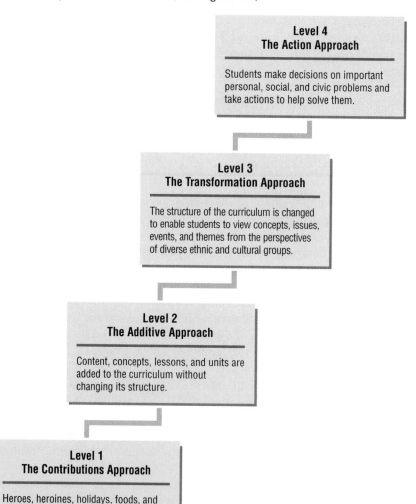

Level 4
The Action Approach

Students make decisions on important personal, social, and civic problems and take actions to help solve them.

Level 3
The Transformation Approach

The structure of the curriculum is changed to enable students to view concepts, issues, events, and themes from the perspectives of diverse ethnic and cultural groups.

Level 2
The Additive Approach

Content, concepts, lessons, and units are added to the curriculum without changing its structure.

Level 1
The Contributions Approach

Heroes, heroines, holidays, foods, and discrete cultural elements are celebrated occasionally.

Source: "Approaches to Multicultural Curriculum Reform" by J.A. Banks, 1997. In J.A. Banks and C.A. Banks (Eds.), *Multicultural Education: Issues and Perspectives*, p. 233, New York: Wiley-Liss, Inc. Reprinted by permission of Wiley-Liss, Inc., a subsidiary of John Wiley & Sons, Inc.

▶ Accountability Issues

Multicultural education—education that promotes equity for all students—is subject to the same assessment questions that any educational approach must answer: What does it cost; that is, what human and material resources are devoted to multicultural education efforts? What happens during the conduct of educational activities? And what are the outcomes of multicultural educational efforts?

Answers to these questions are judged acceptable or unacceptable by comparing them to program claims, to other competing programs, or to standards that describe what might be expected of any educational effort. Useless answers come in response to the question "Is multicultural education effective?" Useful answers about the overall worth of multicultural education, those that can be fairly judged, come in response to the question "Are multicultural programs effective compared to other programs and compared to the goals they were designed to achieve?"

People commonly rely on standardized test scores to judge educational programs, and, through the years, minority-group students have not fared as well on such tests as have majority-group students. There has been considerable within-group variation, however. Overall, the scores of members of minority groups have increased. As Table 9.1 indicates, members of minority groups capitalized on educational opportunities in ways that many had not in the past. Their continued participation is key to learning.

Many other outcomes, however, could be examined to judge the efficacy of multicultural programs. These can be as conveniently and inexpensively acquired as test scores, and they can be extremely useful. For example, high-quality paper-and-pencil measures of student satisfaction with programs and with school generally can be obtained and tracked over time. These can be supplemented with interviews of students, parents, and staff to determine what they do and do not like about multicultural offerings. One also could examine figures on school attendance, dropouts, and participation in extracurricular activities to infer program efficacy. The more these assessments reflect real life in the larger, more inclusive culture outside school, the better. Multicultural education succeeds when it helps students use what they have learned in school in other settings and with other people.

> How would you decide whether multicultural education is effective?

By 2020 more than half the children in public schools will be members of racial or ethnic minorities. Most teachers will be European Americans. As diversity increases, so too will the possibilities for miscommunication and misunderstanding.

What can teachers do to ensure that their curriculum and instruction encourage learning and achievement for all students? Knowing students' backgrounds and giving culturally appropriate responses to students is an important first step.

Instruction. Sensitivity training and cultural awareness programs for both teachers and students are being implemented in schools and communities throughout the nation. For example, the Chicago Children's Museum features an exhibit called "Prejudice Bus," which aims to help children handle discriminatory behavior. The "bus" is a room with enlarged cardboard photos of children sitting on bus seats. People who enter the room hear taped children's voices blurting out racial, ethnic, and other epithets aimed to offend virtually every segment of society. The program, called

▌ **TABLE 9.1**
SAT[1] Scores by Racial/Ethnic Group

Racial–ethnic background	1987	1997	Percent change, 1987 to 1997
1	2	4	5
SAT–Verbal			
All students	**507**	**505**	**–2**
White	524	526	2
Black	428	434	6
Hispanic or Latino	464	466	2
Mexican American	457	451	–6
Puerto Rican	436	454	18
Asian American	479	496	17
American Indian	471	475	4
Other	480	512	32
SAT–Mathematical			
All students	**501**	**511**	**10**
White	514	526	12
Black	411	423	12
Hispanic or Latino	462	468	6
Mexican American	455	458	3
Puerto Rican	432	447	15
Asian American	541	560	19
American Indian	463	475	12
Other	482	514	32

[1]Formerly known as the Scholastic Aptitude Test.

Note: Possible scores on each part of the SAT range from 200 to 800.

Source: Digest of Education Statistics (p. 146), U.S. Department of Education, 1999. Washington, DC: U.S. Government Printing Office.

"Face to Face: Dealing with Prejudice and Discrimination," guides children in strategies for responding to name calling and other discriminatory behavior ("Words that hurt," 1996).

A summary of interviews conducted with 10 Asian American students (Oei & Lyon, 1996, pp. 54–55) suggests ways teachers can respond appropriately to Asian American students and welcome student diversity:

1. Call students by their correct names. Ask for help with pronunciation of unfamiliar names, and help classmates learn to say the names correctly. Do not offer to change or shorten children's names or give them nicknames.

2. Ask students how they identify themselves (such as "Asian American," "Korean American," "Chinese," or just "American"). Do not assume a particular nationality or birthplace. Some students' families will have lived in the United States for many generations; others may be recent immigrants.

3. Do not assume that Asian American students will have particular academic or athletic interests or abilities. Encourage participation in all aspects of school life.

4. Help all students identify and challenge the stereotypes of Asians that might arise in film, literature, textbooks, or TV.

5. If Asian American students express an interest in their Asian heritages, encourage efforts to bring that cultural connection into the classroom. Integrate appropriate literature, arts, and language into the curriculum, and invite students to describe holiday celebrations and religious observances.

> **What are some ways teachers can capitalize on student diversity?**

Manning and Baruth (1996, pp. 212–219) offer guidelines such as the following for teachers in diverse classrooms:

▓ Recognize and accept diversity of culture, gender, ethnicity, race, social class, and religion.

▓ Value diversity as a positive benefit rather than as a problem.

▓ Become informed, not only about students, their families, and their community, but about complex relationships between culture and learning.

▓ Create a classroom environment that demonstrates acceptance and respect.

▓ Encourage students to express diverse views and to take others' perspectives.

▓ Encourage cooperation and positive social interactions and relationships among diverse students.

▓ Develop the skills to plan and implement curriculum and instruction that reflect student cultural diversity and address culturally diverse students' needs.

▓ Value objective perceptions of all learners; base all educational decisions on objective evidence with the student's welfare in mind.

▓ Expect all students to succeed academically.

Perhaps most important is to provide a culture-fair education and to ensure that all students have as many opportunities as possible to demonstrate success.

Curricula. In addition to fostering the development of multicultural instruction, diversity issues in education have led to the creation of new curricula. Blues in the Schools (BITS), for example, is a curriculum shaped over the past 20 years by a variety of individual and cooperative efforts. Goals of the program are to affirm the cultural heritage and contributions of African Americans and to foster understanding across racial and socioeconomic lines. Idlewood Elementary School in Memphis and Minnechaug Regional High School in Wilbraham, Massachusetts, are two of the many schools in the nation using BITS to enrich their curriculum:

> [Memphis sixth-grade] students start the year by practicing the basic 12-bar blues structure on simple instruments such as recorders, xylophones and drums.

How has diversity education shaped the Blues in the School curriculum? What are the advantages of a curriculum like BITS? What are the possible disadvantages?

Through the deep research emphasis of Kids 'N Blues, literature, history and even geography classes bring in information about the cultural and historical experiences that gave birth to the genre. . . . Having hooked them on the music, the fun and the dissection of lyrics, [Hillary Bruch, the music teacher] presents a window on a time and culture even the African American students know little about. . . . Across the country in Massachusetts, Art Tipaldi faces an even greater "history gap" with his all-White classes. He finds that students previously oblivious to racism and discrimination can find in the blues a window on hard truths of the past that still challenge us today. (Millard, 1999, pp. 17, 18, 23)

Black History Month (February) is another example of curricula intended to address diversity issues. There is disagreement about how significant the focus on African American accomplishments during February has been in terms of student learning. There is widespread agreement, however, that Black History Month has affected school curricula.

"Black History Month has in fact, especially in recent years, dramatically changed school curricula from the very beginning all the way through graduate school," said Richard Newman, a researcher at the W.E.B. Du Bois Institute for Afro-American Research at Harvard University (Manzo, 1998).

But Asa Hilliard, a professor of educational psychology at Georgia State University, worries that a cursory examination of history may do more damage than good. "If you have to wait until February to crank up the initiative, you probably are going to get more of a trivial pursuit than anything of substance." (Ibid.)

Banks and others note the importance of presenting "balanced" approaches to multiethnic curriculum, approaches that teach human relations, cultural self-awareness, and multicultural and cross-cultural sensitivity. Such balanced strategies foster understanding of content. They go beyond simple efforts to apprise students of cultural attributes. Balanced approaches promote deeper appreciation of cultures by encouraging students to analyze, evaluate, and synthesize the information they encounter, particularly when the content is complex and contradictory.

Hilliard and others (Asante, 1992; Y. Winn, personal communication, October 9, 1996) have promoted **Afrocentric curricula**, or curricula that emphasize African his-

Benchmarks

Multicultural Education in the United States

1882	George Washington Williams writes *History of the Negro Race in America.*
1896	W.E.B. Du Bois writes *The Suppression of the African Slave Trade to the United States of America, 1638–1870.*
1915	Association for the Study of Negro Life and History is founded in Chicago.
1929	Bruno Lasker writes *Race Attitudes in Children.*
1930	Manuel Gamio writes *Mexican Immigration to the United States.*
1933	Carter G. Woodson writes *The Mis-Education of the Negro.*
1937	*The Negro History Bulletin,* designed for schools, begins publication.
1945	*Democratic Human Relations: Promising Practices and Intergroup and Intercultural Education in the Social Studies,* 16th yearbook of the National Council for the Social Studies, is edited by Hilda Taba and William VanTil.
1965	*Compensatory Education for Cultural Deprivation* is written by Benjamin Bloom, Allison David, and Robert Hess.
1974	"Students' Right to Their Own Language," a position statement, is issued by the National Council of Teachers of English.
1977	*Standards for the Accreditation of Teacher Education,* issued by the National Council for the Accreditation of Teacher Education, includes a requirement for multicultural education in teacher education programs.
1999	Parties in a San Francisco lawsuit reach a settlement replacing a long-standing racial-desegregation scheme for schools with a compromise that emphasizes integration of students by economic status.

Source: Banks, J. A., & Banks, C. A. M. (1995). *Handbook of research on multicultural education.* New York: Macmillan, p. 6. Reprinted by permission of the Gale Group.

tory and culture and the role of African Americans in the formation of the United States. Afrocentrists seek to counteract bias in books and curricula viewed as Eurocentric or that focus exclusively on Europe as the cradle of civilization.

Novelist Francine Prose cautions teachers to examine critically the literature they select for their multicultural classrooms (1999). She notes in particular the "lightweight, mediocre" fiction and autobiography in many high-school English classrooms "taught for reasons that have nothing to do with how well a book is written" (p. 76). These days, Prose contends, racial and ethnic identification of a writer reign supreme, instead of the quality of the writing:

> The question is no longer what the writer has written but rather who the writer is—specifically, what ethnic group or gender identity an author represents. . . . Meanwhile, aesthetic beauty—felicitous or accurate language, images, rhythm, with the satisfaction of recognizing something in fiction that seems fresh and true—is simply too frivolous, suspect, and elitist even to mention . . . (p. 78). [Simplistic lesson plans and assignments have the effect of] blurring the line between reality and fiction (What happened to you that was exactly like what happened to Hester Prynne?) . . . [reducing] our respect for imagination, beauty, art, thought, and the way that the human spirit expresses itself in words. (p. 82)

Critics claim that alternative curricula can lead to education that is exclusionary. In its extreme form, for example, Afrocentric education has led to the founding of special schools or academies for African American males. The Matthew A. Henson School in Baltimore, Maryland, opened in 1989 on the premise that an African American male teacher "could be a positive role model for black boys who may come from female-headed households and may know black men only as drug dealers and idlers on the street corners" (Cooper, 1992). Attempts to start whole schools for African American boys in Milwaukee, Wisconsin, and Detroit, Michigan were criticized as both sexist and separatist, however. In Detroit a U.S. District Court judge ruled that the intentional creation of a race-segregated school or class violates existing federal civil rights law.

While those for and against multicultural education wage rhetorical war, some have opined that multiculturalism is a "middle-class movement," largely irrelevant to life in inner-city schools. According to these opponents, the middle class and privileged have the luxury to consider such issues, because they do not have to suffer the indignities of a life unprotected by money:

> [A]dvocates who put their faith for saving the schools in a multicultural social studies program are as mistaken as those who think multiculturalism means the end of Western Civilization. . . . What most teachers need, more than workshops on diversity, are basic supplies—glue, paper, crayons. (Mosle, 1993)

Barbara Sizemore, former superintendent of the Washington, DC, public schools and dean of the School of Education at De Paul University, warns educators who alter curriculum to teach diversity not to lower their standards:

> What African children who live in poverty need most, she insists, is a highly structured school with firm discipline that is focused on teaching them to take and pass standardized tests. Sizemore . . . is fond of pointing out that students must score 1040 on their SATs to even be considered for admission to her school. (Bradley, 1996, p. 36)

Well-known and highly respected columnist William Raspberry worries that public schools may never be able to help those who need it most.

If I find myself slowly morphing into a supporter of charter schools or vouchers, it isn't because I harbor any illusions that there's something magical about these alternatives. It is because I am increasingly doubtful that the public schools can do (or at any rate will do) what is necessary to educate poor minority children. (1998, p. A8)

Some people believe that efforts to encourage openness to and acceptance of multicultural approaches to teaching and learning have themselves become closed and doctrinaire, yielding what is popularly termed *political correctness*. The debate on this point has focused mainly on teaching and learning in higher education, but the issue is as important for elementary and high school teachers, if not more so (Phillips, 1993; Manzo, Lawton, Bradley, & Archer, 1998). John Searle (1993) argues that extreme proponents of multiculturalism often demand that people choose sides in the debate about the place of various cultures in our society, when we should be helping students to understand different positions and accommodate different ideas. Searle also criticizes multiculturalists for focusing on moral and social issues, thereby distracting people from practical problems, such as adequately funding the programs proposed and finding the time to add, integrate, and deliver the new curricula. The

> **Has multiculturalism become just another form of political correctness?**

Using Technology

The Multicultural Pavilion Web Site

 Paul Gorski at the University of Maryland has created and maintains a remarkably versatile web site called the Multicultural Pavilion. Teachers take advantage of this site to locate poetry, art, songs, book and film reviews, articles, teaching tools, discussions, and more, all relevant to multicultural education. Gorski wants the site to encourage educators to collaborate in their efforts to transform education.

> Multicultural education is a transformative movement in education which produces critically thinking, socially active members of society. It is not simply a change of curriculum or the addition of an activity. It is a movement which calls for new attitudes, new approaches, and a new dedication to laying the foundation for the transformation of society. (Gorski, 1999)

The Council for Exceptional Children (CEC) has created and maintains a site to increase knowledge about educating students with exceptionalities. The CEC is the largest international professional organization dedicated to improving educational outcomes for individuals with exceptionalities, students with disabilities, and/or the gifted. The CEC works to influence governmental policies and professional standards. It provides continual professional development for educators and advocates for newly and historically underserved individuals with exceptionalities.

The site contains information about training programs, events, publications, products, partnerships, public policy, and legislation. It has direct links to the ERIC Clearinghouse on Disabilities and Gifted Education, an extremely useful resource for both general education and special education teachers.

questions remain: What content is most important for students to learn? What standards should be applied for the inclusion and exclusion of content? Who is to decide what stays and what goes?

And so goes the debate, often with little regard for the many ways multicultural education is defined in practice. The challenge has been and continues to be one of finding ways to help all young people succeed—not just separately, but together—and to appreciate one another in the process.

The Future of Multicultural Education.   Just like any other part of the curriculum, both the content and processes of multicultural education will continue to be subject to scrutiny. Does multicultural education foster student engagement in intellectually and socially relevant activities? Does it promote academic achievement? Does multicultural education encourage understanding and acceptance among students? Can multicultural education help forge ties between schools and homes? Answers to these and similar questions will determine the fate of such approaches.

One consequence is certain. If multicultural education efforts come up short, they will be replaced by other strategies that reach out to involve people in schools. For there is general agreement that young people in the United States must be prepared to live and work together in a culturally diverse society.

 ## How Are Educational Services Adapted for Students with Exceptionalities?

Public schools in the United States make special provisions for students to succeed, regardless of their needs and abilities. Schools are morally and legally obligated to create environments that do not restrict but rather enhance children's learning. Adaptations to students' needs and abilities occur in both curricula and instruction. And, increasingly, educators are seeking new and authentic ways of evaluating students' performances as well.

▶ Delivering Services to Students with Disabilities

The law assures individuals with disabilities a right to a free, appropriate education in the least restrictive environment. This means that students with disabilities must be educated in regular classrooms whenever possible. During the 1992–1993 school year, 94 percent of 3- to 21-year-olds with disabilities were served in regular school buildings alongside students without disabilities. Most often, educators place students with disabilities in regular, resource, or separate classroom environments. The government reports that 46 percent are in regular classes, another 29 percent are in resource rooms, and 22 percent are in separate classes (U.S. Department of Education, 1998).

The 1975 Education for All Handicapped Children Act (Public Law 94-142) recognized the rights of students between the ages of 5 and 18 to **equal educational**

opportunity, or access to resources, choices, and encouragement so they might achieve to their fullest potential. Education programs were to be fitted to students' individual needs and were to be carried out in the least restrictive environment. The 1990 **Individuals with Disabilities Education Act (IDEA)** amended the **Education for All Handicapped Children Act,** or Public Law 94-142, by changing the term *handicapped* to *with disabilities* and by extending a free and appropriate public education to every individual between 2 and 21 years of age, regardless of the nature or severity of his disability. The IDEA was reauthorized in 1997 and approved in 1999.

Laws That Support Inclusion.　Today, many students with special needs receive **inclusive education**—education designed and offered to include all people regardless of their physical, social, emotional, or intellectual characteristics. Most often, however, people use the term to refer to education provided in mainstream or general education classrooms to students with disabilities. Inclusive education stands in contrast to special education offerings in separate classrooms or segregated facilities.

Dennis Mithaug (1998) grounds the concept of inclusive education in the moral and legal principles laid down in *Brown* v. *Board of Education* in 1954 and amplified over time. The landmark case established that separating children by race in order to educate them was not only illegal but morally wrong as well. Mitaug situates the concept of inclusive education or *inclusion* in a set of social experiments stimulated by the Brown case. These included busing to desegregate public schools, affirmative action to reduce discrimination in employment, welfare rights to reduce the harmful effects of poverty, and special education to include students with disabilities in the mainstream of public schooling.

Brown v. *Board of Education* stimulated other actions relating directly to students with disabilities. In 1958, the first federal law addressing special education, the Education of Mentally Retarded Children Act, was passed. It created funding to prepare teachers for mentally retarded children. In 1965, the Elementary and Secondary Education Act provided funding to improve the education of disadvantaged children and children with disabilities. Two court cases in particular, both decided in 1972, *The Pennsylvania Association for Retarded Citizens* v. *The Commonwealth of Pennsylvania* and *Mills* v. *Board of Education in the District of Columbia,* have helped advance the rights of students with disabilities (Sack, 1999a).

These laws and court decisions, coupled with actions of parents, civic leaders, and the professional education and health communities, have stimulated the discussion about special education generally and inclusive education specifically. Martha Snell (1998) notes that inclusion should not be thought of as a way of fitting students with special needs into the mainstream. Instead, inclusive education means "creating a mainstream where everyone fits" (p. 76). This presents a new set of challenges requiring special educators and teachers in the mainstream, or in general education settings, to work closely and collaboratively to support children with disabilities.

Maria Sapon-Shevin describes the situation this way:

> What does **inclusion** mean? *Inclusion* means we all belong; it means not having
> to fight for a chance to be part of a classroom or school community; it means
> that all children are accepted. Although the concept of *all children* should be
> fairly self-evident, it is still difficult for many individuals to grasp. "But, of
> course, you don't mean a child like Matthew?" someone will ask. Although chil-

Issues in School Reform

Inclusion of Students with Disabilities

There may be an unwritten social law that any pressure to reform education is sure to meet with equal pressure resisting the reform. Inclusive education for students with disabilities is a good case in point. As the following excerpt from a newspaper suggests, critics of inclusion can be found among both educators and parents of students with disabilities:

The Broward County, Fla., school district is facing criticism from parents of students with disabilities who do not want their children moved from special education centers to regular schools.

The southeastern Florida district is in the process of moving 30 to 40 such students, most of whom have mental retardation, into regular schools, as a result of a December 1997 agreement with federal civil rights officials.

That year, federal officials ordered the 233,000-student district to step up its efforts to include more students with disabilities in regular schools and classes. The officials acted under the federal Individuals with Disabilities Education Act.

Subsequently, the district reviewed the individualized education plans, or IEPs, of about 700 students attending the county's six special education centers and opted to move some of them to regular schools. In addition, the federal agreement required that the county offer additional support services to special education students and teachers in secondary grades, and give parents and IEP team members more options when choosing a student's placement.

The U.S. Department of Education's Office for Civil Rights declined to comment on the case last week because it involves an ongoing investigation, a department spokesman, Rodger Murphey, said. The OCR routinely investigates districts such as Broward County where data show disproportionate numbers of disabled students in segregated classes.

But at least one school board member and many of the parents of the Broward County students whose IEPs are being reviewed are angry. They contend that the OCR has imposed on the district's and parents' judgment.

"Is OCR now becoming the Office of Certain Rights?" said Judie S. Budnick, a member of the county school board who has helped organize parents to push for greater parental control over their children's placements. "They should be looking at all children's rights."

Broward County does have a higher-than-average percentage of students in the special schools—about 18 percent, compared with about 5 percent in the rest of the state, Ms. Budnick acknowledged.

But she maintained that the students' disabilities are so severe that they should be served in a restricted environment. And, she added, many parents with severely disabled children have moved to Broward County because of its high-quality educational services for children with disabilities and state-of-the-art, well-staffed special education centers.

"People are moving from all over the country because of the programs we have," she said. "These parents want these kids to be in the centers." (Sack, 1999, p. 6)

Discussion Questions Why might some parents favor inclusion? Why might others be opposed to inclusion? Where do you stand on this issue? Why?

Source: J. Sack, Fla. district criticized for moving students out of special centers. Reprinted with permission from *Education Week, 18* (30), 6, April 7, 1999b.

dren will require different levels of support and resources, the concept of inclusion does mean all children—*all children,* not just those who are clean, or who have agreeable parents, or who come to school "ready" to learn. *All* means *all.* (1999, p. 4)

How Special Education Is Provided. Schools provide special education services for students with disabilities in a variety of ways. These service options can be described on a continuum ranging from those most physically integrated into general education classrooms to those least integrated.

In some instances the general education teacher meets all the needs of the student. Sometimes a special educator acts as a consultant to the teacher, or an itinerant special education teacher may offer some instruction to a student within the classroom. A student may go to a resource teacher part of the day for specific help. A special education teacher in a center might provide most or all instruction for several days or weeks. When a student is hospitalized, an itinerant general or special educator provides all instruction in the hospital or home before a student returns to school. A student's primary assignment may be to a self-contained special education class, with the student leaving only occasionally to participate in school activities. Sometimes special education students attend separate schools. The least physically integrated arrangement is for a student to be in a residential setting devoted totally to providing a therapeutic environment (Hallahan & Kauffman, 2000).

Students with disabilities are especially at a disadvantage in mathematics and science courses, or so many people believe:

> [P]ersons with disabilities who do not express themselves well are assumed to be unable to understand and do science. Future technological advances and other accommodations are likely to improve the academic performance of children identified with disabilities. Currently, however, 50 to 60% of students with disabilities fail in one or more subjects, and their relative performance in science and mathematics is lower than in other subjects. These results are also reflected in lower SAT scores and other achievement measures. The gaps are not insurmountable, however, because about 8% of all [college] undergraduates report having disabilities. While there are wide disparities in kind and extent of disability that may or may not affect academic achievement, it is clear that many students with disabilities are able to excel in school and go on to higher education. (American Association for the Advancement of Science, 1998, pp. 10–11)

Research conducted in elementary teachers' general education classrooms suggests that effective elementary teachers think and behave in particular ways with children who have disabilities. After conducting an observational study of the behaviors of a large number of such teachers, researchers videotaped and interviewed five teachers to determine why they behaved as they did toward students with special needs (McNergney & Keller, 1999). Table 9.2 shows what researchers learned about effective teachers' actions.

> **What does it take to make inclusion work?**

> How might a classroom teacher and a special education teacher collaborate to teach this student in a general education classroom? What roles might other students in the class take? What might be some advantages and disadvantages of this arrangement?

▌ **TABLE 9.2**
Some Effective Teachers' Actions with Children with Disabilities

1. Teachers watch students as they work on tasks:
   (a) to see if students need help.
   (b) to keep students involved.
   (c) to determine when to move on to the next activity.
2. Teachers give step-by-step directions:
   (a) to help students work independently.
   (b) to avoid interruptions during instructional time.
3. Teachers help learners by giving hints and clarifying misunderstandings:
   (a) to make the content of a lesson more meaningful.
   (b) to help students make connections between old and new material.
   (c) to get students to think.
   (d) to keep students from giving up.
   (e) to give students more time to think.
   (f) to help students succeed so they feel good about themselves.
4. Teachers recognize special needs of learners:
   (a) to give students concrete examples to help them understand.
5. Teachers summarize and review throughout the lesson:
   (a) to help students synthesize information.
   (b) to keep students involved.
6. Teachers praise learners publicly and explain why:
   (a) to encourage student involvement.
   (b) to make students feel good about their achievements.
   (c) to encourage students to behave like others.
   (d) to enhance self-concepts of students.
7. Teachers make connections to students' interests, to the outside world, and to other subjects:
   (a) to increase student attention and interest in the lesson.
   (b) to make content real or meaningful to students.
   (c) to help students see that there is an overlap in content areas.
   (d) to help students form linkages between subjects.
   (e) to reinforce what the teacher and class have just discussed.
8. Teachers urge students to answer or comment:
   (a) to get and keep student involvement.
   (b) to get students to think about the material.
   (c) to give students a chance to answer correctly and feel good about themselves.
   (d) to make students feel that what they have to say is important.
9. Teachers check understanding throughout the lesson:
   (a) to see if students are "with" the teacher.
   (b) to keep students involved in the lesson.
   (c) to get students to think on their own.
10. Teachers question and respond—they praise, acknowledge, approve, redirect, reenter, make eye contact, check status, and so on:
    (a) to keep students involved in the lesson.
    (b) to check understanding.
    (c) to get students to think.
    (d) to review concepts.
11. Teachers work to build students' self-concepts:
    (a) to help students feel that what they have to say is important.
    (b) to help students develop a feeling of power or control—a "can do" attitude.
    (c) to increase student participation.

Source: McNergney, R. & Keller, C. (1999). *Images of Mainstreaming*, Appendix: Some Effective Teachers' Actions, New York: Garland Publishing, Inc. Reprinted by permission.

Special educators and general education classroom teachers are working collaboratively in many ways to understand and help children learn. They are planning programs of professional training together. Consultants in schools are behaving more as advisors and team members and less as supervisors. These teams, in turn, are seeking instructional materials and methods that best fit those students who need special help and the objectives they must achieve. Increasing communication between communities of special educators and general educators will help concentrate resources where they are most needed (McNergney, Hallahan, Trent, and Hockenbury, 1999).

Regardless of where children with disabilities are placed in schools, general and special educators need to work with parents and other professionals to plan an **individualized education program (IEP)** for each child. A child's IEP identifies, for example, current level of performance (strengths and limitations), long- and short-term goals, criteria for success, methods for assessing mastery of objectives (e.g., observation, testing), amount of time that will be spent in general education classrooms, and beginning and ending dates for special services. One IEP appears in Figure 9.4, which was written for Curt, age 15, grade 9.

Who Else Receives Special Education Services?   In some instances, teachers have students in their classrooms who share many of the attributes of exceptional children but who, for one reason or another, are not identified as such. Although teachers are not required to create IEPs for these children, they are obligated to create a learning environment that enables all children to maximize their potentials. When implementing plans, good teachers seek ways to increase students' achievement and to foster positive social relationships between children with disabilities and their nondisabled peers. Many students, disabled or not, have difficulty winning acceptance by their peers; children with disabilities may experience chronic and acute social problems.

Although most students require some instructional adaptation to succeed with some tasks, students with exceptionalities often require more adaptations. People who identify themselves as members of the deaf culture, for example, advocate the use of sign language rather than mechanical aids. Some argue that mechanical hearing devices, particularly those that are surgically implanted, rob deaf people of their self-respect and their group identity. They would prefer to teach children with hearing impairments to communicate with one another as members of a distinct culture by signing. Others spurn the legitimacy or value of a deaf culture and opt for any chance to help children be more like their hearing peers. Some discourage signing, advocate the use of technology to boost children's chances to hear, and encourage speech therapy for all children with hearing impairments.

American Sign Language (ASL), one of the most common sign languages, consists of hand movements that represent concepts or words rather than isolated sounds or letters. Learning ASL is much like learning a foreign language. People learn signs for whole words and complete thoughts, build their vocabulary, and improve their speech through practice. As Figure 9.5 shows, signs vary regionally, like dialects.

The Future of Inclusion.   Two ardent advocates of inclusion, Dorothy Lipsky and Alan Gartner, both at City University of New York, suggest that the increasing implementation of inclusive education programs in schools can be described in terms of

FIGURE 9.4
An IEP for Curt.   How might having an individualized education program (IEP) help the classroom teacher and the special education teacher work together to meet a student's needs?

Individualized Education Program

Student: _____ Curt _____   Age: __ 15 __   Grade: __ 9 __   Date: __ 1998 __

Unique Educational Needs, Characteristics, and Present Level of Performance (PLOPs) *(including how the disability affects the student's ability to progress in the general curriculum)*	Special Education, Related Service, Supplemental Aids & Services, Assistive Technology, Program Modifications, Support for Personnel *(including frequency, duration, and location)*	Measurable Annual Goals & Short-Term Objectives of Benchmarks • To enable student to participate in the general curriculum • To meet other needs resulting from the disability *(including how progress toward goals will be measured)*
Present Level of Social Skills: Curt lashes out violently when not able to complete work, uses profanity, and refuses to follow further directions from adults. **Social Needs:** • To learn anger management skills, especially regarding swearing • To learn to comply with requests	1. Teacher and/or counselor consult with behavior specialist regarding techniques and programs for teaching skills, especially anger management. 2. Provide anger management instruction to Curt. Services 3 times/week, 30 minutes 3. Establish a peer group which involves role playing, etc., so Curt can see positive role models and practice newly learned anger management skills. Services 2 times/week, 30 minutes. 4. Develop a behavioral plan for Curt which gives him responsibility for charting his own behavior. 5. Provide a teacher or some other adult mentor to spend time with Curt (talking, game playing, physical activity, etc.). Services 2 times/week, 30 minutes 6. Provide training for the mentor regarding Curt's needs/goals.	Goal: During the last quarter of the academic year, Curt will have 2 or fewer detentions for any reason. Obj. 1: At the end of the 1st quarter, Curt will have had 10 or fewer detentions. Obj. 2: At the end of the 2nd quarter, Curt will have had 7 or fewer detentions. Obj. 3: At the end of the 3rd quarter, Curt will have had 4 or fewer detentions. Goal: Curt will manage his behavior and language in a reasonably acceptable manner as reported by faculty and peers. Obj. 1: At 2 weeks, asked at the end of class if Curt's behavior and language were acceptable or unacceptable, 3 out of 6 teachers will say "acceptable." Obj. 2: At 6 weeks, asked the same question, 4 out of 6 teachers will say "acceptable." Obj. 3: At 12 weeks, asked the same question, 6 out of 6 teachers will say "acceptable."
Study Skills/ Organizational Needs • How to read text • Note taking • How to study notes • Memory work • Be prepared for class with materials • Lengthen and improve attention span and on-task behavior **Present Level:** Curt currently lacks skill in all these areas.	1. Speech/language therapist, resource room teacher, and content area teachers will provide Curt with direct and specific teaching of study skills, i.e., Note taking from lectures Note taking while reading text How to study notes for a test Memorization hints Strategies for reading text to retain information 2. Assign a study buddy for Curt in each content area class.	Goal: At the end of academic year, Curt will have better grades and, by his own report, will have learned new study skills. Obj. 1: Given a 20–30 min. lecture/oral lesson, Curt will take appropriate notes as judged by that teacher. Obj. 2: Given 10–15 pages of text to read, Curt will employ an appropriate strategy for retaining info.—i.e., mapping, webbing, outlining, notes, etc.—as judged by the teacher.

FIGURE 9.4
An IEP for Curt.   *(Continued)*

Unique Educational Needs, Characteristics, and Present Level of Performance (PLOPs) *(including how the disability affects the student's ability to progress in the general curriculum)*	Special Education, Related Service, Supplemental Aids & Services, Assistive Technology, Program Modifications, Support for Personnel *(including frequency, duration, and location)*	Measurable Annual Goals & Short-Term Objectives of Benchmarks • To enable student to participate in the general curriculum • To meet other needs resulting from the disability *(including how progress toward goals will be measured)*
	3. Prepare a motivation system for Curt to be prepared for class with all necessary materials. 4. Develop a motivational plan to encourage Curt to lengthen his attention span and time on task. 5. Provide aide to monitor on-task behaviors in first month or so of plan and teach Curt self-monitoring. 6. Provide motivational system and self-recording form for completion of academic tasks in each class.	<u>Obj. 3:</u> Given notes to study for a test, Curt will do so successfully as evidenced by his test score. <u>Goal:</u> Curt will improve his on-task behavior from 37% to 80% as measured by a qualified observer at year's end. <u>Obj. 1:</u> By 1 month, Curt's on-task behavior will increase to 45%. <u>Obj. 2:</u> By 3 months, Curt's on-task behavior will increase to 60%. <u>Obj. 3:</u> By 6 months, Curt's on-task behavior will increase to 80% and maintain or improve until end of the year.
Academic Needs/ Written Language: Curt needs strong remedial help in spelling, punctuation, capitalization, and usage. **Present Level:** Curt is approximately 2 grade levels behind his peers in these skills.	1. Provide direct instruction in written language skills (punctuation, capitalization, usage, spelling) by using a highly structured, well-sequenced program. Services provided in small group of no more than four students in the resource room, 50 minutes/day. 2. Build in continuous and cumulative review to help with short-term rate memory difficulty. 3. Develop a list of commonly used words in student writing (or use one of many published lists) for Curt's spelling program.	<u>Goal:</u> Within one academic year, Curt will improve the written language skills by 1.5 or 2 full grade levels. <u>Obj. 1:</u> Given 10 sentences of dictation at his current level of instruction, Curt will punctuate and capitalize with 90% accuracy (checked at the end of each unit taught). <u>Obj. 2:</u> Given 30 sentences with choices of usage, at his current instructional level, Curt will perform with 90% accuracy. <u>Obj. 3:</u> Given a list of 150 commonly used words in writing, Curt will spell with 90% accuracy.

Adaptations to Regular Program:
- In all classes, Curt should sit near the front of the class.
- Curt should be called on often to keep him involved and on task.
- All teachers should help Curt, with study skills as trained by spelling/language specialist and resource room teacher.
- Teachers should monitor Curt's work closely in the beginning weeks/months of his program.

FIGURE 9.5
How One Concept is Expressed in American Sign Language in Different Areas of the Country
Which ASL speakers might have the greatest difficulty in understanding each other?

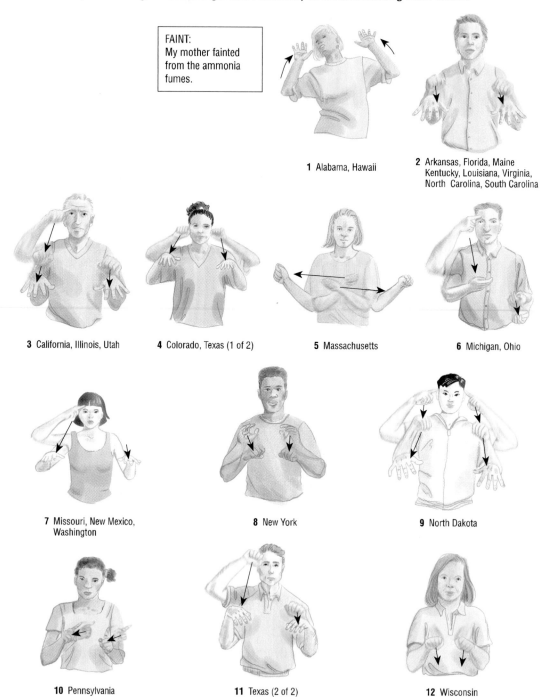

FAINT:
My mother fainted from the ammonia fumes.

1 Alabama, Hawaii

2 Arkansas, Florida, Maine Kentucky, Louisiana, Virginia, North Carolina, South Carolina

3 California, Illinois, Utah

4 Colorado, Texas (1 of 2)

5 Massachusetts

6 Michigan, Ohio

7 Missouri, New Mexico, Washington

8 New York

9 North Dakota

10 Pennsylvania

11 Texas (2 of 2)

12 Wisconsin

Source: Adapted by permission of the publisher, from E. Shroyer and S. Shroyer, *Signs Across America* (1985): 78–80. Washington DC: Gallaudet Universityh Press. Copyright 1984 by Gallaudet University.

two phases or generations (1998). The first phase is one of simply exploring the advisability of establishing inclusive programs; the second is one of exploring how best to implement inclusive programs. The issues that have dominated these generational implementations are shown in Table 9.3. The writers note that many and perhaps most current inclusive education programs are characterized by first-generation practices and attitudes.

▶ Delivering Services to Gifted and Talented Students

Programs for students with exceptional talent have enjoyed varying levels of support over the years. Events such as the launching of Sputnik in 1957 and the publication of *A Nation at Risk* by the National Commission on Excellence in Education in 1983 stimulated educators to put more emphasis on programs for the brightest students. Between the 1960s and 1970s, however, issues of equity often forced gifted education to take a back seat as educators switched their attention to the needs of below-average and disadvantaged students. With increasingly limited resources for public education, people often chose to curtail or eliminate programs for gifted and talented students.

Currently, every state and many school districts have gifted and talented programs. Students who qualify remain in general education classrooms but are assigned accelerated curricula. Or they may be pulled out of the general education classroom for special instruction in a resource room. Sometimes gifted and talented students may attend self-contained classes for talented students. They may also skip a grade in school. Some take Advanced Placement courses and college courses.

When students are selected for gifted and talented programs, studies suggest that economically disadvantaged students are significantly underserved. Examining Table 9.4, it is easy to see why children in poverty might not be able to take advantage of gifted and talented programs; that is, wealth and parental educational background combine to influence student achievement.

Studies also indicate that disproportionately fewer limited English proficient (LEP) students are included in gifted and talented programs. Although schools provide instructional assistance to these students, many people argue that educational programs do not teach the language or higher-order skills that students need to perform well on placement tests. Many gifted LEP students therefore end up in lower-level classes and even are erroneously placed in special education classes (Schmidt, 1993).

Sometimes a stigma is involved in being labeled a high-achieving student. In a survey in three midwestern high schools, students said that they wanted to do well in school but not exceptionally well because they were afraid they would be associated with the "brain crowd" rather than the "in crowd" (U.S. Department of Education, 1993).

The story of one high school student reveals some of the reasons why being bright may be somewhat difficult. In 1993, when Elizabeth Mann was a senior at Montgomery Blair High School in Silver Spring, Maryland, an article in the *Washington Post* bumped her status from "brilliant" to "legendary" (Finkel, 1993). Elizabeth scored 1570 out of a possible 1600 on the SATs, 800 (out of 800) on her achievement test in math, and 800 on her achievement test in physics. Several themes emerged in the story, among them the

Is there a best way to educate students who are gifted and talented?

▌ **TABLE 9.3**
Stages in the Implementation of Inclusive Education

First Generation Issues	*Second Generation Issues*
• Should we do inclusive education?	• How do we do inclusive education?
• Inclusion viewed as a special education issue.	• Inclusion as a schoolwide or districtwide issue.
• Implementation of inclusion the responsibility of special education administrators and staff.	• Implementation of inclusion the responsibility of general education administrators and staff, along with special educators.
• Students placed in general education classes must be "ready."	• Including all students regardless of the intensity of their disability.
• Providing elaborate modifications when a student is included.	• Providing only those supports and accommodations that are educationally necessary.
• Individual paraeducators assigned to students who are included.	• Paraeducators assigned to support all students in the inclusive classroom.
• Inclusive education seen as parallel to general education reforms.	• Inclusive education initiatives are entwined with general education reform.
• Students perceived as "belonging" to general or special educators.	• Special and general education assuming a shared responsibility for all students.
• Assessment focused in student's individual progress.	• Assessment tied to overall curriculum and instruction.
• Teachers who implement inclusive education should be volunteers.	• The teaching of students with disabilities is a normal part of all teachers' roles.
• Staff development focused on transfer of special education skills to general educators.	• Staff development emphasizes development of the discrete and shared knowledge of general and special educators and the development of collaboration between them.
• Emphasis is on helping the student with special needs adjust to general education.	• Emphasis is on empowering all students.
• Focus is on inclusive education at the elementary grades.	• Focus widens to include middle and high school.
• Honoring of parents' due process rights.	• Beyond due process to engagement of parents as partners.
• Related services provided outside regular classroom.	• Related services integrated into the regular program activities.
• Funding tied to placement.	• Funding follows the child.
• Does inclusion benefit the special education student?	• Does inclusion benefit all students.
• Students remain in inclusive environments the entire day.	• General education classrooms provide a common learning base for all students and service delivery and placement decisions are individualized and crafted for children with and without disabilities.

Source: Reprinted with permission from Lipsky, D. K., & Gartner, A. (1998). Factors for successful inclusion: Learning from the past, looking toward the future. In S. J. Vitello & D. E. Mithaug (Eds.), *Inclusive schooling: National and international perspectives*. Mahwah, NJ: Lawrence Erlbaum Associates, Inc., Publishers, 99–100.

▌ **TABLE 9.4**
Scholastic Assessment Test[1] Score Averages by Selected Student Characteristics:
1996 and 1997

Selected characteristics	1996		1997	
	Verbal score	**Mathematics score**	**Verbal score**	**Mathematics score**
1	**2**	**3**	**5**	**6**
All students	505	508	505	511
Family income				
Less than $10,000	429	444	428	445
$10,000 to $20,000	456	464	454	464
$20,000 to $30,000	482	482	480	482
$30,000 to $40,000	497	495	496	497
$40,000 to $50,000	509	507	507	508
$50,000 to $60,000	517	517	515	518
$60,000 to $70,000	524	525	522	526
$70,000 to $80,000	531	533	529	533
$80,000 to $100,000	541	544	540	544
More than $100,000	560	569	559	571
Highest level of parental education				
Less than high school	414	439	412	441
High school diploma	475	474	474	476
Associate degree	489	487	488	489
Bachelor's degree	525	529	524	530
Graduate degree	556	558	556	560

[1]Formerly known as the Scholastic Aptitude Test.

Note: Possible scores on each part of the SAT range from 200 to 800.

Source: Digest of Education Statistics (p. 147), U.S. Department of Education, 1999. Washington, DC: U.S. Government Printing Office.

teachers' near veneration of Elizabeth's talents. The guidance counselor spoke of the "burden" Elizabeth bore because teachers were "absolutely charmed by her" (p. 13). "They are in awe of her. They have set her up as a paragon in their minds, and, I think, in the minds of her peers, which has made her road that much harder" (p. 13).

Some spoke of Elizabeth as likely to be among history's greatest mathematicians or among the smartest people of all time. All of this caused Elizabeth to cringe:

From what I've heard and what I can see, you get the general impression they're all overly enamored of me . . . I guess in and of itself, that's nice. I mean, you can't ever be upset that people like you. So that's fine. The consequences of it are what make me uneasy. (p. 22)

It is not difficult to see why Elizabeth feels this way when a fellow student discusses what he perceives as her favored status:

If you look at what's happened to Elizabeth in her four years in the magnet, there isn't one example of her being disadvantaged. . . . I have a hard time complaining. I've gotten a lot out of the magnet program. But no one has gotten as much out of it as she has. Let me make it clear. Nobody has gotten as much attention out of the program as her. (p. 22)

Elizabeth's closest friend, Valerie Wang, also offered her perspective: "No one dislikes her, because she's not dislikable, but I think there's a lot of resentment" (p. 22).

After finishing third behind two of her classmates in a highly competitive science fair, Elizabeth sat outside her house the next day and expressed her doubts and dreams:

I wish I had beautiful hair. . . . I wish I were better at physics and math than I am. I wish I could stay awake 24 hours a day. I wish I had a car. I wish I could figure out why I've lost so much respect from Josh [a fellow student], and what I could do about it, and what I'm doing wrong. I wish teachers wouldn't single out people. I wish I could be respected for my mind and yet liked as a person regardless of what my mind is like. I wish, well, this is a hard one. I wish people knew about my insecurities, so they wouldn't think I'm conceited, as apparently they do. (p. 27)

Once educators identify giftedness in students, they must decide how to teach them. Some researchers note that participation in gifted and talented programs has positive effects on academic achievement for many gifted and talented students but not for all of them (Marsh, Chessor, Craven, & Roche, 1995). Participation in such programs has negative effects on some gifted students' academic self-concepts. These students suffer from what Marsh and his colleagues call the "big-fish-little-pond effect"; that is, they feel better when they are the most talented students in a class but suffer when they are with others who are equally or more talented.

Do such findings suggest that teachers of the gifted should avoid grouping gifted children together for instruction? Not necessarily:

Of course they get a different view of the world when they are with other bright children—the halos and wings they assumed were their "gift" may seem a little tarnished—this may be a very healthy encounter with reality, but, at the same time, to preserve their sense of power, energy, and effectiveness, they need support in redrawing a healthy vision of themselves. (Marsh, Chessor, Craven, & Roche, 1995, p. 316)

Although the teaching of gifted students defies simple prescriptions, most educators agree on some general guidelines. Definitions of giftedness must be expanded to include criteria other than standardized test scores. Competition is not always conducive to academic and personal growth. Gifted students do better when they pursue projects that are of particular interest to them. They need specific feedback on their performance of tasks, not comparisons of their performances to other students.

How Can Teachers Create Culturally Relevant Classrooms?

From interviews with students, Louis Harris and Associates, Inc. (1996) found three factors that influence positive relations in schools: the quality of teachers' relationships with students, the quality of education, and the social skills teachers impart to students. When these factors are present, students perceive social problems in their schools as less serious and express more confidence that people from different backgrounds receive equal treatment by adults in their community. These factors depend heavily on teachers' knowledge of and attitudes toward their students.

Children (and teachers) who grow up in diverse communities have opportunities to learn about those who differ from themselves and about themselves in relation to others. These opportunities do not always result in social harmony; neither do they inevitably lead to tension and conflict. Without a heterogeneous population of students, however, a school has less human capital upon which to draw when preparing students for life in a diverse world.

What teachers expect from the mix of students they teach and how they act on those expectations are crucial. One way that teachers demonstrate what they expect is through grouping and labeling students. A label sets up expectations in the minds of those who label and those who are labeled; behavior flows from these expectations. Labels can be useful devices; they facilitate the flow of human and material support to students in need. But labels can also foster expectations that are inappropriately low or misguided, nurturing prejudice and fueling discrimination.

When cultural mismatches between teacher and students occur in the classroom—when teacher and students differ racially or ethnically and operate outside each other's normative cultures—the effects can be hard on teachers and their students. In low-income inner-city schools with high proportions of racial and ethnic minorities, low-income students, and at-risk learners, for example, mismatches between teachers' and students' experiences and values are common. Such differences can be frustrating and frightening, particularly to novice teachers. For instance, consider the experience of one teacher:

> The kids in Ruth Sherman's third-grade class loved the books she read to them. . . . [T]heir favorite story was "Nappy Hair," about a black girl named Brenda with the "kinkiest, the nappiest, the fuzziest, the most screwed up, squeezed up, knotted up, tangled up, twisted up" hair. . . . Not all the parents found the story so charming. When one mother stumbled onto a few photocopied pages of the book among her child's school papers . . . , she organized a protest in the neighborhood. Suddenly Ruth Sherman, who is white, was caught in the cross hairs of political correctness. (Clemetson, 1998, p. 38)

Parents in the Bushwick neighborhood of Brooklyn, New York, protested. Sherman was physically threatened to her face. Eventually she resigned. "Everyone—Sherman, administrators and parents—now admits the situation was handled badly." Unfortunately the damage was done.

Mismatches also frustrate students, who believe that teachers do not understand or value them. Too often, "[R]ather than think of minority

What is a "culturally relevant" curriculum?

students as having a culture that is valid and distinct from theirs, [teachers] sometimes think of the youngsters as deficient" (Viadero, 1996, p. 40). Teachers can misinterpret students' responses, believing that students are ignorant or disobedient, for example, when they are only exhibiting subtle and deep-seated cultural differences.

Jeannie Oakes and Martin Lipton (1999) suggest that teachers who are the most successful create "culturally relevant" classrooms—places where curriculum and instruction are "friendly" to difference. "Acquiring these dimensions as part of one's own teaching can be, like foreign travel, daunting at first; but the discovery and adventure are soon difficult to resist" (p. 261). How do teachers develop such settings? Oakes and Lipton suggest teachers begin by getting to know their students and their communities. They also recommend that teachers read some of the literature describing other teachers' experiences in diverse settings.

Gloria Ladson-Billings's book *The Dreamkeepers: Successful Teachers of African American Children* (1994), for example, describes the practices of eight teachers (three white and five African American) who create caring and democratic classroom communities with their inner-city students. One teacher, Ann Lewis, is an Italian American teacher in a largely African American community. Ladson-Billings describes the tack Lewis takes when studying *Charlie Pippin,* a novel about an 11-year-old African American girl who feels alienated from her father, a decorated Vietnam War veteran who has buried all feelings about the war deep inside him:

> *Charlie Pippin* became the centerpiece for a wide range of activities. One group of students began a Vietnam War research group. One group member who assumed a leadership position was a very quiet Vietnamese girl whose relatives had fought in the war. She brought in pictures, maps, letters, even a family member to talk to the class about Vietnam. In the book, the main character—Charlie—had made origami to sell to her classmates. Lewis taught her students how to make origami. She introduced them to Eleanor Coerr's *Sadako and the Thousand Paper Cranes.* A second group of students researched nuclear proliferation. They asked Lewis to rent the video "Amazing Grace," which is about a young boy's and a professional athlete's stand against nuclear weapons. The entire study took place against the backdrop of an impending war between the United States and its allies and Iraq. (p. 110)

When teachers work with students who are bilingual or developing English language proficiency and literacy, making content culturally relevant can be particularly challenging. Some contend that science, for example, reflects the thinking of Western society and that the norms and values of science are more familiar to students from the mainstream middle class than to students from diverse languages and cultures (Eisenhart, Finkel, & Marion, 1996; Lee & Fradd, 1998). They note in particular the emphasis on scientific inquiry—having children act as scientists, asking and answering questions to understand the world—as the recommended strategy for increasing science literacy (National Research Council, 1996). How such an approach might be used with students from diverse language backgrounds has been the subject of much debate (Lee & Fradd, 1998; Rosebery, Warren, & Conant, 1992). Should teachers serve as *knowledge transmitters,* leading students through predetermined lessons and activities, or as *facilitators,* guiding students to ask questions and to investigate their own interests?

Teachers who share the languages and cultures of their students may opt for instructional approaches congruent with students' home cultures. Decisions may also be based on teachers' backgrounds and prior experiences with science. Those from cultures where teachers are expected to exercise authority and serve as knowledge givers may feel comfortable with a direct, explicit approach. In contrast, teachers from cultures emphasizing independence and autonomy may find facilitation comfortable (Fradd & Lee, 1999). A Latino fourth-grade English as a Second Language teacher describes the tension that teachers may experience when using inquiry-based science instruction:

> The students who need to do inquiry the most are those who also need to learn how to observe, measure, and compare things. These students have no idea what to look at, how to hold an instrument, or how to record data in a chart. Sometimes they don't cooperate well because they are shy and don't want others to see their work. Sometimes they want to hide within the group. And sometimes they become boisterous and aggressive when they don't know what to do. Students have to start with simple, concrete activities and basic experiences. Teachers have to be in control in order for students to be successful. Slowly, but very slowly, teachers can let the students take control and work on their own. (p. 19)

The complexity of promoting science inquiry with students and teachers from diverse language backgrounds has prompted researchers to work with teachers to examine the effectiveness of different approaches not just in science, but in other content areas as well (Brown, 1994; Lehrer & Schauble, 1998; Metz, 1995; Rosebery & Warren, 1998; Valdes, 1999). The acquisition of language itself, through reading and language arts, represents another area in which students from different cultures think or process information in different ways. As Sandra Fradd and Ohkee Lee (1999) note, "teachers are . . . in the best position to facilitate as well as transmit insights about how such approaches work and how they may be made applicable for specific groups of students" (p. 20).

SUMMARY

What is multicultural education?

1. There is much confusion about the meaning of multicultural education, yet there is emerging consensus among specialists that multicultural education is a reform movement designed to bring about educational equity for all students from different races, ethnic groups, social classes, abilities, and genders.

2. Multicultural educational approaches have been defined in five ways: (a) teaching the culturally different; (b) human relations; (c) single-group studies; (d) multicultural education; and (e) education that is multicultural and social reconstructionist.

What types of multicultural education curricula exist and how are they evaluated?

3. Sensitivity training and cultural awareness programs for both teachers and students are being implemented in schools and communities throughout the nation. Various types of curricula exist that are integrated into core content or that serve as supplementary units.

4. The appropriateness of multicultural education is defined most often at national and state levels in education standards and in legislation meant to provide equal educational opportunities.

5. James Banks has identified four levels of integrating ethnic content into school curricula that can be used to evaluate multicultural education: contribution, additive, transformation, and action approaches.

6. People judge the efficacy of multicultural education in terms of resources expended, processes of education, and outcomes (standardized test scores, student satisfaction, school attendance, dropout rates, and participation in extracurricular activities).

7. Education for diversity often sparks disagreement and debate. Critics contend that multicultural education is irrelevant to life in inner-city schools, lowers performance standards, encourages people to choose sides rather than help them understand points of view, and overloads the curriculum. Like any other part of the curriculum, both the content and processes of multicultural education will continue to be subject to scrutiny.

How are educational services adapted for students with exceptionalities?

8. The law assures individuals with disabilities a right to a free, appropriate education in the least restrictive environment or in regular classrooms whenever possible.

9. Students with disabilities may have all their needs met by a general education teacher. They may get help from a special education teacher, either in a general education classroom or by being pulled out for services. Some may spend all their time in a self-contained special education classroom or residential setting.

10. Inclusive education is designed and offered in such a way as to include all people regardless of their physical, cultural, emotional, or intellectual characteristics.

11. Some view inclusion not only as an educational issue, but as a logical extension of the civil rights movement.

12. Some teachers are more effective than others in dealing with special education students in mainstreamed or general education settings.

13. Students categorized for special education services must have an individualized education program (IEP).

14. Thinking about and practicing inclusive education can be described in stages or steps.

15. Students who are gifted or talented may be pulled out of the general education classroom for special instruction. They may attend self-contained classes for talented stu-

dents. They may skip a grade in school. Some take Advanced Placement courses and college courses.

16. There is a strong positive relationship between SES and giftedness.

How can teachers create culturally relevant classrooms?

17. Cultural differences between students and teachers may affect how teaching and learning occur.

18. Teachers who are the most successful in working with diverse groups of students develop "culturally relevant" classrooms—places where curriculum and instruction are "friendly" to difference. These teachers get to know their students and their communities, examine other teachers' experiences in diverse settings, and think about the effects of their own beliefs and practices on students who may come from cultures and language backgrounds similar to and different from their own.

TERMS AND CONCEPTS

Afrocentric curricula   344
conflict mediation   334
Education for All Handicapped Children
    Act   349
e pluribus unum   338
equal educational opportunity   348
inclusion   349

inclusive education   349
individualized education program
    (IEP)   352
Individuals with Disabilities Education
    Act (IDEA)   349
multicultural education   333

REFLECTIVE PRACTICE

As part of a class assignment, teachers at an urban high school in Saginaw, Michigan, asked students to reflect on the future of their community by writing letters to local leaders. After reading a newspaper article, "Survival of Blacks Depends on Events in Next 10 Years," students addressed letters to individuals cited in the article, describing issues—education, economic conditions, crime—they considered most critical to African Americans in the 1990s. Their letters revealed to teachers that students often see things in different ways than their teachers or other outsiders do (Fairbanks, 1998). In his letter to the former mayor of Saginaw, for example, Michael, discussed a number of worries:

Dear Dr. Crawford;
    My name is Michael. I am a sophomore at Saginaw High School and a concerned citizen of Saginaw.
    In your comments in The Saginaw News on January 28, I believe that you missed one critical problem, "crimes on blacks committed by blacks." I've seen blacks shoot blacks, blacks sell drugs to blacks, yet nothing is being done about it. This concerns

me because how do I know I won't be the next person to get a bullet from a "Brothers'" [sic] gun?

I agree with the whole article about the economic problems of blacks. Even with a college degree I, being a black male, might have a harder time getting a job than my female counterpart. A company can kill two birds with one stone if they hire a black female and at the same time meet certain hiring requirements.

Education of black children depends on the parents. My parents constantly remind me of my goal to go to college. In my room I have a step by step process and at the end of it is my goal to become a lawyer.

I really hope that I can make people understand that just talking about these problems won't make them go away, we have to work together to get rid of them.

My classmates and I would like you to come to our class and talk about these problems of our race and how we can get them out of our community. Please let me know if you are able to come. Thank you for your time.

Your friend,
Michael (pp. 142–143)

Issues, Problems, Dilemmas, and Opportunities

What concerns does Michael express in his letter? Do you think that he might have other related concerns that are left unvoiced? If so, what might they be?

Perceive and Value

What might a school guidance counselor have to say about Michael's expression of concern?

Know and Act

Michael's thoughts about hiring practices are similar to those that John Ogbu (1987) found among some African Americans who worry that a good education will not guarantee employment opportunities. What do you know about the connections between education and employment opportunities and between education and earnings? Where can you find such information? How might you use this information to help Michael and other students develop a plan of action that would enhance their futures?

Evaluate

Michael mentions that he has already begun to formulate a plan to become a lawyer. How might you encourage him to judge his plan? Are there benchmarks against which he might compare his plan and academic progress toward the attainment of his goal?

 ONLINE ACTIVITY

Children learn through play. They observe and imitate other's actions. Most children use sight to help them gain information quickly and with little effort. For children whose vision is impaired, play and learning can be diminished. This need not be the case, however.

Some commercially available toys are especially well suited to children who are blind or visually impaired. When you go to the McNergney&Herbert home page, you will find a link to the Guide to Toys for Children Who are Blind or Visually Impaired, 1998–1999.

In addition to finding information on all kinds of toys, you will notice this web site has been "Bobby Approved." Bobby is a web-based tool that analyzes web pages for their accessibility to people with disabilities. The Bobby site—also linked to the McNergney&Herbert home page—shows you how to analyze any web site for its accessibility to persons with disabilities.

One more important fact to notice is that the toys carry the endorsement of the American Foundation for the Blind (AFB). The AFB works to enable people who are blind or visually impaired to achieve equality of access and opportunity in their lives. You will find a link to the AFB.

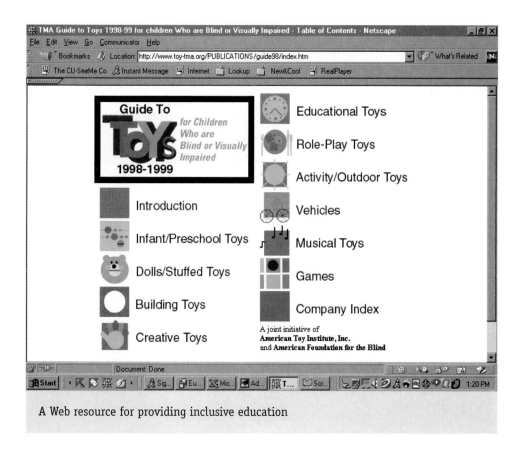

A Web resource for providing inclusive education

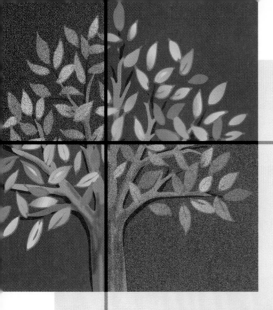

10

Curriculum and Instruction

People typically think of *curriculum* as what is taught in school, and *instruction* as the method by which curriculum is delivered. The word *curriculum*, however, encompasses so many ideas that it defies simple description. We use this chapter to discuss some of the more prominent ways curriculum has been defined through educational practice. We explore some of the forces influencing curriculum content and the aims underlying the curriculum—aims that may be stated explicitly or left implicit. We describe ways educators

369

design curriculum. We also describe models of instruction that can be used for a variety of purposes. Finally, we consider factors that determine the effectiveness of classroom instruction.

PROFESSIONAL PRACTICE QUESTIONS

- ▐ What is curriculum?
- ▐ What forces and change agents affect curriculum content?
- ▐ How are curriculum and instruction planned and organized?
- ▐ What are four general models of instruction?
- ▐ What is effective instruction?
- ▐ How do teachers effectively manage students?

 ## What Is Curriculum?

Most people define **curriculum** in terms of what is taught in school. Books are curriculum. Study guides are curriculum. Movies, newspapers, computer programs, board games, animals, and songs can be curriculum. A good working definition of curriculum is the knowledge and skills that schools are held accountable for helping students to master.

There is a "productive uncertainty" of ideas about the content and aims of school programs, however (Schubert, 1986, p. 8). Peter Oliva (1997) observes that *curriculum* has been used to mean a set of subjects, subject content, a program of studies, a set of materials, a sequence of courses, a set of performance objectives, and a course of study. Curriculum can be regarded as everything that goes on within the school, including extra-class activities, guidance, and interpersonal relationships, as well as everything that is taught both inside and outside school that is directed by the school or planned by school personnel. Curriculum can also be described as a series of experiences undergone by learners in school or that which an individual learner experiences as a result of schooling (Oliva, 1997).

Americans have a variety of conflicting conceptions about what constitutes curriculum, and thus about what children should or should not be taught in classrooms (Kliebard, 1998). The tensions, arguments, and divisions arise in large measure because the population is heterogeneous, and rapid socioeconomic change routinely makes curriculum decisions controversial. Because education is a power reserved to the states, states and localities are left to define curriculum. Beyond some rather vague agreement on the need for students to read, write, and compute, there is considerable variation in people's expectations for how curriculum should be defined.

Who should define the curriculum?

Curriculum is an operative concept outside school as well as inside. Business, industry, churches, prisons, and other organizations provide out-of-school training in topics as diverse as dog obedience, home sales, and natural childbirth. Curriculum is at issue when the agricultural extension agent drops by the rural farmhouse, when children watch *Sesame Street* and attend Scout meetings, and when people study for a real estate license. Curriculum is not the exclusive province of schools.

▶ Explicit and Implicit Curricula

The curriculum contained in policy statements, manuals of procedure, instructional materials, and textbooks that stipulate what and how students are to learn is the **explicit curriculum.** It is a lot like the "public curriculum" of visual images, tours, lectures, and workshops in museums (Vallance, 1995), only more prescriptive. The explicit curriculum expresses in official descriptions of programs, courses, and objectives of study the specific educational expectations held for both teachers and students. Teachers are expected to teach the explicit curriculum; students are supposed to learn it. This is the curriculum for which schools are held publicly accountable.

If the explicit curriculum dominates the public view, another side of the curriculum is unvoiced and often unintended. This side reveals itself in the way teachers present subject matter and in the classroom atmosphere they establish. Philip Jackson (1990, p. 33) calls this curriculum the "hidden curriculum." Elliot Eisner (1985, p. 89) uses the term **implicit curriculum** for essentially the same idea.

Based on observations of teacher–student interactions in elementary classrooms over a period of 2 years, Jackson (1990) perceived a number of institutional expectations that affected a student's success in the classroom. "Trying" was one such expectation taught implicitly, rather than explicitly, through school experiences. If a student "does his homework (though incorrectly), he raises his hand (though he usually comes up with the wrong answer), [and] he keeps his nose in the book during free study period (though he doesn't turn the page very often)," he will likely gain the teacher's approval and be labeled a "model" student (p. 34). Students learn implicitly that mastery of content is not the only road to success in the classroom.

What aspects of the explicit curriculum are evident in this photograph? What aspects of the implicit curriculum might you infer?

Unofficial routines and rituals of schooling also are part of the implicit curriculum. Teacher behavior, such as calling on students with hands raised while ignoring those who verbalize opinions without permission, is but one of the subtle ways that teachers convey what are considered largely middle-class values.

Another type of implicit curriculum relates to teachers' value orientations and to the subject matter they teach. In case studies of four high school teachers (two English teachers and two history teachers), Sigrun Gudmundsdottir (1991) found that teachers' values seeped into the curriculum through personal interpretations of subject matter and through teaching methods.

For example, when English teachers were presenting *Huckleberry Finn,* one teacher viewed the book as an illustration of "an individual rebelling against conventions," while the other considered it "a book about relationships [between Huck and Jim]" (p. 48). In presenting the book, each teacher selected passages for discussion representative of these ideas, thus creating different "texts" for their students.

▶ Null Curriculum

Consequences of school programs are similarly affected by what Eisner (1985, 1994) refers to as the **null curriculum.** This is the curriculum that is *not* taught. Our silence on many matters is purported to have a variety of ramifications, not the least of which is a negative effect on students' abilities to examine critically all sides of an issue and to make informed decisions. The intellectual processes and subject matter areas emphasized and neglected by teachers contribute to this condition.

Should schools be concerned about aspects of the curriculum that are not taught?

For example, James Banks and Cherry McGee Banks contend that many textbooks portray U.S. history and contemporary life experiences in unrealistic ways, glossing over controversial issues and avoiding discussion of discrimination and prejudice. They suggest, as do others (Apple & Beyer, 1988; Sleeter & Grant, 1991), that such texts produce citizens with a narrow sense of reality:

> For example, almost 50 percent of all marriages end in divorce, and one-third of all children will live with a single parent during part of their lives. Yet many textbooks portray the typical U.S. family as one having two adults, two children, a dog, and a house in suburbia. When controversial issues are not presented, students are denied the information they need to confront contemporary problems. (1997, p. 133)

Yet another way that schools convey hidden messages to students is through time schedules for different classes and locations for instruction. Time devoted to the arts, for example, is substantially less than time devoted to such courses as science and math and communicates to students "what counts" in schools (Eisner, 1992, 1994). Moreover, the fact that art teachers are often "floaters"—moving from classroom to classroom—suggests to students that the arts are less permanent and perhaps less important than other courses. Yet if even one generation of students grows up ignorant of architecture, music, paintings, theater, sculpture, dance, poetry, drawing, photography, and graphic and landscape design, the record of human achievement is in jeopardy.

▶ Extracurriculum

Many schools have a well-developed **extracurriculum,** or curriculum that has arisen in and around the core of a student's studies (Berk, 1992). By definition, this extracurriculum is not credit bearing—it is extra, or over and above the required curriculum. Yet it can exert considerable power over students. Students' feelings of self-efficacy, their desire to come to school, their need to belong or be part of a group, and even their performance in other basic curricular areas can be influenced greatly by extracurricular activities.

Sports, band, clubs, study groups, school plays, cheerleading, dance, etc., may fall under the rubric of the extracurriculum. In some schools these activities may be considered *cocurricular* and weighted equally with other academic offerings. In the main, however, most of these activities are viewed as being outside the typical curriculum.

Nevertheless, people make conceptual and policy ties between the curriculum and the extracurriculum. For example, if a student performs poorly on the required curriculum, someone is sure to argue the student should not be allowed to participate in the extracurriculum, at least until there is improvement in her grades. Others will argue the opposite—were it not for the appeal of extracurricular activities, a student with academic problems might be a dropout.

Researchers at the U.S. Department of Education's Office of Research and Improvement (OERI) found a strong connection between extracurricular activities and academic performance. Generally, extracurricular participation rates rose with socioeconomic level, enrollment in an academic curriculum, and attainment of a B+ or better average.

▶ Integrated Curriculum

People across the nation, and in other countries as well, are challenging traditional practices of compartmentalizing subject matter so that teaching and learning bear little resemblance to life outside schools. Instead, they are implementing an **integrated curriculum,** or curriculum that combines concepts and skills from different subject areas (Sowell, 1996). As John Goodlad and Zhixin Su (1992) note, the ultimate integration of curriculum takes place within the learner—in the learner's mind. The way curriculum is organized aids this process.

Efforts to integrate curricula are occurring in different ways in communities all over the country (Virginia Education Association & The Appalachia Educational Laboratory, 1995). Together, teachers of primary-grade students in a California school plan and teach science, social studies, and foreign language as though distinctions among the subjects were real but not insurmountable obstacles. The teaching team helps students acquire concepts, skills, and values by exploring themes that pervade subject matter. They resist chunking the disciplines by the clock and by the classrooms students occupy. Middle-school teachers in North Carolina take the study of science, social studies, language arts, and mathematics beyond school walls to their community—and even to Disney World—to forge connections in young minds between content acquired and content applied. In other efforts, high school teachers and administrators in Illinois restructure blocks of time in their conventional eight-period day into four periods. They assign staff to interdisciplinary teams, change student entrance and exit requirements for courses, and incorporate an entirely new set of instructional models. All of these programs, regardless of grade level and geographical location, intend to raze artificial barriers that separate subject matters to help diverse students work together to solve real problems.

Emerging technologies give impetus to curriculum integration and to the related topics of interdisciplinary teaching and learning. For example, teachers from across the United States and Canada have begun to work together on the Internet to solve real-life problems by analyzing cases of interdisciplinary teaching and learning (Herbert, 1999). One multimedia Web case is entitled "What Did You Learn in School Today?" It features the day-to-day challenges of a kindergarten teacher. She struggles to complete a six-week plan that allows flexibility in teaching yet conforms to her state's standards of learning. The case involves the teaching of language arts, math, and social studies. It explores issues related to ethnicity, culture, parent involvement, cooperative learning, discipline, use of time, and assessment.

What Forces and Change Agents Affect Curriculum Content?

In public education there is a profusion of interests at work to shape the curriculum. Historically, some interests have operated close to and directly on the school itself. Others have exercised power indirectly and from a distance, both conceptually and physically. These interests have wielded considerable authority over what is to be taught and learned. As Figure 10.1 indicates, the forces that shape the curriculum include, for example, national interests, social issues and public opinion, professional groups and individuals, state and local priorities, and mass media and educational publishing.

▶ The National Interest

The influence of national government on the school curriculum has a long and rich history. Passage of the Environmental Education Act (Public Law 91-516), for example, stimulated the modern environmental education movement (DeBoer, 1991). Vocational education (Smith–Hughes Act of 1917), preschool education (Economic Opportunity Act of 1964), and expanded school access for students with disabilities (Education for All Handicapped Children Act of 1975 and final regulations for the Individuals with Disabilities Education Act, 1997) are funded through federal laws. Laws such as these reflect values about education that are in the national interest.

Federal influence on curriculum development also occurs through funding and exhortation. Between 1994 and 1996, for example, the federal government provided financial assistance to states that submitted plans for ways they might help students meet national standards. In 1996, at the second national Education Summit, President Clinton and the governors and 49 executives from some of the largest U.S. companies (e.g., IBM, AT&T, Eastman Kodak) pledged to begin asking for academic transcripts from job applicants and to

What kind of curriculum is in the national interest?

FIGURE 10.1
Forces That Shape the Curriculum   Which forces and groups are most influential in shaping the curriculum in your community's schools?

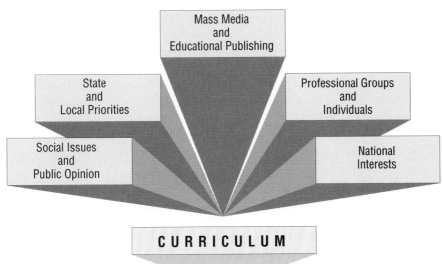

consider a state's educational standards when deciding where to open new plants. In 1999 the U.S. Department of Education sponsored a national conference on how to evaluate the effectiveness of technology, thus indicating national concern about the influence of technology on teaching and learning. The combination of federal, state, and private influences can leverage change in school curriculum simply by their expecting to find evidence of such change in students' transcripts, in the standards that drive curriculum and instruction, and in the way technology is being applied in schools.

▶ Social Issues and Public Opinion

Concerns about issues such as teenage childbearing and the spread of AIDS have been the impetus for a number of curricular efforts. Perhaps the most striking and controversial curriculum aimed unabashedly at restructuring society may be that devoted to what is sometimes called *family life education.* Family life education is an integral part of most school programs. It focuses on topics such as personal health and safety, substance abuse prevention, mental health education, human growth and development (including sex education), and HIV-disease prevention. It is probably the one area of the curriculum that is most closely scrutinized by the public. Parents often must sign a permission form for their children to participate in family life offerings.

To what extent should the curriculum reflect local interests and values?

Family life education programs around the country are alike in that they acknowledge the central role of parents in educating their children. What the curriculum covers, however, varies from place to place. In some localities, for instance, contraceptives are discussed in sex education classes; in other school divisions, educators are prohibited from mentioning condoms or other contraceptives. A provision in the 1996 federal welfare law earmarked $50 million a year for 5 years, beginning in fiscal year 1998, to bring some uniformity to family life education programs. States accepting federal funds for sex education were to teach teenagers to abstain from sex until marriage. Under the law, grantees must inform young people that "sex outside of a marriage can have psychological and physical effects." The law prohibits using funds to teach young people about contraceptives. A report released in 1999 revealed that the year of federal funding had little effect on existing school-based sexuality education programs. Proponents of the law expressed concern that localities were implementing programs that skirted the intent of the legislation (Coles, 1999).

▶ Professional Groups and Individuals

Curriculum in schools has been influenced over time by professional educators, working collectively or as individuals. Some organizations, such as the National Council of Teachers of Mathematics (NCTM), have developed standards intended to guide reform in schools. (See Table 10.1 for other professional groups working on national standards.) The NCTM's *Curriculum and Evaluation Standards for School Mathematics* (1989) comprises 54 value statements. Each is couched in three parts that address (1) what mathematics the curriculum should include, (2) a description of the student activities associated with that mathematics, and (3) instructional examples. Experts assert that the NCTM standards are revolutionary because they "remove computation from its reigning role in the mathematics curriculum and make it serve a more important goal—the development of mathematical thinking" (Association for Supervision and Curriculum Development, 1992, p. 3).

The standards are based on the assumption that "knowing" math means "doing" math. They also recognize the revolution brought about by computers and calculators. The standards set out guidelines for core knowledge, or that knowledge common to all students, as well as special requirements for college-bound students. NCTM has

▌ **TABLE 10.1**
Some Contact Groups for National Standards

English
National Council of Teachers of English (NCTE)
1111 W. Kenyon Road
Urbana, IL 61801-1096

Mathematics
National Council of Teachers of Mathematics
(NCTM)
1906 Association Drive
Reston, Virginia 20191-1593

Physical Education
National Association for Sports and Physical
Education
1900 Association Drive
Reston, VA 22091

Social Studies
National Council for the Social Studies (NCSS)
3501 Newark St. NW
Washington, DC 20016

Science
Office of News and Public Information
National Science Education Standards
2101 Constitution Ave. NW, HA 486
Washington, DC 20418

The Arts
National Association for Music Education
1806 Robert Fulton Drive
Reston, VA 20191

also created a companion volume to accompany the standards entitled *Professional Standards for Teaching Mathematics* (National Council of Teachers of Mathematics, 1991). The teaching standards recognize teachers as central to changing mathematics education in the schools. They emphasize, among other factors, the need to shift instruction toward the use of logic and mathematical evidence for verification and away from a reliance on teachers as sources of right answers. The standards also promote teaching practice that encourages conjecture and problem solving. Standard 1, which follows, addresses how teachers create meaningful instruction:

Standard 1: Worthwhile Mathematics Tasks

The teacher of mathematics should pose tasks that are based on—

- sound and significant mathematics;
- knowledge of students' understanding, interests, and experiences;
- knowledge of the range of ways that diverse students learn mathematics; and that
- engage students' intellect;
- develop students' mathematical understandings and skills;
- stimulate students to make connections and develop a coherent framework for mathematical ideas;
- call for problem formation, problem solving, and mathematical reasoning;
- promote communication about mathematics;
- represent mathematics as an ongoing human activity;
- display sensitivity to, and draw on, students' diverse background experiences and dispositions;
- promote the development of all students' dispositions to do mathematics. (1991)

Figure 10.2 illustrates two teaching activities, one of which the NCTM might consider more "worthwhile" than the other.

Individual teachers also create, select, and transmit curriculum content. Their habits, dispositions, and areas of professional expertise exert powerful influences on what is taught and learned—influences that can be either conservative or boldly innovative. When teachers stick to familiar tools, content, and activities, they operate as conservative—and some believe negative—forces on curriculum (Cuban, 1992). In the 1970s, criticisms of ill-prepared teachers led designers to create what are often referred to as "teacher proof" curricula, or curricula from which students can learn, regardless of the teacher's level of experience, interest, or skill (Grobman, 1970). Today, attitudes toward teachers as professionals are more positive.

> **To what extent should teachers and professional associations determine the curriculum?**

Teachers' creative influences on curricula are many and varied. In language arts or literature-based instruction, for example, teachers who teach with a philosophy of constructivism guide students to define knowledge for themselves, using curricula as stimuli for innovative thinking. These teachers help students select material and act within a social context that molds knowledge but does not determine absolutely what constitutes knowledge (Applebee, 1991; Langer & Applebee, 1986). Teaching in

FIGURE 10.2
Structuring Worthwhile Mathematics Tasks   What skills are required to solve tasks 1 and 2? Why might the National Council for Teachers of Mathematics consider task 2 the more "worthwhile" assignment?

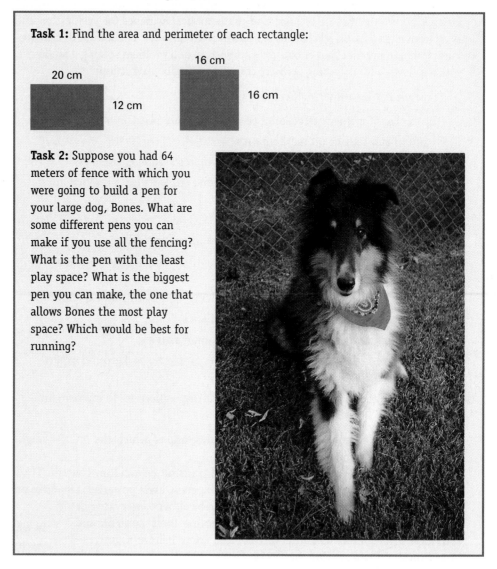

Task 1: Find the area and perimeter of each rectangle:

20 cm

12 cm

16 cm

16 cm

Task 2: Suppose you had 64 meters of fence with which you were going to build a pen for your large dog, Bones. What are some different pens you can make if you use all the fencing? What is the pen with the least play space? What is the biggest pen you can make, the one that allows Bones the most play space? Which would be best for running?

Note. From *Professional Standards for Teaching Mathematics,* March, 1991 (p. 28), Reston, VA: The National Council of Teachers of Mathematics. Reprinted with permission. All rights reserved.

these instances is not a matter of transmitting some objectively formed body of knowledge; it is more a matter of helping students construct and interpret knowledge for themselves.

In other intricate ways, teachers shape what is to be learned by bringing their own personal histories with them into the classroom (Clandinin & Connelly, 1992). Their personalities, their formal academic preparation, and their experiences are all lived out with students through continual interactions. Teachers—and, in turn, students—become the "texts" for study.

Children's needs can and must dictate the nature of some curricula. Indeed, as students' problems increase in number and/or severity, the standard curriculum may be reduced or modified to make room for special curricular offerings. These curricula and the programs organized to deliver them are organized to fit the students instead of the other way around.

Students' needs and interests also are a major consideration when planning instruction. Teachers and curriculum developers recognize the power of the aphorism that success breeds success. When a curriculum stimulates and holds student attention, the curriculum is likely to be copied, extended, promoted, adapted, and used with other students. Also, in noticeable ways, students influence teachers to behave in certain ways in the classroom; that is, students encourage teachers to emphasize or de-emphasize various aspects of the curriculum (Hunt & Sullivan, 1974).

▶ State and Local Priorities

In recent years, state laws and local policies, many promoted by special-interest groups, have influenced everything from textbooks to discipline. Concerns about violence in schools, for example, stimulated the Georgia legislature to sign into law the Improved Student Learning and Discipline Act of 1999. The law requires school districts to teach character education to students at all grade levels, emphasizing the 27 traits listed in Figure 10.3 (Jacobson, 1999). State mandates aimed at overhauling

FIGURE 10.3
Georgia's Character-building Traits Which, if any, of these character traits might be controversial to special-interest groups? Why?

courage	generosity
patriotism	punctuality
citizenship	cleanliness
honesty	respect for the environment
fairness	school pride
respect for others	respect for the creator
kindness	cheerfulness
cooperation	patience
self-respect	creativity
self-control	sportsmanship
courtesy	loyalty
compassion	perseverance
tolerance	virtue
diligence	

Source: Title 20 of the Official Code of Georgia, Section 20-2-145. Available online: http://www.ganet.org/cgi-bin/pub/leg/legdoc?billname=1999/HB84&docpart=full&highlight=character%7Ceducation

In what ways do school curricula reflect state priorities and regional or local interests? What are the other principal sources of influence upon curriculum content?

school curriculum have also resulted in prescribed graduation requirements, an array of state achievement tests, and, in many instances, new textbooks selected to match recommended instructional approaches. In California, for example, students' poor scores on state and national reading tests prompted education officials to revamp their language arts program. Now they emphasize phonics, which teaches children to sound out letters and words. Officials have also revised their mathematics to teach basic skills. Their intent is to diminish attention to real-life application of mathematics and instead to reinforce students' abilities to calculate. California budgeted $1 billion for the purchase of mathematics and language arts textbooks for the turn of the century (Hoff, 1999).

State governments and local education agencies are influenced by political action committees, networks of parents, professional education organizations, civic organizations, and religious groups. Each group develops its own education reform agendas. A state or district may prescribe essential elements for all curricula at all grade levels. Some states—Texas for example—issue essential elements for all subjects from preschool through grade 12 (C. Levinson, personal communication, May 20, 1996).

Whose interests should take precedence in states' curricular reform agendas?

The curriculum that students experience in school also often hinges on local geography and community resources. Students at Longfellow Middle School in La Crosse, Wisconsin, for example, explore life on, in, and around the Mississippi River with the help of teachers and local experts. These include commercial fishermen, officials from the state Department of Natural Resources, and fish and wildlife experts from the National Biological Survey. Students' experiences at the river are the bases for mathematics, science, language arts, and social studies instruction (Pitsch, 1995).

▶ Educational Publishing and Mass Media

Textbooks play an important role in student learning, and the people who select them play an important role in shaping the curriculum (Pinar, Reynolds, Slattery, & Taubman, 1995; Apple, 1998). Various conservative and liberal watchdog organizations routinely urge people to get involved in textbook selection in their states and communities. Nearly half the states have processes by which curricular materials are evaluated and endorsed at the state level. A state-level endorsement in populous states that keep a tight rein on selection, such as Florida, Texas, and California, can be the difference between success and failure for a particular text and, indeed, for its publisher (Apple, 1998).

State textbook adoption policies have influenced the shape of curriculum for years. According to Michael Apple (1998), these policies originated for several reasons. First, there has been an effort to ensure that school districts purchase books at the lowest possible prices. Second, the state has attempted to protect children from being exposed to poor textbooks by relying on experts to make selections. Third, uniformity among texts at the state level enables the establishment of a minimum standard curriculum throughout the state.

Because textbooks may constitute as much as 70 percent of the curriculum, some curriculum experts think that textbooks exert the most powerful influence of all on curriculum (Morrison, 1993; Apple, 1998). They worry about this circumstance because many textbooks lack high quality. They might teach to the "lowest common denominator," or "dumb down" the curriculum; avoid controversy; be pedagogically unsound; or teach inaccurate and erroneous information. In a recent review of textbooks proposed for adoption in California, a panel of mathematicians found hundreds of errors. While the mistakes ranged from a missing equals sign to a muddy explanation of the quadratic equation, it was their pervasiveness that surprised state officials most. . . . "It was shocking," said Cathy Barkett, the administrator of the curriculum frameworks and instructional resources office. "In one 200-page text, 50 of the pages had errors" (Manzo, 1999a, p. 6).

> **To what extent does the textbook publishing industry determine the curriculum?**

Protests about textbooks can erupt into community squabbles. Parent groups in Canadian and U.S. schools, for example, protested the use of a K–6 elementary reading series that uses themes such as Halloween to present fiction, nonfiction, and poetry by well-known English, American, and Canadian authors. Curricula based on Halloween are offensive to fundamentalist groups, who contend that they teach children witchcraft (McConaghy, 1992). When such interest-group protests are reported by the mass media, they affect the way textbooks are written.

Beyond serving informational and public oversight functions, the media are involved directly in producing their own curricula. Channel One Network, the leading provider of television news and educational programs for students, delivers programs by satellite to some 12,000 middle schools and high schools in the United States. Participating schools receive a satellite dish and classroom television monitors in exchange for showing the programming. In turn, schools agree by contract to make Channel One available to 90 percent of their students on 90 percent of school days. In 1999, Channel One claimed 8 million students as regular viewers. The program has not been without its critics. Both liberals and conservatives worry about Channel One's effects on students, criticizing in particular Channel One's introduction of commercials into the classroom. In 1999, the channel charged advertisers as much as $200,000 per 30-second commercial (Walsh, 1999).

The New York Times Learning Network on the Web is a remarkable example of what the media can do to advance teaching and learning. The web site contains daily lesson plans fitted to each day's edition of the newspaper, an archive of previous plans, a special section on education news, discussion topics for parents and students, education product reviews, science quizzes, special news packages on current events and historic events, and many more engaging and intellectually stimulating curricular materials. *New York Times* employees also conduct professional development sessions for teachers.

Voices

On Building the Curriculum

Steven Levy, a teacher with 22 years experience, has won several awards for his work with students of all ages. In his book *Starting from Scratch,* Levy considers the question of who should determine the curriculum taught in schools:

> In most schools, the district or the state provides the framework of required studies. The subjects we are to teach, the skills we are to develop, and the content we are to master [are] outlined to a lesser or greater degree. How can authentic projects arise from the learning community when the curriculum is dictated from above? On the other hand, if we teach what we want to or allow projects to emerge from children's interests, how can the district ensure that the children will be exposed to a thorough and comprehensive program across the grades?
>
> I do think we need some curriculum guidance from the central administration. We need to have a framework so that in the course of the children's education they will be exposed to an integrated and coherent course of study. We also need to coordinate the subjects across the grades so that the children do not learn about electricity three years in a row. We need an outline of when the children are expected to master sentence structure, fractions, scientific procedure. What I want from my system is a very broad sketch of subjects to teach and the freedom to teach them out of my own design. Tell me the children should learn about China, the Civil War, botany, or New England geography. Define the habits of mind, heart, and work that the community decides are important for all children to develop. Then let me have room to explore the topic with the children. I don't think it is necessary that every teacher teach in the same way or that every child have the same experience. If you told twenty artists to paint a river scene, you would get twenty very different renditions. In the same way, if you told twenty teachers to teach about rivers, you would get twenty different lessons. An exhibition of the river paintings in a gallery is enhanced by their similarities and differences. Likewise, the different experiences the children receive from year to year enhance rather than diminish discussions and activities that build on their understanding of rivers.
>
> I want to teach out of the natural activity of the class. I want the children to see how learning is the natural activity of people coming together. I want to begin with the students' experience and their own questions. I want them to follow their own interests. But I also need to address the content and skills prescribed in the curriculum. Herein lies the art of teaching; leading the students from their own experiences and interests to the depth and breadth of the world within the framework of the subjects I am supposed to teach. I need to find the link that leads the children from their own interests and questions to the areas of the required curriculum.

CRITICAL THINKING

According to Levy, how much control should the school system have over curriculum decisions? What role, from Levy's perspective, should teachers play in such decisions? Do you agree with Steven Levy? Why or why not?

Source: Reprinted by permission of Steven Levy: *Starting from scratch: One classroom builds its own curriculum* (Heinemann, a division of Reed Elsevier, Portsmouth, NH, 1996), pp. 28–29.

Commercial textbook publishers influence the curriculum through the authors they hire and the books and materials they produce. Publishers argue that in fact they do not influence the curriculum as much as do the people who buy the books. In their attempt to read the market, publishers provide what they believe people will buy. And buy they do—elementary and secondary textbooks gross nearly $3.3 billion a year (Association of American Publishers, 1999).

 # How Are Curriculum and Instruction Planned and Organized?

When planning for instruction, teachers must consider the destination—the aims of education and goals of the curriculum—as well as the best way to reach the destination. As Nancie Atwell (1987) and Steven Levy (1996) suggest, these decisions cannot be made in a vacuum. To organize curriculum in ways that maximize students' opportunities for success, teachers must also be learners, interacting with students to shape curriculum in ways that meet the students' needs and interests.

▶ Aims of Education

Curriculum and instruction are planned and organized to reflect commitment to specific aims or goals of education. Over the years, differing ideas about the aims of education, roles of teachers and students, and the nature of knowledge have resulted in different orientations toward curriculum. As illustrated in Figure 10.4, orientations include development of cognitive processes; academic rationalism; personal relevance; social adaption, change, and outcomes-based views; and curriculum as technology. The different orientations illustrate how different goals of education influence curriculum development.

▶ Teacher Planning for Instruction

Teacher planning has been described as "the thread that weaves the curriculum, or the *what* of teaching, with the instruction, or how of teaching" (Frieberg & Driscoll, 1996, p. 22). When planning instruction, teachers consider the curriculum, state and local goals and objectives for student learning, instructional strategies for meeting those goals, and means of assessing students' understanding. It is difficult to overestimate the importance of planning how to evaluate student learning and the effectiveness of a lesson.

When identifying goals and objectives, teachers "define the true purpose of the curriculum" (Wiles, 1999, p. 89). They determine what students should learn or be able to do as a result of instruction (e.g., from examples and nonexamples, students should be able to identify similes). Decisions about the desired results of learning help teachers clarify their thinking about methods and materials to use during instruction. Although objectives typically are influenced by state and local mandates,

FIGURE 10.4

Five Aims of Education and Corresponding Curricular Orientations Which aims of education and curricular orientations interest you the most at this time?

Aims of Education	Curriculum Orientation	Roles of Students and Teachers	Examples of Curriculum Content	Examples of Instructional Approaches
Teach students how to learn	Development of Cognitive Processes	Student-centered: Students think about academic tasks and construct meaningful knowledge in relationship to prior experiences. Teachers mediate and facilitate students' learning.	Thinking skills; study skills; problem-solving skills	Scaffolding; inquiry learning
Impart culture to students	Academic Rationalism	Teacher-centered: Students receive instruction and demonstrate competencies.	Great ideas; great works of art; literary classics; basic skills	Direct instruction
Help students find self-fulfillment, develop effective learning styles	Personal Relevance	Student-centered: Students and teachers collaborate to create or match curricula to individual and group interests and needs. Teachers provide opportunities for student reflection and self-evaluation.	Opportunities for personal expression; clarification of personal values	Individualized instruction; nondirective teaching
Help students become productive citizens capable of changing the social order	Social Adaptation, Change, & Outcomes-based views	Teacher-centered: Teachers present facts, issues, problems, and learning challenges for students to act upon or apply in life.	Citizenship; communication skills; environmental, social issues, & job-related skills	Questioning; cooperative learning; project-based learning; internships
Give students the tools they need to master subjects; deliver instruction efficiently	Curriculum as Technology	Subject-centered: Teachers preestablish developmentally appropriate learning goals, outcomes, objectives, and criteria for assessment for a subject area. Students demonstrate minimum competencies.	Traditional subjects; basic skills	Direct instruction; mastery learning

they also are shaped by teachers' perceptions of students' needs and abilities before, during, and after instruction.

To maximize students' opportunities to learn, teachers plan both individually and in teams. Sometimes team planning occurs across grade levels and even across schools. As teachers consider goals and objectives, they may create time lines indicating approximate dates when concepts and skills will be introduced. According to Heidi Jacobs (1997), the resulting documents, sometimes referred to as **curriculum maps,** help teachers to identify gaps and repetitions in the curriculum as well as potential areas in which content areas can be integrated.

When planning for instruction, teachers also think about classroom management. By establishing clear rules and routines, teachers minimize confusion and maximize instructional time. This aspect of planning is particularly important at the beginning of the year, when teachers establish patterns, limits, and expectations that often persist for the remainder of the year (Clark & Dunn, 1991).

When thinking about instruction, teachers also consider ways to motivate students. According to Thomas Good and Jere Brophy (2000), teachers can achieve this goal by (1) establishing a supportive classroom environment in which students feel comfortable taking intellectual risks, (2) selecting activities at an appropriate level of difficulty "that teach things that are worth learning," and (3) using a variety of motivational strategies (p. 223). Such strategies include characterizing the lesson to be taught in familiar terms so that students can conceptualize what they will be learning and explaining goals and objectives for a lesson and their relevance to students' personal lives.

What Are Four General Models of Instruction?

There is no single best way to teach all people for all purposes. Professional teachers develop a repertoire of teaching strategies or models that they can use when conditions warrant (Joyce & Calhoun, 1996). As learners vary in needs and abilities and as goals change, instructional models must change:

> If a teacher creates a single environment in the classroom or repeatedly uses the same instructional approach, only those students who learn well in that environment or with that approach will succeed. The teacher who utilizes a variety of instructional approaches is more likely to reach all students in the classroom; moreover, students are encouraged to learn in a variety of ways. (Gunter, Estes, & Schwab, 1999, p. 60)

Many **instructional models,** or teaching strategies, exist for reaching a variety of desired goals. In their classic work on instruction, *Models of Teaching,* Bruce Joyce and Marsha Weil cluster the strategies in four groups based on the models' purposes (see Figure 10.5). The Behavioral Systems Family of models uses ideas about manipulating the environment to modify students' behaviors. The Social Family capitalizes on people's nature as social beings to learn from and relate to one another. The Information-Processing Family focuses on increasing students' abilities to think—to seek, organize, interpret, and apply information both inductively and deductively. The Personal Family encourages self-exploration and the development of personal identity.

> **How should decisions be made about what teaching methods to use?**

FIGURE 10.5

Examples of Teaching Strategies that Contribute to a Teacher's Instructional Repertoire   Effective teachers employ strategies and combinations of strategies from all four "families."

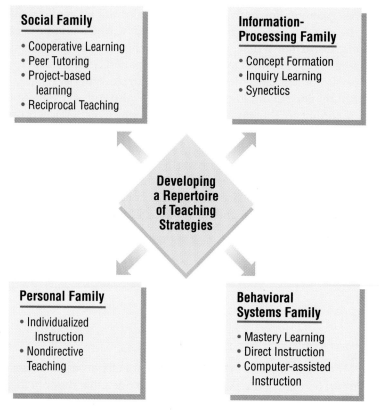

Social Family
- Cooperative Learning
- Peer Tutoring
- Project-based learning
- Reciprocal Teaching

Information-Processing Family
- Concept Formation
- Inquiry Learning
- Synectics

Developing a Repertoire of Teaching Strategies

Personal Family
- Individualized Instruction
- Nondirective Teaching

Behavioral Systems Family
- Mastery Learning
- Direct Instruction
- Computer-assisted Instruction

Note. Adapted from *Models of Teaching* (5th ed.) by B. R. Joyce, and M. Weil, 1996, Boston: Allyn and Bacon.

▶ **Behavioral Systems Strategies**

Mastery learning, one of several behavioral models that has enjoyed widespread use, was developed through the work of Benjamin Bloom (1971), John Carroll (1971), and their colleagues. The basic strategy suggests that student learning is a function of a student's aptitude, his or her motivation, and the amount and quality of instruction. Instead of defining student aptitude as native ability, proponents of mastery learning define it as the amount of time a student requires to master an objective. Given enough time, the inclination to learn, and instruction fitted to a student's needs, students are thought to be capable of mastering a range of subject matter. Teachers must organize instruction into manageable units, diagnose students' needs with respect to the material, teach in ways that meet those needs, and evaluate progress regularly.

Teachers following Bloom's model select objectives that traverse a hierarchy of simple to complex thought processes (recall, comprehension, application, analysis,

▌ **TABLE 10.2**
Bloom's Taxonomy of Educational Objectives

Level	Learner Objectives	Teacher Tasks
1.00 Knowledge	To define, distinguish, acquire, identify, recall, or recognize various forms of information.	To present and/or elicit facts, conventions, categories in ways that enable learners to demonstrate knowledge.
2.00 Comprehension	To translate, transform, give in own words, illustrate, prepare, read, represent, change, rephrase, or restate various forms of information.	To present and/or elicit definitions, words, phrases, relationships, principles in ways that enable learners to demonstrate comprehension.
3.00 Application	To apply, generalize, relate, choose, develop, organize, use, transfer, restructure, or classify various forms of information.	To present and/or elicit principles, laws, conclusions in ways that enable learners to apply what they have learned.
4.00 Analysis	To distinguish, detect, identify, classify, discriminate, recognize, categorize, or deduce various forms of information.	To present and/or elicit elements, hypotheses, assumptions, statements of intent or fact in ways that encourage learners to critically analyze information.
5.00 Synthesis	To write, tell, relate, produce, originate, modify, or document various forms of information.	To present and/or elicit structures, patterns, designs, relationships in ways that encourage learners to form new structures of knowledge.
6.00 Evaluation	To judge, argue, validate, assess, appraise various forms of information.	To present and/or elicit from learners different qualitative judgments.

Source: Teacher Development (p. 57) by R. F. McNergney and C. A. Carrier, 1981, New York: Macmillan.

synthesis, and evaluation). Bloom's taxonomy of learning objectives has guided the development of many curriculum packages. Table 10.2 shows Bloom's taxonomy and the kinds of tasks teachers must undertake if they are to encourage students to accomplish the objectives.

Like mastery learning, **direct instruction** is a highly structured, teacher-centered strategy. It capitalizes on behavioral techniques such as modeling, feedback, and reinforcement to promote basic skill acquisition, primarily in reading and mathematics. Teachers using this model must set high but not unattainable goals for students. The model prescribes classroom organization and processes that maximize the amount of time students spend on academic tasks at which they can succeed with regularity. Policy emphases on the assessment of students' minimum competency on basic reading and mathematics objectives, rather than complex or advanced learning objectives, have stimulated interest in direct instruction.

Behavioral Objectives. In the 1960s and 1970s, Robert Mager (1962) taught educators to write instructional **behavioral objectives**—goal statements, conditions under which learning will occur, and criteria for success. Teaching objectives, and, later, learning objectives, became the backbone of curriculum development, particularly in subject areas in which learning can be measured in quantifiable terms. Statements about what students should know or be able to do after completing a unit of study form the basis of what is taught and how success is judged. As the following example illustrates, outcomes specify the intended result or product of instruction instead of the process of instruction.

An Instructional Behavioral Objective in Mager's Terms:

Conditions of Performance:	Given a definition and examples of an adjective as a part of speech,
Behavior:	students will identify adjectives in sentences
Criteria for Performance:	correctly in at least 8 of 10 instances.

According to Jon Wiles (1999), schools can sometimes overemphasize behavioral objectives to the point that teaching becomes simplistic and mechanized. He suggests that many educators, however, philosophically resist strict adherence to behavioral approaches so that they can remain open to spontaneous opportunities for learning that occur during instruction.

▶ Social Strategies

Instructional models in the social family are intended to help students work together in productive ways to attain both academic and social goals. Teachers serve as guides, encouraging students to express their ideas and to consider others' perspectives as they deal with a variety of problems and issues. Cooperative learning, project-based learning, and reciprocal teaching are just a few examples of approaches to classroom teaching and learning that develop positive school cultures.

Cooperative Learning. **Cooperative learning** is more social in nature than teaching methods in behavioral systems models. Methods for implementing cooperative learning have been articulated by Robert Slavin (1995), Yael Sharan (1990), Shlomo and Yael Sharan (1992), and David and Roger Johnson (1999) and their colleague Zhining Qin (1995).

When used as intended, cooperative learning promotes the careful, purposeful formation of heterogeneous groups of students within classrooms to accomplish social, personal, and academic objectives. Cooperative learning has grown in popularity because of its positive effects on student self-esteem, intergroup relations, acceptance of students with academic and physical limitations, attitudes toward school, and ability to work cooperatively (Slavin & Fashola, 1998).

One cooperative learning technique, Students Teams–Achievement Divisions (STAD), has the teacher use direct instruction to teach students concepts or skills. Students then work in four-member, heterogeneous learning teams to help each other master the content by using study guides, worksheets, and other materials. Following group work, students take quizzes, on which they may not help one another. Teams earn recognition or privileges based on the improvement made by each team member over his or her own past record (Slavin & Fashola, 1998). Thus the success of groups depends on the individual learning of all group members, not on a single group product (Slavin, 1995).

The Education Department of the Metropolitan Opera Guild has created its own cooperative learning model. Teachers can use "Creating Original Opera" to integrate curriculum and to encourage students of all backgrounds and experiences to work collaboratively. The program, designed for students in grades 3 through 6, emphasizes personal responsibility, constructive criticism, and the development of communication skills. Through its emphasis on the formation of an opera company, the program also demands that students work effectively in groups. During an interview, one young actress explained the critical role of cooperation:

> When you act you are part of a company of people putting on the opera. Say like someone forgets their line, and you notice it. Then it is up to you not to make a face or whisper or anything. You have to think fast and make up a new line that your character might say. And that gets the same information said out loud. So imagine that Takisha is supposed to say that she knows the boys are coming, but she forgets her line. Then I have to say, " I think I hear the boys coming," or maybe something like, "We better get going, because this is when the boys usually come to the park." And she should be doing the same thing for me. That's why sometimes when we rehearse you see her or me saying each other's lines. (Wolf, 1994, p. 30)

Teachers using "Creating Original Opera" serve as guides or coaches, helping students learn to work within a company structure. Students select a name for their company; then the company's student public relations officers develop a company logo, press release, mailing lists, flyers, posters, invitations, media contacts, and interviews. Student teams write the script and music while other teams take responsibility for numerous other tasks: building stage models, wiring lights, applying makeup, and so on. By 1999, more than 1,000 classroom teachers and music teachers from around the world had participated in the Creating Original Opera Teacher Training Program (Education at the Met, 1999). You can learn more about "Creating Original Opera" at the Education at the Met web site.

Other Forms of Peer-Mediated Instruction.　**Project-based learning** involves students in relatively long-term, problem-based units of instruction. Students pursue solutions to nontrivial problems posed by the students, teachers, or curriculum developers. Students approach the problems by "asking and refining questions, debating ideas, making predictions, designing plans and/or experiments, collecting and analyzing data, drawing conclusions, communicating ideas and findings to others, asking new questions, and creating artifacts" (Blumenfeld, Soloway, Marx, Krajcik, Guzdial, & Palcinsar, 1991, p. 371). Artifacts are concrete, specific products (e.g., models, reports, videotapes, computer programs), representing students' problem solutions. These can be shared with others and critiqued. Feedback from others allows students to reflect on their work and to revise their solutions as needed. Examples of projects that have been successfully used with middle and high school students include designing a solar house and modeling the effect of water pollution on a stream (Guzdial, 1998).

> Is peer-mediated instruction as effective as teacher-mediated instruction?

As students deal with real-life problems and issues, they have opportunities to draw on many different curricular areas, making connections between subject matter disciplines. Also, technology allows students to work with computerized databases to conduct research and with video technology to construct products using computerized design.

Reciprocal teaching is an instructional method often used to teach poor readers specific comprehension strategies (Brown & Palincsar, 1989). Teachers present students with written material, which they read together, paragraph by paragraph. While reading, students learn four strategies:

1. formulating questions about the reading;
2. summarizing what has been read;
3. clarifying word meanings or confusing text; and
4. predicting what will happen in the next paragraph.

When introducing the strategies, teachers explain a specific skill, model the skill using a selection of text, then coach students as they try to use the strategy on a paragraph of text. As students take turns demonstrating newly learned skills, the teacher supports their efforts by offering feedback, additional modeling, and coaching. The teacher also encourages students in the group to react to one another's statements by elaborating or commenting on another student's summary, suggesting other questions, commenting on another's predictions, and requesting clarification of material they do not understand (Rosenshine & Meister, 1994; Alfassi, 1998). As teacher and students work together, responsibility for much of the work shifts from teacher to students. In this way, teacher and students work cooperatively to bring meaning to text.

> The practice becomes a dialogue: one student asks questions, another answers, and a third comments on the answer; one student summarizes and another comments on or helps to improve the summary; one student identifies a difficult word and the other students help to infer the meaning and give reasons for the inferences they made. (Rosenshine & Meister, 1994, p. 481)

▶ Information-Processing Strategies

Models in this family stimulate the development of thinking skills such as observing, comparing, finding patterns, and generalizing while also teaching specific concepts or generalizations (Eggen & Kauchak, 1996). Information-processing models are built on the ideas of information-processing theorists and modern constructivists. Information-processing models take their cues for instruction from theory that explains how people think.

Forming Concepts and Generalizations. When using the **concept formation** method of instruction, teachers want students to analyze and synthesize data to construct knowledge about a specific concept or idea. A science teacher using concept formation during a unit on plants would likely ask students to (1) examine a variety of plant specimens, (2) place the plants into groups based on structural characteristics, and (3) generate labels for each of the plant groups. The teacher might then provide additional specimens for students to classify. While most of these plants would probably fit existing classifications, students might have to create new categories for some of the plants. In a lesson of this type, students are not passive recipients of information; rather, they are active "creators" or "inventors" of knowledge.

Thinking and Creativity.   **Synectics** is a teaching model that seeks to increase students' problem-solving abilities, creative expression, empathy, and insight into social relations. Developed by William Gordon, a businessman from Cambridge, Massachusetts, synectics is designed to "make the familiar strange," or to force distance between the student and the object or subject matter being investigated. Through a series of exercises, students work as a team to stretch and transpose traditional ways of thinking so as to discover new metaphors and to gain new perspectives on topics from a wide range of fields.

Synectics activities begin with a statement of a problem or topic and a series of *stretching exercises,* or activities, to familiarize students with using analogies in new ways. A teacher might pose a problem about water pollution, for example, and ask students to consider the effects of pollution and ways they might prevent water pollution. For stretching exercises, students might then brainstorm responses to such questions as "Which is more dangerous to water—chemicals or construction waste? Why?" or "Which is a more powerful agent of change—regulations or education? Why?" (McAuliffe & Stoskin, 1993, p. 23).

Can creativity be taught?

During the next phase of the synectics model, students create direct, personal, and symbolic analogies. In the lesson on pollution, for example, the teacher might help students create direct analogies by saying, "An oil slick is like what animal? Why?" or "Toxic waste is like what machine? Why?" (McAuliffe & Stoskin, 1993, p. 24). Personal analogies call for empathetic identification with a person, plant, animal, or nonliving thing or idea. The teacher might suggest, for example, that students "be" a duck:

> One bright morning while swimming in the bay you suddenly spot something strange sparkling in the water. It is black and shiny. Being a rather curious creature you decide to investigate. Tell what happens to you as you enter the area of the oil spill. Are you saved or lost? Tell your feelings as well as what happens to you. (McAuliffe & Stoskin, p. 25)

After students share their ideas, they develop symbolic analogies involving unusual juxtapositions of ideas. For example, students might think of word combinations, such as "awful beauty," "heavy flight," or "helpful panic" (McAuliffe & Stoskin, 1993, p. 27). By the time students return to their original problem, water pollution, they can think about solving the problem in new and creative ways.

Inquiry Learning.   When students engage in **inquiry learning,** they try to answer questions and solve problems based on facts and observations. They think as scientists do while analyzing data and creating and testing theories and hypotheses to expand the conceptual system with which they process information. The Suchman Inquiry Model, one of several ways to structure inquiry lessons, conveys to students that knowledge is tentative. That is, as new information is discovered and new theories evolve, old ideas are modified or pushed aside.

What model of instruction does this learning activity reflect? How does it fit into Joyce and Weil's four-part classification of instructional models? Why do experts recommend that teachers develop and practice a diverse repertoire of teaching methods?

Teachers using Suchman Inquiry present students with a problem. For example, a biology teacher who has been focusing instruction on prey–predator relationships in the balance of nature might provide students with the following information:

> In the mountains of the Southwest a number of years ago, deer were plentiful, although the population would fluctuate somewhat. There were also wolves in the mountains. Some people from a small town witnessed a wolf pack pull down two of the smaller deer in the herd and were horrified. As a result, the people launched a campaign to eliminate the wolves. To the dismay of many of the people, the years following the elimination of the wolves showed a marked decrease in the population of the deer. Why, when the wolf is the deer's natural predator, should this have happened? (Eggen & Kauchak, 1996, p. 250)

The teacher then guides students through five steps:

1. defining the problem;
2. formulating hypotheses;
3. gathering data;
4. organizing data and modifying hypotheses accordingly; and
5. generalizing about findings.

▶ Personal Sources Strategies

Teachers who use personal models of instruction want to involve students actively in the determination of what and how they will learn. The ultimate goal is to develop long-term dispositional changes rather than short-term instructional effects (Joyce, Weil, & Calhoun, 2000). The emphasis is on developing effective learning styles and healthy self-concepts. The nondirective teaching model, based on the work of Carl Rogers (1971) and other advocates of nondirective counseling, is one approach to attaining these goals.

When implementing the **nondirective model,** teachers act both as facilitators and as reflectors. They encourage students to define problems and feelings, to take responsibility for solving problems, and to determine how personal goals might be reached. Problems that the students address may relate to personal, social, or academic issues. When focusing on personal problems, students generally explore feelings about themselves. If considering social issues, students investigate their feelings about others and how their thoughts can influence relationships. Academic concerns generally center around students' feelings about their competence and interests (Joyce, Weil, & Calhoun, 2000).

Thus classroom activities are determined by the learner as she interacts with the teacher and with peers. Acting as a facilitator, the teacher follows five steps when employing the nondirective model:

1. The teacher describes the helping situation, and teacher and student agree on procedures for meeting and interacting with one another. During this phase the student may also identify a problem.

2. The teacher, using strategies such as paraphrasing and asking open questions ("Can you say more about that?"), encourages the student to express positive and negative feelings and to clarify the problem.

3. The teacher uses supportive language ("Yes, it is difficult to be alone") to encourage the student to explore the problem and to develop new insight.

4. The teacher clarifies a student's plan for dealing with the problem.

5. The teacher listens as the student explains the actions she has taken and helps the student to consider other things that might be done to solve the problem.

The five phases of the model might occur in one day or across time. Meetings between teacher and student typically are one-on-one, allowing for privacy and time to explore problems and issues important to the student (Joyce, Weil, & Calhoun, 2000).

 ## What Is Effective Instruction?

Teachers are students, too. Even the best among them do not always know how or why they are successful. With experience, however, they grow accustomed to not having all the answers and to relying instead on the best information available about teaching and learning—information acquired from successful (and unsuccessful) practice. Because the best have stretched themselves time and again to be creative and technically proficient, they know they can call on their abilities when the need arises. They are not afraid to fail, because they have done that too and have lived to teach and learn another day. A good teacher, like a good student, enjoys the work.

Creative teaching, like creative learning, capitalizes on the inspiration of judgment, sensitivity, and intuitive insight. Stanford professor Elliot Eisner (1991) put it well:

> My work in the arts as a painter made it perfectly clear that cognition, by which I mean thinking and knowing, is not limited to linguistically-mediated thought, that the business of making a picture "that works" is an awesome cognitive challenge, and that those who limit knowing to science are naive about the arts and in the long run injurious to the children whose educational programs were shaped by their ideals. (p. 13)

Technically correct or scientific teaching, like scientific learning, takes advantage of information acquired from careful observation and analysis of phenomena in the surrounding world. This information deals with what goes into teaching and learning, what goes on during the course of instruction, and what results from the delivery of instruction. Social scientists who try to unravel the complexities of teaching and learning often focus on variables such as student characteristics and abilities, teaching behaviors, and measures of students' learning. They seek information that will maximize teachers' chances of being successful.

The ongoing debate about how best to teach reading illustrates well the distinction between technical and creative views of teaching (Manzo, 1999b). Some educators advocate the use of phonics, a systematic method of teaching based on the belief that children learn best when taught small components of words (letters) before being taught larger components (sounds, words, sentences). Specialists diagnose students' weaknesses and prepare prescriptions for remediating these deficiencies. Reading specialists in laboratories and carefully designed curricular materials aim to develop hierarchies of skills deemed necessary to master the process of reading.

How should students be taught to read?

In contrast, advocates of *whole language* do not think that reading should be taught separately from other language arts. Whole language is more an inventive philosophy than a specific method for teaching reading and writing, and whole language advocates contend that teachers should use phonics methods only when they think a child will benefit. Students start with stories and learn sentences, words, and sounds as needed.

Good teachers know that science reveals some simple truths about the connection of teaching to learning. Teachers must apply these principles artfully, and on the run, as they construct knowledge applicable to their own unique situations. Attending to both the creative and technical sides of teaching requires that teachers rely on neither creativity nor technical expertise exclusively. Good teachers, like good students, push all their capabilities to the limits to build their knowledge.

The literature on educating teachers is brimming with lists of skills—abilities to use one's knowledge—that one expert or another has advanced as the essential components of teachers' repertoires. As knowledge has grown and as philosophies have changed, programs have required that teacher education students demonstrate far fewer yet more complex skills, such as those described in the sections that follow. Once teachers distinguish themselves as professionals by applying personal, theoretical, and empirical knowledge, they are ready to develop complementary planning and interactive teaching skills, such as those listed in Figure 10.6.

FIGURE 10.6
Teachers' Skills These skills underlie teachers' abilities to understand students, set goals, create learning environments, evaluate student learning, and communicate.

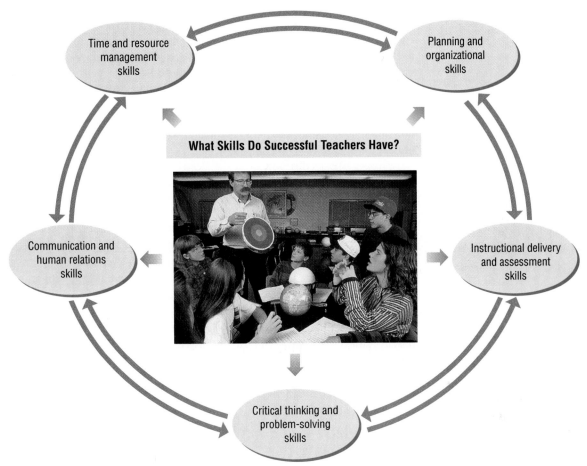

▶ Understanding Students

Good teachers learn about their students so that they can teach in ways that are culturally and developmentally appropriate. Teachers use a variety of methods to understand the influences of students' ages, abilities, and cultural backgrounds to find out what students know, what they can do, how they think, what they value, and what gets in the way of their learning. Teachers can shape their skill of understanding students formally by reading and studying student artifacts, such as tests and projects. They can also informally observe, talk with, and listen to students and their parents.

According to Philip Winne and Ronald Marx (1979), the most frequent, the most critical, and the most generous evaluators of teaching are students. Students watch what teachers do and listen to what teachers say. They take meaning away from their observations, and they assign meaning to what they see and hear. Good teachers understand that when they help students become discerning, reasonable, compassionate adults they also encourage students to become perceptive, sensible, considerate evaluators of teachers and teaching.

Winne and Marx (1979) argue that people too often overlook students' perceptions in trying to understand how and why teaching works as it does:

> Sometimes, when we have arranged the most stellar teaching imaginable, students do not get the point. And, fortunately, even when we feel we have botched instruction, they often learn in spite of our failure. Why? . . . neither the teacher nor the educational psychologist can fully explain these mismatches of instructional prowess and instructional effectiveness. Perhaps one reason for this gap in the ability to explain effects of teaching stems from neglecting an essential feature of school learning, namely, how students perceive how to learn from teaching. (pp. 210–211)

Research on students' mental activities during instruction has examined factors such as student motivations, beliefs, perceptions, and learning strategies. In one study, sixth graders were shown a videotape of a mathematics lesson in which they had just participated. They were asked to recall what they were thinking at various points during the session. Students proved to be fairly sophisticated thinkers. Besides paying attention to what the teacher was saying, mentally responding to the teacher's question, and hearing what other students were saying, students also were getting feedback on the correctness of mental responses by listening to the teacher's reaction.

To what extent should students be the judges of teacher effectiveness?

There are great differences, even among able students, in their abilities to demonstrate self-management strategies during instruction (Corno, 1987). Teachers who attempt to understand how students think about learning may be able to fine-tune instruction as needed. They can also give students opportunities to practice strategies for becoming independent learners.

▶ Communicating

At its core, professional teaching is an intellectual enterprise; thus, good teachers are good communicators. They communicate clearly, both verbally and in writing. They transmit information about subject matter and communicate with parents, administrators, and other teachers. Good teachers also use their skills to communicate expectations for student performance, empathy, positive regard, and willingness to help.

Skillful teachers know how to establish, negotiate, and help students set reasonable goals for learning. Goals typically relate to the development of students' knowledge, skills, and attitudes. Teachers sometimes select goals from existing curricula and match the goals to a student's needs and abilities. This means teachers must help different students accomplish different goals. Sometimes goals are established within a curriculum, and teachers must help all students accomplish the same goals. At yet other times, teachers must help students set their own goals.

Communicating expectations for success and reinforcing success when it occurs are two of the most important functions a teacher serves. Teachers must state their expectations clearly so that students perceive their intent. Teachers also must provide students with feedback about their work, thereby helping students judge their own

Cultural Awareness

Éxito para Todos, a program designed for use with classes of Spanish-speaking children in the elementary grades, employs the same research-based instructional strategies as the Success for All program. The materials used in Éxito para Todos are in Spanish. The curricula are not translations from English, but consist of books and materials appropriate to the children's culture and language. Éxito has reading materials appropriate for kindergarten through grade 6 students.

Like the Success for All model, Éxito para Todos is predicated on research stressing the importance of early academic success. Éxito incorporates a number of prevention and intervention strategies designed to ensure that the Spanish-speaking children in a school develop strong foundations in reading in Spanish in the early grades. English as a Second Language instruction is closely coordinated with reading instruction in Éxito para Todos. The Éxito program is designed around research findings suggesting that Spanish-dominant students perform better when they succeed in learning to read and write in Spanish in the early grades and then are supported in making a transition to English reading in the upper elementary grades.

Source: Éxito para Todos (Spanish Bilingual Adaptation of Success for All). Downloaded from the World Wide Web (September 12, 1999). Available online: (http://www.ed.gov/pubs/ToolsforSchools/ept.html).

Note: This illustration is a registered trademark of the Success For All Foundation, Inc. Reprinted by permission.

progress. If feedback is infrequent or unclear, students have no way of knowing whether they have met or exceeded teachers' or their own expectations.

▸ Creating Learning Environments

In addition to understanding students and communicating effectively, good teachers typically plan for teaching and for interacting with students during the course of instruction. As we have noted, planning involves a variety of activities: selecting appropriate content, designing activities that maximize opportunities for students to succeed, and informing parents and other school personnel (e.g., librarians, fine arts teachers, other classroom teachers) of curricular plans so they might help reinforce concepts being taught. Planning also entails arranging the classroom and organizing necessary materials. Good planners provide for student motivation, reinforcement of good work, and management of people, ideas, and resources. Good plans well implemented can inspire students to do their best work.

Effectively implementing one's instructional plans is a subtle blend of art and science (Gage, 1978). Successful teachers adapt general principles of effective teaching to help students engage in meaningful work, to think for themselves, and to succeed. There is no single all-purpose teaching model or strategy; good teachers have many ways of helping students succeed (Fielding & Pearson, 1994).

From her experience of teaching mathematics, Marilyn Burns (1995) offers a set of practical lessons for teachers that seem relevant to the creation of learning environments in all curricular areas:

1. Whatever you do, create a clear structure at the beginning of the year. (Spend the first month helping children learn how to be effective learners.)

2. For sane planning, organize your year into units (whole-class lessons; a menu of independent activities for partners, individuals, or groups to work on).

3. Give students choices; this helps to motivate them.

4. Remember that children can often do more than you think they can.

5. Focus on basic facts and emphasize reasoning; these are not mutually exclusive activities.

6. Talk less in class; have children talk more.

7. Want to know what children are learning? Ask them to write about it.

8. Use homework as a vehicle to inform parents about children's learning. (1995, pp. 87–88)

▸ Adapting Instruction for Students with Special Needs

In their efforts to help students succeed, effective teachers find ways to capitalize on students' strengths, interests, and related backgrounds. Good teachers also attempt to help students circumvent or compensate for weaknesses in their academic, socio-emotional, or physical development. Students with poor fine motor skills, for example, might need access to a computer to complete assignments. Students who have

Using Technology

Global Links

Teachers like Clare Kilbane integrate technology in their classrooms in a variety of ways. While teaching at St. James the Less, an elementary school in Columbus, Ohio, Kilbane used technology to help students make connections with learners in other locations. Her Global Links project partnered each class in grades kindergarten through 8 with a school somewhere around the globe. Students communicated electronically throughout the year, using e-mail to share original writings and drawings with students in Ireland, Sweden, Canada, and Romania. Kilbane's students also collected songs, folktales, and myths from partner classes to learn about their cultures. To prepare students for the Global Links program, Kilbane took children out to the blacktop in the schoolyard and used a physical model to demonstrate how computers connect to a server and to each other.

difficulty organizing their thoughts and completing assignments might need to learn self-management and learning strategies.

Lyn Corno (1987) and Philip Winne (1991) think teachers should plan to show students how to take notes from lectures, how to organize their thoughts when writing a paper, and how to monitor and control their concentration during instruction. By providing students with the tools for becoming independent learners, teachers welcome students as "integral, conscious, and rational participants in instructional activities" (Winne, 1991, p. 311). These and other skills, in combination with content knowledge, prepare students to continue learning throughout their lifetimes.

Homework assignments allow students opportunities to practice skills learned in class. When fitted to the needs and abilities of students, homework promotes high rates of success. Appropriate assignments also help children develop self-discipline, responsibility, and a love of learning. When parents are involved in the homework experience, assignments help bridge the connection between schoolwork and the real world (OERI, 1995).

What aspects of effective teaching are evident in this picture? What other knowledge and skills do effective teachers demonstrate?

▶ Evaluating Student Learning

Teachers must be able to decide what works in teaching and what does not. Formative assessment is conducted to discover information about students' errors, misunderstandings, understandings, and progress, so that teachers can shape new plans that will improve student performance (Frieberg & Driscoll, 1996). Summative assessment is conducted at the end of a lesson, unit, or course to allow students to demonstrate what they have learned (Frieberg & Driscoll, 1996).

Teachers have access to a variety of information about students. They can use formal measures such as tests and quizzes and informal measures such as questionnaires, interviews, and observations of in-class behaviors. Teachers make judgments daily about students' academic performance, their attitudes and interests, and their ability to work with others. Such information enables teachers to (1) determine what students already know and want to know about topics, (2) plan instruction that is appropriately challenging, (3) motivate student performance, (4) assess progress toward affective and cognitive goals, and (5) communicate progress to others.

Teachers have a responsibility to use the best information available about students before making evaluative decisions. This means assessing students frequently, using procedures that allow students to demonstrate what they can do. After collect-

Issues in School Reform

Policy-Minded Reform

Joseph McDonald, professor of education at New York University (New York City) and co-director of the Cross-Site Research Project of the Annenberg Challenge, muses about reform efforts to date:

> Behind today's interest in school reform lies a variety of concerns. Among them is the fear that the American workforce will be ill-equipped to face international economic competition once it turns up again. Another is a fear that the revitalization of big cities like Chicago will be blocked if the schools in these places are not made more attractive to middle-class families. There is also the worry that even the best public schools provide a superficial and impersonal education for most students. And there is the outrage at the abiding inequalities in American schooling—more than 40 years after President Eisenhower sent troops to Little Rock, Ark. Finally, there is a concern rarely acknowledged explicitly: The sense among aging baby boomers that hardly anything is as good today as when

> they were young, including schools, teachers, and children.

> Politicians exploit the overlap in these concerns in order to build a coalition. Many want an issue to run on in 2000 that sounds suitably "millennial," but promises to be less difficult (in terms of endangering campaign contributions) than, say, health-care reform. Policy activists design the platforms these politicians run on. One result is that the interest in school reform tends to be focused on policy-minded strategies. The good news in this is that policy is implicated in all the problems that bedevil schools and must be part of the solutions. The bad news is that it's a long, long way from Sacramento or Albany to the Hernandez School in Oakland or Seward Park High School on the Lower East Side. Longer still from California and New York to the nation's capital. Where the stretch is so long, the touch can be untrue.

> The dominant policy-minded strategy today involves the stimulation of what is called accountability. Testing is its principal tool. State- or district-directed testing

ing information teachers are obligated to "protect its privacy, recognize the limits of its use in decision making, and not use it to demean or ridicule a pupil" (Airasian, 1996, p. 24).

Measurement and Evaluation.   When their offspring are very young, parents begin informally to assess their potential. When children enter school, assessment becomes formalized as **measurement,** the collection of data relevant to personal characteristics, and **evaluation,** interpreting and attaching value to the data. Diagnostic tests are used to identify specific problems, needs, or disabilities to be considered when making placement decisions about individual students. For example, there are tests for identifying hearing impairment, visual–perceptual problems, and coordination problems. Academic progress or lack thereof is gauged most often by **standardized tests**—commercially-prepared tests designed to obtain uniform samples of student behavior. These tests are usually, but not always, multiple-choice,

is an old American school habit. What's new today is the sheer volume of testing (every grade, every year in some jurisdictions), the efforts to link the tests to curriculum through the use of standards, and the stakes. These are high for students, schools, and districts. They include promotion and graduation decisions, "school report card" scores published in local newspapers and on the World Wide Web, school reconstitution, and state or city takeovers of districts. In some cases, the impulse behind all this is crudely behaviorist, as if teachers and students simply need the right prods to do better. In other cases, there is an explicit acknowledgment that more is involved: Classes may be too large; teachers may need to learn new skills; schools may need restructuring. Still, in what I am calling policy-minded reform, the assumption is that policy can directly solve such problems, and that solving is enough. It is a faulty assumption. Thus, when the governor of California tries in a single summer to reduce class sizes in all California primary classrooms, or Massachusetts tries to improve teaching with a teaching exam, or the U.S. Congress specifies which school reform designs are worthy for schools to adopt, good intentions go awry. California creates a massive teacher shortage, Massachusetts demoralizes its teachers, and Congress undercuts reform creativity.

In fact, even more factors than overcrowding, teacher skill gaps, and faulty school structures impede genuine accountability in American schooling. Accountability-based reform must also deal with inadequate financing, the effects on school of family poverty, the intransigence of district bureaucracy, the reluctance of students to embrace the goals set for them, many teachers' utter inexperience with the kind of learning policymakers promote, and many teachers' doubts about their students' learning capacities. Overcoming such problems requires close tending and on-the-spot design. Remote control is insufficient. . . .

Discussion Questions Describe what one "on-the-spot design" might look like in a school with which you are familiar. How do your and your classmates' visions differ? What do they have in common?

Source: J. P. McDonald, "The Trouble with Policy-Minded School Reform." Reprinted with permission from *Education Week, 19* (1), 1999. Available online: http://www.edweek.org/ew/vol-19/01mcdonal.h19

paper-and-pencil tests administered and scored under conditions uniform to all students. Standardized tests do not necessarily measure what should be taught or the levels at which students should perform.

Standardization is important, because it helps equalize opportunities to take a test and to make test scores comparable. The scores students acquire on these tests are estimates of what they know or can do. These scores are imprecise, however, because they are only samples of students' learned behaviors at a particular point in time. Good teachers know that a variety of circumstances, such as testing conditions (e.g., a cold or crowded room), lucky guesses, illness, test anxiety, and disruption at home, can influence how well a child does on a formal assessment (Airasian, 1996). When making judgments about a student's achievement or potential for learning, these teachers are careful to consider both informal (e.g., teacher-made tests, observations) and formal measures of learning. They also must determine that students have had an opportunity to learn content included on formal assessments. In school, the consequences of "measuring up" are significant: results determine the course of one's educational career (U.S. Congress, 1992).

Those who interpret test results have two ways to answer the question, How well did so-and-so do? On a **norm-referenced test,** they compare a student's test score to the scores of other students. On a **criterion-referenced test,** they judge a student's performance by comparing it to some clearly defined criterion for mastering a learning task or skill.

To be useful, scores must be reliable; that is, a student's score today must be the same as or close to a score she would get tomorrow. The score also must generalize to skills similar to those assessed on the test. And if the test is not machine scored, scorers must be able to agree on their estimates of student performance. Test scores also must be valid; that is, they must measure what they are supposed to measure. For example, if a test claims to assess students' understanding of the workings of an internal combustion engine, it should not be a test of their reading ability.

What ethical considerations should guide testing and grading practices?

Grading. Teachers often use assessment results to assign grades to students. As we note below, some school systems are beginning to use collections of students' work to describe and report students' progress. But using such methods to replace grades entirely is rare. Most school districts continue to use grades to reward students, report to parents, and provide estimates of students' potential for postsecondary study.

Grades take various forms: the familiar letter grades (A+, A, A–, B+, etc.); pass/fail (P/F) or satisfactory/unsatisfactory (S/U); and numerical values (90–100 = A; 80–89 = B, etc.). Grades are frequently supplemented with teachers' comments or estimates of student effort, attitude, work habits, and the like, to provide a fuller representation of students' performances. These comments might be written directly on report cards.

Teachers often feel pulled by opposing desires: to use grades to build students' confidence by rewarding effort and progress, and to assign value to students' performances in some "objective" fashion. These sometimes contradictory demands can force teachers to examine their own ethical reasoning with respect to acceptable and unacceptable grading practice. Planning for evaluation and grading early on helps teachers resolve such dilemmas when and if they arise.

▶ Providing Authentic Assessment

In recent years, reformers have argued that if schools are to be held accountable for student learning, the instruments of assessment—the tests themselves—must be improved. To many, multiple-choice tests that de-emphasize reading, writing, and calculating inhibit learning. Reformers argue that schools need to depend more on authentic assessment: assessment concerned less with students' recognition and recall of facts and more with students' abilities to analyze, apply, evaluate, and synthesize what they know in ways that address real-world concerns. Albert Shanker, former leader of the American Federation of Teachers, for instance, argued for the creation of tests that "test for things that are really important: reading, writing, computing, history" ("Shanker asks," 1989). If this were to happen, of course, it would mean a move away from the use of standardized tests toward some form of authentic assessment.

More educators are beginning to use portfolios to assess student performance. While there is no standard definition of the term *portfolio,* and thus no consensus on what should be in one, Judith Arter and Vicki Spandel (1992) have offered this working definition:

> A portfolio is a purposeful collection of student work that tells the story of the student's efforts, progress, or achievement in (a) given area(s). This collection must include student participation in selection of portfolio content; the guidelines for selection; the criteria for judging merit, and evidence of student self-reflection (1992, p. 36).

Based on a first-time peek into the classroom practices of a nationally representative group of teachers at all levels of schooling, nearly 75 percent of primary grade teachers and 60 percent of intermediate grade teachers use portfolios to assess skills in at least one content area. In contrast, 41 percent of high school teachers use portfolios in at least one subject area (U.S. Department of Education, 1999). Figure 10.7 shows the percentage of K–12 teachers who use portfolios to assess student work in various subject areas.

Although they are not without controversy, portfolios have been promoted as means for evaluating higher-order, complex skills and for providing opportunities for student goal setting and self-evaluation of progress (Arter & Spandel, 1992; McNeil, 1999). People recognize the value of judging students' higher-order thinking skills and practical skills. However, the cost of performance assessment can be immense, both financially and in terms of the time it requires of teachers. Moreover, disagreements over assessment standards will mean that some people do not view such assessments as rigorous (Nuthall, 1992).

Mary Catherine Ellwein (1992, pp. 2, 4) argued persuasively that assessment is a process that is "intertwined with the daily life of teachers" and as much a "state of mind as it is a toolbox." In her efforts to understand teachers' typical evaluative behaviors, she identified two primary activities that teachers use to evaluate: "gathering intelligence" and "kidwatching." By engaging in these activities, teachers learn to understand students in their contexts, determine their strengths and learning strategies, tailor instruction, promote students' awareness of their learning, document their learning and change, and communicate with others connected with the students.

FIGURE 10.7

Percentage of Teachers Who Used Portfolios to Assess Student Work in Various Subject Areas During the Last Semester By teachers' participation in professional development program on student assessment between spring 1993 and completing the 1993–94 questionnaire: 1993–94 and 1994–95.

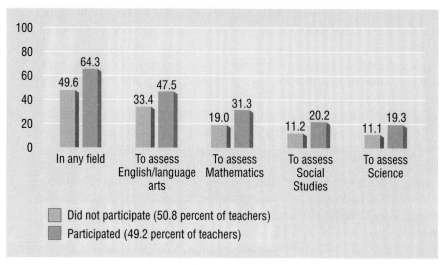

Note. Teachers responded to the survey items on instructional practices in terms of a "designated class" of students for whom they had primary responsibility during the previous semester or grading period. For teachers who were responsible for a single group of students all day, that group was the designated class. For teachers who were responsible for multiple classes or groups of students each day, their first instructional class or group of the day was the designated class. See tables A2–A11 for further data regarding practice use and participation in professional development on student assessment. Standard errors for estimates in figure 15 are provided in Table B8.

Source: U.S. Department of Education, National Center for Education Statistics, Schools and Staffing Survey: 1993–94 (School and Teacher Questionnaires) and Teacher Follow-up Survey: 1994–95, 1999.

How Do Teachers Manage Students Effectively?

Classrooms are often "crowded, competitive, contradictory, multidimensional, simultaneous, unpredictable, public . . . [places where] teachers work with captive groups of students on academic agendas that students have not helped to set" (Weinstein & Mignano, 1997, pp. 5–6). Teachers who understand the complexity of classrooms realize the importance of finding ways to gain students' cooperation and involvement in the educational activities. Through careful planning with many other people, these teachers also take steps to prevent problems from occurring. **Classroom management,** then, is the collective ability of teachers, students, administrators, school boards, and even police and the courts to agree on and implement a common framework for social and academic interactions (Doyle, 1986; Frieberg, Stein, & Huang, 1995; and Wolfgang, Bennett, & Irvin, 1999).

What is the key to effective classroom management?

Classroom management is not only about discipline, however (Jones & Jones, 1998). Successful teachers create total systems of management that address various aspects of behavior. As Jere Brophy (1988, 1996) has argued, a classroom management system is designed to maximize student engagement, not merely to minimize misconduct. Teachers who emphasize the creation and maintenance of learning environments as caring communities are more successful than teachers who assert their roles as authority figures and disciplinarians.

▶ Research Informs Teacher Management Behavior

Jacob Kounin's (1970) classic research on classroom management and discipline remains as some of the most important work ever done on these subjects. He shot hundreds of hours of kinescopes of classroom interactions, preschool through college levels. He learned that often teachers created problems for themselves; that is, they behaved in ways that actually encouraged students to become uninvolved in classroom activities and to misbehave.

Kounin suggests that good classroom managers do not "satiate" students; that is, they prevent boredom by varying learning tasks and by maintaining lesson momentum. They avoid giving too many directions or lengthy explanations. They stop activities when students become restless and make smooth transitions from one activity to the next. The intent is to maximize student involvement and to minimize disruptions.

When disruptions occur, Kounin suggests tactics that teachers can use to prevent problems from escalating—tactics such as "with-it-ness" and "overlapping" behaviors. A teacher who is "with it" seems to have eyes in the back of her head. Aware of what is going on, this teacher stops students who are misbehaving and does so in a timely manner. Overlapping, which is a teacher's ability to handle more than one thing at a time, can occur when a teacher who is working with a small group of students also manages a disruption in another part of the room.

Ed Emmer and his colleagues (Emmer, Evertson, & Anderson, 1980) observed 28 third-grade classrooms during the first few weeks of school. They found that the tone that teachers set in the beginning of the year tended to affect the way the rest of the year proceeded. When teachers planned and organized themselves to begin the year smoothly, they created a set of expectations in the minds of students that became self-fulfilling. When teachers taught and retaught behaviors deemed desirable, such as maintaining classroom rules, they reinforced a classroom community where people respected each other. Teachers who taught what is meant to function effectively in the classroom and made consequences clear and applied them consistently met with success. These researchers found that the same general principles held in junior high and high school settings (Evertson, 1985; Evertson & Emmer, 1982).

▶ Relationships Between Teachers and Students

There is an affective component to managing classrooms, a dimension of personal relationships that helps shape how people behave and get along with one another. The literature is full of examples of counseling and personal development approaches to defining and managing how classrooms should function. Indeed, as any guidance counselor would attest, to be effective, any classroom management system must be based on respectful relationships between teachers and students (Henderson and Gysbers, 1998).

Among the ideas promoted to build or enhance positive student–teacher relationships is the notion that what teachers expect from students is what they will get.

Benchmarks

A Sample of Contributions to the Conceptualization of Curriculum and Instruction (1900–2000)

1900–1920 Alfred Binet develops a systematic procedure in France for assessing learning aptitudes. Later, at Stanford University in the United States, Binet's test is revised and a formula for determining IQ added.

Research on teaching concentrates on characteristics of learners and on more and less effective teachers.

In experiments with cats, Edward Thorndike describes the law of effect—that any behavior resulting in satisfaction will tend to be repeated. This and similar work influences development of teaching approaches.

Franklin Bobbitt's *The Curriculum* (1918) marks the birth of curriculum as a professional field of study.

The Commission on the Reorganization of Secondary Education issues its celebrated *Cardinal Principles of Secondary Education* (1918).

1920–1940 In behavioral experiments with dogs, Russian scientist Ivan Pavlov discovers classical conditioning.

Swiss psychologist Jean Piaget describes the stages of cognitive development in children from infancy through adolescence.

Russian Lev S. Vygotsky describes the roles of social learning and language in the cognitive development of children.

W. W. Charters's *Curriculum Construction* (1923) shifts curriculum theorists' focus from content alone to the means for determining curriculum content.

Harold Rugg and Ann Shumaker's *The Child-Centered School* (1928) argues for the involvement of teachers in curricular decisions.

George Counts's pamphlet *Dare the Schools Build a New Social Order?* argues that curriculum and instruction should be less child-centered and more prescriptive, shaping attitudes, developing tastes, and imposing ideas.

1940–1960 Research on teaching begins to concentrate on what teachers do in classrooms rather than on their personal characteristics.

Lewis Terman begins a long-term study of 1,528 gifted American children. This classic study is slated to end in 2010.

In experiments with pigeons and rats, B. F. Skinner develops the concept of operant conditioning, in which learning is based on the consequences of behavior. This work profoundly influences the development of behavioral teaching approaches.

David Wechsler develops the Adult Intelligence Scale, testing different kinds of aptitude, on which the Wechsler Intelligence Scale for Children (WISC-R) is based. This view of learners' abilities shapes teaching approaches.

Humanist psychologists such as Harry Stack Sullivan describe child and adolescent development in terms of interpersonal interaction.

Abraham Maslow describes human motivation in terms of the satisfaction of needs.

Curriculum and teaching reflect concerns for personal development and interpersonal interactions.

The Harvard Committee on the Objectives of Education in a Free Society publishes *General Education in a Free Society* (1945), a report that questions the appropriateness of curricular materials for high school students who are not college bound.

Benjamin Bloom publishes a taxonomy of educational objectives for the cognitive domain.

John Carroll develops the theory of effective instruction, on which mastery learning is based.

Ralph Tyler's *Basic Principles of Curriculum and Instruction* (1949) stimulates the format of curriculum guides, teachers' editions of textbooks, lesson plan books, and evaluation instruments.

1960–1980	Research on primate communication advances the study of human language. Noam Chomsky theorizes that children acquire language through transformational grammar and other deep structures of the brain.

In human development studies, Erik Erikson describes stages requiring resolutions of psychological crises, and Lawrence Kohlberg describes stages of moral development based on children's responses to moral dilemmas. Dilemmas themselves become teaching materials.

Research on human memory by R. C. Atkinson and others leads to the development of the information-processing theory of learning. Robert Gagné, Madeline Hunter, and others develop models of direct instruction based on task analysis and information-processing theory.

Albert Bandura and others describe the behavioral principles of modeling and observational learning.

Jacob Kounin and others describe teacher behaviors that relate to teaching effectiveness and efficacious classroom management.

Robert Mager proposes behavioral objectives stating precisely what students should know or be able to do at the end of a lesson or unit of study.

Jerome Bruner and others develop discovery learning and instructional models based on cognitive learning theory.

A Sample of Contributions to the Conceptualization of Curriculum and Instruction (1900–2000) (Continued)

1980–2000   Social and cooperative models of teaching are promoted by individuals such as Robert Slavin, David and Roger Johnson, and Schlomo Sharan.

Global issues, such as the ecological crisis and economic interdependency, receive increasing attention in curriculum and instruction.

National standards for curriculum are produced by various professional associations.

The 1994 Ready-To-Learn Act (Public Law 102-545) establishes Ready-To-Learn Television programs to support educational programming and instructional materials for preschool and elementary schoolchildren and their parents, child care providers, and educators.

The School-To-Work Opportunities Act of 1994 (Public Law 103-239) provides money to states and communities to develop programs that prepare young people for first jobs and continuing education. The Departments of Education and Labor create a school-to-work home page on the Web.

The 1994 Goals 2000: Educate America Act (Public Law 103-227) establishes a new federal partnership to reform the nation's education system through a system of grants to states and local communities.

1998 marks the first year of funding for a 5-year federally initiated family life education program. States accepting federal monies agree to teach teenagers to abstain from sex until marriage.

In 1999 the Kansas Board of Education votes to delete evolution from the state's science curriculum.

During the summer of 1999, the U.S. Department of Education sponsors a national conference on evaluating the effectiveness of technology.

Robert Rosenthal and Leonore Jacobson's (1968) observation that teachers' expectations for students became self-fulfilling prophecies has helped fuel the misperception that teachers' expectations were the sole or most important determinant of student performance. Jere Brophy and Tom Good (1971, 1974; Good and Brophy, 2000) have done much to clarify the influence of teacher expectations not only on personal relationships and student classroom behavior, but on student achievement as well. Like Kounin before them, Good and Brophy suggest that teachers may create problems for themselves and for student by communicating their expectations differently—sometimes inappropriately—to high and low achievers. They call the teacher behaviors listed in Table 10.3 "danger signals" if the differentiation is large and occurs on many dimensions rather than on one or two dimensions.

▌ **TABLE 10.3**
How Teachers May Treat High and Low Achievers Differently

1. Waiting less time for lows to answer a question before giving the answer or calling on someone else

2. Giving lows answers or calling on someone else, rather than trying to improve their responses by giving clues or repeating or rephrasing questions

3. Inappropriate reinforcement: rewarding inappropriate behavior or incorrect answers by lows

4. Criticizing lows more often for failure

5. Praising lows less often for success

6. Failing to give feedback to the public responses of lows

7. Generally paying less attention to lows or interacting with them less frequently

8. Calling on lows less often to respond to questions or asking them only easier, nonanalytic questions

9. Seating lows farther away from the teacher

10. Demanding less from lows

11. Interacting with lows more privately than publicly, and monitoring and structuring their activities more closely

12. Differential administration or grading of tests or assignments, in which highs but not lows are given the benefit of the doubt in borderline cases

13. Less friendly interactions with lows, including less smiling and fewer other nonverbal indicators of support

14. Briefer and less informative feedback to questions of lows

15. Less eye contact and other nonverbal communication of attention and responsiveness

16. Less use of effective but time-consuming instructional methods with lows when time is limited.

17. Less acceptance and use of lows' ideas

18. Exposing lows to an impoverished curriculum

Source: Good, T. L., & Brophy, J. E. (2000). *Looking in classrooms* (8th ed.). New York: Addison Wesley Longman, Inc., pp. 85–86.

▶ Classroom Management as Self-Control

Teachers support student self-control in a variety of ways. Effective managers involve students in self-management to help them learn to monitor their own behavior. If a student is having difficulty staying in his seat, for example, a teacher might help the student observe and record his behaviors to create a level of awareness. Then, over time, the student might gradually assume greater responsibility for his self-control.

As C. M. Charles (1999) suggests, teachers demonstrate many techniques to encourage student self-control. They use nonverbal signals to alert students that they know what is going on is inappropriate. Teachers use physical proximity—they move closer to students—to communicate disapproval. They show interest in students' appropriate behavior, and they ignore inappropriate student behavior. Teachers help students who need it, thus helping students help themselves, while diminishing the likelihood of misbehavior. Teachers often help students by restructuring or rescheduling activities, removing seductive objects, or removing students from troubling situations. Teachers establish and adhere to routines and, in doing so, help students know what to expect. Good humor goes a long way toward making classrooms desirable, productive places to be—places where students control themselves. Teachers who motivate students to take an interest in their work do their best to head off student misbehavior and encourage student involvement.

SUMMARY

What is curriculum?

1. Curriculum is generally thought of as knowledge and skills that schools are held accountable for helping students master. The development of curricula is driven by a variety of competing values and philosophies about goals, content, and organization of education programs.

2. Curriculum is an operative concept outside school in business, industry, and private organizations, where training and education are important.

3. Arguments about curriculum arise frequently because the population is heterogeneous, and rapid socioeconomic change routinely makes curriculum decisions controversial.

4. Because education is a power reserved to the states, states and localities are left to define the curriculum. Thus curriculum can be contextually defined. Beyond some rather vague agreement on the need for students to read, write, and compute, there is considerable variation in people's desires and expectations for what the curriculum should deliver.

5. Curricula can be characterized as explicit (visible or public), implicit (unvoiced, often unintended), null (untaught), extra (beyond the required), and integrated (interdisciplinary, thematic, team taught, etc.).

What forces and change agents affect curriculum content?

6. A variety of forces have shaped curriculum through the years, including national interests, social issues and public opinion, professional groups and individuals, state and local priorities, and mass media and educational publishing.

How are curriculum and instruction planned and organized?

7. Curriculum and instruction relate to the aims of education in five ways: (1) development of cognitive processes, (2) academic rationalism, (3) personal relevance, (4) social adaptation and social reconstruction, and (5) mastery of learning objectives.

8. When planning for instruction, teachers consider a variety of factors: the curriculum, state and local goals and objectives for student learning, instructional strategies for meeting those goals, means of assessing students' understanding, qualities of the learning environment, students' individual needs, classroom management, ways to motivate students, and methods for teaching students learning and self-management strategies.

What are four general models of instruction?

9. The behavioral systems family uses ideas about manipulating the environment to modify students' behaviors. Mastery learning, direct instruction, behavioral objectives, and outcomes-based education are based on this model.

10. The social family capitalizes on people's nature as social beings to learn from and relate to one another. The many forms of cooperative learning, project-based learning, and reciprocal teaching are based on this model.

11. The information-processing family focuses on increasing students' abilities to think—to seek, organize, interpret, and apply information both inductively and deductively. Concept formation, synectics, and inquiry learning are based on this model.

12. The personal sources family encourages self-exploration and the development of personal identity through nondirective teaching methods.

What is effective instruction?

13. Successful teachers exhibit skills of understanding students, setting goals, creating environments conducive to learning, judging those environments, and communicating about teaching and learning to others. Successful teachers also manage classrooms to avoid problems and to handle problems when they arise.

14. Teachers use formal measures such as tests and quizzes and informal measures, such as questionnaires, interviews, and observations of in-class behaviors to judge students' academic performance, their attitudes and interests, and their ability to work with others. Teachers also use authentic assessments concerned with students' abilities to analyze, apply, evaluate, and synthesize what they know in ways that address real-world concerns.

How do teachers effectively manage students?

15. Teachers design classroom management systems to maximize student engagement, not merely to minimize misconduct. Those who are most successful emphasize the creation and maintenance of learning environments as caring communities.

16. Research supports many tactics that teachers use to increase student involvement and to decrease misbehavior.

TERMS AND CONCEPTS

REFLECTIVE PRACTICE

Careful planning does not always prevent problems. On June 22, 1993, Adele Jones, a high school algebra teacher in Georgetown, Delaware, was fired over grades (McCarthy, 1993). Jones had failed 27 percent of her Algebra II class in 1991–92 and 42 percent the year before. When the Indian River School Board first announced its decision, some 200-plus students, including some who had failed the course, marched in protest against the dismissal. Jones's colleagues backed her with enthusiasm—43 of 48 signed a letter condemning the board for its action. The Delaware affiliate of the National Education Association paid for a lawyer to take the case to court. Jones claimed to have rebelled against the practice of rewarding students with grades they did not earn; the board interpreted the failure of so many students as an indication of her incompetence.

Issues, Problems, Dilemmas, and Opportunities

Why and for whom is it problematic when large numbers of students fail? Can you think of other situations in which maintaining high academic standards while encouraging all students to succeed becomes a dilemma?

Perceive and Value

Why might the Indian River School Board consider high rates of student failure unacceptable? Can you argue from the board's point of view that high rates of student failure are an indication of teacher failure? In contrast to the board, why might Adele Jones's colleagues be so supportive of her? If you were a parent of one of the students who failed, why might you be angry? Why might you be supportive of the teachers' actions? If you were a student who had been failed, why might you nevertheless support the teachers? What might be the stake of a professional organization such as the NEA or the AFT in this case?

Know and Act

Assume you were the teacher hired to take Ms. Jones's place. What more might you want to know about the definition of failure in this instance and the circumstances that led to so many students failing the course? What might you want to know about the previous teacher's instructional planning, teaching methods, and measurement and evaluation practices? What might you need to do to improve student performance while meeting curriculum goals and the district's curriculum standards? How could you justify your actions to your principal if asked to do so?

Evaluate

How might you determine whether students understood the practical value of the material you were teaching and whether they compared favorably to other students in their mastery of key concepts?

 ## ONLINE ACTIVITY

Some teachers create WebQuests, or problem-based lessons, that encourage students to use the World Wide Web as an educational resource. The model was developed in 1995 at San Diego State University by Bernie Dodge and Tom March. WebQuests can be adapted to address objectives in every curricular area and can be designed for children in grades 3–12. To learn more about this inquiry-based model, go to the WebQuest site and investigate ways that teachers are structuring web sites to help students use electronic information to solve problems.

11

Education and the Law

Government shapes education through its legal apparatus. Legislatures make laws that guide the practice of education, and chief executives enforce these laws. In their efforts to settle disagreements, courts through the years have interpreted the law in a series of decisions. The specific types of disagreements we describe here have at one time or another been played out in courts across the land. Specifically, we consider five categories of rights and responsibilities as they have been elaborated by court actions—those of parents, students, teachers, administrators, and school boards.

We have structured the chapter a bit differently from the others. In each general category, vignettes or slices of educational life are presented as they might occur in schools. Some of these situations are similar, but not identical, to cases heard in federal and state courts. Issues and problems follow each vignette. We then provide relevant points of law to help you judge actions you propose.

We encourage consideration of the relevance of the law as it applies in real situations. It is important to note that points of law discussed in this chapter are illustrative, not definitive. New rulings make it necessary for educators to stay abreast of courtroom events so as to make informed professional decisions.

PROFESSIONAL PRACTICE QUESTIONS

- How does government influence education?
- What legal principles affect public education?
- What are parents' rights and responsibilities?
- What are students' rights and responsibilities?
- What are teachers' rights and responsibilities?
- What are the rights and responsibilities of school districts?

 ## How Does Government Influence Education?

Choose your answer to this question from one of the following: (1) slowly, (2) with haste, (3) minimally if at all, (4) profoundly, or (5) all of the above. The astute observer will probably argue that the answer depends heavily on the definitions of government, influence, and maybe education, too.

Government is organized into federal, state, and local units. As we note below, the constitutional authority for making educational decisions is reserved to the states, and they, in turn, encourage localities to assume much responsibility for schools. The federal government, however, can and does exert powerful sway over the conduct of education. At the federal and state levels, Congress and the state legislatures pass laws meant to constrain people's most base instincts and to encourage all that is good about teaching and learning. The chief executives (the president and the governors) are bound to enforce these laws. And the courts interpret the laws when disagreements arise.

At one level or another, and in one or more branches, government functions to decide who should go to school, how a school building is constructed, how children travel to and from school, what subjects they take, what they eat for lunch and when they eat it, who teaches the children, how, if, and when they progress, and so forth. *Government,* then, can be defined by its organizational structure and by the functions it performs.

The term *influence* is probably best measured on a continuum from little or none to strong or profound. Legislation that allocates and appropriates funds for educational programs may be the easiest way to think about influence. Here, influence can be defined in dollars—the more dollars, the more likely the influence will be strong. The caveat in this deceptively simple example is that more money buys more *potential* influence, but not necessarily more *kinetic* influence or educational power. Real influence depends on how the money is spent.

The influence of government on education might be defined in other ways. For instance, the president of the United States and the governors of 50 states champion a set of national standards for education. They advocate adoption by local schools and tout the benefits to the economy of world-class education. Congress and state legislatures regulate the development and use of tests meant to assess teachers' and students' success in meeting these standards. City and town councils and local school boards look to school employees to deliver results. Here influence might be defined in terms of the resources that go into the activities of these governmental officials, the activities in which they engage, and the results that emanate from these activities, all rather difficult and costly to measure with any precision.

Education in the vernacular usually refers to public education or that education supported by public money and governmental institutions. Public schools serve slightly less than 90 percent of the K–12 population and have long ago become institutionalized in our society. But this seemingly clear definition, like so many others, can be misleading. Public schools may get support for all kinds of programs from private sources. Individuals buy jerseys for the football team; local businesses and service organizations raise money for computers; large corporations give discounts and outright grants for facilities, programs, equipment, training, and scholarships. And private schools, too, may get public funds in support of their efforts. In some communities children who attend private religious schools ride public school buses paid for by public funds. In 1999 the state of Florida began issuing vouchers that allow children to attend private schools of their choice at taxpayer expense. When one stretches the definition of education to include educational activities that occur outside school walls, such as online access to public educational services, the definition of what constitutes education becomes even murkier.

But what of the influence of the third branch of government, the judiciary? How and to what degree do the courts influence education? The courts remain the one governmental authority through which individuals or groups of people, often from outside the political mainstream, can exert palpable influence on the conduct of education. The courts exercise their influence by settling disputes and by interpreting the law in the process.

What Legal Principles Affect Public Education?

The United States Constitution does not mention education. All state constitutions, however, specify that the legislature has the power to establish and maintain free public schools. States' legal control over education is authorized by the 10th Amendment's provision that "powers not delegated to the United States by the Constitution, nor prohibited by it to the States, are reserved to the States respectively, or

FIGURE 11.1
Levels at Which Disputes Are Heard   In settling disputes, why is it important for the "extra-legal" grievance system to function effectively?

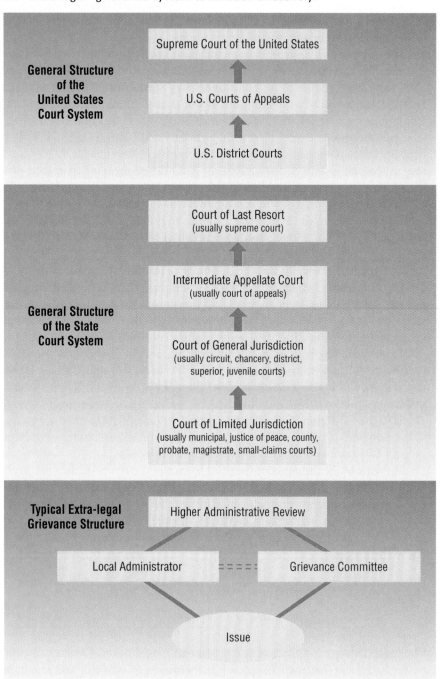

to the people." Such control must be exercised in a manner consistent with the Constitution's provisions for the basic rights of individuals.

When disputes arise over educational practices or policies, the parties involved make every effort to settle differences at the local level of governance, most always informally before formal entry into the judicial system. Either state courts or the federal judiciary system hear unresolved cases. At the state level, statutes prescribe where cases should be taken and which ones should be heard by the highest court. As Figure 11.1 illustrates, the Supreme Court of the United States is the highest court in the land, beyond which there is no redress. Most cases heard by the Supreme Court are cases in which the validity of a state or federal statute is questioned in light of the federal Constitution or cases in which title, right, privilege, or immunity is claimed under the Constitution (Alexander & Alexander, 1998).

The Supreme Court frequently considers several statutory and constitutional provisions when rendering decisions about educational matters. One is the First Amendment to the Constitution, which contains two clauses often cited in lawsuits: the **establishment clause,** which prohibits recognition of the primacy of one religion, and the **free exercise clause,** which ensures religious freedom.

▨ The First Amendment states that

> Congress shall make no law respecting an establishment of religion, or prohibiting the free exercise thereof; or abridging the freedom of speech, or of the press; or the right of the people peaceably to assemble, and to petition the government for a redress of grievances.

This amendment is the basis for a number of lawsuits challenging aid to and regulation of nonpublic schools, public school policies that advance or inhibit religion, and actions that impair expression by teachers and students.

▨ The Fourth Amendment guarantees citizens that the right

> to be secure in their persons, houses, papers, and effects, against unreasonable searches and seizures, shall not be violated, and no warrants shall issue, but upon probable cause, supported by oath or affirmation, and particularly describing the place to be searched, and the persons or things to be seized.

When a student's bookbag, locker, or person is searched for illegal or dangerous items, this amendment usually serves as the basis for judgments about the legality of such actions.

▨ The 14th Amendment is the most widely invoked constitutional provision in school-related cases (McCarthy, Cambron-McCabe, & Thomas, 1998). Section 1 states that

> [N]o State shall make or enforce any law which shall abridge the privileges or immunities of citizens of the United States; nor shall any State deprive any person of life, liberty, or property, without due process of law; nor deny to any person within its jurisdiction the equal protection of the laws.

This clause, the **equal protection clause,** is significant in litigation related to school finance, the expulsion and suspension of students, the dismissal of teachers, and discrimination on the basis of race, gender, and disabilities.

FIGURE 11.2
Groups with Rights and Responsibilities under the U.S. Constitution and Federal Laws What do overlapping areas in this diagram represent?

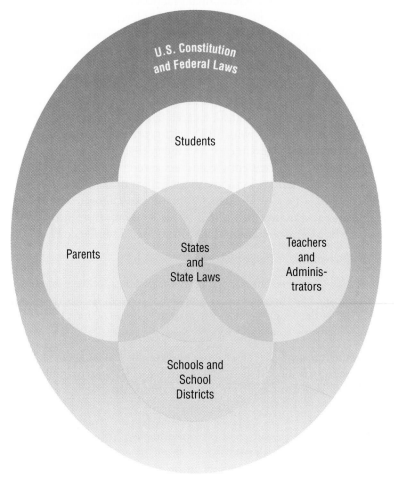

When disputes relate to contractual situations, Article I, Section 10 of the Constitution typically comes into play. This article states in part that "no State shall . . . pass any . . . ex post facto law, or law impairing the obligation of contracts." Interpretations of this constitutional provision enable the courts to determine the validity of contracts and possible breaches of contracts. Figure 11.2 suggests why disputes may arise.

In the scenarios that follow, note that disputes are resolved on the basis of constitutional provisions, state and federal legislation, rules and regulations of state and local boards, and case law (common law) emanating from the judicial system. Note also that Supreme Court decisions have brought some uniformity to educational practices and policies across the land.

What Are Parents' Rights and Responsibilities?

A number of cases decided by the courts have dealt directly with parents' rights and responsibilities as parents and as guardians of their children. As the following scenarios suggest, knowledge of such rulings is just as important for teachers as for parents.

▶ A Question of Religious Principle

At the end of the school day, Betty Anne Mason fell into stride with three of her ninth-grade students weaving their way to the locker room. The students—James, Lashanta, and Miranda—were so engrossed in conversation that they didn't notice Betty Anne until they reached the locker room. Normally friendly and outgoing in class, the students seemed suddenly fidgety and nervous when Betty Anne asked good-naturedly if they planned to attend the ninth grade dance Friday night. Miranda muttered something about having to stay home to "do some stuff," then made a beeline for the front door. As Betty Anne turned toward the other two students, James blushed and whispered something to Lashanta who bobbed her head in agreement. "Hey, what's with you guys today?" asked Betty Anne.

"Mrs. Mason," said Lashanta, "I don't know if you heard or not, but there is a meeting at 7:00 tonight after the Bible study session at Miranda's house. A bunch of parents who don't like what is going on here at Walden High are getting together to talk about taking their kids out of school and teaching them at home. Miranda's parents have already told her this is her last week at Walden. Can you believe it?"

As she headed for the principal's office, Betty Anne was upset. Miranda was one of her most promising students. Surely her parents wouldn't try to pull something like this. If they did, wouldn't they be violating the compulsory attendance law? By the time she reached the office, Betty Anne's mind was racing. She headed straight for the principal's office, hoping to get some answers to her questions.

Analysis of "A Question of Religious Principle."   If parents have religious or philosophical objections to a school program, can they exempt their children from school? The Supreme Court's 1972 decision in *Wisconsin* v. *Yoder* allowed members of the Old Order Amish religious community to exempt their children from school attendance beyond eighth grade, even though home instruction provided by the Amish was not equivalent to instruction in public schools. (The Amish had argued that compulsory attendance in the upper grades would have a detrimental effect on the established way of life in their farm-based, traditional community.) The Court's decision was based on the religious freedom clause of the First Amendment and on evidence that the Amish way of life was an acceptable alternative to formal education (Zirkel, Richardson, & Goldberg, 1995).

Litigation since *Wisconsin* v. *Yoder* suggests that the "Amish exception" cannot be used by parents who wish to exempt their children from schools for philosophical or religious reasons unless evidence suggests that such schooling might destroy their religion. For those dissatisfied with the public schools, however, compulsory atten-

What are the rights and responsibilities of parents who claim that public school curricula or the public school experience violates their religious principles?

dance requirements may be fulfilled in private, denominational, or parochial schools. In all states and the District of Columbia, home-schooling is yet another option.

An examination of data collected by the Home School Legal Defense Association (1999) indicates, however, that the way states regulate homeschooling varies widely. Only 37 states specifically regulate home schooling, and the vast majority (41) do not require parents to have specific qualifications to teach. Only 26 require students to have regular evaluations or take standardized tests (C. Klicka, personal communication, July 20, 1999). In Kentucky, for example, state law specifies that students must spend 185 days per year focusing on five areas: reading, writing, spelling, math, and library research. There are no teacher qualifications for parents. Parents are expected to maintain an attendance register and scholarship reports, but no student testing is required (Home School Legal Defense Association, 1999).

In contrast, North Dakota law requires home-schooled students to study a prescribed curriculum 175 days per year, 4 hours per day. The elementary curriculum stretches beyond the Kentucky curriculum to include English grammar, geography, U.S. history, civil government, nature, elements of agriculture, physiology and hygiene, effects of alcohol, prevention of contagious diseases, and the U.S. Constitution. Curriculum at the secondary level is equally specific. To continue studying at home, North Dakota students must meet cutoff scores on standardized tests. Parents serving as teachers must also meet standards. Those who do not possess a teaching certificate or a baccalaureate degree are required to meet or exceed the cutoff score for a national teacher exam or to possess a high school diploma or GED and be monitored by a certified teacher during the first 2 years of home instruction or until the parent's child completes third grade, whichever is later; monitoring must continue thereafter if the child performs below the 50th percentile on standardized achievement tests (Home School Legal Defense Association, 1999).

In the past few years several states, including Arizona, Colorado, Florida, Maine, Washington, and Wyoming, have passed laws requiring public schools to open sports and other extracurricular activities to home-schooled students. Other states are considering such policies, but most states leave decisions on whether to open activities to home schoolers to local districts (White, 1998).

▶ You Can't Spank My Child!

Steve Donovan's face was flushed as he escorted Brian's parents to the door. In his role as principal, he suspected that there might be some backlash from his actions the day before; but, as he had explained to Brian's parents, he had warned Brian several times that if he kept spitting on other students, he was going to be spanked. When Brian repeated the offense yesterday, Steve made good on his promise. Brian's parents were furious. "We know Brian has some behavior problems," they said, "but we sent a note to Brian's teacher telling her that

Can teachers use physical punishment on a child?

spanking was not to be used as a disciplinary measure. Your behavior was an infringement on our rights as parents, and we're going to see that you don't get away with something like this again!"

Analysis of "You Can't Spank My Child!"   Given that Brian's parents requested formally that their child not be spanked, would a court of law support Steve's actions? In *Ingraham* v. *Wright* (1977), the Supreme Court ruled that the Constitution does not prohibit the use of corporal punishment in the schools. In so ruling, the Court concluded that cases dealing with corporal punishment should be handled at the state rather than the federal level. Whether Brian's parents have a legitimate complaint, then, depends on state and local school board policies.

In states that allow corporal punishment, parental objection to the practice does not necessarily prevail. In *Baker* v. *Owen* (1975), a case challenging a North Carolina state law permitting reasonable corporal punishment, the federal district court recognized parents' basic right to supervise the upbringing of their children. The court also recognized the importance of maintaining order in the schools, ultimately deciding that parents' wishes should not interfere with methods chosen by school officials for maintaining discipline.

Some states and localities do have laws requiring written permission from parents before students can be spanked. If there is no state or local regulation to the contrary, however, schools are not required to seek parental permission before administering corporal punishment. Educators must be aware of state laws and board policies banning or restricting the use of corporal punishment in the classroom.

A common restriction is that principals are the only ones who can use corporal punishment, doing so only in the presence of an adult witness. Educators who violate such policies may face monetary fines, dismissal, and even imprisonment (McCarthy, Cambron-McCabe, & Thomas, 1998). Corporal punishment, though often equated with paddling, is more broadly defined as "reasonable physical force used by school authorities to restrain unruly students, to correct unacceptable behavior, and to maintain the order necessary to conduct an educational program" (Data Research, Inc., 1998, p. 139). Sometimes teachers who have demonstrated excessive force when disciplining a student (e.g., throwing a student against a chalkboard and then pulling him upright by his hair) have been dismissed for cruelty or charged with criminal assault and battery.

Nathan Essex (1999) warns teachers working in school systems where corporal punishment is allowed to avoid excessive force and to adhere to local guidelines when administering such punishment. Corporal punishment is unacceptable in most states. Those that allow it do so only as a last resort, to be avoided if at all possible.

▶ Do Some Parents Have Special Rights?

Kenneth and Karen Rothschild, deaf parents of non-hearing-impaired students, used American sign language as their primary means of communication. When the school system denied their request to hire a sign language interpreter for school-sponsored functions, the Rothschilds were forced to obtain their own interpreter at great personal expense. Subsequently, they brought action against the school district and the superintendent for violating section 504 of the Rehabilitation Act of 1973, which prohibits discrimination on the basis of a disability. School officials denied the charge, arguing that they had made good-faith efforts to accommodate the Rothschilds' needs by providing special seating arrangements at all school-sponsored functions.

Analysis of "Do Some Parents Have Special Rights?"   Must a school system provide special services, such as sign language interpreters, to parents who are disabled? In *Rothschild* v. *Grottenthaler* (1990), the United States Court of Appeals ruled that a public school system receiving federal financial assistance is obligated to provide a sign language interpreter at school district expense to deaf parents attending school-initiated events. In explaining its decision, the court said that without an interpreter, people like the Rothschilds do not have equal opportunity to participate in activities incidental to their children's education. The court also noted that the Rehabilitation Act specifies that access to necessary accommodations for individuals with disabilities should not impose undue financial or administrative burdens on them. Accordingly, the school system was ordered to (1) reimburse the Rothschilds for monies spent on interpreters, and (2) hire an interpreter to assist the Rothschilds at school-initiated activities directly involving their children's academic or disciplinary progress.

What Are Students' Rights and Responsibilities?

In *Tinker* v. *Des Moines Independent Community School District* (1969), the Supreme Court emphasized that students do not lose their rights when they pass through the schoolhouse door. Under the Constitution they continue to be persons "possessed of fundamental rights which the state must respect." Although school authorities are vested with broad powers for the development and implementation of an educational program, then, they must avoid unreasonable, vague, arbitrary actions or actions in direct conflict with students' constitutional rights and freedoms.

▶ In God Somebody Trusts

Jack Mills sat at his desk grading papers late one afternoon. He heard singing down the hall in the direction of the principal's office. He recognized the strains of "Onward Christian Soldiers" being sung by what sounded like a fairly large group of students. Students often sang in the building after the final bell; Omega High had many after-school activities. But they did not usually sing hymns. When Ellie Ferro, the sophomore English teacher, stormed into his room, Jack was surprised by her anger.

Can students conduct religious practices in school?

"Jack, the Young Crusaders for Christ are holding a prayer meeting in the gymnasium again. Apparently the principal said they could meet there whenever the basketball team was not practicing. It really ticks me off that they get to stay here when nobody else gets to use the building for church meetings. The principal has been cuddling up to those fundamentalists every chance she gets. It isn't fair. I want you to come with me to her office. I think we need to call her on this one."

Analysis of "In God Somebody Trusts."   Jack feels nervous about Ellie's anger, largely because the law on prayer clubs in schools is a mystery to him. Given the number of court cases focusing on the wall of separation between church and state since the mid-20th century, Jack's confusion is understandable. In the tug-of-war over where the lines of separation should be drawn, some argue that the First Amendment's establishment clause prohibits religious observance of any type in schools. Others contend that the Amendment's provisions for free speech, free exercise, and association rights prohibit schools from religious discrimination.

In *Widmar* v. *Vincent* (1981), the Supreme Court ruled that refusing religious groups access to facilities while allowing other groups use of the same facilities was a violation of students' rights of free speech. Furthermore, the Court deemed college students less impressionable than high school students. As adults, college students could be expected to perceive that the university was neutral in granting permission to a prayer club to meet on public property. With passage of the **Equal Access Act (EAA)** in 1984, Congress indicated that secondary-school students were also mature enough to understand that a school does not condone religion merely by allowing prayer clubs on public property.

The EAA stipulates that secondary public schools accepting federal aid must treat student religious groups in the same way as other extracurricular clubs. That is, if a school allows noncurriculum student groups (e.g., the baseball card collecting club or the chess club) to meet on school property during noninstructional time, other student-initiated groups, regardless of their religious, philosophical, or political views, must have equal access to school premises. In *Board of Education of the Westside Community Schools* v. *Mergens* (1990), the Supreme Court upheld the constitutionality of the EAA.

Given the Supreme Court's ruling, the sanctioning of any student club not directly tied to the curriculum prohibits schools from discriminating against other student organizations, such as the Young Crusaders for Christ, or even groups having little community support, such as satanists or skinheads. If schools do permit noncurriculum student group meetings during noninstructional time, teachers or other school employees may be present only in a nonparticipatory capacity. Furthermore, meetings may not be coordinated or led by nonschool persons (La Morte, 1998).

Rulings on other major cases dealing with separation of church and state contain implications for educators:

- *West Virginia State Board of Education* v. *Barnette* (1943)—Educators cannot require students to salute/pledge allegiance to the American flag when those students choose not to for personal or religious reasons.

- *Goetz* v. *Ansell* (1973)—Requiring students to stand quietly or to leave the room during the pledge of allegiance is unconstitutional. According to the Court, the first action compels an act of acceptance of the pledge over deeply held convictions, while the latter is a benign form of punishment for nonparticipation.

> *School District of Abington Township* v. *Schempp* (1963)—Prayer and Bible reading in public school classrooms are unconstitutional. However, study of the Bible as part of a secular program of education focusing on its literary and historic value may occur.

> *Wallace* v. *Jaffree* (1985)—Educators cannot require students to pause for a moment of silence for meditation or voluntary prayer.

> *Lee* v. *Weisman* (1992)—Prayers at a high school graduation ceremony are unconstitutional. (Since *Weisman,* however, school systems in some states have skirted the ban on prayer at graduation services by allowing students to initiate, plan, and lead invocations.)

Does the Lemon test really work?

Since 1971, Supreme Court justices have often applied the tripartite **Lemon test,** a test emanating from the case *Lemon* v. *Kurtzman* (1971), when deciding whether specific practices or policies constitute an establishment of religion. Under the Lemon test, each of the following questions must be answered affirmatively to satisfy the Constitution:

1. Does the challenged practice or policy have a secular purpose?

2. Does it have the effect of neither advancing nor inhibiting religious practices? and

3. Does practice or policy avoid an excessive entanglement between government and religion?

How much longer the Lemon test will survive as the yardstick for settling establishment clause disputes is questionable. As Justice Antonin Scalia noted, there are several problems with the Lemon test:

> It is so easy to kill. It is there to scare us (and our audience) when we wish it to do so, but we can command it to return to the tomb at will. . . . For my part, I agree with the long list of constitutional scholars who have criticized *Lemon* and bemoaned the strange Establishment Clause geometry of crooked lines and wavering shapes its intermittent use has produced. (Bureau of National Affairs, 1993)

 To learn more about the Lemon test, visit the web site for the Freedom Forum First Amendment Center and search there for "Lemon Test."

▶ Playing Fairly

At the end of the school day, Mary Ellen, Joe, and David went to the principal's office, where Anne Jeffrey, the assistant principal, handed each of them a sealed envelope addressed to their parents. "As I understand it," she said, "each of you is suspended for three days. This notice of suspension should be given to your parents."

"Are you kidding?" said Joe. "Nobody said anything to me about this. What are the charges against us?"

"Wait a minute," interrupted Mary Ellen. "Does this have anything to do with what happened during lunch today? If it does, this is a bunch of crap. We weren't the ones who started that fight."

Using Technology

The Law Online

One way educators can stay current on changes in the law is to get online. For instance, use a search engine to find "Oyez Oyez Oyez," a U.S. Supreme Court multimedia database maintained by Northwestern University. Click on "Cases" and then "Search by Title." When prompted for text, enter the words "Edwards v. Aguillar," a case decided in 1987.

This case dealt with a Louisiana law entitled the "Balanced Treatment for Creation Science and Evolution Science in Public School Instruction Act." The law prohibited the teaching of the theory of evolution in the public schools unless that instruction was accompanied by the teaching of creation science, a biblical belief that all forms of life appeared abruptly on Earth at about the same time. Schools were not forced to teach creation science, but if either topic was to be addressed, evolution or creation, teachers were obligated to discuss the other as well. The Court decided the case in a 4 to 3 vote (with 2 abstentions).

Nancy Willard, a specialist in computer law and education law, has created a web site entitled "K–12 Acceptable Use Policies" to help K–12 school systems develop effective Internet policies and practices. Use a search engine to find this site. School districts everywhere are moving quickly to provide Internet access for their students and employees. With such access comes unfiltered information and opportunities to communicate with people from around the world.

Willard's site evaluates some of the basic constitutional issues, as well as educational issues, that arise in the context of K–12 acceptable use policies for Internet access. She bases her analysis on past court decisions in other environments. "Use of the Internet in the K–12 environment is so new that there are no court cases that are directly on point." Visit the site and read the "Student Acceptable Use Policy Template" to learn what kind of restrictions a school might legally place on student access to the Internet.

"Yeah," said David. "It was that bunch of rednecks. They're always mouthing off and getting in your face. How come they aren't getting suspended? They cause trouble every day! You guys just never see them!"

"Look, I don't want to hear it," said Anne. "The principal asked me to give you these forms and that's it. Now go get on the bus before you get into any more trouble."

"You mean we don't even get to tell our side of the story?" asked Joe. "Man, this is really wrong!"

If you were the teacher of these students, how would you respond to their complaints about the way their suspension was handled?

> **Can students ever be denied the right to due process of law?**

Analysis of "Playing Fairly." In *Goss* v. *Lopez* (1975), the Supreme Court addressed the grievances of Dwight Lopez and several of his peers, who were suspended by the principal for 10 days without being given a hearing, a practice sanctioned by Ohio law. Because the principal did not follow mandated legal procedures, the Court ruled that the students were denied **due process of law.** Specifically, the

Court noted that the principal's actions were in violation of the 14th Amendment and subsequently ordered school officials to remove references to the students' suspensions from school records. The Court held that students facing temporary suspension from school must be given oral or written notice of the charges, an explanation of evidence if they disagree with the charges, and an opportunity to present their side of the story. Whenever possible, the notice and hearing are to precede suspension from school (La Morte, 1999).

In instances when student behavior is serious enough to warrant long-term suspension or expulsion, prudent educators provide students with a written notice describing the charges, time and place of a hearing, and procedures to be followed in the hearing. Students have the right to know what evidence will be presented and who will testify, as well as the substance of such testimony. They also have the right to cross-examine witnesses and to present witnesses to testify on their behalf. Written or taped records of proceedings and the decision of the group conducting the hearing are to be made available to students. Students are also to be made aware of the right of appeal (Essex, 1999).

▶ Show Me What's in There!

When David Adams, the assistant principal, stepped outside, his attention was drawn to three students walking across the school courtyard. As he moved toward them, he noticed that the boys were looking at a small black bag held by William, one of the students. The bag, a vinyl calculator case, had a suspicious bulge in its side.

When he questioned the boys about where they were going and why they were late to class, William, palming the leather case and hiding it behind his back, responded that his classes had ended and he was on his way home. Curious about what William was hiding, the assistant principal insisted, to no avail, that William show him the object in his hand. "It's nothing," said William. "Leave me alone. You have a search warrant or something?"

After sending the other two boys back to class, David took William to the office and asked an aide to witness his efforts to look at the calculator case. When William refused to let him see it, David pried it out of William's hand, unzipped it, and found marijuana and other drug paraphernalia. David called the police, and William was arrested. As he was being escorted out of the office, William turned to David and said, "You haven't seen the end of this. I know my rights. You can't be searching me or anybody else without a warrant!"

Analysis of "Show Me What's in There!" Does a school official have the right to search students? The scenario of William follows closely the events as they occurred in a California public school. After being convicted in juvenile court, William appealed the decision, saying that the evidence against him had been procured by an illegal search and thus should have been excluded from the hearing. In *In re William G.* (1985), the Supreme Court of California agreed, basing its decision on the reasonable suspicion standard set forth in *New Jersey* v. *T.L.O.* (1985).

In *New Jersey* v. *T.L.O.* (1985), the Supreme Court stated that school officials are acting not **in loco parentis** (in place of the parents) but as agents of the state when they search students under their authority. While this means that school officials are subject to the Fourth Amendment, the Court ruled that schools are special settings and thus there should be some "easing of the restrictions" normally placed on public authorities when conducting searches. Accordingly, school officials need not obtain a warrant or show "probable cause" when searching a student suspected of violating school rules or the law. Instead, when determining the legality of school searches, school officials can rely on "reason" and "common sense." Tests for determining reasonableness are whether (1) at the inception of the search there are reasonable grounds for suspecting that evidence will be found to prove a student is in violation of the law or school rules, and (2) the scope of the search is reasonably related to the objectives of the search, the age and sex of the student, and the nature of the infraction.

Such guidelines allow for much latitude among courts when interpreting Fourth Amendment rights (McCarthy, Cambron-McCabe, & Thomas, 1998). In the case of William, the court decided that the assistant principal had insufficient grounds for conducting a search. First, the assistant principal had no prior knowledge of William using or selling illegal drugs. Second, suspicion that William was late to class and William's attempt to hide the leather object provided no reasonable basis for a search. Third, William's demand for a warrant merely indicated that he wanted to preserve his constitutional rights (National Organization on Legal Problems of Education, 1988).

In *New Jersey* v. *T.L.O.,* the situation differed markedly. In this case a student claimed that her Fourth Amendment rights were violated when a school official searched her purse. The student (T.L.O.) was one of two girls sent to the office for smoking in the girl's restroom (a violation of school rules). When questioned by the assistant vice principal, T.L.O. denied having smoked at all. However, when T.L.O. complied with the request to open her purse, the assistant vice principal found marijuana and drug paraphernalia, $40.98 in single dollar bills and change, plus a handwritten note to a friend, requesting that she sell marijuana at school. Subsequently, the school official notified T.L.O.'s mother and the police, and T.L.O., after being advised of her rights, admitted to selling marijuana at the high school.

When the state brought delinquency charges against T.L.O., she claimed that the assistant vice principal had violated her Fourth Amendment rights, and thus evidence from her purse and her confession should be suppressed. The Supreme Court disagreed, saying that the search met the criteria for reasonableness; that is, a teacher had witnessed T.L.O.'s smoking, and thus the school official had a duty to investigate whether a school code had been broken (La Morte, 1999).

More recently, the Supreme Court's ruling in *Veronia School Dist. 47J* v. *Acton* (1995) gave school officials the right to screen student athletes for drug use. In

What was the Supreme Court's reasoning in ruling that school officials have the right to screen student athletes for drug use? Why is such screening not an invasion of the athletes' privacy?

explaining its decision, the Court noted that random urinalysis drug testing is not a violation of students' protection against unreasonable search and seizure, because schoolchildren have fewer rights than adults. The Court further held that students who participate voluntarily in sports have low expectations for privacy, because teammates undress together and shower in communal locker rooms. Furthermore, privacy rights compromised by urine samples are considered negligible, because conditions of collection are similar to public restrooms, and the results are viewed only by limited authorities. Finally, the Court emphasized that governmental concern over the safety of minors under their supervision overrides the minimal, if any, intrusion in student athletes' privacy. In 1999, more than 100 districts in at least 20 states required students to submit to urine tests if they wanted to play sports (Portner, 1999).

▶ Are There Limits on Student Expression?

Can school administrators censor student publications?

Students at Kirkwood High School in suburban St. Louis, Missouri, had enjoyed much freedom in the production of the school newspaper. When the students agreed to run an ad for Planned Parenthood, Birthright (an organization concerned with reproductive issues) requested that students run an antiabortion ad to counteract Planned Parenthood's message. Several parents and local citizens considered such advertisements inappropriate and insisted that principal Franklin McCallie ban the ads from the student newspaper (Conkling, 1991).

Analysis of "Are There Limits on Student Expression?"   Students had reason to cheer when in 1969 the Supreme Court ruled on *Tinker* v. *Des Moines Independent Community School District,* a case in which three public school students, suspended for wearing armbands to protest the war in Vietnam, won their court battle. Deciding in favor of the students, the Court declared that public school authorities do not have the right to silence students' political or ideological viewpoints simply because they disagree with students' ideas. Under *Tinker,* only in instances when student behavior could result in disorder or disturbance or interfere with the rights of others may students' verbal or symbolic expression be restricted.

In 1988, the Supreme Court restricted students' First Amendment rights in *Hazelwood School District* v. *Kuhlmeier* when it ruled that principals could censor school-sponsored publications. The basis for the Court's decision emanated from a case involving students in a high school journalism class who claimed that their First Amendment rights were violated when the principal reviewed their material and removed two stories—one on divorce, the other on three students' experiences with pregnancy—from the school-sponsored newspaper. According to the Supreme Court, a student newspaper does not represent a forum for public expression when it is part of the school curriculum. Thus, school officials can censor material considered inconsistent with the educational mission of the school. This includes material that is ungrammatical, poorly researched, biased or prejudiced, vulgar, or inappropriate for an immature audience.

If schools have clearly established, either through practice or policy, students' rights to control editorial content, the publication is considered an open forum and restrictions under Hazelwood do not apply. At Kirkwood High School, principal Franklin McCallie firmly believed that the newspaper should be an open forum for student expression. Thus he allowed student journalists to decide what to do about the controversial ads.

▌ Treating Different Students Differently—Illegal Discrimination?

As Sam Miller's fifth-grade class lined up to leave the gymnasium, Tyrone grabbed Tony's hat and ran to the end of the line. Tony, a mainstreamed student with emotional disturbance, raced after Tyrone, knocked him to the gym floor, and punched Tyrone hard enough to bloody his nose. When Sam pulled Tony away from Tyrone, Tony swung his fist and hit another child in the stomach. Sam wrapped his arms

Cultural Awareness

Both students' and teachers' freedom of expression can be limited by dress codes imposed by school districts. School officials suspended a 13-year-old boy living in rural, north Indiana, for wearing an earring to school. The case posed an unusual contest between family and community values, as the student contended that he wanted to wear an earring like the one his dad wears. The student's parents argued that the school district's policy violated their son's rights under the due process and equal protection clauses. The Indiana Civil Liberties Union also contended that the district's dress code constituted gender discrimination, because girls were allowed to wear earrings. In *Hines* v. *Caston School Corporation* (1995), an Indiana appellate court held that the school district's dress code mirrored the community's conservative standards and served to instill discipline in students. The court also rejected the equal protection claim, stating that, without respect to gender, the dress code prohibits all students from wearing jewelry that conflicts with community standards (Data Research, 1999).

In Mississippi, a teacher who was a member of the African Hebrew Israelites sometimes wore a head-wrap to school as an expression of her religious and cultural heritage. When the teacher transferred of her own volition to a different school, her new principal instructed the teacher not to wear the head-wrap. Concerned that she might lose her job, the teacher complied with the principal's wishes until she attended a district-wide session on multicultural education and learned that the school system valued diversity. When she began wearing her head-wrap again, the administration terminated her employment. The teacher filed a grievance, claiming she wore her head covering in compliance with her religious beliefs. The district denied her grievance and offered her reemployment if she would agree to remove her head covering. The teacher rejected the offer and appealed her case to the U.S. District Court for the Southern District of Mississippi. In *McGlothin* v. *Jackson Municipal* (1993), the court ruled in favor of the school district. Although the teacher was deemed to have sincere religious beliefs, she had failed to communicate these beliefs until the final stage of her grievance. Thus the court ruled that the school district was not required to accommodate the teacher's beliefs under the First Amendment or Title VII (Data Research, Inc., 1999).

Can students with disabilities be expelled for dangerous conduct?

around Tony's waist and carried him to the back of the gym before he could do any more damage and sent one of his students to get the principal. This wasn't the first time Tony had exploded, but it was the most serious and dangerous of incidents.

Sam was nearing his wit's end. He had talked with the resource teacher about ways to diffuse Tony's anger, but it was sometimes impossible to intervene before Tony's quick temper caused incidents like the one in the gym. In Sam's mind, Tony threatened other students and needed to be disciplined for his misbehavior. Sam decided to ask the principal either to expel Tony or to give him a long-term suspension so that Tony's Individual Educational Plan (IEP) team could have sufficient time to rethink Tony's placement.

Analysis of "Treating Different Students Differently—Illegal Discrimination?"

Can students with disabilities be expelled or given long-term suspensions for dangerous conduct? Disciplining students with disabilities has been a controversial and confusing issue for educators and parents. Under the 1975 Education for All Handicapped Children Act (EAHCA), now called the Individuals with Disabilities Education Act (IDEA), students with disabilities are guaranteed a free and appropriate education. In 1988 the Supreme Court ruled in *Honig* v. *Doe* that expulsion of students with disabilities for behavior attributable to their disabilities would be a violation of EAHCA provisions (Data Research, Inc., 1998). The Court did agree, however, that students with disabilities exhibiting behavior dangerous to self or others could be temporarily suspended for up to 10 days if such punishment were the same that would be used for a nondisabled student. The 1997 IDEA amendments altered this ruling by allowing school officials to establish a 45-day interim educational placement for students carrying weapons, using drugs, or demonstrating behavior that might result in injury to themselves or others.

Final IDEA regulations established in 1999 offer schools even more leeway in disciplining disruptive students with disabilities by allowing school officials to suspend a student for up to 10 days at a time and for additional removals of up to 10 days for separate acts of misconduct, as long as the removals do not constitute a pattern. Special education services do not need to be provided during the first 10 days of suspension. However, if a child is subsequently removed for up to 10 school days for other violations of school conduct codes, services must be provided. Administrators and the special education teacher determine services that are needed. Furthermore, decisions as to whether a student's behavior is related to his or her disability are now required only for a suspension that results in a change of placement (U.S. Department of Education, 1999).

▶ Would You Check These Papers for Me?

The terse phone call from Amy Aller's mother, a local lawyer, should have alerted Charles Armstrong to the possibility of an unpleasant parent conference, but Amy was a good student, and as far as Charles knew, she had been quite happy in school. Amy had left school that afternoon a little upset by the low score on her math quiz, but her grades in general were so good that he couldn't imagine one assignment prompting a parent conference; it had to be something else.

As Charles sat facing Mrs. Aller that afternoon, she explained the reason for her conference. Amy was in fact upset—not so much because of her low math score but because of the "unkind" comments about her paper made by classmates. "How did anyone else know Amy's grade on this quiz?" asked Mrs. Aller. Charles shifted uncomfortably in his chair. "I have student helpers who grade papers for me when they finish their work," said Charles. "I guess one of them must have told the others about Amy's paper today. I'm sorry. This has never been a problem before. I'll be sure to say something to my students tomorrow so this type of thing doesn't happen again."

> **Is posting grades an invasion of students' privacy?**

As she stood to leave, Mrs. Aller said, "I like you, Mr. Armstrong, but I want to tell you I don't think you should use this system anymore. I believe it violates the Buckley Amendment. No student should have knowledge of another student's progress in school."

Later that night Charles pulled out his college textbook, read about the Buckley Amendment, and reflected on his conference with Mrs. Aller. If Mrs. Aller was right, did he also violate students' rights of privacy when he displayed some students' papers as examples of good work? What about when he asked students to raise their hands to indicate whether they got something right or wrong on written assignments? Was he in violation of the law when he had students work problems at the board in front of their peers? Charles made a mental note to call the legal advisor to the teachers' organization the next day to get some answers to these questions.

Analysis of "Would You Check These Papers for Me?" Is it an invasion of privacy when a student checks or corrects a peer's school work? Charles may very well be in violation of the Buckley Amendment when he allows students to grade classmates' papers. Part of the Family Educational Rights and Privacy Act (commonly referred to as the **Buckley Amendment**) prohibits schools from releasing information about a student to third parties without parental or student permission. This ruling suggests that teacher practices such as permitting students to grade or correct other students' papers, reading aloud or posting grades, and asking students to raise their hands if they responded correctly or incorrectly to a problem violate students' rights to privacy, potentially causing students embarrassment or shame (Chase, 1976). To learn more about the Family Educational Rights and Privacy Act, visit the web site of the Electronic Privacy Information Center.

 ## What Are Teachers' Rights and Responsibilities?

Teachers enjoy a number of rights also extended to students. For example, they may be excused from saluting or pledging allegiance to the flag if such actions violate their beliefs and commitments. However, as with students, there are times when teachers' constitutional rights must be considered in light of important educational goals. Because of the nature of their jobs, teachers usually are held to higher standards of behavior than are ordinary citizens (Imber & van Geel, 1993). The scenarios that follow examine some of the issues decided by the courts in this delicate balance between teachers' rights as citizens and their rights as state employees. The scenarios also suggest some of the responsibilities inherent in teachers' jobs, particularly with regard to student safety.

▶ To Join or Not to Join

Megan beamed when she received a contract from the Detroit public schools in July. Although her college advisor had warned her that it might be midsummer or later before anyone heard about their job applications, Megan had been on pins and needles since graduation. For as long as she could remember, Megan had wanted to be a teacher. Now she also had school loans to repay, so she needed to be employed as soon as possible.

> **Do teachers have to pay dues to teachers' unions if they are not members?**

A few days after signing her contract, Megan received a letter from the Detroit Federation of Teachers (DFT) describing the benefits of belonging to the professional association and the cost of joining. Megan tossed the letter in the trash, deciding that she would wait until she had some financial stability before spending money she didn't have. During the first week of school, a representative of the DFT announced at a faculty meeting that those who had not paid dues to the DFT needed to do so or risk being dismissed from their jobs. Megan was confused. Perhaps she had misunderstood the announcement. Surely nonmembers of the DFT would not be required to pay dues.

Analysis of "To Join or Not to Join."   Can teachers who are not union members be required to pay dues to the organization? Federal law recognizes teachers' constitutional rights to advocate, organize, and join a teacher union. In many states, teachers also have the right to engage in collective bargaining, a procedure for resolving disagreements between employers and employees. Teachers negotiate with their school boards, usually through their union representative, about such issues as contract hours, salaries, and fringe benefits. There are no constitutional guarantees that school boards must bargain with teachers' unions, however, so restrictions on the scope of bargaining vary greatly from state to state.

By 1991 about 80 percent of public school teachers belonged to either the National Education Association (NEA) or the American Federation of Teachers (AFT). At the same time, more than half of the states had laws requiring nonmembers of unions to pay dues to the union as a condition of employment. Several Supreme Court rulings uphold the constitutionality of such laws. In a case (*Abood* v. *Detroit Board of Education*) heard in 1977, Christine Warczak and a number of other teachers challenged a Michigan law requiring teachers who had not become union members within 60 days to pay an amount equal to union dues or face discharge. The teachers argued that because they did not believe in collective bargaining or agree with union activities unrelated to collective bargaining, such a law violated their right to freedom of association as guaranteed in the First and Fourteenth Amendments. The Supreme Court disagreed, noting that union activities benefit every employee, union member or not, thus all should share the cost of the union's collective bargaining activities. The Court also decided, however, that it was a violation of First Amendment rights to require public employees to support financially a union's political activities.

In 1984 the Supreme Court clarified this last portion of the *Abood* decision by ruling in *Ellis* v. *Brotherhood of Railway, Airline, and S.S. Clerks* that a union's non-political publications, conventions, and social activities are sufficiently related to the union's work in collective bargaining to justify the charging of nonunion members for such services. Litigation expenses not involving the negotiation of agreements or settlement of grievances, or charges for general organizing efforts, however, cannot be charged to dissenting employees. In its 1986 ruling in *Chicago Teachers Union, Local No. 1 AFL–CIO* v. *Hudson,* the Supreme Court also stated that unions must explain the basis for the dues amount, allow a prompt opportunity to contest the fee before an impartial decision maker, and hold in escrow disputed amounts until the parties reach consensus (Fischer, Schimmel, & Kelly, 1995).

▶ There's Got to be a Way to Keep This Job!

Sandra Allen, a second-year teacher, loved her teaching job. With the exception of two or three students who had difficulty controlling their actions, her class was well behaved and motivated to learn. Most students consistently completed assignments on time, and their work was accurate and neat. Sandra knew that parents had been ambivalent about their children having the "new" teacher at school, but their comments during parent conferences indicated that they, too, were pleased with their children's academic progress.

When Sandra received notice in May that she would not be rehired for the upcoming academic year, she felt shocked and angry. Because her principal's midyear evaluation rated Sandra as "above average" or "outstanding" in all categories, Sandra had assumed that her contract would be renewed. She needed only 1 more year of teaching in the system to earn tenure. Surely the school board could not force her out of the system without giving her reasons for doing so, or could it?

Analysis of "There's Got to be a Way to Keep This Job!"   Sandra's story is much like that of David Roth, an assistant professor of political science at Wisconsin State University–Oshkosh, who was hired for a fixed term of 1 academic year. When Roth was notified at the end of the academic term that he would not be rehired for the following year, he went to court, claiming that the decision infringed on his Fourteenth Amendment rights. In ruling on *Board of Regents of State Colleges* v. *Roth* (1972), the Supreme Court disagreed with Roth's charge, explaining that a probationary teacher does not have the same rights as a tenured teacher.

According to the Court, tenured teachers may not be removed from their positions without specific or good cause, nor may they be dismissed for capricious or arbitrary reasons (e.g., political beliefs and activities). Thus, tenured teachers have a property interest meriting due process protection. In most states, however, the contract of a teacher with probationary status can be terminated at the end of the year (state statute generally specifies a date by which teachers must be notified of such action) without cause. This means that a probationary teacher maintains property interest only for the duration of a 1-year term. However, if the probationary teacher can present evidence to suggest that nonrenewal is in retaliation for exercise of constitutional rights (e.g., freedom of speech), the employer must follow due process (Essex, 1999).

If the school board resorts to **dismissal** (removing a probationary or tenured teacher before the completion of his or her contract), the board must provide a notice, hearing, or notification of reasons for dismissal. State statutes typically list broad causes for dismissal, such as incompetency, immorality, unprofessional conduct, and neglect of duty. Lack of funding and a decline in student enrollment may also be just cause for the midyear dismissal of both tenured and nontenured teachers (La Morte, 1999). Many state laws also stipulate that nontenured teachers must be dismissed before tenured teachers, and, among tenured teachers, the least experienced must be dismissed first.

▶ A Line Between Personhood and Professionalism

Jason O'Hara enjoyed his most-popular-teacher status at Baker Middle School. Students, parents, and colleagues respected him for his innovative ideas, sharp wit, and ability to interest students in learning. Now in his fourth year of teaching, Jason had tenure in the school system and was chair of the English department.

> **Can a teacher be dismissed for private conduct?**

When Jason received a note from John Wright, the principal, requesting that he come to the office that afternoon, Jason thought nothing of it. Mr. Wright had been very supportive of Jason and his efforts to upgrade the English curriculum. As he stepped through the office door, however, Jason knew that something was amiss. Mr. Wright, a grim look on his face, handed Jason a two-page letter addressed to the superintendent. The letter, written by a teacher with whom Jason had had a brief homosexual relationship the year before, made explicit the nature of their relationship. Jason read it in stunned silence.

"Jason," said Mr. Wright, "this letter was also mailed to members of the school board. Several of them are really uptight about this. They want to dismiss you for immoral behavior. I think this is going to be an ugly battle. I'll do everything I can to help you, but I think you also need legal assistance. Do you have a good lawyer?"

Analysis of "A Line Between Personhood and Professionalism"

Can a teacher be dismissed for private conduct? As noted in Chapter 2, teachers in earlier times were held to rigid codes of conduct. Those who crossed the line between moral and immoral behavior resigned or were dismissed immediately from their teaching duties. In recent times, however, the line of demarcation has blurred because it is often difficult to get community consensus about what constitutes immoral conduct. Moreover, many educators believe that when the school day ends, what occurs in the privacy of their homes is their own business and should not affect negatively their status as professionals. Those who disagree argue that being a private person does not relieve educators of their duty to serve as role models for children.

Ambiguity about what constitutes moral and immoral behavior is reflected by court decisions in different states. In making employment decisions based on a teacher's sexual orientation, courts usually consider "the adverse effect on students or fellow teachers, adversity anticipated within the school system, surrounding circumstances, and possible chilling effects on discipline" (Alexander & Alexander, 1998, p. 611).

Depending on public reaction to Jason's case, then, he may or may not be dismissed from his teaching position. In 1969 the California Supreme Court heard a case (*Morrison* v. *State Board of Education*) involving a teacher, Marc Morrison, whose circumstances were much like those of Jason. When the superintendent received a letter from a male teacher who had been involved sexually with Morrison the year before, the school board voted to dismiss Morrison on grounds of immoral and unprofessional behavior. The court disagreed with the school board's actions, saying that the board's definition of immoral behavior was dangerously vague and could implicate many educators. Ruling in favor of Morrison, the court also stated that disapproval of an educator's private conduct was insufficient reason for dismissal, particularly when there was no proof that the educator's professional work was affected negatively by the conduct.

However, eight years later in *Gaylord* v. *Tacoma School District No. 10* (1977), a case heard by the supreme court of Washington, the court upheld the dismissal of a teacher who admitted his homosexuality to the vice principal of the school. Based on the fact that at least one student and several teachers and parents had challenged the teacher's fitness to teach, the court held that the teacher's continuance in the system would likely disrupt the educational process.

Such cases end differently in different localities because the U.S. Supreme Court has not yet recognized a constitutional privacy right to engage in homosexual behavior. Based on the 1984 ruling in *National Gay Task Force* v. *Board of Education of Oklahoma City,* however, teachers have the right to advocate publicly for legalization of homosexuality as long as such activity is not disruptive to the educational process. As indicated in the 1984 ruling in *Rowland* v. *Mad River Local School District,* advocacy does not include talking with co-workers about personal sexual preferences or those of students. In this case, an Ohio guidance counselor who had been dismissed by the school board for admitting her bisexuality to several members of the staff argued that her First and Fourteenth Amendment rights had been violated. The Court disagreed, saying that the guidance counselor's statements were not protected by the First Amendment because they were not made as a citizen on matters of public concern; rather, the counselor's statements were a matter of private concern. Furthermore, the court held that, absent evidence that heterosexual employees had been or would be treated differently for discussing sexual preferences, nonrenewal of the counselor's contract did not violate the Fourteenth Amendment (Essex, 1999).

▶ What Do You Mean I'm Violating Copyright Laws?

During summer vacation, Robert Wells, the newly appointed chair of the mathematics department at Central High, videotaped a two-part series on "Mathematics in Today's Workplace" and added it to his growing collection of tapes. Robert's students had responded well to his occasional use of a videotape to illustrate concepts being taught in class. He believed that these newest tapes would be especially effective in the spring, when math analysis students planned projects showing real-life applications of mathematics.

As he thought about the upcoming inservice program he would conduct for department members, Robert also realized that his videotapes might be an excellent tool for helping others think about ways to vary instruction. Excited by the prospect, Robert contacted Dorothy James at the media center to see if she would make copies of his videotapes and place them on reserve in the school library. When Dorothy asked Robert if he had permission to

What constitutes fair use?

videotape the copyrighted television programs, he was caught off guard. "What do you mean?" Robert said. "I'm using these tapes for teaching purposes. Lots of people do that. What's the big deal?"

"I used to think it was okay myself," said Dorothy, "but now I'm not so sure. I'll call central office and see what I can find out. Until we know, we'd better not copy any of those videotapes."

Analysis of "What Do You Mean I'm Violating Copyright Laws?" Can teachers videotape television programs and use them for educational purposes? Although the Supreme Court has not decided whether it is illegal for teachers to tape television broadcasts on home video recorders for later classroom use, 1981 congressional guidelines for off-the-air taping suggest that such activities may in fact constitute copyright infringement. Guidelines specify that copyrighted television programs may be videotaped by nonprofit educational organizations but that videotapes must be destroyed or erased after 45 calendar days if the institution has not obtained a license for such videotaping. Teachers may use the videotapes with students at school, or with students receiving homebound instruction, one time during the first 10 school days after recording occurs. One additional showing is allowed during the 10-day period, but only for instructional reinforcement. Additional use is limited to evaluation of the videotape's usefulness as an instructional tool (McCarthy, Cambron-McCabe, & Thomas, 1998).

In *Encyclopedia Britannica Educational Corporation* v. *Crooks* (1982), a New York federal district court found a school system guilty of violating fair use standards by engaging in extensive off-the-air taping and replaying of programs broadcast on public television. The court found that such taping interfered with the marketability of producers' films. In 1984, in *Sony Corporation of America* v. *Universal City Studios,* the Supreme Court ruled that personal videorecording for the purpose of "time shifting" (recording of a program for later viewing), however, did not harm the television market (McCarthy, Cambron-McCabe, & Thomas, 1998).

Until the Supreme Court decides whether home taping for broader viewing by students in classrooms constitutes fair use of copyrighted materials, teachers are well advised to adhere to congressional guidelines. Another option, of course, is to seek written permission from copyright owners to videotape programs for classroom use.

The Internet offers an exciting array of motion media, music, text material, graphics, illustrations, and photographs for educational purposes. When incorporating others' electronic materials in multimedia projects, however, teachers and students are obligated to act responsibly. The same level of care is expected when using print materials from textbooks, magazines, and other sources. To learn more about copyright as applied to multimedia, visit the University of Virginia's Copyright Guidelines site on the Web.

▶ Maybe She Is Just a Sickly Child

Theresa chose a desk near the back of the room, not near anyone in particular. She was quiet and somewhat plain in her dress, but her long brown hair was striking. Joan Mason didn't know much about 8-year-old Theresa because Theresa had just moved to town in August. Her permanent records indicated that she was above average in ability. While she had missed a lot of school last year, her grades were about average, maybe a little low in math.

Another parent told Joan that Theresa's mother had been divorced last year and had moved here, at least in part, to get away from her former husband. The family— Theresa's mother and her younger sister; a man she called Jim, whom she described as her mother's friend; and Jim's 17-year-old son—lived in a small ranch house in a nice neighborhood on the outskirts of town.

As Joan worked with Theresa the first few weeks of school, Theresa seldom missed a day of school and kept up with daily assignments. By mid-October, however, things had begun to change. Theresa's attendance became sporadic, and Joan noticed that Theresa often was passive and uncommunicative, both with Joan and with classmates. During seatwork, Theresa chewed her fingernails, her constant gnawing sometimes drawing blood. When Joan talked with Theresa's mother during a parent conference, she did not seem overly concerned by Joan's observations. She indicated that Theresa's behavior at home had not changed and attributed Theresa's recent absences and withdrawn manner to her tendency to be a "sickly child." After the conference, Joan still worried about Theresa, but she didn't know what to do.

What about this situation concerns you? What, if anything, would you do if you were Theresa's teacher?

Analysis of "Maybe She Is Just a Sickly Child." Educators, unlike physicians, social workers, and law enforcement officers, have a unique opportunity to monitor students' social behaviors, academic progress, and attitudes over time. Some patterns of behavior, especially sudden, dramatic changes, can be a warning sign of something gone awry in a child's life. Teachers need to be particularly alert to patterns of behavior that could indicate that a child is the victim of abuse or neglect.

As defined by the Child Abuse Prevention and Treatment Act, child abuse and neglect include physical or mental injury, sexual abuse or exploitation, negligent treatment, or maltreatment (1) of a child younger than 18 years of age (unless state law specifies a younger age), (2) by any person responsible for a child's welfare, (3) under circumstances that harm or threaten a child's health or welfare.

Sexual abuse is defined as

> [(1)] the employment, use, persuasion, inducement, enticement or coercion of any child to engage in, or assist any other person to engage in, any sexually explicit conduct (or any simulation of such conduct) for the purpose of producing any visual depiction of such conduct, or (2) rape, molestation, prostitution, or other form of sexual exploitation of children, or incest with children. (U.S. Department of Health and Human Services, 1999)

As noted in Chapter 7, abuse can occur at any socioeconomic level to both males and females. In every state, educators must report cases of abuse or neglect resulting in physical injury to a child, and, in the majority of states, educators must report instances of emotional, mental, or sexual abuse. Failure to report suspected abuse and neglect constitutes a misdemeanor in most states and, with a few exceptions, teachers are identified among the professionals required to make such reports. Certain behaviors or signs occurring repeatedly or in combination may cue an educator that child abuse is present in a family (see Table 11.1).

▌ **TABLE 11.1**
Signs of Child Abuse

Signs of Physical Abuse

Consider the possibility of physical abuse when the child:

- has unexplained burns, bites, bruises, broken bones, or black eyes;
- has fading bruises or other marks noticeable after an absence from school;
- seems frightened of the parents and protests or cries when it is time to go home from school;
- shrinks at the approaches of adults; or
- reports injury by a parent or another adult caregiver.

Consider the possibility of physical abuse when the parent or other adult caregiver:

- offers conflicting, unconvincing, or no explanation for the child's injury;
- uses harsh physical discipline with the child; or
- has a history of abuse as a child.

Signs of Emotional Maltreatment

Consider the possibility of emotional maltreatment when the child:

- shows extremes in behavior, such as overly compliant or demanding behavior, extreme passivity or aggression;
- is either inappropriately adult (parenting other children, for example) or inappropriately infantile (frequently rocking or head-banging, for example);
- is delayed in physical or emotional development;
- has attempted suicide; or
- reports a lack of attachment to a parent.

Consider the possibility of emotional maltreatment when the parent or other adult caregiver:

- constantly blames, belittles, or berates the child;
- is unconcerned about the child and refuses to consider offers of help for the child's school problems; or
- overtly rejects the child.

Signs of Neglect

Consider the possibility of neglect when the child:

- is frequently absent from school;
- begs or steals food or money from classmates;
- lacks needed medical or dental care, immunizations, or glasses;
- is consistently dirty and has severe body odor;
- lacks sufficient clothing for the weather;
- abuses alcohol or other drugs; or
- states that there is no one at home to provide care.

Consider the possibility of neglect when the parent or other adult caregiver:

- appears to be indifferent to the child;
- seems apathetic or depressed;
- behaves irrationally or in a bizarre manner; or
- abuses alcohol or other drugs.

Signs of Sexual Abuse

Consider the possibility of sexual abuse when the child:

- has difficulty walking or sitting;
- suddenly refuses to change for gym or to participate in physical activities;
- demonstrates bizarre, sophisticated, or unusual sexual knowledge or behavior;
- becomes pregnant or contracts a venereal disease, particularly if under age 14;
- runs away; or
- reports sexual abuse by a parent or another adult caregiver.

Consider the possibility of sexual abuse when the parent or other adult caregiver:

- is unduly protective of the child, severely limits the child's contact with other children, especially of the opposite sex;
- is secretive and isolated; or
- describes marital difficulties involving family power struggles or sexual relations.

Source: Reprinted with permission from *Educators, Schools, and Child Abuse,* by D. D. Broadhurst, © 1994, by permission of the publisher, Prevent Child Abuse America, Chicago, Illinois.

State statutes specify procedures for reporting child abuse or neglect. Many localities also have school board policies and procedures to encourage effective reporting of suspected child abuse. Under the Child Abuse and Neglect Act, educators are assured immunity from civil liability if reports of abuse and neglect are made in good faith.

▶ You Should Have Known Better

Two teachers organized a trip to a museum of natural history for a group of about 50 students ranging in age from 12 to 15 years. When they arrived at the museum, students divided into small groups to tour the museum without supervision. One student, Roberto Mancha, of his own volition joined a group and proceeded with them to the various exhibits. While out of his teacher's sight, Roberto alleged that he was accosted by a group of youths not connected with the school, beaten by them, and as a result suffered serious injuries. In *Mancha* v. *Field Museum of Natural History* (1972), Roberto's father initiated action against the school district, the two teachers, and the museum for the injuries suffered by his son at the museum.

Were the teachers negligent? Should they have been expected to supervise students at all times?

Analysis of "You Should Have Known Better."   Suits brought by students injured during school-related activities are the most common type of litigation in education (Imber & van Geel, 1993). A teacher who demonstrates **negligence** (failure to exercise reasonable care to protect students from injury) may be held liable for damages if an injured student can prove the following:

1. the teacher had a legal duty to offer a standard of care that would have prevented the injury from occurring,

2. the teacher did not live up to the standard of care,

3. the teacher's carelessness resulted in harm to the student, and

4. the student sustained an actual injury that could be measured in monetary terms (Imber & van Geel, 1993).

When accused of negligence, a teacher can try to prove that a student's injury was a mere accident, that her action or inaction was not the cause of such injury, and that some other act intervened and was the cause of the injury. Other rejoinders against negligence include contributory negligence, comparative negligence, and assumption of risk (Alexander & Alexander, 1998).

Contributory negligence occurs when the student who was injured failed to exercise the required standard of care for his own safety. When this condition exists, depending on such things as a child's age and mental maturity, the teacher may be absolved from liability. A high school student, for example, who has been taught how to use a power saw and observed to determine that she can operate the machine safely may be guilty of contributory negligence if injured while removing a piece of wood from the machine with her hands—a violation of safety practices that the students have been taught.

When can a teacher be sued for negligence?

What are teachers' responsibilities toward children's health and safety? If one of these children were to be injured by another child during recess, can the teacher supervising the playground be sued for negligence?

In situations in which teacher and student are both held liable for an injury, there may be a charge of **comparative negligence.** Generally, this means that a teacher is held accountable for a proportion of damages commensurate with the degree to which he contributed to the injury. **Assumption of risk,** rarely applicable except in cases of competitive athletics, means that people who are aware of possible risks involved in an activity voluntarily participate, thus agreeing to take their chances.

In *Mancha* v. *Field Museum of Natural History* (1972), an Illinois court dismissed charges of negligence brought against the school, museum, and teachers. Although the lower courts viewed the teachers' action of letting students tour the museum in an unsupervised group as an intentional act, given the nature of the environment (a museum), it was not an act that teachers should have anticipated would result in harm to a student. In explaining their verdict, the court argued that a museum is very different from a factory, a stone quarry, or a place where there might be dangerous machinery, or a place where there might be a shooting or an assault:

> The Museum in question is itself a great educational enterprise which enables teachers, parents, and children to learn much that could be learned at school. . . . To say that the teachers had a duty to supervise and discipline the entire Museum trip would be to ignore the realities of the situation and to make such trips impossible. (*Mancha* v. *Field Museum of Natural History,* 1972, p. 902)

However, there have been several cases in which students were injured and educators were found to have breached duty of care:

- A group of students with mental retardation were left unattended for a half hour, and a student received an eye injury when another pupil threw a wooden pointer (*Gonzalez* v. *Mackler,* 1963).

- A student who was permitted to wear mittens fell while climbing on a jungle gym (*Ward* v. *Newfield Central School District No. 1,* 1978).

- A student was burned when she and her peers were working on a project for the science fair. The accident occurred when the students tried to light a defective burner that had gone out, and alcohol exploded. Although the teacher had set up the experiment and checked to see that it worked properly, the teacher was not in the room when the students lit the burner. Because the students were not advised to wait until the teacher's return to light the fire and were not personally supervised, the teacher was held liable for negligence (*Station* v. *Travelers Insurance Co.*, 1974).

What Are the Rights and Responsibilities of School Districts?

Although the courts have consistently asserted that the authority for public education resides in the state legislature, schools for the most part are locally administered. As mentioned in Chapter 6, school boards deal with a variety of educational issues and problems. A number of court cases, in conjunction with federal and state statutes, have clarified the special responsibilities and rights of local school boards.

▶ Balancing Academic Freedom

The school board meeting raged on for several hours. Three English teachers from the high school and a number of parents voiced their opinions about the list of texts used in elective high school literature courses. When the board voted to eliminate 10 texts from the diverse list of 1,285 books, the teachers were enraged. They believed that all the books were necessary components of a curriculum designed to stimulate debate and broaden student knowledge. Viewing the board's action as an invasion of their First Amendment right to academic freedom, the three English teachers decided to seek legal counsel. They could not believe that a local school board had ultimate authority to determine what textbooks would be used in schools.

> **Do school boards have the power to ban textbooks?**

Analysis of "Balancing Academic Freedom." Since the U.S. Supreme Court ruling in *Hazelwood School District* v. *Kuhlmeier* (1988), the Court has indicated a willingness to allow local school boards the final decision regarding the curriculum and the availability of books, films, and materials in elementary and secondary classrooms. However, if school boards' actions contract rather than expand knowledge, judicial intervention is not uncommon (Alexander & Alexander, 1998). When deciding individual cases, the courts usually consider the educational relevance of controversial material, teaching objectives, and the age and maturity of the intended audience.

In *Virgil* v. *School Board of Columbia County, Florida* (1989), the Supreme Court upheld a local school board's right to remove two readings from the curriculum because of objections to the material's vulgarity and sexual explicitness. Although the Court did not endorse the decision, stating that they seriously questioned how young people could be harmed by reading the masterpieces of Western literature, the Court acknowledged that the school board's decision was reasonably related to "legitimate pedagogical concerns." That is, as in *Hazelwood,* school officials considered the emotional maturity of the intended audience when determining the appropriateness of readings dealing with potentially sensitive topics (Alexander & Alexander, 1998).

How much freedom does a teacher have in the selection of material for her students? In 1989 a Fifth Circuit Court of Appeals ruling held that teachers cannot assert a First Amendment right to replace an official supplementary reading list with their own list of books without first getting administrative approval. Nor may teachers delete parts of the curriculum that conflict with their personal beliefs. A kindergarten teacher, for example, who refuses to teach a unit on patriotic topics may be dismissed by the school board for not covering prescribed material (La Morte, 1999).

Teachers do have freedom in selecting teaching strategies, however. Teachers who want to assign controversial materials may usually do so as long as the selected materials are relevant to the topic of study, appropriate to the age and maturity of the students, and unlikely to cause disruption. When a high school psychology teacher in a conservative Texas community was fired for having her students read a masculinity survey from *Psychology Today,* the court ruled that the school violated the teacher's constitutional rights. In the eyes of the court, there was no evidence that the material caused substantial disruption, and there was no clear, prior prohibition against the use of such materials (Fischer, Schimmel, & Kelly, 1995).

▶ Equal Treatment

Fifteen African American preschool and elementary students living in a low-income housing project in Ann Arbor, Michigan, brought suit against the board of education

Voices

On Teachers' Freedom of Speech

Court cases such as *Boring* v. *Buncombe Co. Board of Education* (1998) help define teachers' freedom of speech. In this case a high school drama teacher in Buncombe County, North Carolina, was punished for producing Lee Blessing's *Independence,* a play about a dysfunctional, single-parent family that includes a divorced mother and three daughters. One adult daughter is a college professor and a lesbian, a second adult daughter is pregnant and unwed, and the third child is a high school senior who gave up her illegitimate child for adoption several years earlier.

The drama teacher informed her principal of the play's title, and she sent home scripts with the cast of four students. None of the actresses' parents complained, then or later, about the content of the play. At a regional competition, the production won 17 of 21 awards. Prior to the state competition, the four girls performed one scene in an English class. Although English students were to obtain permission

slips from their parents, one viewer apparently did not do so. The student's parent complained to the principal about the play, and the principal censored portions of the script. (The production still won second place in the state competition.) When the drama teacher received her end-of-the-year evaluation, it was very positive. Just a few days later, however, the superintendent approved the principal's request that the drama teacher be transferred to a junior high school, where she would teach introductory drama.

The drama teacher regarded her transfer as retaliation for her play selection and a violation of her First Amendment rights. Three federal courts ruled on the drama teacher's lawsuit. In an **en banc** hearing—a proceeding involving all judges—the U.S. Court of Appeals for the Fourth Circuit ruled 7 to 6 in favor of the school board's decision. Judge Widener wrote the majority opinion:

for practices they claimed denied them equal educational opportunities. According to the students, their language (African American English) differed from standard English that was spoken by teachers and used in written materials of the school. The students claimed a violation of Title 20 of the U.S. Code, which provides that no state can deny individuals educational opportunities due to their race, gender, or national origin by failing to overcome language barriers that might inhibit learning (*Martin Luther King, Jr., Elementary School Children* v. *Michigan Board of Education*, 1979).

Analysis of "Equal Treatment."   Are school boards legally obligated to make special provisions for students who speak "black English"? In its 1954 landmark decision *Brown* v. *Board of Education of Topeka, Kansas,* the Supreme Court addressed for the first time issues of educational inequality when it repudiated the "separate but equal" doctrine, attempting to put an end to racial segregation in schools. As the courts worked, and continue to work, to effect unitary school systems, many have questioned the quality of educational opportunities for minority-group students in such settings. One area of concern has been classification of students for special services. Sometimes courts and legislatures have directed attention to discriminatory classifications of minority-group students; in other situations, such as those involving linguistic minority-group students, the courts have addressed the absence of student classifications.

Plaintiff's selection of the play *Independence,* and the editing of the play by the principal, who was upheld by the superintendent of schools, [do] not present . . . matter[s] of public concern and [are] nothing more than an ordinary employment dispute. That being so, plaintiff has no First Amendment rights derived from her selection of the play *Independence.* . . .

Although the concept of academic freedom has been recognized in our jurisprudence, the doctrine has never conferred upon teachers the control of public school curricula. . . .

The question before us is not new. From Plato to Burke, the greatest minds of Western civilization have acknowledged the importance of the very subject at hand and have agreed on how it should be treated. . . . Someone must fix the curriculum of any school, public or private. In the case of a public school, in our opinion, it is far better public policy, absent a valid statutory directive on

the subject, that the makeup of the curriculum be entrusted to the local school authorities who are in some sense responsible, rather than to the teachers, who would be responsible only to the judges, had they a First Amendment right to participate in the makeup of the curriculum.

As stated by the majority: The only issue in this case is whether a public high school teacher has a First Amendment right to participate in the makeup of the school curriculum through the selection and production of a play. We hold that she does not.

CRITICAL THINKING

Do you think this court's decision might have a chilling effect on a teacher's willingness to be innovative? Why or why not?

Source: Boring v. *Buncombe Co. Board of Education,* 136 F.3d 364 [124 Ed.Law Rep. [56]] (4th Cir. 1998). Available online: http://lw.bna.com/lw/19980303/952593.htm

In *Lau* v. *Nichols* (1974), the only Supreme Court decision involving English-deficient students, the Court held that a school district receiving federal aid must provide special instruction for non-English-speaking students whose opportunities to learn are restricted because of language barriers. This particular case centered around the plight of about 1,800 Chinese American students in San Francisco public schools who spoke little or no English yet were offered no remedial English language instruction or other special compensatory program by the school system. According to the Court, such treatment of students violated Title VI of the **Civil Rights Act of 1964,** which specifies that no one, regardless of race, color, or origin, can be discriminated against or denied participation in programs receiving federal assistance.

Following *Lau,* Congress offered further protection to students when it passed the **Bilingual Act of 1974,** amended in 1988. This act calls for parental involvement in the planning of appropriate educational programs for children with limited English-speaking ability. Neither the Bilingual Act nor Title VI, however, specifies what types of programs are appropriate for addressing the needs of students with limited English-speaking abilities. Types of assistance offered to students who have difficulty understanding standard English vary greatly from state to state.

Since the *Lau* ruling, many cases have been heard by the courts, one of which was *Martin Luther King, Jr., Elementary School Children* v. *Michigan Board of Education* (1979). As described above, African American students who protested the use of standard English as the sole medium of instruction brought this suit before the court.

In ruling on the case, the Court acknowledged that Michigan schools had provided special assistance to these and other students through learning consultants, a speech therapist, a psychologist, a language consultant, tutors, and parent helpers. Evidence existed of good faith efforts to meet the needs of students who spoke black English. The Court noted, however, that teachers seemed to lack knowledge about black English and thus were restricted in their ability to educate African American students. To remedy this, the Court did not order the establishment of a bilingual program, as was done in the Lau case. Instead, the Court required the school board to develop a plan whereby teachers would learn to recognize the home language of students and to use that knowledge to teach reading skills and standard English more effectively.

▶ How Could You Let This Happen to a Student?

When Peter graduated from high school, he sought $500,000 in damages from the San Francisco Unified Schools for failing to provide him with an adequate education. According to Peter, the school system was at fault for his poor skills because it had (1) failed to apprehend his reading disabilities, (2) assigned him to classes in which curricular materials were not geared to his reading level, (3) allowed him to pass from grade to grade without seeing that he mastered basic skills necessary for success at succeeding levels, (4) assigned him to teachers who did not know how to meet his learning needs, and (5) allowed him to graduate without being able to read at the eighth-grade level as required by the Education Code. Moreover, Peter said that his mother had been told that his reading ability was not much below the school's average.

Are schools liable for educational malpractice?

Given the sequence of events, can the school system be held liable for educational malpractice?

Analysis of "How Could You Let This Happen to a Student?"   Although teachers and educational institutions have historically been exempt from legal responsibility and accountability, increasing numbers of educational malpractice claims have forced the courts to deal frequently with issues of academic negligence. A precedent-setting case occurred in California in 1976, when Peter W., the high school graduate described above, accused the school system of negligently and intentionally depriving him of basic skills.

The state appellate court dismissed Peter W.'s suit, contending that there were no explicit "standards of care" by which schools or classroom teachers could be judged negligent in their duties. Besides conflicting ideas about the best way to educate students, the Court noted that there were a variety of physical, neurological, emotional, cultural, and environmental factors that influenced learning yet were beyond a classroom teacher's control. In addition, the Court reasoned that attempts to hold school districts to a "duty of care" in academic matters would likely result in a flood of malpractice suits that would only inhibit their ability to discharge their academic functions (*Peter W. v. San Francisco Unified School District,* 1976).

For the most part, the California court's decision has been followed in educational malpractice litigation. However, in instances when educators have maliciously or intentionally caused injury to children by furnishing false information about a child's learning problems and altering information to cover their actions (*Hunter* v. *Board of Education of Montgomery County,* 1982) or placing a child in a program despite scores showing a placement to be inappropriate (*B.M. by Berger* v. *State of Montana,* 1982), courts have allowed parents to bring action against school officials (La Morte, 1999).

▶ Somebody Will Pay!

Christine Franklin, a 10th-grade student, felt uncomfortable around Andrew Hill, a sports coach and economics teacher at her high school in suburban Atlanta. According to Christine, Hill sexually harassed her by doing such things as asking if she would be willing to have sex with an older man, calling her at home to ask her out, and forcibly kissing her on the mouth in the school parking lot. During Christine's junior year, things got much worse; on at least three occasions, Hill allegedly pressured her into having sex. When Christine reported Hill's actions to school officials, they took no immediate steps to curtail Hill's behavior. By the time Christine had lodged a complaint with the U.S. Education Department's office for civil rights, however, Hill had resigned and the school had adopted a grievance procedure to avoid future violations.

Still angry about the abuse she had suffered at the high school, Christine decided to sue the school district for monetary damages. She argued that Hill's behavior toward her violated Title IX (a law prohibiting schools supported with federal monies from discriminating on the basis of gender). In school officials' eyes, Christine didn't stand a chance in court; they had resolved the problem and it was unlikely to occur again.

Can students who are victims of sexual harassment sue for damages?

Can students who are victims of sexual harassment and other forms of sex discrimination sue for monetary damages?

Analysis of "Somebody Will Pay!" In 1992, when the Supreme Court heard Christine Franklin's case (*Franklin* v. *Gwinnett County Public Schools*), the Court ruled unanimously that Christine had suffered sexual harassment. Furthermore, the Court stated for the first time that schools supported by federal funds were susceptible to lawsuit and, in instances of sexual harassment and other forms of sex discrimination, liable under Title IX for monetary damages to the victims of such mistreatment. Because *Franklin* was about a teacher's harassment of a student, some lower courts concluded that the Supreme Court's decision did not apply to student-to-student harassment. With *Davis* v. *Monroe County Board of Education* (1999), however, this assumption was proved erroneous.

LaShonda Davis, on whose behalf the recent case was filed, was only 10 years old when a classmate, G. W., sexually harassed her by touching her breasts and genitals, telling her he wanted to have sex with her, and rubbing up against her. Despite LaShonda's complaints to teachers, no one intervened on her behalf. One teacher even refused for more than 3 months to let LaShonda change seats, so she could distance herself from G. W. in the classroom. Only after LaShonda's mother filed a criminal complaint against G. W., alleging sexual battery, did the harassment stop. Concerned by her daughter's declining grades and a suicide note, LaShonda's mother next filed a lawsuit against the district, alleging that Title IX had been violated.

Benchmarks

Selected Supreme Court Cases on School-Related Issues

1943	*West Virginia State Board of Education* v. *Barnette*. Requiring students to salute or pledge to the American flag becomes unconstitutional.
1963	*School District of Abington Township* v. *Schempp*. Prayer and Bible reading in public school classrooms become unconstitutional.
1969	*Tinker* v. *Des Moines Independent School District*. Students do not lose their constitutional rights and freedoms when they pass through the schoolhouse door.
1971	*Lemon* v. *Kurtzman*. States may not provide direct aid for secular services to parochial schools, including teacher salaries and instructional materials.
1974	*Lau* v. *Nichols*. School districts receiving federal aid must provide special instruction for non-English-speaking students whose opportunities to learn are restricted because of language barriers.

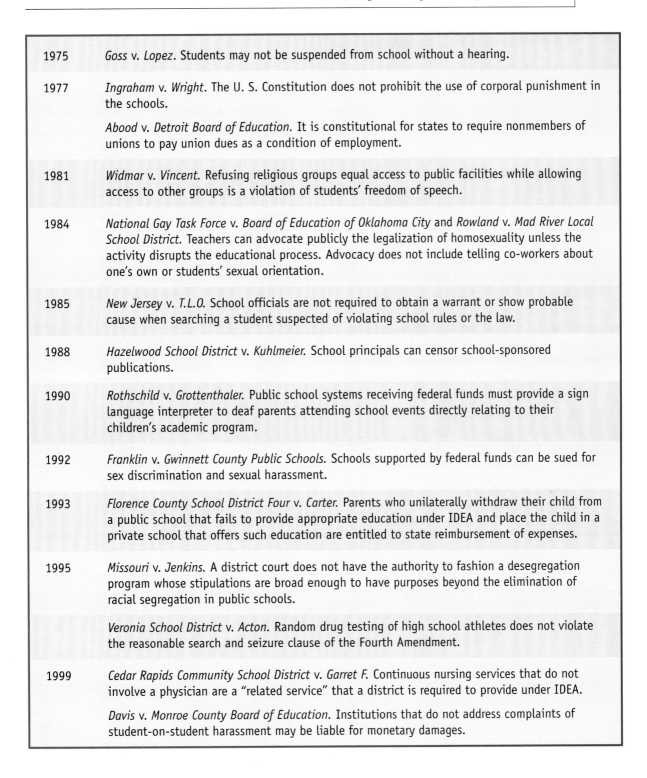

1975	*Goss* v. *Lopez*. Students may not be suspended from school without a hearing.
1977	*Ingraham* v. *Wright*. The U. S. Constitution does not prohibit the use of corporal punishment in the schools.
	Abood v. *Detroit Board of Education*. It is constitutional for states to require nonmembers of unions to pay union dues as a condition of employment.
1981	*Widmar* v. *Vincent*. Refusing religious groups equal access to public facilities while allowing access to other groups is a violation of students' freedom of speech.
1984	*National Gay Task Force* v. *Board of Education of Oklahoma City* and *Rowland* v. *Mad River Local School District*. Teachers can advocate publicly the legalization of homosexuality unless the activity disrupts the educational process. Advocacy does not include telling co-workers about one's own or students' sexual orientation.
1985	*New Jersey* v. *T.L.O.* School officials are not required to obtain a warrant or show probable cause when searching a student suspected of violating school rules or the law.
1988	*Hazelwood School District* v. *Kuhlmeier*. School principals can censor school-sponsored publications.
1990	*Rothschild* v. *Grottenthaler*. Public school systems receiving federal funds must provide a sign language interpreter to deaf parents attending school events directly relating to their children's academic program.
1992	*Franklin* v. *Gwinnett County Public Schools*. Schools supported by federal funds can be sued for sex discrimination and sexual harassment.
1993	*Florence County School District Four* v. *Carter*. Parents who unilaterally withdraw their child from a public school that fails to provide appropriate education under IDEA and place the child in a private school that offers such education are entitled to state reimbursement of expenses.
1995	*Missouri* v. *Jenkins*. A district court does not have the authority to fashion a desegregation program whose stipulations are broad enough to have purposes beyond the elimination of racial segregation in public schools.
	Veronia School District v. *Acton*. Random drug testing of high school athletes does not violate the reasonable search and seizure clause of the Fourth Amendment.
1999	*Cedar Rapids Community School District* v. *Garret F.* Continuous nursing services that do not involve a physician are a "related service" that a district is required to provide under IDEA.
	Davis v. *Monroe County Board of Education*. Institutions that do not address complaints of student-on-student harassment may be liable for monetary damages.

Issues in School Reform

Charter Schools

In the 1990s, concepts of *charter schools,* publicly funded alternatives to existing public school systems, began to appear as devices to promote educational reform. Advocates have described charter schools as opportunities to escape state regulation that controls K–12 public schools, thus freeing educators to concentrate on innovative ways to produce student learning. Legislatures in 35 states have passed laws to lift public school regulations for charter schools, while limiting the number and nature of charters that can be granted. Charters, proponents argue, will operate more as private schools left free to rise or fall on their merits and less as heavily subsidized public bureaucracies intent on their own preservation.

The Center for Education Reform (2000), an organization that promotes charter schools, describes how some 1,700 of them differ from traditional public schools:

Accountability: Charter schools are held accountable for how well they educate children in a safe and responsible environment, not for compliance with district and state regulations. They are judged on how well they meet the student achievement goals established by their charter, and how well they manage the fiscal and operational responsibilities entrusted to them. Charter schools must and do operate lawfully and responsibly, with the highest regard for equity and excellence. If they fail to deliver, they are closed.

Choice: Parents, teachers, community groups, organizations, or individuals interested in creating a better educational opportunity for children can start charter schools. Local and state school boards, colleges and universities, and other community agencies interested in fostering innovation and excellence in schools sponsor them. Students choose to attend, and teachers choose to teach at charter schools.

Autonomy: Charter schools are freed from the traditional bureaucracy and regulations that divert a school's energy and resources toward compliance rather than excellence. Instead of jumping through

Reversing the decision of the U.S. Court of Appeals for the 11th Circuit, which in 1998 ruled that institutions have no obligation to address complaints of student-on-student harassment, the Supreme Court held that schools can in fact be held liable for monetary damages if they are deliberately indifferent to known sexual harassment (Williams, 1999).

▶ What Kind of Choice Is This?

When the special education teacher and Anita Leopold met at the end of second grade to construct Miranda Leopold's IEP, they agreed that Miranda was at a point where she could benefit academically and socially from interactions with regular education students. Accordingly, they created a plan that would allow Miranda to be mainstreamed into a regular third-grade classroom. With the exception of daily tutorial sessions with a resource teacher, Miranda would experience the regular curriculum for third-grade students.

procedural hoops and over paperwork hurdles, educators can focus on setting and reaching high academic standards for their students.

The jury is still out on whether charter schools will yield improved student performance or models of practice to be emulated by others. There is little doubt, however, that charter schools and other simultaneous efforts to reform public education have often contributed to confusing, contradictory public policy. Frederick Hess (1999) has argued that the special case of urban school reform in particular has created what can best be described as "policy churn." Instead of stimulating improvement of student performance in public schools, charters and other reform initiatives have frequently served to legitimize poor educational practice in urban school districts.

By embracing reform, policy makers recognize public dissatisfaction with urban school performance and promise that improvement is around the corner. Not only are districts pursuing an immense number of reforms, they recycle initiatives, constantly modify previous initiatives, and

adopt innovative reform A to replace practice B even as another district is adopting B as an innovative reform to replace practice A.

The collective exercise of reform has become a spinning of wheels. More and more energy is expended in an effort that goes nowhere. Like a car stuck on a muddy road, urban school districts have not benefited from simply spinning the wheels more and more rapidly. (1999, p. 5)

Discussion Questions

1. Find out whether the community you live in has any charter schools. How many are there and what are their goals? Compare the charter schools in your community with those of your classmates' communities.

2. Discuss the advantages and disadvantages of accepting a first teaching position in a charter school rather than a regular public school.

Source: Spinning wheels: The politics of urban school reform, by F. M. Hess, 1999 (p. 5). Washington, DC: Brookings Institution Press and the Center for Education Reform's web page: http://www.edreform.com/pubs/chglance.htm

Anita liked her daughter's new placement. When she learned, however, that Miranda also qualified for the Milwaukee Parental Choice Program, she didn't know what to think. One of the private schools on the choice list focused on art and music, both of which Miranda loved. The idea of sending Miranda to such a school appealed to Anita. When she phoned the school for information about the program, however, Anita learned that the choice school had no resource teacher to help Miranda with her reading skills. Anita was perplexed. Didn't choice schools have to offer the same services to students with disabilities as did the public schools? How could state taxes be used for educational programs that, in a sense, discriminate against certain students? Are choice schools held to the same standards as public schools?

Analysis of "What Kind of Choice is This?"   On March 3, 1992, the Wisconsin Supreme Court voted 4 to 3 to overturn a court of appeals ruling that the Milwaukee Parental Choice Plan (MPCP) was unconstitutional. Established in March 1990, the Choice Plan allowed up to 1,000 low-income students in Milwaukee to receive a voucher worth $2,500 each year to attend certain private, nonsectarian schools in the city. According to Shirley S. Abrahamson, one of the dissenting Justices, the majority opinion on this issue "permits the legislature to subvert the unifying, democratizing purpose of public education by using public funds to substitute private education for public education without the concomitant controls exerted over public education" (*Davis* v. *Grover,* 1992).

In 1995, the legislature approved a budget proposal initiated by Wisconsin Governor Thompson that would expand the program to include religious schools and 15 percent of the public school population, or roughly 15,000 students. Thompson's proposal was immediately challenged by the Milwaukee Teachers' Education Association and the American Civil Liberties Union. In 1998 the Wisconsin Supreme Court upheld the constitutionality of the revised MPCP, which at the time provided vouchers of $4,400 to some 1,500 children (Walsh, 1998).

What Miranda's mother needs to realize when determining which school her daughter will attend is that private schools in the MPCP are not held to the same standards as public schools. As Barbara Miner (1998) noted, under Milwaukee's plan, private schools do not, for example, have to obey the state's open meetings and records laws; do not have to hire certified teachers or even require teachers to have college degrees; do not have to administer statewide tests required of public schools; and do not have to release publicly data such as test scores, attendance figures, and suspension and dropout rates. Furthermore, unlike public schools, private schools can control whom they accept and the terms under which students stay enrolled.

Aside from controversy surrounding the inclusion of parochial schools in the MCPC, one of the more contentious issues in Milwaukee involves students with special education needs. Voucher proponents argue that private schools do not have sufficient funding to support these students; thus public schools should be responsible for meeting their needs. Although a private school may constitutionally provide services, such as a sign-language interpreter, they are not required to do so.

SUMMARY

How does government influence education?

1. At federal and state levels, Congress and the state legislatures pass laws that affect teaching and learning. Chief executives enforce these laws. When disagreements arise, the courts interpret the laws.

2. The government also influences education by allocating and appropriating educational funds and setting standards.

What legal principles affect public education?

3. States' legal control over education is authorized by the Tenth Amendment.

4. When educational disputes arise, the parties involved make every effort to resolve differences at the local level. Most cases heard by the Supreme Court of the United

States, the highest court in the land, are cases in which the validity of a state or federal statute is questioned.

What are parents' rights and responsibilities?

5. In many states, parents may exempt their children from attending school if they meet certain requirements for providing education at home.

6. The legality of corporal punishment varies from state to state and district to district.

7. Public schools receiving federal financial assistance must afford special educational assistance to students categorized as having special learning needs.

What are students' rights and responsibilities?

8. As long as the school building is available for use by other noncurriculum clubs, and as long as the school does not sponsor or conduct club meetings, religious clubs are permissible on school grounds.

9. Students cannot be suspended or expelled without due process.

10. School searches must be guided by "reason" and "common sense"; that is, at the inception of the search, there must be reasonable grounds for suspecting that evidence will be found to prove a student is in violation of the law or school rules, and the scope of the search must be reasonably related to the objectives of the search, the age and gender of the student, and the nature of the infraction.

11. School officials can censor school-sponsored student-produced material that they consider inconsistent with the educational mission of the school.

12. Schools can institute dress codes.

13. Schools cannot expel students with disabilities for behavior attributable to their disabilities; however, schools may temporarily suspend students with disabilities who exhibit behavior dangerous to self or others.

14. Schools cannot release information about a student to third parties without parental or student permission, except in the event of an emergency.

What are teachers' rights and responsibilities?

15. Teachers may be required to share in the cost of the union's collective bargaining activities even though they do not belong to the union.

16. Tenured teachers cannot be dismissed without specific or good cause. Teachers with probationary status, however, generally have no constitutional right to due process when their contract is terminated at the end of the school year.

17. The Supreme Court has not yet recognized a constitutional privacy right to engage in homosexual behavior. Teachers do have the right to advocate publicly for legalization of homosexuality as long as such activity is not disruptive to the educational process. Advocacy does not include talking with co-workers about sexual preference.

18. Until the Supreme Court decides whether home videotaping for broader viewing by students in classrooms constitutes fair use of copyrighted materials, teachers are well

advised to adhere to Congressional guidelines. Another option is to seek written permission from copyright owners to videotape programs for classroom use.

19. Educators must report cases of abuse or neglect resulting in physical injury to a child, and, in most states, educators must report instances of emotional, mental, or sexual abuse.

20. Educators are expected to demonstrate care that a reasonable and prudent person would take when supervising students. When unusual dangers exist, special caution must be employed to prevent injury or harm to students.

What are the rights and responsibilities of school districts?

21. School boards generally have the right to determine curriculum to be taught, even if teachers disagree with the board's decision.

22. School districts receiving federal aid must provide special instruction for non-English-speaking students whose opportunities to learn are restricted because of language barriers.

23. Educational malpractice suits do not fare well in the courts. However, educators cannot maliciously or intentionally injure children by furnishing false information about a child's learning problems and altering information to cover their actions, or by placing a child in a program despite scores showing a placement to be inappropriate.

24. Public schools can be sued for sexual harassment and other forms of sex discrimination.

25. The relationship between public and private schools may be redefined in the future in cases involving the funding of school choice programs.

TERMS AND CONCEPTS

assumption of risk   442
Bilingual Act of 1974   446
Buckley Amendment   433
Civil Rights Act of 1964   446
comparative negligence   442
contributory negligence   441
dismissal   436
due process of law   427

en banc   444
Equal Access Act (EAA)   425
equal protection clause   419
establishment clause   419
free exercise clause   419
in loco parentis   428
Lemon test   426
negligence   441

REFLECTIVE PRACTICE

Lexington, North Carolina, September 26, 1996—First grader Johnathan Prevette is accused of sexual harassment of a classmate. Johnathan kissed a female classmate on the cheek, and the girl's mother charged sexual harassment. The superintendent suspended Johnathan from school.

If Jane Ottinger, a teacher at Lincoln Middle School, had read this headline in her Sunday paper a year ago, she would have believed that it was some kind of cruel joke. Since when did a little boy kissing a little girl become sexual harassment?

But that was before she had lived through what was to become known as the Amy Christopher Incident. Amy was a bright, pretty girl in Jane's sixth-grade class. Mr. and Mrs. Christopher argued that the boys in Amy's class had treated her so badly that she had become an emotional wreck. When the Christophers complained to Jane about the behavior, Jane went immediately to the principal and recounted her conversation with them. The principal said that he would handle the matter and that Jane should be alert to signs of inappropriate behavior but not to worry too much. As nearly as Jane could remember, he said something like, "The hormones begin to rage about this time in kids' lives. Sometimes the boys, and the girls too, get carried away. This is natural. Although the school does not want and would never condone such behavior, you need to understand that some parents are fanatics who blow everything out of proportion. Flirting and teasing are part of life in the sixth grade."

Six months later the Christophers moved to another school district. Their move was accompanied by a front-page story in the local paper, in which they were quoted as saying that they "had complained repeatedly to the teacher and school officials about the sexual harassment of their daughter and other children, but gotten no results."

Now, some four months later, when Jane read the story about little Johnny she felt sad. Had times changed so much since she was a child? Where would all these claims and counterclaims end?

Issues, Problems, Dilemmas, and Opportunities

How do issues such as the Amy Christopher Incident offer opportunities for teaching and learning? How do incidents of possible sexual harassment impede learning?

Perceive and Value

If you were Amy's parents, what might you say to your daughter's teacher and principal if you suspected other children of sexual harassment? If you were Amy's teacher, what would you think of the principal's response?

Know and Act

If you were a teacher faced with a situation like that presented by Amy Christopher, what more would you want to know? Assuming that you reported incidents between students and told your principal about parents' concerns, what more—if anything—might you do? Rank the following activities in the order in which you might undertake them. Explain your reasoning.

- Weave prevention of sexual harassment throughout the curriculum.
- Train peer leaders in awareness and prevention, and use them to teach workshops for other children.
- Provide students with safe avenues to report harassment.

■ Involve parents in lessons and homework on sexual harassment (LRP Publications, 1996a, p. 3).

Evaluate

Examine your own perceptions about sexual harassment. What standards guide your assessment of acceptable and unacceptable behaviors among young people? Examine a school's faculty handbook. Does it mention sexual harassment among students? If so, what does it communicate?

ONLINE ACTIVITY

Use a search engine to find the "Learning Network," a web site developed by the *New York Times* for students, teachers, and parents. Students can read the day's top stories, take a news quiz, write a letter to the editor, or ask a reporter a question. Teachers can read the latest education news, access a daily lesson plan (written in partnership with the Bank Street College of Education in New York City), and access previous lessons from the archive. Parents can join an online discussion and participate with their children in activities in the student section.

12

Global and Comparative Education

We are a country of immigrants. Even though we have slowly and reluctantly begun to recognize some historical native influences, we have been and continue to be shaped by the values and lessons of life that people bring with them to this land. When we slip unconsciously into ethnocentric self-satisfaction, some individual from another country or international group makes us realize that people everywhere share many of the same dreams and fears. The people, cultures, and languages of the world shape our national self-image and influence our collective expectations for schools and teachers.

We use this chapter to explore how education in other countries and cultures compares to education in the United States. We discuss how our educational lives are similar to and different from those lived by people around the world. We look beyond comparisons of educational systems in various nations to consider what values and issues unite people on a global scale.

PROFESSIONAL PRACTICE QUESTIONS

▌ Why should we learn about educational life outside the United States?

▌ What do we know about education in other countries?

▌ How might we enhance understanding of global interdependence?

 ## Why Should We Learn About Educational Life Outside the United States?

From one corner of the globe to the other, people are confronting increasing cultural, economic, political, and social diversity. Progress in transportation and communication systems is compelling people within and between nations to interact with one another in ways never before imaginable. Schools around the world both shape and reflect this diversity by attending to such concepts as multicultural education, intercultural education, cross-cultural education, international education, comparative education, and global studies. Each concept has its own particular definition, but all tend to share the assumptions that human life is interdependent and that such mutual dependence has important implications for how we teach and learn (Cushner, 1998).

It has been estimated that there are some 10 million guest workers or migrant laborers in Europe alone and more than 24 million people around the world who live within the borders of a nation they do not call home (Childers & Urquart, 1994). In 1997, nearly 1 in 10 residents of the United States (25.8 million) was foreign born, and almost 1 in 3 of these foreign-born residents was a naturalized citizen, according to a report released by the U.S. Department of Commerce Census Bureau (1998). When educators plan curriculum, instruction, and assessment for their conception of "typical" students in their systems, and when the populations of these schools change by the addition of even a few students from other nations and cultures, what worked in the past may no longer be appropriate.

▶ To Prepare for the Future

Educators must anticipate the future. To do so with any sense of confidence requires that we learn what others value, how they think, what they are likely to do and not do. As we gain such knowledge, we can enhance our chances to perform our professional roles with sensitivity and intelligence. To learn about the diversity of life today and to imagine what it might be like tomorrow, we have only to look in schools around the world. There we will find the future leaders and followers who in one way or another will affect our own lives.

We can urge ourselves to be more open, less parochial, and more global in our views, but the inhabitants of Newcomers High School in the New York City borough of Queens do so every day. Newcomers High, a school devoted to meeting the special needs of immigrant children, opened its doors to about 60 immigrant students in September 1995. Less than a year later, staff at Newcomers were educating nearly 600 students who spoke some 20 languages and came from more than 40 countries. The world literally comes to the door of Newcomers High.

Imagine what it must feel like to face a group of 30 high school students who have just assembled in the middle of the most populous city in the country. You must be able to communicate with them, to say nothing of being able to teach them. Diversity of language, thought, religion, custom, and values just might stretch a teacher to rethink the meaning of the word *education*. Figure 12.1 contains examples of some major holidays celebrated by students at Newcomers High School.

At Newcomers High School, teachers and administrators try to provide students with the skills necessary to function effectively in mainstream schools and in the larger community. Students participate in an orientation program, for example, that focuses on such basic skills as how to make change and how to use the subway system. To stay competitive with students in mainstream schools, enrollees attend classes in core content areas that are taught in their home languages. For about 9 hours each week, students also attend English as a Second Language (ESL) classes that focus on listening, writing, reading, and speaking skills. In the different classes students work individually and cooperatively on a variety of assignments.

The program at Newcomers High School includes learning opportunities for parents as well. At least one afternoon a week, the school offers ESL classes for parents. Several times during the school year, parents may also attend information sessions that focus on such issues as immigration laws, as well as local, state, and national laws.

The International Baccalaureate Organisation (IBO), a nonprofit educational foundation based in Switzerland, takes another approach to making comparative education relevant to teachers and students around the world. Founded in the 1960s, the IBO grew out of international school efforts to establish a common curriculum and university entry credentials for geographically mobile students. International educators also hoped that a shared academic experience that emphasized critical thinking and exposure to a variety of viewpoints would foster tolerance and intercultural understanding among young people.

The IBO's diploma program for students in their last two years of high school and the middle years program for students ages 11 to 16 are offered in English, French, and Spanish. Both programs seek to enhance international understanding and academic excellence.

The desired profile of the IBO student is that of a critical and compassionate thinker, an informed participant in local and world affairs who values the shared humanity that binds all people together while respecting the variety of cultures

FIGURE 12.1

Selections from An Immigrant Calendar This figure shows major holidays for selected months, celebrated in the countries of origin of New York City's largest immigrant groups. What approach does Newcomers High School take to the education of immigrants?

January

1 New Year's Day
  Independence Day (Haiti)
  Founding Day of Republic of China (Taiwan)
2 Day of the Ancestors (Haiti)
6 Day of the Kings (Dominican Republic)
  Epiphany (Greece)
7 Christmas (Russia)
13 New Year (Russia)
15 Shabebarat (Pakistan)
26 Republic Day (India)
31* Lunar New Year's Day (China, Korea, Taiwan, Vietnam)

February

1* Beginning of Ramadan
5 Constitution Day (Mexico)
21 Martyrs Day (Bangladesh)
23 Anniversary of the Republic (Guyana)
27 Independence Day (Dominican Republic)
28* Fat Tuesday

March

1* Ash Wednesday
  Independence Movement Day (Korea)
2 Eid al Fitr
8 International Women's Day (Russia)
17 St. Patrick's Day (Ireland)
20 Feast of San Jose (Colombia)
21 Benito Juarez's Birthday (Mexico)
23 Pakistan Day
25 Independence Day (Greece)
26 Independence Day (Bangladesh)
29 Youth Day (Taiwan)

April

1 Children's Day (Taiwan)
5 Arbor Day (Korea)
  Tomb Sweeping Day (Taiwan)
9* Palm Sunday
  Day of Valor (Philippines)
14* Good Friday
  Pan American Day
15* Festival of Passover
  Pahela Baishakh-First Day of Bangla Year (Bangladesh)
16* Easter
17* Easter Monday
23* Easter (Russia)
25 Liberation Day (Italy)
27 Holocaust Memorial Day

May

1 Labor Day (Bangladesh, Colombia, Ecuador, Greece, Haiti, Ireland, Italy, Mexico, Philippines, Poland, Russia, Taiwan)
  May Day (China, Pakistan)
  *Orthodox Easter (Greece)
3 Anniversary of the Constitution (Poland)
4 Independence Day (Isreal)
5 Children's Day (Korea)
  Cinco de Mayo-Battle of Puebla (Mexico)
9 Victory Day WWII (Russia)
10 Eid-al-Adha
18 Flag Day (Haiti)
23 Labor Day (Jamaica)
29* Ascension Day (Colombia)
30* Muslim New Year

June

2 Dragon Boat Festival (Taiwan)
4* Whit Sunday
5* Whit Monday (Ireland)
8 Ashura
12 Independence Day (Philippines)
15* Corpus Christi
19 Sacrado Corazon (Colombia)
  Labor Day (Trinidad & Tobago)
26 Ascension del Senor (Colombia)

July

1 Communist Party Anniversary (China)
4 U.S. Filipino Friendship Day (Philippines)
5 Caribbean Day (Guyana)
17 Constitution Day (Korea)
20 Independence Day (Colombia)
24 Simon Bolivar Day

August

1 Army Day (China)
5 National Day (El Salvador)
7 August Bank Holiday (Ireland)
  Freedom Day (Guyana)
  Battle of Bojaco (Colombia)
  Independence Day (Jamaica)
8 Birth of Mohammed
10 Independence Day (Ecuador)
14 Independence Day (Pakistan, India)
15 Feast of the Assumption
  Ferragosto (Italy)
  Liberation Day (Korea)
16 Restoration of Independence (Dominican Republic)
20 Holiday of the Perfect Moment (Bangladesh)
21 Corpus Christi (Colombia)
29 Janmastni (India, Bangladesh)
31 Independence Day (Trinidad & Tobago)

September

6 Defense Day (Pakistan)
8 Chusoc (Korea)
9 Mid-Autumn Festival (Taiwan)
11 Death of Quaid-e-Azam (Pakistan)
15 Independence Day (El Salvador, Guatemala, Costa Rica)
16 Independence Day (Mexico)
24 Virgin de la Mercedes (Dominican Republic)
25* Rosh Hashanah
28 Confucius' Birthday (Taiwan)
30 Republic Day (Trinidad & Tobago)

October

1 National Day (China)
3 National Foundation Day (Korea)
4* Yom Kippur
10 Double Tenth National Day (Taiwan)
12 Columbus Day
17 National Heroes Day (Jamaica)
23 Diwali (India)
25 Taiwan's Retrocession Day (Taiwan)
30 October Bank Holiday (Ireland)
31 Chiang Kai-Shek's Birthday (Taiwan)

November

1 All Saints Day
2 Day of the Dead (Mexico, El Salvador)
5 First Cry of Independence (El Salvador)
7 State Holiday (Russia)
  National Day (Bangladesh)
9 Birthday of Allama Iqba (Pakistan)
11 National Independence Day (Poland)
12 Sun Yat-Sen's Birthday (Taiwan)
13 Cartagena Independence Day (Colombia)
30 National Heroes Day (Philippines)

December

5 Discovery of Haiti (Haiti)
12 Virgin de Guadalupe (Mexico)
  Constitutional Day (Russia)
16 Victory Day (Bangladesh)
18* First Day of Chanukah
25 Christmas Day
  Shab-e-Maira (Pakistan)
26 Boxing Day
  St. Stephen's Day (Ireland)
30 National Hero Jose Riza Day (Philippines)

*Holiday that occurs on a different date each year.

and attitudes that makes for the richness of life. (International Baccalaureate Organisation, 1996)

The IBO provides numerous services to some 800 participating schools in 100 countries. These include curriculum and assessment development, teacher preparation and information seminars, and electronic networking. As you will note from Figure 12.2, the IBO offers programs suitable for children ages 3 to 19. You can learn more about the IBO at its web site.

▶ To Become Globally Aware

The extent to which students recognize their connections to other countries and people of the world constitutes an estimate of their **global awareness.** Such awareness is important, as Tye and Tye (1992) observe, because the welfare of the United States is tied to the welfare of other countries by economics, the environment, politics, culture, and technology. When there is unusual activity on the New York stock market, people watch to see what effect it will have in Tokyo, Bonn, and London. Acid rain, depletion of the ozone layer, ocean pollution, and disposal of nuclear waste are multinational concerns. The fall of the Soviet Union and reorganization of Eastern

FIGURE 12.2
You can learn more about how the IBO is organized by going to their web site (http:www.ibo.org.uk/ibo/english/index.cfm)

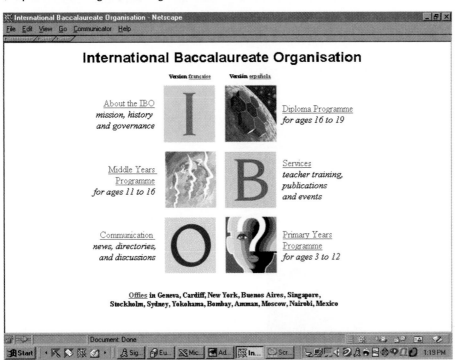

Source: Reproduced with the permission of the International Baccalaureate Organisation.

Europe have had reverberations in military spending, labor policies, capital investment, and, most immediately, in the immigration of children into the classrooms of the world.

As more people travel and work in countries other than those in which they were born, and as more people employ advances in communications technology, the interplay of cultures increases. In some instances increased contact leads to competition and conflict. In other cases, familiarity breeds cooperation, for different people realize that they must work together if they are to survive and prosper. Everywhere, people call on schools to promote technical skills to communicate and wisdom to use these technological skills for enhancing mutual understanding. Schools around the world must help tomorrow's adults learn languages, understand cultures, and use a host of electronic communication systems in order to function in today's world. A global society is no longer the pipedream of the futurist. It is an idea that people define each day as they reach around the world with their computers and fax machines.

Unfortunately it is difficult to discuss global challenges and the potential of modern education without using grandiose language—the kind that glazes people's eyes. Clare Booth Luce—journalist, diplomat, playwright, and politician—once referred to such language as "globaloney." The simple truth, however, is that the implications of joining education and technology on a global scale are nothing short of breathtaking.

Tye and Tye (1992) argue that a global perspective, aided by technology, forces people to consider problems that cut across national boundaries. Educators who think about the world also cultivate students' abilities to decenter and to view the world from others' perspectives. Elise Boulding (1988) noted that this process has occurred naturally for years through voluntary associations referred to as *nongovernmental organizations,* or **NGOs.** These transnational associations—groups such as churches, scouts, farmers, chambers of commerce, physicians, athletes, and

Why is global awareness important? What are some implications of joining education and technology on a global scale?

educators—grew in number from 176 in 1909 to more than 18,000 in the mid-1980s. They all advance agendas that focus on problems and issues of common interest, regardless of national borders.

Futures For Children (FFC) is an INGO (or International NGO) with its home-base in Albuquerque, New Mexico. For more than 40 years the organization has worked to improve the well-being of children and communities by helping people help themselves. For example, they offer leadership programs for young Native Americans in New Mexico, Arizona, North Dakota, and Oregon. The FFC Leadership Program encourages young people to

- work in their communities to discover their leadership abilities;
- carry out projects in their communities;
- build relationships with adults whom they respect;
- choose and achieve a fund-raising goal to assist the next group of students; and
- meet and share experiences on a regular basis.

FFC also collaborates with four sister organizations that work in more than 150 communities in Central and South America. The FFC counselors and volunteers build schools, hospitals, roads, bridges, water sanitation systems, latrines, and wells and offer cholera prevention education programs, agricultural improvements, and small business development in Medellin, Colombia; Tegucigalpa, Honduras; San Jose, Costa Rica; and Oaxaca, Mexico.

For educators to enlarge their views of the world, or to think globally and encourage their students to do the same, the basic curriculum and instruction in most schools must change. Change with regard to a school's attention to global education must overcome a number of obstacles or competing demands. Historically, school leaders have not considered global perspective to be very important. Teachers' limited time is already devoted to existing curricula, standardized testing, and accreditation demands. Leadership is essential if people are to attend to global issues.

When a critical mass of educators thinks globally, they can make global thinking come alive for students. For example, in one school—along with engaging in regular activities, such as using library materials and listening to guest speakers—teachers and students instituted a simple set of special projects and materials:

- a set of folk literature, poetry, and music from around the world for grades 1 and 2;
- a collection of books dealing with cultural commonalities among families of the world for grades 7 and 8;
- an endangered species unit for the middle grades;
- a special global education section in the school library; and
- an all-school display of "Our Earth" that represented interdisciplinary work at all grade levels (Tye & Tye, 1992).

Not only do teachers and interesting curricula foster attention to global issues; money and jobs also fuel interest in international and worldwide issues. Business leaders have been among the more vocal parties in encouraging schools to think

Voices

On Teaching Abroad

Sheryl Cohen and Jennifer Post, U.S. and Canadian citizens respectively, were colleagues at the Colegio Bolivar in Cali, Colombia. The school, a prekindergarten through 12th-grade private, bicultural, bilingual American school, enrolls nearly 1,200 students, the vast majority of whom are Colombian nationals. Sheryl taught third grade; Jenn taught high school English. Both have recently resumed their careers in the United States and Canada. Why did they decide to teach in Colombia? How were their experiences both disappointing and rewarding?

JENN: I had been teaching in Canada for 8 years and felt like I needed new challenges. I had always traveled, but I wanted to be more than just a tourist for a couple of weeks. I also wanted to live and work in a non-English-speaking country.

SHERYL: I was burned out after 5 years of teaching in an inner-city Los Angeles school. I had just enrolled in a master's program at Pepperdine and turned 30—I needed a change. I also wanted to improve my Spanish and

Sheryl Cohen

learn more about the Spanish culture. I went to a job fair, and the principal from Colegio Bolivar sold me on the school.

JENN: My first year, I had problems with differences between the culture I was used to and my new Colombian culture. For example, my conceptions of truth, fairness, and sharing differed greatly from those of my students. I thought students were cheating, they thought they were sharing. I had to build into my teaching strategies techniques to minimize shared work so I could get an account of what an individual knew independently of the group.

Classroom management also differed from Canadian schools. The idea of quiet work did not exist. My students talked all the time—constant mumbling. What I perceived as rudeness, they perceived as normal. I never felt as though I bonded with my students, largely because they saw me as an outsider, which, of course, I was. They did not confide in me, and I missed that in students.

I loved the idea of rising to the challenge in Colombia. Creative writing

globally, for they view schools as vital to the production and maintenance of the workforce that will be called upon to compete in a wider world.

An example of one state's commitment to the connection between schooling and competitiveness in the global marketplace can be found in South Carolina. The state established special schools to train workers, free of charge, for any company that agrees to create new jobs in the area. Workers with no experience learned to use the metric system, computers, and blueprints. South Carolina has been unusually successful in attracting internationally owned corporations such as Michelin and other European high-end machining and high-technology manufacturing firms. BMW, the forty-sixth German company to invest in South Carolina's Spartanburg County, employs 2000 workers and represents an $800 million investment.

For what kind of future should schools in the United States prepare students?

The real challenge for American public education is to educate workers today for careers and jobs they will fill tomorrow. In other words, educators

was especially exciting. The natural poetry of the Spanish language helped my students be excellent writers. The quality of work done by second-language learners in my traditional introductory British literature class was incredible. I could see that my Colombian students were far better prepared to work in the global marketplace than are my Canadian students. The material I covered at Bolivar was much more difficult than I can cover in Canada.

SHERYL: While the opportunity was there to work with others on my grade level, I felt isolated from teachers above and below me. For example, I remember how much my third-grade students liked my reading of *Charlie and the Chocolate Factory*. When a fourth-grade teacher found out I was reading the book, she really got upset. She was going to teach it to my students the following year, and she thought I had destroyed the chance for her to motivate them. I had no idea of what she or the other teachers in fourth grade taught. This was different from my experience in Los Angeles schools.

Despite the lack of communication across grade levels, my creative freedom as an elementary teacher in Colombia was unlimited. I could try new programs, new techniques; my principal always encouraged and supported me. I had only 16 children in my class. I gave

Jennifer Post

my students a lot of personal attention—I knew them very well. My kids were much more affectionate than my students in the United States. The younger children were particularly affectionate, but that changed as they grew older. Even though the official language of instruction was English, my Spanish improved dramatically. A child would come to me and say in Spanish "I want to say [something] in English" so I told them how to say it. We talked in Spanish about how to talk in English. While my kids in LA spoke Spanish at home and at school, I did not teach in Spanish, nor did I encourage them to use their Spanish. My own Spanish wasn't good enough, and it was always a struggle to find resources to support ESL speakers. In Cali, a city that was not a tourist destination, the minute I walked out of the school gate, my world was in Spanish.

CRITICAL THINKING

What challenges did Sheryl Cohen and Jennifer Post encounter when working with students and colleagues in Colombia? What unexpected opportunities arose during their teaching experiences in Colombia?

Note. From S. E. Cohen & J. Post, personal communications, April 10, 1996.

must identify and teach knowledge and skills now, in hopes of preparing students for a future they can only vaguely imagine. If you were asked to identify knowledge and skills deemed critical for today's students to master, what would you say?

What Do We Know About Education in Other Countries?

The concept of **international comparative education** suggests that (1) problems of educational development are common in many societies, and (2) by studying education in different societies, educators develop new insights into these societies, and they also derive innovative understanding of their own society (Thomas, 1990). The discourse in the United States on multicultural education, for example, has been framed in purely American terms. International comparative perspectives have largely been missing. The United States, however, is not the only country that has experienced the phenomenon of being home to a diversity of cultural groups within its national borders. Nor is the United States the only country addressing problems that arise from close interaction among diverse cultural groupings. In many instances, the problems Americans face are not unique to U.S. society. People in other countries face them too, often with considerable success. Their experiences can help us reflect on our own assumptions and actions in ways that would be impossible without a point of comparison.

With the North American Free Trade Agreement (NAFTA), the General Agreement on Tariffs and Trade (GATT), the European Union (EU), and other multinational pacts, multicultural understanding becomes increasingly important for all people and all nations. Indeed, the ancient Greeks recognized the importance of learning about and from others. For Plutarch, people who studied life's lessons wherever they found them demonstrated their strength of character. Thucydides suggested that people who learn from others may prepare themselves to avoid some of life's pitfalls and to capitalize on success.

▶ Education in Canada

In 1995, the rebellion of French-speaking Canadians, centered in Quebec, nearly split the country in two with a secession vote. Yet we Americans appeared inured to the troubles of our best trading partner and most trusted military ally. One wonders if we could pass a multiple-choice quiz on basic facts on Canada. If asked, could we explain why the propagation of culture through schooling matters so much in Canadian society?

What makes the propagation of culture through schooling a problem in any country?

Canada's land mass makes it the second largest country in the world. Its economy is diverse and successful. Nearly two-thirds of the population live in metropolitan areas along the border with the United States. Some 60 percent of Canada's population live in 2 of its 12 provinces and territories—English-speaking Ontario and French-speaking Quebec. Until recently, Canada had one of the highest birth rates in the industrialized world. Canada has been a refuge, a home for immigrants from around the world (Fowler, 1998).

Although Canada is a federal state, provincial governments control education. Canada has neither a national system of education nor a central office of education. Each province has its own Ministry of Education headed by an elected minister. In all provinces schools are operated by local boards of education; the degree of decentralization varies across provinces. Both provincial governments and local governmental units fund the educational enterprise. Typically, children start school at age 6 or 7. They must attend for at least 10 years, or until the age of 15 or 16. The organization of school levels (elementary, middle, high) varies by province, with some using a system of 7 years in elementary, 2 in middle, and 3 in high school. Others use a 7–5, 8–4, or, as in Quebec, a 6–5–2 system. The school year runs between 180 and 200 days per year.

Promotion through the elementary grades is more or less automatic. At the secondary level, variation exists among the provinces, but most use the credit system, with children taking varying levels of courses to accumulate credits for graduation. Students in British Columbia, Alberta, and Quebec must pass a graduation diploma examination. Many schools offer general and advanced levels of diplomas. An average of more than 60 percent of high school graduates go on to some form of post-secondary education (Berg, 1995).

The Canadian educational system, like many others in modern economic states, faces the challenges of the information age and an increasingly competitive global economy. Consequently, many Canadian educators recognize the need to improve and make relevant the kind and quality of education young people receive. Movements for teacher accountability, strengthening basic skills education, accommodating increasing cultural diversity, and addressing gender inequality characterize current Canadian education reform.

Because Canada has 12 systems of education, it is not surprising that the response to these demands has been piecemeal. Efforts to define the role of education in a complex society and to determine priorities will consume educators, parents, and government officials into the next century. An estimated two-thirds of the jobs created between 1989 and 2000 will require a minimum of 12 years of schooling, and about 40 percent will require more than 16 years of school (Berg, 1995).

Canadian schools have reflected the cultural similarities among Canadians as well as the deep division that exists between French speakers and English speakers in Quebec. In 1977, Bill 101 was passed into law, with support of the Parti Quebecois, a separatist party in Quebec. The bill established French as the only official language in the province and imposed many restrictions on the use of English or any other language in business and education. French was the only language allowed to be displayed by businesses on outdoor signs. Language police from the Office de la Langue Francaise were appointed to ensure that businesses were not violating the law. A ruling of the Supreme Court of Canada has since eased such restrictions.

Bill 101 had a profound effect on education in Quebec, because all (nonanglophone and even some anglophone) immigrants to Quebec had to attend French language schools. The bill was an attempt by the government of Quebec to preserve the prominence of francophones in the province in the face of the increasing number of immigrants entering the province since 1990, the majority of whom spoke no French. The Montreal Catholic School Commission, which operates more than 300 schools in Montreal, has considered an outright ban on any language but French in its schools. (Public schools in Quebec are designated as either Protestant or Catholic and are supported financially by the government.) This ban would include all school-sponsored activities, as well as speech in the halls and on schoolyards. Offenders would be transferred to other schools, and repeat offenders would be expelled.

If we relied only on the sensational events in Quebec, we would have an unrealistic view of life in the majority of Canadian schools. Most school jurisdictions have developed and now use multicultural curricula, particularly in social studies. The ministries of education, teachers, university professors, and publishers have cooperated to develop learning resources and instruction appropriate for the richness of ethnicity and culture that characterize Canadian schools across all the provinces and territories (Fowler, 1998). You can visit some Canadian schools online by accessing them through the EduNet web site.

Many educators in the United States, particularly those in the West and Southwest, would have difficulty reading about events in Quebec schools without drawing parallels between their situation and the English-only movement in California. How are the positions of students with English as their primary language similar to and different from one another in the two countries? How do the positions of the language-minority students compare in both countries?

▶ Education in Mexico

The images of Mexico we receive from movies, television, and the popular press seem to alternate between extremes: culturally rich, socially warm, and humanly inviting versus stunningly poor, socially archaic, and openly hostile to outsiders. Both suggest that image exists largely in the eye of the beholder.

The United States of Mexico is a country of 31 states that shares its borders with the United States of America, Guatemala, and British Honduras. The nation has one of the highest population growth rates in the world. Population density varies greatly among the states. The capital, Mexico City, and one of its neighboring states account

What effects does the United States have on education in Mexico?

for more than 22 percent of the total population. Mexico City is the second largest city in the world, with 24 million people. Overall the Mexican population is becoming more urbanized: the percentage of the population living in urban areas increased from 42 percent in 1950 to 71 percent in 1990. The Mexican economy has been hit by a series of economic crises in the past several decades that have resulted in a continued and radical uneven distribution of wealth. High expectations surround the signing of the NAFTA agreement, which reduces Mexico's trade barriers with Canada and the United States of America.

Spanish is the official language of Mexico, although more than 93 languages and dialects are present (Reyes, 1995). Nearly 1 million Mexican citizens do not speak Spanish, and 10 percent are illiterate.

Since 1993 the state governments have controlled the running of preschools, primary and secondary schools, and teacher-training institutes, except in the Federal District. This decentralization of power represents a major shift in education policy.

In 1992 the length of compulsory education was increased from six to nine years. The Mexican education system is structured in a 6–3–3 configuration: six years of primary school; three years of lower secondary school; and either passing of an entrance examination to gain entry to three years of upper secondary school (*bachillerato*) leading to a higher education qualification, or transferring to a three- or four-year technical school.

Mexican schools contain a large percentage of overage students in each grade because of students repeating grades and/or dropping out and then re-enrolling in school. Overage students account for up to 30 percent of enrollment in some grades, particularly in the fifth and sixth grades. Because overage students inflate enrollment numbers in elementary schools, pupil–teacher ratios are high, at 30 to 1. Many Mexican students do not advance to the upper secondary school level. According to the 1990 census, only 54 percent of the 20- to 24-year-olds in Mexico had completed ninth grade. Among 40- to 44-year-olds, only 25 percent had completed ninth grade (Reyes, 1995).

David Lorey (1995) has argued that by far the most serious problem at the basic level of education is the high and persistent dropout rate, a consequence of family poverty. "Only about 50% of entering students at any level complete their studies. In rural areas of the country, approximately 75% of school children do not finish the first six years of primary education" (1995, p. 1).

The rapid increase in the number of school-age children has placed a heavy burden on the educational system nationwide. Overall, the emphasis of national basic-education programs has been on access rather than on relevance or quality (Lorey, 1995). There has been a demand to accommodate an additional 500,000 students per year since 1950, although this trend has slowed since the mid-1980s. Since 1978, on average, 42 classrooms have been added to the public education system each day. This expansion of the educational system has not been equal in all regions of Mexico; the northern part of Mexico and Mexico City attain high enrollment ratios, but states in the southeast regions have lower rates (Reyes, 1995). Twenty-three percent of Mexican elementary schools are one-teacher schools, and 15 percent do not offer all six grades. Although accommodations are made for students with special needs, only about 10 percent of such students enroll.

According to Aurora Elizondo Huerta (1999) in 1990 there were about 15 million Mexican Americans, between 2 and 3 million of whom were illegal workers; that number has been increasing by 100,000 to 200,000 each year. In 1990 in Los Angeles

Cultural Awareness

As Marleen Pugach (1998) discovered in her study of life in the pseudonymous town of Havens on the United States–Mexican border, it often takes time, lots of time, for people to accept one anothers' culture. The Latinos of Havens recognize the problem, but they also perceive progress.

This recognition of progress in matters of participation and leadership on the part of Mexican-American and Mexican students is noted with a sense of modest optimism for the future. Both at school and in the community, the shift away from the "old days," when discrimination was everywhere and it was virtually impossible for visible numbers

of Mexican-origin people to get ahead, is greeted quietly, as a long awaited incremental step toward a more just division of power and authority. . . . As the principal of HHS, Daniel Martinez sees the progress but not the eradication of the problem. "As a general rule we all get along well. Both Anglos and Mexicans have been very supportive of me in my job. As a general rule people are good and kind here in Sonora County. I love my community. I love the people I work for and I love the kids I work with. But there will always be some discrimination." (1988, p. 122)

Source: Pugach, M. C. (1998). *On the border of opportunity: Education, community, and language at the U.S.–Mexico Line.* Mahwah, NJ: Lawrence Erlbaum Associates, Publishers.

Latino children represented 63 percent of the total student body. On average, third-grade students scored 500 on the California Assessment Program, while white and non-Latino students scored 614. Eighth-grade Latino students scored 414, and whites and non-Latinos scored 567. Some 45 percent of Latino teenagers who enter ninth grade in California do not graduate. One-third of them drop out of school in the tenth grade. Across the state, the dropout rate for Latinos is double that for whites and non-Latinos.

So how might teachers in the United States increase Latino students' chances for success? Some argue that educators must confront the problem of illiteracy in the home before students can succeed in school. Others favor scaling back or eliminating bilingual education programs to limit Latino students' reliance on Spanish, thus forcing them to learn English. Still others contend that more bilingual programs and intercultural education for all students would help break prejudices held about Latinos, changing how others view them and how they view themselves. Some believe teachers need to encourage Latino students to be more competitive, to concentrate less on skill training and more on the values needed to succeed in the workplace. And these are just a few ideas. The variation among students, however, prohibits simple prescriptions for teaching and learning.

▶ Education in Japan

Critics of American education often hail Japan as an example to be emulated. The Japanese, they argue, demand educational excellence, and they get it. At the same time, others contend that Japan's schools foster conformity and reward obedience. Our knowledge of and feelings about Japanese education most often are mixed.

Japan is a country of more than 3000 islands in East Asia, with a population of more than 125 million. This densely populated country of city dwellers is ethnically homogeneous (with only 1 percent minorities). Tokyo, the capital, is the largest city in the world, with more than 28 million inhabitants.

From the time of its defeat in World War II until 1990, Japan enjoyed extraordinary economic success. Between 1990 and 1994, however, land values fell dramatically and industrial giants, such as Nissan, closed factories, as car production fell about 22 percent. While Japanese citizens struggled with the realities of increasing unemployment and the social problems accompanying it, they continued to place a high priority on the development of a well-educated and skilled populace (Desmond, 1996).

Structurally, the Japanese education system closely resembles the U.S. system. The vast majority of Japanese students attend public schools in mixed-ability classrooms. Unlike the United States, there is no external examination scheme in Japan—no public or private testing service that creates, sells, distributes, and scores a set of examinations common to students across the country. Internal, school-system assessments determine promotion and certification of completion. Students at all levels wear uniforms. They begin school at age 6, attending elementary schools (grades 1–6) with an average pupil–teacher ratio of 20 to 1. After completion of elementary school, students attend a 3-year lower-secondary school, with 50-minute class periods and an average pupil–teacher ratio of 17.4 to 1. Nearly all lower-secondary school students study English as a foreign language.

Although not compulsory, 96 percent of the children who complete lower-secondary school attend upper-secondary school. Some 70 percent of these students attend public school, the remainder pay to attend private schools. In upper-secondary schools, 75 percent of the students pursue a general, academic course of study, and the remainder enroll in specialized (streamed) tracks, such as technology, foreign languages, and computers. Students with special needs can complete secondary school by correspondence. Since 1988, some students with special needs can attend credit-system upper-secondary schools, or schools that award diplomas for courses taken instead of requiring students to pass a graduation examination. Thirty-four percent of Japanese upper-secondary school graduates continue in higher education after passing a competitive entrance examination (Kanaya, 1995).

At the end of the school day, many young people in Japan attend a private after-school class. Classes may be of two types: **okeiko-goto** (enrichment classes in areas such as music, the arts, and physical education) and **juku** (supplementary classes in academic subjects). Together, *juku* and *okeiko-goto* are a multimillion-dollar industry. *Okeiko-goto* often begin during children's elementary years and may continue throughout their lives. *Juku,* however, are taken exclusively during children's elementary and secondary years. *Juku* classes help young people keep up with the demanding school curriculum, provide remedial instruction in areas of weakness, and prepare students for various entrance exams.

Juku range from classes of one to three students meeting in a teacher's home to multiple schools all over the country with dozens of classes at each site. Classes meet two to three times a week and may last two to three hours or more. Unlike teachers in the public schools, *juku* teachers often group their students by ability rather than by grade level. Phases of drill and individual assistance by the teacher also are common in *juku* schools. Some people contend that the instruction young people receive in these settings closes the "sensitive gap" between what is learned in public schools and what students must know to move up the educational ladder (Harnisch, 1994). Presumably, as in other cultures, this gap represents the difference between explicit curriculum (what is set forth for public consumption) and the implicit curriculum (the more subtle but quite powerful adult expectations of student performance). (See Figure 12.3.)

There are different perspectives on what transpires in Japanese public schools. Some reports suggest that schools demand intense rote learning and conformity (Desmond, 1996). Other studies suggest that teachers in the public schools generally function more as facilitators and "knowledge guides" than dispersers of information and facts. Teachers are described as believing that students must construct knowledge, not merely receive it from teachers (Sato and McLaughlin, 1992). Harold Stevenson and James Stigler demonstrate the constructivist approach with the following example of a fifth-grade mathematics class:

> **How does Japan's educational system compare to the U.S. system?**

The teacher walks in carrying a large paper bag full of clinking glass. Her entry into the classroom. . . . by the time she has placed it on her desk, the students are regarding her with rapt attention. What's in the bag? She begins to pull out items, placing them one by one on her desk. She removes a pitcher and a vase. A beer bottle evokes laughter and surprise. She soon has six containers lined up on her

FIGURE 12.3

Is there an American equivalent to *juku*? SCORE! Educational Centers affiliated with the immensely successful Kaplan Educational Centers—the company that brings you preparation courses for the SAT and many other tests—may come close. In the spring of 1999 SCORE! had more than 70 sites across the United States and more on the way each week. These for-profit tutoring centers prepare elementary and secondary students in reading, mathematics, and language arts.

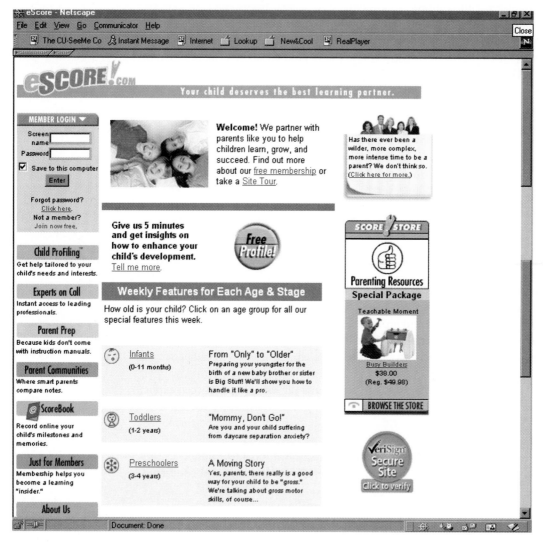

desk. . . . The teacher, looking thoughtfully at the containers, poses a question: "I wonder which one would hold the most water?" This leads to a great deal of experimentation on the part of the students—filling and measuring with buckets and cups of water. Groups of students record their results. Finally the teacher returns to the question she posed at the beginning of the lesson: Which container holds the most water? She reviews how they were able to solve the problem, and points out that the answer is now contained in the bar graph on the board [which she constructed from their results]. (Stevenson & Stigler, 1992, pp. 177–178)

See Table 12.1 for Joel Spring's (1998) perspective on Japanese education.

As Berliner and Biddle (1995) have noted, the mass media frequently compare American public education to Japanese education, resulting in a distorted view of both systems. Many news reports proclaim the Japanese system superior in producing higher achievement among its students. These reports often suggest that Japanese students attend school more days per year than do American students and produce higher mathematics and science test scores. Much emphasis also has been placed on Japanese schools' adherence to national standards that are enforced through nationwide examinations.

But these "facts" can be misleading. When eighth-grade American students' mathematics abilities were compared to their Japanese counterparts who had been exposed to similar curricula, American students' scores were found to match or exceed those of the Japanese students (Westbury, 1992). Although Japanese students spend more days in school than do American students (240 days and 180 days, respectively), the difference in the amount of academic instruction is not profound (Stevenson & Stigler, 1992). A typical school year in Japan includes 65 to 70 afternoons of either free time or nonacademic activities. Three or four days a year also are devoted to cleaning the school (Goya, 1993). Japanese students enjoy longer lunch periods and breaks between classes than do American students. Entrance into upper secondary school requires passing an examination but it is a test of elimination. If

TABLE 12.1
One View of the Attributes of the Japanese Educational Model

Joel Spring (1998) describes the basic elements of the Japanese school system as follows:	8. Mathematics and mathematical thinking are central to the school curriculum. Mathematics provides the language for technical development.
1. The government assumes the role of moral and social educator.	9. Students are taught English along with the national language. The teaching of English is considered essential for the global economy.
2. Nationalism and patriotism are taught in the schools to promote economic goals.	
3. The goal of moral and social education is the virtuous and cooperative worker and citizen.	10. Critical thinking about political, economic, and social issues is constricted by distinctions between education and scholarship and practical learning and moral discourse.
4. Economic development is a major purpose of the school system.	
5. An examination system is used to sort human resources for the labor market.	11. Creativity is considered important for work and not for personal pleasure.
6. Income and status are a function of performance on national examinations.	If, on a scale of 1 to 5, you assume that Japan is a 5 on all items, where would you rate public schools in the United States? Can you explain your reasoning?
7. The examination system controls the curriculum by encouraging teaching to the test and a reliance on private cram schools. Student life centers around exam wars.	

Source: Spring, J. (1998). *Education and the rise of the global economy.* Mahwah, NJ: Lawrence Erlbaum Associates, Inc., p. 65.

there are 300 freshman slots and 304 students apply, the test is given to eliminate 4 students. Passing scores can be as low as 5 percent (Goya, 1994).

▶ Education in India

India, a nation of nearly 1 billion people, in addition to being the world's largest democracy, may be the most culturally and ethnically diverse country in the world. It is in a region known historically for its tolerance of diversity; nonetheless, regional and ethnic tension continue. Because the language of commerce and of instruction in India is English, while more than a dozen regional languages (such as Hindi, Urdu, and Tamil) and local dialects are used in everyday speech in all but the major cities, the nation offers unique opportunities to educate others about diversity. Bilingualism is the norm, and trilingualism is common.

The Indian constitution set forth in 1950 directs the government to provide free and compulsory education for all children up to age 14. It also provides for equal educational opportunity and protection of religious and linguistic minority groups. The school system, which varies from state to state, is generally organized as 2 to 3 years of private kindergarten (beginning at about age 3), followed by 10 years of private or public basic education, perhaps followed by 2 years of private or public higher secondary education, and then perhaps followed by 3 years of tuition-free higher education. School holidays include 20 religious festivals from Hindu, Muslim, Christian, Sikh, Parsi, and Jain traditions.

In 1986 the federal parliament adopted its National Policy for Education and Policy of Action, which have served as the bases for the development of the National Curriculum for Elementary and Secondary Education. The intent of the common core is to cut across subject areas and to promote "India's common cultural heritage, egalitarianism, democracy and secularism, equality of the sexes, protection of the environment, removal of social barriers, observance of the small family norm, and the encouragement of a scientific outlook" (Bordia, 1988, p. 351). In advancing this agenda, the central government makes explicit the need to encourage attention to similarities among Indians, not to exploit their differences.

The realities of schooling in India often vary considerably from the official intent and formal proclamations. The illiteracy rate has more than tripled since independence in 1947, from 15 to 52 percent (Lloyd, 1999). Enrollment rates are greater in the cities than in the rural areas and greater for boys than for girls, especially girls from disadvantaged groups (people of low castes, tribal people, and religious minorities). In 1990 to 1991, the enrollment rate in primary schools was reported as 115 percent for boys and 86 percent for girls (Theobald, 1995). (Boys exceeded 100 percent because under- and overage children attended school.) Theobald notes that enrollment figures are especially important, because they determine the number of teachers assigned, the number of books provided, and the number of classrooms available, all of which typically are insufficient. Nonattending students should be removed from the rolls, but this rarely happens. "Participation is therefore much lower than many of the raw statistics would lead one to believe" (Theobald, 1995, p. 144).

What are the preconditions for universal literacy in any society?

Improvements in Indian teaching methods are difficult to effect, in part because classes often have more than 50 students. Many students are plagued

The KATHA school was founded in a New Delhi, India, slum by Geeta Dharmarajan in 1990. She believes that children's mothers can help their children succeed by becoming empowered themselves. How might this belief be expressed in the KATHA school curriculum?

by poverty (some 45 percent of the people live below the poverty line and another 20 percent barely above it). "[T]he young teacher inevitably succumbs to the advice of older colleagues and settles into a pattern of delivering sermons and a stylized catechism of question-and-answer exchanges" (Taylor, 1991, p. 331).

Life can be especially difficult for women and girls in India, because they have been forced historically to play the role of caregiver and often denied formal education in the process. The KATHA school in Delhi is one example of an organization created specifically to address their problems. Some 600 students—Hindus, Muslims, Christians, Jains, Parsis, and others—learn to work together on common literacy and life skills necessary for survival. The school began as a creche, or nursery for babies. The teachers care for babies and thus free the older girls to get an education in the Girl/Child Program, a program designed to address gender oppression in the slums of Delhi. The mothers come for classes and learn how to cook, bake, and sell their wares to support their families. Teachers provide the women not only with life skills but also with the confidence necessary to earn a living for themselves and their children (McNergney, Regelbrugge, & Harper, 1997).

Indian schools, like schools in the United States and elsewhere, are subject to many outside political pressures. Since the Hindu nationalist Bharatiya Janata Party (BJP) came to power in 1998, a radical Hindu-revivalist movement has promoted the idea of the "Hinduization" of education in India (Lloyd, 1999). In part the movement is an effort to counter the influence of Christian missionaries, who Hindu fundamentalists believe tricked people into conversion. Christians comprise 2.5 percent of India's nearly 1 billion people. Hindus account for 80 percent and Muslims for 12 percent.

One goal of the movement is to rewrite history. For instance, "Did you know that Homer's *Iliad* was actually written by an Indian? Or that the 1947 partition of the Indian subcontinent was part of a Christian plot to divide and conquer Hindus and Muslims?" (Lloyd, 1999, p. A56)

How do struggles over the influence of religion on curriculum play themselves out in public schools in the United States?

Another goal is to institute compulsory courses in Indian values from preschool through graduate school. These would include Hindu religious texts in all syllabi and would infuse education in Indian values and culture at all levels of teacher education.

Critics acknowledge that the schools need to be reformed, but they argue the content favored by the BJP would fuel tensions in India by stripping religious minorities of their constitutional rights. Supporters of the proposed reforms believe they are trying to right past wrongs.

Figure 12.4 shows the home page of a multimedia case study about education in India.

FIGURE 12.4

A Multimedia Case Study of Life in New Delhi Schools You can learn more about education in India's schools from *Project New Delhi: A Multimedia Teaching Case,* available as a CD from Allyn and Bacon Publishers.

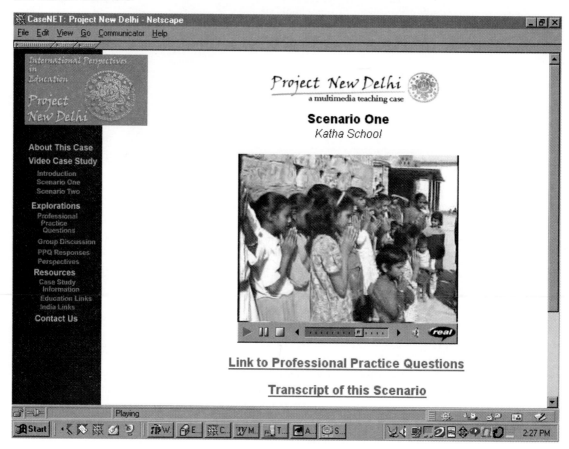

▶ Education in the United Kingdom

Children between ages 5 and 16 in the United Kingdom (England, Scotland, Wales, and Ireland) must attend school. At 16, students take main secondary school examinations. Advanced-level examinations typically follow after two additional years of schooling and constitute the entrance standard for higher education. Publicly supported schools often are called *state schools, government schools,* or *council schools* (run by borough government councils) to differentiate them from the privately funded schools, called *public schools.* (Note the completely opposite meaning of the term *public* as it is used in the United States.)

Schools are organized into two or three tiers. The two-tier system is composed of primary schools (ages 5 to 11), occasionally subdivided into infant (ages 5 to 7) and junior (ages 7 to 11), and secondary schools (ages 11 to 16 or 18), which resemble American comprehensive high schools. The three-tier system, used only in England, consists of first schools (ages 5 to 8 or 9), middle schools (ages 8 to 12 or 9 to 13), and upper schools, which usually are nonselective (ages 12 or 13 to 16 or 18). Churches help operate some primary and secondary schools even though these schools are supported by public funds (Booth, 1988).

How does the existence of a state religion affect education in any country?

The United Kingdom is characterized by great ethnic and cultural diversity. More than half of London's 10 million inhabitants were born outside Great Britain. Immigrant settlement has not been limited to London; many immigrants have settled in other cities, towns, and villages.

Unlike schools in the United States, those in England include religious education (RE) as a core subject. The focus of RE is on the officially established Church of England. With the diversity of cultures and religions in schools, the practice has not been without its critics. In January 1996 more than 1,500 junior school students in 40 schools were withdrawn from RE courses by their Muslim parents ("Muslim parents," 1996). The boycott, one of the largest mass exercises to date, was prompted by parents' concern over the dominance of Christianity in RE syllabuses taught by non-Muslims. Parents worried that their children would receive inaccurate information about Islam and be confused by other faiths introduced in religious classes.

Until recently, the British educational system had a long tradition of noninterference by the central government. In 1988, however, the Education Reform Act emphasized two themes in the education of all students in the British system: back to the basics and the link between education and the economy (Judge, 1989). The act was followed by pressure for a national curriculum and teacher accountability (i.e., the alignment of teaching performance with the curriculum). It also promoted the idea of giving parents a greater voice in managing schools and stimulated the creation of a new system of national compulsory and universal examinations. As Liz Bondi (1991) observed, the shift in mood in the British system from expansion and optimism to one of retrenchment and redefinition has mirrored the mood in the United States. The reasons for this shift have largely to do with demographic changes, public disenchantment, and a shortage of public funds to support education.

The United Kingdom hopes to improve student learning by infusing technology into the curriculum. In Scotland, for instance, national educational guidelines for students ages 5 to 14 resulted in an environmental studies program that actively involves students in problem-solving situations. According to results from a cross-national case-study project sponsored by the Organization for Economic Co-Operation and Development, primary schools implement the technology curriculum in various ways. In one rural school, for example, student tasks include activities such as constructing a lookout tower and observation platform using only recycled materials and designing a model of an earth-moving machine that could clear a level path for a new airport runway. Among teachers' objectives are to make learning practical and to create an interdisciplinary approach that incorporates contributions from teachers of art, design, and home economics ("A Global Revolution," 1996).

As Figure 12.5 illustrates, one way the United Kingdom is taking advantage of technology to advance connections among its own people and with others across Europe is through an online project called Netd@ys sponsored by the European Commission. Students create multimedia projects and link them to the Netd@ys site. Then students and their teachers are encouraged to "meet" one another online and to learn more about participants' communities. In Scotland, for example, students from five primary schools are exploring and describing their local community

FIGURE 12.5
The Eoropean Commission's Netd@ys Web Site

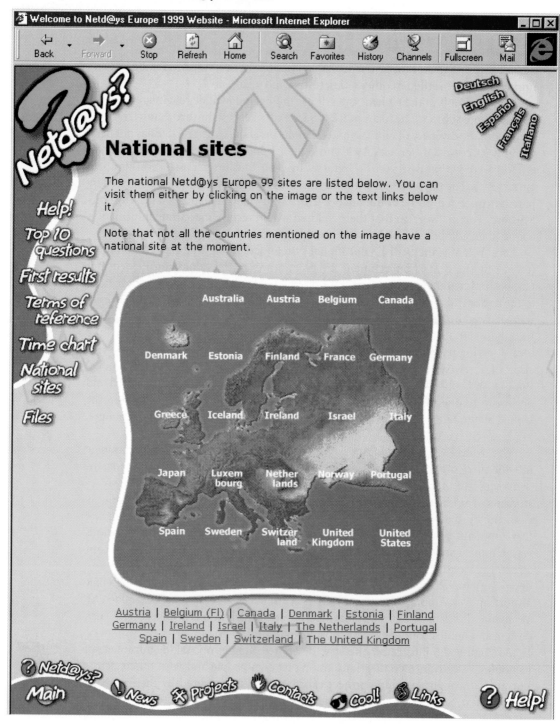

Note: From About Netd@ys. Available online: http://www.netdays99.org/ downloaded 7/22/99
Note: This screen capture has been published by permission of the Eurpoean Commission.

histories. They will partner with students at other geographical locations to learn what they have in common.

It remains to be seen if, when, and how the UK's education system might be affected by its participation in the European Union (EU). At present, the 28 countries in the EU encompass four types of status. The United Kingdom is a full member state. One EU idea that could revolutionize education and employment is the European Personal Skills Card. "The European Personal Skills Card would accredit work skills that were not covered by paper diplomas from schools including vocational schools. In other words, the goal is to bring all workers into a credentialing system" (Spring, 1998, p. 107). The Personal Skills Cards would record people's qualifications—the skills or outcomes of learning and working. As employers across Europe recognize and use these cards, they might promote European unity. The cards might also begin to influence how educators in the United Kingdom design and deliver education.

▶ Education In Denmark

Denmark offers an interesting contrast to the United Kingdom. It is small and has a homogeneous population of slightly more than 5 million. Danish citizens exhibit open, liberal politics and sentiments. They have one of the most highly developed social welfare systems in the world. Immigration is a relatively recent phenomenon in Denmark. Since about 1970, most immigrants have come from Turkey and the Indian subcontinent. Recently, however, people have moved to Denmark from virtually all over the world.

The Danish Ministry of Education takes an activist, interventionist approach to educational and social problems. Yet schools in Denmark have an exceptionally high degree of local control, similar to schools in the United States. The Ministry of Education sets school objectives, but local schools decide how to meet them. Individual schools determine their own curricula, and teachers teach however they please. Highly experienced teachers write the learning materials. There is no control over the scope, sequence, and content of textbooks. While Danish is the first and most important language, English is widely spoken and at a very high level by the well-educated professional classes. Classes taught in English are common at the upper-secondary level.

Education in Denmark is free and compulsory for students from 7 to 16 years of age. Students attend school for 20 more days than U.S. students, but their school day is somewhat shorter. Approximately 90 percent of the students go to the **Folkeskole,** or public school as it is called in the United States. The remainder go to "private" schools supported by the government. Most 3- to 6-year-olds go to kindergartens. For the first 7 years, the Folkeskole teaches all subjects. In grades 8 through 10, the Folkeskole is comprehensive except in mathematics, English, German, physics, and chemistry; students in these courses attend either basic or advanced classes. Grade 10 in the Folkeskole is optional, after which students enter various forms of vocational–technical education and commercial training programs or attend a gymnasium—a higher preparatory course of study.

Evaluation of student progress in Danish schools is quite different from that in other countries. Children do not take end-of-the-year examinations in primary education and receive no grades for the first seven years of compulsory education. Students enrolled in grades 8 through 10 receive marks generally based on a scale of 1 to 10. Students in grades 9 and 10 also take a *leaving examination* at the end of the year. Exams are optional, and there is no cutoff score or minimal mark that a student must receive in order to pass. The relatively casual nature with which examinations are given and used ensures the promotion of most students (Jansen & Kreiner, 1995).

To handle the diversity of student needs in classrooms, the Danish have increasingly relied on special education services. About 12.5 percent of students enrolled in Danish public schools receive special education services; twice as many boys as girls are in this group. Overall, approximately 13 percent of children are referred for behavioral problems, 14 percent for intelligence problems, 6 percent for speech impairments, 7 percent for sensory or physical impairments, and 60 percent for learning problems. The majority of students with learning disabilities receive support in Danish, particularly in reading. Special education services also are extended to adults with physical and mental disabilities (Jansen & Kreiner, 1995).

During their professional training program, future teachers become qualified to teach Danish and two special subjects of their choosing at all levels in primary and secondary education. For this reason, it is possible for Danish teachers, working together in teams, to follow the same group of students throughout their 9 or 10 years in the Folkeskole. The class teacher, or lead teacher, for the team is generally the same person throughout this period of time (Bjerg et al., 1995). The lead teacher is usually a teacher of Danish or mathematics and serves as the primary link between students, parents, and the school (McAdams, 1993).

Students are involved in planning the content of lessons and making decisions about classroom issues. A pupil council at each school makes recommendations to the school board on matters of schoolwide concern. The school board at each Folkeskole includes five to seven parents elected by parents of children enrolled in the school. Two teacher representatives, two students, a member of the municipal council, and the lead teacher participate as nonvoting members of the board (McAdams, 1993).

Like people of other nations, the Danes seek to prepare students to be qualified technically to function effectively in society. They also try to socialize young people to the importance of common moral concepts and social solidarity (Florander, 1988). Like many Western countries, Denmark has lost unskilled jobs in recent years. As a consequence, the Danes are eager to boost the knowledge and skills of citizens to remain economically competitive in the emerging European Union.

For this reason, education of adults is also a priority in Denmark. Evening schools are common, and they cover a wide range of subjects. To reduce the expense of such courses, the state awards a grant to approved evening schools. Educational offerings for adult immigrants are required by the 1990 Open Education Act and are financed through counties' education budgets. Courses focus on Danish language, Danish culture, and Danish social conditions (Jansen & Kreiner, 1995).

Denmark has a long tradition of teaching about international topics. This tradition is understandable, given the size and location of the country. Danish society is generally more internationally oriented than many other, larger countries. The study of international topics occurs in geography, history, and social studies, but also in the teaching of foreign languages, where classes spend some 25 percent of their time. Also, the frequency of teacher exchanges among countries has increased in recent years, largely because of Denmark's Observer Status in the European Union. On an average, 20 Danish teachers have taken part in the teacher exchange program each year since it was established in 1989 (Danish Ministry of Education, 1999).

▶ Education in Singapore

The Republic of Singapore, a city-state on the southern tip of continental Southeast Asia, is considered the world's laboratory for experiments in social engineering. It is a multicultural society, comprising people of Chinese (77%), Malay (14%), Indian (7%), and Eurasian (2%) ancestries. Just under 3 million people inhabit the 231 square miles of Singapore (Gopinathan, 1994). The city-state, with one of the highest living standards in Asia, bills itself as the Switzerland of Asia, the Gateway to the Future. Singapore is a city of business opportunity and a hub of high-tech development. The government tries to assure all citizens that, no matter what their ethnic or cultural background, they are first and foremost Singaporean.

Singapore consists mainly of immigrants and their descendants. While Singapore was a British colony, Singaporean education required English as the language of government and advanced schooling. The system also fostered ethnic segregation and had separate schools taught in Chinese, Tamil, and Malay. Since Singapore's establishment as a republic in 1965, however, life has changed. Today, most tourists to Singapore know that it is illegal to chew gum (actually, it is illegal to import chewing gum) and that extinguishing a cigarette on the sidewalk can draw a large fine. But few realize that the Singaporean educational system has developed innovative approaches to multicultural education. For example, even though Singapore maintains four official languages, the government has unified the English- and non-English-speaking schools (Chinese, Malay, and Tamil) into a single educational system. The unification of schools, undertaken in the late 1950s, was viewed by leaders as an essential ingredient in their strategy to build a nation with its own unique identity.

> **Would other countries' solutions for multilingual education work for the United States?**

By 1968, as a result of a strong family planning program and a large investment in school facilities and teacher education, all children of primary-school age were enrolled in school. In 1973, educational authorities required all students to know English as either their first or second language and to know one other major language of the community. In the 1980s, authorities backed off this overly ambitious goal. Most students try to become bilingual, and many seek the English track as a first choice because of the access it offers to jobs and higher education (Thomas, 1988).

Children begin school at age 6. During their 6 years of primary education, they focus on English, mathematics, their mother tongue (Chinese, Malay, Tamil), music, art and crafts, and physical education. In Primary Six, all students sit for the Primary

Singaporean teachers from Anderson Secondary School work together to develop multicultural curricula for their students. Why are multicultural curriculum and instruction so important to these Southeast Asian teachers?

In Cape Town, South Africa, students leave Queen's Park High School. Their diversity reflects modest progress toward racial integration following the abolishment of apartheid. What educational challenges does South Africa face?

School Leaving Examination (PSLE) and then move on to the next stage of secondary education.

Students spend 4 to 5 years in Secondary School. They take curricula based on their aptitudes and interests. In general, the subjects studied in secondary schools include English, the mother tongue, mathematics, science, literature, history, geography, art, technical studies, home economics, civics and moral education, music, and physical education. At the end of secondary school, students either take examinations that screen them for postsecondary education or training.

Unlike the United States, in Singapore there are close relationships among government, industry, and secondary and postsecondary education. Annual surveys estimate workforce needs, and the schools and informal educational organizations respond with programs to fill those needs. These connections are especially important to a country that has few natural resources and must depend on the talents of its people for its place in the world.

▶ Education in South Africa

In 1996 a court ruled that a white school in an Afrikaner town 180 miles north of Johannesburg had to admit three black students it had tried previously to bar (Associated Press, 1996). In doing so, the court knocked down what many believed was one of the most blatant challenges to South Africa's first constitution that promised equal rights. Nelson Mandela helped establish this constitution and took the lion's share of responsibility for facing such challenges. Now that burden belongs to Mandela's successor, Thabo Mbeki, South Africa's second democratically elected president.

South Africa is one of the most multicultural societies in the world. From 1949 to 1991, the structure of society was shaped by an official policy of **apartheid** (pronounced "a·par·tate" or "a·par·tite"), or separation of the races. This meant that blacks lived in *homelands, black states,* and segregated *townships* outside the major cities. Under apartheid, whites were not allowed to enter the townships without permission, and nonwhites were not permitted to stay overnight in white urban areas without special permission. People had to carry passes at all times. Schools for whites got money, facilities, and teachers, while black schools were, for the most part, neglected.

Although the United States is marked by a history of slavery, it is difficult for most Westerners to imagine how a policy such as apartheid could be justified in recent history anywhere in the world. The former language of apartheid in South Africa, however, must sound hauntingly familiar to western ears: The ultimate goal of apartheid was to create "a mosaic of peoples, each with a separate national identity. They will be politically independent but economically interdependent" (King, 1988, p. 600).

The open challenge to segregated education began in 1976 to 1977 with riots in Soweto, a black township outside Johannesburg (Lemmer, 1993). This revolt was triggered by an attempt to impose instruction in Afrikaans (an amalgam of Dutch, French, German, African, and Malay) instead of English (King, 1988). The apartheid legislation was repealed in 1991, initiating what promises to be a dramatic restructuring of society, including a restructuring of the segregated education system that has supported it. A new constitution was adopted in 1993, opening the door to free elections in which all South Africans may participate. In daily life, however, segregation continues to be reinforced by great disparities in wealth, personal attitudes, and historically separate and unequal education systems.

Almost all South African school systems are organized with 4 years of junior primary, 3 of senior primary, 3 of junior secondary, and 2 of senior secondary. Schools have been oriented toward the western view of a liberal education, that is, students are to be well grounded in history, languages, mathematics, the sciences, and the arts. Teaching typically is teacher-centered, and learning is passive, with a heavy emphasis on rote and academics. As such, education has been perceived as irrelevant to black children, who generally live bleak lives. School is compulsory for whites until age 16, Asians until 15, so-called coloureds (mixed race) until age 14. School attendance is not yet compulsory for black South Africans. Figure 12.6 shows the distribution of students by race.

The white, so-called coloured, and Indian schools use either English or Afrikaans as the primary languages of instruction. Many black students whose mother tongue is not English or Afrikaans, and who are enrolled at these schools, do not have a sufficient command of either language (particularly in secondary schools) to cope with the academic demands made on them.

> If Black students are to cope in languages that are not their home languages, then special programs for accelerating the acquisition of the language used as the medium of instruction at an open school is an urgent necessity. Lack of profi-

FIGURE 12.6
Composition of Primary and Secondary School Enrollment in South Africa, 1995
What student groups are minorities in South Africa? How does minority status differ in South Africa compared to the United States?

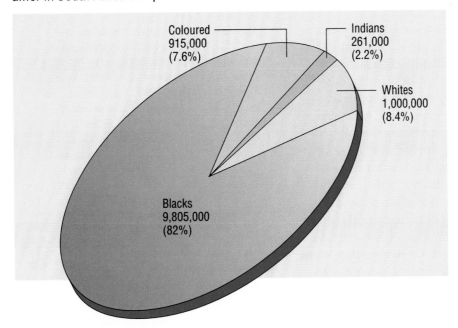

Coloured
915,000
(7.6%)

Indians
261,000
(2.2%)

Whites
1,000,000
(8.4%)

Blacks
9,805,000
(82%)

Source: Statistics: South Africa (1996). Pretoria, South Africa: Statistics Council. Retrieved July 7, 1999, http://www.statssa.gov.za/SABrief/table6.htm

ciency in either English or Afrikaans often results in Black students being regarded as linguistically inadequate. This is obviously a false assumption because a poor performance in a second or third language does not imply general linguistic deprivation. Nevertheless the tendency to make such an assumption affects the teachers' general expectation of the students' chances of success. . . . (Stonier, 1998, p. 229)

For 10 years or more before Nelson Mandela's election, blacks in large numbers boycotted schools and destroyed school property. The morale and authority of black teachers was seriously damaged. Many black students literally forgot how to learn and how to study. Influential black leaders fear that the crisis in education may have cost the nation a generation of young people (Hartshorne, 1990). The government is in the process of reconceptualizing the school system from top to bottom in an effort to clarify the legal status of different categories of schools and to establish national norms and standards for governance, finance, and the effectiveness of schooling (Committee to Review the Organization, Governance and Funding of Schools, 1995). Change cannot be achieved overnight, however. "A very complex system has its own momentum, and the authorities have stated that although it is important to effect changes with all speed, care must be exercised to make certain that the system does not collapse. Consequently, the changes taking place have been

---

Using Technology

South African Students Speak Out

Today in South Africa some black students find themselves in formerly all-white schools. They live in a period of disequilibrium between a stage of apartheid and an ensuing stage of mutual social and educational development, not yet defined clearly in thought or practice. Black, white, and so-called coloured students can be seen in the same buildings, but they are not often seen or heard talking, laughing, or working together outside classrooms. In other words, the system has begun to desegregate, but students within these schools are not yet working and living together as friends.

All students come to school with assumptions and preconceptions about one another. They attend classes together, wear the same school colors, and cheer for school teams. Yet, as a high school senior at Westerford High School explains, students often choose not to associate across racial lines:

Although we have open schools, we still find that the black children sort of group around and form friendships with the blacks, and the same with the coloureds and the white children. And this is not because people set out to exclude themselves. I think because we've been so divided, we don't know enough about each other to understand one another. It is easy to talk about acceptance and tolerance of each other's differences. But if we don't understand each other's cultures, how can we really accept them, let alone respect them?

You can see and hear this young woman speak on the Web in an offering entitled *Project Cape Town: Education and Integration in South Africa*. To find the site, enter the following address: **http://curry .edschool. Virginia.EDU/go/capetown/**

interpreted by some as being too rapid and by others as being too slow" (Stonier, 1998, p. 212).

How Might We Enhance Understanding of Global Interdependence?

People in the United States always seem to be asking, "How are we doing, educationally speaking, compared to people in other nations?" The question too often forces discussion into a descending spiral of invidious comparisons—a series of attempts to make the United States look better, or worse, than other countries by examining students' test scores, dollars spent on education, and other factors. We can foster understanding and interdependence only by making reasonable comparisons and by seeking common conceptual ground.

▶ The Third International Mathematics and Science Study

The Third International Mathematics and Science Study, or TIMSS, is the largest, most comprehensive, and most rigorous study of schools and students ever conducted. During the 1995 school year, some half-million students from 41 nations were assessed at the fourth, eighth, and final year of secondary school. Researchers examined students' mathematics and science achievement by studying schools, curricula, instruction, lessons, textbooks, policy issues, and the lives of teachers and students to understand the educational contexts in which mathematics and science learning occur.

Grade 4 Mathematics and Science Achievement.   Twenty-six nations participated at this grade level. The U.S. students scored above the international average in mathematics and were outperformed by 11 countries, with Singapore in first place. In mathematics, U.S. students' performance exceeded the international average in Whole Numbers; Fractions and Proportionality; Digital Representation, Analysis and Probability; Geometry; and Patterns, Relations and Functions. The U.S. students scored below the international average in Measurement, Estimation, and Number Sense.

In science, U.S. students were outperformed only by Korea and Japan; U.S. fourth-grade students were outperformed by one or two other nations in Earth Science, Life Science, and Environmental Issues and the Nature of Science. In Physical Science, five other nations outperformed U.S. students.

The number of topics included in U.S. textbooks and curriculum guides was at or above the international average in fourth-grade mathematics and slightly below the international average in fourth-grade science.

Grade 8 Mathematics and Science Achievement.   United States students scored below the international average of 41 nations in mathematics; they scored at about the international average in Data Representation, Analysis and Probability, Algebra, and Fractions and Number Sense, and below the international average in Geometry, Measurement, and Proportionality.

United States students exceeded the international average in science; they scored above the international average in Earth Science, Life Science, and Environmental Issues and the Nature of Science. They scored at the international average in Chemistry and in Physics.

The U.S. eighth-grade mathematics curriculum is less focused than that of other countries, based on an analysis of the intended curriculum in each of the 41 TIMSS countries. The U.S. eighth-grade science curriculum more closely reflects international practices.

Grade 12 Mathematics and Science Achievement.   Researchers assessed a sample of all students at the end of secondary school (twelfth grade in the United States) in mathematics and science general knowledge. These assessments were tests of what is purported to be the mathematics and science needed to function effectively in society as adults.

The content of the mathematics general knowledge assessment represented about a seventh-grade level of curriculum for most TIMSS nations, but was most like the ninth-grade curriculum in the United States. The science general knowledge content was most like the ninth-grade curriculum internationally and the eleventh-grade curriculum in the United States.

United States twelfth graders scored below the international average and among the lowest of the 21 participating nations in both mathematics and science general knowledge (Figures 12.7 and 12.8). The United States outperformed only South Africa and Cyprus on both assessments. The U.S. students' scores on the general knowledge assessments of TIMSS were better in science than in mathematics.

United States students in the twelfth grade were less likely to be taking mathematics or science than were their counterparts in other countries. While 66 percent of graduating students in the United States were currently taking mathematics, the average in all the countries participating in the general knowledge assessment was 79 percent. The same general pattern held for science (53 percent for the United States and 67 percent for all the TIMSS countries).

▶ The Big Dog Syndrome

With a kind of my-dog's-bigger-than-your-dog mentality, people are eager to compare educational systems around the world. Gerald Bracey (1996) believes that while international comparisons of schooling are commonly used to rank educational systems, they are just as routinely abused. He contends that students from the United States are often found wanting when there are no statistically or educationally significant differences between them and students in other nations. In a similar vein, Cynthia Patrick and Robert Calfee argue that such comparisons are a "textbook case of hype" (1996, p. C4). To them, international comparisons detract schools from the real issue: "how to prepare our students for the future."

Robert Mislevy (1995) cautions against comparing students who appear similar on the surface but really are very different from one another. Choosing a specific age group to compare across countries, such as all 13-year-olds, can be problematic.

FIGURE 12.7
Final Year of Secondary School Nations' average mathematics general knowledge performance compared with the U.S.

Nation	Average
(Netherlands)	560
Sweden	552
(Denmark)	547
Switzerland	540
(Iceland)	534
(Norway)	528
(France)	523
New Zealand	522
(Australia)	522
(Canada)	519
(Austria)	518
(Slovenia)	512
(Germany)	495
Hungary	483
(Italy)	476
(Russian Federation)	471
(Lithuania)	469
Czech Republic	466
(United States)	**461**
(Cyprus)	446
(South Africa)	356

International Average = 500

Source: National Center for Education Statistics (1998). *Pursuing Excellence: A Study of U.S. Twelfth-Grade Mathematics and Science Achievement in International Context.* Figure 1. Washington DC: NCES.

Notes:
1. Nations not meeting international guidelines are shown in parentheses.
2. The international average is the average of the national averages of the 21 nations.

⬆ Nations with average scores significantly higher than the U.S.

= Nations with average scores not significantly different from the U.S.

⬇ Nations with average scores significantly lower than the U.S.

FIGURE 12.8
Final Year of Secondary School Nations' average science general knowledge performance compared with the U.S.

Nation	Average
Sweden	559
(Netherlands)	558
(Iceland)	549
(Norway)	544
(Canada)	532
New Zealand	529
(Australia)	527
Switzerland	523
(Austria)	520
(Slovenia)	517
(Denmark)	509
(Germany)	497
(France)	487
Czech Republic	487
(Russian Federation)	481
(United States)	**480**
(Italy)	475
Hungary	471
(Lithuania)	461
(Cyprus)	448
(South Africa)	349

International Average = 500

Source: National Center for Education Statistics (1998). *Pursuing Excellence: A Study of U.S. Twelfth-Grade Mathematics and Science Achievement in International Context.* Figure 5. Washington DC: NCES.

Notes:
1. Nations not meeting international guidelines are shown in parentheses.
2. The international average of the national averages of the 21 nations.

⬆ Nations with average scores significantly higher than the U.S.

= Nations with average scores not significantly different from the U.S.

⬇ Nations with average scores significantly lower than the U.S.

Only 20 percent of U.S. eighth-grade students take algebra, but nearly 80 percent of Japanese students enroll in algebra.

Mislevy notes that the strictly timed, no-talking-no-help format tasks of most international assessments favor students and nations where such assessments are common. "An American student excused from gym class to take a pencil-and-paper test may have a different motivation for doing well than a 'champion of the school' selected to take the same test in Korea" (1995, p. 422). If a Belgian student learns early on to answer only if he is sure, not to guess at answers, and an American student learns from an early age to guess to obtain a higher score, then the student from Belgium is likely to have fewer wrong answers than the American.

The French teach mathematics without the constant reviewing that characterizes U.S. teaching methods. The Japanese divide students into academic and nonacademic tracks at much older ages than do schools in the United States. The Poles teach chemistry, biology, and physics together from grade 6 on; they do not switch subjects each year, as schools in the United States typically do (Gladwell, 1991). Some countries organize mathematics into units of algebra, geometry, trigonometry, and calculus and offer them from the seventh grade onward. The kind of calculus taught to seventh graders in another country is not the calculus taught to U.S. students in an AP calculus course.

Any international comparison of achievement must account for students' opportunities to learn the material on which they are tested. Such opportunities relate positively to money spent on education. If students in different countries do not have opportunities to learn the same things at the same time or by the same age, we must question the value of comparing these students in terms of academic achievement. When spent wisely, money can create many opportunities for students to learn. Figure 12.9 contains comparative information on national spending on education.

For some time now, critics of U.S. public education have used international comparisons to condemn U.S. schools. Others have dismissed these comparisons as mean spirited and wrong headed. Lawrence Stedman argues for a more balanced perspective:

> Our students have been world class in some subjects at certain ages. This message should be repeated frequently so it can penetrate a national media that often ignores the good news about U.S. schools. We must not shy away from the harsh realities, however. There are deep and long-standing problems in U.S. educational achievement. The international assessments are not so flawed that we can afford to ignore the often poor position of U.S. students. (1994, p. 30)

▶ Comparisons That Foster a Global View

Concepts of global and comparative education need not be restrictive. They can stretch far beyond the narrow focus of the big dog syndrome to address commonalities among people, regardless of where they live. People are naturally curious about what it is we share as a result of our humanness. Are there activities in which we all engage that make us more alike than we are different from one another? How and what can we learn about ourselves by learning about others who live in markedly different cultures? Questions such as these stimulate us to look well beyond our familiar surroundings to investigate life in other places.

FIGURE 12.9
Government Spending for Education   In this sample, Sweden and Finland rank first in the world in terms of government support for education. How does the United States rank? What factors influence nations' comparative spending on education?

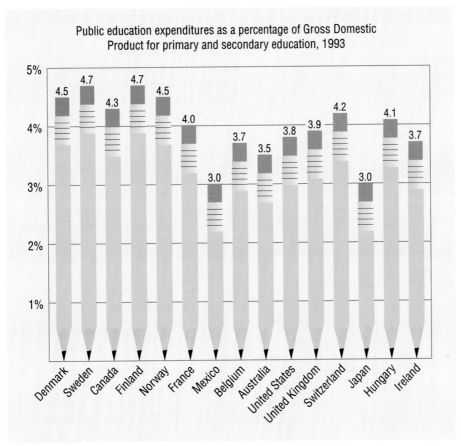

Source: The Condition of Education 1997. (Table 55-1) by U.S. Department of Education, 1997. Washington, DC: U.S. Government Printing Office.

Some studies of teaching and learning across cultures suggest how much educators share, regardless of where they live and work. For example, the educational construct of *wait-time* has been investigated in many settings in many international contexts and with different kinds of students.

Professor Mary Budd Rowe (1986) originated the concept of wait-time as a way to describe the pauses in a classroom teacher's verbal activity. One type of wait-time occurs when a teacher asks a question of a student and then waits for a student to respond. The other type occurs after the student responds. If a teacher can learn to wait for at least 3 seconds before filling the void with her talk, then the quantity and quality of students' responses increase dramatically, regardless of where in the world these events take place.

Issues in School Reform

Do U.S. Teachers Expect Too Little?

TIMSS researchers conducted in-depth investigations of curricular, instructional, and contextual differences among three nations—the United States, Japan, and Germany. Here is part of what they concluded:

▪ Some 95 percent of U.S. teachers stated they were "very aware" or "somewhat aware" about current ideas in the teaching and learning of mathematics. But the videotape study of classrooms revealed only a few teachers applying the key concepts of current reform measures. Japanese lessons, in contrast to U.S. or German lessons, more often resembled the recommendations of experts. The U.S. lessons typically focused on acquiring mathematical skills instead of conceptual understanding and were less coherently presented.

▪ In comparison to German and Japanese teachers, U.S. teachers rarely developed mathematical concepts, that is, proved, derived, or explained them in depth. The average percentage of topics developed was 22 percent in the United States, 77 percent in Germany, and 83 percent in Japan.

▪ Independent mathematics and mathematics education experts judged none of the U.S. lessons evaluated in the TIMSS videotape study as containing a high-quality sequence of mathematical ideas. In contrast, 39 percent of Japanese lessons and 28 percent of German lessons were judged to contain such ideas.

▪ New teachers in the United States receive less on-the-job training and mentoring than do new teachers in Japan and Germany.

Discussion Questions

Are school reformers in the United States correct when they claim that teachers expect too little of students? Why might the information in the following figure lead you to suspect as much? Why might you be cautious in reaching any hard-and-fast conclusions about teachers' expectations based on this information?

Source: National Center for Educational Statistics. (1999). *The TIMMS Videotape Classroom Study: Methods and Findings from an Exploratory Research Project on Eighth-Grade Mathematics Instruction in Germany, Japan, and the United States.* Figure 34. Washington, DC: NCES.

Percentage of Lessons Rated as Having Low, Medium, and High Quality of Mathematical Content (Grade 8)

- Low
- Medium
- High

	Low	Medium	High
Germany	34	38	28
Japan	11	51	39
United States	89	11	0

Graham Nuthall and his colleague Adrienne Alton-Lee from New Zealand explored how students think about tests—in particular, achievement tests in science and social studies (1995). When students were asked to describe how they got their answers and to recall experiences and activities that were relevant to the formulation of those answers, the students described using direct knowledge, deduction and inference, and plain old guessing, much like students everywhere. As the following exchange between an interviewer and 10-year-old Jan suggests, students often remember events that surrounded learning long after the events occur. Students are also more or less likely to take the word of their peers in class discussions.

Interviewer: Where did you learn that?

Jan: Last year, Mr. B. said, does anyone know what mercury is? And Tony put up his hand and said . . . Oh, no! . . . Mr. B. said, what's in a thermometer? And Tony put up his hand and said it was mercury. And it was right, and since then I have remembered.

(The researchers' original recording of the event shows that Jan's memory was essentially correct. But when she was asked if she remembered what she thought at the time, her recollection was more complicated.)

Jan: I thought, you [Tony] have got to be wrong. I thought mercury was sort of a jewel or something like that. Or just a planet.

Interviewer: So you thought he was wrong?

Jan: Mm. I thought it was ink or water. (1995, pp. 196–97)

Jan went to school in a New Zealand community, but she might as well have been from San Diego, Cleveland, or Albany. Like other students around the world, she could visualize past classroom events and transport herself back in time to reconstruct the interactions. Many learning principles and teaching strategies do have cross-cultural validity.

Other studies of classroom interactions point to common concerns among educators working around the globe, while highlighting culture-based differences in the ways they respond to those concerns. Research on the evaluative behaviors of Asian teachers, for example, suggests that they, like their American counterparts, learn much by watching their students. Their learning differs, however, in important ways from that of American teachers particularly when interpreting students' mistakes.

For Americans, errors tend to be interpreted as an indication of failure in learning the lesson. For Chinese and Japanese, they are an index of what still needs to be learned. These divergent interpretations result in very different reactions to the display of errors—embarrassment on the part of American children, calm acceptance by Asian children. They also result in differences in the manner in which teachers utilize errors as effective means of instruction. (Stigler & Stevenson, 1991, p. 27)

Ernest Boyer (1992) identified eight fundamental characteristics that bind all people together as teachers and learners. Boyer suggested that these characteristics might serve as the core of a curriculum for global and comparative studies.

Imagine how teachers might use these ideas to stimulate learners to search for common ground.

1. As human beings we share the mysteries of the life cycle—birth, growth, and death. We do so, of course, without fully understanding or appreciating how these phenomena are alike and different from culture to culture. What milestone events do you celebrate in your culture? How are these events and celebrations similar to and different from such events in another culture that is distant geographically (or philosophically) from your culture?

2. We all use symbols to express feelings and ideas. Language, both written and spoken, shapes how we think and behave. Do you speak, write, and/or read a language other than English? How many of your friends and family are bilingual or multilingual? What encourages or discourages you from learning other languages?

3. The aesthetic forms a kind of universal language that transcends words. We connect with others through music, dance, painting, sculpture, and the many visual arts. Is there a particular form of artistic expression that is especially important to you? How might you be affected explicitly and implicitly by artists from other nations and various cultures?

4. So far as we know, we are unique among living creatures in our abilities to recall the past and to anticipate the future. This sense of time is not uniform from culture to culture, but the present we occupy allows us to look forward and back at the same time. What do you imagine your future might hold? Personally or professionally speaking, how is your future likely to be similar to and different from an aspiring teacher in another nation? How might you test your assumptions?

5. Every person belongs to groups. Some memberships are assigned and some are freely chosen. Some memberships are brief, others last a lifetime. People are social beings. To what groups do you belong? To what groups have you been assigned? Do you share membership in any of these groups with people from different nations or cultures?

6. We are all connected to planet Earth. For some of us the direct connections are more apparent—living and working on a farm as opposed to dwelling in a city. Regardless of the immediacy of our connections, we all depend on the natural world for our survival. What, if any, environmental issues are important to you in your own locale? Do you know whether these issues are important in other locations? What, if any, environmental events in your immediate locale affect people who are distant from you? How might environmental events in other places be felt in your own neighborhood?

7. Work occupies our lives. We all produce, and we all consume. We all must take to survive, but we all must give back if people are not only to survive but to prosper. What do you give back?

8. Although we must meet our basic human needs for food, shelter, and the like, people everywhere want more from life. In every corner of the globe, we can find people searching for a larger purpose in life. Sometimes educators describe

Benchmarks

Developments in International Education

1940s	United Nations Educational, Scientific, and Cultural Organization (UNESCO) is founded to broaden the base of education throughout the world and to encourage cultural interchange.

The International Telecommunication Union (ITC) becomes a part of the United Nations to promote international cooperation in telecommunications.

1960s   National Academy of Education (NAE) is founded to stimulate research in education and includes a division in comparative education.

International Baccalaureate Organization (IBO) and the Institute of International Education are founded in the United States for international teacher education and the study of comparative education.

1970s   Telecommunications satellites, cable television, information processing, and fiber-optic technologies are developed for commercial use.

1980s   European Center for Higher Education (ECHE) implements new programs to increase student mobility across national education systems and to develop databases to facilitate transnational exchange of information.

The Internet becomes a loosely organized, research-based network of computer users at major universities in Europe and the United States. The world's first distance learning collaborations are set up based on telecommunications and computer technologies.

1990s   National Security Education Act triples federal spending on undergraduate study abroad, overseas graduate research, and grants to support programs in international studies.

UNESCO begins efforts to standardize educational credential reporting, licensing, and certification.

The Internet expands to colleges, businesses, governments, individual users, and elementary and secondary schools in more than 65 countries.

2000   Schools in developed countries are wired for direct access to the Internet. Wireless communications and satellite technology use text, audio, and video to link people around the globe from schools to mountaintops, from offices to rain forests.

their desire to "make a difference" or to "be part of something bigger than themselves." Do you have these thoughts? How might you act on them?

Boyer's eight fundamental characteristics do not begin to exhaust the list of people's commonalities. Others unite people generally around the globe, and teachers and students more specifically. We might be surprised, for example, to find out how teachers and students think about the concept of learning. How rich and varied are their definitions? How strongly do they hold their perceptions? Do these perceptions change over time and across borders?

SUMMARY

Why should we learn about educational life outside the United States?

1. Teachers in the United States often teach immigrants and their children. Immigrants' languages, cultural mores, and other factors require that teachers be attuned to life in other countries.

2. Teachers can enhance global awareness—the recognition among people that they are connected to other countries and people of the world—by attending to the concept in any or virtually all subject-matter domains.

3. Nongovernmental organizations (NGOs) also cultivate people's abilities to view the world from others' perspectives. These transnational associations—groups such as churches, scouts, farmers, chambers of commerce, physicians, athletes, and educators—focus on problems and issues that transcend national borders. The number of NGOs is increasing.

What do we know about education in other countries?

4. International comparative education suggests that problems of educational development are common across societies, and that by studying education in different societies, people develop new insights into these societies and an improved understanding of their own society.

5. People in nations as different from one another as Canada, Mexico, Japan, India, the United Kingdom, Denmark, Singapore, South Africa, and the United States can learn much from one another about teaching and learning.

How might we enhance understanding of global interdependence?

6. International comparisons of education systems can serve useful educational purposes. As we examine conceptions of students, teaching, and learning in other countries, we can better understand and, in some instances, change our own practices. Because of differences in measures, students being compared, and the contexts in which education occurs, comparisons among the school systems of the world must be undertaken with care.

7. People are bound to one another by many fundamental characteristics, including—but not limited to—their use of symbols, their appreciation for aesthetic forms, and their ability to recall the past and to anticipate the future.

TERMS AND CONCEPTS

apartheid   482
Folkeskole   479
global awareness   461
international comparative
   education   465

juku   495
NGO   462
okeiko-goto   495

REFLECTIVE PRACTICE

Newcomers High School teacher Diana Cabot discusses the challenges of teaching physical education to Newcomers students:

> I was born and raised in Queens and graduated from Newtown High School. Students there speak many languages, so I was used to being around people from different cultures. English is my primary language, but I also speak Spanish. Many of my students speak Spanish, but some do not, so I try to speak English only. One of the biggest challenges I face as a classroom teacher is how to deal with the different languages. I teach physical education, and one thing I have to be concerned about is safety. To be sure students understand the rules, I try to use a lot of visuals when I teach. I even bring in a T-shirt and pants to show them what they are supposed to wear for class.
>
> I also have to find out about students' cultures. Girls from the Indian cultures, for example, must wear long-sleeved blouses. I am concerned that they might get too hot during aerobics and dehydrate, so I keep an eye on them. They can't have contact with males either, so in the beginning when we had coed classes that was difficult. I had to work with them separately while someone else taught the boys.
>
> I learn about students' religions too. Recently, for example, some of my students were celebrating Ramadan, and they were fasting. I was concerned that they would be too weak to do anything physical, so I had them help me with attendance. I would tell them to do as much as they could but to sit down if they got tired and I would excuse them, because I wasn't sure who was or wasn't fasting. So I had to get parents' permission to excuse students from some of the activities. It's a learning experience. Every time somebody says, "Oh, I can't do this," I do some research to find out about religious holidays or cultural expectations. Of course, sometimes students are shy, and they won't say anything. They will just take a zero rather than participate. So I ask them questions or talk to their teachers to find out if what I am doing conflicts with their religion.

The biggest challenge for students is probably the language. We do a lot of group work here. I assign students to groups, because if I allow them to pick their own partners, students work only with the people they know. I want them to communicate with others. They tend to be shy, so I mix the language groups. My goal is not only for students to learn physical skills but also to learn English. If they don't understand each other they can't do the work.

Issues, Problems, Dilemmas, and Opportunities

Ms. Cabot notes several challenges—both for her and her students—in the physical education classes at Newcomers High School. List them, and rank them in terms of their likely importance from Ms. Cabot's point of view.

Perceive and Value

Assume a point of view other than Ms. Cabot's. For example, imagine yourself as a student in a physical education class at Newcomers High School. Imagine that you do not speak English, or at least not very well. How might you feel? Why? What might you be most worried about in the class? Why? Do you hold any personal values that might make you more or less successful in this class? What values might you share with Ms. Cabot?

Know and Act

Suppose you are co-teaching with Diana or serving as a teaching assistant in her class. How might you help her (1) get to know the students better, (2) communicate better with all the students, (3) modify curriculum and instruction appropriately and comfortably for both herself and the students, and (4) infuse a coherent multicultural approach into the program? How might you help the students to (1) know one another better, (2) communicate better with each other and with you and Diana, and (3) succeed in meeting curriculum goals in culturally appropriate contexts?

Evaluate

In what ways specifically could you evaluate the effectiveness of each possible solution or strategy you identified? What criteria could you and Diana use to determine the success of your program?

 ONLINE ACTIVITY

Do you have any idea how many and what percentage of U.S. students study abroad each year? More than 20 percent of international students enroll in U.S. institutions in just ten U.S. counties; can you guess where these counties are located? What nation sends the most scholars to study in the U.S.? Answers to these questions can be found on the web site for the International Institute of Education.

You might be especially interested to know that the site carries information for college and university students about how to apply for Fulbright grants to study abroad. The

U.S. Congress created the Fulbright Program in 1946 to foster understanding among nations through educational and cultural exchanges. Senator J. William Fulbright, sponsor of the legislation, viewed the program as an investment in peace.

Each year the Fulbright program allows Americans to study or conduct research in over 100 nations. Congress and participating nations fund the program. Under the policy guidance of the presidentially-appointed J. William Fulbright Foreign Scholarship Board, the United States Department of State sponsors the program in cooperation with binational Fulbright commissions and foundations abroad, and with the help of U.S. embassies.

The Institute of International Education (IIE) coordinates the activities relevant to the U.S. graduate student program and conducts an annual competition for the scholarships, most of which are for one academic year of study or research.

Source: Reproduced with permission from the Institute for International Education.

13

The Future of Education in a Changing World

Only fools and fortune tellers predict the future with assurance. We need no special powers, however, to conclude that two broad trends in teaching are certain. First, the days of the lone-wolf teacher are over. Professional educators of tomorrow will know where and how to connect with many others who share resources and interests in educating young people. Educators will depend more on each other and on people with special knowledge and talents. They will collaborate to solve educational problems and create new educational opportunities.

Second, professional educators will have greater opportunities to construct their own careers. They will assume new roles and take on new tasks, redefining their jobs and themselves in the process. Teachers will conduct classroom research; create curriculum; participate in school- and system-level decision making; design, implement, and report evaluations of educational progress; work with other service providers in the context of their communities; and master technology. No single skill will be more important for educators than the ability to think on one's feet.

In this chapter we describe how forces in society, often outside the control of teachers themselves, affect their professional lives. We explain how one influence in particular—technology—seems to be shifting the educational foundation under our feet. We also describe how collaborative networks of people can transform teaching, learning, and the professional development of educators. Finally, we look forward to teachers constructing a promising future for themselves and their students.

PROFESSIONAL PRACTICE QUESTIONS

▋ What trends are changing teachers' professional roles?

▋ How are links to technology changing the foundations of education?

▋ How are collaborative networks transforming teaching and learning?

▋ How are collaborative networks transforming the professional development of teachers?

▋ How can professional educators prepare for the future?

 ## What Trends Are Changing Teachers' Professional Roles?

Stand up straight. Somebody is leaning on you. People are trying to push you to offer something called a "world-class education." Never mind that there is little agreement on the meaning of the phrase, beyond a vague consensus that we have to be the best—as though we are not the best now, even if we could all agree on the definition of best. Modern educational reformers have put you on the front page. Although the discussion is often confusing and contradictory, it is clear that education is news. And both critical and casual observers alike are alert to the fact that teachers make a difference—make *the* difference—in young people's lives.

There has never been a better time to be a teacher. Teachers are emerging from a thicket of goals, objectives, standards, curricula, outcomes, competencies, performances, and the like as leaders of a movement to advance educational well-being. From the outside looking in, many people have much to say about how teaching and learning should be improved. But teachers are there at the center of activity every day, working to inspire, inform, and support young people. Teachers will be there when everybody else has gone home.

Several obvious trends mark the conduct of public education in the United States—trends toward the use of common goals and standards, toward comprehensive curriculum development and performance assessment, and toward the development of human talent in inclusive settings. Teachers can help shape these trends if they choose to do so.

▶ Trends Toward Common Goals and Standards

In 1989 and 1990 Presidents Bush and Clinton and other political leaders established the first National Education Goals (see Chapter 1). Prompted by public dissatisfaction with "low levels of student performance, increasing global economic competition, and consistently poor showings on international assessments," the creators of the Goals sought to rally national attention to achieving high-performance education results (National Education Goals Panel, 1994, p. 12). The values and attitudes driving their efforts are epitomized in the quote from Vince Lombardi that appears above the introduction to the 1994 National Education Goals Report: "If you're not keeping score, you're just practicing" (p. 13). States' progress as measured by 26 national and 33 state indicators is made public routinely through the National Education Goals Panel (1999).

On March 26 to 27, 1996, President Clinton and 40 of the nation's governors met in Palisades, New York, for the second national Education Summit. Their task was to advance progress on improving academic **standards,** or the benchmarks against which student progress can be judged. They also addressed how student assessment should proceed and how technology should be used in the public schools. They were joined by a select number of chief executive officers (CEOs) from major corporations who have argued that they too have a stake in the success of the nation's schools.

Despite some disagreements, the governors agreed to develop and establish within 2 years internationally competitive standards, assessments to measure progress toward meeting them, and accountability systems of consequence (Lawton, 1996a). The 49 CEOs committed themselves to establishing within a year new hiring standards that require applicants to demonstrate academic achievement through such school-based records as transcripts and diplomas. Christopher Cross, long-time civil service employee and highly respected president of the Council for Basic Education, was quoted as saying "I think there's a good deal of facile commitment to standards and not a lot of understanding of what that means" (Lawton, 1996a, p. 23).

> **Will national goals and standards raise academic standards nationwide?**

At the time the National Education Goals were conceived, with the exception of mathematics, no subject area had national standards to guide educational practice. The push to set demanding expectations for students in grades kindergarten through 12 has since resulted in the development of national standards in all academic areas.

The standards themselves have been formulated by a collection of nonprofit and professional associations of educators. They are designed to be used on a voluntary basis. The federal government, however, has underwritten the cost of creating many of these documents and has provided financial incentives to states that implement them. Figure 13.1 shows an example taken from the National Council of Teachers of Mathematics standards.

FIGURE 13.1
Example of National Standards

STANDARD 1: MATHEMATICS AS PROBLEM SOLVING

In grades K–4, the study of mathematics should emphasize problem solving so that students can—use problem-solving approaches to investigate and understand mathematical content; formulate problems from everyday and mathematical situations; develop and apply strategies to solve a wide variety of problems; verify and interpret results with respect to the original problem; acquire confidence in using mathematics meaningfully.

Focus

Problem solving should be the central focus of the mathematics curriculum. As such, it is a primary goal of all mathematics instruction and an integral part of all mathematical activity. Problem solving is not a distinct topic but a process that should permeate the entire program and provide the context in which concepts and skills can be learned.

This standard emphasizes a comprehensive and rich approach to problem solving in a classroom climate that encourages and supports problem-solving efforts. Ideally, students should share their thinking and approaches with other students and with teachers, and they should learn several ways of representing problems and strategies for solving them. In addition, they should learn to value the process of solving problems as much as they value the solutions. Students should have many experiences in creating problems from real-world activities, from organized data, and from equations.

In the early years of the K–4 program, most problem situations will arise from school and other everyday experiences. When mathematics evolves naturally from problem situations that have meaning to children and are regularly related to their environment, it becomes relevant and helps children link their knowledge to many kinds of situations. As children progress through the grades, they should encounter more diverse and complex types of problems that arise from both real-world and mathematical contexts.

When problem solving becomes an integral part of classroom instruction and children experience success in solving problems, they gain confidence in doing mathematics and develop persevering and inquiring minds. They also grow in their ability to communicate mathematically and use higher-level thinking processes.

Discussion

Classrooms with a problem-solving orientation are permeated by thought-provoking questions, speculations, investigations, and explorations; in this environment, the teacher's primary goal is to promote a problem-solving approach to the learning of all mathematics content. The following example illustrates this meaning.

FIGURE 13.1
(Continued)

A lesson designed to develop the characteristics of parallelograms can be approached from a problem-solving perspective. The teacher, who has a collection of quadrilaterals like the ones shown below, has the children discover the teacher's rule for sorting the shapes. One rule is to have all parallelograms in one loop and all nonparallelograms in the other.

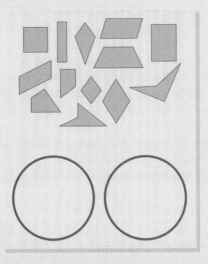

In turn, each child picks a shape and decides in which loop to put it. The teacher says yes or no as each student places a shape. Throughout the process, the children are asked to think about the common characteristics of the shapes in each loop; after all shapes are placed, these common characteristics are discussed. As a result, the children learn to define parallelograms and name their characteristics in the context of a thought-provoking activity.

School districts have also made special efforts to make their practice congruent with national standards. Putnam Valley, a small community north of Westchester County in New York, is a good example. Their web site emphasizes the place of standards in their own schools.

> Good teachers have standards in mind when they set their lessons up, where the idea of a "standard" represents a specific idea of what the teacher expects a student to recall, replicate, manipulate, understand, or demonstrate at some point down the road—and of how the teacher will know how close a student has come to meeting that standard. (Hill, 1999)

How are teachers' and students' roles changing in today's classrooms? What trends in curriculum standards and assessment might account for those changes?

Outcome-Centered Learning.　Critics of existing education programs, especially business leaders, frequently voice concern about the need to demonstrate "results" in education. Outcome-centered learning considers the products of learning as a reflection of students' time spent in school. The argument for the idea is simple: The nation must be able to assess student progress systematically, that is, to evaluate student performance across locales and over time. This is the only way of knowing (1) how well or how poorly students are performing, (2) what might be done to improve weak results, and (3) whether various reform measures actually make any difference.

The focus on educational outcomes or products is not new. In the 1920s efforts were made to apply scientific principles to education problems and to assess these applications by examining students' work. Accountability has always been associated with demands to demonstrate evidence of student competence—test scores, compositions, times clocked in races. What makes recent emphases on accountability different from past efforts is the role of the teacher. Today's teachers assume greater responsibility for student competence and exert more influence over the kinds of outcomes used to assess students as opposed to relying so heavily on tests created outside schools. The intent is to enhance the authenticity of student evaluations.

At the local level, students' outcomes are also measured through teacher-made and standardized tests. Educators may use test results to make instructional and placement decisions and also to compare performances of students from school to school and from district to district. Schools across the nation supplement information from so-called objective tests with samples of student work, portfolios, demonstrations, and other student products so as to measure not only what students know, but also what they can do and how they reason.

Will accountability for national standards cause schools to teach to the test?

National Assessments of Educational Progress (NAEP).　Student assessments such as the *National Assessments of Educational Progress* (NAEP) have become benchmarks of the reform process in the United States. The NAEP is a congressionally mandated set of tests developed by the Educational Testing Service. Since 1969, the NAEP has been administered nationally to samples of students in grades 4, 8, and 12 to measure their knowledge and skills in a variety of subject areas.

Education reformers view the NAEP as a stimulus to change in teaching practice. The U.S. Department of Education refers to the National Assessments of Educational Progress as the Nation's Report Card. Table 13.1 shows the percentages of fourth-grade public school students who performed at or above the *Proficient* achievement level in 1992, 1994, and 1998. Significant differences are noted in the third column.

As the table reveals, between 1992 and 1998, the percentage of public school fourth graders who attained or exceeded the *Proficient* level increased significantly in Colorado, Connecticut, Kentucky, Louisiana, Maryland, Minnesota, Mississippi, and the Virgin Islands. There were no significant decreases for any other state or jurisdiction.

▌ **TABLE 13.1**
Percentage of Grade 4 Students at or above the *Proficient* Level for Public Schools Only: 1992, 1994, and 1998

	Percentage of students at or above *Proficient*						
	1992	**1994**	**1998**		**1992**	**1994**	**1998**
Nation	27	28	29				
States				Nevada	—	—	21
Alabama	20	23	24	New Hampshire†	38	36	38
Arizona	21	24	22	New Mexico	23	21	22
Arkansas	23	24	23	New York†	27	27	29
California†	19	18	20	North Carolina	25	30	28
Colorado	25	28	34**†	Oklahoma	29	—	30
Connecticut	34	38	46**†	Oregon	—	—	28
Delaware	24	23	25	Rhode Island	28	32	32
Florida	21	23	23	South Carolina	22	20	22
Georgia	25	26	24	Tennessee	23	27	25
Hawaii	17	19	17	Texas	24	26	29
Iowa†	36	35	35	Utah	30	30	28
Kansas†	—	—	34	Virginia	31	26	30
Kentucky	23	26	29*	Washington	—	27	29
Louisiana	15	15	19*†	West Virginia	25	26	29
Maine	36	41	36	Wisconsin†	33	35	34
Maryland	24	26	29*	Wyoming	33	32	30
Massachusetts†	36	36	37				
Michigan	26	—	28	**Other Jurisdictions**			
Minnesota†	31	33	36*	District of Columbia	10	8	10
Mississippi	14	18	18*	DDESS	—	—	32
Missouri	30	31	29	DoDDS	—	28	34†
Montana†	—	35	37	Virgin Islands	3	—	8**

*Indicates that the percentage in 1998 was significantly different from that in 1992 if only one jurisdiction is being examined.

**Indicates that the percentage in 1998 was significantly different from that in 1992 using a multiple comparison procedure based on 43 jurisdictions.

†Indicates that the percentage in 1998 was significantly different from that in 1994 if only one jurisdiction is being examined.

†Jurisdiction did not satisfy one or more of the guidelines for school participation rates.

Source: National Center for Education Statistics (1999). *The NAEP 1998 reading report card: National and state highlights.* Washington, DC: U.S. Government Printing Office, p. 15.

Between 1994 and 1998, the percentage of public school fourth graders at or above *Proficient* increased significantly in Colorado, Connecticut, Louisiana, and Department of Defense overseas schools. There were no significant declines.

The Minimum Competency Movement.   If public schools are designed for all of society's children, is there some common body of knowledge and minimal level of learning that can and should be expected of all students? Those who answer this question affirmatively support minimum competency programs, or curriculum and instruction geared toward the successful completion of **minimum competency tests.** These tests are designed to assess the lowest acceptable levels of student performance.

The minimum competency movement began in the 1970s as a reaction against (1) what some have perceived as a diminished emphasis on content and academic rigor in schools; (2) the practice of social promotion—promoting children through the grades to keep them with their agemates even if they could not keep pace academically; and (3) decreasing performance in the use of public funds to foster **literacy**—defined most often as scores on tests of reading, writing, and calculation. The minimum competency movement has advanced an agenda for educational and social change. "Minimums" are often defined in terms of what some adults believe children will need to know and be able to do in order to get and keep a job in later life. By concentrating on the "minimums" in curriculum, proponents intend to raise, indirectly, maximum standards (Lerner, 1991). The movement promotes curriculum, instruction, and evaluation that prepare students for the future. Advocates emphasize technology in the workplace and concentration on basic skills.

Is a focus on minimum competency a disservice to students?

Proponents of minimum competence want to help children from poverty-stricken areas, shortchanged by poor schools, receive the preparation they need to build secure futures. They often define security in terms of job skills and self determination.

Many states have developed lists of minimum competencies for students. Arizona, for example, has developed lists of skills in seven subjects for the eighth and twelfth grades. The following skills are examples from Arizona's list of 87 skills in health for eighth-grade students.

- Identifies personal care practices. Example: washing hands before eating, brushing teeth.
- Communicates symptoms of his/her physical illness.
- Lists some of the ways communicable diseases are transmitted.
- Identifies and describes a variety of foods.
- States the importance of eating breakfast and describes a healthful breakfast. (Oliva, 1992, p. 122)

Critics contend that the minimum competency movement has led to an overemphasis on **high-stakes tests**—tests used to evaluate school performance—that determine students' grade promotion, graduation, and access to specific fields of study. High-stakes tests, critics argue, limit the curriculum to simplistic ideas. These tests also punish students who simply "do not get it" (Cooper, 1999). This punishment can have high costs not only in self-esteem, but also in dollars. In Chicago, for instance, students who fail the third, sixth, or eighth grade go to summer school. The school district is spending $50 million per year on summer school and other remedial programs intended to help students move to the next grade.

Opportunity-to-Learn Standards Critics of minimum competency tests have advanced the concept of **opportunity-to-learn (OTL) standards.** OTL standards are meant to hold schools accountable for giving students a fair chance to succeed by providing them with appropriate support—books, materials, machines, teachers, time to learn, and other tools.

For a school to meet an opportunity-to-learn standard, it must provide a sufficient quantity and quality of resources, practices, and the conditions necessary for student success. Responsibility to meet such standards, proponents argue, must fall not only to schools but also to districts and to states as well. Students must be given the opportunity to learn by the adults who run the educational systems if students are to be held accountable for their performance later in life.

As Andrew Porter (1995) has observed, however, the OTL standards are strictly voluntary; they will not be used to hold states or localities accountable.

> If they have any influence on school improvement, it will be through persuasion provided by visions of good education practice and information from OTL indicators on progress [viz., evidence of resources devoted to creating favorable conditions for learning] schools are providing toward school improvement. (Porter, 1995, p. 27)

▶ Trends Toward Comprehensive Curriculum and Assessment

There is little doubt that educators and other citizens of the United States are engaged in a struggle to control curriculum in the public schools. It has raged since the inception of the common school and continues in many forms today. Policymakers at all levels of government, parents, philosophers, educational practitioners, citizens, and would-be citizens want to influence what is to be taught and learned in schools. This will be an ongoing struggle.

Evolving educational standards emanating from changes in the public's expectations will stimulate reform of curriculum, methods of teaching and learning, and processes of assessment. These reforms will occur slowly in some places and rapidly in others; when viewed together, they will constitute a noticeable trend in the way teachers will perform their jobs.

Many educators recognize that curricular reform requires more than continually adding information to courses of study. Processes of curriculum integration must blend old and new material, form links between concepts, structure content so students will make connections in their minds, organize people and ideas by themes, and team students and teachers.

Reformed educational systems will look different from one another; but the integration of knowledge, people, and thinking—not the mere addition of information to the curriculum—is likely to be a common attribute among systems. Students who will graduate in 2004 from Maryland schools, for example, will be expected to pass a battery of 10 tests: three in English, three in social studies, and two each in mathematics and science. Exams for each content area will assess students' abilities to work

Are integrated curricula and comprehensive, authentic assessments feasible?

with others, communicate, use technology, and think critically. The notion behind the new tests is to hold all students, regardless of which school they attend, to the same high standards (Lawton, 1996b).

Concerns about student progress have prompted educators to rethink time-honored practices of defining achievement solely or even mainly in terms of standardized achievement tests. Tests that yield information on students' abilities to pick "right" and "wrong" answers will diminish in importance in the years ahead. In their place, educators want to develop a **comprehensive assessment** of student progress that will provide information on students' capacities for reasoning, thinking divergently, and solving problems creatively.

To be useful, such a comprehensive assessment will need to reflect more accurately the kinds of challenges students will face in real life than do multiple-choice tests of knowledge acquisition. A truly comprehensive assessment will provide estimates of students' abilities to complete a variety of life's tasks and to function effectively in many contexts. To develop such an assessment for a future that is, at best, difficult to predict is a challenging task, but it is also a task that teachers, in collaboration with other professionals, will undertake.

Student assessment in the United States, especially at state and local levels, relies on short-answer tests that do not promote reflective thinking on the part of students. As Table 13.2 indicates, the American Association for the Advancement of Science (1998) promotes assessment that capitalizes on a variety of tasks and methods.

New authentic assessment, or assessment that is connected to what students must be able to do in the real world, will offer opportunities for teachers to assert their expertise in assessment. Educators will place less emphasis on having outside measurement experts create tests, which separates assessment from teaching. Consequently, assessment will more often emphasize having teachers identify logical student outcomes, will communicate expectations for student performance, and will tie evaluation directly to instruction (Stiggins, 1994).

TABLE 13.2
Characteristics of Good Classroom Assessments

- They produce measurable evidence of learning.
- They are relevant to the student and to the learning goal.
- They involve close transfer of learning gained through the curriculum.
- They accommodate a variety of developmental levels and intelligences.
- They account for prior knowledge about the task context or provide preassessment activities to familiarize all students with the content.
- They give students and teachers options to have tasks completed individually or cooperatively.
- They allow the student to select the best approach to the task.
- They assess tasks consistently.

Source: American Association for the Advancement of Science (1998). *Blueprints for reform. Science, mathematics, and technology education. Project 2061.* New York: Oxford University Press, p. 170.

Just as she teaches continually, the teacher who demonstrates comprehensive, authentic methods of assessment will be engaged continually in processes of assessment. She will teach material, and she will create opportunities for students to demonstrate their mastery of that material in various ways. For example, if students are studying the compass points, the teacher might have them playing games on the playground that require them to demonstrate their knowledge of direction by moving from place to place; she might turn them loose on a football field with compasses in hand and maps to be charted; or she might put them at computers with opportunities to "travel" from place to place on the globe. In any or all instances, she will observe their abilities to perform their tasks. She might also have students judge the difficulty of the problems they face and estimate their own understanding of these problems, while she makes the same judgments. As processes of assessment and learning become more comprehensive and authentic, then, they also will become more interrelated.

Too often, students do not see connections between tests and what they do in school, thus diminishing the value of teaching and learning in their minds. The American Association for the Advancement of Science suggests ways teachers and students can work together to make instruction and assessment complementary activities:

> A typical scenario, especially in secondary school, is to read the text, listen to lectures, perhaps do some lab work, and then be tested on the week's work on Friday. This process is not unlike assessment procedures in most colleges and universities. Classroom science instruction and assessment can be brought together through observations and checklists of students' performance in activities such as solving problems and conducting lab experiments, assessment of individual and group projects using several criteria, and the use of portfolios that reflect student growth and achievement on a variety of activities over time. In all these, students can have a role in selecting the criteria for evaluating their work, in making choices about what will be assessed, and in making improvements on performances. (1998, p. 171)

▶ Trends Toward Education for Diversity

Standards are uniform, but children are different. If they are to achieve the same or similar outcomes, children need different levels and kinds of support. Increasingly, in the years ahead, teachers will be called on to make informed decisions about students' needs and abilities and to deliver support fitted to individual and group needs. In addition to developing multicultural and inclusive curricula and instructional approaches, educators will plan interventions for gender equity and adaptations for mainstreamed students with disabilities.

Gender Sensitivity Training. One trend prevents gender bias in the classroom and offers **gender sensitivity training** to students. Gender-fair education provides curricula that avoid sex role stereotyping and promotes equal educational opportunities for girls and women. Standard textbooks now draw attention to women's relevant contributions. Teachers routinely encourage girls to take and to master mathematics and science courses throughout their educational careers. Education texts avoid the generic use of male terms.

A number of educators have created curricula that avoid sex role stereotyping and identify opportunities for girls and women to take advantage of all their possibilities for education. The *Civitas* curriculum offers the following objectives for gender sensitivity training.

The citizen should be able to:

1. explain the similarities and differences between men's and women's political participation throughout American history.

2. explain how the changing roles that have been deemed appropriate for men and women have affected their participation in American politics.

3. explain how the effects of public policies vary by gender, affecting men and women differently.

4. take, defend, and evaluate positions on constitutional and public policy issues regarding gender and political participation. (Quigley & Bahmueller, 1991, p. 258)

Overall, *Civitas* examines gender from three frames of references—conceptual, historical, and contemporary—suggesting directions for sharply defined study. The conceptual frame draws attention to such factors as the basis for past exclusion of

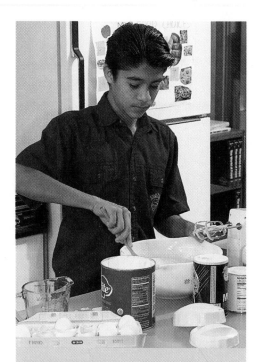

How can gender-fair education be provided in all classrooms? What role can gender sensitivity training play in addressing problems of gender bias?

women from politics, the role of feminism, arguments for and against changing women's roles in society, women's changing place in politics, and women's relatively small role in the exercise of formal political power. The historical perspective emphasizes the place of women in politics at the founding of the nation, the beginning of women's political activism, the campaign for women's suffrage, and the various phases of the feminist movement. The contemporary perspective looks out on gender issues as they have been articulated in the 1990s, including wage inequality and job segregation, and considers women in politics in present-day America.

Civitas is constructed to be sensitive to the raging controversy over multicultural issues in the social sciences. The writers and editors have tried to respond to critics of other curricula who have argued that too often Western values and European contributions to the United States and to the world have been overstressed. Certainly, the gender section of the curriculum, and other sections, are geared toward change.

Equity between males and females might be realized as people adopt a more caring attitude toward others. Nel Noddings (1984, 1992), Madeline Grumet (1987), and others have argued that society's prevailing conceptions of gender will be changed only by "transforming" what and how children are taught about caring and ethics.

I have argued for a curriculum aimed at producing people who will not intentionally harm others; a transformed structure of schooling that will encourage the development of caring relations; a moral education that emphasized maternal interests in preserving life, enhancing growth, and shaping acceptable children; and the development of a morality of evil that should help all of us understand and control our own tendencies toward evil. (Noddings, 1992, p. 678)

How far should schools go in attempting to ensure gender equity?

Teaching All Students in Inclusive Classrooms.   The inclusion movement in special education has encouraged the teaching of children with disabilities in general education classrooms instead of teaching them in self-contained classrooms or separate facilities. Inclusion carries the force of law and considerable public support. At the same time, disagreement abounds about which settings are most appropriate for which students and about how to provide instruction for students with disabilities in inclusive classrooms.

As a classroom teacher you will face the following. First, teaching children with disabilities requires that you understand the needs and abilities of all students as fully as possible. Students' characteristics may well dictate what they can accomplish and how they are to be taught. Second, you must set tasks or objectives that are worthwhile and that students with disabilities can accomplish. All students may not be able to achieve all of the same objectives at the same level of proficiency. Third, you must fit instruction to individuals' goals, needs, and strengths. This means more than simply varying the amount of work or the amount of learning time; you may also need to structure teaching and assignments for special students in different ways. Fourth, you will have to assess students in ways that allow them to demonstrate what they know and can do. You will have to rely less on standard measures of learning for students with disabilities and more on alternative assessments of what they have learned.

▶ Trends Toward Character Education

There were always cats at Mark Twain's farm, and favorite cats had their own names—Blatherskite, Sour Mash, Stray Kit, Sin, Satan. His children inherited his love of them. His daughter Susy once said, "The difference between Papa and Mamma is, that Mamma loves morals and Papa loves cats." (Fadiman, 1985, p. 555)

To call the search for some space between moral absolutes and everyday life a "trend" hardly seems right; if so, it is probably the longest-standing trend on record. Yet not a day passes without teachers and children negotiating the line between the way it is and the way it is supposed to be. If anything, this sometimes kind-hearted, sometimes not-so-gentle character formation will require more of teachers in the future. Although Mr. and Mrs. Clemens (Twain) may have been able to help their children love both cats and morals, times have changed. Altered family structures and increasing demands on caregivers to earn a living will impel teachers to take up the slack that may exist in young people's character education.

Clarifying or teaching values, sometimes referred to as **character education,** has been highly controversial since the 1960s. According to Thomas Likona, the values clarification teaching of the 1960s and 1970s "led students to believe whatever values they had were O.K., as long as they were clarified, even if it was shoplifting or

Satanism" (Viadero, 1992, p. 12). Likona believes that students were misled when teachers opened lessons on values by saying that there is no right or wrong answer. Instead, teachers need to say that there may be more than one answer and that students must be prepared to support their answers with sound moral reasoning.

Kevin Ryan and Karen Bohlin (1999) acknowledge an increasingly sophisticated set of educational approaches for dealing with a range of youth pathologies—crime, suicide, drug use, and promiscuity. Ryan and Bohlin describe three approaches to character education that dominate activities in schools: values, views, and virtues. Each approach, while somewhat different, is meant to help young people develop good character.

> **How far should schools go in teaching moral values?**

The *values approach* is most popular in schools. The idea is that values drive what people want, or they are the concepts to which people assign worth. Teachers' actions in this approach are variations on the educational strategy that gives students opportunities to learn how to establish good values so that they might make wise choices in their lives.

The *views approach* concentrates on making explicit intellectual positions on laws, politics, wealth, poverty, religion, and the like. Teachers and students examine relative goodness or evil of various positions for the purpose of developing one's own views and attitudes.

The *virtues approach,* according to Ryan and Bohlin, fosters moral commitments leading to a good life. For instance, it is not enough to value the Bible if one fails to act compassionately when compassion is called for in the Bible. It is insufficient to be able to articulate a point of view, while being unable to develop habits of hard work, sincerity, courage, and personal responsibility evolving from that point of view.

To give students a sense of belonging and to encourage them to participate in the responsibilities of community, state, and nation, a number of schools have developed curricula to encourage volunteerism, or **service learning.** Joseph Kahne and Joel Westheimer (1996) contend that service learning programs fall into two general categories: those that encourage the goal of change and those that foster the goal of charity. Change programs encourage students to adopt a moral stance of caring, a political view of the value of reconstructing society, and an intellectual stance on the importance of engaging in experiences that transform the way people think. Charity programs are organized around the moral principle of giving, the political ideal of performing one's civic duty, and the added intellectual value of gaining experience from engaging in service activities.

In many instances, volunteer groups such as the 300-member service club at Fallston High School in Harford County, Maryland, perform their services outside school hours and receive no credit, awards, or certificates of appreciation from their school. Individual service projects, such as tutoring peers or younger children or working with residents in nursing homes, foster communication and intergenerational understanding. Group service projects, such as repairing bleachers or cleaning up the local park, help students learn to plan and cooperate with others to get a job done. Students who volunteer also become more responsible and develop more favorable attitudes toward the people they work with than do other young people.

Service learning often includes environmental stewardship. From instructional units that teach students about water conservation in the West, to programs that educate young people about controlling soil erosion in the Midwest, to curriculum

Cultural Awareness

Service learning can take many forms. The experience of students from across the country who participate in New York's Youth Services Opportunities Project (YSOP) goes a long way toward breaking down stereotypes.

Howard Juris, 69, admits he used to think of many teenagers as ruffians.

Travis Lowder, 16, says he used to believe homeless people were generally strange. But over a chicken dinner and a conversation about theology last month, the stereotypes began to fall away.

"It is a very pleasant experience, being with the younger generation," said Mr. Juris as he finished a brownie sundae for dessert. "All we hear about in the papers are the rotten apples."

Mr. Lowder, who attends Pleasantville (N.Y.) High School, added: "There's a general stereotype that [homeless people] are crazy. But just sitting down to talk with them dispels the myth."

Some 1,400 students from across the nation attend YSOP work camps each year. Many are high school students who are required to perform community service and who attend the program as a part of a school group. Others are affiliated with churches or attend on their own.

Meghan O'Gorman, 14, a student at the Convent of the Sacred Heart, a private Roman Catholic school in Greenwich, Conn., described the program as life-changing. "When I came home, I wanted to tell everyone everything that I'd done," she said. "I am telling all my friends. I was, like, so moved."

Source: Blair, J. (1999, March 10). Teens and homeless share dinner, discussion, insight. (*Education Week, 18*(26), 6.

---

aimed at raising consciousness about acid rain in the East, science and social studies teachers work to sensitize young people to the importance of preserving the delicate balance of forces in their environment. Schools regularly encourage student participation in such activities as Arbor Day, recycling programs, and wildlife preservation projects. In so doing, schools play an important but indirect role in educating parents about environmental issues.

Should schools make service learning mandatory?

 ## How Are Links to Technology Changing the Foundations of Education?

Nothing better proves the adage that the more things change the more they stay the same than the technology boom. While technological innovation grows exponentially, people call increasingly for indications of the worth of the investment. With each new digital wonder come questions about how it might affect teaching and learning (Trotter, 1998). There is a kind of healthy tension between wanting to use technology to turn schools upside down and worrying about how to measure bene-fits and costs (Kent & McNergney, 1999).

New teacher roles are emerging through links to technology. As schools develop capacities to deliver video, audio, data, and text to classrooms through electronic media, teachers will face multiple challenges beyond the problems of operating the machinery. They will have to use technology both as a means of direct instruction that focuses on basic skills and as a way to help students construct their own knowl-edge and develop a deep understanding of the subject matter. Teachers will also teach students to use technology for themselves. Now computers often are used only for drill and practice or as rewards for students who finish their "real work" early. In some schools, lack of funds and a shortage of trained personnel will limit access to computers. Even with an ample supply, the challenge will be to use computers in ways that actually help students to think and learn.

Most experts agree that some basic conditions must exist if computers are going to be used effectively to link students with information and people in the larger world. Computers must be available in sufficient number so that work stations can be provided for every two to three students. Teachers need training and opportuni-ties to use computers if they are going to help students use them. Teachers also need time to restructure their curricula around computers if the machines are going to be used for anything other than drill and practice. Teachers will have difficulty inte-grating technology with classroom instruction when students must go to a lab to access a computer.

Mark and Cindy Grabe (1998) have identified five themes that describe the dif-ferent uses of technology in classrooms. When students use technology to study a particular content area, and the technology is secondary to learning the content, then the technology has been "integrated into content-area instruction." As teachers encourage students to learn to apply general-purpose software, such as word-pro-cessing programs, they are using a "tools approach" to technology instruction. The Grabes also write of using technology to promote "an active role for students." By "active," they mean the mental behavior of students as they use technology to con-struct meaning for themselves or to solve complex problems. When students become more active, teachers may use technology to step back from their role of dispenser of information to play a *facilitative* role, or one of assisting students. Technology also can be used to facilitate "an integrated or multidisciplinary approach" to teaching and learning involving a broad range of skills. Finally, technology can enhance inter-actions among students, providing the benefits of *cooperative learning*.

▶ The Internet and the World Wide Web

Teachers will use the Internet to promote any or all of the Grabes's themes. The **Internet** is a global telecommunications network that began as a military effort to ensure communications in case of a nuclear attack. Sometimes referred to as the information superhighway, the Internet now carries both public and private/com-mercial information to an estimated 36 million people, a number that grows daily. More than 9,000 smaller networks are connected to each other via the Internet by **modem** (a device that allows one to connect a computer to a network using special software and a regular telephone line), through direct fiber-optic or copper links, and/or over radio and light waves.

People use the Internet in a number of ways (Hofstetter, 1998). Services are defined by protocols, or programs, that specify how information moves over the Internet. These are listed next.

Electronic mail (e-mail) is the most popular application of the Internet. Users can send e-mail to individuals or to groups of individuals at the same time. Teachers often establish a mailing list, or **listserv,** that allows them to send a message to all of their students in a class at the same time with a single keystroke. **Chat** is a form of real-time or **synchronous communication** on the Internet; that is, the chat program allows people to send and receive typed messages almost instantaneously. Another form of synchronous communications is **videoconferencing,** or seeing and hearing one another over computers.

News groups are electronic message services that post to servers locally, regionally, nationally, and/or internationally. People subscribe to a news group to gain access to the messages and to post their own messages. News groups are widely used in education. News groups, like e-mail, are forms of **asynchronous communication,** or communication that occurs at times convenient for any of the parties involved; that is, they do not have to be present online at the same time.

A **file transfer protocol (FTP)** lets people move, or download, files from computers anywhere on a network to their own computers. A teacher might locate files of pictures, documents, or raw data at NASA and wish to use them with her students in a science class studying outer space. She might use an FTP to capture the files, put them on her computer, and use them whenever she or the students need them.

The **World Wide Web** (also called the Web or WWW) is a subset of the Internet. The Web consists of tens of thousands of documents that often have text and still images, as well as audio and video. These documents are called **hypermedia.**

With appropriate software and an Internet connection, one can access virtually any of the Web's documents. The range of information accessible on the Web is remarkable. One can travel to points all around the world, as well as find some truly phenomenal educational resources. Getting information from the Web requires no permission, and users can also share what they have with the rest of the world.

A **Web browser** is the software that enables the user to retrieve and see what is on the Web. Popular browsers include Internet Explorer, Netscape, and Mosaic. A **home page,** the first page of a Web document, is much like a textbook's table of contents. Besides indicating who or what organization has posted the document, the page suggests what might be found within the web site.

▶ Distance Learning

Televised instruction has been a fact of life for decades, but new technology designed to promote **distance learning** provides possibilities for teachers and students to connect with each other and to make content areas and topics come alive by communicating interactively over long distances (Institute for Higher Education Policy, 1999). In its most advanced form, distance learning allows people to interact with one another as if they were in the same room. Students can see and hear teachers, and teachers can answer students' questions and react to students' comments instantaneously. These features are especially useful when students are located in geographically remote areas.

The Star Schools Program, established by the Department of Education in 1988, has been instrumental in promoting distance education. You can connect to any of the Star Schools web sites through the U.S. Department of Education web site. The purpose of the Star Schools Program is to encourage improved instruction in mathematics, science, and foreign languages, as well as other areas, such as literacy skills and vocational education. The program uses telecommunications to teach underserved populations, including low-income and nonliterate students, students with limited English proficiency, and students with disabilities. By the end of the decade about 2 million students in all states, the District of Columbia, and the territories had enrolled in courses in math, science, foreign language, and other subjects funded in part by Star School grants. In addition, thousands of teachers had taken courses and participated in staff development programs offered through the Star Schools Program. Regional partnerships exist in cities and states across the nation (U.S. Department of Education, 1999b).

Distance learning projects are especially important for many small, isolated school districts that, because of cost constraints, have had to exclude all but basic-level courses from their curriculum. As financial support goes down and state education standards go up, distance learning offers attractive possibilities for making connections with people and ideas.

▶ Telecommunications Capabilities in the Schools

To understand how technology is changing the foundations of education, we need to know how and where technology is being used. Do educators and their students enter the "information age" when they enter schools, or do they drop back in time, technologically speaking? As illustrated in Figure 13.2, a growing number of students have access to computers at school. Is the technology revolution touching everyone or only those in wealthy areas and in certain geographic regions of the country? How is technology affecting the formation, acquisition, and, most important, the use of knowledge?

It is always difficult to know, relatively speaking, what constitutes appropriate and sufficient use of technology. The CEO Forum on Education and Technology (1998) created a "STaR Chart" to help people gauge School Technology and Readiness (hence the acronym STaR) to use technology. The chart describes six areas: hardware, connectivity, content, professional development, integration and use, and educational benefits. It is possible to profile a school as low-tech, mid-tech, or high-tech in each of the six categories and to set targets for improvement. The chart can serve as both an evaluation and a planning device for technology use in schools. Figure 13.3 contains the STaR Chart standards for hardware.

Efforts by the federal government have done much to stimulate the use of technology in schools, particularly those in need. The Universal Service program for schools and libraries, better known as the **E-rate,** is a federal program that provides discounts on telecommunications and Internet technologies to elementary and sec-

FIGURE 13.2
Student Use of Computers   The percentage of students using a computer at school has increased dramatically in recent years. Why is it so important for access to computers to be higher in schools than in homes?

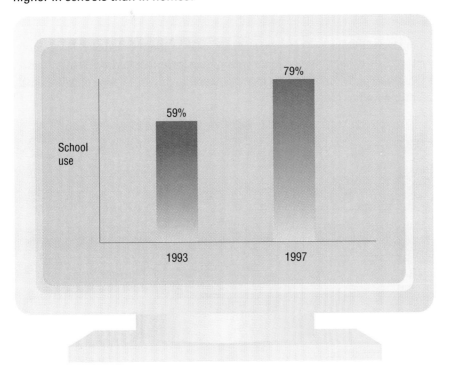

Source: U.S. Department of Education (1999). *Digest of Education Statistics.* Washington, DC: U.S. Government Pringing Office.

ondary schools and public libraries. Thousands of libraries and schools, from every state in the nation, have participated in this program.

Congress authorized the E-rate discount program as part of the Telecommunications Act of 1996. The idea was to bring affordable access to the Internet, distance learning, and other telecommunications-based learning technologies to schoolchildren and library users. The program provides discounts ranging between 20 and 90 percent, with the poorest schools and libraries receiving the highest discounts. The discounts apply to Internet, telecommunications, and internal connections services.

In 1997, the average public school contained 75 computers. With these computers, more schools and more classrooms are getting on the Internet. As Figure 13.4 indicates, the proportion of schools with Internet access increased rapidly from 35 percent in 1994 to 89 percent in 1998 (U.S. Department of Education, 1999a). Although some access is now widespread, most schools are not extensively connected. About 51 percent of instructional rooms had access to the Internet in 1998. Some estimates put the number of children (ages 3 to 17) who regularly access the Internet at 38 million by the year 2002 (eMarketer, 1999).

Using Technology

Internet-Based Videoconferencing

Teachers use the Internet to connect with one another and with government officials to concentrate on common problems. With his dog Trifle in tow, Lowell P. Weicker, Jr., former governor of Connecticut, held an Internet-based videoconference with preservice and inservice teachers from across the nation to discuss a range of educational issues.

Professor Patricia Millman of Fairmont State College and one of her students query Weicker about the use of technology in schools.

Professor Neal Topp and his students at the University of Nebraska, Omaha, quiz Weicker on school funding inequities and school integration.

Trifle steals the show offline.

FIGURE 13.3
1998 School Technology and Readiness

Star Indicators	Hardware			
	Students per computer	Students per multimedia computer	Students per CD-Rom	Maintenance
LOW Tech	10–26	More than 36	More than 333	Off-site irregular maintenance
MID Tech	7–14	12–59	More than 83	Off-site irregular maintenance
HIGH Tech	4–9	7–17	21–250	Off-site regular maintenance
TARGET Tech	2–5	3–8	7–71	On-site continual maintenance

Source: CEO Forum on Education and Technology (1998). STaR Chart: A tool for assessing school technology and readiness. Focus on professional development. Washington, DC: Author. Reprinted with permission.

There are important educational, cultural, and economic reasons why schools are likely to promote telecommunications technologies as learning tools to be placed in the hands of students. As Todd Kent (1999) argues, chief among these reasons are the preservation and extension of democracy. Speaking of recent court decisions that are beginning to clarify the parameters of free speech on the Internet, Kent observes:

If judges are correct in their description of the Internet as an unprecedented market place for free speech, educators must examine their responsibility in educating students in its use. The education community must find a way to allow all children to participate actively in the Internet without falling prey to the distractions of an environment of free speech that includes inappropriate or low-quality material currently protected under the law. Public education has the potential to help ensure that access is not restricted to those children whose families can financially afford it. (1999, p. 30)

FIGURE 13.4
Percent of All Public Schools and Instructional Rooms Having Internet Access: Fall 1994 to Fall 1998

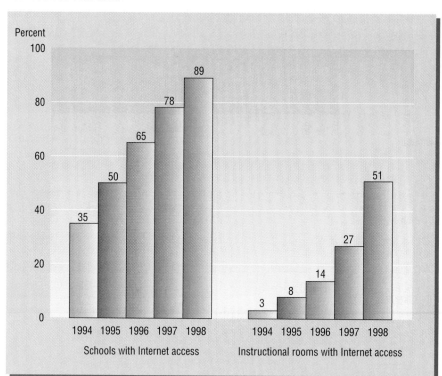

Source: U.S. Department of Education, National Center for Education Statistics, Fast Response Survey System, *Advanced Telecommunications in U.S. Elementary and Secondary Public Schools*, Fall 1996, and *Internet Access in Public Schools and Classrooms: 1994–98.*

 In short, technology in the hands of ordinary people is democratizing the foundations of education. Technology brings opportunities for a person anywhere with a computer and a telephone line to make, acquire, interpret, and apply knowledge. (If you visit the AskERIC Virtual Library on the web you can see just how quickly and easily knowledge is available to those who seek it online.)

But what price must people pay for this new freedom? With increasing opportunities for people to make themselves public electronically comes the necessity of sorting the good information from the poor. The kind of quality control exercised in traditional publishing does not exist in electronic communication and publication, except in a few instances. Moreover, issues of censorship that have been settled legally and practically in traditional publishing must be reexamined with regard to the new communication technologies. Are the creators and managers of the Internet to censor materials? Are school leaders to con-

Could the Internet have a negative impact on education?

trol what is appropriate and inappropriate for young people to read, see, and hear online? Who will decide?

Because much of schooling is controlled and funded by state education authorities, it is important to know what state policymakers are thinking with regard to the use of technology. As part of the *Technology Counts* report based on a national survey, writers working for *Education Week* formulated a set of policy recommendations for using technology effectively in schools. See these recommendations in Figure 13.5. State by state responses to these recommendations appear on the *Education Week* web site.

By its very nature, technology forces people to look forward, to anticipate not only what is important at the moment but what is likely to be important later. When teachers consider how technology might be used to collaborate on their own professional development, they can get a sense of what their students will need to know and be able to do if they are to work together effectively.

FIGURE 13.5
Recommendations for State Policymakers

- States should regularly update their technology plans and evaluate how well they are being implemented.
- States should periodically collect data on the presence and use of technology in schools.
- Because technology must be maintained and updated to remain useful, states should pay for technology as an ongoing commitment, rather than as a one-time expense.
- States should take steps to make sure technology is equitably distributed.
- States should help schools update the physical infrastructure of their buildings to support technology.
- States should adopt standards for what students should learn about technology and be able to do with it.
- States should require incoming teachers to have technology training or expertise to obtain a teaching license.
- States should create opportunities for teachers to learn how to use technology.
- States should disseminate information about effective or innovative uses of education technology.

Source: Technology Counts '98 (undated). Reprinted with permission from *Education Week on the Web.* Available online: http://www.edweek.org/sreports/tc98/st/st-s1.htm

Issues in School Reform

Wired in Boston

The rapid development of technology for educational purposes has made a dramatic impact on schools across the nation. In the following you will see highlights from the technology plan for the Boston Public Schools. As of Spring 1999, in the third year of the plan, Boston can attest to the following accomplishments and immediate goals.

Networked Schools

Every one of Boston's 130 schools has a "starter network" (computer lab, library, principal's office, and 4–8 classrooms) connected to a wide-area network based at Court Street, our central administrative office. Eleven schools are completely networked, with plans to complete the networking of all schools by 2002. Boston is the first major urban school district in the country to have networks and high-speed Internet access throughout every school.

Hardware and Software

In June 1995, Boston had a 1:63 computer student ratio for new computers. By June 1999, we will have installed 10,500 additional state of the art computers, bringing Boston to a 1:6 computer to student ratio. This accomplishment puts Boston well on the way to reaching the goal of one computer for every four students and a computer for each teacher, a commitment made by Mayor Menino in his State of the City Address in January 1996. All computers come "loaded" with software;

Microsoft Office on all machines, and in addition, ClarisWorks, KidPix, and HyperStudio on all elementary and middle school equipment. Each school also receives a budget to purchase additional curriculum software.

Assistive Technology

Boston Public Schools, supported by funding from city, state, and federal funds, has made a major commitment to providing computers and appropriate assistive technology to all special needs classrooms by 2002, as teachers participate in professional development to understand how to use these technologies to support student learning.

Professional Development

Boston has developed Technology Competencies to be achieved by all staff. These competencies, based on those recognized by the International Society for Technology in Education (ISTE), and supported by the Boston Teachers Union, have five levels of proficiency. At each level, BPS offers free on-site courses to teachers, principals, and other staff to help them achieve those competencies. In addition, teachers are awarded computers for their classrooms, once they have completed competencies at each level, and have been "coached" by one of their colleagues to produce technology-based materials for their classrooms.

Student Competencies

In September 1998, a team of Lead Teachers representing all grade levels and including subject area

 ## How Are Collaborative Networks Transforming Teaching and Learning?

Collaborative networks are groups of people gathered voluntarily to help each other explore and advance particular educational issues. Such groups are at the hub of

teachers, bilingual, SPED, and computer instructors began to work to develop a set of Student Technology Competencies. . . . They based their work on the standards recommended and recognized nationally by the International Society for Technology in Education. . . .

Curriculum Integration

Boston Public Schools, supported by grants from the federal and state governments, as well as by IBM, is developing Web-based resources to support the dissemination of exemplary curriculum material which support[s] Boston's Citywide Learning Standards, as well as on-line rubrics to support the assessment of student work. Hundreds of teachers participate in technology-based curriculum workshops and coaching to share the development of best teaching practices.

Libraries

All Boston Public High School libraries, as well as 10 elementary and middle school libraries, are automated in a unique partnership with the Boston Public Library. . . .

Support

The greatest challenge for all school systems developing technology programs is providing adequate support for the technology. To address this concern, Boston has worked on several fronts, including the development of a remote management system for all its networks, and implementation of a sophisticated Help Desk system which responds to many problems over the phone and deploys

teams of technicians to resolve others. Boston anticipates that a major source of support for its technology will be its BPS students. Through partnerships with Microsoft, 3Com, Cisco and other technology companies, Boston's Offices of School-to-Career and Instructional Technology have developed courses and apprenticeships for students ranging from A+ computer repair to networking and systems operation. After school and during vacations, students work as apprentices to BPS technicians, supporting the technology in schools. BPS is developing a 13th and 14th year program in collaboration with CityYear and Americorps for our graduates to continue their work as paid interns in the schools, and at the same time continuing their technical training.

Partnerships

Boston Public Schools has received tremendous support for its technology programs. The LINC Plan has raised more than $38.75 million, including $15.75 million from private partners and $23 million in grants. Major business partners include 3Com, Microsoft, HiQ, Intel, Bell Atlantic, Boston Edison, and more than 100 other companies.

Critical Thinking Are some parts of a technology plan more important than others? Who might be included in the development of such a plan?

Source: Massachusetts LINC Boston, the technology plan for Boston Public Schools. The Secretary's National Conference on Education Technology (July 12–13, 1999). Washington, DC: U.S. Department of Education, pp. 32–34.

efforts to improve the education of targeted student groups, such as students at risk of school failure. One innovative approach is to form *learning communities* that provide children with rich experiences and connect their schools with the children's experiences, their culture, and their community. This approach is part of Stanford Professor Henry Levin's **Accelerated Schools** program, which he instituted in two elementary schools in San Francisco in 1986. The program now serves more than 1,000 schools in 40 states (Northwest Regional Educational Laboratory, 1997).

Instead of trying to remediate perceived deficiencies in children's learning abilities, Levin encourages educators to capitalize on students' strengths, giving at-risk students the kind of rich and challenging instruction typically reserved for gifted and talented children.

> This notion of viewing all children as deserving of and benefiting from the same approach that had been reserved exclusively for those who were labeled gifted and talented was certainly a strange perspective a decade ago when the Accelerated Schools Project was launched. At the time, the standard fare for children in at-risk situations was to immerse them in remedial experiences that emphasized basic skills and repetitive drills in a simplified curriculum. The result was that the longer they attended school, the farther they lagged behind the mainstream in their academic development. (Levin, 1996, p. 3)

For Levin, collaboration is important in the process of transforming a school into an Accelerated School: 90 percent of the staff must agree on the concept before he will work with them. He encourages them to "take stock" of what they are doing and to form a "deep vision" for the future (Brandt, 1992). Always, the adults who run schools must ask themselves a simple question: Is this what we would want for our own children? The answer to the question can spur people to behave in new and creative ways.

Levin argues that people must begin changing schools by developing a deep vision of the future. Sometimes this process can take weeks or months. This vision is not often found in the typical mission statement of a school—a document that, according to Levin, frequently lacks vision. Instead, he wants to help people work together to develop a set of beliefs that drive their daily behavior.

When Beth Keller and Pilar Soler (1996) investigated the effects of the Accelerated Schools philosophy on teachers' beliefs and practices, they found changed attitudes, but they did not know how these attitudes might have filtered into classroom life. Teachers they surveyed reported changes in how they conceptualized teaching styles, expectations for students, accountability, collaboration, reflection, and participation. The investigators also noted that teachers viewed the principal's support and encouragement as crucial to the success of translating the philosophy into action.

▶ Developing Schools for Reform

Levin's concept of Accelerated Schools constitutes only one model of reform. Many others have emerged in recent years. The American Association of School Administrators (AASA) has described 24 notable approaches along a number of dimensions. With the help of the American Institutes for Research, the AASA has also rated their effectiveness in terms of raising student achievement—students' test scores, grades, and graduation rates. Their review found only a few school reform models that have documented their positive effects in such terms. It is important to remember that some approaches have not been operating long enough to have produced this information. And these student achievement measures are not the sole criteria by which the public or the educational community judges school success.

The summary in Table 13.3 provides a snapshot of the approaches' relative strengths in three areas: (1) evidence of positive effects on student achievement, (2) support developers provide schools as they adopt the approaches, and (3) first-year adoption costs.

▶ Targeting Students at Risk

There are other school reform strategies meant especially for children at risk. Since the 1970s James B. Comer of Yale University and his colleagues have been working with teachers, principals, parents, and community members to help children at risk to beat the odds and succeed. Comer uses a collaborative process to create programs that foster child development. He calls the process the School Development Program. It, too, appears in Table 13.3.

Comer's strategy has been tried and found successful in some of the toughest schools in Washington, DC; Camden, New Jersey; Brooklyn; Dade County; Chicago; Dallas; Detroit; New Orleans; and many other communities. David Squires and Robert Kranyik (1995/1996) characterize the Comer approach as a form of site-based management, in which teams of professionals engage in "no-fault problem solving" and "consensual or collaborative decision making." In other words, people do not blame one another for problems; they work together to solve them.

When Dallas adopted Comer's approach in 10 schools, they called it School-Centered Education to convey the idea that it was their own special adaptation. They used principals, teachers, and parents to help train others in the approach. They redirected resources to local schools from the central office and restructured the central office staff to focus on providing services to schools. The lesson in the Dallas experience, and in other places, as well, is that success depends heavily on public ownership of the ideas. People in the school community need to "own" the ideas if they are to take root and grow.

Collaborative networks also are transforming teaching and learning in American high schools. In 1984 to 1985, for example, Theodore Sizer of Brown University organized the **Coalition of Essential Schools,** with nine member schools. Sizer's intent was to build and maintain viable networks of parents, students, and educators who could transform high schools into better places to teach and learn. By 1999, more than 1,000 schools were members of the Coalition. Each school defines for itself what constitutes a "good school," but the coalition of all schools expresses allegiance to nine common principles, shown in Figure 13.6.

One challenge for Essential Schools is to link or integrate everything from curricula to people. In their effort to live up to the motto Less is more, Essential Schools encourage high school teachers who view themselves as subject matter specialists to think about stripping down their own discipline to essentials and linking instruction between the disciplines. Coalition members advocate "adopting common themes or aligning parallel courses, either separately or in teams" (Cushman, 1993b, p. 4) and then combining the content of two or more courses—for instance, linking history, literature, government, and the arts in an American studies course (Cushman, 1993a).

TABLE 13.3
Summary of All 24 Approaches to School Reform[1]

	Evidence of positive effects on student achievement[2]	Year introduced in schools	Number of schools	Support developer provides schools	First year costs[3]	First-year costs with current staff reassigned
Accelerated Schools (K–8)	◔	1986	1000	◑	$27	$14
America's Choice (K–12)	?	1998	300	●	$190	$90
ATLAS Communities (PreK–12)	?	1992	63	◑	$98	$90
Audrey Cohen College (K–12)	?	1970	16	◑	$161	$86
Basic Schools Network (K–12)	?	1992	150	◑	$12	NC
Coalition of Essential Schools (K–12)	○	1984	1000	◔	NA	NA
Community for Learning (K–12)	◑	1990	92	●	$157	$82
Co-NECT (K–12)	?	1992	75	●	$588	NC
Core Knowledge (K–8)	◑	1990	750	◑	$56	NC
Different Ways of Knowing (K–7)	◑	1989	412	●	$84	NC
Direct Instruction (K–6)	●	Late '60s	150	◑	$244	$194
Expeditionary Learning Outward Bound (K–12)	◑	1992	65	●	$81	NC
The Foxfire Fund (K–12)	?	1966	NA	◔	$65	NC
High Schools That Work (9–12)	●	1987	860	●	$48	NC
High/Scope (K–3)	◔	1967	27	●	$130[4]	NC
League of Professional Schools (K–12)	◔	1989	158	◑	$13	NC
Modern Red Schoolhouse (K–12)	?	1993	50	●	$215	NC

When studying five Coalition high schools, Patricia Wasley and her colleagues (Wasley, Hampel & Clark, 1997) found that the Coalition strategy involved the whole school in discussion about how to help students, but that no two good Coalition schools look alike.

> [T]he intellectual work of figuring out what needs redesigning falls specifically to the local community. The principles, which at first may appear simple and straightforward, challenge the traditional American high school in profound ways. As such, they stimulate healthy controversy both in schools and out. (1997, p. 4)

▌ **TABLE 13.3**
(Continued)

	Evidence of positive effects on student achievement[2]	Year introduced in schools	Number of schools	Support developer provides schools	First year costs[3]	First-year costs with current staff reassigned
Onward to Excellence (K–12)	◔	1981	1000	●	$72	$60
Paideia (K–12)		1982	80	◐	$146	$96
Roots and Wings (PreK–6)	◔	1993	200	●	$270	$70
School Development Program (K–12)	◐	1968	700	◐	$45	$32
Success for All (PreK–6)	●	1987	1130	●	$270	$70
Talent Development High School (9–12)	◔	1994	10	●	$57	$27
Urban Learning Centers (PreK–12)	?	1993	13	◐	$169	$159

Key

● = Strong evidence of positive effects on student achievement

◐ = Promising evidence of positive effects on student achievement

◔ = Marginal evidence of positive effects on student achievement

○ = Evidence of mixed, weak, or no effects on student achievement

? = No research on effects on student achievement

[1]This table summarizes information from *An Educator's Guide to Schoolwide Reform*.

[2]Although many types of student outcomes are important, evidence of positive effects on student achievement is a key consideration in selecting schoolwide reforms. However, some schools may wish to consider a new approach that has not yet developed strong evidence of effectiveness, but provides the strongest match with school goals.

[3]Costs are in thousands of dollars (e.g., $62=$62,000).

[4]The estimate for High/Scope assumes a school of 25 K–3 teachers.

Source: American Institutes for Research, 1999. *An educators' guide to schoolwide reform.* Arlington, VA: Educational Research Service. Retrieved August 24, 1999, from the web site of the American Association of School Administrators: http://www.aasa.org/reform

Strategies for involving parents and community members in an Essential School run the gamut of possibilities: sponsoring evening study groups in which adults explore the same educational issues, holding public exhibitions of student work, paying parents as classroom aides, organizing parent advisory groups, holding small-group sessions with the principal, publishing a newsletter, encouraging the local newspaper to cover educational issues, and so forth.

The Cadillac of the line of school reform models is **Success for All,** developed by Robert Slavin and Nancy Madden at Johns Hopkins University. (It is also listed in Table 13.3.) The program operates in more than 1,100 schools in the United States and five other countries. It is expensive, comparatively speaking, and effective, espe-

FIGURE 13.6
Principles of Essential Schools   If you were asked to rank by importance the attributes of an Essential School listed at left, what would be your top two or three?

The Essential School should

✓ focus on helping adolescents learn to use their minds;

✓ have a simple mission requiring students to master essential skills and knowledge;

✓ help all students strive for the same goals, but vary means according to students' needs;

✓ personalize teaching and learning;

✓ be guided by the metaphor of student as worker, not teacher as deliverer of instruction;

✓ prepare students to exhibit their language and mathematical skills;

✓ set a tone that communicates expectations, trust, and decency; use incentives; and encourage parents to collaborate;

✓ help staff think of themselves first as generalists and next as specialists; and

✓ provide for planning time, competitive salaries, and per-pupil costs of no more than 10% above traditional schools.

Source: Horace's School: Redesigning the American High School by T. R. Sizer. Boston: Houghton Mifflin. All rights reserved.

cially for urban students at risk for academic failure. The main goal of Success for All is to ensure success in reading. The program also strives to reduce referrals to special education, reduce the number of students who are retained, increase daily attendance, and address family needs. Its companion program, Roots and Wings, deals with content and experiences for children in reading and language arts, mathematics, science, and social studies.

Success for All has nine components: (1) a reading curriculum that provides at least 90 minutes of daily instruction in classes regrouped across age lines according to reading performance; (2) assessment of student progress at least once very eight weeks; (3) one-to-one reading tutors; (4) a program for prekindergarten and kindergarten children that emphasizes language development and reading; (5) an emphasis on cooperative learning as a key teaching strategy; (6) a family support team to encourage parent support and involvement and to address problems at home; (7) a local facilitator to provide mentoring, counseling, and support to the school as needed; (8) staff support teams that assist teachers during the implementation; and (9) training and technical assistance on reading assessment, classroom management, and cooperative learning.

Should all students be exposed to the same basic curriculum?

▶ Increasing Parental Involvement

Collaborative approaches must involve parents to succeed. Children's futures are inextricably linked to their parents. When parents take an interest in their children's progress, when parents hold high but reasonable expectations for their children's performance and support them by meeting basic needs, good things happen: Students' school attendance improves, their self-esteem and achievement spiral upward, and their long-term prospects for living successful, productive lives increase.

Educators work to forge and maintain strong ties to families. Connections can be seen in the thousands of parent–teacher organizations across the country. The most famous, the National Parent Teacher Association (National PTA), celebrated its 100th anniversary in 1996. In 1896, when Alice McLellan Birney founded the organization as the National Congress of Mothers in Washington, DC, she did so with refreshing clarity of purpose: "Let us have no more croaking as to what cannot be done; let us see what can be done" (National PTA, 1995–1996). What had to be done was to establish and tend lines of communication between home and school. The PTA and other such organizations sanctioned connections between families and schools; they made it appropriate and possible for adults in and out of the educational system to work together for children.

Too often, however, it is difficult to meet and work with the parents and guardians of children most in need of a strong home–school support network—single parents, those working at more than one job, those pulled in so many directions by so many problems that they are struggling just to survive. Many of these single parents are children themselves. Despite the small number of glowing exceptions, far too many of these young parents fail in school, thus relegating themselves and their children to a bleak future. Fewer than one-third of teens who start families before they reach the age of 18 complete high school. Children of teenage parents often perform more poorly in school than other students and are 50 percent more likely to repeat a grade (Sandham, 1999). (See Figure 13.7.)

 ## How Are Collaborative Networks Transforming the Professional Development of Teachers?

One visible attempt to encourage education professionals to work together on relevant tasks has been the concept of the **professional development school,** or PDS. A PDS is a college–school partnership that stimulates cooperation among professors, teachers, student teachers, and young people.

William Johnson (1990) likens the notion of a professional development school to the image of the teacher promoted by John Dewey as an "interpreter of culture to active children, not the scientific classroom manager guiding children through hierarchically organized curricula" (1990, p. 584). Paul Dixon and Richard Ishler call the professional development school movement "the inventing of a new institution mixing the best of theory, research, and practice at the precollege level and among teacher preparatory programs" (1992, p. 28). The concept of a professional development school is very similar to what others have called a "professional practice school" (Levine, 1992).

FIGURE 13.7
Barriers to Effective Parent Involvement

- Parents may have a low literacy level and may have difficulty reading newsletters or notes that are sent home.

- Non-English-speaking or limited-English-speaking parents may have difficulty communicating with the schools.

- Parents with nonmajority cultural and linguistic backgrounds may be uncomfortable about becoming involved in the school. Or parents who have been discriminated against previously may feel alienated and hesitate to get involved.

- Parents may not feel welcome at school.

- Parents who have had unsuccessful or stressful school experiences may feel uncomfortable interacting with personnel in their children's school.

- Parents who have not finished school may feel uncomfortable about entering the school setting.

- Some families are under acute economic stress; their basic needs take precedence over involvement in their children's education.

- When both parents work outside the home, they may have difficulty attending school events that are held during the workday.

- Parents' child-care responsibilities may prevent them from participating in programs held at school.

- Parents may lack transportation to participate in school activities, or parking may be a problem.

- Many parents are raising their children alone. Financial and time limitations can make it difficult to be involved at school.

- Time limitations for both parents and teachers make it difficult to participate readily in parent involvement activities. A large percentage of employed parents feel they do not have enough time with their children. Teachers also have limited time. They are usually not provided time for parent involvement programs; they have to make time. Teachers' after-school time is limited; often they are parents themselves.

Source: Stein, M. R., & Thorkildsen, R. J. (1999). *Parent involvement in education: Insights and applications from the research.* Bloomington, IN: Phi Delta Kappan International, pp. 64–66.

While schools as places are the prominent feature in the PDS picture, a professional-development school is not simply a particular school. The name is misleading. A PDS is a unique college–school partnership, and a concept that spurs cooperation among professors, teachers, student–teachers, and yes, youngsters. Reform is cultivated in colleges as well as schools. The PDS enthusiast values the team theme that has sparked change in business, engineering, and medicine. In these fields, as in professional-development-school alliances, teamwork is essential to professional practice. This approach is uncommon in traditional professor–teacher relationships. (Schwartz, 1999, p. 41)

Researchers at the Center for Research on the Context of Teaching at Stanford University suggest that "teachers' professional communities—be they academic departments, schools, or teacher networks—are powerful mechanisms for stimulating innovation, reflection, experimentation, and reform" (McLaughlin & Talbert, 1993, p. 3). Despite encouraging and highly visible attempts to foster collaboration between universities and public schools, however, people are probably more likely to read about such efforts than to experience them.

Why is there not more collaboration between universities and public schools?

▶ Advancing Subject Area Studies

Collaborative networks for teachers as professionals also focus on content areas and mutual professional development through collegial activities. In 1985 and 1986 the Ford Foundation targeted more than $6 million to 11 cities across the United States to establish collaborative networks of mathematics teachers, school administrators, and mathematicians from colleges and universities and industry. These 11 cities were Cleveland, Durham, Los Angeles, Memphis, Minneapolis–St. Paul, New Orleans, Philadelphia, Pittsburgh, St. Louis, San Diego, and San Francisco. Since 1990 four more cities have been added to the group: Dayton, Ohio; Columbus, Georgia; Worcester, Massachusetts; and Milwaukee, Wisconsin.

The networks have attempted to break teacher isolation and encourage professionalism by providing activities such as industrial internships for teachers, symposia, workshops, dinner meetings, and site visits. They have also funded trips to conferences and professional meetings for teachers.

Evaluation of the collaboratives' activities suggest that of the approximately 3,000 high school mathematics teachers in the original sites, about 20 percent have become frequent participants in activities offered at their sites. More than 80 percent of those teachers thought that the network had enriched their professional lives and that, in fact, they were valued by a larger community (Webb & Romberg, 1994).

▶ Enhancing Collegiality Among Educators

John Goodlad and others have led efforts to institutionalize some new opportunities for teachers to interrelate as colleagues with common interests and to function cooperatively. Goodlad and his colleagues established the **National Network for Educational Renewal,** consisting of 34 colleges and universities and more than 100 school districts in 14 states. The intent of this network is to renew schools and teacher education. Members of the National Network for Educational Renewal agree to address a set of 19 postulates, the first of which sets the tone for the organization:

How are new collaborative networks for teachers extending collegiality beyond school walls? What other collaborative networks are transforming education in the United States?

Programs for the education of the nation's educators must be viewed by institutions offering them as a major responsibility to society and be adequately supported and promoted and vigorously advanced by the institution's top leadership. (National Network for Educational Renewal, 1999)

Without support, of course, even the best ideas, like seed cast on stone, never take hold. The give and take of colleagues who at some level share a commitment to deal openly with difficult issues contributes to a climate that is hospitable to educational growth and development.

American schools have long been polite places where no one confronts anyone else too directly. Teachers who disagree with policies complain in private and ignore the policy in practice. Administrators congratulate themselves on their accomplishments without seeking evidence of success or failure from those they know to be skeptical. Those schools that consistently paper over areas of disagreement hardly ever build educational programs that truly develop their students' potential.

Schools that do engage in rigorous discourse have many advantages that increase and persist over time. The climate of the school becomes more professional, centered around dialogue about teaching and learning. Those usually labeled as resisters can win the regard of their peers because of their ability to ask the most difficult questions. In turn, the resisters find legitimate avenues for involvement. All staff members feel relieved they can speak openly instead of covertly, and they begin to see that direct conversation, straight shooting, can improve their capacity to work with students. (Hampel, 1999, p. 47)

How Can Professional Educators Prepare for the Future?

It would be natural for educators to be overwhelmed by the complexity and pace of our rapidly changing world. There is so much to know, so much to do. Faced with the diversity of interests that contend for attention in public education, it would be easy to take one of two actions: leap headfirst into the maelstrom of problems or sit back, paralyzed with indecision. But professionals must chart another course. They must distinguish themselves from nonprofessionals in two important ways: by what they know and by what they know how to do. Those who will prevail will do so by participating in collaborative networks for the purposes shown in Figure 13.8, by building their store of knowledge, and by refining their repertoire of skills.

▶ Using Professional Knowledge

Can collaborative networks contribute to the professionalization of teaching?

Both informal and formal sources of knowledge inform the successful practice of teaching. The formal knowledge base of a profession exists in books, periodicals, and other writings. This knowledge serves as a foundation for teacher education programs, as a basis for licensure and certification exami-

FIGURE 13.8
Uses of Collaborative Networks   People are more likely to collaborate when they have reasons to do so and opportunities for working together. What barriers, other than time and opportunity, might restrict collaboration among teachers? What other factors might enhance the likelihood of collaboration?

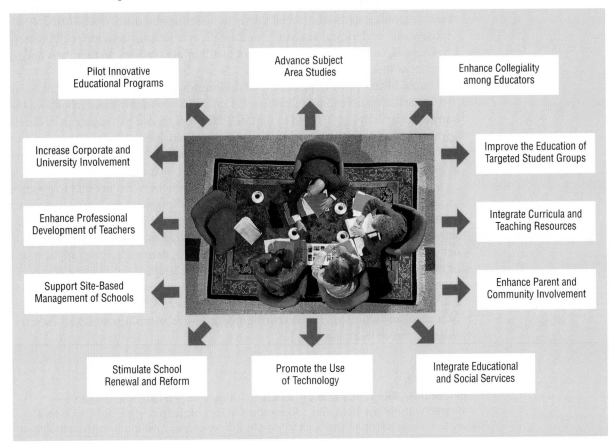

nations and as a benchmark by which teachers gauge their own practice. The informal knowledge base is an uncodified body of knowledge that exists in the minds and hearts of those who practice the profession. For many teachers this personal source of knowledge can be richer and more immediately applicable than the recorded knowledge (Clandinin & Connelly, 1996).

The formal knowledge base for teaching consists of two general kinds of knowledge: theory-driven conceptions of effective teaching, and results of empirical research. These two kinds of knowledge often complement each other. Theory helps to explain how teaching and learning occur; research provides results of observations or experiments that help to explain relationships between teaching and learning. The most useful theories for educators explain what teachers should do and why (Joyce & Weil, 1996).

For example, Jean Piaget formulated a theory of intellectual development that has implications for guiding teachers' actions. He described intellectual development in terms of stages (sensorimotor, preoperational, concrete operational, formal operational). In his theory, the teacher's role is threefold: (1) to create environments where children can spontaneously construct knowledge for themselves in ways that match their stages of cognitive development, (2) to assess children's thinking, and (3) to organize group activities for social interaction among children (Wadsworth, 1978). Teachers who understand and can articulate the relationship between such theoretical knowledge and practice demonstrate that they are ready to do their best and to do better as their knowledge improves.

Harold Mitzel (1960) first described the empirical research on teaching in a way that made it accessible to practitioners. He gave us a way to think and talk about the knowledge underlying our field so that we could apply it and participate in its development. Mitzel depicted a set of four instructional variables to describe teaching and learning as interrelated activities. These instructional variables include presage characteristics, teaching processes, student products, and instructional contexts.

Presage characteristics are the characteristics of teachers that are said to presage, or precede, acts of teaching—for example, teachers' personalities and background knowledge. Teaching process variables are demonstrated by teachers during a lesson—the questions they ask, the feedback they provide, and the like. Student product variables are student outcomes measured by tests, demonstrations, applications of knowledge, and other measurable indications of learning. Instructional context variables are factors both inside and outside the classroom that impinge on teaching and learning, such as students' characteristics, school leadership, money spent on education, and children's home environments. The relationships among these variables are shown in Figure 13.9.

FIGURE 13.9
Model for Describing Research on Teaching   Research on teaching cannot be conducted without the help and cooperation of lots of people—teachers, students, parents, administrators. What factors might influence your willingness to participate in research studies either as an investigator or as the subject of investigation?

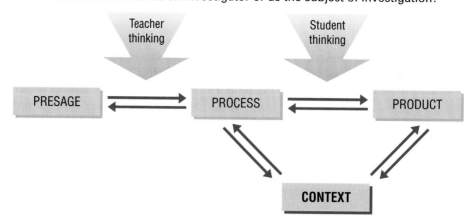

Source: Adapted from "Teacher Effectiveness: Criteria of Teacher Effectiveness" by H. E. Mitzel, 1960. In *Encyclopedia of Educational Research* (3rd ed.) (pp. 1481–1486) by C. S. Harris (Ed.) Copyright 1960 and renewed 1988, by American Research Association. Used by permission of Macmillan Publishing Company.

Herbert Walberg (1991) summarized some 8,000 studies of teaching and learning in elementary and secondary schools to provide an overview of more and less effective educational practices. Using a statistical process of calculating "effect sizes," he revealed the relative power of different instructional behaviors to boost student achievement. For instance, Table 13.4 shows the greater effectiveness of using manipulative materials in the teaching of mathematics over problem-solving approaches and the new math of the 1960s and 1970s.

As Thomas Good and Jere Brophy (2000) have noted, current research builds on findings that indicate how important teachers are when it comes to stimulating student learning. This new research also focuses on the role of the student and recognizes that students do not passively receive or copy input from teachers.

> Instead they actively mediate it by trying to make sense of it and to relate it to what they already know (or think they know) about the topic. This is precisely what we want them to do, because unless students build representations of the new learning, "making it their own" by paraphrasing it in their own words and considering its meanings and implications, the learning will be retained only as relatively meaningless and inert rote memories. (2000, p. 416)

The teachers best prepared to face the future are those armed not only with empirical and theoretical knowledge but with practical knowledge of teaching, as well. This knowledge is constructed through teachers' own experiences. In many ways practical knowledge held tacitly by teachers is far ahead of theory and research. Teachers have always constructed their own knowledge by intuiting or experiencing what it takes to work with others to help them learn.

Researchers who study teachers' and students' thinking sometimes use concept maps to describe implicit knowledge. Concept maps are ways of organizing ideas about a particular topic so that relationships among subtopics can be displayed visually. When Tina created her own concept maps of "teacher planning" at the beginning and end of a semester, they turned out to be very different, because her thinking had changed over time. Her beginning-of-semester concept map of teacher planning appears in Figure 13.10. Tina said this about her maps and her thinking:

> For the first map, I had recently completed a job working at a student computer lab at a high school (over the summer). I did not know much about teacher

▌ TABLE 13.4
Effects of Mathematics Methods

Method	Number of Studies	Effect Size	Graphic Representation of Effect Size
Manipulative materials	64	1.04	.xxxxxxxxxx
Problem solving	33	0.34	.xxxx
New mathematics	134	0.24	.xx

Source: Effective Teaching: Current Research (p. 58) by Hersholt C. Waxman and Herbert J. Wahlberg (Eds.), 1991. Berkeley, CA: McCutchan. Copyright 1991 by McCutchan Publishing Corporation, Berkeley, CA 94702. Permission granted by the publisher.

FIGURE 13.10

Tina's Concept Map of Teacher Planning What thoughts about planning seemed most important to this teacher?

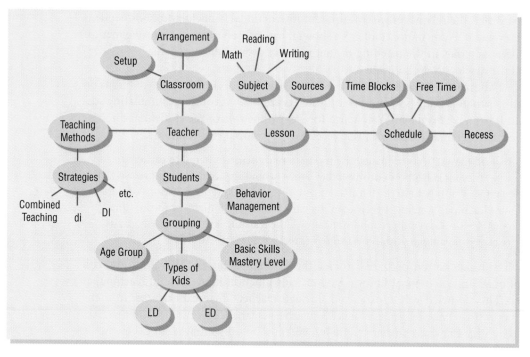

planning except for what I had experienced or what had been touched on in class. Because of my lack of education on teacher planning, the map was very general in most areas. The newer map is more developed, more specific simply because I know more about planning than I did then. I have had many classes and field experiences this semester that have shown me some of the necessities and pitfalls associated with planning instruction and classroom management. I was able to be more specific at the end of the semester and even join items, because I have learned first-hand that most of these planning ideas are intertwined.

Successful teachers possess both general and specific teaching knowledge, but apply their knowledge differently with different students. Jere Brophy and Mary McCaslin (1992) underscore the importance of teaching to individual students' needs in a series of studies they did on teachers' perceptions of and strategies for dealing with "problem students" (students exhibiting unsatisfactory achievement, personal adjustment, or classroom behavior). Teachers who had been identified by their principals as less successful in dealing with "problem students" described those students as underachievers, low achievers, aggressive, defiant, distractible, immature, shy, or rejected by peers. Brophy and McCaslin found no magic formula for teaching problem students, but they did identify some notable differences between successful and unsuccessful teachers. Typically, successful teachers demonstrated more willingness to become personally involved with students, showed more confidence in their own abilities to help the students improve their behaviors, and were better able to articulate strategies for helping students to change their behavior and increase their learning.

What teachers need to know about teaching is also closely allied to their disciplines. It is not enough to possess general teaching knowledge at the expense of content knowledge any more than it is to know the content and be ignorant of teaching. To teach mathematics successfully, for example, a teacher must master the subject matter, but must also possess the teaching knowledge necessary for creating environments where students can learn mathematics. This blending of content knowledge and teaching knowledge has been called **pedagogical content knowledge** (Shulman, 1986).

▶ Reflecting on Professional Practice

We have tried to encourage the idea that the best preparation for a future in teaching is to learn from work on the job. Those who can reflect intelligently on their own practice have the greatest chance of continuing to progress as teachers and to achieve some reasonable sense of professional self-determination. The five steps of professional practice noted in this text promote such behavior.

In any field, professionals *perceive* problems and opportunities; because they are awake—they are mentally alert to what is going on around them. Professionals also can articulate their *values* in relation to the values of others they work with and serve. People's values help determine whether professionals' actions will be accepted or rejected.

In addition, professionals possess some specialized knowledge that nonprofessionals do not. Professional educators *know* their content, and they know how to communicate in ways that students will understand and accept. They possess knowledge about teaching and learning. Exceptionally talented teachers, both experienced and novice, also often know when they need to know more.

Acting on the basis of one's perceptions, values, and knowledge is the bread-and-butter of professional life. Professionals continually apply their knowledge and demonstrate their skills in ways that nonprofessionals cannot.

Finally, professionals *evaluate* their actions to determine their effectiveness and to plan for the future. People who can reflect intelligently on their practice—and who enjoy doing important work as best they can—turn jobs into careers.

Teachers are students, too. Even the best among us do not always know how or why we are successful. With experience, however, we grow accustomed to not having all the answers and to relying, instead, on the best information available, information acquired from successful and unsuccessful practice. No matter how professionally capable or personally adept teachers become, we will never single-handedly teach our students all that they need to know and be able to do. Nor can we anticipate all the

Voices

On How Great Teachers Influence Students

Teachers strongly influence students' habits of mind. Edward R. Ducharme, editor of the Journal of Teacher Education *and himself a teacher educator, reflects on his experiences as a student of Muriel Ragsdale, his high school art teacher.*

I often find it valuable to speculate on what I call great teachers: what makes them the way they are? How are they alike? What do they have in common? I frequently ask students in teacher preparation classes to write about great teachers they may have had. A number of years ago I wrote about a great teacher I had in high school even more years ago. She remains dear in my memory years later.

I begin by arguing that we should surround our children with great people. In general we have not surrounded kids with great people; nice people, maybe, but not great people. What are great people? They are those with a passion for something, with a high degree of tolerance for all kinds of difficulties, with finely honed talents or skills, people with a desire to engender and help develop the best in others, and with a love for the variety that is humankind.

Let me reflect on Muriel Ragsdale who was my high school art teacher when I was a high school student. She taught an art class in which we started with pencils and sheets of paper when we were in the 10th grade and by the time we graduated three years later we had worked in just about every imaginable medium. Most of us had some degree of competency

in our work, so I guess it would have to be said that Muriel Ragsdale was a pretty good teacher of her subject matter of art.

But art became a class in which hundreds of things other than drawing, sketching, and painting went on. Muriel Ragsdale fostered all manner of conversations in that room as we worked on our projects. She talked of the power of dreams, fashions in dress, life in Manhattan (where she'd lived for a while). We did oil paintings of our favorite phobias (mine was falling off cliffs) so as to exorcise them from our consciousness and thus avoid bad dreams (not all schemes of gifted teachers work; I still have that occasional dream of falling!); we played a game inviting any five people in the history of the world to a dinner party and telling the reasons for our choices. I remember inviting Leonardo Da Vinci, Robert Frost, Joan of Arc, Ted Williams, and Franklin Roosevelt. (Now, that would have been some dinner!) I'm not sure I would make many changes if I were asked to play the same game today. We planned school dances sponsored by the Art Club which she advised. She showed slides and copies of famous paintings. To this day, when I walk into a museum like the National Gallery in Washington there is always a moment when I see the original of a painting and I remember Muriel Ragsdale showing us a copy.

Trust and warmth developed among us kids, some of whom saw one another only in this class. One day we talked and laughed and made noise

problems students will face. We must learn to work together with others, to work democratically, to maximize our effects. And the most important people with whom we must collaborate are students. By working together we model for students what we hope they in turn will model for others. We also transmit a set of democratic values that form the cultural bedrock of society.

The best teachers stretch themselves time and again to be creative and technically proficient; they know they can call on their abilities when the need arises. They are not afraid to fail, because they have done that too and have lived to teach and learn another day. A good teacher, like a good student, gains power from doing the work.

beyond Muriel Ragsdale's tolerance. She asked us to stop and we thought she was kidding, so we continued. She asked again; we kept on. She wept, looked at us, and left the room. We sat in shame for five minutes or so and then went and got her. I still feel shame recalling that moment when we made her cry through our own callousness and insensitivity.

My favorite art activity was producing sports cartoons. I was pretty good, and by my senior year, I was considering art school. One day I went to Muriel Ragsdale and asked her: "Am I good enough that, with schooling and more training, I can make a living at art?" (Yes, a very practical question; but what do you expect of a French Canadian, callow youth whose parents were limited to 6th and 7th grade education, who worked in a grocery store every day after school and all day Saturday, and saw college only through the images presented in Hollywood musicals of the time?) She looked at me—I am sure I was her favorite student (one instinctively knows that)—a long time and then said: "No. You see, you cannot do with your hands what you see in your head and you probably wouldn't be satisfied with that kind of life." Those of us who teach know what courage it takes to discourage our favorite students from pursuing what we do for a living.

You may now see why I loved Muriel Ragsdale and cherish her memory. She gave us a sense of dignity and importance; she didn't ridicule our occasional adolescent whining and pains. I saw Muriel Ragsdale twice after graduating from high school, the first time when I was a senior in college, majoring in English, not art. The second time was years later; she had retired, and I was a professor at the University of Vermont. She had read what I had written. She said to me, "All those years I taught, I never knew anyone understood what I was doing." I was glad I had written what I had and sad that only in her retirement had she read words of love and praise and understanding.

Children of all ages should have people like Muriel Ragsdale around them. She goaded us, inspired us, wept in front of us. She told jokes, talked about great literature, dared us to be ourselves, and—most importantly—she loved us.

I have walked a long distance since my school days. Many other teachers have taught me; I have taught many teachers; I have taught high school students, undergraduates, masters students, and doctoral students. Always I look in others and in myself for the qualities that made Muriel great as a teacher and as a human being.

All these thoughts reduce to one: schools should have many people in them whom kids would go out of their way to spend time with and still remember years later.

CRITICAL THINKING

What great teachers have you known? How were they similar to and different from Muriel Ragsdale? What characteristics did Muriel Ragsdale possess, if any, that would help her succeed in today's schools? If, sometime, somewhere in the future, one of your former students was writing about you as a teacher, how would you want to be remembered?
Source: In Praise of Muriel Ragsdale by E. Ducharme, September, 1996, unpublished manuscript, Drake University.

SUMMARY

What trends are changing teachers' professional roles?

1. The role of teacher is changing because of public attention to a variety of educational factors—performance standards, goals, instructional objectives, curriculum, measurable student outcomes, concepts of minimum competence and comprehensive assessment, as well as students' opportunities to learn the material for which they will be held accountable.

2. Minimum competency tests and other high-stakes tests focus educators and the lay public on educational outcomes, or what students know and can do. Some people argue that if such tests are to be used to hold students accountable then school systems must be held accountable for providing opportunities for students to learn.

3. There are several notable efforts to change how students are taught and assessed: integrating curriculum rather than simply adding more information; assessing students' skills, knowledge, and attitudes using comprehensive measures; and making assessment reflect what students must be able to do and how they will need to behave in real life if they are to be successful.

4. A number of other trends also promise to alter the role of teacher, including gender issues, inclusion of students with disabilities in general education classrooms, and attention to the character education of children in forms of service learning.

How are links to technology changing the foundations of education?

5. Technology can be integrated into content area instruction or taught as tools to perform tasks. Technology can promote an active role for students by encouraging them to use technology to construct meaning for themselves and to solve complex problems. Technology also can be used to facilitate an integrated or multidisciplinary approach to teaching and learning involving a broad range of skills. Technology can enhance interactions among students, providing the benefits of cooperative learning.

6. The Internet and World Wide Web are opening many new educational possibilities, including distance education.

7. Technology in the hands of ordinary people is democratizing the foundations of education, because technology brings opportunities for a person anywhere with a computer and a telephone line to make, acquire, interpret, and apply knowledge. Technology also forces people to look forward, to anticipate not only what is important at the moment but what is likely to be important later.

How are collaborative networks transforming teaching and learning?

8. Collaborative networks of parents, educators, business leaders, government bureaucrats, and others, are at the hub of efforts to improve the education of targeted student groups, such as students at risk of school failure. Other collaborative networks intent on changing current educational practice target schools and subject matter areas.

9. Strong empirical support for some school reform models is emerging.

How are collaborative networks transforming the professional development of teachers?

10. Professional development schools represent one approach to advancing the development of teachers. These organizations are meant to function much as teaching hospitals in the medical field, or to be places where novice and experienced professionals work together to demonstrate and share their expertise.

11. Collaborative networks for teachers as professionals also focus on content areas and mutual professional development through collegial activities. These networks try to break teacher isolation and encourage professionalism by providing activities such as industrial internships for teachers, symposia, workshops, dinner meetings, site visits, conferences, and professional meetings for teachers.

How can professional educators prepare for the future?

12. Professional teachers prepare themselves to continue learning by steeping themselves in the foundational knowledge base of the profession, knowledge that emanates from many sources, including theory, research, and practice.

13. The teachers best prepared to continue learning on the job are those who can reflect on their work. Reflection means recognizing issues, taking perspectives or examining values, calling up relevant professional knowledge upon which to base one's actions, taking such actions, and evaluating their effects.

TERMS AND CONCEPTS

Accelerated Schools   521
asynchronous communication   515
character education   511
chat   515
Coalition of Essential Schools   525
collaborative network   521
comprehensive assessment   508
distance learning   515
electronic mail (e-mail)   515
E-rate   516
file transfer protocol (FTP)   515
gender sensitivity training   509
high-stakes test   506
home page   515
hypermedia   515
Internet   514
listserv   515
literacy   506

minimum competency test   506
modem   514
National Assessments of Educational Progress (NAEP)   504
National Network for Educational Renewal   531
news groups   515
opportunity-to-learn (OTL) standards   507
pedagogical content knowledge   537
professional development school   529
service learning   512
standards   501
Success for All   527
Synchronous communication   515
videoconferencing   515
Web browser   515
World Wide Web   515

REFLECTIVE PRACTICE

In the following case, Sarah, a classroom teacher, attends a faculty meeting on teachers' use of lab computers. After reading this case, apply the steps of professional practice as outlined in the questions that follow.

After students left for the day, Sarah returned to her classroom, exhausted and frustrated. She wondered what she might do to minimize the difficulty she experienced when conducting a structured computer activity. She wasn't sure how to remedy that with all the other demands on her time. Tom Howard doubled as the computer coordinator. He had already been generous with his time, and she didn't feel right about asking for more. Sarah wished there were other support for teachers.

As she was straightening her classroom and preparing to return to the computer lab, the intercom came to life with a squeal and a thump. Mr. Greenway addressed the faculty:

"Good afternoon teachers! Our faculty meeting will begin promptly in 10 minutes. Refreshments are available in the conference room. Please come now and grab a bite to eat so that we can begin and end on time."

Sarah had forgotten there was a meeting this afternoon. All she wanted to do was to go home and relax before dinner. She had planned to do some errands and make a couple of calls to parents, which would consume most of her evening. . . .

Mr. Greenway began the meeting soon after Sarah arrived by reading a letter from a parent, praising teachers for providing a nurturing environment for students at Andrew Jackson. As the meeting continued, Sarah struggled to keep her mind focused on the topic of discussion until Mr. Greenway mentioned a concern about the computer lab.

"It has come to my attention that the computers in the lab are being used inappropriately. When we were asked last year to identify our greatest need, everyone agreed on more computers for instruction. As all of you know, funding for the three computers needed to complete the lab was provided in large part by the PTA. Now that we have the computers we asked for, it is time that we begin integrating them into our instructional program, not using them for fun and games."

Mr. Greenway continued: "Specifically, I want each grade-level team to meet in the next couple of weeks to establish goals for using computers to supplement instruction. I will be working with Tom and a few others to develop inservice programs to address some existing training needs. All faculty will be expected to attend. When you do develop computer-related projects, be sure to showcase them when parents visit. Products developed by children on computers should be set out for parents to see on PTA nights and on other special occasions. If you are not taking your class to the lab on a weekly basis, do so. There is a schedule on the lab door. Just sign up for an open block. Finally, when you take your class to the lab, you should be prepared to teach a lesson that makes meaningful use of the applications available on those computers. I do not want to hear of teachers taking their classes to the lab to play while they grade papers. The computer lab was set up at great expense to function as an educational resource to our students. It was not intended to be a video arcade."

Immediately Sarah recalled Mr. Harris's visit to the lab. (He was the father of one of her students.) She drove home after the meeting, worried that Mr. Harris had complained to Mr. Greenway about students playing games on the computer. If so, Sarah wondered, what, if anything, she should do to rectify the situation. She also wondered what counted as "instructional use" of computers. Would Mr. Greenway perceive keyboarding as frivolous activity? Sarah felt like a first-year teacher all over again.

Source: Becker, F. (undated). The webs we weave. Charlottesville, VA: CaseNET, University of Virginia. Available online: http://casenet.edschool.virginia.edu

Issues, Problems, Dilemmas, and Opportunities

Identify as many problems and issues as you can in this brief episode, and try to group them as "chronic" and "acute." Chronic problems tend to persist and are not easily resolved, while acute problems require immediate attention.

Perceive and Value

Think about this situation from Sarah's point of view. Why might she feel like a first-year teacher again? What, specifically, might Sarah be thinking as she muses about the need for "other support" for teachers?

Think about the situation from Mr. Greenway's point of view. Why might Mr. Greenway be so concerned about making "meaningful use of the applications available on [the] computers"? And why is he so concerned about showcasing students' work?

If you were Mr. Harris or the parent of another child in Sarah's room, what might lead you to think that too much time is spent playing games on the computers? As a parent, what actions might you take if you were concerned about this possibility?

Know and Act

What would Sarah need to know to address the problems you identified as acute? How could she best obtain the information she would need to address those problems effectively?

Assume that you are Sarah. What might you do to address the problem you identified as most acute, and what rationale would you develop for your action? Answer in first person, as if you were Sarah (e.g., "I would call Mr. Harris and invite him to our classroom as soon as possible").

Evaluate

What might be some positive and negative consequences of the particular actions you identified in the previous paragraph? For instance, if you immediately invited Mr. Harris to your classroom, and your students or you were unprepared for his visit, his perceptions might go from bad to worse. On the other hand, if Mr. Harris came to your class and saw the students working together on computers to study some interesting and important content, his impressions might improve.

Use the case as the basis for an essay in which you (1) tie your judgments to your actions, (2) consider that most actions typically have both positive and negative consequences, and (3) speculate on several different ways to judge success.

 ## ONLINE ACTIVITY

There are many search engines that can be used to locate useful web sites. Here is an example created by Kay Cutler at the University of Virginia to illustrate how you can use AltaVista (http://altavista.com) to find anything that interests you. Once you have read through the questions and answers in Tips for Effective Search Results below, why not see what the Web has to offer in the way of teaching jobs?

Tips for Effective Search Results

Question: What is the function of quotation marks in a search strategy?

Answer: Double quotation marks are used to find an exact phrase. For example, if I am looking for **lesson plans,** I must type "lesson plans." If I type **lesson plans** and do not use quotation marks, the engine will look for the word **lesson** *and* the word **plans.** Thus, I might retrieve a web page with information about how a teacher learned a lesson about the effect of floor plans on classroom management.

Question: When should you use uppercase or lowercase?

Answer: When in doubt, use lowercase text in your searches. When you use lowercase text, the search service finds both upper- and lowercase results. When you use uppercase text, the search service finds only uppercase. For example, to find articles about the American Civil War, the preferred search strategy would be to use "**Civil War,**" not "**civil war.**" Lowercase "**civil war**" would yield links on all civil wars.

Question: What does the asterisk (*) indicate in a search strategy?

Answer: By typing an * at the end of a key word or word's stem, you can search for the word with multiple endings. For example, diar* finds web sites with the word **diary** and the word **diaries.**

Question: What does the plus sign (+) indicate in a search strategy?

Answer: A + in front of a key word or phrase instructs AltaVista that the key word or phrase must be included in the resulting links. In this strategy, I want only web sites that have **Civil War, lesson plans,** and **diaries** mentioned. If a web site mentions **Civil War** and **lesson plans** but does not feature information about **diaries,** I do not want it.

Question: What function does adding the domain **edu** play in a search?

Answer: It instructs AltaVista to retrieve web sites created by schools or universities. You can also restrict a search to governmental (**gov**), commercial (**com**), or organizational (**org**) sites.

Question: Should I use synonyms in a search?

Answer: Yes. If you are looking for lesson plans for high school mathematics, you can try any or all of the strategies below, substituting a synonym for the word **mathematics:**

"lesson plans" + mathematics + high school*
"lesson plans" + geometry + "high school*"
"lesson plans" + trigonometry + "high school*"

Glossary

Accelerated Schools: schools designed to improve the speed of learning economically disadvantaged students; based on the work of Henry Levin.

accreditation: the review and approval of education programs by outside experts.

Adoption and Safe Families Act of 1997: act of Congress designed to enhance the services and extend the scope of child welfare agencies.

aesthetics: the branch of philosophy concerned with beauty.

Afrocentric curriculum: educational program that places African culture and history at the center of what students are expected to learn, illustrating the important role that Africa has played in the development of Western civilization.

alternative certification: granting of approval to teach to individuals who have not participated in a traditional, state-approved teacher education program.

alternative school: any school operating within the public school system that has programs addressing the specific needs or interests of targeted student groups.

American Federation of Teachers (AFT): political organization of 800,000 members devoted to the advancement of educational issues and affiliated with the American Federation of Labor/Congress of Industrial Organizations (AFL/CIO). The organization has sponsored such projects as Dial-a-Teacher and Learning Line. It has also supported teacher internship programs, adopt-a-school programs, and national conferences for paraprofessionals and other school personnel.

apartheid: separation of the races.

apprenticeship: practical work experience under the supervision of skilled workers in the trades and the arts.

assimilation: the process of educating and socializing a group to make it similar to the dominant culture.

assumption of risk: implicit responsibility assumed by people who are aware of the possible risks involved in an activity in which they voluntarily participate, thus agreeing to take their chances.

asynchronous communication: communication on the Internet that occurs at times convenient for any of the parties involved (e.g., newsgroups, e-mail).

at-risk students: children who are unlikely to complete high school; have failed one or more grades; are enrolled in special education classes; speak a language other than English; and/or are affected adversely by life- and health-threatening factors, such as poverty, disease, abuse and neglect, substance abuse, teenage pregnancy, and physical violence.

attention-deficit/hyperactivity disorder (ADHD): a neurobiologically based disorder characterized by inappropriate levels of inattention, impulsivity, and hyperactivity.

authentic assessment: assessment concerned less with students' recognition and recall of facts and more with students' abilities to analyze, apply, evaluate, and synthesize what they know in ways that address real-world concerns.

axiology: a branch of philosophy that seeks to ascertain what is of value.

behavioral objectives: objectives that describe conditions for teaching and learning, what is to be learned, and criteria for success.

behaviorism: a philosophical orientation based on the belief that human behavior is determined by forces in the environment that are beyond human control rather than by the exercise of free will.

Bilingual Act of 1974: a law requiring parental involvement in the planning of appropriate educational programs for children with limited English-speaking ability.

bilingual education: instruction in both English and a student's native language.

black codes: conduct codes established by southerners that allowed African Americans to hold property, to sue and be sued, and to marry, but forbade them to carry firearms, to testify in court in cases involving European Americans, or to leave their jobs.

block grant: money provided in a lump sum for several education programs in a locality.

block scheduling: organizing class schedules typically to provide longer instructional periods during the school day.

Blue-Backed Speller: Webster's *American Spelling Book,* first published in 1783.

Brown v. Board of Education: the Supreme Court case that determined that segregation of students by race is unconstitutional and that education is a right that must be available to all Americans on equal terms.

Buckley Amendment: part of the Family Educational Rights and Privacy Act that prohibits schools from releasing information about a student to third parties without parental or student permission.

Bureau of Indian Affairs (BIA): a governmental agency established to, among other activities, oversee education programs for Native Americans.

▶ C

career ladder: incentive program designed to acknowledge differences in the skills of teachers.

categorical grant: funding for an education program designed for a particular group and a specific purpose (e.g., bilingual education).

central office staff: superintendents and their associates and assistants.

certification: recognition by the state that a teacher has met minimum standards for competent practice.

character education: a curricular approach driven by personal relevance that focuses on clarifying or unifying teaching values.

charter school: an independent public school supported by state funds but freed from many regulations and run by individuals who generally have the power to hire and to fire colleagues and to budget money as they see fit.

chat: a form of real-time or synchronous communication on the Internet.

Chautauqua movement: an adult education movement that began in the late 1800s and led to the establishment of civic music associations, correspondence courses, lecture-study groups, youth groups, and reading circles.

chief state school officer: the chief administrator of the state department of education and the head of the state board of education, sometimes referred to as the state superintendent or the commissioner of education.

Child Abuse Prevention and Treatment Act: passed by Congress in 1974 to provide financial support to states that implement programs for identification, prevention, and treatment of instances of child abuse or neglect.

Civil Rights Act of 1964 (Title VI): a law that specifies that no one, regardless of race, color, or origin, can be discriminated against or denied participation in programs receiving federal assistance.

classroom management: the collective ability of teachers and students to agree upon and implement a common framework for social and academic interactions.

Coalition of Essential Schools: alternative high schools serving targeted students through school-based educational reform initiatives; based on Theodore Sizer's work.

cognitivism: a philosophical orientation based on the belief that people actively construct their knowledge of the world through experience and interaction rather than through behavioral conditioning.

collaborative network: a group of people who have come together voluntarily to help each other explore and advance specific educational issues.

collective bargaining: the negotiation of the professional rights and responsibilities of workers (e.g., teachers) as a group.

collegiality: relationships based on the sharing of power.

Committee of Fifteen: a committee that addressed the curriculum of elementary schools in 1895. Its curriculum focused on "the five windows of the soul"—grammar, literature and art, mathematics, geography, and history. It believed the role of school to be an efficient transmitter of cultural heritage through a curriculum that was graded, structured, and cumulative.

Committee of Ten on Secondary School Studies: a committee established by the NEA in 1892 to standardize high school curricula.

common school: a tax-supported school established in colonial times to allow all boys and girls to receive three free years of education focused on reading, writing, arithmetic, and history; predecessor of public schools.

comparative negligence: a situation in which teacher and student are both held liable for an injury.

compensatory education program: a program that provides children from low-income families with education opportunities beyond those offered in a school's standard program to compensate for factors (e.g., teachers, curricula, time, and materials) missing in young people's lives.

comprehensive assessment: assessment that measures students' capacities for reasoning, thinking divergently, and solving problems creatively.

concept formation: a method of instruction used by teachers when they want students to analyze and synthesize data to construct knowledge about a specific concept or idea.

constructivism: a view of knowledge as constructed or built up by individuals acting within a social context that molds knowledge but does not determine absolutely what constitutes knowledge.

contributory negligence: failure of a person who is injured to exercise the required standard of care for his or her own safety.

cooperative learning: a teaching model that encourages heterogeneous groups of students to work together to achieve such goals as mastery of subject matter and understanding and acceptance of one another.

cosmology: the study of nature and origin of the cosmos, or universe.

Council of Chief State School Officers: a non-policy-making organization composed of leaders of state departments of elementary and secondary education in the 50 states, the District of Columbia, the Department of Defense Dependents Schools, and 5 U.S. extra-state jurisdictions—Virgin Islands, Puerto Rico, Northern Mariana Islands, Guam, and American Samoa.

criterion-referenced test: a test by which a student's performance is judged by comparing it to some clearly defined criterion for mastering a learning task or skill. The quality of a student's performance is measured against an absolute standard.

cultural literacy: shared information or common knowledge of a culture supposedly needed to function fully in that culture.

cultural pluralism: a state in which people of diverse ethnic, racial, religious, and social groups maintain autonomous participation within a common civilization.

culture: the sum of the learned characteristics of a people (e.g., language, religion, social mores, artistic expression, sexual behavior), which may be tied to geographical region. *Culture* also can be used in a "micro" sense to describe more conceptually discrete groups of people-cultures within cultures, subcultures, or microcultures.

curriculum: what is taught inside and sometimes outside school.

▸ D

dame school: an educational program for boys and girls run by local women in a colonial community that typically focused on rudimentary reading skills.

direct instruction: highly structured, teacher-centered strategy that capitalizes on such behavioral techniques as modeling, feedback, and reinforcement to promote basic skill acquisition, primarily in reading and mathematics.

discrimination: differential treatment associated with labels.

dismissal: removal of a probationary or tenured teacher before the completion of his or her contract.

distance learning: the capacity for teachers to communicate interactively with students or with one another over long distances.

district power equalization: a relationship between state and local government in which localities establish the tax rate for educational spending and the state guarantees a set amount of money proportional to local revenue.

due process of law: mandated legal procedures designed to protect the rights of individuals.

▶ E

early intervention: providing care and support from the prenatal period through the first years of life to enable children to enter school ready to learn.

Education for All Handicapped Children Act (Public Law 94-142): federal law that requires all states to provide a free and appropriate public education to children between the ages of 5 and 18 with disabilities . Education is to be planned through an individualized education program (IEP) and carried out in the least restrictive environment.

Education Consolidation and Improvement Act (ECIA): the 1981 act of Congress that consolidated many education programs into two major programs.

electronic-mail (e-mail): messages sent and received via computers.

Elementary and Secondary Education Act (ESEA) of 1965: the single most comprehensive extension of federal involvement in education, which resulted in policy-making power shifting to the federal level. The Act provided funds to alleviate the effects of poverty through a variety of programs. It supported school libraries, the purchase of textbooks and other instructional materials, guidance, counseling, health services, and remedial instruction. It also established research centers and laboratories to advance educational practice.

emergency certification: certification granted temporarily until requirements and standards required for becoming a practicing teacher are met.

English academy: a school established in Philadelphia in 1749 by Benjamin Franklin that emphasized the acquisition and application of knowledge thought to be most useful to the modern man.

English as a Second Language (ESL): an instructional program designed to teach English to speakers of other languages.

epistemology: a branch of philosophy concerned with the nature of knowledge or how we come to know things.

Equal Access Act: a 1984 law passed by Congress that recognizes that secondary-school students are mature enough to understand that a school does not condone religion by merely allowing prayer clubs on public property.

equal educational opportunity: access to the resources, choices, and encouragement each student needs to achieve his or her fullest potential through education, regardless of race, color, national origin, gender, disability, or socioeconomic status.

equal protection clause: Section 1 of the Fourteenth Amendment, which prevents states from making or enforcing laws that abridge the privileges or immunities of citizens of the United States; deprive people of life, liberty, or property without due process of law; or deny equal protection of the laws.

E-rate: a federal program that provides discounts on telecommunications and Internet technologies to elementary and secondary school and public libraries.

essentialism: a philosophical orientation that acknowledges the existence of a body of knowledge that all people must learn if they are to function effectively in society.

establishment clause: the clause in the First Amendment prohibiting Congress from making laws respecting the establishment of religion or prohibiting the free exercise of religion.

ethics: a branch of philosophy concerned with issues of morality and conduct.

ethnicity: a term describing a group of people with a common tradition and a sense of identity that functions as a subgroup within the larger society; membership is largely a matter of self-identification.

ethnocentric: unable to see and understand society from points of view different from one's own.

Eurocentric: of curriculum and/or teaching, depicting Europe as the cradle of Western culture.

evaluation: interpreting and attaching value to data relevant to people, programs, teaching, and learning.

exceptional learner: a child who has a special ability or disability that sets him or her apart from other children.

exclusion act: an act based on race passed by Congress to stop unwanted immigration.

existentialism: a philosophy that emphasizes the subjectivity of human experience and the importance of individual creativity and choice in a nonrational world.

explicit curriculum: curriculum contained in policy statements, manuals of procedure, instructional materials, books, and other printed matter that explicate what and how students are to learn.

extracurriculum: non-credit-bearing activities, such as debate club and cheerleading, that are over and above the required curriculum.

▶ F

file transfer protocol (FTP): a means for moving, or downloading, files from computers anywhere on a network to a specific computer.

flat grant: a uniform or variable grant provided by the state to the school districts.

Folkeskole: a Danish public school.

formative assessment: evaluation conducted for the purpose of shaping, forming, and improving knowledge and performance.

for-profit school: school that does not have tax-exempt status because it is run by a company to make money.

foundation program: a program by which the state guarantees school districts a certain amount of money for educational expenditures and determines what proportion of that cost should be shouldered by localities.

free exercise clause: a clause in the First Amendment prohibiting Congress from making laws abridging the freedom of speech or of press or the right to peaceably assemble or to petition the government for a redress of grievances.

Freedman's Bureau: a government-sponsored organization established one month before the end of the Civil War to provide food, medicine, and seed to destitute southerners.

full-service school: a school that attempts to meet basic needs of students by providing such things as food, clothing, showers, medical care, and family counseling.

full state funding: payment by the state of all educational expenses of school districts through a statewide tax.

funding equity: equal amounts of financial support for students, regardless of where they live.

▶ G

gender bias: discriminatory treatment, often subtle or unconscious, that unfairly favors or disfavors individuals because they are females or because they are males.

gender sensitivity training: use of curricula that avoid sex-role stereotyping and the creation of educational opportunities for females to take advantage of all their opportunities for education.

giftedness: the potential for high performance due to strengths in one or more of the following areas: general intellectual ability, specific academic aptitude, creative or productive thinking, leadership ability, ability in the visual or performing arts, and psychomotor ability.

global awareness: the recognition of people's connections to other countries and peoples of the world

▶ H

habits of mind: the shared skills, attitudes, and values transmitted by custom or convention from one generation to the next.

Head Start: the first major early childhood program subsidized by the federal government; provides comprehensive services to low-income 3- and 4-year-olds and their families.

hearing impairment: degree of deafness; uncorrectable inability to hear well.

hidden passage: educational activities that provided slaves with the intellectual power to escape bondage and to make lives for themselves after the Civil War.

high stakes test: test used to evaluate school performance that determines students' grade promotion, graduation, and/or access to specific fields of study.

Hispanic: having Spanish colonial origins or being Spanish-speaking.

holding power: the ability to keep students in school until they receive a high school diploma or an equivalency certificate.

home page: the first page of a Web document.

hornbook: an instructional material used during colonial days. Letters, numerals and other information were affixed to a piece of wood and covered with transparent material made from the horns of cattle that served as a protective layer.

humanism: a philosophy that, in terms of education, calls for respect and kindness toward students and developmentally appropriate instruction in liberal arts, social conduct, and moral principles.

hypermedia: documents that consist of text and still images, as well as audio and video.

▶ I

idealism: a philosophy that suggests that ultimate reality lies in consciousness or reason.

implicit curriculum: the unvoiced and often unintended lessons influenced by teachers' value orientations.

Improving American Schools Act: reauthorizes and revamps the Elementary and Secondary Education Act. Legislation includes Title 1, professional development and technical assistance programs, safe and drug-free schools and communities provision, and provisions promoting school equity.

incentive program: program that offers outside incentives for good attendance and good grades.

inclusive education: education designed and offered to include all people regardless of their physical, social, emotional, or intellectual characteristics; most often used to refer to education provided in mainstream or general educational classrooms to students with disabilities.

Indian Self-Determination and Educational Assistance Act: the decision by Congress in 1975 to terminate federal reservations for Native Americans.

individualized education program (IEP): a plan approved by parents or guardians that spells out what teachers will do to meet a student's individual needs.

Individuals with Disabilities Education Act (IDEA): a 1990 act of Congress that amended the Education for All Handicapped Children Act by changing the term *handicapped* to *with disabilities* and by extending a free and appropriate public education to every individual between 3 and 21 years of age, regardless of the nature or severity of his or her disability.

induction program: program that provides special assistance, monitoring from experienced colleagues, and feedback on teaching performance to beginning teachers in the first one to three years on the job.

in loco parentis: a term meaning "in place of the parent" that suggests that educators possess a portion of a parent's rights, duties, and responsibilities.

inquiry learning: answering and solving problems by analyzing data and creating and testing theories and hypotheses to expand the conceptual system with which one processes information.

institution: an established organization with an identifiable structure and a set of functions meant to preserve and extend social order.

instructional models: deliberate, explicit, complete plans for teaching that can be fitted to students and objectives.

integrated curriculum: curriculum that combines concepts and skills from different subject areas so that they are mutually reinforcing.

intelligence quotient (IQ): score calculated by dividing an individual's mental age by his or her chronological age and multiplying the result by 100.

intermediate educational unit (IEU): collaborative organization maintained by separate districts to provide educational services (e.g., joining together to construct and maintain a technical training center for students).

international comparative education: the study of education in different societies to develop new insights into these societies and to derive innovative understanding of one's own society.

Internet: an electronic network with the capacity to span the globe.

interpersonal power: the ability to influence others due to one's position in an organization or one's personal attributes (e.g., possession of special knowledge or skills).

▶ J

juku: after-school classes offered to elementary and secondary students in Japan to help them keep up with the demanding school curriculum.

▶ K

kindergarten: an educational program for young children; first established by Friedrich Froebel in 1837.

▶ L

land grant school: a public school established through federal assistance, the first of which was provided by the Northwest Ordinance of 1785.

language disorder: receptive, expressive, or language processing problem; and/or difficulty with the meaning of words (semantics), the sequential organization of words according to their relationship to each other (syntax), and/or the purpose of or uses for language.

latchkey child: a child who is without adult supervision for several hours each day.

Latin grammar school: the first formal type of secondary school in the colonies, established in Boston in 1635 for boys from 9 to 10 years of age who could read and write English.

learning disability: a disorder in one or more of the basic psychological processes involved in understanding or in using language, spoken or written, which may manifest itself in an imperfect ability to listen, think, speak, read, write, spell, or do mathematical calculations.

Lemon test: a tripartite test used to decide whether specific practices or policies are an establishment of religion.

license: a certificate that indicates a teacher has demonstrated minimal teaching competence.

limited English proficient (LEP): a categorization of students are qualified for instruction in English as a Second Language.

listserv: a mailing list that allows a person to send a message to a group of individuals with a single keystroke.

literacy: one's ability to read, write, and calculate.

local property taxes: taxes on land and improvements firmly attached to the land (e.g., fences, barns) and on personal property, such as automobiles.

local school board: the primary policy-making body for public schools, composed of elected or appointed public servants.

lyceum: out-of-school program, such as a reading circle or debating club, designed to improve the education of children and adults.

▶ M

magnet school: an alternative school within a public school system that draws students from its whole district instead of drawing only from its own neighborhood and that offers a curriculum based on a special theme or instructional method.

Marxism: a philosophy based on Karl Marx's belief that the human condition is determined by forces in history that prevent people from achieving economic freedom and social and political equality.

mastery learning: one of several behavioral models that suggest that, given enough time, the inclination to learn, and instruction fitted to a student's needs, students are capable of mastering a range of subject matter.

McGuffey Reader: a book first produced in 1836 by William Holmes McGuffey to teach literacy skills and to advance the Protestant ethic through stories and essays.

measurement: the collection of data from individual students from a variety of sources (e.g., tests and quizzes, interviews, questionnaires, observations of in-class behaviors).

mentoring program: a support system aimed at enhancing academic success and self-esteem of at-risk students; also, a program to help new teachers.

merit pay: an incentive program designed to encourage teachers to strive for outstanding performance by rewarding such practice.

metaphysics: the branch of philosophy that focuses on the study of reality.

minimum competency test: a test designed to assess the lowest acceptable level of student performance.

minority: a term that carries both a quantitative meaning (e.g., a group or subgroup in society that is identifiably fewer in number than another group) and/or a political connotation (e.g., the relative political power or influence that perceptions of a group exert in society).

mission school: a school established by priests to convert Native Americans to Catholicism.

modem: a device that allows one to connect a computer to a network using special software and an ordinary telephone line.

monitorial method: a method devised by Lancaster for teaching large groups of students, by which a master teacher instructed monitors, and they, in turn, instructed younger children.

moral development: changes, relating to age and intelligence, in the way an individual makes reasoned judgments about right and wrong.

multicultural education: a reform movement designed to bring about educational equity for all students, including those from different races, ethnic groups, social classes, abilities, and genders.

multiple intelligences: a large number of cognitive abilities, each slightly different from the next, that constitute one's intellectual ability.

▶ N

National Assessment of Educational Progress (NAEP): a congressionally mandated battery of achievement tests operated by the Educational Testing Service to assess the effects of schooling.

National Association for the Advancement of Colored People: established in 1934, the first nationwide special-interest group for African Americans.

National Association for the Education of Young Children (NAEYC): one of the largest professional associations for early childhood educators.

National Board for Professional Teaching Standards (NBPTS): a nonprofit organization charged with the task of creating a national system of certification to be used to designate truly outstanding teachers.

National Center for Education Statistics (NCES): an arm of the executive branch responsible for collecting and analyzing education statistics for the nation.

national certification: recognition for individual teachers, based on a national sample.

National Congress of Parents and Teachers (PTA): the largest volunteer education organization in the United States; it has long supported legislation at the state and national levels designed to benefit children.

National Defense Education Act (NDEA): a federal law passed in 1958 to provide funds for upgrading the teaching of mathematics, science, and foreign languages and for establishing guidance services.

National Education Association (NEA): an organization with two million members guided by the vision of enabling students to develop themselves as people, to practice human relations skills, to learn how to be economically productive citizens, and to be responsible for their community and nation. It was instrumental in creating the National Council for Accreditation of Teacher Education (NCATE), a national organization that monitors the quality of collegiate teacher education programs.

National Education Goals: national goals established by President George Bush and the 50 governors in 1989 to ensure readiness for school; high school completion; student achievement and citizenship; excellence in science and mathematics; adult literacy and lifelong learning; and safe, disciplined, and drug-free schools. Extended by President Clinton in 1994 to include teacher education and parental involvement.

National Governors' Association: a coalition of state chief executives.

National Network for Educational Renewal: a network consisting of universities and partner schools designed to simultaneously renew schools and teacher education.

negligence: failure to exercise reasonable care to protect students from injury.

news groups: electronic message services that post to servers locally, regionally, nationally, and/or internationally.

NGO: an international nongovernmental organization that advances agenda focused on problems and issues of common interest, regardless of national interest.

nondirective model: a teaching strategy in which teachers act as facilitators and as reflectors to encourage students to define problems and feelings, to take responsibility for solving problems, and to determine how personal goals might be reached.

nongraded classroom: a classroom in which children are grouped heterogeneously by ability, sometimes with students of various ages.

normal school: an educational program established in the 1800s dedicated solely to training teachers so that they could perform according to high standards, or "norms."

norm-referenced test: a test used to compare the quality of a student's performance to that of other students.

null curriculum: the curriculum that is not taught in schools.

▶ O

okeiko-goto: enrichment classes in areas such as music, the arts, and physical education that people in Japan may continue throughout their lives.

ontology: the study of nature, existence, or being.

opportunity-to-learn standards: standards meant to

hold schools accountable for giving students a fair chance to succeed by providing them with appropriate support: books, materials, machines, teachers, time to learn, and other tools.

▶ P

parochial school: school established by one of various religious groups to inculcate their beliefs and ideas in children.

pedagogical content knowledge: the particular teaching knowledge necessary to impart content knowledge.

people's profession: a designation for the teaching profession that recognizes that teachers generally come from the middle-class and seek approval of and support for their practice from the people themselves.

perennialism: a philosophy that exalts the great thoughts and accomplishments of the past for their own sake and for what they can offer to future generations.

per-pupil expenditure: money allocated for educational services divided by the number of pupils to be served.

personal property: property that is movable, either tangibles (e.g., machinery, livestock, crops, automobiles) or intangibles (e.g., money, stocks, bonds).

philosophy: a set of ideas about the nature of reality and about the meaning of life.

Plessy* v. *Ferguson: the 1896 Supreme Court case that legalized separate but equal public facilities for African Americans and served to legalize school segregation.

portfolio: a purposeful collection of student work that tells the story of the student's efforts, progress, or achievement in (a) given area(s).

practical knowledge: knowledge constructed through teachers' own experiences about what works with students in classrooms.

pragmatism: a philosophical method that defines the truth and meaning of ideas according to their physical consequences and practical value.

Praxis Series: an examination battery that purports to assess skills and knowledge at each stage of a beginning teacher's career from entry into teacher education to actual classroom performance.

prejudice: an adverse opinion formed without just grounds or without sufficient knowledge.

primer: a textbook for children designed to impart rudimentary reading skills that also reflected the religious values of the colonies.

principal: the person responsible for managing a school at the building level.

private school: a nonprofit, tax-exempt institution governed by a board of trustees and financed through private funds, such as tuitions, endowments, and grants; sometimes called a *for-profit school.*

professional development school: a school in which university and public school people work together to explore problems of teaching and learning.

progressive taxation: taxes, such as income taxes, that require people who earn more to pay more.

progressivism: a movement aimed at using human and material resources to improve the American's quality of life as an individual; in schools this meant focusing on the needs and interests of students rather than on those of teachers. The movement was characterized by a willingness to experiment with methods of teaching and learning.

project-based learning: the involvement of students in relatively long-term, problem-based units of instruction that allow students to pursue solutions to problems posed by students, teachers, or curriculum developers.

pull-out program: program in which individual students are removed from regular classes for a period of time each day for special instruction.

▶ R

race: a classification that is not typically chosen but is instead assigned by others; defined most often by physical characteristics.

realism: a philosophy that suggests that objects of sense or perception exist independently of the mind.

real property: property that is not readily movable (e.g., land, buildings, improvements).

reciprocal teaching: an instructional method used to teach poor readers specific comprehension-monitoring strategies.

reciprocity agreement: a pact by which professional licensure for educational practice in one state makes one eligible for licensure in another state.

reduction in force (RIF): a layoff of teachers.

regressive taxation: a method of taxing citizens that requires those with limited incomes to spend a greater percentage of their income on taxes than wealthy people spend.

remediation: curriculum designed to correct students' weaknesses.

retention: nonpromotion from one grade to the next at the expected time because of school failure.

⟩ S

scaffolding: a method of teaching in which a teacher provides assistance, guidance, and structure to enhance student learning and self-regulation.

school-based budgeting: allocating resources at the building level rather than at the level of central administration.

school choice: the idea that people should be free to choose schools for their children.

school district: a state-defined geographical area assigned responsibility for public instruction within its borders.

school governance: establishment and overseeing of the structure and functions of public education.

school restructuring: efforts to encourage site-based management.

seminary: academy for girls that was the primary means for advancing the educational skills of future teachers.

service learning: learning that results from volunteer work performed outside school hours.

site-based management: the involvement of people at the school level in decisions about teaching and learning, budgeting, and hiring personnel.

social promotion: the passing of children to successive grades to keep them with others of their age, regardless of their past performance or academic abilities.

social reconstructionism: a philosophy based on the belief that people are responsible for social conditions and can improve the quality of human life by changing the social order.

socioeconomic status: a combination of one's income, occupation, values, education, and lifestyle.

Socratic method: teaching through inquiry and dialogues in which students discover and clarify knowledge.

special-interest group: a group of people who coalesce around particular interests and try to exert pressure for the advancement of their causes.

speech impairment: a fluency disorder (such as stuttering), articulation disorder (abnormality in the production of sounds), voice disorder (such as hoarseness or hypernasality—too many sounds produced through the nose), and/or delayed speech.

standardized tests: tests, often multiple choice paper-and-pencil tests, administered and scored under conditions uniform to all students.

standards: benchmarks against which progress can be judged.

state board of education: regulatory agency that controls standards for educational practice in most states and advises governors and legislators about the conduct of educational business.

state education department (SED): a bureaucracy that acts as an advisor to the executive and legislative branches of a state government. An SED is organized to carry out a state's education business, including regulating or overseeing elementary and secondary schools' and colleges' and universities' conduct of teacher and administrator preparation.

state standards boards: commissions established to regulate professional practice in education that either have final authority or serve only in advisory capacity to policymakers.

student-teacher ratio: an estimate of average class size, calculated by dividing the total number of students in a school by the total number of staff (often including noninstructional staff).

student teaching: a field experience in which preservice teachers plan, organize, and provide instruction to students full-time over a period of weeks.

Success for All: a school reform model whose main goal of is to ensure success in reading, especially for urban students at risk for academic failure.

summative assessment: assessment designed to inform a summary decision, for example, an assessment of a teacher's strengths and weaknesses to be used to make decisions about such matters as tenure and termination of contract.

superintendent of schools: executive officer of the local school board, appointed by the board.

synectics: a teaching model that seeks to increase students' problem-solving abilities, creative expression, empathy, and insight into social situations.

▶ T

teacher planning: consideration of such things as curriculum, state and local goals and objectives for student learning, instructional strategies for meeting those goals, and methods for assessing students' understanding.

teacher portfolio: a compilation of products displaying a teacher's knowledge and skills, such as teacher-created tests and videotapes of one's own teaching.

teacher union: a confederation of educators joined politically to advance their cause.

tenure: a continuing contract that guarantees a teacher's employment unless just cause for termination can be demonstrated.

Thomism: a philosophy based on the writings of Saint Thomas Aquinas that suggests that reality is an ordered world created by God that humans can come to know. Life is temporary, and humans strive for eternity with God.

Title I: one of the largest federally funded education programs for at-risk elementary and secondary students; begun in 1965 as the first bill of President Johnson's War on Poverty.

Title IX: a provision of the 1972 Education Amendments Act that guarantees that individuals may not be excluded on the basis of sex from any education program or activity receiving federal financial assistance.

tracking: a process of segregating students by ability.

tuition tax credit: a provision that allows a taxpayer to subtract educational costs from taxes owed.

tuition tax deduction: a provision that allows a taxpayer to subtract educational costs from taxable income before computing taxes.

▶ U

universal schooling: education of all citizens for the common good.

▶ V

videoconferencing: a form of synchronous communication that involves seeing and hearing one another via computer.

visual impairment: degree of blindness; uncorrectable inability to see well.

voucher: scrip used to purchase education for a child.

▶ W

Web browser: the software that enables a person to retrieve and see what is on the World Wide Web.

Women's Educational Equity Act (WEEA): a 1974 law that expanded programs for females in mathematics, science, technology, and athletics; mandated nonsexist curriculum materials; implemented programs for increasing the number of female administrators in education and raising the career aspirations of female students; and extended educational and career opportunities to minority-group, disabled, and rural women.

World Wide Web: a subset of the Internet consisting of tens of thousands of multimedia documents.

▶ Y

year-round school: educational program that runs through the summer months as well as during the academic year.

▶ Z

zero-base budgeting: a process of budgeting that requires all expenditures to be justified each fiscal year.

References

▶ Chapter 1

Associated Press (1999, March 31). Governor aims to ease teacher licensing. *Daily Progress*, pp. B1, B2.

Barber, L. W. (1990). Self-assessment. In J. Millman & L. Darling-Hammond (Eds.), *The new handbook of teacher evaluation: Assessing elementary and secondary school teachers* (pp. 216–228). Newbury Park, CA: Sage.

Basinger, J. (1999, April 21). States are urged to de-emphasize teacher training, give more power to principals. *The Chronicle of Higher Education*. Available online: http://chronicle.com/daily/99/04/99042105n.htm

Bradley, A. (1998). Expiring "Troops to Teachers' Project" outfits classrooms with professionals in demand. *Education Week, 18*(7), 1, 13.

Brandt, R. M. (1990). *Incentive pay and career ladders for today's teachers: A study of current programs and practices.* Albany, NY: State University of New York Press.

Bureau of Labor Statistics (1999). *1998–99 Occupational outlook handbook.* Washington, DC: Department of Labor. Available online: http://stats.bls.gov/ocohome.htm

Choy, S. P., Bobbitt, S. A., Henke, R. R., Medrich, E. A., Horn, L. J., & Lieberman, J. (1993). *America's teachers: Profile of a profession.* Washington, DC: U.S. Department of Education.

Counsel for Learned Societies in Education (1998, June). Academic standards in education. Available online: http://members.aol.com/caddogap/clsehome.htm

Darling-Hammond, L. (1995, Summer). The condition of teaching in America. Resources for restructuring. New York: National Center for Restructuring Education, Schools, and Teaching, Teachers College, Columbia University.

Darling-Hammond, L., & Berry, B. (1998). Investing in teaching. *Education Week, 17*(37), 34, 48.

Department of Defense (1999, February). Troops to Teachers: Program overview. Available online: http://voled.doded.mil/dantes/ttt/overview.htm

Dewey, J. (1910). How we think. Lexington, MA: D. C. Heath.

Duke, D. L., & Stiggins, R. J. (1990). Beyond minimum competence: Evaluation for professional development. In J. Millman & L. Darling-Hammond (Eds.), *The new handbook of teacher evaluation: Assessing elementary and secondary school teachers* (pp. 116–132). Newbury Park, CA: Sage.

Education Week (1999, March 17). *This week's news: Across the nation.* Available online: http://www.edweek.org/ew/current/thisweek.htm#across

Eraut, M. (1994). *Developing professional knowledge and competence.* London: Falmer Press.

Feiman-Nemser, S. (1996, July). Teacher mentoring: A critical review. *ERIC Digest.* ERIC Clearinghouse on Teaching and Teacher Education, Washington, DC. ERIC Document Reproduction Service No. ED 397 060.

Feiman-Nemser, S., Parker, A., & Zeichner, K. (1993). Are mentor teachers teacher educators? *ERIC Digest.* ERIC Clearinghouse on Teaching and Teacher Education, Washington, DC. ERIC Document Reproduction Service No. ED 353 251.

Feistritzer, C. E. (1997). *Alternative teacher certification: A state-by-state analysis 1997.* Washington, DC: National Center for Education Information.

Hoff, D. J. (1999). With 2000 looming, chances of meeting National Goals iffy. *Education Week, 18*(18), 1, 28–30.

Kelley, C., & Odden, A. (1995, September). Reinventing teacher compensation systems. *CPRE finance briefs.* New Brunswick, NJ: Rutgers University.

Little, J. W. (1990). The mentor phenomenon and the social organization of teaching. In C. Cazden (Ed.), *Review of research in education*, Vol. 16 (pp. 297–351). Washington, DC: American Educational Research Association.

Meyer, J. W., & Rowan, B. (1978). The structure of educational organizations. In J. Meyer (Ed.), *Environment and organizations* (pp. 78–109). San Francisco, CA: Jossey-Bass.

Meyer, D. K., & Tusin, L. F. (1999, March–April). Preservice teachers' perceptions of portfolios: Process versus product. *Journal of Teacher Education, 50*(2), 131–139.

National Board for Professional Teaching Standards (1999). *About the National Board.* Available online: http://www.nbpts.org/http://www.nbpts.org/

National Center for Education Information (1998). *Profile of Troops to Teachers.* Available online: http://voled.doded.mil/dantes/ttt/profile.htm

National Education Association (1999). *Beginning teacher coaching program.* Available online: http://www.nea.org/newunion/mtdiablo.html

National Education Goals Panel (1999, February 22). National Education Goals Panel recommends that Goals be renamed "America's Education Goals," and continue beyond year 2000. Available online: http://negp.gov/nepg/webpg75.htm

New Jersey Department of Education (1999, May 20). *Professional licensure and standards.* Available online: http://www.state.nj.us/njded/adopted/license/license.htm

Olebe, M., Jackson, A., & Danielson, C. (1999, May). Investing in beginning teachers—The California model. *Educational Leadership, 56*(8), 41–44.

Ruark, J. K. (1999). Redefining the good life: A new focus in the social sciences: Psychologists lead movement to shift scholars' attention away from societal ills and toward studying what works. Available online: http://chronicle.com/colloquy/99/goodlife/background.htm

Teach for America, Statistics (1999). Recruiting history. Available online: http://www.teachforamerica.org

Teacher Magazine (1995). Controversial corps regroups, 6 (5), 11.

Thomas B. Fordham Foundation (1999). The teachers we need and how to get more of them. Available online: http://www.edexcellence.net/library/teacher.html

Tryneski, J. (1998). Requirements for certification of teachers, counselors, librarians, administrators for elementary and secondary schools (63rd ed.) Chicago: University of Chicago Press.

U.S. Department of Education (1994). *Public elementary teachers' views on teacher performance evaluations*. Washington, DC: U.S. Government Printing Office.

U.S. Department of Education (1996). *Digest of education statistics, 1996*. Washington, DC: U.S. Government Printing Office.

U.S. Department of Education (1998a). The condition of education 1998. NCES 98-013, by John Wirt, Tom Snyder, Jennifer Sable, Susan P. Choy, Yupin Bae, Janis Stennett, Allison Gruner, & Marianne Perie. Washington, DC: Office of Educational Research and Improvement.

U.S. Department of Education (1998b). Projections of education statistics to 2008. Available online: http://nces.ed.gov/pubs98/pj2008/index.html

U.S. Department of Education (1998c). Digest of education statistics, 1998. NCES 1999-036, by Thomas D. Snyder, Charlene Hoffman, Claire M. Geddes. Washington, DC: U.S. Government Printing Office.

▶ Chapter 2

Ambrose, S. E. (1996). *Undaunted courage: Meriwether Lewis, Thomas Jefferson, and the opening of the American West*. New York: Simon & Schuster.

Axelrod, A., & Phillips, C. (1968). *What every American should know about American history: 200 events that shaped the nation*. Holbrook, MA: Adams Media Corporation.

Ayers, E. L. (1999). *History in hypertext*. Available online: http://jefferson.village.virginia.edu/vcdh/Ayers.OAH.html

Barman, J., Hebert, Y., & McCaskill, D. (1986). *Indian education in Canada* (Vol. I). Vancouver: University of British Columbia.

Barnard, H. (1857, March). The public high school. *American Journal of Education*, pp. 185–189.

Berlin, I. (1974). *Slaves without masters: The free negro in the antebellum South*. New York: Vintage.

Best, J. H. (Ed.) (1962). *Benjamin Franklin on education*. New York: Teachers College Press, Columbia University.

Blum, J. M., McFeely, W. S., Morgan, E. S., Schlesinger, A. M., Jr., Stampp, K. M., & Woodward, C. V. (1997). *The national experience: A history of the United States* (8th ed.). San Diego, CA: Harcourt Brace Jovanovich.

Boyd, W. (Ed.) (1962). *The Emile of Jean Jacques Rousseau*. New York: Bureau of Publications, Teachers College, Columbia University.

Boyer, P. S., Clark, C. E., Kett, J. F., Salisbury, N., Sitkoff, H., & Woloch, N. (2000). *The enduring vision: A history of the American people* (4th ed.). Boston: Houghton Mifflin Co.

Bullock, H. A. (1967). *A history of Negro education in the South: From 1619 to the present*. Cambridge, MA: Harvard University Press.

Coleman, M. C. (1993). *American Indian children at school, 1850–1930*. Jackson: University Press of Mississippi.

Cremin, L. A. (1970). *American education: The colonial experience, 1607–1783*. New York: Harper & Row.

Cremin, L. A. (1980). *American education: The national experience, 1783–1876*. New York: Harper & Row.

Cross, B. M. (1965). *The educated woman in America: Selected writings of Catharine Beecher, Margaret Fuller, and M. Carey Thomas*. New York: Teachers College Press, Columbia University.

Deighton, L. C. (Ed.) (1971). *The encyclopedia of education* (Vol. 9). New York: Macmillan Company and The Free Press.

Dolan, J. P. (1985). *The American Catholic experience: A history from colonial times to the present*. Garden City, NY: Doubleday.

Douglass, F. (1882). *Life and times of Frederick Douglass*. Hartford, CT: Park.

Douglass, F. (1974). Frederick Douglass describes his self-education (c. 1830). In S. Cohen (Ed.), *Education in the United States: A documentary history* (Vol. 3) (pp. 1624–1625). New York: Random House.

Downs, R. B. (1978). *Friedrich Froebel*. Boston: Twayne.

Edwards, P. (Ed.) (1972). *Encyclopedia of philosophy* (Vol. 7). New York: The Macmillan Company and The Free Press.

Elsbree, W. S. (1939). *The American teacher: Evolution of a profession in a democracy*. New York: American Book.

Emerson, R. W. (1884). *Lectures and biographical sketches*. Cambridge, MA: Riverside.

Flynn, G. (1971). *Sor Juana Ines de la Cruz*. New York: Twayne.

Fogel, D. (1988). *Junipero Serra, the Vatican, and enslavement theology*. San Francisco, CA: Ism.

Ford, P. L. (Ed.) (1899). *The New England primer*. New York: Dodd, Mead.

Franklin, J. H. (1980). *From slavery to freedom: A history of negro Americans* (5th ed.). New York: Alfred A. Knopf.

Gay, P. (Ed.) (1964). *John Locke on education*. New York: Bureau of Publications, Teachers College, Columbia University.

Gutek, G. L. (1968). *Pestalozzi and education*. New York: Random House.

Hahner, J. (1976). *Women in Latin American history*. Los Angeles: University of California.

Hallahan, D. P., & Kauffman, J. M. (2000). *Exceptional children: Introduction to special education* (8th ed.). Boston: Allyn and Bacon.

Hewett, F. M., & Forness, S. R. (1984). *Education of exceptional learners* (3rd ed.). Boston: Allyn and Bacon.

Jefferson, T. (1931). Report of the commissioners appointed to fix the site of the University of Virginia. In R. J. Honeywell (Ed.), *The educational work of Thomas Jefferson* (pp. 248–260). Cambridge, MA: Harvard University Press.

Kaestle, C. F. (1983). *Pillars of the republic: Common schools and American society, 1780–1860*. New York: Hill and Wang.

Kauffman, J. (1981). Introduction: Historical trends and contemporary issues in special education in the United States. In J. M. Kauffman & D. P. Hallahan (Eds.), *Handbook of special education* (pp. 3–23). Upper Saddle River, NJ: Prentice Hall.

Krug, E. A. (1964). *The shaping of the American high school, 1880–1920*. New York: Harper & Row.

Lannie, V. P. (1968). *Public money and parochial education: Bishop Hughes, Governor Seward and the New York school controversy*. Cleveland, OH: Press of Case Western Reserve.

Mann, L. (1979). *On the trail of process: A historical perspective on cognitive processes and their training*. New York: Grune & Stratton.

Manuel, H. T. (1965). *Spanish-speaking children of the Southwest: Their education and the public welfare*. Austin: University of Texas Press.

Pestalozzi, J. H. (1898). *How Gertrude teaches her children* (2nd ed.). Syracuse, NY: C. W. Bardeen.

Reigart, J. F. (1969). *The Lancasterian system of instruction in the schools of New York City*. New York: Arno Press & the *New York Times*.

Riesman, D. (1954). *Individualism reconsidered*. Glencoe, IL: Free Press.

Rury, J. L. (1989). Who became teachers?: The characteristics of teachers in American history. In D. Warren (Ed.), *American teachers: Histories of a profession at work* (pp. 9–48). New York: Macmillan.

Spacks, P. M. (1995). *Boredom: The literary history of a state of mind*. Chicago: University of Chicago Press.

Steinhardt, M. A. (1992). Physical education. In P. W. Jackson (Ed.), *Handbook of research on curriculum* (pp. 964–1001). New York: Macmillan.

The Sun. (1833a, December 19). p. 2.

The Sun. (1833b, December 20). p. 3.

Tocqueville, A. (1840). *Democracy in America: Part the second, the social influence of democracy* (H. Reeve, Trans.). New York: J. & H. G. Langley.

Tyack, D. (1967). *Turning points in American educational history*. Lexington, MA: Xerox College.

Ulich, R. (1968). *History of educational thought*. New York: D. Van Nostrand.

Zitkala-Sa. (1921). *American Indian stories*. Washington, DC: Hayworth.

▶ Chapter 3

Adams, L. L. (1977). *Walter Lippmann*. Boston: Twayne Publishers.

Agee, J., & Evans, W. (1960). *Let us now praise famous men* (2nd ed.). New York: Ballantine.

Alba, R. D. (1991). *Ethnic identity: The transformation of white America*. New Haven, CT: Yale University Press.

Ayres, L. P. (1909). *Laggards in our schools*. New York: Charities Publication Committee.

Barton, C. (1999). *Teaching and learning in architecture.* Available online: http://curry.edschool.virginia.edu/go/mcnergney/architecture

Bennett, C. (1999). Comprehensive multicultural education: Theory and practice (4th ed.). Boston: Allyn and Bacon.

Berliner, D. C., & Biddle, J. J. (1998). The lamentable alliance between the media and school critics. In G. I. Maeroff (Ed.), *Imaging education: The media and schools in America.* New York: Teachers College Press, pp. 26–45.

Bestor, A. E. (1953). *Educational wastelands: The retreat from learning in our public schools.* Urbana: University of Illinois Press.

Blum, J. M., McFeely, W. S., Morgan, E. S., Schlesinger, A. M., Jr., Stampp, K. M., & Woodward, C. V. (1997). *The national experience: A history of the United States* (8th ed.), San Diego, CA: Harcourt Brace Jovanovich.

Bond, H. M. (1934). *The education of the Negro in the American social order.* Upper Saddle River, NJ: Prentice Hall.

Bossert, S. T. (1985). Effective elementary schools. In R. J. Kyle (Ed.), *Reaching for excellence* (pp. 39–53). Washington, DC: U.S. Government Printing Office.

Bracey, G. W. (1998). *Put to the test: An educator's and consumer's guide to standardized testing.* Bloomington, IN: Phi Delta Kappa International.

Brown, C. L., & Pannell, C. W. (1985). The Chinese in America. In J. O. McKee (Ed.), *Ethnicity in contemporary America: A geographical appraisal* (pp. 195–216). Dubuque, IA: Kendall/Hunt.

Callahan, R. E. (1962). *Education and the cult of efficiency.* Chicago: University of Chicago Press.

Carlson, R. A. (1975). *The quest for conformity: Americanization through education.* New York: John Wiley & Sons.

Carnegie, D. (1936). *How to win friends & influence people.* New York: Simon and Schuster.

Cole, J. Y. (1979). *For Congress and the nation: A chronological history of the Library of Congress.* Washington, DC: Library of Congress.

Commission on the Reorganization of Secondary Education. (1918). *Cardinal principles of secondary education* (Bulletin No. 35). Washington, DC: U.S. Government Printing Office.

Covello, L. (1958). *The heart is the teacher.* New York: McGraw-Hill Book Co.

Cremin, L. A. (1988). *American education: The metropolitan experience.* New York: Harper & Row.

Cuban, L. (1984). *How teachers taught: Constancy and change in American classrooms 1890–1980.* New York: Longman.

Dabney, C. W. (1969). *Universal education in the South: Vol. II.* New York: Arno Press & the *New York Times.*

Daily Report Card (1996, June 26). *Children and television, watching television: The new racial divide.* Vol. 6, No. 58. Available online: http://www.utopia. com / mailings / reportcard / DAILY. REPORT. CARD218. html#Index10.

Degler, C. N. (1959). *Out of our past: The forces that shaped modern America.* New York: Harper & Row.

Du Bois, W. E. B. (1903). *The souls of black folk: Essays and sketches.* Chicago: A. C. McClurg. Available online: http://etext.lib.virginia.edu/modeng/modeng0.browse.html.

Du Bois, W. E. B. (1904). *The souls of black folk.* Chicago: A. C. McClurg.

Edwards, J. (1991). To teach responsibility, bring back the Dalton Plan. *Phi Delta Kappan,* 72 (5), 398–401.

Efron, S. (1990, April 29). Few Viet exiles find U.S. riches. *Los Angeles Times,* p. 1.

Franklin, J. H. (1967). *From slavery to freedom* (3rd ed.). New York: Alfred A. Knopf.

Fuchs, L. H. (1990). *The American kaleidoscope: Race, ethnicity, and the civic culture.* Middletown, CT: Wesleyan University Press.

General Accounting Office (1995). *School facilities: Condition of America's schools. Report to Congressional requesters.* Washington, DC: General Accounting Office, Health, Education, and Human Services Division. Available online: http://frwebgate.access.gpo.gov/

Goodman, J. M. (1985). The Native American. In J. O. McKee (Ed.), *Ethnicity in contemporary America: A geographical appraisal* (pp. 195–216). Dubuque, IA: Kendall/Hunt.

Gould, J. E. (1961). *The Chautauqua movement.* Albany: State University of New York Press.

Hallahan, D. P., & Kauffman, J. M. (2000). *Exceptional learners: Introduction to special education* (8th ed.). Boston: Allyn and Bacon.

Harris, K. A. (1984). *Profiles of Detroit's high schools: 1975 to 1984.* Detroit: Detroit School District, U.S. District Court Monitoring Commission.

Jackson, H. H. (1977). *A century of dishonor: A sketch of the United States government's dealings with some of the Indian tribes.* St. Clair Shores, MI: Scholarly Press. (Original work published 1880)

James, W. (1899). *Talks to teachers on psychology: And to the students on some of life's ideals.* New York: Henry Holt and Company.

Jennings, J. F. (1998). *Why national standards and tests? Politics and the quest for better schools.* Thousand Oaks, CA: Sage Publications.

Kauffman, J. M. (1981). Historical trends and contemporary issues in special education in the United States. In J. M. Kauffman & D. P. Hallahan (Eds.), *Handbook of special education.* Upper Saddle River, NJ: Prentice Hall.

Kliebard, H. M. (1986). *The struggle for the American curriculum, 1893–1958.* Boston: Routledge & Kegan Paul.

Kunen, J. S. (1996, April 29). The end of integration. *Time,* 147(118) pp. 39–45.

Lazarus, E. (1888). *The poems of Emma Lazarus: Vol. 1.* Boston: Houghton Mifflin.

Link, A. S., & Catton, W. B. (1963). *American epoch: A history of the United States since the 1890s.* New York: Alfred A. Knopf.

Lodge, H. C. (1891). The restriction of immigration. *North American Review,* pp. 27–36.

Minzey, J. D., & LeTarte, C. (1979). *Community education, from program to process to practice: The schools' role in a new educational society.* Midland, MI: Pendell.

Murphy, J. (1990). The educational reform movement of the 1980s: A comprehensive analysis. In J. Murphy (Ed.), *The educational reform movement of the 1980s* (pp. 3–55). Berkeley, CA: McCutchan.

National Commission on Excellence in Education. (1983). *A nation at risk: The imperative for education reform.* Washington, DC: U.S. Department of Education.

National Education Goals Panel (1999, February 22). National Education Goals Panel recommends that goals be renamed "America's Education Goals" and continue beyond year 2000. Available online: http://negp.gov/negp/webpg75.htm

Nifong, C. (1996, August 6). Hispanics and Asians change the face of American South. *Christian Science Monitor,* sec. 1, p. 4.

Painter, N. I. (1977). *Exodusters: Black migration to Kansas after Reconstruction.* New York: Alfred A. Knopf.

Parkhurst, H. (1922). *Education on the Dalton Plan.* New York: Dutton.

Peabody, E. P. (1886). *Sara Winnemucca's practical solution of the Indian problems: A letter to Dr. Lyman Abbot of the "Christian Union."* Cambridge, MA: John Wilson and Son.

Powell, A. G., Farrar, E., & Cohen, D. K. (1985). *The shopping mall high school: Winners and losers in the educational marketplace.* Boston: Houghton Mifflin.

Public Agenda (1997, May). *Good news, bad news: What people really think about the educational press.* Paper presented at the meetings of the Educational Writers Association, Washington, DC.

Raven, S., & Weir, A. (1981). *Women in history.* London: Weidenfeld and Nicolson.

Rice, J. M. (1969). *The public-school system of the United States.* New York: Arno Press.

Riis, J. A. (1890). *How the other half lives.* New York: Charles Scribner's Sons.

Schnaiberg, L. (1999). Calif.'s year on the bilingual battleground. *Education Week, 18*(38), 1, 9–10.

Travers, R. M. (1983). *How research has changed American schools: A history from 1840 to the present.* Kalamazoo, MI: Mythes.

Tyack, D., & Hansot, E. (1982). *Managers of virtue.* New York: Basic Books.

U.S. Bureau of Indian Affairs (1974). Government schools for Indians (1881). In S. Cohen (Ed.), *Education in the United States: A documentary history* (Vol. 3, pp. 1754–1756). New York: Random House.

U.S. Bureau of the Census. (1975). *Historical statistics of the United States: Colonial times to 1970 (Part 1).* Washington, DC: U.S. Government Printing Office.

U.S. Bureau of the Census. (1990). *Statistical abstract of the United States* (110th ed.). Washington, DC: U.S. Government Printing Office.

U.S. Census Bureau (1995, August). *American Indian and Alaska Native populations: Selected social and economic characteristics for the 25 largest American Indian tribes, 1990.* Washington, DC: U.S. Government Printing Office. Available online: http://www.census.gov/population/socdemo/race/indian/ailang2.txt

U.S. Census Bureau (1997). *Money income in the United States, 1997 current population reports, consumer income,* P60-197. Washington, DC: U.S. Government Printing Office.

U.S. Department of Education (1998). *The condition of education 1998.* NCES 98-013, by John Wirt, Tom Snyder, Jennifer Sable, Susan P. Choy, Yupin Bae, Janis Stennett, Allison Gruner, and Marianne Perie. Washington, DC: Office of Educational Research and Improvement.

U.S. Department of Education (1999). *Digest of education statistics, 1998.* NCES 1999-036, by Thomas D. Snyder, Charlene Hoffman, Claire M. Geddes. Washington, DC: U.S. Government Printing Office.

U.S. Federal Register (1999, January 5). Notices. *64*(2), 484.

Walley, C. W., & Gerrick, W. G. (Eds.) (1999). *Affirming middle grades education.* Boston: Allyn and Bacon.

Washington, B. T. (1907). *The future of the American Negro.* Boston: Small, Maynard.

Weinberg, D. H. (1997). *Press briefing on 1997 income and poverty estimates.* Washington, DC: U.S. Census Bureau. Available online: http://www.census.gov/hhes/income/income97/prs98asc.html

Zhou, M. (in press). Straddling different worlds: The acculturation of Vietnamese refugee children. In R. G. Rumbaut & A. Portes (Eds.), *Ethnicities: Coming of age in immigrant America.* Berkeley: University of California Press. Available online: http://migration.ucdavis.edu/mm21/1999/Zhou.html

▶ Chapter 4

Achebe, C. (1968). *Things fall apart.* London: Heinemann Educational Books.

Adler, M. (1982). *The Paideia proposal: An educational manifesto.* New York: Macmillan.

Apple, M. (1995). *Education and power.* New York: Routledge.

Asante, M. K. (1987). *The Afrocentric idea.* Philadelphia: Temple University Press.

Asante, M. K. (1992). Learning about Africa. *Executive Educator, 14*(9), 21–23.

Banks, J. A. (1994). *Multiethnic education: Theory and practice* (3rd ed.). Boston: Allyn and Bacon.

Banville, J. (1998, August 13). The last days of Nietzsche. *New York Review of Books,* vol. 45, No. 13, pp. 22–25.

Bestor, A. (1985). *Educational wastelands: The retreat from learning in our public schools* (2nd ed.). Urbana: University of Illinois Press.

Bloom, A. (1987). *The closing of the American mind.* New York: Simon and Schuster.

Brameld, T. (1950). *Patterns of educational philosophy: A democratic interpretation.* New York: World Book.

Brophy, J. (1999). Perspectives of classroom management: Yesterday, today, and tomorrow. In H. J. Freiberg (Ed.), *Beyond behaviorism: Changing the classroom management paradigm* (pp. 43–58). Boston: Allyn and Bacon, 43–58.

Bryk, A. S., Lee, V. E., & Holland, P. B. (1993). *Catholic schools and the common good.* Cambridge, MA: Harvard University Press.

Buber, M. (1970). *I and thou* (W. Kaufman, Trans.). New York: Charles Scribner's Sons. (Original work published 1937)

Clark, C. M. (1995). *Thoughtful teaching.* London: Cassell.

Clark, C. M., & Peterson, P. L. (1986). Teachers' thought processes. In M. C. Wittrock (Ed.), *Handbook of research on teaching* (3rd ed.) (pp. 255–296). New York: Macmillan.

Clive, J. (1989). *Not by fact alone: Essays on the writing and reading of history.* Boston: Houghton Mifflin.

Cohen, S., & Hearn, D. (1988). Reinforcement. In R. F. McNergney (Ed.), *Guide to classroom teaching* (pp. 43–66). Boston: Allyn and Bacon.

Corbin, H. (1993). *History of Islamic philosophy.* London: Kegan Paul International.

Counts, G. S. (1928). *School and society in Chicago.* New York: Harcourt, Brace.

Dewey, J. (1916). *Democracy and education: An introduction to the philosophy of education.* New York: Macmillan Co.

Durant, W. (1961). *The story of philosophy: The lives and opinions of the great philosophers.* New York: Simon and Schuster.

Ewert, G. D. (1991). Habermas and education: A comprehensive overview of the influence of Habermas in educational literature. *Review of Educational Research, 61*(3) 345–378.

Fakhry, J. (1983). *A history of Islamic philosophy* (2nd ed.). New York: Columbia University Press.

Fenstermacher, G. D. (1986). Philosophy of research on teaching: Three aspects. In M. C. Wittrock (Ed.), *Handbook of research on teaching* (3rd ed.) (pp. 37–49). New York: Macmillan.

Fine, M. (1987). Silencing in public schools. *Language Arts, 64*(2), 157–174.

Freire, P. (1970). *Pedagogy of the oppressed.* New York: Seabury Press.

Fukuyama, F. (1992). *The end of history and the last man.* New York: Free Press.

Giroux, H. A. (1984). Public philosophy and the crisis in education. *Harvard Educational Review, 54*(2), 186–194.

Green, T. (1976). Teacher competence as practical rationality. *Educational Theory, 26,* 249–258.

Haberman, M. (1995). *Star teachers of children in poverty.* West Lafayette, IN: Kappa Delta Pi.

Hanson, V. D., & Heath, J. (1998). *Who killed Homer? The demise of classical education and the recovery of Greek wisdom.* New York: Free Press.

Herbert, J. M., & Keller, C. E. (1999). Marcia Sampson: "If you're not teaching, the students are not learning." In R. F. McNergney & C. E. Keller (Eds.), *Images of mainstreaming: Educating students with disabilities* (pp. 29–48). New York: Garland Publishing.

Hirsch, E. D., Jr. (1987). *Cultural literacy: What every American needs to know.* Boston: Houghton Mifflin.

Hirsch, E. D., Jr. (1996). *The schools we need and why we don't have them.* Garden City, NY: Doubleday.

Hirsch, E. D., Jr., Rowland, W. G., Jr., & Stanford, M. (Eds.) (1989). *A first dictionary of cultural literacy: What our children need to know.* Boston: Houghton Mifflin.

Holtom, D. C. (1984). *The political philosophy of modern Shinto: A study of the state religion of Japan.* Chicago: University of Chicago Libraries.

Horizon Instructional Systems (1997). *Horizon school charter.* Available online: http://www.nccn.net/hnycmbpd/Horizon/estabdoc/charter.html

Hunt, D. E. (1987). *Beginning with ourselves: In practice, theory, and human affairs.* Cambridge, MA: Brookline Books.

Hutchins, R. M. (1936). *The higher learning in America.* New Haven: Yale University Press.

James, W. (1907). *Pragmatism and four essays from The Meaning of Truth.* New York: Longmans, Green and Co.

Kent, T. W., & McNergney, R. F. (1999). *Will technology really change education? From blackboard to web.* Thousand Oaks, CA: Corwin Press.

King, M. L., Jr. (1964). *Stride toward freedom: The Montgomery story.* New York: Harper and Row.

Kneller, G. F. (1971). *Introduction to the philosophy of education* (2nd ed.). New York: Wiley.

Lesko, N. (1988). *Symbolizing society: Stories, rites, and structure in a Catholic high school.* New York: Falmer Press.

Moore, M. (1997). The history of our mothers' dreams. In M. Moore, *Spirit voices of bones.* Candler, NC: rENEGADE pLANETS pUBLISHING, p. 18.

Morine-Dershimer, G. (1990, April). *To think like a teacher.* Vice-presidential address presented at the annual meeting of the American Educational Research Association, Boston.

Nietzsche, F. (1924). *On the future of our educational institutions.* New York: Macmillan.

Nietzsche, F. (1961). *Thus spake Zarathustra: A book for everyone and no one.* (R. J. Hollingdale, Trans.). New York: Penguin. (Original work published 1883)

Noddings, N. (1984). *Caring: A feminine approach to ethics & moral education.* Berkeley: University of California Press.

Norman, D. A. (1992). *Turn signals are the facial expressions of automobiles.* Reading, MA: Addison-Wesley.

O'Neill, W. F. (1981). *Educational ideologies: Contemporary expressions of educational philosophy.* Santa Monica, CA: Goodyear.

Organ, T. W. (1974). *Hinduism: Its historical development.* Woodbury, NY: Barron's Educational Series.

Paley, V. (1979). *White teacher.* Cambridge, MA: Harvard University Press.

Parziale, J., & Fischer, K. W. (1998). The practical use of skill theory in classrooms. In R. F. Sternberg & W. M. Williams (Eds.), *Intelligence, instruction, and assessment: Theory into practice* (pp. 95–110). Boston: Allyn and Bacon.

Perkins, D. (1998). What is understanding? In M. S. Wiske (Ed.), *Teaching for understanding* (pp. 39–57). San Francisco: Jossey-Bass.

Perrone, V. (1998). *Teacher with a heart: Reflections on Leonard Covello and Community.* New York: Teachers College Press.

Pinar, W. F. (1998). Understanding curriculum as gender text: Notes on reproduction, resistance, and male–male relations. In W. F. Pinar (Ed.), *Queer theory in education* (pp. 221–243). Mahwah, NJ: Lawrence Erlbaum.

Rambachan, A. (1992). *The Hindu vision.* Delhi: Motilal Banarsidass.

Rorty, R. (1991). *Objectivity, relativism, and truth: Philosophical papers: Vol. 1.* Cambridge, MA: Cambridge University Press.

Sartre, J.-P. (1947). *Existentialism.* New York: Philosophical Library.

Schön, D. A. (1987). *Educating the reflective practitioner: Toward a new design for teaching and learning in the professions.* San Francisco: Jossey-Bass.

Shishu Bharati (1999). Shishu Bharati: School of Languages and Cultures of India. Available online: http://www.shishubharati.org/

Shulman, L. S. (1987). Knowledge and teaching: Foundations of the new reform. *Harvard Educational Review, 57,* 1–22.

Skinner, B. F. (1971). *Beyond freedom and dignity.* New York: Alfred A. Knopf.

Sleeter, C. E., & Grant, C. A. (1993). *Making choices for multicultural education: Five approaches to race, class, and gender* (2nd ed.). New York: Merrill.

Snelling, J. (1987). *The Buddhist handbook: A complete guide to Buddhist teaching and practice.* London: Century.

Wasley, P. A., Hampel, R. L., & Clark, R. W. (1997). *Kids and school reform.* San Francisco: Jossey-Bass.

Westbrook, R. B. (1991). *John Dewey and American democracy.* Ithaca, NY: Cornell University Press.

Winkler, K. J. (1994). An African writer at a crossroads. *The Chronicle of Higher Education, 40*(19), A9, A12.

X, Malcolm. (1965). *The autobiography of Malcolm X.* New York: Grove Press.

▶ Chapter 5

Achilles, C. M. (1996). Students achieve more in smaller classes. *Educational Leadership, 53,* 76–79.

Ackerman, R., Donaldson, G. A., Jr., & Van der Bogert, R. (1996). *Making sense as a school leader: Persisting questions, creative opportunities.* San Francisco: Jossey-Bass.

Alexander, K. L., & Entwisle, D. R. (1996) Schools and children at risk. In A. Booth & J. F. Dunn (Eds.), *Family-school links: How do they affect educational outcomes?* (pp. 67–88). Mahwah, NJ: Lawrence Erlbaum.

Ames, N. L. (1996). Creating secure school environments through total school reform: The Harshman story. *Middle School Journal, 2*(3), 4–13.

Archer, J. (1998). Breaking the tradition. *Education Week.* Available online: http://www.edweek.org/ew/1998/27jewish.h17

Bafumo, M. E. (1998, March). The roots of learning. *Educational Leadership, 55*(6), 66–69.

Barnes, H. (1991, October). Learning that grows with the learner. An introduction to Waldorf education. *Educational Leadership,* pp. 52–54.

Barth, R. S. (1990). *Improving schools from within: Teachers, parents and principals can make the difference.* San Francisco: Jossey-Bass.

Belluck, P. (1999). Board for Kansas deletes evolution from curriculum. *New York Times, CXLVII*(51,247), A1.

Boyer, E. L. (1995). *The basic school: A community for learning.* Princeton, NJ: Carnegie Foundation for the Advancement of Teaching.

Campbell, D., Cignetti, P. B., Melenyzer, B., Nettles, D. H., & Wyman, R. (1997). *How to develop a professional portfolio for teachers.* Boston: Allyn and Bacon.

David, J. L. (1995/1996). The who, what, and why of site-based management. *Educational Leadership, 53*(4), 4–9.

Deal, T. E., & Peterson, K. D. (1991, June). *The principal's role in shaping school culture.* Washington, DC: U.S. Department of Education.

Decker, L. E., Gregg, G. A., & Decker, V. A. (1995). *Teacher's manual for parent and community involvement.* Fairfax, VA: National Community Education Association.

Dornbusch, S. M., & Glasgow, K. L. (1996). The structural context of family–school relations. In A. Booth & J. F. Dunn (Eds.), *Family–school links: How do they affect educational outcomes?* (pp. 35–44) Mahwah, NJ: Lawrence Erlbaum.

Eaton, W. E. (Ed.). (1990). *Shaping the superintendency: A reexamination of Callahan and the cult of efficiency.* New York: Teachers College Press.

Eccles, J. S., & Harold, R. D. (1996). Family involvement in children's and adolescents' schooling. In A. Booth & J. F. Dunn (Eds.), *Family–school links: How do they affect educational outcomes?* (pp. 3–34) Mahwah, NJ: Lawrence Erlbaum.

Fichter, F. H. (1958). *Parochial school: A sociological study.* Notre Dame, IN: University of Notre Dame Press.

Finn, J. D., & Achilles, C. M. (1990). Answers and questions about class size: A statewide experiment. *American Educational Research Journal, 27*(3), 557–577.

Ford, R. (1995). Critical perspective on the case of Hans Christian Andersen School. *Guide to foundations in action: Videocases of teaching and learning in multicultural settings* (pp. 161–174). Boston: Allyn and Bacon.

Geske, T. G., Davis, D. R., & Hingle, P. L. (1997). Charter schools: A viable public school choice option? In E. Cohn (Ed.), *Market approaches to education: Vouchers and school choice.* Tarrytown, NY: Elsevier Science.

Glass, G. V. (1988). *At last—A better way to measure class size: A step-by-step guide for local associations.* Washington, DC: National Education Association.

Glickman, C. D. (1998). *Revolutionizing America's schools.* San Francisco: Jossey-Bass.

Grubb, W. N. (1996). The new vocationalism: What it is, what it could be. *Phi Delta Kappan, 77*(8), 535–546.

Guskey, T. R. & Peterson, K. D. (1995/1996), The road to classroom change. *Educational Leadership, 53*(4), 10–14.

Gutiérrez, R., & Slavin, R. E. (1992). Achievement effects of the nongraded elementary school: A best evidence synthesis. *Review of Educational Research, 62*(4), 333–376.

Hadley, W. H. (1996). Teacher preparation and certification in middle grades education. *Journal of Instructional Psychology, 23*(1), 21–25.

Hanushek, E. A. (1995). Moving beyond spending fetishes. *Educational Leadership, 53*(3), 60–64.

Holmes County Chamber of Commerce (1999). Many Amish attend parochial, one-room schools. Available online: http://www.visitamishcountry.com/amish/schls.htm

Home School Legal Defense Association (1997). Home education across the United States: How many home schoolers are there? Available online: http://www.hslda.org/nationalcenter/statsandreports/ray1997/03.stm

Hoy, W. K., & Miskel, C. G. (1996). *Educational administration: Theory, research, and practice* (5th ed.). New York: McGraw-Hill.

HSLDA. (1997). Home education across the United States: How many home schoolers are there? Available online: http://www.hslda.org/national/center/statsandreports/ray1997/03.stm

Information for Delaware Education Alumni (1997). School notes. Capuano receives UD presidential citation. Available online: http://www.udel.edu/chep/idea/notes.html

Judson, G. (1996, February 1). Education company banned from Hartford schools. *New York Times, 5,* p. B3.

Keen, M. (1999). Three semesters for learning. *School Administrator, 3*(56), 27–30.

Kennedy, J. (Ed.) (1996). Making all schools charter schools is more likely to change systems. *R & D Watch, 1*(2), 4.

Keough, R. (1999). What's up, Doc? *Education Week, 18*(33), 26–31.

Lareau, A. (1996). Assessing parent involvement in schooling: A critical analysis. In A. Booth & J. F. Dunn (Eds.) *Family–school links: How do they affect educational outcomes?* (pp. 57–66). Mahwah, NJ: Lawrence Erlbaum.

Lee, V. E., Smith, J. B., & Croninger, R. G. (1996). Restructuring high school helps improve student achievement. *WCER Highlights, 8*(1), 4, 5, 9.

Leithwood, K., Steinbach, R., & Begley, P. (1992). Socialization experiences: Becoming a principal in Canada. In F. W. Parkey & G. E. Hall (Eds.), *Becoming a principal: The challenges of beginning leadership* (pp. 284–307). Boston: Allyn and Bacon.

Litow, S. S. (1999). Problems of managing a big-city school system. In D. Ravitch, *Brookings Papers on Education Policy 1999* (pp. 185–230). Washington, DC: Brookings Institution Press.

Loveless, T. (1998). *The tracking wars: State reform meets school policy.* Washington, DC: Brookings Institute Press.

Maehr, M. L., & Midgley, C. (1999). Declining motivation after the transition to middle schools: Schools can make a difference. *Journal of Research and Development in Education, 32*(3), 131–147.

Mathews, J. (1999, April 7). School firm reports rise in test scores. *Washington Post,* p. A3. Available online: http://newslibrary.krmediastream.com/cgi-bin/document/wp_auth?DBLIST=wp99&DOCNUM=18057

National Association for the Education of Young Children & the National Association of Early Childhood Specialists in State Departments of Education (NAECS/SDE) (1992). Guidelines for appropriate curriculum content and assessment in programs serving children ages 3 through 8. *Young Children, 46*(1), 21–38.

National Association for Year-Round School (1999). History of year-round education. Available online: http://www.NAYRE.org/

National Association of Elementary School Principals. (1994). *Best Ideas from America's blue ribbon schools: Vol. 2.* Thousand Oaks, CA: Corwin Press.

National Association of Secondary School Principals (1996). *Breaking ranks: Changing an American institution.* Reston, VA: NASSP.

New York City Public Schools (1992, February 10). *Qualities of the New York City schools chancellor.* Facsimile of an unofficial document.

Norton, M. S., Webb, L. D., Dlugosh, L. L., & Sybouts, W. (1996). *The school superintendency: New responsibilities, new leadership.* Boston: Allyn and Bacon.

Oakes, J. (1995). More than meets the eye: Links between tracking and the culture of schools. In H. Pool & J. A. Page (Eds.), *Beyond tracking: Find success in inclusive schools.* Bloomington, IN: Phi Delta Kappa Educational Foundation.

Oakes, J. & Lipton, M. (1999). Teaching to change the world. Boston: McGraw-Hill Companies, Inc.

Ordovensky, P. (1996). What makes an excellent school? *USA Today,* p. D19–20.

Parks, D., & Barrett, T. (1994). Principals as leaders of leaders. *Principal, 74*(2), 11–12.

Pate-Bain, H., Achilles, C. M., Boyd-Zaharias, J., & McKenna, B. (1992). Class size does make a difference. *Phi Delta Kappan, 74,* 253–256.

Phelan, P., Davidson, A. L, & Cao, H. T. (1992). Speaking up: Students' perspectives on school. *Phi Delta Kappan, 73*(9), 695–704.

Ponessa, J. (1996). Catholic school enrollment continues to increase. *Education Week, 15*(30), 5.

Pool, H., & Page, J. A. (Eds.) (1995). Introduction. *Beyond tracking: Finding success in inclusive schools.* Bloomington, IN: Phi Delta Kappa Educational Foundation.

Popham, J. W. (1995). School-site assessment: What principals need to know. *Principal, 75*(8), 38–40.

Reeves, K. (1999). The four-day school week. *School Administrator, 3*(56), 30–34.

Rettig, M., & Canady, R. L. (1999). The effects of block scheduling. *School Administrator, 3*(56), 14–20.

Rotherham, A. (1999). When it comes to school size, smaller is better. *Education Week, 18*(24), 52, 76.

Sandham, J. (1998, November 4). Program puts teachers online. *Education Week, 18*(10), 39.

Scarpati, S., & Silver, P. G. (1999). Readiness for academic achievement in preschool children. In E. V. Nuttall, I. Romero, & J. Kalesnik (Eds.), *Assessing and screening preschoolers: Psychological and educational dimensions* (pp. 262–280). Boston: Allyn and Bacon.

Schnaiberg, L. (1999). Study finds home schoolers are top achievers on tests. *Education Week, 18*(25), 9.

Sernak, K. (1998). *School leadership—Balancing power with caring.* New York: Teachers College Press.

Shepard, L. A. (1997). Children not ready to learn? The invalidity of school readiness testing. *Psychology in the Schools, 34*(2), 85–89.

Sommerfeld, M. (1995). Under the big top. *Educational Week, 15*(14), 22–29.

Stone, S. J. (1998). Creating contexts for middle-age learning. *Childhood Education, 74*(4), 234–236.

Til, W. V., Vars, G. F., & Lounsbury, J. H. (1967). *Modern education for the junior high school years* (2nd ed.). Indianapolis: Bobbs-Merrill.

U.S. Department of Education (1998a). *Characteristics of the 100 largest public elementary and secondary school districts in the United States: 1995–96,* NCES 98-214, by Beth A. Young. Washington, DC: U.S. Government Printing Office.

U.S. Department of Education (1998b). *1998 Regional Conferences on Improving America's Schools.* Available online: http://www.ncbe.gwu.edu/iasconferences/1998/casestudies/denver.htm#Chicago

U.S. Department of Education (1999a). *Digest of education statistics, 1998.* NCES 1999-036, by Thomas D. Snyder, Charlene Hoffman, Claire M. Geddes. Washington, DC: U.S. Government Printing Office.

U.S. Department of Education (1999b). *Reducing class size: What do we know?* By Ivor Pritchard, National Institute on Student Achievement, Curriculum and Assessment. Washington, DC: Office of Educational Research and Improvement.

Wagner, M. B. (1990). *God's schools: Choice and compromise in American society.* New Brunswick, NJ: Rutgers University Press.

Walsh, D. J., Ellwein, M. C., Eads, G. M., & Miller, A. (1991). Knocking on kindergarten's door: Who gets in? Who's kept out? *Early Childhood Research Quarterly, 6,* 89–100.

Walsh, M. (1999). Most Edison Schools report rise in test scores. *Education Week, 18*(31), 9.

Wasley, P. A., Hampel, R. L., & Clark, R. W. (1997). *Kids and school reform.* San Francisco: Jossey-Bass.

White, K. A. (1999). Ahead of the curve. *Education Week, 18*(18), 32, 36.

Whitebook, M., Howes, C., & Phillips, D. (1998). *Worthy work, unlivable wages: The national child care staffing study, 1988–1997.* Washington, DC: Center for the Child Care Workforce.

Wolfgang, C. H., Bennett, B. J., Irvin, J. L. (1999). Strategies for teaching self-discipline in the middle grades. Boston: Allyn and Bacon.

Zill, N. (1996). Family change and student achievement: What we have learned, what it means for schools. In A. Booth & J. F. Dunn (Eds.), *Family–student links: How do they affect educational outcomes?* (pp. 139–176). Mahwah, NJ: Lawrence Erlbaum.

▶ Chapter 6

Americans with Disabilities Association, Inc. (1999). ADA mission statement. Available online: http://www.ada-pac.org/#campnews

Appalachia Educational Laboratory (1990). Rural school finance, fiscal policies for rural schools, a conference summary [Special issue]. *The Link, 9*(4).

Bales, R. F. (1954). In conference. *Harvard Business Review,* No. 32, 41–49.

Becker, G. S. (1964). *Human capital: A theoretical and empirical analysis, with special reference to education.* New York: Columbia University Press.

Berliner, D. C. (1992, February). *Educational reform in an era of disinformation*. Paper presented at the annual meeting of the American Association of Colleges for Teacher Education, San Antonio, TX.

Berliner, D. C., & Biddle, B. J. (1995). *The manufactured crisis: Myths, fraud, and the attack on America's public schools*. Reading, MA: Addison-Wesley.

Berliner, D. C., & Biddle, B. J. (1998). The lamentable alliance between the media and school critics. In G. I. Maeroff (Ed.), *Imaging education: The media and schools in America* (pp. 26–45). New York: Teachers College Press.

Bowers, D. G., & Seashore, S. E. (1966). Predicting organizational effectiveness with a four-factor theory of leadership. *Administrative Science Quarterly, 11*, 238–264.

Bracey, G. W. (1991). Why can't they be like we were? *Phi Delta Kappan, 73*(2), 105–117.

Bradley, B. (1996). Toward civic-minded media. *Media Studies Journal, 10*(1), 40–41.

Burrup, P. E., & Brimley, V. (1982). *Financing education in a climate of change*. Boston: Allyn and Bacon.

Burrup, P. E., Brimley, V., & Garfield, R. R. (1999). *Financing education in a climate of change*. Boston: Allyn and Bacon.

Business Owner's Toolkit (1999, August 2). What are sales taxes? Available online: http://www.toolkit.cch.com/text/p07_4010.asp

Carson, C. C., Huelskamp, R. M., & Woodall, T. D. (1991). *Perspective on education in America* (3rd draft). Albuquerque, NM: Sandia National Laboratories.

Chubb, J. E., & Moe, T. M. (1990). *Politics, markets, and America's schools*. Washington, DC: The Brookings Institute.

Clune, W. H. (1995). Educational adequacy: A theory and its remedies. *University of Michigan Journal of Law Reform, 28*(3), 481–491.

Cohn, E., & Geske, T. G. (1990). *The economics of education* (3rd ed.). Oxford: Pergamon Press.

Cooper, K. J., & Pressley, S. A. (1999, April 29). Florida house approves school vouchers; senate votes today. *Washington Post*, p. A02. Available online: http://newslibrary.krmediastream.com/cgi-bin/document/wp_auth?DBLIST=wp99&DOCNUM=22363

Darling-Hammond, L., & McLaughlin, M. W. (1995). Policies that support professional development in an era of reform. *Phi Delta Kappan, 76*(8), 597–604.

Fiedler, F. E. (1967). *A theory of leadership effectiveness*. New York: McGraw-Hill.

Friedman, M. (1955). The role of government in education. In R. A. Solo (Ed.), *Economics and the public interest* (pp. 123–144). New Brunswick, NJ: Rutgers University Press.

Friedman, M. (1995, June 23). *Public schools: Make them private*. Washington, DC: CATO Institute.

Glickman, C. D. (1998). *Revolutionizing America's schools*. San Francisco: Jossey-Bass.

Guthrie, J. W., Garms, W. I., & Pierce, L. C. (1988). *School finance and education policy: Enhancing educational efficiency, equality, and choice*. Upper Saddle River, NJ: Prentice Hall.

Hambrick, D. C. (1998). Corporate coherence and the top management team. In D. C. Hambrick, D. A. Nadler, & M. L. Tushman (Eds.), *Navigating change: How CEOs, top teams, and boards steer transformation* (pp. 123–140). Boston: Harvard Business School Press.

Hanushek, E. (1989). Expenditures, efficiency, and equity in education: The federal government's role. *American Economic Review, 79*, 46–51.

Hendrie, C. (1999a, May 17). Survey finds gap between public, board members on urban schools. *Education Week, 18*(27), 9.

Hendrie, C. (1999b, May 5). Battle over principals in Chicago: Administration vs. local councils. *Education Week, 34*(18), 8–9.

Hentschke, G. C., Dembowski, F. L., Faux, J. H., Hansen, S. J., Kehoe, E., Meno, L., Murphy, M. J., Vigilante, R. P., & Yagielski, J. (1986). *School business administration: A comparative perspective*. Berkeley, CA: McCutchan.

Hoy, W. K., & Miskel, C. G. (1996). *Educational administration: Theory, research, and practice* (5th ed.). New York: McGraw-Hill.

Kozol, J. (1991). *Savage inequalities: Children in America's schools*. New York: Crown.

Leithwood, K. A. (1992). The move toward transformational leadership. *Educational Leadership, 49*(5), 8–12.

Levin, H. M. (1987, June). *Finance and governance: Implications of school-based decisions*. Paper presented at the National Advisory Committee of the Work in America Institute, New York.

Lindle, J. C. (1996). Lessons from Kentucky about school-based decision making. *Educational Leadership, 53*(4), 20–23.

Lucas, J. (1999, June 9). "Old girl" network of superintendents bucks prevailing statistics nationwide. *AASA Online. Leadership News*. Available online: http://www.aasa.org/LN/Misc/6-9-99oldgirl.htm

McCormick, K. (1984). These tried-and-true alliances have paid off for public schools. *American School Board Journal, 10*, 24–26.

National Association of Manufacturers (1999). The situation: Your training needs are growing. Your budget isn't. The solution: NAM VIRTUAL UNIVERSITY. Available online: http://www.nam.org/Training/namvu.html

National Association of State Boards of Education (1996, January). *State education governance at-a-glance*. Alexandria, VA: National Association of State Boards of Education.

National Education Goals Panel (1998). *Notes about the 1998 findings: Illinois*. Available online: http://www.negp.gov/issues/publication/98statefact/il.htm/

National Organization for Women Legal Defense and Education Fund (1993, Fall). *NOW LDEF challenges St. Louis board of education* (p. 2). NOW Legal Defense and Education Fund.

Odden, A. (1984). Financing educational excellence. *Phi Delta Kappan, 65*(5), 311–318.

Peterson, P. E. (1999). Top ten questions asked about school choice. In D. Ravitch (Ed.), *Brookings papers on education policy 1999* (pp. 371–418). Washington, DC: Brookings Institution Press.

Putka, G. (1991, May 15). Whittle develops plan to operate schools for profit. *Wall Street Journal*, p. B8.

Pyhrr, P. A. (1973). *Zero-base budgeting: A practical management tool for evaluating expenses*. New York: John Wiley & Sons.

Rose, L. C., & Gallup, A. M. (1998, September). The 30th annual Phi Delta Kappa/Gallup poll of the public's attitudes toward the public schools. *Phi Delta Kappan, 80*(1), 41–56.

Sadowski, M. (1995, March/April). The numbers game yields simplistic answers on the link between spending and outcomes. *Harvard Education Letter, 11*(2), 1–4.

Schultz, T. W. (1981). *Investing in people: The economics of population quality*. Berkeley: University of California Press.

Stearns, T. M., Hoffman, A. N., & Heide, J. B. (1987). Performance of commercial television stations as an outcome of interorganizational linkages and environmental conditions. *Academy of Management Journal, 30*, 71–90.

Stogdill, R. M. (1981). Traits of leadership: A follow-up to 1970. In B. M. Bass (Ed.), *Stogdill's handbook of leadership* (pp. 73–97). New York: Free Press.

Thro, W. E. (1990). The third wave: The impact of the Montana, Kentucky and Texas decisions on the future of public school finance reform litigation. *Journal of Law & Education, 19*(2), 219–250.

U.S. Department of Education. (1989). *Making sense of school budgets*. Washington, DC: Office of Educational Research and Improvement.

U.S. Department of Education (1997, October) *Cane Run Elementary School: A parent-friendly, family focused urban school*. Available online: http://www.ed.gov/pubs/FamInvolve/cane.html

U.S. Department of Education (1998). *The condition of education 1998*. NCES 98-013, by John Wirt, Tom Snyder, Jennifer Sable, Susan P. Choy, Yupin Bae, Janis Stennett, Allison Gruner, & Marianne Perie. Washington, DC: Office of Educational Research and Improvement.

U.S. Department of Education (1999). *Digest of education statistics, 1998*. NCES 1999-036, by Thomas D. Snyder, Charlene Hoffman, & Claire M. Geddes. Washington, DC: U.S. Government Printing Office.

Verstegen, D. (1990). Efficiency and economies-of-scale revisited: Implications for financing rural school districts. *Journal of Education Finance, 16*, 159–179.

Verstegen, D., & McGuire, C. K. (1991). The dialectic of reform. *Educational Policy, 5*(4), 386–411.

Ward, J. G. (1992). Schools and the struggle for democracy: Themes for school finance policy. In J. G. Ward & P. Anthony (Eds.), *Who pays for student diversity?* (pp. 241–250). Newbury Park, CA: Corwin Press.

Wartts, N. (1998, August 21). More school partnerships sought. Green appeals to civic, business leaders. *Detroit Free Press*. Available online: http://www.freep.com/news/education/qsum21.htm

Webb, L. D. (1990). New revenues for education at the state level. In J. K. Underwood & D. A. Verstegen (Eds.), *The impacts of litigation and legislation on public school finance: Adequacy, equity, and excellence* (pp. 27–58). New York: Harper & Row.

Weiss, C. (1995). The four "I"s of school reform: How interests, ideology, information, and institution affect teachers and principals. *Harvard Educational Review, 65*(4), 571–592.

White, K. A. (1999, June 14). Summer brings building boom in city schools. *Education Week, 18*(42), 1, 16.

Williams, J. (1992). The politics of education news. In R. F. McNergney (Ed.), *Education research, policy, and the press: Research as news* (pp. 177–200). Boston: Allyn and Bacon.

Zaleznick, A. (1977). Managers and leaders: Are they different? *Harvard Business Review, 55*(3), 67–78.

▶ Chapter 7

American Psychological Association & Music Television (undated). *Warning signs. Fight for your rights: Take a stand against violence.* Washington, DC: American Psychological Association.

Astor, R. A., Meyer, J. A., & Behre, W. J. (1999). Unowned places and times: Maps and interviews about violence in high schools. *American Educational Research Journal, 36*(1), 3–42.

Balli, S. J. (1996, Winter). Family diversity and the nature of parental involvement. *Educational Forum, 60*, pp. 149–155.

Barr, R. D., & Parrett, W. H. (1995). *Hope at last for at-risk youth.* Boston: Allyn and Bacon.

Calfee, C., Wittwer, F., & Meredith, M. (1998). *Building a full-service school: A step-by-step guide.* San Francisco: Jossey-Bass.

Centers for Disease Control and Prevention (1996, June). *HIV/AIDS surveillance report.* Atlanta, GA: Author.

Children's Defense Fund. (1996, April 9). *Child gun deaths up 94 percent.* Washington, DC: Author.

Children's Defense Fund (1999). Child care basics. Available online: http://www.childrensdefense.org/childcare/cc_basics.html#15

Coleman, J., Lyon, J., & Piper, R. (1995). *Teenage suicide and self harm.* Brighton, England: TSA Publishing Ltd.

Coles, A. D. (1999a, January 20). Discontented, some districts shifting gears on anti-drug programs. *Education Week, 18*(19), 5.

Coles, A. D. (1999b, May 12). Health update. *Education Week, 8*(35), 13.

Dryfoos, J. G. (1994). *Full-service schools: A revolution in health and social services for children, youth, and families.* San Francisco: Jossey-Bass.

Elkind, D. (1988). *The hurried child: Growing up too fast too soon.* Reading, MA: Addison-Wesley.

Finn, C. E., Jr. (1991). *We must take charge: Our schools and our future.* New York: Free Press.

Friedli, L., & Scherzer, A. (1996). *Positive steps: Attitudes and awareness among 11–24 year olds.* London: Health Education Authority Publications.

Froschl, M., & Gropper, N. (1999). Fostering friendships, curbing bullying. *Educational leadership, 56*(8), 72–75.

Gallup Organization, Inc. (1991). *Teenage suicide study executive summary.* Princeton, NJ: Author.

Garbarino, J., Dubrow, N., Kostelny, K., & Pardo, C. (1992). *Children in danger.* San Francisco: Jossey-Bass.

Georgia Student Finance Commission (1999). *Building cornerstones for students: Annual report 1998.* Available online: http://www.gsfc.org/

Girls' substance abuse. (1996). *Education Week, 15*(38) 7.

Gladding, S. T. (1996). *Counseling: A comprehensive profession* (3rd ed.) (p. 389) Upper Saddle River, NJ: Prentice Hall.

Green, J. (1991, October 13). This school is out: At Harvey Milk, a high school for gay students, lessons are taught in grammar, algebra and survival. *New York Times Magazine*, pp. 32, 33, 36, 59, 60, 68.

Groopman, J. E. (1993, March 8). T.B. or not T.B.? *New Republic*, pp. 18–19.

Harp, L. (1994, September). Who's minding the children? *Education Week, 14*, 28–33.

Hofferth, S. L. (1998). *Healthy environments, healthy children.* Ann Arbor, MI: Child Development Supplement, Panel Study of Income Dynamics, Institute of Social Research, University of Michigan.

Intercultural Development Research Association (1999). Coca-Cola Valued Youth Program. Available online: http://www.idra.org/ccvyp/default.htm

Jacobson, L. (1998, November 18). Study tracks how children spend their time. *Education Week, 18*(12), 8.

Jalongo, M. R., Isenberg, J. P., & Gerbracht, G. (1995). *Teachers' stories: From personal narrative to professional insight.* San Francisco: Jossey-Bass.

Kann, L., Warren, W., Collins, J. L., Ross, J., Collins, B., & Kolbe, L. J. (1993). Results from the national school-based 1991 Youth Risk Behavior Survey and progress toward achieving related health objectives for the nation. *Public Health Reports, 108*, Supplement 1, pp. 47–55.

Kozol, J. (1995). *Amazing grace.* New York: Random House.

Landau, S., Pryor, J. B., & Haefli, K. (1995). Pediatric HIV: School-based sequelae and curricular interventions for infection prevention and social acceptance. *School Psychology Review, 24*(2), 213–229.

Lawton, M. (1995, May). Suicide rate among youths soaring, C.D.C. reports. *Education Week, 14*(32), 5.

Leighninger, M., & Niedergang, M. (1995). Good news at Fairbanks Elementary. *Education: How can schools and communities work together to meet the challenge?* Pomfret, CT: Topsfield Foundation.

Loosli, A. R., & Ruud, J. S. (1998). Meatless diets in female athletes: A red flag. *Physician and Sportsmedicine, 26*(11), 45.

Louis Harris and Associates, Inc. (1996). *The Metropolitan Life survey of the American teacher, 1996: Students voice their opinions on: Violence, social tension and equality among teens, part I.* New York: MetLife.

McCarthy, M. M., & Cambron-McCabe, N. (1998). *Public school law: Teachers' and students' rights* (4th ed.). Boston: Allyn and Bacon.

Mullet, J. H., & Groves, C. C. (1996, March). Second chance university. *American School Board Journal*, pp. 23–25.

National Association for the Education of Young Children (1998). *Learning to read and write: Developmentally appropriate practices for young children, pt. 1.* Available online: http://www.naeyc.org/about/position/position_index.htm

National Commission on Children. (1991). *Beyond rhetoric: A new American agenda for children and families.* Washington, DC: Author.

National Research Council. (1993). *Understanding child abuse and neglect.* Washington, DC: National Academy Press.

Neuman, S. B., Hagedorn, T., Celano, D., & Daly, P. (1995, Winter). Toward a collaborative approach to parent involvement in early education: A study of teenage mothers in an African-American community. *American Educational Research Journal, 32*(4), 801–827.

Panel on High-Risk Youth, Commission on Behavioral and Social Sciences and Education, National Research Council (1993). *Losing generations: Adolescents in high-risk settings.* Washington, DC: National Academy Press.

Payne, K. J., & Biddle, B. J. (1999). Poor school funding, child poverty, and mathematics achievement. *Educational Researcher, 28*(6), 4–13.

Portner, J. (1993, June 16). Prevention efforts in junior high found not to curb drug use in high school. *Education Week*, p. 9.

Riley, R. (1996, March 7). *Riley Touts National Read, Writing Partnership as Reading Report Card is Issued.* Available online: http://inet.ed.gov/PressReleases/03-1996/readfin.html

Russell, L. (1998). *Child maltreatment and psychological distress among urban homeless youth.* New York: Garland Publishing.

Sanchez, R. (1999, September 17). Gates to give $1 billion for minority scholarships. *Washington Post*, p. A01.

Sandham, J. L. (1999). Father figures. *Education Week, 18*(35), 26–31.

Sidel, R. (1996). *Keeping women and children last: America's war on the poor*. New York: Penguin.

Slavin, R. E., & Fashola, O. S. (1998). *Show me the evidence! Proven and promising programs for America's schools*. Thousand Oaks, CA: Corwin Press.

Smith, T., Polloway, E., Patton, J., & Dowdy, C. (1995). *Teaching students with special needs in inclusive settings*. Boston: Allyn and Bacon.

Stein, M. R. S., & Thorkildsen, R. J. (1999). *Parent involvement in education: Insights and applications from the research*. Bloomington, IN: Phi Delta Kappa International.

Strapp, L. (1996). Teen parenting: One school system's efforts to help mothers and their babies. *Equity and Excellence in Education, 29*(1), 86–90.

Tonks, D. (1992, December/1993, January). Can you save your students' lives? Educating to prevent AIDS. *Educational Leadership*, pp. 48–54.

U.S. Bureau of the Census. (1996). *Income and poverty: 1994*. Available online: http://www.census.gov/hhes/income/povregn.html

U.S. Bureau of the Census (1997). Table 2. Characteristics of grandchildren who are coresidents with grandparents: 1997. *Current population survey*, pp. 23–198. Washington, DC: Author.

U.S. Bureau of the Census (1998a). Table A. People and families in poverty by selected characteristics: 1989, 1996, and 1997, *The official statistics*, p. vii. Washington, DC: Author.

U.S. Bureau of the Census (1998b). Table A-1. Average poverty threshold for a family of four and the consumer price indexes: 1947–1997. *The official statistics*, p. A-3. Washington, DC: Author.

U.S. Bureau of the Census (1998c). Table 4. Household relationship and presence of parents for persons under 18 years, by age, sex, race, and Hispanic origin: March 1998, p. 26. Available online: http://www.census.gov/population/www/soldemo/ms-1a.html

U.S. Bureau of the Census (1998d), Table 2. Selected characteristics—households by total money income in 1997. *The official statistics*, p. 5. Washington, DC: Author.

U.S. Bureau of the Census (1998e). *Married couples by labor force, status of spouses: 1986 to present*. Washington, DC: Author.

U.S. Bureau of the Census (1998f). Table 8: Deaths and death rates for the 10 leading causes of death in specified age groups, by race and sex: United States, 1996. *National vital statistics report, 47*(9), 27–37.

U.S. Department of Education (1993). *Reinventing Chapter 1: The current Chapter I program and new directions, final report of the National Assessment of the Chapter 1 Program*. Washington, DC: Author.

U.S. Department of Education (1995a). *Indicator of the month: Welfare recipiency, by educational attainment*. Washington, DC: U.S. Government Printing Office.

U.S. Department of Education (1995b). *National education longitudinal study of 1988: Two years later: Cognitive gains and school transitions of NELS: 88 eighth graders*. Washington, DC: U.S. Government Printing Office.

U.S. Department of Education (1998). *The condition of education 1998*. NCES 98-013, by John Wirt, Tom Snyder, Jennifer Sable, Susan P. Choy, Yupin Bae, Janis Stennett, Allison Gruner, & Marianne Perie. Washington, DC: Office of Educational Research and Improvement.

U.S. Department of Education (1999a). *Dropout rates in the United States: 1997*, NCES 1999-082, by P. Kaufman, S. Klein, & M. Frase. Washington, DC: National Center for Education Statistics. Available online: http://nces.ed.gov/pubs99/quarterlyjul/3-Elem-Sec/3-esq12-g.html

U.S. Department of Education (1999b, June 1). Study of education resources and federal funding: Preliminary report. Washington, DC: Author.

U.S. Department of Education (1999c, August 1). Targeting schools: Study of Title I allocations within school districts. Washington, DC: Author.

U.S. Department of Education (1999d). *The impacts of Upward Bound: Final report for phase I of the national evaluation—analysis and highlights*. Washington, DC: Author.

U.S. Department of Health and Human Services (1988). *Study findings: Study of national incidence and prevalence of child abuse and neglect*. Washington, DC: National Center on Child Abuse and Neglect.

U.S. Department of Health and Human Services (1994). *1992 national annual incidence and prevalence of child abuse and neglect*. Washington, DC: National Center on Child Abuse and Neglect.

U.S. Department of Health and Human Services (1997). *Head Start program performance measures: Second progress report, including data from the Family and Child Experiences Survey (FACES) spring 97 pilot study*. Washington, DC: Author.

U.S. Department of Health and Human Services (1998). *Performance improvement 1998. LEAP: Final report on Ohio's welfare initiative to improve school attendance among teenage parents*. Available online: http://aspe.os.dhhs.gov/progsys/98eval/intro.htm#executive_summary

U.S. Department of Health and Human Services (1999a). *Births: final data for 1997, Vol. 47*. Available online: http://www.cdc.gov/nchswww/releases/99news/99news/97natal.htm

U.S. Department of Health and Human Services (1999b, June 16). *HHS fact sheet: Clinton administration record on HIV/AIDS*. Available online: http://www.hhs.gov

Von Drehle, D. (1999, April 25). To killers, model school was cruel. *Washington Post*, Sunday, Final Edition, p. A1.

Waxman, H. C. (1992). Introduction: Reversing the cycle of educational failure for students in at-risk environments. In H. C. Waxman, J. Walker de Felix, J. E. Anderson, & H. P. Baptiste, Jr. (Eds.), *Students at risk in at-risk schools: Improving environments for learning* (pp. 1–9). Newbury Park, CA: Corwin Press.

Wisconsin Legislative Audit Bureau (1997). *An evaluation of effects of the learnfare program, 1993–1996*. Madison, WI: State of Wisconsin Legislative Audit Bureau Madison, WI. Available online: http://dpls.dacc.wisc.edu/learnfare/index.html

▶ Chapter 8

AAUW Educational Foundation (1998). *Gender gaps: Where schools still fail our children*. Washington, DC: American Association of University Women Educational Foundation.

AAUW Educational Foundation and the National Education Association. (1992). *The AAUW report: How schools shortchange girls: A study of major findings on girls and education*. Washington, DC: Authors.

Abramowitz, R. H., Petersen, A. C., & Schulenberg, J. E. (1984). Changes in self-image during early adolescence. In D. Offer, E. Ostrov, & K. Howard (Eds.), *Patterns of adolescent self-image* (pp. 19–28). San Francisco: Jossey-Bass.

American Association of Mental Retardation (1999). Fact sheet: What is mental retardation? Available online: http://www.aamr.org/Policies/faqmentalretardation.html

Associated Press (1999, April 16). Calif. governor asks mediation on prop. 187. *Washington Post*, p. A08. Available online: http://newslibrary.krmediastream.com/cgi-bin/document/wp_auth?DBLIST=wp99&DOCNUM=19813

Avery, P. G., & Walker, C. (1993). Prospective teachers' perceptions of ethnic and gender differences in academic achievement *Journal of Teacher Education, 44*(1), 27–37.

Bafumo, M. E. (1998, March). The roots of learning. *Educational Leadership, 55*(6), 66–69.

Banks, J. A. (1996). The historical reconstruction of knowledge about race: Implications for transformative teaching. In J. A. Banks (Ed.), *Multicultural education, transformative knowledge, and action: Historical and contemporary perspectives* (pp. 64–87). New York: Teachers College Press.

Banks, J. A. (1997). Multicultural education: Characteristics and goals. In J. A. Banks & C. A. McGee Banks (Eds.), *Multicultural education: Issues and perspectives* (3rd ed.) (pp. 3–28). Boston: Allyn and Bacon.

Barkley, R. A. (1998). *Attention-deficit hyperactivity disorder: A handbook for diagnosis and treatment*. New York: Guilford Press.

Bernstein, R. (1990, October 14). In U.S. schools: A war of words. *New York Times Magazine*, pp. 44–47.

Bouchard, J. J., Jr., Lykken, D. T., McGue, M., Segal, N., & Tellegen, A. (1990). Sources of human psychological differences: The Minnesota study of twins reared apart. *Science, 250,* 223–228.

Brooks-Gunn, J., Graber, J. H., & Paikoff, R. L. (1994). Studying links between hormones and negative affect: Models and measures. *Journal of Research on Adolescence, 4*(4), 469–486.

Bullivant, B. M. (1993). Culture: Its nature and meaning for educators. In J. A. Banks & C. A. McGee Banks (Eds.), *Multicultural education: Issues and perspectives* (2nd ed.) (pp. 29–47). Boston: Allyn and Bacon.

Cameron, J., & Pierce, W. D. (1994, Fall). Reinforcement, reward, and intrinsic motivation: A meta-analysis. *Review of Educational Research, 64*(3), 363–423.

Caplan, N., Choy, M. H., & Whitmore, J. K. (1991). *Children of the boat people: A study of educational success.* Ann Arbor: University of Michigan Press.

Carey, N., & Farris, E. (1996, March). *Racial and ethnic classifications used by public schools.* Washington, DC: National Center for Education Statistics, Office of Educational Research and Improvement, Department of Education.

Carlson, D. (1998). Who am I? Gay identity and a democratic politics of the self. In W. F. Pinar (Ed.), *Queer theory in education* (pp. 107–120). Mahwah, NJ: Lawrence Erlbaum.

Caudell, L. S. (1996). Research review. *NW Education, 1*(1), 31–34.

Ceci, S. J., & Ruiz, A. (1993). Transfer, abstractness, and intelligence. In D. Detterman & R. J. Sternberg (Eds.), *Transfer on trial: Intelligence, cognition, and instruction* (pp. 168–191). Norwood, NJ: Ablex.

Children's Defense Fund. (1992). *The state of America's children 1992.* Washington, DC: Author.

Clark, C. M. (1995). *Thoughtful teaching.* London: Cassell.

Cohen, D. L. (1993, April 7). New study links lower I.Q. at age 5 to poverty. *Education Week,* p. 4.

Cremin, L. A. (1957). *The republic and the school.* New York: Teachers College Press.

Daily Report Card (1996, June 19). Single-sex classes: A return to the turn of the century? Available online: http://www.utopia.com/mailings/reportcard/DAILY.REPORT.CARD217. html#Index2

Elliott, D. V. M. (1999). The sacred willow: Four generations in the life of a Vietnamese family. New York: Oxford University Press.

Fine, M. (1995). *Habits of mind: Struggling over values in America's classrooms.* San Francisco: Jossey-Bass.

Friend, M., & Bursuck, W. D. (1999). *Including students with special needs: A practical guide for classroom teachers* (2nd ed.). Boston: Allyn and Bacon.

Gardner, H. (1995, November). Reflections on multiple intelligences: Myths and messages. *Phi Delta Kappan, 77*(3), 200–209.

Gardner, H. (1999). *The disciplined mind: What all students should understand.* New York: Simon & Schuster.

Gardner, H., & Hatch, T. (1989). Multiple intelligences go to school: Educational implications of the theory of multiple intelligences. *Educational Researcher, 18*(8), 4–10.

Gilligan, C. (1982). *In a different voice: Psychological theory and women's development.* Cambridge, MA: Harvard University Press.

Gilligan, C., & Attanucci, J. (1988). Two moral orientations: Gender differences and similarities. *Merrill-Palmer Quarterly, 34,* 223–237.

Guilford, J. P. (1988). Some changes in the structure-of-intellect model. *Educational and Psychological Measurement, 48,* 1–4.

Hallahan, D. P., & Kauffman, J. M. (2000). *Exceptional learners: Introduction to special education* (8th ed.). Boston: Allyn and Bacon.

Hammill, D. D., Leigh, J. E., McNutt, G., & Larsen, S. (1988). A new definition of learning disabilities. *Learning Disability Quarterly, 11*(3), 217–232.

Hansen, D. T. (1996, January). Teaching and the moral life of classrooms. *Journal for a Just and Caring Education, 2*(1), 59–74.

Harrison, R., & Bennett, C. (1995). Racial and ethnic diversity. In R. Farley (Ed.), *State of the union: America in the 1990s: Vol. 2. Social trends.* New York: Russell Sage Foundation.

Heath, D. H. (1999). *Morale, culture, and character: Assessing schools of hope.* Bryn Mawr, PA: Cornrow Publishing House.

Hendrie, C. (1999, April 16). U.S. schools lapsing into "resegregation," Orfield warns. *Education Week on the Web.* Available online: http://www.edweek.org/ew/vol-16/29deseg.h16

Henry, S. L., & Pepper, F. C. (1990). Cognitive, social, and cultural effects on Indian learning style: Classroom implications. *Journal of Educational Issues of Language Minority Students, 7,* 85–97.

Herbert, J. M., & McNergney, R. F. (1996). *The case of Columbus, New Mexico: Educational life on the border.* Washington, DC: American Association of Colleges for Teacher Education and ERIC Clearinghouse on Teaching & Teacher Education.

Hill, D. (1990, June/July). A theory of success and failure. *Teacher Magazine,* pp. 40–45.

Hilliard, A. G., III. (1990). Back to Binet: The case against the use of IQ tests in the schools. *Contemporary Education, 61*(4), 184–189.

Kohn, A. (1996, Spring). By all available means: Camero and Pierce's defense of extrinsic motivators. *Review of Educational Research, 66*(1), 1–4.

Kunen, J. S. (1996). The end of integration. *Time, 147*(18), 38–45.

Lawton, M. (1995). More children becoming overweight, study finds. *Education Week, 15*(6), 6.

Lawton, M. (1996). Effort to improve diet, exercise of students results in some gains. *Education Week, 15*(27), 14.

Lepper, M. R., Keavney, M., & Drake, M. (1996, Spring). Intrinsic motivation and extrinsic rewards: A commentary on Camero and Pierce's meta-analysis. *Review of Educational Research, 66*(1), 5–32.

Lewin, T. (1998, December 13). How boys lost out to girl power. *New York Times, 148* (51,370), section 4, p. 3.

Martelle, S. (1999, July 28). Technology replacing Braille. *Los Angeles Times,* ID: 0990067041, p. A1.

Matute-Bianchi, M. E. (1991). Situational ethnicity and patterns of school performance among immigrant and nonimmigrant Mexican-descent students. In M. A. Gibson & J. U. Ogbu (Eds.), *Minority status and schooling: A comparative study of immigrant and involuntary minorities* (pp. 205–248). New York: Garland.

Morin, R. (1995, October 8). A distorted image of minorities. *Washington Post,* pp. A1, A27.

Mwamwenda, T. S. (1992). Comment: Universality of formal operational thought. *Perceptual and Motor Skills, 78*(2), 78.

National Information Center for Children and Youth with Disabilities. (1996). Definition of learning disabilities. Available online: http://www.ldonline.org/ld_indepth/general_info/gen-2.html#anchor1083490

Office of Federal Statistical Policy and Standards. (1978). *Statistical policy handbook.* Washington, DC: U.S. Department of Commerce.

Ogbu, J. U., & Simons, H. D. (1998). Voluntary and involuntary minorities: A cultural–ecological theory of school performance with some implications for education. *Anthropology & Education Quarterly, 29*(2), 155–188.

Palmer, J. M., & Yantis, P. A. (1990). *Survey of communication disorders.* Baltimore, MD: Williams & Wilkins.

Pollina, A. (1995). Gender balance: Lessons from girls in science and mathematics. *Educational Leadership, 53*(1), 30–33.

Ponessa, J. (1995). NEA backing for gay month sparks firestorm. *Education Week, 15*(8), 3.

Porter, R. P. (1995). The New York City study. *READ Perspectives, 2*(2), 1–5.

Power, F. C., Higgins, A., & Kohlberg, L. (1989). *Lawrence Kohlberg's approach to moral education.* New York: Columbia University Press.

Ramirez, J. D. (1992, Winter/Spring). Executive summary. *Bilingual Research Journal, 16,* 1–245.

Renzulli, J. S. (1982). Dear Mr. and Mrs. Copernicus: We regret to inform you. . . . *Gifted Child Quarterly, 26,* 11–14.

Rierdan, J., & Koff, E. (1991). Depressive symptomology among very early maturing girls. *Journal of Youth and Adolescence, 20,* 415–25.

Ruenzel, D. (1999, April 14). Pride & prejudice. *Education Week on the Web.* Available online: http://www.edweek.org/ew/1999/31gay.h18

Rutherford, F. J., & Ahlgren, A. (1994). *Science for All Americans* (2nd ed.). New York: Oxford University Press.

Sadker, M., & Sadker, D. (1993, March). Fair and square? *Instructor,* pp. 45, 46, 67, 68.

Schmidley, D., & Alvarado, H. A. (1997, March). *The foreign-born population in the United States: March 1997 (update)*. Washington, DC: U.S. Government Printing Office.

Schnaiberg, L. (1999a). Immigrants: Providing a lesson in how to adapt. *Education Week, 18*(20), 34–35.

Schnaiberg, L. (1999b). Calif.'s year on the bilingual battleground. *Education Week, 18*(38), 1, 9–10.

Sockett, H. (1993). *The moral base for teacher professionalism*. New York: Teachers College Press.

Sothern, M. S., von Almen, T. K., Schumacher, H. D., Suskind, R. M., & Blecker, U. A. (1999, June). Multidisciplinary approach to the treatment of childhood obesity. *Delaware Medical Journal, 71*(6), 255–261.

Spearman, C. (1927). *The abilities of man*. New York: Macmillan.

Steele, S. (1990). *The content of our character: A new vision of race in America*. New York: Harper Perennial.

Sternberg, R. J. (1996, March). Myths, countermyths, and truths about intelligence. *Educational Researcher, 25*(2), 11–16.

Sternberg, R. J., & Detterman, D. K. (Eds.). (1986). *What is intelligence?: Contemporary viewpoints on its nature and definition*. Norwood, NJ: Ablex.

Sternberg, R. J., & Williams, W. M. (1998). *Intelligence, instruction and assessment: Theory into practice*. Mahwah, NJ: Lawrence Erlbaum.

Stroup, K. (1998). *Proceedings for the Policy Panel on Racial/Ethnic Data Collection, March 17–18, 1998*. Washington, DC: National Center for Education Statistics. Available online: http://nces.ed.gov/npec/papers/race-ethnic3.htmlSummary

Suro, R. (1998, July 19). The next wave: How immigration blurs the race discussion. *Washington Post*, p. C1.

Sutherland, P. (1992). *Cognitive development today: Piaget and his critics*. London: Paul Chapman.

Terkel, S. (1992). *Race: How blacks and whites think and feel about the American obsession*. New York: New Press.

Tomlinson, C. A. (1999). *The differentiated classroom: Responding to the needs of all learners*. Alexandria, VA: Association for Supervision and Curriculum Development.

U.S. Department of Education (1993). *National excellence: A case for developing America's talent*. Washington, DC: U.S. Government Printing Office.

U.S. Department of Education (1996, June). *Announcement: NCES releases proceedings of the Conference on Inclusion Guidelines and Accommodations for limited English proficient students in the National Assessment of Educational Progress*. Washington, DC: U.S. Government Printing Office.

U.S. Department of Education (1999). *Digest of education statistics 1998*. Washington, DC: U.S. Government Printing Office.

U.S. Department of Health, Education, and Welfare (1977, August 23). *Federal Register, 42*(163), 42478.

Wolf, B., Pratt, C., & Pruitt, P. (1990). *Human exceptionality: Society, school and family* (3rd ed.). Boston: Allyn and Bacon.

▶ Chapter 9

American Association for the Advancement of Science (1998). Blueprints for reform. Science, mathematics, and technology education: Project 2061. New York: Oxford University Press.

Asante, M. K. (1992). Learning about Africa. *Executive Educator, 14*(9), 21–23.

Banks, J. A. (1996). The historical reconstruction of knowledge about race: Implications for transformative teaching. In J. A. Banks (Ed.), *Multicultural education, transformative knowledge, and action: Historical and contemporary perspectives* (pp. 64–87). New York: Teachers College Press.

Banks, J. A. (1997). Multicultural education: Characteristics and goals. In J. A. Banks & C. A. McGee Banks (Eds.), *Multicultural education: Issues and perspectives* (3rd ed.) (pp. 3–28). Boston: Allyn and Bacon.

Bennett, C. (1999). *Comprehensive multicultural education: Theory and practice* (4th ed.). Boston: Allyn and Bacon.

Bigler, E. (1999). *American conversations: Puerto Ricans, white ethnics, and multicultural education*. Philadelphia: Temple University Press.

Bodine, R. J., & Crawford, D. K. (1998). *The handbook of conflict resolution education: A guide to building quality programs in schools*. San Francisco: National Institute for Dispute Resolution and Jossey-Bass Publishers.

Bradley, A. (1996, March 13). Unconventional wisdom: Two distinguished African-American educators dissent from the progressive ideology of contemporary school reform. *Education Week, 15*(25), 34–43.

Brown, A. (1994). The advancement of learning. *Educational Researcher, 23*(8), 4–12.

Clemetson, L. (1998, December 14). Caught in the cross-fire. A young teacher finds herself in a losing racial battle with parents. *Newsweek*, pp. 38–39.

Cooper, K. J. (1992, November 27). Broadening horizons: Afrocentrism takes root in Atlanta schools. *Washington Post*, p. A1.

Eisenhart, M., Finkel, E., & Marion, S. F. (1996). Creating the conditions for scientific literacy: A re-examination. *American Educational Research Journal, 33*, 261–295.

Fairbanks, C. M. (1998). Imagining neighborhoods: Social worlds of urban adolescents. In C. Fleischer & D. Schaafsma (Eds.), *Literacy and democracy: Teacher research and composition studies in pursuit of habitable spaces* (pp. 135–156). Urbana, Ill.: National Council of Teachers of English.

Finkel, D. (1993, June 13). The wiz. *Washington Post Magazine*, pp. 8–13, 22–27.

Fradd, S. H. & Lee, O. (1999). Teachers' roles in promoting science inquiry with students from diverse language backgrounds. *Educational Researcher, 28*(6), 14–20.

Gay, G. (1995). Curriculum theory and multicultural education. In J. A. Banks & C. A. Banks (Eds.), *Handbook of research on multicultural education* (pp. 25–43). New York: Macmillan.

Gollnick, D. M. (1995). National and state initiatives for multicultural education. In J. A. Banks & C. A. Banks (Eds.), *Handbook of research on multicultural education* (pp. 44–64). New York: Macmillan.

Gorski, P. (1999). *Multicultural pavilion: Mission and working definition*. Available online: http://curry.edschool.virginia.edu/go/multicultural

Grant, C. A., & Gomez, M. L. (1996). *Making schooling multicultural: Campus and classroom*. Upper Saddle River, NJ: Prentice Hall.

Hallahan, D. P., & Kauffman, J. M. (2000). *Exceptional children: Introduction to special education* (8th ed.). Boston: Allyn and Bacon.

Johnson, D., & Johnson, R. (1997). Teaching students to be peacemakers: Results of five years of research. *Peace and conflict: Journal of peace psychology, 1*(4), 417–438.

Johnson, D. W., Johnson, R., Dudley, B., Ward, M., & Magnuson, D. (1995). The impact of peer mediation training on the management of school and home conflicts. *American Educational Research Journal, 32*(4), 824–844.

Kleinfeld, J. (1995). Critical perspective on the case of Hans Christian Andersen School. In *Guide to foundations in action: Videocases: Teaching and learning in multicultural settings* (pp. 191–208). Boston: Allyn and Bacon.

Ladson-Billings (1994). *The dreamkeepers: Successful teachers of African American students*. San Francisco: Jossey-Bass.

Lee, O., & Fradd, S. H. (1998). Science for all, including students from non-English language backgrounds. *Educational Researcher, 27*(4), 12–21.

Lehrer, R., & Schauble, L. (1998). Reasoning about structure and function: Children's conceptions of gears. *Journal of Research in Science Teaching, 35*, 3–25.

Lipsky, D. K., & Gartner, A. (1998). Factors for successful inclusion: Learning from the past, looking toward the future. In S. J. Vitello & D. E. Mithaug (Eds.), *Inclusive schooling: National and international perspectives* (pp. 98–112). Mahwah, NJ: Lawrence Erlbaum.

Louis Harris and Associates, Inc. (1996). *The Metropolitan Life survey of the American teacher: 1996: Students voice their opinions on violence, social tension and equality among teens, part I*. New York: Author.

Manning, M. L., & Baruth, L. G., 1996. *Multicultural education of children and adolescents* (2nd ed.). Boston: Allyn and Bacon.

Manzo, K. K. (1998, February 11). Black history month has left mark on curriculum, but to what extent? *Education Week on the Web*. Available online: http://www.edweek.org/ew/1998/22hist.h17)

Manzo, K. K., Lawton, M., Bradley, A., & Archer, J. (1998, June 17). Report assails new social studies texts. *Education Week, 17*(40), 14.

Marsh, H. W., Chessor, D., Craven, R., & Roche, L. (1995). The effects of gifted and talented programs on academic self-concept: The big fish strikes again. *American Educational Research Journal, 32*(2), 285–319.

McNergney, R., & Keller, C. (1999). Appendix. Some effective teachers' actions. In R. McNergney & C. Keller (Eds.), *Images of mainstreaming: Educating students with disabilities* (pp. 211–212). New York: Garland Publishing.

McNergney, R. F., Hallahan, D. P., Trent, S. C., & Hockenbury, J. C. (1999). Working together to help teachers and students. In R. McNergney & C. Keller (Eds.), *Images of mainstreaming: Educating students with disabilities* (pp. 193–209). New York: Garland Publishing.

Metz, K. E. (1995). Reassessment of developmental constraints on children's science instruction. *Review of Educational Research, 65*, 93–127.

Millard, B. (1999, Spring). School house blues: An African-American art form offers new lessons in harmony. *Teaching Tolerance, 15*, 17–23.

Mills v. *Board of Education of District of Columbia* 348 F. Supp. 866 (1972).

Mithaug, D. E. (1998). The alternative to ideological inclusion. In S. J. Vitello & D. E. Mithaug (Eds.), *Inclusive schooling: National and international perspectives* (pp. 1–23). Mahwah, NJ: Lawrence Erlbaum.

Mosle, S. (1993, August 1). Scissors, not sermons. *Washington Post Education Review*, p. 5.

National Research Council (1996). *National science education standards*. Washington, DC: National Academy Press.

Oakes, J., & Lipton, M. (1999). *Teaching to change the world*. Boston, MA: McGraw-Hill.

Oei, T., & Lyon G. (1996). In our own words. *Teaching Tolerance, 5*(2), 46–59.

Ogbu, J. U. (1987). Variability in minority school performance: A problem in search of an explanation. *Anthropology & Education Quarterly, 18*, 312–334.

Phillips, W. (1993). Introduction. *Partisan Review, 60*(4), 509.

Prose, F. (1999). I know why the caged bird cannot read: How American high school students learn to loathe literature. *Harper's Magazine, 299*(1792), 76–84.

Raspberry, W. (1998, June 26). Public schools are unable to educate minority children. *Daily Progress*, p. A8.

Rosebery, A. S., & Warren, B. (Eds.) (1998). *Boats, balloons, and classroom video*. Westport, CT: Heinemann.

Rosebery, A. S., Warren, B., & Conant, F. R. (1992). Appropriating scientific discourse: Findings from language minority classrooms. *Journal of the Learning Sciences, 21*, 61–94.

Sack, J. (1999a, January 27). Bringing special education students into the classroom. *Education Week, 18*(20), 36–37.

Sack, J. (1999b, April 7). Fla. district criticized for moving students out of special centers. *Education Week, 18*(30), 6.

Sapon-Shevin, M. (1999). *Because we can change the world: A practical guide to building cooperative, inclusive classroom communities*. Boston: Allyn and Bacon.

Schmidt, P. (1993, May 26). Seeking to identify the gifted among L.E.P. students. *Education Week*, pp. 1, 12–13.

Searle, J. R. (1993). Is there a crisis in American higher education? *Partisan Review, 60*(4), 693–708.

Sleeter, C. E. (1993). Multicultural education: Five views. *Education Digest, 58*(7), 53–57.

Sleeter, C. E., & Grant, C. A. (1994). *Making choices for multicultural education: Five approaches to race, class, and gender* (3rd ed.). Upper Saddle River, NJ: Merrill/Prentice-Hall.

Snell, M. E. (1998). Characteristics of elementary school classrooms where children with moderate and severe disabilities are included: A compilation of the findings. In S. J. Vitello & D. E. Mithaug (Eds.), *Inclusive schooling: National and international perspectives* (pp. 76–97). Mahwah, NJ: Lawrence Erlbaum.

Pennsylvania Association for Retarded Children v. *Commonwealth of Pennsylvania*, 343 F. Supp. 279 (1972).

U.S. Department of Education (1993). *National excellence: A case for developing America's talent*. Washington, DC: U.S. Government Printing Office.

U.S. Department of Education (1998). *Twentieth annual report to Congress on implementation of the Individuals with Disabilities Act*. Washington, DC: Author.

Valdes, G. (1999). Incipient bilingualism and the development of English language writing abilities in the secondary school. In C. J. Faltis & P. Wolfe (Eds.), *So much to say: Adolescents, bilingualism, and ESL in the secondary school* (pp. 138–176). New York: Teachers College Press.

Viadero, D. (1996, January). Expert testimony. *Teacher Magazine*, pp. 24–25.

Words that hurt: Chicago exhibit forces kids to confront prejudice. (1996, May/June). *Teacher Magazine*, p. 13.

▶ Chapter 10

Airasian, P. W. (1996). *Assessment in the classroom*. New York: McGraw-Hill.

Alfassi, M. (1998). Reading for meaning: The efficacy of reciprocal teaching in fostering reading comprehension in high school students in remedial reading classes. *American Educational Research Journal, 35*(2), 309–332.

Apple, M. W. (1998). The culture and commerce of the textbook. In *The curriculum: Problems, politics, and possibilities* (2nd ed.), pp. 157–166. Albany, NY: State University of New York Press.

Apple, M. W., & Beyer, L. E. (1988). Social evaluation of curriculum schooling. In L. E. Beyer & M. W. Apple (Eds.), *The curriculum: Problems, politics, and possibilities* (pp. 334–349). Albany: State University of New York Press.

Applebee, A. N. (1991). Environments for language teaching and learning. In J. Flood, J. Jensen, & J. R. Squire (Eds.), *Handbook of research on teaching the English language arts* (pp. 549–558). New York: Macmillan.

Arter, J. A., & Spandel, V. (1992). NCME instructional module: Using portfolios of student work in instruction and assessment. *Educational Measurement, 11*, 36–44.

Association for Supervision and Curriculum Development. (1992, January). What the NCTM standards say. *Curriculum Update*, p. 3.

Association of American Publishers (1999). Industry statistics: 1998 preliminary estimated industry net sales. Available online: http://www.publishers.org/home/stats/index.htm

Atwell, N. (1987). *In the middle: Writing, reading, and learning with adolescents* (pp. 3–4). Portsmouth, NH: Boynton/Cook.

Banks, J., & McGee Banks, C. A. (1997). *Multicultural education: Issues and perspectives* (3rd ed.). Boston: Allyn and Bacon.

Berk, L. E. (1992). The extracurriculum. In P. W. Jackson (Ed.), *Handbook of research on curriculum* (pp. 1002–1043). New York: Macmillan.

Beyer, L. E., & M. W. Apple (Eds.) (1998). *The curriculum: Problems, politics, and possibilities* (2nd ed.). Albany, NY: State University of New York Press.

Bloom, B. (1971). Mastery learning. In J. H. Block (Ed.), *Mastery learning: Theory and practice* (pp. 13–28). New York: Holt, Rinehart and Winston.

Blumenfeld, P., Soloway, E., Marx, R., Krajcik, J., Guzdial, M., & Palcinsar, A. (1991). Motivating project-based learning: Sustaining the doing, supporting the learning. *Educational Psychologist, 26*(3 & 4), 369–398.

Brophy, J. (1988). Educating teachers about managing classrooms and students. *Teaching and Teacher Education, 4*(1), 1–18.

Brophy, J. (1996, April). Classroom management as socializing students into clearly articulated roles. Paper presented at the Annual Meeting of the American Educational Research Association, New York.

Brophy, J., & Good, T. (1971). Teacher's communication of differential expectations for children's classroom performance: Some behavior data. *Journal of Educational Psychology, 61*, 365–374.

Brophy, J., & Good, T. (1974). *Teacher–student relationships: Causes and consequences*. New York: Holt, Rinehart and Winston.

Burns, M. (1995). The 8 most important lessons I've learned about organizing my teaching year. *Instructor, 105*(2), 86–88.

Carroll, J. B. (1971). Problems of measurement related to the concept of learning for mastery. In J. H. Block (Ed.), *Mastery learning: Theory and practice* (pp. 29–46). New York: Holt, Rinehart and Winston.

Charles, C. M. (1999). *Building classroom discipline* (6th ed.). New York: Longman.

Clandinin, D. J., & Connelly, F. M. (1992). Teacher as curriculum maker. In P. W. Jackson (Ed.), *Handbook of research on curriculum* (pp. 363–401). New York: Macmillan.

Clark, C. M., & Dunn, S. (1991). Second-generation research on teachers' planning. In H. C. Waxman & H. J. Walberg (Eds.), *Effective teaching: Current research* (pp. 183–201). Berkeley, CA: McCutchan.

Coles, A. D. (1999). Report on abstinence funds raises questions. *Education Week, 18*(31), 6.

Corno, L. (1987). Teaching and self-regulated learning. In D. C. Berliner & B. V. Rosenshine (Eds.), *Talks to teachers* (pp. 249–266). New York: Random House.

Cuban, L. (1992). Curriculum stability and change. In P. W. Jackson (Ed.), *Handbook of research on curriculum* (pp. 216–217). New York: Macmillan.

DeBoer, G. E. (1991). *A history of ideas in science education: Implications for practice*. New York: Teachers College Press.

Doyle, W. (1986). Classroom organization and management. In M. C. Wittrock (Ed.), *Handbook of research on teaching* (3rd ed.) (pp. 392–431) New York: Macmillan.

Education at the Met (1999). *Creating original opera*. Available online: http://operaed.org/

Eggen, P. D., & Kauchak, D. P. (1996). *Strategies for teachers: Teaching content and thinking skills* (3rd ed.). Boston: Allyn and Bacon.

Eisner, E. W. (1985). *The educational imagination: On the design and evaluation of school programs* (2nd ed.). New York: Macmillan.

Eisner, E. W. (1991, September). What the arts taught me about education. *Art Education*, pp. 11–19.

Eisner, E. W. (1992). The misunderstood role of the arts in human development. *Phi Delta Kappan, 73*(8), 591–595.

Eisner, E. (1994). *Cognition and curriculum reconsidered* (2nd ed.). New York: Teachers College Press.

Ellwein, M. C. (1992). Research on classroom assessment meanings and practices. *Commonwealth Center News, 5*(1), 2, 4.

Emmer, E., Evertson, C. & Anderson, L. (1980). Effective management at the beginning of the school year. *Elementary School Journal, 80,* 221–231.

Evertson, C. (1985). Training teachers in classroom management: An experimental study in secondary school classrooms. *Journal of Educational Research, 79,* 51–58.

Evertson, C., & Emmer, E. (1982). Effective management at the beginning of the school year in junior high school classes. *Journal of Educational Psychology, 74,* 485–498.

Fielding, L. G., & Pearson, R. D. (1994). Reading comprehension: What works. *Educational Leadership, 51*(5), 62–68.

Frieberg, H. L., & Driscoll, A. (1996). *Universal teaching strategies* (2nd ed.). Boston: Allyn and Bacon.

Frieberg, H. L., Stein, T. A., & Huang, S. (1995). Effects of a classroom management intervention on student achievement in inner-city elementary schools. *Educational Research and Evaluation, 1*(1), 36–66.

Gage, N. L. (1978). *The scientific basis of the art of teaching*. New York: Teachers College Press.

Good, T. L., & Brophy, J. E. (2000). *Looking in classrooms* (8th ed.). New York: Addison Wesley Longman.

Goodlad, J. I., & Su, Z. (1992). Organization of the curriculum. In P. W. Jackson (Ed.), *Handbook of research on curriculum* (pp. 327–344). New York: Macmillan.

Grobman, H. (1970). *Developmental curriculum projects: Decision points and processes*. Itasca, IL: Peacock.

Gudmundsdottir, S. (1991). Values in pedagogical content knowledge. *The Journal of Teacher Education, 41*(3), 44–52.

Gunter, M. A., Estes, T. H., & Schwab, J. (1999). *Instruction: A models approach* (3rd ed.). Boston: Allyn and Bacon.

Guzdial, M. (1998). Technological support for project-based learning. In C. Dede (Ed.), *ASCD year book 1998: Learning with technology*. Alexandria, VA: Association for Supervision and Curriculum Development.

Henderson, P., & Gysbers, N. C. (1998). *Leading and managing your school guidance program staff*. Alexandria, VA: American Counseling Association.

Herbert, J. M. (1999). An online learning community: Technology brings teachers together for professional development. *American School Board Journal, 186*(3), 39–41.

Hoff, D. (1999). Calif. approves math, English textbooks tied to standards. *Education Week, 18*(41), 10.

Hunt, D. E., & Sullivan, E. V. (1974). *Between psychology and education*. Hinsdale, IL: Dryden Press.

Jackson, P. W. (1990). *Life in classrooms*. New York: Teachers College Press.

Jacobs, H. H. (1997). *Mapping the big picture: Integrating curriculum & assessment K–12*. Alexandria, VA: Association for Supervision and Curriculum Development.

Jacobson, L. (1999). A kinder, gentler student body. *Education Week, 18*(42), 1, 22–23.

Johnson, D. W., & Johnson, R. T. (1999). *Learning together and alone: Cooperative, competitive, and individualistic learning*. Boston: Allyn and Bacon.

Jones, V. F., & Jones, L. S. (1998). *Comprehensive classroom management: Creating communities of support and solving problems* (6th ed.). Boston: Allyn and Bacon.

Joyce, B. R., & Calhoun, E. E. (1996). *Creating learning experiences: The role of instructional theory and research*. Alexandria, VA: Association for Supervision and Curriculum Development.

Joyce, B., & Weil, M. (1996). *Models of teaching* (5th ed.). Boston: Allyn and Bacon.

Kliebard, H. M. (1998). The effort to reconstruct the modern American curriculum. In L. E. Beyer & M. W. Apple (Eds.), (pp. 21–33). *The curriculum: Problems, politics, and possibilities* (2nd ed.). Albany, NY: State University of New York Press.

Kounin, J. S. (1970). *Discipline and group management in classrooms*. New York: Holt, Rinehart and Winston.

Langer, J. A., & Applebee, A. N. (1986). Reading and writing instruction: Toward a theory of teaching and learning. In E. Z. Rothkopf (Ed.), *Review of research in education: Vol. 13* (pp. 171–194). Washington, DC: American Educational Research Association.

Levy, S. (1996). *Starting from scratch: One classroom builds its own curriculum*. Portsmouth, NH: Heinemann.

Mager, R. F. (1962). *Preparing instructional objectives*. Palo Alto, CA: Fearon.

Manzo, K. K. (1999a). States setting strategies to reduce mistakes in textbooks. *Education Week, 18*(38), 6.

Manzo, K. K. (1999b). Reading experts question if "balance" is the answer. *Education Week, 18*(35), 8.

McAuliffe, J., & Stoskin, L. (1993). *What color is Saturday? Using analogies to enhance creative thinking in the classroom*. Tucson, AZ: Zephyr Press.

McCarthy, C. (1993, July 3). Firing the messenger. *Washington Post*, p. A23.

McConaghy, T. (1992). A witch hunt bedevils a Canadian reading series. *Phi Delta Kappan, 73*(8), 649.

McNeil, J. D. (1999). *Curriculum: The teacher's initiative* (2nd ed.). Upper Saddle River, NJ: Prentice Hall.

Morrison, G. S. (1993). *Contemporary curriculum K–8*. Boston: Allyn and Bacon.

National Council of Teachers of Mathematics (1989). *Curriculum and evaluation standards for school mathematics*. Reston, VA: Author.

National Council of Teachers of Mathematics (1991). *Professional standards for teaching mathematics*. Reston, VA: Author.

Nuthall, D. D. (1992, May). Performance assessment: The message from England. *Educational Leadership*, pp. 54–57.

Office of Educational Research and Improvement (OERI) (1995, October). *Announcement: Helping your child with homework*. Washington, DC: U.S. Department of Education.

Oliva, P. F. (1997). *Developing the curriculum* (4th ed.). New York: Addison Wesley Longman.

Pinar, W. F., Reynolds, W. M., Slattery, P., Taubman, P. M. (1995). *Understanding curriculum: An introduction to the study of historical and contemporary curriculum discourses*. New York: Peter Lang Publishing, Inc.

Pitsch, M. (1995, February). Life on the Mississippi. *Teacher Magazine, 6,* 14–15.

Qin, Z., Johnson, D. W., & Johnson, R. T. (1995). Cooperative versus competitive efforts and problem solving. *Review of Educational Research, 65*(2), 129–144.

Rogers, C. (1971). *Client centered therapy.* Boston: Houghton Mifflin.

Rosenshine, B., & Meister, C. (1994). Reciprocal teaching: A review of the research. *Review of Educational Research, 64*(4), 479–530.

Rosenthal, R., & Jacobson, L. (1968). *Pygmalion in the classroom: Teacher expectation and pupils' intellectual development.* New York: Holt, Rinehart and Winston.

Schubert, W. H. (1986). *Curriculum: Perspective, paradigm, and possibility.* New York: Macmillan.

Shanker asks end to some standard tests. (1989, October 29). *Washington Post,* p. A13.

Sharan, S. (1990). Cooperative learning and helping behavior in the multiethnic classroom. In H. C. Foot, M. J. Morgan, & R. H. Shute (Eds.), *Children helping children* (pp. 151–176). New York: John Wiley & Sons.

Sharan, Y., & Sharan, S. (1992). *Group investigation: Expanding cooperative learning.* New York: Teachers College Press.

Slavin, R. E. (1995). *Cooperative learning* (2nd ed.). Boston: Allyn and Bacon.

Slavin, R. E., & Fashola, O. S. (1998). *Show me the evidence! Proven and promising programs for America's Schools.* Thousand Oaks, CA: Corwin Press.

Sleeter, C. E., & Grant, C. A. (1991). Race, class, gender, and disability in current textbooks. In M. W. Apple & L. K. Christian-Smith (Eds.), *The politics of the textbook* (pp. 78–110). New York: Routledge.

Sowell, E. J. (1996). *Curriculum: An integrative introduction.* Upper Saddle River, NJ: Prentice Hall.

U.S. Congress, Office of Technology Assessment (1992). *Testing in American schools: Asking the right questions* (OTA-SET-519). Washington, DC: U.S. Government Printing Office.

U.S. Department of Education (1999). *What happens in classrooms? Instructional practices in elementary and secondary schools, 1994–95,* NCES 1999-348. By R. R. Henke, X. Chen, & G. Goldman. Project Officers, M. Rollefson & K. Gruber. Washington, DC: Author.

Vallance, E. (1995). The public curriculum of orderly images. *Educational Researcher, 24*(2), 4–13.

Virginia Education Association & The Appalachia Educational Laboratory. (1995, April). *Interdisciplinary units with alternative assessments: A teacher-developed compendium.* Washington, DC: U.S. Department of Education, Office of Educational Research and Improvement.

Walsh, M. (1999). Conservatives join effort to pull the plug on Channel One. *Education Week, 18*(30), 5.

Weinstein, C. S., & Mignano, Jr., A. J. (1997). *Elementary classroom management: Lessons from research and practice* (2nd ed.). New York: McGraw-Hill.

Wiles, J. (1999). *Curriculum essentials: A resource for educators.* Boston: Allyn and Bacon.

Winne, P. H. (1991). Motivation and teaching. In H. C. Waxman & H. J. Walberg (Eds.), *Effective teaching: Current research* (pp. 210–230). Berkeley, CA: McCutchan.

Winne, P. H., & Marx, R. W. (1979). Perceptual problem solving. In P. L. Peterson & H. J. Walberg (Eds.), *Research on teaching: Concepts, findings, and implications* (pp. 210–230). Berkeley, CA: McCutchan.

Wolf, D. P. (1994). *An assessment of "Creating Original Opera."* Cambridge, MA: Performance Assessment Collaboratives for Education.

Wolfgang, C. H., Bennett, B. J., & Irvin, J. L. (1999). *Strategies for teaching self-discipline in the middle grades.* Boston: Allyn and Bacon.

▶ Chapter 11

Abood v. *Detroit Board of Education,* 431 U.S. 209, 97 S.Ct. 1782 (1977).

Alexander, K., & Alexander, M. D. (1998). *American public school law* (4th ed.). Belmont, CA: Wadsworth Publishing Co.

Baker v. *Owen,* 395 F. Supp. 294 M.D.N.C. (1975).

B.M. by Berger v. *State of Montana,* 649 P.2d 425 (Mont. 1982).

Board of Education of the Westside Community Schools v. *Mergens,* 496 U.S. 226 (1990).

Board of Regents of State Colleges v. *Roth,* 408 U.S. 564 (1972).

Boring v. *Buncombe Co. Board of Education,* 136 F.3d 364 [124 Ed. Law Rep. [56]] (4th Cir. 1998).

Brown v. *Board of Education of Topeka, Kansas,* 347 U.S. 483 (1954).

Bureau of National Affairs. (1993). Lamb's Chapel and John Seigerwald, petitioners v. Center Moriches Union Free School District et al. *United States Law Week, 61*(46), 4549–4554.

Cedar Rapids Community School District v. *Garret F.* (1999). 106 F.3d 822.

Center for Education Reform (2000). Answers to frequently asked questions about charter schools. Available online: http://www.edreform.com/school_reform_faq/charter_schools.htm

Chase, C. I. (1976). Classroom testing and the right to privacy. *Phi Delta Kappan, 58,* 331–332.

Chicago Teachers Union, Local No. 1 AFL–CIO v. *Hudson,* 475 U.S. 292, 106 S.Ct. 1066 (1986).

Conkling, W. (1991, November/December). The big chill. *Teacher Magazine,* pp. 46–53.

Data Research, Inc. (1999). *1999 deskbook encyclopedia of American school law.* Rosemount, MN: Author.

Davis v. *Grover,* 480 N. W. 2d 460, (Wis. 1992).

Davis v. *Monroe County Board of Education* (1999). 97-843, 526 U.S. 629; 119 S.Ct. 1661.

Ellis v. *Brotherhood of Railway, Airline, and S.S. Clerks,* 466 U.S. 435, 104 S. Ct. 1885 (1984).

Encyclopedia Britannica Educational Corporation v. *Crooks,* 542 F. Supp. 1156 (W.D. N.Y. 1982).

Essex, N. L. (1999). *School law and the public schools: A practical guide for educational leaders.* Boston: Allyn and Bacon.

Fischer, L., Schimmel, D., & Kelly, C. (1995). *Teachers and the law* (4th ed.). White Plains, NY: Longman.

Florence County School District Four v. *Carter,* 510 U.S. 7 (1993).

Franklin v. *Gwinnett County Public Schools,* 112 S.Ct. 1028 (1992).

Gaylord v. *Tacoma School District No. 10,* 88 Wa.2d 286, 559 P.2d 1340 (1977).

Goetz v. *Ansell,* 477 F.2d 636 (2nd Cir. 1973).

Gonzalez v. *Mackler,* 241 N.Y.S.2d 254 (N.Y. App. Div. 1963).

Goss v. *Lopez,* 419 U.S. 565, 95 Ct. 729, 42 L.Ed.2d 725 (1975).

Hazelwood School District v. *Kuhlmeier,* 484 U.S. 260 (1988).

Hess, F. M. (1999). *Spinning wheels: The politics of urban school reform.* Washington, DC: Brookings Institution Press.

Hines v. *Caston School Corporation,* 63 USLW 2799 (Ind. App. 1995).

Home School Legal Defense Association (1999). Across the states. Available online: http://www.hslda.org/

Honig v. *Doe,* 484 U.S. 305, 108 S.Ct. 592 (1988).

Hunter v. *Board of Education of Montgomery County,* 425 A.2d 681 (Md.App. 1981), *aff'd in part and rev'd in part on other grounds,* 439 A.2d 582 (Md. App.1982).

Imber, M., & van Geel, T. (1993). *Education law.* New York: McGraw-Hill.

Ingraham v. *Wright,* 430 U.S. 651, 97 S.Ct 1401, 51 L.Ed.2d 711 (1977).

In re William G., 221 Cal. Rptr. 118 (1985).

La Morte, M. W. (1999). *School law: Cases and concepts* (6th ed.). Boston: Allyn and Bacon.

Lau v. *Nichols,* 414 U.S. 563 (1974).

Lee v. *Weisman,* 69 U.S.L.W. 4723 (1992).

Lemon v. *Kurtzman,* 403 U.S. 602, 91 S.Ct. 2105, 29 L.Ed.2d 745 (1971).

LRP Publications. (1996a, May). Five ways to prevent peer sexual harassment. *Your School and the Law, 26*(5), 10.

Mancha v. *Field Museum of Natural History,* 283 N.E.2d 899 (Ill. App. 1972).

Martin Luther King, Jr., Elementary School Children v. *Michigan Board of Education,* 473 Federal Supplement, 1371 (1979).

McCarthy, M. M., & Cambron-McCabe, N. H., & Thomas, S. B. (1998). *Public school law: Teachers and students' rights* (4th ed.). Boston: Allyn and Bacon.

McGlothin v. *Jackson Municipal,* 999 F. 2d 1580 (1993).

Miner, B. (1998). Why I don't vouch for vouchers. *Educational Leadership, 56*(2), 40–42.

Missouri v. *Jenkins,* 115 S.Ct. 2038, 132 L. Ed. 2d 63 [100 Ed. Law Rep. [506]] (1995).

Morrison v. *State Board of Education,* 1 Cal.3d 214, 82 Cal.Rptr. 175, 191, 461 P. 2d.375, 391 (1969).

National Gay Task Force v. *Board of Education of Oklahoma City,* 729 F.2d 1270 (10th Cir. 1984), *aff'd by divided court,* 470 U.S. 903 (1985).

National Organization on Legal Problems of Education (1988). *Education Law Update 1987–1988.* USA: Author.

New Jersey v. *T.L.O.,* 221 Cal. Rptr. 118 (1985).

Peter W. v. *San Francisco Unified School District,* 131 Cal.Rptr. 854 (1976).

Portner, J. (1999, April 7). Drug testing latest tactic in prevention. *Education Week, 18*(30), 1, 16–17.

Rowland v. *Mad River Local School District, Montgomery County, Ohio,* 730 F.2d 444 (6th Cir. 1984).

Rothschild v. *Grottenthaler,* 907 F. 2nd, 286, (1990, June 27).

School District of Abington Township v. *Schempp,* 374 U.S. 203, 300,83 S.Ct 1560, 1620 (1963).

Sony Corporation of America v. *Universal City Studios, Inc.,* 464 U.S. 417 (1984) *reh'g denied,* 465 U.S. 1112 (1984).

Station v. *Travelers Insurance Co.,* 292 So.2d 289 (La. Ct. App. 1974).

Tinker v. *Des Moines Independent Community School District,* 393 U.S. 503, 89 S.Ct. 733, 21 L.Ed.2d 731 (1969).

U.S. Department of Health and Human Services (1999). Child Abuse Prevention and Treatment Act. Available online: http://www.acf.dhhs.gov /programs/cb/policy/capta.htm

U.S. Department of Education (1999, April 14). IDEA Regulations Published. Available online: http://www.ed.gov/pubs/EDInitiatives/99/99-03-18.html#4

Veronia School Dist. 47J v. *Acton,* 515 U.S. 646 (1995).

Virgil v. *School Board of Columbia County Florida,* 862 F.2d 1517 (1989).

Wallace v. *Jaffree,* 427 U.S., 38 (1985).

Walsh, M. (1998, June 17). Court allows vouchers in Milwaukee. *Education Week, 17*(40), 1, 16.

Ward v. *Newfield Central School District No. 1,* 412 N.Y.S.2d 57 (N.Y. App. Div. 1978).

West Virginia State Board of Education v. *Barnette,* 319 U.S. 624; 642 (1943).

White, K. A. (1998, January 14). Conn. Home schooler wants chance to play basketball with school team. *Education Week on the Web,* Available online: http://www.edweek.org/ew/vol-17/18home.h17

Widmar v. *Vincent,* 454 U.S. 263 (1981).

Williams, V. L. (1999). A new harassment ruling: Implications for colleges. *Chronicle of Higher Education, 65*(41), A56.

Wisconsin v. *Yoder,* 406 U.S. 205 (1972).

Zirkel, P. A., Richardson, S. N., & Goldberg, S. S. (1995). *A digest of Supreme Court decisions affecting education* (3rd ed.). Bloomington, IN: Phi Delta Kappa Educational Foundation.

▶ Chapter 12

Associated Press (1996, February 17). Court orders S. African school to admit blacks. *Washington Post,* p. A28.

Berg, D. L. (1995). Canada. In T. N. Postlethwaite (Ed.), *The encyclopedia of comparative education and national systems of education* (2nd ed.) (pp. 180–189). Oxford: Pergamon Press.

Bondi, L. (1991). Choice and diversity in school education: Comparing developments in the United Kingdom and the USA. *Comparative Education, 27*(2), 125–34.

Booth, C. (1988). United Kingdom. In T. N. Postlethwaite (Ed.), *The encyclopedia of comparative education and national systems of education,* (2nd ed.) (pp. 691–698). Oxford: Pergamon Press.

Bordia, A. (1988). India. In T. N. Postlethwaite (Ed.), *The encyclopedia of comparative education and national systems of education* (pp. 350–358). Oxford: Pergamon Press.

Boulding, E. (1988). *Building a global civic culture: Education for an interdependent world.* Syracuse, NY: Syracuse University Press.

Boyer, E. (1992). Educating in a multicultural world. In D. Bragaw & W. S. Thomson (Eds.), *Multicultural education: A global approach* (pp. 48–53). New York: The American Forum for Global Education.

Bracey, G. W. (1996). International comparisons and the condition of American education. *Educational Researcher, 25*(1), 5–11.

Childers, E., & Urquhart, B. (1994). *Renewing the United Nations system.* Geneva: United Nations.

Committee to Review the Organization, Governance and Funding of Schools (1995, August 31). *Report of the committee to review the organization, governance and funding of schools.* Pretoria: Department of Education.

Cushner, K. (1998). Intercultural education from an international perspective: An introduction. In K. Cushner (Ed.), *International perspectives on intercultural education* (pp. 1–4). Mahwah, NJ: Lawrence Erlbaum.

Danish Ministry of Education (1999, July 2). *The European dimension of education.* Available online: http://www.uvm.dk/gammel/kap11.htm

Desmond, E. W. (1996). The failed miracle. *Time, 147*(17), 60–64.

Florander, J. (1988). Denmark: System of Education. In T. Husen & T. N. Postlethwaite (Eds.), *The International encyclopedia of education: Research and studies: Vol. 3* (pp. 1354–1360). New York: Pergamon Press.

Fowler, R. (1998). Intercultural education in Canada: Glimpses from the past, hopes for the future. In K. Cushner (Ed.), *International perspectives on intercultural education* (pp. 302–318). Mahwah, NJ: Lawrence Erlbaum.

Gladwell, M. (1991, December 2–8). Apples plus 4 oranges equals 1 uproar over math skills. *Washington Post Weekly Edition,* p. 33.

A global revolution in science, mathematics and technology. (1996, April 10). *Education Week, 15*(29), Special Forum Section, 1–8.

Gopinathan, S. (1994). Education and development: The Singapore experience. In P. Morris & A. Sweeting (Eds.), *Education and development: The East Asian experience* (pp. 1–25). New York: Greenwood Press.

Goya, S. (1993). The secret of Japanese education. *Phi Delta Kappan, 75*(2), 126–129.

Goya, S. (1994). Japanese education: Hardly known facts. *Education Digest, 59*(8), 8–12.

Harnisch, D. L. (1994). Supplemental education in Japan: Juku in schooling and its implications. *Journal of Curriculum Studies, 26*(3), 323–334.

Hartshorne, K. (1990). Post-apartheid education: A concept in process (opportunities within the process). In R. Schrire (Ed.), *Critical choices for South Africa: An agenda for the 1990s.* New York: Oxford University Press, 168–185.

Huerta, A. E. (1999). *Las Trampas de la identidad en un mundo de mujeres.* Mexico: Editorial Itaca.

International Baccalaureate Organisation (1996). *Welcome to the International Baccalaureate Organization.* Available online: http://www.ibo. org/Geneva, Switzerland.

Jansen, M., & Kreiner, S. (1995). Denmark. In T. N. Postlethwaite (Ed.), *The encyclopedia of comparative education and national systems of education* (2nd ed.) (pp. 31–47). Oxford: Pergamon Press.

Judge, H. (1989, June). Is there a crisis in British secondary schools? *Phi Delta Kappan, 70*(10), 813–815.

Kanaya, T. (1995). Japan. In T. N. Postlethwaite (Ed.), *International encyclopedia of national systems of education* (pp. 482–488). New York: Elsevier Science.

King, E. J. (1988). South Africa. In T. N. Postlethwaite (Ed.), *The encyclopedia of comparative education and national systems of education* (2nd ed.) (pp. 600–605). Oxford: Pergamon Press.

Lemmer, E. M. (1993). Educational renewal in South Africa: Problems and prospects. *Compare, 23*(1), 53–62.

Lloyd, M. (1999, February 19). Hindu nationalists campaign to remake education in India: Ruling party and its allies enlist academics to revise the canon. *Chronicle of Higher Education,* p. A56.

Lorey, D. E. (1995, March–April). Education and the challenges of Mexican development. *Challenge, 38:*51–55.

MayaQuest (undated). *Back by popular demand—MayaQuest '96: Students around the country log onto the Internet, lead expedition into Central America.* Minneapolis, MN: MayaQuest Interactive Expedition.

McAdams, R. P. (1993). *Lessons from abroad: How other countries educate their children.* Lancaster, PA: Technomic.

McNergney, R. F., Regelbrugge, L. A., & Harper, J. P. (1997). Multicultural education in a global context. In J. McIntyre & D. M. Byrd (Eds.), *Teacher education yearbook* (pp. 7–25). Thousand Oaks, CA: Corwin Press.

Mislevy, R. J. (1995). What can we learn from international assessments? *Educational Evaluation and Policy Analysis, 17*(4), 419–437.

Muslim parents boycott religious classes. (1996, January). *The Times Educational Supplement,* p. 3.

Nuthall, G., & Alton-Lee, A. (1995). Assessing classroom learning: How students use their knowledge and experience to answer classroom achievement test questions in science and social studies. *American Educational Research Journal, 32*(1), 185–223.

Patrick, C. L., & Calfee, R. C. (1996, April 7). A textbook case of hype. *Washington Post,* p. C1.

Pugach, M. C. (1998). *On the border of opportunity: Education, community, and language at the U.S.-Mexico line.* Mahwah, NJ: Lawrence Erlbaum.

Reyes, M. E. (1995). Mexico. In T. N. Postlethwaite (Ed.), *International encyclopedia of national systems of education* (2nd ed.) (pp. 643–652). New York: Elsevier.

Sato, N., & McLaughlin, M. W. (1992). Context matters: Teaching in Japan and the United States. *Phi Delta Kappan, 73*(5), 359–366.

Spring, J. (1998). *Education and the rise of the global economy.* Mahwah, NJ: Lawrence Erlbaum.

Stedman, L. (1994). Incomplete explanations: The case of U.S. performance in the international assessment of education. *Educational Researcher, 23*(7), 24–32.

Stevenson, H. W., & Stigler, J. W. (1992). *The learning gap: Why our schools are failing and what we can learn from Japanese and Chinese education.* New York: Summit.

Stigler, J. W., & Stevenson, H. W. (1991, Spring). How Asian teachers polish each lesson to perfection. *American Educator,* pp. 20–30.

Stonier, J. (1998). Breaking out of a separatist paradigm: Intercultural education in South Africa. In K. Cushner (Ed.), *International perspectives on intercultural education* (pp. 210–236). Mahwah, NJ: Lawrence Erlbaum.

Taylor, W. H. (1991). India's national curriculum: Prospects and potential for the 1990s. *Comparative Education, 27*(3), 325–344.

Theobald, D. (1995, June). Investing in grandchildren: Basic education in the Indian sub-continent. *Asian Affairs, 26* (Part 2), 141–151.

Thomas, R. M. (Ed.) (1990). *International comparative education: Practices, issues, & practices.* Oxford: Pergamon Press.

Tye, B. B., & Tye, K. A. (1992). *Global education: A study of school change.* Albany, NY: State University of New York Press.

United States Department of Commerce (1998, April 6). *Foreign-born Population Reaches 25.8 Million, According to Census Bureau.* Washington, DC. Available online: http://www.census.gov/Press-Release/cb98-57.html

Westbury, I. (1992). Comparing American and Japanese achievement: Is the United States really a low achiever? *Educational Researcher, 21*(5), 18–24.

▶ Chapter 13

American Association for the Advancement of Science (1998). *Blueprints for reform. Science, mathematics, and technology education. Project 2061.* New York: Oxford University Press.

American Association of School Administrators (1999). *An educator's guide to school reform.* Arlington, VA: Author. Available online: http://www.aasa.org/reform/index.htm

Blair, J. (1999, March 10). Teens and homeless share dinner, discussion, insight. *Education Week, 18*(26), 6.

Brandt, R. S. (1992). On building learning communities: A conversation with Hank Levin. *Educational Leadership, 50*(1), 19–23.

Brophy, J., & McCaslin, M. (1992). Teachers' reports of how they perceive and cope with problem students. *Elementary School Journal, 93*(1), 3–68.

Clandinin, D. J., & Connelly, F. M. (1996). Teachers' professional knowledge landscapes: Teacher stories—stories of teachers—school stories—stories of schools. *Educational Researcher, 25*(3), 24–30.

CEO Forum on Education & Technology (1998). *1998 STaR Chart: A tool for assessing school technology and readiness.* Washington, DC: Author.

Cooper, K. (1999, August 1). Pupils sweat out the 'big test': End of social promotions forces Chicagoans into summer school. *Washington Post,* pp. A3, A19.

Cushman, K. (1993a). Essential collaborators: Parents, school, and community. *Horace, 9*(5), 1–8.

Cushman, K. (1993b). What's essential? Integrating the curriculum in essential schools. *Horace, 9*(4), 1–8.

Dixon, P. N., & Ishler, R. E. (1992). Professional development schools: Stages in collaboration. *Journal of Teacher Education, 43*(1), 28–34.

Ducharme, E. (1996). *In praise of Muriel Ragsdale.* Unpublished manuscript, Drake University.

eMarketer (1999). *Net user demographics: Children online.* Retrieved from the World Wide Web, August 26, 1999. Available online: http://www.emarketer.com/estats/demo_child.html

Fadiman, C. (Ed.) (1985). *The Little, Brown book of anecdotes.* Boston: Little, Brown & Co.

Good, T. L., & Brophy, J. E. (2000). *Looking in classrooms* (8th ed.). New York: Addison Wesley Longman.

Grabe, M., & Grabe, C. (1998). *Learning with Internet tools: A primer.* Boston: Houghton Mifflin Co.

Grumet, M. (1987). Women and teaching: Homeless at home. *Teacher Education Quarterly, 14*(2), 39–46.

Hampel, R. L. (1999, April 21). The power and peril of idea-driven reform. *Education Week, 18*(32), 44–47.

Hill, C. (1999, August 19). *Developing educational standards: An annotated list of Internet sites with K–12 educational standards and curriculum frameworks documents.* Available online: http://putwest.boces.org/Standards.html

Hofstetter, F. T. (1998). *Internet library.* Boston: Irwin/McGraw-Hill.

Institute for Higher Education Policy (1999, April). *What's the difference? A review of contemporary research on the effectiveness of distance learning in higher education.* Washington, DC: Institute for Higher Education Policy.

Johnson, W. R. (1990). Inviting conversations: The Holmes Group and tomorrow's schools. *American Educational Research Journal, 27*(4), 581–588.

Joyce, B. R., & Weil, M. (1996). *Models of teaching.* Boston: Allyn and Bacon.

Kahne, J., & Westheimer, J. (1996). In the service of what? The politics of service learning. *Phi Delta Kappan, 77*(9), 593–599.

Keller, B. M., & Soler, P. (1996). The influence of the Accelerated Schools philosophy and process on classroom practices. In C. Finnan, E. P. St. John, J. McCarthy & S. P. Slovacek (Eds.), *Accelerated schools in action: Lessons from the field* (pp. 273–290). Thousand Oaks, CA: Corwin Press.

Kent, T. W. (1999). Making connections: The democratic classroom and the Internet. In R. F. McNergney, E. D. Ducharme, & M. K. Ducharme (Eds.), *Educating for democracy: Case-method teaching and learning* (pp. 29–44). Mahwah, NJ: Lawrence Erlbaum.

Kent, T. W., & McNergney, R. F. (1999). *Will technology really change education? From blackboard to web.* Thousand Oaks, CA: Corwin Press.

Lawton, M. (1996a). Board approves plans for NAEP civics test. *Education Week, 15*(25), 6.

Lawton, M. (1996b). States move to toughen exit exams: Educators, employers, seek to set bar higher. *Education Week, 15*(22), 1, 23.

Lerner, B (1991, March). Good news about American education. *Commentary,* pp. 19–25.

Levin, H. M. (1996). Accelerated schools : The background. In C. Finnan, E. P. St. John, J. McCarthy & S. P. Slovacek (Eds.), *Accelerated schools in action: Lessons from the field* (pp. 3–23). Thousand Oaks, CA: Corwin Press.

Levine, M. (Ed.). (1992). *Professional practice schools: Linking teacher education and school reform.* New York: Teachers College Press.

McLaughlin, M. W., & Talbert, J. E. (1993). *Contexts that matter for teaching and learning.* Stanford, CA: Center for Research on the Context of Secondary School Teaching.

Mitzel, H. E. (1960). Teacher effectiveness. In C. W. Harris (Ed.), *Encyclopedia of educational research* (3rd ed.) (pp. 1481–1486). New York: Macmillan.

National Center for Education Statistics (1999). *The NAEP 1998 reading report card: National and state highlights* (p. 15). Washington, DC: U.S. Government Printing Office.

National Education Goals Panel (1999, January). *Building a nation of learners. State comparisons of the data volume to the 1998 national education goals report.* Available online: wysiwyg://37/http://www.negp.gov/webpg80.htm

National Education Goals Panel. (1994). *The national education goals report 1994.* Washington, DC: U.S. Government Printing Office.

National Network for Educational Renewal (1999). *19 Postulates necessary for the simultaneous renewal of schools and the education of educators.* Retrieved from the World Wide Web, August 26, 1999. Available online: http://depts.washington.edu/cedren/NationalNetworkForEducationalRenewal.html

National PTA. (1995–1996). *National PTA 100 Years.* Available online: http://www.pta.org.

Noddings, N. (1984). *Caring: A feminine approach to ethics and moral education.* Berkeley: University of California Press.

Noddings, N. (1992). Gender and the curriculum. In P. W. Jackson (Ed.), *Handbook of research on curriculum* (pp. 659–686). New York: Macmillan.

Northwest Regional Educational Laboratory. (1997). *Catalog of school reform models* (1st ed.). Available online: http://www.nwrel.org/scpd/natspec/catalog/index.html

Oliva, P. F. (1992). *Developing the curriculum* (3rd ed.). New York: HarperCollins.

Porter, A. C. (1995). The uses and misuses of opportunity-to-learn standards. *Educational Researcher, 24*(1), 21–27.

Quigley, C. N., & Bahmueller, C. F. (Eds.) (1991). *Civitas: A framework for civic education.* Calabasas, CA: Center for Civic Education.

Ryan, K., & Bohlin, K. (1999, March 3). Values, views, or virtues? *Education Week, 18*(25), 72, 49.

Sandham, J. L. (1999, May 12). Father figures. *Education Week, 18*(35), 26–31.

Schwartz, F. (1999, June 16). Milestone or millstone? *Education Week, 18*(40), 41, 44.

Shulman, L. S. (1986). Paradigms and research programs in the study of teaching. In M. C. Wittrock (Ed.), *Handbook of research on teaching* (3rd ed.) (pp. 3–36). New York: Macmillan.

Squires, D. A., & Kranyik, R. D. (1995/1996). The Comer program: Changing school culture. *Educational Leadership, 53*(4), 29–32.

Stein, M. R., & Thorkildsen, R. J. (1999). *Parent involvement in education: Insights and applications from the research.* Bloomington, IN: Phi Delta Kappa International.

Stiggins, R. J. (1994). *Student-centered classroom assessment.* Upper Saddle River, NJ: Prentice Hall.

Trotter, A. (1998). Technology counts. Introduction. A question of effectiveness. *Education Week on the Web.* Available online: http://www.edweek.org/sreports/tc98/intro/in-n.htm

U.S. Department of Education (1999a). *Digest of education statistics 1998.* Washington, DC: U.S. Government Printing Office.

U.S. Department of Education (1999b, January 11). Star Schools—What is the Star Schools Program? Washington, DC: U.S. Government Printing Office. Available online: http://www.ed.gov/prog_info/StarSchools/whatis.html

Viadero, D. (1992, November 25). Survey finds young people more likely to lie, cheat, steal. *Education Week,* p. 5.

Wadsworth, B. (1978). *Piaget for the classroom teacher.* New York: Longman.

Walberg, H. J. (1991). Productive teaching and instruction: Assessing the knowledge base. In H. C. Waxman & H. J. Walberg (Eds.), *Effective teaching: Current research* (pp. 33–62). Berkeley, CA: McCutchan.

Wasley, P. A., Hampel, R. L., & Clark, R. W. (1997). *Kids and school reform.* San Francisco: Jossey-Bass.

Webb, N. L., & Romberg, T. A. (Eds.) (1994). *Reforming mathematics education in America's cities: The urban mathematics collaborative project.* New York: Teachers College Press.

Name Index

Subject Index

581

▶ D